NAVAL TRAINING UNIT
CALIFORNIA INSTITUTE OF TECHNOLOGY
PASADENA, CALIFORNIA

Pp 583-588

F. W. Treat

R E V I S E D   E D I T I O N

E D I T E D   B Y   **SHARON BROWN**

PROFESSOR OF ENGLISH, BROWN UNIVERSITY

N E W   Y O R K · 1 9 4 5
HARCOURT, BRACE AND COMPANY

This complete edition is produced in full compliance with the government's regulations for conserving paper and other essential materials.

PREFACE

Present Tense, originally published in three volumes, appears now in a single volume. The revision involves much more than change of format. Selections carried over from the first edition have had to meet two tests: the test of classroom usefulness, as reported by teachers; and the test of contemporaneousness, as determined by the course of events. Many of the selections have a timeless relevance and so they have been kept; others were significant only for their own time and have been replaced. Much of the material, especially in Section VI, Portrait of a World, is new.

Fully recognizing the war as the pivotal phenomenon of our time, we have tried to see it in perspective, to place it in proportion to other great turning points of history. This is not to agree with Bernard Shaw that the war is merely a bubble on the froth of history, but to take it as a tragic interruption of the normal, healthy ways of peace.

This book is, then, in large part, a reassertion of those ideas and convictions which, in time of peace, we are all too ready to take for granted but which, in time of war, we are quick to defend. What we would defend we must justify. What we would justify we must understand.

Present Tense is a survey of contemporary ideas as interpreted by a number of the best minds of our time. What they have to say is of present and immediate interest to the generation which will use this book. *Present Tense* takes account of the needs of men and women returning from military service who will ask of the colleges the means for rebuilding their philosophies. Fully aware of the defects in our social structure, it stresses the better impulses of the present and encourages a hopeful outlook upon the future.

The arrangement of material, as described hereafter in the Foreword, has been simplified. Introductions to the seven sections, designed to orient the reader to their general meaning and direction, are new or largely rewritten. The notes which precede the selections are rewritten, too, with the purpose of bringing out the sequence of ideas which has dictated their arrangement. The overall purpose has been to make a readable, human, stimulating, integrated collection of living literature.

In so far as it achieves this purpose the book should promote the student's powers of self-expression. The best teacher of composition is helpless before the student who has nothing to say. Sometimes this want of ideas arises from the feeling that it is not worth while to have any ideas. Confronted in these pages by the provocative features of his own time, the student should find that he has something to say after all.

Furthermore, as a preliminary to composition, reading is essential. As we learn to talk by hearing other people talk, so do we learn to write by reading what other people write. As matter for the student's unconscious assimilation, these specimens represent modern writing at its best, writing marked by that sincerity and directness which is the special virtue of the modern arts.

Theme assignments, loosely related to the readings, have been added at the end of this edition. Unlike the conventional lists of topics, these assignments are stated with sufficient fullness so that the student has a real situation or problem to work on.

So far as practicable, complete selections or self-sufficient units have been chosen. The several forms of writing have not been segregated. Prose and verse—fiction, biography, lyric, drama—every field is presented in an order apparently casual but actually planned to follow a natural sequence of ideas. For the teacher of the types course, whose first concern must be form, an alternative table of contents by types has been provided on page x.

I gratefully acknowledge the co-operation of authors and publishers who have permitted the use of copyrighted material; of the staff of the Providence Athenaeum; of Professor Newman B. Birk of Tufts College, who first prompted this revision; and of the many teachers whose experiences with *Present Tense* have guided the making of a new edition. Deepest is my appreciation for the good judgment of my wife, Elizabeth Duryea Brown, who has been an ever present help in the resolution of critical questions.

S. B.

CONTENTS

CONTENTS

CONTENTS BY TYPES

ESSAYS

FICTION

BIOGRAPHY

POETRY

DRAMA

FOREWORD

"NO man is an *Iland,* intire of it selfe; every man is a peece of the *Continent,* a part of the *maine;* if a *Clod* bee washed away by the *Sea, Europe* is the lesse, as well as if a *Promontorie* were, as well as if a *Mannor* of thy *friends* or of *thine own* were; any mans *death* diminishes *me,* because I am involved in *Mankinde;* And therefore never send to know for whom the *bell* tolls; It tolls for *thee.*"

So John Donne long ago described the way in which the one, sharing the experiences of the many, is "involved in mankind." So the reader of this book, sharing the experiences of many writers, will discover that their stories are his own, that the many and the one are identical. Here you have the life of a man, a woman—a pilgrim on a progress through a world he never made but which he seeks to understand—and the tense is present.

In this book we have a chance to look upon some seven aspects of the life of Everyman: his youth and schooling, his marriage and home making, his work, his play, his citizenship in the nation, his larger citizenship in the world, and his final judgment on it all—"the last of life, for which the first was made." Here, if you like, is a new Seven Ages presented page by page in steady growth, from the child wrapped in his own concerns to the mature mind fixed upon the everlasting questions of our race.

Between the beginning and the end we shall find ourselves involved in that mingling of bravery and beastliness, of ecstasy and bitterness, which, in our prouder moments, we call civilization. But we make a grievous error if we measure bad and good on the same scale. The good, in the long run, has a way of surviving. The true values are permanent, however the world may batter or ignore them. The poems of Athens outlive the spears of Sparta.

In the long run . . . it is a needed reassurance in our time. It means that we see the present in the light of past and future. We live in the present, are most immediately concerned with it, but we see it as no more than it is: a point at which the future instantly and mysteriously becomes the past, "the still point of the turning world." In the long run . . . it means the perspective of the educated mind which sees history as a cavalcade of events which is all eternity in passing a given point. Some minds are short-run minds, easily cast down. Some minds are long-run minds, indifferent to despair. The intelligent man or woman will not allow his mind to stop in the short-run present but will be constantly projecting it into the long-run future. In appraising human behavior, he will ask, "What is this act worth—in the long run?"

In the following pages we shall try to reach some long-run judgments about humanity. What values may we find that hold true through the thick and thin of experience? Are there enough true values here to justify a faith in life? Man lives his life but once. What is it worth, ultimately? We all know that it has its darker aspects, disloyalty and hate and cowardice and cruelty. But we cheat ourselves of our birthright of courage if we fail to give due weight to faith and love and charitableness. These qualities we shall find again and yet again in the profound and universal experiences of life, experiences which fill the essays, stories, poems, and plays of the ensuing pages.

I. FIRST PERSON SINGULAR

WE begin at the beginning. Out of mystery man appears. Present tense, first person singular—*I am*. But who am I? What is this Me that so insistently declares its identity, that straddles every page of the book of life? In our present questioning is the echo of all the askers who have gone before us. We will not be satisfied by the sound of our own voices. To the men and women of a scientific age there is no such thing as the Unknowable, there is only the Unknown.

But for a little blessed space of years, no doubts assail the child. He accepts his personality as he accepts the universe; in fact the two are much the same thing. About his ego revolve the stars in their courses; for his delight the sun rises and sets. For the universe is an exceedingly pleasant place, a place of games and devices, of impulses and dreams.

Already in your college years you are beginning to look back to your childhood with the wistfulness of age remembering youth. These things are relative. You don't have to be old to know that memory is one of the best things life affords. In memory the events of childhood stand out with special distinctness despite the romantic trappings with which we adorn them. These, of all memories, we would least readily let go. "In a world that is old and cold and bright with frost and stars, bliss is a little thing like a spark in the night, and the cozy and quiet folk are few—rabbits in their burrows, birds in their nests, and children in their beds. If one could draw a magic circle around their 'infant joy' and keep it young forever! . . . Who could desire to be very great that had the choice of being very little?"

How fragile yet immortal are these first years—this has been the burden of many a poet's song. The first chapters of an autobiography are usually the happiest. A man remembers the boyhood he used to know as the best that life had to give. Then the good moment goes.

Presently the time arrives when a child is suddenly conscious of the world outside himself, of the shapes of things in that world of reality. He may even, for an adolescent moment, think himself in love with another being. But this is passing fancy. The main business of his increasing years is still singular—the education of the self, a lonely business, after all.

And now here is college. All the values of youth are heightened and sharpened. If you are lucky you begin to see what it is all about, this process of living—how the present has grown out of the past and how the future is growing out of the present. College means many things to many minds, but to all it can mean this: a favored period when the main concern of earning a living can be postponed and a man or woman can adjust himself to the universe. Just outside the college gates is the world of things, where force wars against spirit. Within the college gates is the world of ideas, so protected from conflict that it is ever in danger of turning into a world of dreams. However much college life may once have encouraged the retreat from reality, it can no longer afford such a luxury. Today's student cannot forget that the true end of study is action. "Good thoughts," wrote Bacon, "are little better than good dreams except they be put in action." Education can only give you the ideas, facts, tools for living. Bit by bit you fit the pieces into the pattern of your future. Word by word you lay up the affirmations of wise men to overcome the denials of a lifetime. Day by day you build a long-run world in which action is sustained by knowledge. For action without knowledge lacks direction, just as knowledge without action lacks purpose.

College is a brief space of privilege when the outside world says to you, "Here, we'll leave you alone until you find yourself. Here is leisure to grow in. In God's name, make the most of it!"

E. B. White

E. B. White (1899-   ) was born in Mount Vernon, New York, and was educated at Cornell University. He joined the staff of The New Yorker *shortly after it was founded and for ten years contributed the miniature essays called "Talk of the Town." In 1938 a growing distrust of city life, with its neuroses, its false values, its worship of speed and hardness and glitter, drove him to abandon the metropolis he had so ably interpreted and move to a farm in Maine. His subsequent adventures on the soil have been told from time to time in essays marked by an unpretentious elegance and a disarming humor. In spite of the third personal pronoun, the spirit of the following essay is clearly first person singular. This is, literally, a personal essay.*

A BOY I KNEW

I AM quite sure that the character I'm least likely to forget is a boy I grew up with and nowadays see little of. I keep thinking about him. Once in a while I catch sight of him—down a lane, or just coming out of a men's washroom. Sometimes I will be gazing absently at my own son, now nine years old, and there in his stead this other boy will be, blindingly familiar yet wholly dreamlike and unapproachable. Although he enjoys a somewhat doubtful corporality, and occurs only occasionally, like a stitch in the side, without him I should indeed be lost. He is the boy that once was me.

The most memorable character in any man's life, and often the most inspiring, is the lad that once he was. I certainly can never forget him, and, at rare intervals when his trail crosses mine, the conjunction fills me with elation. Once, quite a while ago, I wrote a few verses which I put away in a folder to ripen. With the reader's kind permission I will exhume these lines now, because they explain briefly what I am getting at:

> In the sudden mirror in the hall
> I saw not my own self at all,
> I saw a most familiar face:
> My father stood there in my place,
> Returning, in the hall lamp's glare,
> My own surprised and watery stare.
> In thirty years my son shall see
> Not himself standing there, but me.

This bitter substitution, or transmigration, one generation with another, must be an experience which has disturbed men from the beginning of time. There comes a moment when you discover yourself in your father's shoes, saying his say, putting on his act, even looking as he looked; and in that moment everything is changed, because if you are your father, then your son must be you. Or something like that—it's never quite clear. But anyway you begin to think of this early or original self as someone apart, a separate character, not someone you once were but someone you once knew.

I remember once taking an overnight journey with my son in a Pullman compartment. He slept in the lower berth, handy to the instrument panel containing fan and light controls; I slept in the upper. Early in the morning I awoke and from my vantage point looked down. My boy had raised the shade a few inches and was ingesting the moving world. In that instant I encountered my unforgettable former self: it seemed as though it were I who was down there in the lower berth looking out of the train window just as the sky was growing light, absorbing the incredible wonder of fields, houses, bakery trucks, the before-breakfast world, tasting the sweetness and scariness of things seen and only half understood—the train penetrating the morning, the child penetrating the meaning of the morning and of the future. To this child the future was always like a high pasture, a little frightening, full of herds of steers and of intimations of wider prospects, of trysts with fate, of vague passionate culminations and the nearness to sky and to groves, of juniper smells and sweet-fern in a broiling noon sun. The future was one devil of a fine place, but it was a long while on the way.

This boy (I mean the one I can't forget) had a good effect on me. He was a cyclist and an early riser. Although grotesque in action, he was of noble design. He lived a life of enchantment; virtually everything he saw and heard was being seen and heard by him for the first time, so he gave it his whole attention. He took advantage of any slight elevation of ground or of spirit, and if there was a fence going his way, he mounted it and escaped the commonplace by a matter of four feet. I discovered in his company the satisfactions of life's interminable quest; he was always looking for something that had no name and no whereabouts, and not finding it. He either knew instinctively or he soon found out that seeking was more instructive than finding, that journeys were more rewarding than destinations. (I picked up a little of that from him, and have found it of some use.)

He was saddled with an unusual number of worries, it seems to me, but faith underlay them—a faith nourished by the natural world rather than by the supernatural or the spiritual. There was a lake, and at the water's edge a granite rock upholstered with lichen. This was his pew, and the sermon went on forever.

He traveled light, so that he was always ready for a change of pace or of direction and was in a position to explore any opportunity and become a part of any situation, unhampered. He spent an appalling amount of time in a semidormant state on curbstones, pier-heads, moles, stringpieces, carriage blocks, and porch steps, absorbing the anecdotes, logic and technique of artisans. He would travel miles to oversee a new piece of construction.

I remember this boy with affection, and feel no embarrassment in idealizing him. He himself was an idealist of shocking proportions. He had a fine capacity for melancholy and the gift of sadness. I never knew anybody on whose spirit the weather had such a devastating effect. A shift of wind, or of mood, could wither him. There would be times when a dismal sky conspired with a forlorn side street to create a moment of such profound bitterness that the world's accumulated sorrow seemed to gather in a solid lump in his heart. The appearance of a coasting hill softening in a thaw, the look of backyards along the railroad tracks on hot afternoons, the faces of people in trolley cars on Sunday—these could and did engulf him in a vast wave of depression. He dreaded Sunday afternoon because it had been deliberately written in a minor key.

He dreaded Sunday also because it was the day he spent worrying about going back to school on Monday. School was consistently frightening, not so much in realization as in anticipation. He went to school for sixteen years and was uneasy and full of dread the entire time—sixteen years of worrying that he would be called upon to speak a piece in the assembly hall. It was an amazing test of human fortitude. Every term was a nightmare of suspense.

The fear he had of making a public appearance on a platform seemed to find a perverse compensation, for he made frequent voluntary appearances in natural amphitheaters before hostile audiences, addressing himself to squalls and thunderstorms, rain and darkness, alone in rented canoes. His survival is something of a mystery, as he was neither very expert nor very strong. Fighting natural disturbances was the only sort of fighting he enjoyed. He would run five blocks to escape a boy who was after him, but he would stand up to any amount of punishment from the elements. He swam from the rocks of Hunter's Island, often at night, making his way there alone and afraid along the rough, dark trail from the end of the bridge (where the house was where they sold pie) up the hill and through the silent woods and across the marsh to the rocks. He hated bathing beaches and the smell of bathhouses, and would go to any amount of trouble to avoid the pollution of undressing in a stall.

This boy felt for animals a kinship he never felt for people. Against considerable opposition and with woefully inadequate equipment, he managed to provide himself with animals, so that he would never be without something to tend. He kept pigeons, dogs, snakes, polliwogs, turtles, rabbits, lizards, singing birds, chameleons, caterpillars and mice. The total number of hours he spent just standing watching animals, or refilling their water pans, would be impossible to estimate; and it would be hard to say what he got out of it. In spring he felt a sympathetic vibration with earth's renascence, and set a hen. He always seemed to be under some strange compulsion to assist the processes of incubation and germination, as though without him they might fail and the earth grow old and die. To him a miracle was essentially egg-shaped. (It occurs to me that his faith in animals has been justified by events of recent years: animals, by comparison with men, seem to have been conducting themselves with poise and dignity.)

In love he was unexcelled. His whole existence was a poem of tender and heroic adoration. He harbored delusions of perfection, and with consummate skill managed to weave the opposite sex into them, while keeping his distance. His search for beauty was always vaguely identified with his search for the ideal of love, and took him into districts which he would otherwise never have visited. Though I seldom see him these days, when I do I notice he still wears that grave inquiring expression as he peers into the faces of passers-by, convinced that some day he will find there the answer to his insistent question.

As I say, I feel no embarrassment in describing this character, because there is nothing personal in it—I have rather lost track of him and he has escaped me and is just a strange haunting memory, like the memory of love. I do not consider him in any way unusual or special; he was quite ordinary and had all the standard defects. They seem unimportant. It was his splendor that matters—the unforgettable splendor. No wonder I feel queer when I run into him. I guess all men do.

William Alexander Percy

William Alexander Percy (1885-1942) was born, lived, and died in Greenville, Mississippi. Lanterns on the Levee, published a month before his death, is the story of his life. Although he was never strong in body, Will Percy had a will that carried him through the University of the South and Harvard Law School, made him a Captain in World War I, led him to campaign for his father, a United States Senator, against the forces of the Klan, and made him dictator of flood relief when disaster struck his community. Author of four books of distinguished verse, he yet found time to operate a model plantation of 3,000 acres. His autobiography has made its way by the quiet distinction of its style and the inner flame of its writer's integrity. Mère and Père, referred to below, were his mother's parents, natives of New Orleans.

PLAYMATES

ANY little boy who was not raised with little Negro children might just as well not have been raised at all. My first boon-companion was Skillet, the small dark son of Mère's cook. He was the best crawfisher in the world and I was next. Instead of closed sewers our town had open ditches, which after an overflow swarmed with crawfish, small clear ones, quite shrimp-like, whose unexpected backward agility saved them from any except the most skilful hands, and large red ones, surly and whiskered, with a startling resemblance to the red-nosed old reprobates you saw around the saloons when you were looking for tobacco tags in the sawdust. When these rared back and held their claws wide apart, Skillet said they were saying: "Swear to God, white folks, I ain't got no tail." Theoretically it was for their tails that we hunted them, because when boiled and seasoned and prayed over they made that thick miraculous pink soup you never experience unless you have French blood in the family or unless you dine at Prunier's. Of course anyone could catch crawfish with a string and a lump of bacon, and anyone knows their family life is passed in holes, like snake-holes, from which they must be lured; but who except Skillet had ever observed that a hollow bone lying on the bottom of a ditch is bound to be occupied by one? Maybe he sat there as in a summerhouse thinking or catching a nap or saying to himself: "These boys will never think of this." If you waded up noiselessly and clapped both hands suddenly and simultaneously over both ends of the bone, he was yours and went into the bucket outraged and blowing bubbles, nothing appeased that his high destiny was to contribute his bit to a bisque d'écrevisses.

Skillet's sister Martha was a virago. Like Goneril she never reformed and so kept the plot boiling. She constantly threatened to do away with our crawfish in some low diabolical manner. This led to a painful incident. After an especially successful day we decided to hide from Martha our water-bucket brim-full of the simmering live catch and chose for that purpose an obscure corner behind the bookcase in Mère's parlor. Black fate decreed that on that very night Mère should give what was called a soirée. Now, the parlor was the hallowed place to receive guests, gay and beribboned and with splendid bustles. Fruit punch seemed to make them as lively as cocktails do now (I think Père spiked it). Mrs. Holland sang the Jewel Song from *Faust* and as an encore "Three Little Pigs Went to Market." Everyone said she should have joined the New Orleans Opera instead of marrying Mr. Holland, as obviously she would have had a succès fou in *Mignon* or *L'Africaine,* but Mother insisted she was a natural comédienne and would have been irresistible in *Orphée aux Enfers* or *Les Cloches de Corneville.* Then someone began playing dance music, which, if I recollect accurately, was as enticing and stimulating as the radio, but in a nice way, and without interpolations concerning liver pills and tooth paste. After the dancing, Mother and Mr. Harry Ball were to have sung a duet—they had "parlor voices, but sweet"—and it may have been sung, but I was not destined to hear it. At that moment a ladylike scream stopped the music and threw the gathering into consternation. Mrs. Holland had stepped on a large red crawfish in the attitude of "Swear to God, white folks." It made a crunchy sound. Another was discovered and another; they were all over the place. Mère was indignant, but Mother, though she retired me hastily, and in bad odor, really wanted to laugh. Skillet and I were in disgrace; Martha—need I say?—escaped unscathed.

Crawfishing was not Skillet's only excellence. As a conversationalist he outdistanced any white child in inventiveness, absurdity, and geniality. In Mère's back yard we would sit in a row-boat, a relic of the last overflow, and for hours ply imaginary oars toward an imaginary land that we described and embellished as we approached. These voyages afforded endless opportunity for discussions. One in particular drifts back to me across long years. It was one of those still, hot days when earth things lie tranced at the bottom of a deep sea of summer sun. We were resting on our oars at the moment. Far, far up buzzards circled dreamily, their black wings motionless, tilting, banking, coasting in wide arcs, somnambulistic symbols of the drowse and delight of deep summer. Watching them, Skillet observed in a singsong: "If they was to ever light, the world would burn up." As the birds seemed fixed at their vast altitude, this was a safe prophecy. But I was skeptical, as could have been expected of any horrid little white realist. Skillet, though, was so eloquent in citing reasons and authorities that my disbelief weakened and by degrees I was convinced, for the old excellent reason that I wanted to be. As we watched, the buzzards, careening and narrowing their circles, began to descend. It was exciting to see them drop lower and lower and to think what might happen. At last we could discern their horrible necks and heads. Skillet rose in a kind of ecstasy, thrusting out his arms, flexing his knees, and chanting: "Don't let 'em light, God, don't let 'em light." The flames of a consuming world were practically around us. Only the fire music as it came to Mime about the time Siegfried rushed in with the bear could have expressed our abject and delicious terror. They were hovering over our own back yard and, last touch of horror, there lay one of Mère's chickens dead—indeed, more than dead—their target, stark and untidy on the crust of the earth so unconcerned and so doomed. One of the ghastly creatures suddenly rocked, flapped its wings, and settled down awkwardly on the fence between us and the Fergusons'. "Look, I told you so, the world didn't burn up," I almost sobbed, torn between relief and disappointment. "He lit on a fence. He ain't never teched the ground," whispered Skillet. The buzzard gave an ungainly bound and landed on the too, too solid earth. "Look," I wailed. "He lit on a chip," Skillet observed affably. I was outraged.

Calling to mind with gratitude those to whom we are indebted on our journey is not only a sort of piety, but one of the few pleasures that endure without loss of luster to the end. I like to imagine that Skillet is not in jail or dead, but that he lords it in a Pullman car or pulpit, or perhaps has a farm of his own and many little crawfishers—in fine, that the swooping dark wings continue for him to light on a chip. He is all my memory records of what must have been long months of my childhood; all others it seems were lay figures.

Equally treasurable were Amelia's children on Aunt Nana's farm in Virginia, where I was deposited so many summers. I don't remember the house well except that it was square, airy, and very old, with a corridor behind leading to the kitchen, storerooms, and Amelia's sleeping-quarters; the old furniture and woodwork made no impression whatever. All around were cornfields and dabs of woods, and a few hundred yards in front the small cool river. I must have seen it rain there often, but like a sun-dial I remember only sunlight, acres and acres of it: sometimes merely pale and fresh and still on the pasture; or heavy like a great depth of blue sea-water on the undulating rows of corn, which, tired of the weight, sagged limply; or in splotches and scarves and sudden widths of glitter on the river; or, best, early in the morning, when it slanted in long gray panels through the orchard and barely silvered the small yellow pears with a sweat of cold dew on them and dew on the grass where they lay. Quantities of little wiggly paths, cow-paths likely, meandered everywhere and nowhere, bordered by straggling colonies of tawny lilies and bushes of pokeberry, indispensable for war-paint on our Indian days. They too were sunny, but managed to make every patch of shade a port of call, and two of them met in the little wood where an old fox-grape vine with the kindliness and humor of old age crooked one arm into a perfect swing. The swing itself would be in shadow, of the breezy arrowy kind, all shreds and patches on you as you swung through it, but you looked out from under the branches across all that shining clearness that lay on the fields and the aspen woodland to the old house far off to the left, and you knew you needed nothing else. When your peace is without grayness, it comes seldom and does not stay long; some are still hunting for it and some are trying to find it again, but know they won't.

At Aunt Nana's there were so many fascinating spots you couldn't make the round of them in a week, and all of them smelled good. The dairy, round, with thick walls and no windows, where the crocks of milk and clabber and cream stood in live spring-water, smelled cold and slightly sour. The corn-bin had a warm yellow smell like a loaf of bread at the moment Amelia opened the oven and pawed it out with the edge of her apron. The barn, from the pile of manure in front (which Père said Uncle George was too lazy to scatter over the fields, and it was beautiful manure) to the stalls, soggy with corn-shucks and urine, had an exciting smell, like autumn, but the smell was definitely good. Of course the kitchen was so full of things to whiff and sniff and inhale with eyes closed that you could stay there all day, only you were always being shooed out, on lucky occasions with the batter-bowl to lick. The best smell, however, was undoubtedly at the mill. That mill was none of your modern contraptions, spotless and intricate and unintelligible. You saw how it worked when it worked, which was occasionally. There was the dam, and the mill-pond above and behind it; there was the huge water-wheel which sloshed and turned when the sluice was opened; there were the great millstones, likely the very ones the gods used to use, between which the corn filtered to its golden doom; and there was the miller, a bit sweaty and covered with a lovely creamy dust of meal, especially his eyebrows and mustache. Sometimes I was allowed to ride behind Reuben when he took a sack of corn to be ground. We would wait till the resulting sack of meal was ready to be put over the pommel and jogged home to Amelia, by her to be manipulated into corn-pones of unspeakable crunchiness and savor. The meal would be still damp and warm when turned over to us, and it was hard not to eat it raw, like chickens, so rich and sweet and really fundamental it smelled.

Reuben was too old to be interesting, perhaps eighteen, but Amelia's children—Ligey, Martha, Cora, Friday, and a few more I've forgotten—

were exactly the right ages. They seem to have arrived precisely a year apart and all were dark, but some were darker, and no two of them looked alike. I often wondered who and where their father was, and once put the question to Aunt Nana, but she developed one of those little attacks of hurry and said, as well as I could gather, he was a traveling man. However, it must have been a fine father or set of fathers, because they were fine children and as playmates perfection. Small satyrs and fauns could not have been more instructive or resourceful or absurd.

We harried the hillsides for arrow-heads and found many splendid ones—training I found invaluable years later when between showers I hunted sea-shells in Bora-Bora. Sometimes we spent days on end in full flight from a murderous band of gypsies. Cora's cries on one occasion when she was almost captured were so blood-curdling we rushed off down the road and abandoned her to her fate, quite forgetting the plot she furthered with such histrionic fervor. Friday had a genius for discovering hornet-nests. Silvery and rather Burmese in design, one would be hanging on a tree conveniently low, its irascible inmates in a stew and a lather, storming in and out. Led by Friday, we would approach as near as we dared and let fly our barrage against the patiently built castle of the poor earnest insects. But they, un-advised of the other-cheek doctrine we have so long been beseeching one another to follow, would sally forth in the best modern echelon formation, armed to the tip, and we, sounding precipitate and individual retreat, would scatter yowling. If someone was not badly stung, to be borne lamenting loudly to Amelia's soda and scarifying invective, it was a disappointing adventure.

In our milder moods the river was a favorite haunt. It was the right sort of river. With the dam closed, it could be waded and was all pools and trickles and slimy shelving rocks. Although not scorning such lesser quarry as eels, leeches, water-snakes, and frogs, our constant ambition was to dis-cover a giant sturgeon. This ambition was unlikely but not impossible of fulfillment, because one had found its way into our river as a result of the Johnstown flood and we had seen it with our own eyes hanging from the ceiling of the tool-house, its tail sweeping the floor, glittering in the lamp-light, magnificent even in death. We noticed when it was split open that with just a little more room Jonah could have sat inside. We discussed this and kindred issues for days afterwards.

During one of these theological sessions I swallowed a persimmon seed. Doctors had recently discovered appendicitis, attributed it to the swallowing of a seed, and considered it fatal. Solemn with this medical erudition, I explained the grisly situation and announced my approaching demise. All accepted the news with delight and prepared for the end. I lay on the ground and my faithful retainers knelt around me, in the manner of sundry ver-sions of the Assumption of the Virgin. I closed my eyes, and fervent prayers rose loudly. Nothing happened. Nothing ever did happen. Reviving was undignified and bitterly disappointing to all concerned. As a corpse I was a fiasco, but as mourners my colored entourage displayed genius. Racially they are the best diers in the world anyway: they put more force and enthusiasm into the scene, being seriously aware it is the climax of the show, their curtain. If Friday had swallowed my persimmon seed, he would beyond question have died outright and to perfection, although it's a role one can't rehearse.

So many things to do and each summer so short. To chase rats in the barn, a dangerous and slightly sickening enterprise; to teach the kitten to play circus (our cats were Manx, with stubs for tails and bouncing rabbit motions); to climb the roof of the corridor and watch the ducks file out to the pond, cracking dry mirthless jokes to one another and sometimes laying an egg, shamelessly and without stopping, on the bare ground with no thought of a nest; to be allowed to help with the cider press where all the apples with a rotten spot, those claimed and contended for by the yellow-jackets, disappeared into the hopper and gushed out the sides in a seethe of bubbly brown liquor, fit for Ceres; to hunt in the mold of the wood-pile for the turquoise bits that were fox-fire and find instead a land-terrapin closed up safe from the mad world in his neat hinged box, and to devise means to make him come out—so many things to do, and summer so short.

Supervised play and summer camps came after my time. I missed learning the principles of team work and many games which must be helpful if you can think of nothing to do. Instead, Friday's accent, Cora's intonation, and Ligey's grammatical uses contaminated beyond hope of purification the wells of what should have been my pure English undefiled. That was their only evil influence. Of nastiness and bad manners they taught me nothing; older boys of my own color and caste were later to be my instructors in those subjects. From Amelia's children I learned not only gaiety and casualness and inventiveness, but the possibility that mere living may be delightful and that natural things which we ignore unless we call them scenery are pleasant to move among and gracious to recall. Without them it would probably never have occurred to me that to climb an aspen sapling in a gale is one of those ultimate experiences, like experiencing God or love, that you need never try to remember because you can never forget. Aspens grow together in little woods of their own, straight, slender, and white. Even in still weather they twinkle and murmur, but in a high wind you must run out and plunge among them, spattered with sunlight, to the very center. Then select your tree and climb it high enough for it to begin to wobble with your weight. Rest your foot-weight lightly on the frail branches and do most of your clinging with your arms. Now let it lunge, and gulp the wind. It will be all over you, slapping your hair in your eyes, stinging your face with bits of bark and stick, tugging to break your hold, roaring in your open mouth like a monster sea-shell. The trees around you will thrash and seethe, their white undersides lashed about like surf, and sea-music racing through them. You will be beaten and bent and buffeted about and the din will be so terrific your throat will invent a song to add to the welter, pretty barbaric, full of yells and long calls. You will feel what it is to be the Lord God and ride a hurricane; you will know what it is to have leaves sprout from your toes and finger-tips, with satyrs and tigers and hounds in pursuit; you will never need again to drown under the crash of a maned wave in spume and splendor and thunder, with the white stallions of the sea around you, neighing and pawing. That must have been the very wood old Housman had in mind when he sang "We'll to the woods no more." But when he found his way to it he was alone, and it was autumn.

H. L. Mencken

As we gather from the following flavorsome account, Henry Louis Mencken (1880-   ) grew up in Baltimore. He still lives there, in the house where, at the age of three, he was just emerging from "the unfathomable abyss of nonentity"—a fate which he has been conspicuously successful in avoiding ever since. Through his long association with the Baltimore Evening Sun *and the* American Mercury *he has stamped his personality and opinions on the consciousness of the reading public. Although he assures us that "I have no purpose in writing save to express my own ego," his works wage a relentless war on middle-class inanities. Yet his insurgent manner disguises a basic conservatism, especially in politics. In* The American Language *he has made an impressive study of American word-ways without ever being guilty of dullness or pedantry.*

INTRODUCTION TO THE UNIVERSE

AT the instant I first became aware of the cosmos we all infest I was sitting in my mother's lap and blinking at a great burst of lights, some of them red and others green, but most of them only the bright yellow of flaring gas. The time: the evening of Thursday, September 13, 1883, which was the day after my third birthday. The place: a ledge outside the second-story front windows of my father's cigar factory at 368 Baltimore street, Baltimore, Maryland, U. S. A., fenced off from space and disaster by a sign bearing the majestic legend: *Aug. Mencken & Bro.* The occasion: the third and last annual Summer Nights' Carnival of the Order of

Orioles, a society that adjourned *sine die,* with a thumping deficit, the very next morning, and has since been forgotten by the whole human race.

At that larval stage of my life, of course, I knew nothing whatever about the Order of Orioles, just as I knew nothing whatever about the United States, though I had been born to their liberties, and was entitled to the protection of their army and navy. All I was aware of, emerging from the unfathomable abyss of nonentity, was the fact that the world I had just burst into seemed to be very brilliant, and that peeping at it over my father's sign was somewhat hard on my still gelatinous bones. So I made signals of distress to my mother and was duly hauled into her lap, where I first dozed and then snored away until the lights went out, and the family buggy wafted me home, still asleep.

The latter details, you will understand, I learned subsequently from historians, but I remember the lights with great clarity, and entirely on my own. They constitute not only the earliest of all my earthly recollections, but also one of my most vivid, and I take no stock in the theories of psychologists who teach that events experienced so early in life are never really recalled, but only reconstructed from family gossip. To be sure, there is a dead line beyond which even the most grasping memory does not reach, but I am sure that in my own case it must have run with my third birthday. Ask me if I recall the occasion, probably before my second, when I was initiated into the game of I-spy by a neighbor boy, and went to hide behind a wire screen, and was astonished when he detected me—ask me about that, and I'll admit freely that I recall nothing of it whatever, but only the ensuing anecdote, which my poor mother was so fond of telling that in the end I hid in the cellar every time she started it. Nor do I remember anything on my own about my baptism (at which ceremonial my father, so I have heard, made efforts to get the rector tight, and was hoist by his own petard), for I was then but a few months old. But not all the psychologists on earth, working in shifts like coal-miners, will ever convince me that I don't remember those lights, and wholly under my own steam.

They made their flash and then went out, and the fog again closed down. I don't recall moving to the new house in Hollins street that was to be my home for so many years, though we took possession of it only a few weeks later. I don't recall going into pants at about a quarter to four years, though it must have been a colossal experience, full of pride and glory. But gradually, as my consciousness jelled, my days began to be speckled with other events that, for one reason or another, stuck. I recall, though only somewhat vaguely, the deck of an excursion-boat, *circa* 1885, its deafening siren, and the wide, gray waters of Chesapeake Bay. I recall very clearly being taken by my father to a clothing-store bright with arc-lights, then a novelty in the world, and seeing great piles of elegant Sunday suits, and coming home with one that was tight across the stern. I recall a straw hat with flowing ribbons, a cat named Pinkie, and my brother Charlie, then still a brat in long clothes, howling like a catamount one hot Summer night, while my mother dosed him with the whole pharmacopoeia of the house, and frisked him for outlaw pins. I recall, again, my introduction to the wonderland of science, with an earthworm (*Lumbricus terrestris*) as my first subject, and the experiment directed toward finding out how long it would take him, laid out in the sun on the backyard walk, to fry to death. And I recall my mother reading to me, on a dark Winter afternoon, out of a book describing the adventures of the Simple Simon who went to a fair, the while she sipped a cup of tea that smelled very cheerful, and I glued my nose to the frosty window pane, watching a lamplighter light the lamps in Union Square across the street and wondering what a fair might be. It was a charming, colorful, Kate Greenaway world that her reading took me into, and to this day I can shut my eyes and still see its little timbered houses, its boys and girls gamboling on village greens, and its unclouded skies of pale blue.

I was on the fattish side as an infant, with a scow-like beam and noticeable jowls. Dr. C. L. Buddenbohn, who fetched me into sentience at 9 P.M., precisely, of Sunday, September 12, 1880, apparently made a good (though, as I hear, somewhat rough) job of it, despite the fact that his surviving bill, dated October 2, shows that all he charged "to one confinement" was ten dollars. The science of infant feeding, in those days, was as rudimentary as bacteriology or social justice, but there can be no doubt that I got plenty of calories and vitamins, and probably even an overdose. There is a photograph of me at eighteen months which looks like the pictures the milk companies print in the rotogravure sections of the Sunday papers, whooping up the zeal of their cows. If cannibalism had not been abolished in Maryland some years before my birth I'd have butchered beautifully.

My mother used to tell me years afterward that my bulk often attracted public notice, especially when it was set off dramatically against her own lack of it, for she was of slight frame and less than average height, and looked, in her blue-eyed blondness, to be even younger than she actually was. Once, hauling me somewhere by horse-car, she was confronted by an old man who gaped at her and me for a while with senile impertinence, and then burst out: "Good God, girl, is that baby *yours?*" This adiposity passed off as I began to run about, and from the age of six onward I was rather skinny, but toward the end of my twenties my cross-section again became a circle, and at thirty I was taking one of the first of the anti-fat cures, and beating it by sly resorts to malt liquor.

My gradually accumulating and clarifying memories of infancy have to do chiefly with the backyard in Hollins street, which had the unusual length, for a yard in a city block, of a hundred feet. Along with my brother Charlie, who followed me into this vale when I was but twenty months old,

I spent most of my pre-school leisure in it, and found it a strange, wild land of endless discoveries and enchantments. Even in the dead of Winter we were pastured in it almost daily, bundled up in the thick, scratchy coats, overcoats, mittens, leggings, caps, shirts, over-shirts and under-drawers that the young then wore. We wallowed in the snow whenever there was any to wallow in, and piled it up into crude houses, forts and snow-men, and inscribed it with wavering scrolls and devices by the method followed by infant males since the Würm Glaciation. In Spring we dug worms and watched for robins, in Summer we chased butterflies and stoned sparrows, and in Autumn we made bonfires of the falling leaves. At all times from March to October we made a Dust Bowl of my mother's garden.

The Hollins street neighborhood, in the eighties, was still almost rural, for there were plenty of vacant lots near by, and the open country began only a few blocks away. Across the street from our house was the wide green of Union Square, with a fishpond, a cast-iron Greek temple housing a drinking-fountain, and a little brick office and tool-house for the square-keeper, looking almost small enough to have been designed by Chick Sale. A block to the westward, and well within range of our upstairs windows, was the vast, mysterious compound of the House of the Good Shepherd, with nuns in flapping habits flitting along its paths and alleys, and a high stone wall shutting it in from the world. In our backyard itself there were a peach tree, a cherry tree, a plum tree, and a pear tree. The pear tree survives to this day and is still as lush and vigorous as it was in 1883, beside being thirty feet higher and so large around the waist that its branches bulge into the neighboring yards. My brother and I used to begin on the cherries when they were still only pellets of hard green, and had got through three or four powerful bellyaches before the earliest of them was ripe. The peaches, pears and plums came later in the year, but while we were waiting for them we chewed the gum that oozed from the peach-tree trunk, and practiced spitting the imbedded flies and June bugs at Pinkie the cat.

There was also a grape-arbor arching the brick walk, with six vines that flourished amazingly, and produced in the Autumn a huge crop of sweet Concord grapes. My brother and I applied ourselves to them diligently from the moment the first blush of color showed on them, and all the sparrows of West Baltimore helped, but there was always enough in the end to fill a couple of large dishpans, and my mother and the hired girl spent a hot afternoon boiling them down and storing them away in glass tumblers with tin tops. My brother and I, for some reason or other, had no fancy for the grape jelly thus produced with so much travail, but we had to eat it all Winter, for it was supposed, like camomile tea, to be good for us. I don't recall any like embalming of the peaches, plums and pears; in all probability we got them all down before there were any ripe enough to preserve. The grapes escaped simply because some of them hung high, as in the fable of the fox. In later years we collared these high ones by steeple-jacking, and so paid for escape from the jelly with a few additional bellyaches.

But the show-piece of the yard was not the grape-arbor, nor even the fruit-trees; it was the Summer-house, a rococo structure ten feet by ten in area, with a high, pointed roof covered with tin, a wooden floor, an ornate railing, and jig-saw spirals wherever two of its members came together. This Summer-house had been designed and executed by my mother's father, our Grandfather Abhau, who was a very skillful cabinet-maker and had also made some of the furniture of the house. Everything of his construction was built to last, and when, far on in the Twentieth Century, I hired a gang of house-wreckers to demolish the Summer-house, they sweated half a day with their crowbars and pickaxes. In the eighties it was the throne-room and justice-seat of the household, at least in Summer. There, on fair Sunday mornings, my father and his brother Henry, who lived next door, met to drink beer, try out new combinations of tobacco for their cigar factory, and discuss the credit of customers and the infamies of labor agitators. And there, on his periodical visitations as head of the family, my Grandfather Mencken sat to determine all the delicate questions within his jurisdiction.

My mother was an active gardener, and during her forty-two years in Hollins street must have pulled at least a million weeds. For this business, as I first recall her, she had a uniform consisting of a long gingham apron and an old-time slat-bonnet—a headdress that went out with the Nineteenth Century. Apron and slat-bonnet hung on nails behind the kitchen door, and on a shelf adjoining were her trowels, shears and other such tools, including always a huge ball of twine. My brother Charlie and I, as we got on toward school age, were drafted to help with the weeding, but neither of us could ever make out any difference between weeds and non-weeds, so we were presently transferred to the front of the house, where every plant that came up between the cobblestones of Hollins street was indubitably verminous. The crop there was always large, and keeping it within bounds was not an easy job. We usually tackled it with broken kitchen knives, and often cut our hands. We disliked it so much that it finally became convict labor. That is to say, it was saved up for use as punishment. I recall only that the maximum penalty was one hour, and that this was reserved for such grave offenses as stealing ginger-snaps, climbing in the pear-tree, hanging up the cat by its hind leg, or telling lies in a gross and obvious manner.

Charlie was somewhat sturdier than I, and a good deal fiercer. During most of our childhood he could lick me in anything approximating a fair fight, or, at all events, stall me. Civil war was forbidden in Hollins street, but my Grandfather Mencken, who lived in Fayette street, only three blocks away, had no apparent objection to it, save of course when he was taking his afternoon nap. I remember a glorious day when eight or ten head of his grandchildren called on him at once, and began raising hell at once. The affair started as a more or less decorous pillow-fight, but proceeded quickly to much more formidable weapons, including even bed-slats. It ranged all over the house, and must have done a considerable damage to the bric-a-brac, which was all in the Middle Bismarck mode. My grandmother and Aunt Pauline, fixed by my grandfather's pale blue eye, pretended to be amused by it for a while, but when a large china thunder-mug came bouncing down the third-story stairs and a black hair-cloth sofa in the parlor lost a leg they horned in with loud shrieks and lengths of stove-wood, and my grandfather called time.

Charlie and I were very fond of Aunt Pauline, who was immensely hospitable, and the best doughnut cook in all the Baltimores. When the creative urge seized her, which was pretty often, she would make enough doughnuts to fill a large tin wash-boiler, and then send word down to Hollins street that there was a surprise waiting in Fayette street. It was uphill all the way, but Charlie and I always took it on the run, holding hands and pretending that we were miraculously dashing car-horses. We returned home an hour or so later much more slowly, and never had any appetite for supper. The immemorial tendency of mankind to concoct rituals showed itself in these feasts. After Charlie had got down his first half dozen doughnuts, and was taking time out to catch his breath and scrape the grease and sugar off his face, Aunt Pauline would always ask "How do they taste?" and he would always answer "They taste like more." Whether this catechism was original with the high contracting parties or had been borrowed from some patent-medicine almanac or other reference-work I don't know, but it never varied and it was never forgotten.

There were no kindergartens, playgrounds or other such Devil's Islands for infants in those innocent days, and my brother and I roved and rampaged at will until we were ready for school. Hollins street was quite safe for children, for there was little traffic on it, and that little was slow-moving, and a cart approaching over the cobblestones could be heard a block away. The backyard was enough for us during our earliest years, with the cellar in reserve for rainy days, but we gradually worked our way into the street and then across it to Union Square, and there we picked up all the games then prevailing. A few years ago, happening to cross the square, I encountered a ma'm in horn-rimmed spectacles teaching a gang of little girls ring-around-a-rosy. The sight filled me suddenly with so black an indignation that I was tempted to grab the ma'm and heave her into the goldfish pond. In the days of my own youth no bossy female on the public payroll was needed to teach games to little girls. They taught one another—as they had been doing since the days of Neanderthal Man.

Nevertheless, there was a constant accretion of novelty, at least in detail. When we boys chased Indians we were only following the Sumerian boys who chased Akkadians, but the use of hatchets was certainly new, and so was the ceremony of scalping; moreover, our fiends in human form, Sitting Bull and Rain-in-the-Face, had been as unknown and unimagined to the Sumerian boys as Henry Ward Beecher or John L. Sullivan. The group songs we sang were mainly of English provenance, but they had all degenerated with the years. Here, precisely, is what we made of "King William" in Hollins street, *circa* 1885:

> King William was King James's son;
> Upon a ri' a race he won;
> Upon his breast he wore a star,
> The which was called the life of war.

What a ri' was we never knew and never inquired, nor did we attach any rational concept to *the life of war*. A favorite boys' game, called "Playing Se*bast*apool" (with a heavy accent on the *bast*), must have been no older in its outward form than the Crimean War, for Sebastapool was plainly Sevastopol, but in its essence it no doubt came down from Roman times. It could be played only when building or paving was going on in the neighborhood, and a pile of sand lay conveniently near. We would fashion this sand into circular ramparts in some friendly gutter, and then bristle the ramparts with gaudy tissue-paper flags, always home-made. Their poles were slivers of firewood, and their tissue-paper came from Newton's toy store at Baltimore and Calhoun streets, which served the boys and girls of West Baltimore for seventy years, and did not shut down at last until the Spring of 1939. The hired girls of the block cooked flour paste to fasten the paper to the poles.

To the garrison of a Sebastapool all the smaller boys contributed tin soldiers, including Indians. These soldiers stood in close and peaceful ranks, for there was never any attempt at attack or defense. They were taken in at night by their owners, but the flags remained until rain washed the Sebastapool away, or the milkman's early morning horse squashed it. There were sometimes two or three in a block. Girls took a hand in making the flags, but they were not allowed to pat the ramparts into shape, or to touch the tin soldiers. Indeed, for a little girl of that era to show any interest in military affairs would have been as indecorous as for her to play leap-frog or chew tobacco. The older boys also kept rather aloof though they stood ready to defend a Sebastapool against raiders. Tin soldiers were only for the very young. The more elderly were beyond such inert and puerile simulacra, which ranked with rag dolls and paper boats. These elders fought in person, and went armed.

In the sacred rubbish of the family there is a specimen of my handwriting dated 1883—two signatures on a sheet of paper now turned a dismal brown, the one small and rather neat and the other large and ornamented with flourishes. They seem somehow fraudulent, for I was then but three years old, but there they are, and the date, which is in my mother's hand, is very clear. Maybe she guided my stubby fingers. In the same collection there is another specimen dated January 1, 1887. It shows a beginning ease with the pen, though hardly much elegance. My mother also taught me many other humble crafts—for example, how to drive a nail, how to make paper boats, and how to sharpen a lead pencil. She even taught me how to thread a needle, and for a time I hoped to take over darning my own stockings and patching the seats of my own pants, but I never managed to master the use of the thimble, and so I had to give up. Tying knots was another art that stumped me. To this day I can't tie a bow tie, though I have taken lessons over and over again from eminent masters, including such wizards as Joe Hergesheimer and Paul Patterson. When I go to a party someone has to tie my tie for me. Not infrequently I arrive with the ends hanging, and must appeal to my hostess.

This incapacity for minor dexterities has pursued me all my life, often to my considerable embarrassment. In school I could never learn to hold a pen in the orthodox manner: my handwriting satisfied the professors, but my stance outraged them, and I suffered some rough handling until they finally resigned me to my own devices. In later life I learned bricklaying, and also got some fluency in rough carpentering, but I could never do anything verging upon cabinet-work. Thus I inherited nothing of the skill of my Grandfather Abhau. All my genes in that field came from my father, who was probably the most incompetent man with his hands ever seen on earth. I can't recall him teaching me anything in my infancy, not even marbles. He would sometimes brag of his youthful virtuosity at all the customary boys' games, but he always added that he had grown so old (he was thirty-one when I was six) and suffered so much from dead beats, noisy children and ungrateful cigarmakers, drummers and bookkeepers that he had lost it. Nor could he match the endless stories that my mother told me in the years before I could read, or the many songs. The only song I ever heard him sing was this one:

> Rain forty days,
> Rain forty nights,
> Sauerkraut sticking out the smokestack.

Apparently there were additional words, but if so he never sang them. The only Märchen in his repertoire had to do with a man who built a tin bridge. I recall nothing of this tale save the fact that the bridge was of tin, which astonished my brother and me all over again every time we heard of it. We tried to figure out how such a thing was possible, for the mention of tin naturally made us think of tomato-cans. But we never learned.

Archibald MacLeish

Archibald MacLeish (1892-   ) was born in Glencoe, Illinois; was educated in New England; and attended Yale and the Harvard Law School. After a brief law practice he went abroad for five years during which he was constantly traveling, reading, and writing poetry. Since his return to the United States in 1928 he has visited Mexico to collect material for Conquistador, *has been an editor of* Fortune, Librarian of Congress, and in 1944 was appointed Assistant Secretary of State. His poems show an interesting course of growth, from the subjective lyricism of "Eleven" or " 'Not Marble nor the Gilded Monuments' " to the intense social consciousness of "Speech to a Crowd" or "The Western Sky."*

ELEVEN

And summer mornings the mute child, rebellious,
Stupid, hating the words, the meanings, hating
The Think now, Think, the O but Think! would leave
On tiptoe the three chairs on the verandah
And crossing tree by tree the empty lawn
Push back the shed door and upon the sill
Stand pressing out the sunlight from his eyes
And enter and with outstretched fingers feel
The grindstone and behind it the bare wall
And turn and in the corner on the cool
Hard earth sit listening. And one by one,
Out of the dazzled shadow in the room
The shapes would gather, the brown plowshare, spades,
Mattocks, the polished helves of picks, a scythe
Hung from the rafters, shovels, slender tines
Glinting across the curve of sickles—shapes
Older than men were, the wise tools, the iron
Friendly with earth. And sit there quiet, breathing
The harsh dry smell of withered bulbs, the faint
Odor of dung, the silence. And outside
Beyond the half-shut door the blind leaves
And the corn moving. And at noon would come,
Up from the garden, his hard crooked hands
Gentle with earth, his knees still earth-stained, smelling

22

Of sun, of summer, the old gardener, like
A priest, like an interpreter, and bend
Over his baskets.
                    And they would not speak:
They would say nothing. And the child would sit there
Happy as though he had no name, as though
He had been no one: like a leaf, a stem,
Like a root growing—

William Saroyan

William Saroyan (1908-   ) is rather closely related to Aram Garo-ghlanian, the irresponsible Armenian brat whose adventures he tells in My Name Is Aram. *Nobody knows where one ends and the other begins. Saroyan was born in California, the son of an Armenian immigrant. Given only a public school education he has made himself, by sheer industry and impudence, one of the most discussed writers of the day. His stories are obviously no more than impromptus, and sometimes they are inexcusably less; yet his best work achieves a careless comedy and a mad vitality that override criticism.*

THE CIRCUS

ANY time a circus used to come to town, that was all me and my old pal Joey Renna needed to make us run hog-wild, as the saying is. All we needed to do was see the signs on the fences and in the empty store windows to start going to the dogs and neglecting our educations. All we needed to know was that a circus was on its way to town for me and Joey to start wanting to know what good a little education ever did anybody anyway.

After the circus *reached* town we were just no good at all. We spent all our time down at the trains, watching them unload the animals, walking out Ventura Avenue with the wagons with lions and tigers in them and hanging around the grounds, trying to win the favor of the animal men, the workers, the acrobats, and the clowns.

The circus was everything everything else we knew wasn't. It was adventure, travel, danger, skill, grace, romance, comedy, peanuts, popcorn, chewing-gum and soda-water. We used to carry water to the elephants and stand around afterwards and try to seem associated with the whole magnificent affair, the putting up of the big tent, the getting everything in order, and the worldly-wise waiting for the people to come and spend their money.

One day Joey came tearing into the classroom of the fifth grade at Emerson School ten minutes late, and without so much as removing his hat or trying to explain his being late, shouted, Hey, Aram, what the hell are you doing here? The circus is in town.

And sure enough I'd forgotten. I jumped up and ran out of the room with poor old Miss Flibety screaming after me, Aram Garoghlanian, you stay in this room. Do you hear me, Aram Garoghlanian?

I heard her all right and I knew what my not staying would mean. It would mean another powerful strapping from old man Dawson. But I couldn't help it. I was just crazy about a circus.

I been looking all over for you, Joey said in the street. What happened?

I forgot, I said. I knew it was coming all right, but I forgot it was today. How far along are they?

I was at the trains at five, Joey said. I been out at the grounds since seven. I had breakfast at the circus table. Boy, it was good.

Honest, Joey? I said. How were they?

They're all swell, Joey said. Couple more years, they told me, and I'll be ready to go away with them.

As what? I said. Lion-tamer, or something like that?

I guess maybe not as a lion-tamer, Joey said. I figure more like a work-man till I learn about being a clown or something, I guess. I don't figure I could work with lions right away.

We were out on Ventura Avenue, headed for the circus grounds, out near the County Fairgrounds, just north of the County Hospital.

Boy, what a breakfast, Joey said. Hot-cakes, ham and eggs, sausages, coffee. Boy.

Why didn't you tell me? I said.

I thought you knew, Joey said. I thought you'd be down at the trains same as last year. I would have told you if I knew you'd forgotten. What made you forget?

I don't know, I said. Nothing, I guess.

I was wrong there, but I didn't know it at the time. I hadn't really forgotten. What I'd done was *remembered*. I'd gone to work and remembered the strapping Dawson gave me last year for staying out of school the day the circus was in town. That was the thing that had kind of kept me sleeping after four-thirty in the morning when by rights I should have been up and dressing and on my way to the trains. It was the memory of that strapping old man Dawson had given me, but I didn't know it at the time. We used to take them strappings kind of for granted, me and Joey, on account of we wanted to be fair and square with the Board of Education and if it was against the rules to stay out of school when you weren't sick, and if you were supposed to get strapped for doing it, well, there we were, we'd done it, so let the Board of Education balance things the best way they knew how. They did that with a strapping. They used to threaten to send me and Joey to Reform School but they never did it.

Circus? old man Dawson used to say. I see. *Circus*. Well, bend down, boy.

So, first Joey, then me, would bend down and old man Dawson would get some powerful shoulder exercise while we tried not to howl. We wouldn't howl for five or six licks, but after that we'd howl like Indians coming. They used to be able to hear us all over the school and old man Dawson, after our visits got to be kind of regular, urged us politely to try to make a little less noise, inasmuch as it was a school and people were trying to study.

It ain't fair to the others, old man Dawson said. They're trying to learn something for themselves.

We can't help it, Joey said. It hurts.

That I know, old man Dawson said, but it seems to me there's such a thing as modulation. I believe a lad can overdo his howling if he ain't thoughtful of others. Just try to modulate that awful howl a little. I think you can do it.

Then he gave Joey a strapping of twenty and Joey tried his best not to howl so loud. After the strapping his face was very red and old man Dawson was very tired.

How was that? Joey said.

That was better, old man Dawson said. By far the most courteous you've managed yet.

I did my best, Joey said.

I'm grateful to you, old man Dawson said.

He was tired and out of breath. I moved up to the chair in front of him that he furnished during these matters to help us suffer the stinging pain. I got in the right position and he said, Wait a minute, Aram. Give a man a chance to get his breath. I'm not twenty-three years old. I'm *sixty*-three. Let me rest a minute.

All right, I said, but I sure would like to get this over with.

Don't howl too loud, he said. Folks passing by in the street are liable to think this is a veritable chamber of tortures. Does it really hurt that much?

You can ask Joey, I said.

How about it, Joey? old man Dawson said. Aren't you lads exaggerating just a little? Perhaps to impress someone in your room? Some girl, perhaps?

We don't howl to impress anybody, Mr. Dawson, Joey said. We wouldn't howl if we could help it. Howling makes us feel ashamed, doesn't it, Aram?

It's awfully embarrassing to go back to our seats in our room after howling that way, I said. We'd rather not howl if we could help it.

Well, old man Dawson said, I'll not be unreasonable. I'll only ask you to try to modulate it a little.

I'll do my best, Mr. Dawson, I said. Got your breath back?

Give me just a moment longer, Aram, Mr. Dawson said.

When he got his breath back he gave me my twenty and I howled a little louder than Joey and then we went back to class. It was awfully embarrassing. Everybody was looking at us.

Well, Joey said, what did you expect? The rest of you would fall down and die if you got twenty. You wouldn't *howl a little,* you'd die.

That'll be enough out of you, Miss Flibety said.

Well, it's true, Joey said. They're all scared. A circus comes to town and what do they do? They come to school. They don't go out to the circus.

That'll be enough, Miss Flibety said.

Who do they think they are, giving us dirty looks? Joey said.

Miss Flibety lifted her hand, hushing Joey.

Now the circus was back in town, another year had gone by, it was April again, and we were on our way out to the grounds. Only this time it was worse than ever because they'd seen us at school and knew we were going out to the circus.

Do you think they'll send Stafford after us? I said.

Stafford was truant officer.

We can always run, Joey said. If he comes, I'll go one way, you go another. He can't chase *both* of us. At least one of us will get away.

All right, I said. Suppose one of us gets caught?

Well, let's see, Joey said. Should the one who isn't caught give himself up or should he wreck Stafford's Ford?

I vote for wreck, I said.

So do I, Joey said, so wreck it is.

When we got out to the grounds a couple of the little tents were up, and the big one was going up. We stood around and watched. It was great the way they did it. Just a handful of guys who looked like tramps doing work you'd think no less than a hundred men could do. Doing it with style, too.

All of a sudden a man everybody called Red hollered at me and Joey.

Here, you Arabs, he said, give us a hand.

Me and Joey ran over to him.

Yes, sir, I said.

He was a small man with very broad shoulders and very big hands. You didn't feel that he was small, because he seemed so powerful and because he had so much thick red hair on his head. You thought he was practically a giant.

He handed me and Joey a rope. The rope was attached to some canvas that was lying on the ground.

This is going to be easy, Red said. As the boys lift the pole and get it in place you keep pulling the rope, so the canvas will go up with the pole.

Yes, sir, Joey said.

Everybody was busy when we saw Stafford.

We can't run now, I said.

Let him come, Joey said. We told Red we'd give him a hand and we're going to do it.

I'll tell you what, I said. We'll tell him we'll go with him after we get the canvas up; then we'll run.

All right, Joey said.

Stafford was a big fellow in a business suit who had a beef-red face and looked as if he ought to be a lawyer or something. He came over and said, All right, you hooligans, come along with me.

We promised to give Red a hand, Joey said. We'll come just as soon as we get this canvas up.

We were pulling for all we were worth, slipping and falling. The men were all working hard. Red was hollering orders, and then the whole thing was over and we had done our part.

We didn't even get a chance to find out what Red was going to say to us, or if he was going to invite us to sit at the table for lunch, or what.

Joey busted loose and ran one way and I ran the other and Stafford came after *me*. I heard the circus men laughing and Red hollering, Run, boy, run. He can't catch *you*. He's soft. Give him a good run. He needs the exercise.

I could hear Stafford, too. He was very sore and he was cussing.

I got away, though, and stayed low until I saw him drive off in his Ford. Then I went back to the big tent and found Joey.

We'll get it this time, Joey said.

I guess it'll be Reform School this time, I said.

No, Joey said, I guess it'll be thirty. We're going to do some awful howling if it is. Thirty's a lot of whacks even if he *is* sixty-three years old. He ain't exactly a weakling.

Thirty? I said. Ouch. That's liable to make me cry.

Maybe, Joey said. Me too, maybe. Seems like ten can make you cry, then you hold off till it's eleven, then twelve, and you think you'll start crying on the next one, but you don't. We haven't so far, anyway. Maybe we will when it's thirty.

Oh, well, I said, that's tomorrow.

Red gave us some more work to do around the grounds and let us sit next to him at lunch. It was swell. We talked to some acrobats who were

Spanish, and to a family of Italians who worked with horses. We saw both shows, the afternoon one and the evening one, and then we helped with the work, taking the circus to pieces again; then we went down to the trains, and then home. I got home real late. In the morning I was sleepy when I had to get up for school.

They were waiting for us. Miss Flibety didn't even let us sit down for the roll call. She just told us to go to the office. Old man Dawson was waiting for us, too. Stafford was there, too, and very sore.

I figured, Well, here's where we go to Reform School.

Here they are, Mr. Dawson said to Stafford. Take them away, if you like.

It was easy to tell they'd been talking for some time and hadn't been getting along any too well. Old man Dawson seemed irritated and Stafford seemed sore at him.

In *this* school, old man Dawson said, I do any punishing that's got to be done. Nobody else. I can't stop you from taking them to Reform School, though.

Stafford didn't say anything. He just left the office.

Well, lads, old man Dawson said. How was it?

We had lunch with them, Joey said.

Let's see now, old man Dawson said. What offense is this, the sixteenth or the seventeenth?

It ain't that many, Joey said. Must be eleven or twelve.

Well, old man Dawson said, I'm sure of one thing. This is the time I'm supposed to make it thirty.

I think the next one is the one you're supposed to make thirty, Joey said.

No, Mr. Dawson said, we've lost track somewhere, but I'm sure this is the time it goes up to thirty. Who's going to be first?

Me, I said.

All right, Aram, Mr. Dawson said. Take a good hold on the chair, brace yourself, and try to modulate your howl.

Yes, sir, I said. I'll do my best, but thirty's an awful lot.

Well, a funny thing happened. He gave me thirty all right and I howled all right, but it *was* a modulated howl. It was the most modulated howl I ever howled; because it was the *easiest* strapping I ever got. I counted them and there were thirty all right, but they didn't hurt, so I didn't cry as I was afraid I might.

It was the same with Joey. We stood together waiting to be dismissed.

I'm awfully grateful to you boys, old man Dawson said, for modulating your howls so nicely this time. I don't want people to think I'm killing you.

We wanted to thank him for giving us such easy strappings, but we couldn't say it. I think he knew the way we felt, though, because he smiled in a way that gave us an idea he knew.

Then we went back to class.

It was swell because we knew everything would be all right till the County Fair opened in September.

Hans Zinsser

Hans Zinsser (1878-1940) did not, to be sure, call As I Remember Him *an autobiography. But the initials of the sub-title,* The Biography of R. S., *are supposed to stand for "romantic self." At any rate, the life of R. S. parallels that of the eminent and beloved bacteriologist whose unresting efforts to better the lot of his fellows took him into the plague-ridden regions of Serbia and Russia and won him high honors here and abroad. In the light of the more or less amorous adventures below it is hard to understand how Zinsser ever succumbed to matrimony. But, with a scientist's devotion to truth of definition, he is driven to de-romanticize his first infatuations.*

CALF LOVE

THE first girl I ever noticed in what, later, I recognized as a sentimental emotion was called Mamie. She was the daughter of a truck driver in my father's chemical factory. We used to play in the large factory yard, where hundreds of barrels of resin were stored on end, and it was great fun to jump from barrel top to barrel top. Mamie had a brother who became a bosom friend, and games of tag on the barrels were organized in which Mamie—being several years younger—was patronizingly allowed to participate. She and her brother were sweet children, amiable and gentle, and I loved them both very dearly. Their lives were hard. At twelve and ten, respectively, they were called upon for severe domestic service, and their poor mother,—a stout, red-faced woman,—kind enough when she was sober, was less so when drunk. Their happy moments were the ones they spent with me, playing on the barrels; but when I went back to my playroom to have my feet dried and to be fed my supper, they went back to a little frame house where dirt, noise, unmerited abuse, and frugal tolerance were their lot.

Mamie was blue-eyed and blonde, with a bright blondeness that shone through the dirt on her face and the squalor of her clothes. And how humbly grateful she was to be allowed to be "It," chasing us over the barrels. There must have been a faint dawning of the endocrines in me even then, baneful prophecy of a long life of struggle, for while I was sorry for Jimmy when I happened to think of being so, there was always a protective tenderness in my heart for Mamie.

One day—it was drizzling—the wet drove us from our playground into a little shed where carboys of sulphuric acid were stored. I dug a nickel out of my pocket and Jimmy was dispatched to the store on the corner to buy some barber-pole candy sticks. Mamie and I sat close together, for we were damp and a little chilly. She stuck up her wet face to be kissed, and I gazed down at her with the warm intention of kissing her. But when I looked into her face, I saw two little rivulets running from Mamie's nose to her pouted upper lip. I had never noticed them before, although I had often observed her sticking her tongue out and upward whenever she sniffed. For ours was a catarrhal climate. Now I looked and saw. But I have always been proud in later days that, even at this early age, I mastered my repulsion and kissed Mamie on her salty lips. Dear Mamie! What has become of you since? You were a lovely child, in spite of the rivulets on your upper lip, and—no doubt—you deserved more consideration than the world has given you. What happened to me at that moment has never left me since and is perhaps the only achievement that may eventually entitle me to some measure of self-approbation—namely, the mastery of arrogance and disgust by tenderness and pity.

We played in the great court of my father's chemical factory and the atmosphere was redolent with odors of resin, sulphuric acid, and amyl acetate. I never pass a chemical factory or smell amyl acetate without thinking of Mamie and our games on the barrels. Yes, the sense of smell is the most nostalgic of our senses. I recall a charming lady from the West who stayed with us in New York, but left suddenly—long before she had intended to. She was in the recently cleaned bathroom one morning and, smelling the household ammonia, got so homesick for her twins that she couldn't stand it and had to go home.

2

It is strange that after all these years I should remember their names. They were called Galeoti, and came from Florence; and the name of the English governess was Miss Satterthwaite. For a month, in the late spring, we played together, the two little girls and I, in the garden of the hotel at Pegli, on the Italian Riviera. Everything was bursting into flower, and the garden had bushes blazing with white and red; there were gravel walks, and a fountain with a spout in the middle, and goldfish which were fed conscientiously every morning by the fat proprietress. We skipped and laughed in the garden, for the little Galeoti girls—one of them my age, the other two years younger, which would make her ten—were merry and great chatterboxes in a mixture of Italian and English that was frequently corrected by the governess. We took long walks together into the hills, and came home with great bunches of violets. Late in the afternoon, Miss Satterthwaite often read to us. Among other things, she read an English translation of De Amicis. She was only a child herself, about seventeen, I should judge, and pretty as blonde, high-colored British girls so often are at that age. To me, she seemed a young goddess. I sat very quiet when she read, and followed her about like a little dog. She was very lonely—probably it was the first time she had been away from home and isolated, as a young English governess would be in an Italian family. The parents Galeoti were away most of the time on excursions and at night played cards with my father and mother and other people in the hotel, drinking large quantities of *Asti spumante* and having very jolly times, as we children could hear after we had gone to bed.

I slept in a room that faced the garden, and the warm fragrance from many flowers and shrubs came into my window. I used to pretend that I was going to bed outside, among the bushes. One night, I remember I could not sleep because the moon was white in the window; and, feeling restless and adventurous, I tiptoed through the hall and crept out into the garden. There, on a bench, Miss Satterthwaite was sitting, and when I slipped up beside her, I saw that she was weeping. I was very sorry for her, but she took my hand between hers and told me that it was only the moonlight, that she had felt lonesome and was crying only because it was so terribly beautiful. And suddenly she said: "Hush!" and I heard my first nightingale. But it was a great disappointment. I was thinking of Miss Satterthwaite and the terrible grief I thought she was enduring when she led me to the door and told me to be a good boy and go to bed.

3

Of course I have been more or less in love all my life. But in the golden, adolescent days I fell in and out much faster than I did later. A look, a touch of the hand, a word, or—as in one case—only the sound of a snatch of song heard through a window on a summer night, and I was off on the new, sometimes before I was out of the old. Even this was not embarrassing, because the ladies in question had been fallen in love with, adored in half a dozen execrable sonnets, taken on honeymoons to Spanish castles that I kept always ready and fully equipped for such purposes, and dropped again for a new love before they themselves had become aware that they were participating in a romantic adventure. I used them, so to speak, as lay figures for my sentimental education. It did me a lot of good, and them no harm.

There was Marie-Louise, the New York society girl, ten years older than I, indeed approaching thirty, an accomplished musician with a magnificent, almost Wagnerian soprano, but a figure pathologically—that is, incapacitatingly—fat. She would have made four of me, and she thought I was "a nice boy but a little funny."

There was Maud, the harness maker's daughter, a young Diana, but always suspecting melodramatic perils to her virtue from the rich man's son.

There was the Smith girl, who really had no particular attractions except that she lived in a hotel across the lake and tempted my Hero and Leander complex by sitting out on the wharf with a lantern at night; knowing that I would swim across a half mile of cold, black, starlit water just because of the stage setting. I might have been drowned half a dozen times, and no one the wiser till the next day; and when I did arrive and sat dripping and cold on the dock, we had nothing to say to each other—she, because she was a stupid little doll, and I because I was blown. Yet even she served a purpose, and I used to swim home and climb up the hill through the woods, half-frozen but feeling elatedly heroic and devoted.

There was—but why catalogue them? They were all appropriate in their individual ways, and played passive, usually unconscious rôles in my development. Unlike François Villon, I know more or less what life made of them—poor things. Not one turned out to be a princess, and those I've seen within the last ten years had become just as one would have expected— quite commonplace, with no signs whatever of having lived for a time in a cloud-swept castle somewhere between Barcelona and Bourg Madame.

In all this there was—I should say, in my own justification—a minimum of the physical. In defense of romanticism, which in so many of its aspects appears silly and affected, one should not underestimate the service it does, at a certain age, in sublimating into its lovely hocus-pocus what might otherwise, and, in its absence, often does, become a gross or careless attitude toward physical love. The romanticism which had me in its grip at that age was associated with hard riding, frugal living,—as far as food and drink were concerned,—and intellectual intoxication, under George Woodberry's influence, with the English romantic poets and their idealization of love. The cult of physical hardness helped considerably in keeping this state of mind from becoming, as it might so easily have done, a morbid one; for by instinct I knew the wisdom of Guarnerius's prescription for love-melancholy: "To go with haircloth, etc., as monks do, but above all to fast."

Also, the ladies as a rule were far from sentimental themselves. One of them, now the mother of four and the still attractive grandmother of two or three,—Ella,—how lovely, but, withal, how sensible she was! She was the daughter of the principal of a well-known boys' boarding school, and had an apartment of her own, on the corner of the big barrack-like school building, high above the road. I used to serenade her at night, riding under her window on my big gray horse, Harry, and singing softly to the twang of a lute—with many a sour chord, for Harry was young and lively. The first time, Ella came to the window for a moment in a lovely pink nightgown. The second time, she didn't come to the window at all. She pretended to be asleep, and didn't mention my visit the next day. The third time, just as I was really finding my voice, the window just above her own was thrown open and a bucket of cold soapsuds came smack down on my horse's head. For a mile, I just hung on, trying not to drop the lute. I was halfway to Shruboak before I had the horse under control. Ella didn't mention this the next day, either. The boy who threw the water was, I believe, the one whom she married a few years later. I trust she had little comfort of him. He had a depraved sense of humor.

4

There was a chestnut girl, who lived over the grocery store in the village. In those days, I classified girls as chestnut, sorrel, or bay. Her father was quite a celebrity. He was very old, a carpenter by trade, and had fought in the Civil War. When my father once complimented him on his hale-and-hearty appearance, and asked him how he had managed to live to such a healthy old age, he made a remark which I then thought original with him: "Ye want to know why I've lived so long, mister? Well, it's because I had sense enough to run like hell at the second battle o' Bull Run." Pansy was the apple of his eye. She was pretty, in the slightly oversolid, bucolic manner, and was what was called "pert" in her conversation. On warm summer evenings, when the roads were fragrant with locust blossoms, I often rode down to the store to sit on the piazza with her and the old man, who would tell us stories of what was still known as "the War." He often told the same tale, but since he was a great liar and never told it the same way twice, it was never stale. Pansy was amorously inclined, and in this case, at least, any ideas I got into my head were initiated by her. She was something of a local belle, and had acquired the habit, in a gently bovine manner, of exercising, in male company, beguilements which were highly effective with the young farmer boys, grooms, and store clerks throughout the township. This is not to insinuate that she was not a thoroughly nice girl, and if I was flattered and inclined to dangerous plays of imagination in her regard, I was probably like the foolish one of the verse:—

Stultus quando videt
Quod pulchra puellula ridet
Tum fatuus credit
Se quod amare velit—

which is to say that when a fool sees a fair maid smile at him, he thinks it love when it's only flirtation. At any rate, Pansy in her way was a dear girl, and I might have made a fool of myself with her as with others had it not been for one of those fortunate flashes of common sense which have so often snatched me, by mere accident, from precipices of imbecility.

One evening we were sitting on the porch. The old man had talked himself to sleep, and began to snooze right in the middle of the Wilderness. Invention had tired him. Pansy and I were sitting closer together than the temperature warranted, and her arm was pressed caressingly against my shoulder. There was a crescent moon, and a gentle breeze enfolded us with the fragrance of the honeysuckle vine. If her head had followed her arm at that moment, God knows what might have happened. But Pansy, though—I still truly believe—a good girl, possibly intent on a bolder yet—I insist—entirely innocent (innocent in the conventional sense) attack upon my emotions, asked me suddenly whether I would like to see their new calf. It was so *darling,* she said, and had such lovely eyes and such a soft, wet nose. It was a temptation, for the calf of course was in the barn; and the barn was isolated and dark and full of hay. I fell, and said I'd love to see the calf. Merely for convention's sake, I think, Pansy lighted a stable lantern, so that we might at least fulfill the ostensible purpose of really looking at the calf. Oh, how sweet and aphrodisiacally caressing is the odor of a cow-barn at night, with its indescribable blending of clover, cow manure, sour milk, and animal! A gentle tremor ascended my spine as I stepped over the threshold, and I drew Pansy's soft form closer to my side as we stumbled over the rough boards by the dim and swinging light in her hand. I had lost all interest in the calf, and dear Pansy I believe had completely forgotten it. Yet we dared not *not* look at it—half craving, half dreading what might happen when we had seen it. But here Pallas Athene—ever my guardian goddess—intervened. Pansy walked into the stall, put her chubby arm about the calf's neck, and held the stable lantern at arm's length in front of her. And here they were—both confronting me, the dim rays of the lantern illuminating both their faces. Fascinated, I gazed upon them. They appeared like two sisters—helpless, bovine, kindly; infinite vacuity looked out at me from these two pairs of large, swimming eyes. The expression of Pansy's warm and moist lips was not more invitingly tender than the soft, velvety nozzle of the calf. There they stood,—poor innocents,—two calves together; and I gazed and gazed, hypnotically held in the light of the lamp, until I did not know which was Pansy and which calf. And I bent down and kissed the calf tenderly on the nose. Then I went out quietly, and untied my horse from the hitching post. Pansy followed me out. There were tears in her eyes when she said good-night, as I mounted and rode away—sadly, but not without a sense of relief.

John V. A. Weaver

*John V. A. Weaver (1893-1938) was for some years a newspaperman in
Chicago and New York. As a poet he defined his medium in the title
of his first collection: In American. He tried to express the inarticulate
little man in the language of the streets. "To Youth" shows that sometimes his feelings broke through the restrictions of the vernacular.*

TO YOUTH

This I say to you.
Be arrogant! Be true!
True to April lust that sings
Through your veins. These sharp springs
Matter most . . . Afteryears
Will be time enough for sleep . . .
Carefulness . . . and tears.

Now, while life is raw and new,
Drink it clear, drink it deep!
Let the moonlight's lunacy
Tear away your cautions. Be
Proud, and mad, and young, and free!
Grasp a comet! Kick at stars
Laughingly! Fight! Dare!

Arms are soft, breasts are white,
Magic's in the April night—
Never fear. Age will catch you,
Slow you down, ere it dispatch you
To your long and solemn quiet . . .

What will matter then the riot
Of the lilacs in the wind?
What will mean—then—the crush
Of lips at hours when birds hush?

Purple, green, and flame will end
In a calm, gray blend.

Only . . . graven in your soul
After all the rest is gone
There will be the ecstasies . . .
Those alone . . .

Lincoln Steffens

*Lincoln Steffens (1866-1936) was born in San Francisco and grew up,
a boy on horseback, in the robust air of pioneer days. He attended the
University of California, where he won a reputation for non-conformity
which lasted the rest of his life. After studying philosophy at five European universities he took up the life of an American journalist. But he
was no mere reporter. For forty crowded years he threw himself into
the reform of government and business corruption.* The Shame of the
Cities *(1904) is the most notable of his muckraking exposures. The
selection which follows is an early chapter from the remarkable* Autobiography *which he wrote toward the end of his life.*

I GET A COLT TO BREAK IN

COLONEL CARTER gave me a colt. I had my
pony, and my father meanwhile had bought a pair of black carriage horses
and a cow, all of which I had to attend to when we had no "man." And
servants were hard to get and to keep in those days; the women married,
and the men soon quit service to seize opportunities always opening. My
hands were pretty full, and so was the stable. But Colonel Carter seemed to
think that he had promised me a horse. He had not; I would have known
it if he had. No matter. He thought he had, and maybe he did promise
himself to give me one. That was enough. The kind of man that led immigrant trains across the continent and delivered them safe, sound, and together where he promised would keep his word. One day he drove over
from Stockton, leading a two-year-old which he brought to our front door
and turned over to me as mine. Such a horse!

She was a cream-colored mare with a black forelock, mane, and tail and
a black stripe along the middle of her back. Tall, slender, high-spirited, I
thought then—I think now—that she was the most beautiful of horses.
Colonel Carter had bred and reared her with me and my uses in mind. She
was a careful cross of a mustang mare and a thoroughbred stallion, with
the stamina of the wild horse and the speed and grace of the racer. And
she had a sense of fun. As Colonel Carter got down out of his buggy and

went up to her, she snorted, reared, flung her head high in the air, and, coming down beside him, tucked her nose affectionately under his arm.

"I have handled her a lot," he said. "She is as kind as a kitten, but she is as sensitive as a lady. You can spoil her by one mistake. If you ever lose your temper, if you ever abuse her, she will be ruined forever. And she is unbroken. I might have had her broken to ride for you, but I didn't want to. I want you to do it. I have taught her to lead, as you see; had to, to get her over here. But here she is, an unbroken colt; yours. You take and you break her. You're only a boy, but if you break this colt right, you'll be a man—a young man, but a man. And I'll tell you how."

Now, out West, as everyone knows, they break in a horse by riding out to him in his wild state, lassoing, throwing, and saddling him; then they let him up, frightened and shocked, with a yelling broncho-buster astride of him. The wild beast bucks, the cowboy drives his spurs into him, and off they go, jumping, kicking, rearing, falling, till by the weight of the man, the lash, and the rowels, the horse is broken—in body and spirit. This was not the way I was to break my colt.

"You must break her to ride without her ever knowing it," Colonel Carter said. "You feed and you clean her—you; not the stable man. You lead her out to water and to walk. You put her on a long rope and let her play, calling her to you and gently pulling on the rope. Then you turn her loose in the grass lot there and, when she has romped till tired, call her. If she won't come, leave her. When she wants water or food, she will run to your call, and you will pet and feed and care for her." He went on for half an hour, advising me in great detail how to proceed. I wanted to begin right away. He laughed. He let me lead her around to the stable, water her, and put her in the stable and feed her.

There I saw my pony. My father, sisters, and Colonel Carter saw me stop and look at my pony.

"What'll you do with him?" one of my sisters asked. I was bewildered for a moment. What should I do with the little red horse? I decided at once.

"You can have him," I said to my sisters.

"No," said Colonel Carter, "not yet. You can give your sisters the pony by and by, but you'll need him till you have taught the colt to carry you and a saddle—months; and you must not hurry. You must learn patience, and you will if you give the colt time to learn it, too. Patience and control. You can't control a young horse unless you can control yourself. Can you shoot?" he asked suddenly.

I couldn't. I had a gun and I had used it some, but it was a rifle, and I could not bring down with it such game as there was around Sacramento— birds and hares. Colonel Carter looked at my father, and I caught the look.

So did my father. I soon had a shotgun. But at the time Colonel Carter turned to me and said:

"Can't shoot straight, eh? Do you know what that means? That means that you can't control a gun, and that means that you can't control yourself, your eye, your hands, your nerves. You are wriggling now. I tell you that a good shot is always a good man. He may be a 'bad man' too, but he is quiet, strong, steady in speech, gait, and mind. No matter, though. If you break in this colt right, if you teach her her paces, she will teach you to shoot and be quiet."

He went off downtown with my father, and I started away with my colt. I fed, I led, I cleaned her, gently, as if she were made of glass; she was playful and willing, a delight. When Colonel Carter came home with my father for supper, he questioned me.

"You should not have worked her today," he said. "She has come all the way from Stockton and must be tired. Yes, yes, she would not show her fatigue; too fine for that, and too young to be wise. You have got to think for her, consider her as you would your sisters."

Sisters! I thought; I had never considered my sisters. I did not say that, but Colonel Carter laughed and nodded to my sisters. It was just as if he had read my thought. But he went on to draw on my imagination a centaur; the colt as a horse's body—me, a boy, as the head and brains of one united creature. I liked that. I would be that. I and the colt: a centaur.

After Colonel Carter was gone home I went to work on my new horse. The old one, the pony, I used only for business: to go to fires, to see my friends, run errands, and go hunting with my new shotgun. But the game that had all my attention was the breaking in of the colt, the beautiful cream-colored mare, who soon knew me—and my pockets. I carried sugar to reward her when she did right, and she discovered where I carried it; so did the pony, and when I was busy they would push their noses into my pockets, both of which were torn down a good deal of the time. But the colt learned. I taught her to run around a circle, turn and go the other way at a signal. My sisters helped me. I held the long rope and the whip (for signaling), while one of the girls led the colt; it was hard work for them, but they took it in turns. One would lead the colt round and round till I snapped the whip; then she would turn, turning the colt, till the colt did it all by herself. And she was very quick. She shook hands with each of her four feet. She let us run under her, back and forth. She was slow only to carry me. Following Colonel Carter's instructions, I began by laying my arm or a surcingle over her back. If she trembled, I drew it slowly off. When she could abide it, I tried buckling it, tighter and tighter. I laid over her, too, a blanket, folded at first, then open, and, at last, I slipped up on her myself, sat there a second, and as she trembled, slid off. My sisters held her for me, and when I could get up and sit there a moment or two, I tied her at a block, and we, my sisters and I, made a procession of mounting and dismounting. She soon got used to this and would let us slide off over her rump, but it was a long, long time before she would carry me.

That we practiced by leading her along a high curb where I could get on as she walked, ride a few steps, and then, as she felt me and crouched, slip off. She never did learn to carry a girl on her back; my sisters had to lead her while I rode. This was not purposeful. I don't know just how it happened, but I do remember the first time I rode on my colt all the way round the lot and how, when I put one of the girls up, she refused to repeat. She shuddered, shook and frightened them off.

While we were breaking in the colt a circus came to town. The ring was across the street from our house. Wonderful! I lived in that circus for a week. I saw the show but once, but I marked the horse-trainers, and in the mornings when they were not too busy I told them about my colt, showed her to them, and asked them how to train her to do circus tricks. With their hints I taught the colt to stand up on her hind legs, kneel, lie down, and balance on a small box. This last was easier than it looked. I put her first on a low big box and taught her to turn on it; then got a little smaller box upon which she repeated what she did on the big one. By and by we had her so that she would step up on a high box so small that her four feet were almost touching, and there also she would turn.

The circus man gave me one hint that was worth all the other tricks put together. "You catch her doing something of herself that looks good," he said, "and then you keep her at it." It was thus that I taught her to bow to people. The first day I rode her out on to the streets was a proud one for me and for the colt, too, apparently. She did not walk, she danced; perhaps she was excited, nervous; anyhow I liked the way she threw up her head, champed at the bit, and went dancing, prancing down the street. Everybody stopped to watch us, and so, when she began to sober down, I picked her up again with heel and rein, saying, "Here's people, Lady," and she would show off to my delight. By constant repetition I had her so trained that she would single-foot, head down, along a country road till we came to a house or a group of people. Then I'd say, "People, Lady," and up would go her head, and her feet would dance.

But the trick that set the town talking was her bowing to anyone I spoke to. "Lennie Steffens' horse bows to you," people said, and she did. I never told how it was done; by accident. Dogs used to run out at us and the colt enjoyed it; she kicked at them sometimes with both hind hoofs. I joined her in the game, and being able to look behind more conveniently than she could, I watched the dogs until they were in range, then gave the colt a signal to kick. "Kick, gal," I'd say, and tap her ribs with my heel. We used to get dogs together that way; the colt would kick them over and over and leave them yelping in the road. Well, one day when I met a girl

I knew I lifted my hat, probably muttered a "Good day," and I must have touched the colt with my heel. Anyway, she dropped her head and kicked—not much; there was no dog near, so she had responded to my unexpected signal by what looked like a bow. I caught the idea and kept her at it. Whenever I wanted to bow to a girl or anyone else, instead of saying "Good day," I muttered "Kick, gal," spurred her· lightly, and—the whole centaur bowed and was covered with glory and conceit.

Yes, conceit. I was full of it, and the colt was quite as bad. One day my chum Hjalmar came into town on his Black Bess, blanketed. She had had a great fistula cut out of her shoulder and had to be kept warm. I expected to see her weak and dull, but no, the good old mare was champing and dancing, like my colt.

"What is it makes her so?" I asked, and Hjalmar said he didn't know, but he thought she was proud of the blanket. A great idea. I had a gaudy horse blanket. I put it on the colt and I could hardly hold her. We rode down the main street together, both horses and both boys, so full of vanity that everybody stopped to smile. We thought they admired, and maybe they did. But some boys on the street gave us another angle. They, too, stopped and looked, and as we passed, one of them said, "Think you're hell, don't you?"

Spoilsport!

We did, as a matter of fact; we thought we were hell. The recognition of it dashed us for a moment; not for long, and the horses paid no heed. We pranced, the black and the yellow, all the way down J Street, up K Street, and agreed that we'd do it again, often. Only, I said, we wouldn't use blankets. If the horses were proud of a blanket, they'd be proud of anything unusually conspicuous. We tried a flower next time. I fixed a big rose on my colt's bridle just under her ear and it was great—she pranced downtown with her head turned, literally, to show off her flower. We had to change the decoration from time to time, put on a ribbon, or a bell, or a feather, but, really, it was not necessary for my horse. Old Black Bess needed an incentive to act up, but all I had to do to my horse was to pick up the reins, touch her with my heel, and say, "People"; she would dance from one side of the street to the other, asking to be admired. As she was. As we were.

I would ride down to my father's store, jump off my prancing colt in the middle of the street, and run up into the shop. The colt, free, would stop short, turn, and follow me right up on the sidewalk, unless I bade her wait. If anyone approached her while I was gone, she would snort, rear, and strike. No stranger could get near her. She became a frightened, frightening animal, and yet when I came into sight she would run to me, put her head down, and as I straddled her neck, she would throw up her head and pitch me into my seat, facing backwards, of course. I whirled around right, and off we'd go, the vainest boy and the proudest horse in the State.

"Hey, give me a ride, will you?" some boy would ask.

"Sure," I'd say, and jump down and watch that boy try to catch and mount my colt. He couldn't. Once a cowboy wanted to try her, and he caught her; he dodged her forefeet, grabbed the reins, and in one spring was on her back. I never did that again. My colt reared, then bucked, and, as the cowboy kept his seat, she shuddered, sank to the ground, and rolled over. He slipped aside and would have risen with her, but I was alarmed and begged him not to. She got up at my touch and followed me so close that she stepped on my heel and hurt me. The cowboy saw the point.

"If I were you, kid," he said, "I'd never let anybody mount that colt. She's too good."

That, I think, was the only mistake I made in the rearing of Colonel Carter's gift-horse. My father differed from me. He discovered another error or sin, and thrashed me for it. My practice was to work hard on a trick, privately, and when it was perfect, let him see it. I would have the horse out in our vacant lot doing it as he came home to supper. One evening, as he approached the house, I was standing, whip in hand, while the colt, quite free, was stepping carefully over the bodies of a lot of girls, all my sisters and all their girl friends. (Grace Gallatin, later Mrs. Thompson-Seton, was among them.) My father did not express the admiration I expected; he was frightened and furious. "Stop that," he called, and he came running around into the lot, took the whip, and lashed me with it. I tried to explain; the girls tried to help me explain.

I had seen in the circus a horse that stepped thus over a row of prostrate clowns. It looked dangerous for the clowns, but the trainer had told me how to do it. You begin with logs, laid out a certain distance apart; the horse walks over them under your lead, and whenever he touches one you rebuke him. By and by he will learn to step with such care that he never trips. Then you substitute clowns. I had no clowns, but I did get logs, and with the girls helping, we taught the colt to step over the obstacles even at a trot. Walking, she touched nothing. All ready thus with the logs, I had my sisters lie down in the grass, and again and again the colt stepped over them. None was ever touched. My father would not listen to any of this; he just walloped me, and when he was tired or satisfied and I was in tears, I blubbered a short excuse: "They were only girls." And he whipped me some more.

My father was not given to whipping; he did it very seldom, but he did it hard when he did it at all. My mother was just the opposite. She did not whip me, but she often smacked me, and she had a most annoying habit of thumping me on the head with her thimbled finger. This I resented more than my father's thoroughgoing thrashings, and I can tell why now.

I would be playing Napoleon and as I was reviewing my Old Guard, she would crack my skull with that thimble. No doubt I was in the way; it took a lot of furniture and sisters to represent properly a victorious army; and you might think as my mother did that a thimble is a small weapon. But imagine Napoleon at the height of his power, the ruler of the world on parade, getting a sharp rap on his crown from a woman's thimble. No. My father's way was more appropriate. It was hard. "I'll attend to you in the morning," he would say, and I lay awake wondering which of my crimes he had discovered. I know what it is to be sentenced to be shot at sunrise. And it hurt, in the morning, when he was not angry but very fresh and strong. But you see, he walloped me in my own person; he never humiliated Napoleon or my knighthood, as my mother did. And I learned something from his discipline, something useful.

I learned what tyranny is and the pain of being misunderstood and wronged, or, if you please, understood and set right; they are pretty much the same. He and most parents and teachers do not break in their boys as carefully as I broke in my colt. They haven't the time that I had, and they have not some other incentives I had. I saw this that day when I rubbed my sore legs. He had to explain to my indignant mother what had happened. When he told it his way, I gave my version: how long and cautiously I had been teaching my horse to walk over logs and girls. And having shown how sure I was of myself and the colt, while my mother was boring into his silence with one of her reproachful looks, I said something that hit my father hard.

"I taught the colt that trick, I have taught her all that you see she knows, without whipping her. I have never struck her; not once. Colonel Carter said I mustn't, and I haven't."

And my mother, backing me up, gave him a rap: "There," she said, "I told you so." He walked off, looking like a thimble-rapped Napoleon.

Aldous Huxley

Aldous Huxley (1894-   ), the brother of Julian Huxley, is English-born and was educated at Oxford. He is a prolific writer of novels, stories, and essays, all of them loaded with ideas. From a point of view relentlessly scientific he has passed over to mysticism, but he has no illusions about the society between the two World Wars. "Young Archimedes" reveals the kinship of music and mathematics, and poses the mystery of genius. In Guido's story is the story of every genius whom the world has failed to understand and so brought to grief.

YOUNG ARCHIMEDES

MEN cannot live at ease except where they have mastered their surroundings and where their accumulated lives outnumber and outweigh the vegetative lives about them. Stripped of its dark woods, planted, terraced, and tilled almost to the mountains' tops, the Tuscan landscape is humanised and safe. Sometimes upon those who live in the midst of it there comes a longing for some place that is solitary, inhuman, lifeless, or peopled only with alien life. But the longing is soon satisfied, and one is glad to return to the civilised and submissive scene.

I found that house on the hilltop the ideal dwelling-place. For there, safe in the midst of a humanised landscape, one was yet alone; one could be as solitary as one liked. Neighbours whom one never sees at close quarters are the ideal and perfect neighbours.

Our nearest neighbours, in terms of physical proximity, lived very near. We had two sets of them, as a matter of fact, almost in the same house with us. One was the peasant family, who lived in a long, low building, part dwelling-house, part stables, storerooms and cowsheds, adjoining the villa. Our other neighbours—intermittent neighbours, however, for they only ventured out of town every now and then, during the most flawless weather—were the owners of the villa, who had reserved for themselves the smaller wing of the huge L-shaped house—a mere dozen rooms or so—leaving the remaining eighteen or twenty to us.

They were a curious couple, our proprietors. An old husband, grey, listless, tottering, seventy at least; and a signora of about forty, short, very plump, with tiny fat hands and feet and a pair of very large, very dark black eyes, which she used with all the skill of a born comedian. Her vitality, if you could have harnessed it and made it do some useful work, would have supplied a whole town with electric light. The physicists talk of deriving energy from the atom; they would be more profitably employed nearer home—in discovering some way of tapping those enormous stores of vital energy which accumulate in unemployed women of sanguine temperament and which, in the present imperfect state of social and scientific organisation, vent themselves in ways that are generally so deplorable: in interfering with other people's affairs, in working up emotional scenes, in thinking about love and making it, and in bothering men till they cannot get on with their work.

Signora Bondi got rid of her superfluous energy, among other ways, by "doing in" her tenants. The old gentleman, who was a retired merchant with a reputation for the most perfect rectitude, was allowed to have no dealings with us. When we came to see the house, it was the wife who showed us round. It was she who, with a lavish display of charm, with irresistible rollings of the eyes, expatiated on the merits of the place, sang the praises of the electric pump, glorified the bathroom (considering which, she insisted, the rent was remarkably moderate), and when we suggested calling in a surveyor to look over the house, earnestly begged us, as though our well-being were her only consideration, not to waste our money unnecessarily in doing anything so superfluous. "After all," she said, "we are honest people. I wouldn't dream of letting you the house except in perfect condition. Have confidence." And she looked at me with an appealing, pained expression in her magnificent eyes, as though begging me not to insult her by my coarse suspiciousness. And leaving us no time to pursue the subject of surveyors any further, she began assuring us that our little boy was the most beautiful angel she had ever seen. By the time our interview with Signora Bondi was at an end, we had definitely decided to take the house.

"Charming woman," I said, as we left the house. But I think that Elizabeth was not quite so certain of it as I.

Then the pump episode began.

On the evening of our arrival in the house we switched on the electricity. The pump made a very professional whirring noise; but no water came out of the taps in the bathroom. We looked at one another doubtfully.

"Charming woman?" Elizabeth raised her eyebrows.

We asked for interviews; but somehow the old gentleman could never see us, and the Signora was invariably out or indisposed. We left notes; they were never answered. In the end, we found that the only method of communicating with our landlords, who were living in the same house with us, was to go down into Florence and send a registered express letter to them. For this they had to sign two separate receipts and even, if we chose to pay forty centimes more, a third incriminating document, which was then returned to us. There could be no pretending, as there always was with ordinary letters or notes, that the communication had never been received. We began at last to get answers to our complaints. The Signora, who wrote all the letters, started by telling us that, naturally, the pump didn't work, as the cisterns were empty, owing to the long drought. I had to walk three miles to the post office in order to register my letter reminding her that there had been a violent thunderstorm only last Wednesday, and that the tanks were consequently more than half full. The answer came back: bath water had not been guaranteed in the contract; and if I wanted it, why hadn't I had the pump looked at before I took the house? Another walk into town to ask the Signora next door whether she remembered her adjurations to us to have confidence in her, and to inform her that the existence in a house of a bathroom was in itself an implicit guarantee of bath water. The reply to that was that the Signora couldn't continue to have communications with people who wrote so rudely to her. After that I put the matter into the hands of a lawyer. Two months later the pump was actually replaced. But we had to serve a writ on the lady before she gave in. And the costs were considerable.

One day, towards the end of the episode, I met the old gentleman in the road, taking his big maremman dog for a walk—or being taken, rather, for a walk by the dog. For where the dog pulled the old gentleman had perforce to follow. And when it stopped to smell, or scratch the ground, or leave against a gatepost its visiting-card or an offensive challenge, patiently, at his end of the leash, the old man had to wait. I passed him standing at the side of the road, a few hundred yards below our house. The dog was sniffing at the roots of one of the twin cypresses which grew one on either side of the entry to a farm; I heard the beast growling indignantly to itself, as though it scented an intolerable insult. Old Signor Bondi, leashed to his dog, was waiting. The knees inside the tubular grey trousers were slightly bent. Leaning on his cane, he stood gazing mournfully and vacantly at the view. The whites of his old eyes were discoloured, like ancient billiard balls. In the grey, deeply wrinkled face, his nose was dyspeptically red. His white moustache, ragged and yellowing at the fringes, drooped in a melancholy curve. In his black tie he wore a very large diamond; perhaps that was what Signora Bondi had found so attractive about him.

I took off my hat as I approached. The old man stared at me absently, and it was only when I was already almost past him that he recollected who I was.

"Wait," he called after me, "wait!" And he hastened down the road in pursuit. Taken utterly by surprise and at a disadvantage—for it was engaged in retorting to the affront imprinted on the cypress roots—the dog permitted itself to be jerked after him. Too much astonished to be anything but obedient, it followed its master. "Wait!"

I waited.

"My dear sir," said the old gentleman, catching me by the lapel of my coat and blowing most disagreeably in my face, "I want to apologise." He looked around him, as though afraid that even here he might be overheard. "I want to apologise," he went on, "about that wretched pump business. I assure you that, if it had been only my affair, I'd have put the thing right as soon as you asked. You were quite right: a bathroom is an implicit guarantee of bath water. I saw from the first that we should have no chance if it came to court. And besides, I think one ought to treat one's tenants as handsomely as one can afford to. But my wife"—he lowered his voice— "the fact is that she likes this sort of thing, even when she knows that she's in the wrong and must lose. And besides, she hoped, I dare say, that you'd get tired of asking and have the job done yourself. I told her from the first that we ought to give in; but she wouldn't listen. You see, she enjoys it. Still, now she sees that it must be done. In the course of the next two or three days you'll be having your bath water. But I thought I'd just like to tell you how . . ." But the Maremmano, which had recovered by this time from its surprise of a moment since, suddenly bounded, growling, up the road. The old gentleman tried to hold the beast, strained at the leash, tottered unsteadily, then gave way and allowed himself to be dragged off. ". . . how sorry I am," he went on, as he receded from me, "that this little misunderstanding . . ." But it was no use. "Good-bye." He smiled politely, made a little deprecating gesture, as though he had suddenly remembered a pressing engagement, and had no time to explain what it was. "Good-bye." He took off his hat and abandoned himself completely to the dog.

A week later the water really did begin to flow, and the day after our first bath Signora Bondi, dressed in dove-grey satin and wearing all her pearls, came to call.

"Is it peace now?" she asked, with a charming frankness, as she shook hands.

We assured her that, so far as we were concerned, it certainly was.

"But why *did* you write me such dreadfully rude letters?" she said, turning on me a reproachful glance that ought to have moved the most ruthless malefactor to contrition. "And then that writ. How *could* you? To a lady . . ."

I mumbled something about the pump and our wanting baths.

"But how could you expect me to listen to you while you were in that mood? Why didn't you set about it differently—politely, charmingly?" She smiled at me and dropped her fluttering eyelids.

I thought it best to change the conversation. It is disagreeable, when one is in the right, to be made to appear in the wrong.

A few weeks later we had a letter—duly registered and by express messenger—in which the Signora asked us whether we proposed to renew our lease (which was only for six months), and notifying us that, if we did, the rent would be raised 25 per cent, in consideration of the improvements which had been carried out. We thought ourselves lucky, at the end of much bargaining, to get the lease renewed for a whole year with an increase in the rent of only 15 per cent.

It was chiefly for the sake of the view that we put up with these intolerable extortions. But we had found other reasons, after a few days' residence, for liking the house. Of these, the most cogent was that, in the peasant's youngest child, we had discovered what seemed the perfect playfellow for our own small boy. Between little Guido—for that was his name—and the youngest of his brothers and sisters there was a gap of six or seven years. His two elder brothers worked with their father in the fields; since the time of the mother's death, two or three years before we knew them, the eldest sister had ruled the house, and the younger, who had just left school, helped her and in betweenwhiles kept an eye on Guido, who by this time, however, needed very little looking after; for he was between six and seven years old and as precocious, self-assured, and responsible as the children of the poor, left as they are to themselves almost from the time they can walk, generally are.

Though fully two and a half years older than little Robin—and at that age thirty months are crammed with half a life-time's experience—Guido took no undue advantage of his superior intelligence and strength. I have never seen a child more patient, tolerant, and untyrannical. He never laughed at Robin for his clumsy efforts to imitate his own prodigious feats; he did not tease or bully, but helped his small companion when he was in difficulties and explained when he could not understand. In return, Robin adored him, regarded him as the model and perfect Big Boy, and slavishly imitated him in every way he could.

These attempts of Robin's to imitate his companion were often exceedingly ludicrous. For by an obscure psychological law, words and actions in themselves quite serious become comic as soon as they are copied; and the more accurately, if the imitation is a deliberate parody, the funnier—for an overloaded imitation of someone we know does not make us laugh so much as one that is almost indistinguishably like the original. The bad imitation is only ludicrous when it is a piece of sincere and earnest flattery which does not quite come off. Robin's imitations were mostly of this kind. His heroic and unsuccessful attempts to perform the feats of strength and skill, which Guido could do with ease, were exquisitely comic. And his careful, long-drawn imitations of Guido's habits and mannerisms were no less amusing. Most ludicrous of all, because most earnestly undertaken and most incongruous in the imitator, were Robin's impersonations of Guido in the pensive mood. Guido was a thoughtful child, given to brooding and sudden abstractions. One would find him sitting in a corner by himself, chin in hand, elbow on knee, plunged, to all appearances, in the profoundest meditation. And sometimes, even in the midst of his play, he would suddenly break off, to stand, his hands behind his back, frowning and staring at the ground. When this happened Robin became overawed and a little disquieted. In a puzzled silence he looked at his companion. "Guido," he would say softly, "Guido." But Guido was generally too much preoccupied to answer; and Robin, not venturing to insist, would creep near him, and throwing himself as nearly as possible into Guido's attitude—standing Napoleonically, his hands clasped behind him, or sitting in the posture of Michelangelo's Lorenzo the Magnificent—would try to meditate too. Every few seconds he would turn his bright blue eyes towards the elder child to see whether he was doing it quite right. But at the end of a minute he began to grow impatient; meditation wasn't his strong point. "Guido," he called again and, louder, "Guido!" And he would take him by the hand and try to pull him away. Sometimes Guido roused himself from his reverie and went back to the interrupted game. Sometimes he paid no attention. Melancholy, perplexed, Robin had to take himself off to play by himself. And Guido would go on sitting or standing there, quite still; and his eyes, if one looked into them, were beautiful in their grave and pensive calm.

They were large eyes, set far apart and, what was strange in a darkhaired Italian child, of a luminous pale blue-grey colour. They were not always grave and calm, as in these pensive moments. When he was playing, when he talked or laughed, they lit up; and the surface of those clear, pale lakes of thought seemed, as it were, to be shaken into brilliant sun-flashing ripples. Above those eyes was a beautiful forehead, high and steep and domed in a curve that was like the subtle curve of a rose petal. The nose was straight, the chin small and rather pointed, the mouth drooped a little sadly at the corners.

I have a snapshot of the two children sitting together on the parapet of the terrace. Guido sits almost facing the camera, but looking a little to one side and downwards; his hands are crossed in his lap and his expression, his attitude are thoughtful, grave, and meditative. It is Guido in one of those moods of abstraction into which he would pass even at the height of laughter and play—quite suddenly and completely, as though he had all at once taken it into his head to go away and had left the silent and beautiful body behind, like an empty house, to wait for his return. And by his side sits little Robin, turning to look up at him, his face half averted from the camera, but the curve of his cheek showing that he is laughing; one little raised hand is caught at the top of a gesture, the other clutches at Guido's sleeve as though he were urging him to come away and play. And the legs dangling from the parapet have been seen by the blinking instrument in the midst of an impatient wriggle; he is on the point of slipping down and running off to play hide-and-seek in the garden. All the essential characteristics of both the children are in that little snapshot.

"If Robin were not Robin," Elizabeth used to say, "I could almost wish he were Guido."

And even at that time, when I took no particular interest in the child, I agreed with her. Guido seemed to me one of the most charming little boys I had ever seen.

We were not alone in admiring him. Signora Bondi when, in those cordial intervals between our quarrels, she came to call, was constantly speaking of him. "Such a beautiful, beautiful child!" she would exclaim with enthusiasm. "It's really a waste that he should belong to peasants who can't afford to dress him properly. If he were mine, I should put him into black velvet; or little white knickers and a white knitted silk jersey with a red line at the collar and cuffs! or perhaps a white sailor suit would be pretty. And in winter a little fur coat, with a squirrel skin cap, and possibly Russian boots . . ." Her imagination was running away with her. "And I'd let his hair grow, like a page's, and have it just curled up a little at the tips. And a straight fringe across his forehead. Everyone would turn round and stare after us if I took him out with me in Via Tornabuoni."

What you want, I should have liked to tell her, is not a child; it's a clock-work doll or a performing monkey. But I did not say so—partly because I could not think of the Italian for a clock-work doll and partly because I did not want to risk having the rent raised another 15 per cent.

"Ah, if only I had a little boy like that!" She sighed and modestly dropped her eyelids. "I adore children. I sometimes think of adopting one—that is, if my husband would allow it."

I thought of the poor old gentleman being dragged along at the heels of his big white dog and inwardly smiled.

"But I don't know if he would," the Signora was continuing, "I don't know if he would." She was silent for a moment, as though considering a new idea.

A few days later, when we were sitting in the garden after luncheon, drinking our coffee, Guido's father, instead of passing with a nod and the usual cheerful good-day, halted in front of us and began to talk. He was a fine handsome man, not very tall, but well-proportioned, quick and elastic in his movements, and full of life. He had a thin brown face, featured like a Roman's and lit by a pair of the most intelligent-looking grey eyes I ever saw. They exhibited almost too much intelligence when, as not infrequently happened, he was trying, with an assumption of perfect frankness and a childlike innocence, to take one in or get something out of one. Delighting in itself, the intelligence shone there mischievously. The face might be ingenuous, impassive, almost imbecile in its expression; but the eyes on these occasions gave him completely away. One knew, when they glittered like that, that one would have to be careful.

Today, however, there was no dangerous light in them. He wanted nothing out of us, nothing of any value—only advice, which is a commodity, he knew, that most people are only too happy to part with. But he wanted advice on what was, for us, rather a delicate subject: on Signora Bondi. Carlo had often complained to us about her. The old man is good, he told us, very good and kind indeed. Which meant, I dare say, among other things, that he could easily be swindled. But his wife . . . Well, the woman was a beast. And he would tell us stories of her insatiable rapacity: she was always claiming more than the half of the produce which, by the laws of the metayage [1] system, was the proprietor's due. He complained of her suspiciousness: she was forever accusing him of sharp practices, of downright stealing—him, he struck his breast, the soul of honesty. He complained of her short-sighted avarice: she wouldn't spend enough on manure, wouldn't buy him another cow, wouldn't have electric light installed in the stables. And we had sympathised, but cautiously, without expressing too strong an opinion on the subject. The Italians are wonderfully noncommittal in their speech; they will give nothing away to an interested person until they are quite certain that it is right and necessary and, above all, safe to do so. We had lived long enough among them to imitate their caution. What we said to Carlo would be sure, sooner or later, to get back to Signora Bondi. There was nothing to be gained by unnecessarily embittering our relations with the lady—only another 15 per cent, very likely, to be lost.

Today he wasn't so much complaining as feeling perplexed. The Signora had sent for him, it seemed, and asked him how he would like it if she were to make an offer—it was all very hypothetical in the cautious Italian style—to adopt little Guido. Carlo's first instinct had been to say that he wouldn't like it at all. But an answer like that would have been too coarsely committal. He had preferred to say that he would think about it. And now he was asking for our advice.

Do what you think best, was what in effect we replied. But we gave it distantly but distinctly to be understood that we didn't think that Signora Bondi would make a very good foster-mother for the child. And Carlo was inclined to agree. Besides, he was very fond of the boy.

"But the thing is," he concluded rather gloomily, "that if she has really set her heart on getting hold of the child, there's nothing she won't do to get him—nothing."

He too, I could see, would have liked the physicists to start on unemployed childless women of sanguine temperament before they tried to tackle the atom. Still, I reflected, as I watched him striding away along the ter-

[1] share-cropping.

race, singing powerfully from a brazen gullet as he went, there was force there, there was life enough in those elastic limbs, behind those bright grey eyes, to put up a good fight even against the accumulated vital energies of Signora Bondi.

It was a few days after this that my gramophone and two or three boxes of records arrived from England. They were a great comfort to us on the hilltop, providing as they did the only thing in which that spiritually fertile solitude—otherwise a perfect Swiss Family Robinson's island—was lacking: music. There is not much music to be heard nowadays in Florence. The times when Dr. Burney could tour through Italy, listening to an unending succession of new operas, symphonies, quartets, cantatas, are gone. Gone are the days when a learned musician, inferior only to the Reverend Father Martini of Bologna, could admire what the peasants sang and the strolling players thrummed and scraped on their instruments. I have travelled for weeks through the peninsula and hardly heard a note that was not "Salome" or the Fascists' song. Rich in nothing else that makes life agreeable or even supportable, the northern metropolises are rich in music. That is perhaps the only inducement that a reasonable man can find for living there. The other attractions—organised gaiety, people, miscellaneous conversation, the social pleasures—what are those, after all, but an expense of spirit that buys nothing in return? And then the cold, the darkness, the mouldering dirt, the damp and squalor. . . . No, where there is no necessity that retains, music can be the only inducement. And that, thanks to the ingenious Edison, can now be taken about in a box and unpacked in whatever solitude one chooses to visit. One can live at Benin, or Nuneaton, or Tozeur in the Sahara, and still hear Mozart quartets, and selections from the Well-Tempered Clavichord, and the Fifth Symphony, and the Brahms clarinet quintet, and motets by Palestrina.

Carlo, who had gone down to the station with his mule and cart to fetch the packing-case, was vastly interested in the machine.

"One will hear some music again," he said, as he watched me unpacking the gramophone and the disks. "It is difficult to do much oneself."

Still, I reflected, he managed to do a good deal. On warm nights we used to hear him, where he sat at the door of his house, playing his guitar and softly singing; the eldest boy shrilled out the melody on the mandolin, and sometimes the whole family would join in, and the darkness would be filled with their passionate, throaty singing. Piedigrotta [2] songs they mostly sang; and the voices drooped slurringly from note to note, lazily climbed or jerked themselves with sudden sobbing emphases from one tone to another. At a distance and under the stars the effect was not unpleasing.

"Before the war," he went on, "in normal times" (and Carlo had a hope, even a belief, that the normal times were coming back and that life

[2] popular songs of Naples.

would soon be as cheap and easy as it had been in the days before the flood), "I used to go and listen to the operas at the Politeama. Ah, they were magnificent. But it costs five lire now to get in."

"Too much," I agreed.

"Have you got *Trovatore?*" he asked.

I shook my head.

"*Rigoletto?*"

"I'm afraid not."

"*Bohème? Fanciulla del West? Pagliacci?*"

I had to go on disappointing him.

"Not even *Norma?* Or the *Barbiere?*"

I put on Battistini in "La ci darem" out of *Don Giovanni.* He agreed that the singing was good; but I could see that he didn't much like the music. Why not? He found it difficult to explain.

"It's not like *Pagliacci,*" he said at last.

"Not palpitating?" I suggested, using a word with which I was sure he would be familiar; for it occurs in every Italian political speech and patriotic leading article.

"Not palpitating," he agreed.

And I reflected that it is precisely by the difference between *Pagliacci* and *Don Giovanni,* between the palpitating and the nonpalpitating, that modern musical taste is separated from the old. The corruption of the best, I thought, is the worst. Beethoven taught music to palpitate with his intellectual and spiritual passion. It has gone on palpitating ever since, but with the passion of inferior men. Indirectly, I thought, Beethoven is responsible for *Parsifal, Pagliacci,* and the *Poem of Fire;* still more indirectly for *Samson and Delilah* and "Ivy, cling to me." Mozart's melodies may be brilliant, memorable, infectious; but they don't palpitate, don't catch you between wind and water, don't send the listener off into erotic ecstasies.

Carlo and his elder children found my gramophone, I am afraid, rather a disappointment. They were too polite, however, to say so openly; they merely ceased, after the first day or two, to take any interest in the machine and the music it played. They preferred the guitar and their own singing.

Guido, on the other hand, was immensely interested. And he liked, not the cheerful dance tunes, to whose sharp rhythms our little Robin loved to go stamping round and round the room, pretending that he was a whole regiment of soldiers, but the genuine stuff. The first record he heard, I remember, was that of the slow movement of Bach's Concerto in D Minor for two violins. That was the disk I put on the turntable as soon as Carlo had left me. It seemed to me, so to speak, the most musical piece of music with which I could refresh my long-parched mind—the coolest and clearest of all draughts. The movement had just got under way and was beginning to unfold its pure and melancholy beauties in accordance with the laws of the most exacting intellectual logic, when the two children, Guido in front and little Robin breathlessly following, came clattering into the room from the loggia.

Guido came to a halt in front of the gramophone and stood there, motionless, listening. His pale blue-grey eyes opened themselves wide; making a little nervous gesture that I had often noticed in him before, he plucked at his lower lip with his thumb and forefinger. He must have taken a deep breath; for I noticed that, after listening for a few seconds, he sharply expired and drew in a fresh gulp of air. For an instant he looked at me—a questioning, astonished, rapturous look—gave a little laugh that ended in a kind of nervous shudder, and turned back towards the source of the incredible sounds. Slavishly imitating his elder comrade, Robin had also taken up his stand in front of the gramophone, and in exactly the same position, glancing at Guido from time to time to make sure that he was doing everything, down to plucking at his lip, in the correct way. But after a minute or so he became bored.

"Soldiers," he said, turning to me; "I want soldiers. Like in London." He remembered the rag-time and the jolly marches round and round the room.

I put my fingers to my lips. "Afterwards," I whispered.

Robin managed to remain silent and still for perhaps another twenty seconds. Then he seized Guido by the arm, shouting, "Vieni, Guido! Soldiers. Soldati. Vieni giuocare soldati."

It was then, for the first time, that I saw Guido impatient. "Vai!" he whispered angrily, slapped at Robin's clutching hand and pushed him roughly away. And he leaned a little closer to the instrument, as though to make up by yet intenser listening for what the interruption had caused him to miss.

Robin looked at him, astonished. Such a thing had never happened before. Then he burst out crying and came to me for consolation.

When the quarrel was made up—and Guido was sincerely repentant, was as nice as he knew how to be when the music had stopped and his mind was free to think of Robin once more—I asked him how he liked the music. He said he thought it was beautiful. But *bello* in Italian is too vague a word, too easily and frequently uttered, to mean very much.

"What did you like best?" I insisted. For he had seemed to enjoy it so much that I was curious to find out what had really impressed him.

He was silent for a moment, pensively frowning. "Well," he said at last, "I liked the bit that went like this." And he hummed a long phrase. "And then there's the other thing singing at the same time—but what are those things," he interrupted himself, "that sing like that?"

"They're called violins," I said.

"Violins." He nodded. "Well, the other violin goes like this." He hummed again. "Why can't one sing both at once? And what is in that box? What makes it make that noise?" The child poured out his questions.

I answered him as best I could, showing him the little spirals on the disk, the needle, the diaphragm. I told him to remember how the string of the guitar trembled when one plucked it; sound is a shaking in the air, I told him, and I tried to explain how those shakings get printed on the black disk. Guido listened to me very gravely, nodding from time to time. I had the impression that he understood perfectly well everything I was saying.

By this time, however, poor Robin was so dreadfully bored that in pity for him I had to send the two children out into the garden to play. Guido went obediently; but I could see that he would have preferred to stay indoors and listen to more music. A little while later, when I looked out, he was hiding in the dark recesses of the big bay tree, roaring like a lion, and Robin, laughing, but a little nervously, as though he were afraid that the horrible noise might possibly turn out, after all, to be the roaring of a real lion, was beating the bush with a stick, and shouting, "Come out, come out! I want to shoot you."

After lunch, when Robin had gone upstairs for his afternoon sleep, he reappeared. "May I listen to the music now?" he asked. And for an hour he sat there in front of the instrument, his head cocked slightly on one side, listening while I put on one disk after another.

Thenceforward he came every afternoon. Very soon he knew all my library of records, had his preferences and dislikes, and could ask for what he wanted by humming the principal theme.

"I don't like that one," he said of Strauss's *Till Eulenspiegel*. "It's like what we sing in our house. Not really like, you know. But somehow rather like, all the same. You understand?" He looked at us perplexedly and appealingly, as though begging us to understand what he meant and so save him from going on explaining. We nodded. Guido went on. "And then," he said, "the end doesn't seem to come properly out of the beginning. It's not like the one you played the first time." He hummed a bar or two from the slow movement of Bach's D Minor Concerto.

"It isn't," I suggested, "like saying: All little boys like playing. Guido is a little boy. Therefore Guido likes playing."

He frowned. "Yes, perhaps that's it," he said at last. "The one you played first is more like that. But, you know," he added, with an excessive regard for truth, "I don't like playing as much as Robin does."

Wagner was among his dislikes; so was Debussy. When I played the record of one of Debussy's Arabesques, he said, "Why does he say the same thing over and over again? He ought to say something new, or go on, or make the thing grow. Can't he think of anything different?" But he was less censorious about the "Après-Midi d'un Faune." "The things have beautiful voices," he said.

Mozart overwhelmed him with delight. The duet from *Don Giovanni,* which his father had found insufficiently palpitating, enchanted Guido. But he preferred the quartets and the orchestral pieces.

"I like music," he said, "better than singing."

Most people, I reflected, like singing better than music; are more interested in the executant than in what he executes, and find the impersonal orchestra less moving than the soloist. The touch of the pianist is the human touch, and the soprano's high C is the personal note. It is for the sake of this touch, that note, that audiences fill the concert halls.

Guido, however, preferred music. True, he liked "La ci darem"; he liked "Deh vieni alla finestra"; he thought "Che soave zefiretto" so lovely that almost all our concerts had to begin with it. But he preferred the other things. The *Figaro* overture was one of his favourites. There is a passage not far from the beginning of the piece, where the first violins suddenly go rocketing up into the heights of loveliness; as the music approached that point, I used always to see a smile developing and gradually brightening on Guido's face, and when, punctually, the thing happened, he clapped his hands and laughed aloud with pleasure.

On the other side of the same disk, it happened, was recorded Beethoven's *Egmont* overture. He liked that almost better than *Figaro.*

"It has more voices," he explained. And I was delighted by the acuteness of the criticism; for it is precisely in the richness of its orchestration that *Egmont* goes beyond *Figaro.*

But what stirred him almost more than anything was the *Coriolan* overture. The third movement of the Fifth Symphony, the second movement of the Seventh, the slow movement of the Emperor Concerto—all these things ran it pretty close. But none excited him so much as *Coriolan.* One day he made me play it three or four times in succession; then he put it away.

"I don't think I want to hear that any more," he said.

"Why not?"

"It's too . . . too . . ." he hesitated, "too big," he said at last. "I don't really understand it. Play me the one that goes like this." He hummed the phrase from the D Minor Concerto.

"Do you like that one better?" I asked.

He shook his head. "No, it's not that exactly. But it's easier."

"Easier?" It seemed to me rather a queer word to apply to Bach.

"I understand it better."

One afternoon, while we were in the middle of our concert, Signora Bondi was ushered in. She began at once to be overwhelmingly affectionate towards the child; kissed him, patted his head, paid him the most outrageous compliments on his appearance. Guido edged away from her.

"And do you like music?" she asked.

The child nodded.

"I think he has a gift," I said. "At any rate, he has a wonderful ear and a power of listening and criticising such as I've never met with in a child of that age. We're thinking of hiring a piano for him to learn on."

A moment later I was cursing myself for my undue frankness in praising the boy. For Signora Bondi began immediately to protest that, if she could have the upbringing of the child, she would give him the best masters, bring out his talent, make an accomplished maestro of him—and, on the way, an infant prodigy. And at that moment, I am sure, she saw herself sitting maternally, in pearls and black satin, in the lee of the huge Steinway, while an angelic Guido, dressed like little Lord Fauntleroy, rattled out Liszt and Chopin, to the loud delight of a thronged auditorium. She saw the bouquets and all the elaborate floral tributes, heard the clapping and the few well-chosen words with which the veteran maestri, touched almost to tears, would hail the coming of the little genius. It became more than ever important for her to acquire the child.

"You've sent her away fairly ravening," said Elizabeth, when Signora Bondi had gone. "Better tell her next time that you made a mistake, and that the boy's got no musical talent whatever."

In due course, the piano arrived. After giving him the minimum of preliminary instruction, I let Guido loose on it. He began by picking out for himself the melodies he had heard, reconstructing the harmonies in which they were embedded. After a few lessons, he understood the rudiments of musical notation and could read a simple passage at sight, albeit very slowly. The whole process of reading was still strange to him; he had picked up his letters somehow, but nobody had yet taught him to read whole words and sentences.

I took occasion, next time I saw Signora Bondi, to assure her that Guido had disappointed me. There was nothing in his musical talent, really. She professed to be very sorry to hear it; but I could see that she didn't for a moment believe me. Probably she thought that we were after the child too, and wanted to bag the infant prodigy for ourselves, before she could get in her claim, thus depriving her of what she regarded almost as her feudal right. For, after all, weren't they her peasants? If anyone was to profit by adopting the child it ought to be herself.

Tactfully, diplomatically, she renewed her negotiations with Carlo. The boy, she put it to him, had genius. It was the foreign gentleman who had told her so, and he was the sort of man, clearly, who knew about such things. If Carlo would let her adopt the child, she'd have him trained. He'd become a great maestro and get engagements in the Argentine and the United States, in Paris and London. He'd earn millions and millions. Think of Caruso, for example. Part of the millions, she explained, would of course come to Carlo. But before they began to roll in, those millions, the boy would have to be trained. But training was very expensive. In his own interest, as well as in that of his son, he ought to let her take charge of the child. Carlo said he would think it over, and again applied to us for advice. We suggested that it would be best in any case to wait a little and see what progress the boy made.

He made, in spite of my assertions to Signora Bondi, excellent progress. Every afternoon, while Robin was asleep, he came for his concert and his lesson. He was getting along famously with his reading; his small fingers were acquiring strength and agility. But what to me was more interesting was that he had begun to make up little pieces on his own account. A few of them I took down as he played them and I have them still. Most of them, strangely enough, as I thought then, are canons. He had a passion for canons. When I explained to him the principles of the form he was enchanted.

"It is beautiful," he said, with admiration. "Beautiful, beautiful. And so easy!"

Again the word surprised me. The canon is not, after all, so conspicuously simple. Thenceforward he spent most of his time at the piano in working out little canons for his own amusement. They were often remarkably ingenious. But in the invention of other kinds of music he did not show himself so fertile as I had hoped. He composed and harmonised one or two solemn little airs like hymn tunes, with a few sprightlier pieces in the spirit of the military march. They were extraordinary, of course, as being the inventions of a child. But a great many children can do extraordinary things; we are all geniuses up to the age of ten. But I had hoped that Guido was a child who was going to be a genius at forty; in which case what was extraordinary for an ordinary child was not extraordinary enough for him. "He's hardly a Mozart," we agreed, as we played his little pieces over. I felt, it must be confessed, almost aggrieved. Anything less than a Mozart, it seemed to me, was hardly worth thinking about.

✦

He was not a Mozart. No. But he was somebody, as I was to find out, quite as extraordinary. It was one morning in the early summer that I made the discovery. I was sitting in the warm shade of our westward-facing balcony, working. Guido and Robin were playing in the little enclosed garden below. Absorbed in my work, it was only, I suppose, after the silence had prolonged itself a considerable time that I became aware that the children were making remarkably little noise. There was no shouting, no running about; only a quiet talking. Knowing by experience that when children are quiet it generally means that they are absorbed in some delicious mischief, I got up from my chair and looked over the balustrade to see what they were doing. I expected to catch them dabbling in water, making a bonfire, covering themselves with tar. But what I actually saw was Guido, with a burnt stick in his hand, demonstrating on the smooth paving-stones of the path, that the square on the hypotenuse of a right-angled triangle is equal to the sum of the squares on the other two sides.

Kneeling on the floor, he was drawing with the point of his blackened stick on the flagstones. And Robin, kneeling imitatively beside him, was growing, I could see, rather impatient with this very slow game.

"Guido," he said. But Guido paid no attention. Pensively frowning, he went on with his diagram. "Guido!" The younger child bent down and then craned round his neck so as to look up into Guido's face. "Why don't you draw a train?"

"Afterwards," said Guido. "But I just want to show you this first. It's *so* beautiful," he added cajolingly.

"But I want a train," Robin persisted.

"In a moment. Do just wait a moment." The tone was almost imploring. Robin armed himself with renewed patience. A minute later Guido had finished both his diagrams.

"There!" he said triumphantly, and straightened himself up to look at them. "Now I'll explain."

And he proceeded to prove the theorem of Pythagoras—not in Euclid's way, but by the simpler and more satisfying method which was, in all probability, employed by Pythagoras himself. He had drawn a square and dissected it, by a pair of crossed perpendiculars, into two squares and two equal rectangles. The equal rectangles he divided up by their diagonals into four equal right-angled triangles. The two squares are then seen to be the squares on the two sides of any one of these triangles other than the hypotenuse. So much for the first diagram. In the next he took the four right-angled triangles into which the rectangles had been divided and rearranged them round the original square so that their right angles filled the corners of the square, the hypotenuses looked inwards and the greater and less sides of the triangles were in continuation along the sides of the square (which are each equal to the sum of these sides). In this way the original square is redissected into four right-angled triangles and the square on the hypotenuse. The four triangles are equal to the two rectangles of the original dissection. Therefore the square on the hypotenuse is equal to the sum of the two squares—the squares on the other two sides—into which, with the rectangles, the original square was first dissected.

In very untechnical language, but clearly and with a relentless logic, Guido expounded his proof. Robin listened, with an expression on his bright, freckled face of perfect incomprehension.

"Treno," he repeated from time to time. "Treno. Make a train."

"In a moment," Guido implored. "Wait a moment. But do just look at this. *Do*." He coaxed and cajoled. "It's so beautiful. It's so easy."

So easy. . . . The theorem of Pythagoras seemed to explain for me Guido's musical predilections. It was not an infant Mozart we had been cherishing; it was a little Archimedes with, like most of his kind, an incidental musical twist.

"Treno, treno!" shouted Robin, growing more and more restless as the exposition went on. And when Guido insisted on going on with his proof, he lost his temper. "Cattivo Guido," he shouted, and began to hit out at him with his fists.

"All right," said Guido resignedly. "I'll make a train." And with his stick of charcoal he began to scribble on the stones.

I looked on for a moment in silence. It was not a very good train. Guido might be able to invent for himself and prove the theorem of Pythagoras; but he was not much of a draughtsman.

"Guido!" I called. The two children turned and looked up. "Who taught you to draw those squares?" It was conceivable, of course, that somebody might have taught him.

"Nobody." He shook his head. Then, rather anxiously, as though he were afraid there might be something wrong about drawing squares, he went on to apologise and explain. "You see," he said, "it seemed to me so beautiful. Because those squares"—he pointed at the two small squares in the first figure—"are just as big as this one." And, indicating the square on the hypotenuse in the second diagram, he looked up at me with a deprecating smile.

I nodded. "Yes, it's very beautiful," I said—"it's very beautiful indeed."

An expression of delighted relief appeared on his face; he laughed with pleasure. "You see, it's like this," he went on, eager to initiate me into the glorious secret he had discovered. "You cut these two long squares"—he meant the rectangles—"into two slices. And then there are four slices, all just the same, because, because—oh, I ought to have said that before—because these long squares are the same, because those lines, you see . . ."

"But I want a train," protested Robin.

Leaning on the rail of the balcony, I watched the children below. I thought of the extraordinary thing I had just seen and of what it meant.

I thought of the vast differences between human beings. We classify men by the colour of their eyes and hair, the shape of their skulls. Would it not be more sensible to divide them up into intellectual species? There would be even wider gulfs between the extreme mental types than between a Bushman and a Scandinavian. This child, I thought, when he grows up, will be to me, intellectually, what a man is to a dog. And there are other men and women who are, perhaps, almost as dogs to me.

Perhaps the men of genius are the only true men. In all the history of the race there have been only a few thousand real men. And the rest of us— what are we? Teachable animals. Without the help of the real men, we should have found out almost nothing at all. Almost all the ideas with which we are familiar could never have occurred to minds like ours. Plant the seeds there and they will grow; but our minds could never spontaneously have generated them.

There have been whole nations of dogs, I thought; whole epochs in which no Man was born. From the dull Egyptians the Greeks took crude experience and rules of thumb and made sciences. More than a thousand years passed before Archimedes had a comparable successor. There has been only one Buddha, one Jesus, only one Bach that we know of, one Michelangelo.

Is it by a mere chance, I wondered, that a Man is born from time to time? What causes a whole constellation of them to come contemporaneously into being and from out of a single people? Taine thought that Leonardo, Michelangelo, and Raphael were born when they were because the time was ripe for great painters and the Italian scene congenial. In the mouth of a rationalising nineteenth-century Frenchman the doctrine is strangely mystical; it may be none the less true for that. But what of those born out of time? Blake, for example. What of those?

This child, I thought, has had the fortune to be born at a time when he will be able to make good use of his capacities. He will find the most elaborate analytical methods lying ready to his hand; he will have a prodigious experience behind him. Suppose him born while Stonehenge was building; he might have spent a lifetime discovering the rudiments, guessing darkly where now he might have had a chance of proving. Born at the time of the Norman Conquest, he would have had to wrestle with all the preliminary difficulties created by an inadequate symbolism; it would have taken him long years, for example, to learn the art of dividing MMMCCCCLXXXVIII by MCMXIX. In five years, nowadays, he will learn what it took generations of Men to discover.

And I thought of the fate of all the men born so hopelessly out of time that they could achieve little or nothing of value. Beethoven born in Greece, I thought, would have had to be content to play thin melodies on the flute or lyre; in those intellectual surroundings it would hardly have been possible for him to imagine the nature of harmony.

From drawing trains, the children in the garden below had gone on to playing trains. They were trotting round and round; with blown round cheeks and pouting mouth, like the cherubic symbol of a wind, Robin puff-puffed, and Guido, holding the skirt of his smock, shuffled behind him, tooting. They ran forward, backed, stopped at imaginary stations, shunted, roared over bridges, crashed through tunnels, met with occasional collisions and derailments. The young Archimedes seemed to be just as happy as the little tow-headed barbarian. A few minutes ago he had been busy with the theorem of Pythagoras. Now, tooting indefatigably along imaginary rails, he was perfectly content to shuffle backwards and forwards among the flower-beds, between the pillars of the loggia, in and out of the dark tunnels of the laurel tree. The fact that one is going to be Archimedes does not prevent one from being an ordinary cheerful child meanwhile. I thought of this strange talent distinct and separate from the rest of the mind, independent, almost, of experience. The typical child-prodigies are musical and mathematical; the other talents ripen slowly under the influence of emotional experience and growth. Till he was thirty Balzac gave proof of nothing but ineptitude; but at four the young Mozart was already a musician, and some of Pascal's most brilliant work was done before he was out of his teens.

In the weeks that followed, I alternated the daily piano lessons with lessons in mathematics. Hints rather than lessons they were; for I only made suggestions, indicated methods, and left the child himself to work out the ideas in detail. Thus I introduced him to algebra by showing him another proof of the theorem of Pythagoras. In this proof one drops a perpendicular from the right angle on to the hypotenuse, and arguing from the fact that the two triangles thus created are similar to one another and to the original triangle, and that the proportions which their corresponding sides bear to one another are therefore equal, one can show in algebraical form that $c^2 + d^2$ (the squares on the other two sides) are equal to $a^2 + b^2$ (the squares on the two segments of the hypotenuse) $+ 2ab$; which last, it is easy to show geometrically, is equal to $(a + b)^2$, or the square on the hypotenuse. Guido was as much enchanted by the rudiments of algebra as he would have been if I had given him an engine worked by steam, with a methylated spirit lamp to heat the boiler; more enchanted, perhaps—for the engine would have got broken, and remaining always itself, would in any case have lost its charm, while the rudiments of algebra continued to grow and blossom in his mind with an unfailing luxuriance. Every day he made the discovery of something which seemed to him exquisitely beautiful; the new toy was inexhaustible in its potentialities.

In the intervals of applying algebra to the second book of Euclid, we experimented with circles; we stuck bamboos into the parched earth, measured their shadows at different hours of the day, and drew exciting conclusions from our observations. Sometimes, for fun, we cut and folded sheets of paper so as to make cubes and pyramids. One afternoon Guido arrived carrying carefully between his small and rather grubby hands a flimsy dodecahedron.

"E tanto bello!" he said, as he showed us his paper crystal; and when I asked him how he managed to make it, he merely smiled and said it had been so easy. I looked at Elizabeth and laughed. But it would have been more symbolically to the point, I felt, if I had gone down on all fours, wagged the spiritual outgrowth of my *os coccyx,* and barked my astonished admiration.

It was an uncommonly hot summer. By the beginning of July our little Robin, unaccustomed to these high temperatures, began to look pale and tired; he was listless, had lost his appetite and energy. The doctor advised mountain air. We decided to spend the next ten or twelve weeks in Switzerland. My parting gift to Guido was the first six books of Euclid in Italian. He turned over the pages, looked ecstatically at the figures.

"If only I knew how to read properly," he said. "I'm so stupid. But now I shall really try to learn."

From our hotel near Grindelwald we sent the child, in Robin's name, various post cards of cows, Alp-horns, Swiss chalets, edelweiss, and the like. We received no answers to these cards; but then we did not expect answers. Guido could not write, and there was no reason why his father or his sisters should take the trouble to write for him. No news, we took it, was good news. And then one day, early in September, there arrived at the hotel a strange letter. The manager had it stuck up on the glass-fronted notice-board in the hall, so that all the guests might see it, and whoever conscientiously thought that it belonged to him might claim it. Passing the board on the way in to lunch, Elizabeth stopped to look at it.

"But it must be from Guido," she said.

I came and looked at the envelope over her shoulder. It was unstamped and black with postmarks. Traced out in pencil, the big uncertain capital letters sprawled across its face. In the first line was written: AL BABBO DI ROBIN, and there followed a travestied version of the name of the hotel and the place. Round the address bewildered postal officials had scrawled suggested emendations. The letter had wandered for a fortnight at least, back and forth across the face of Europe.

"Al Babbo di Robin. To Robin's father." I laughed. "Pretty smart of the postmen to have got it here at all." I went to the manager's office, set forth the justice of my claim to the letter and, having paid the fifty-centime surcharge for the missing stamp, had the case unlocked and the letter given me. We went in to lunch.

"The writing's magnificent," we agreed, laughing, as we examined the address at close quarters. "Thanks to Euclid," I added. "That's what comes of pandering to the ruling passion."

But when I opened the envelope and looked at its contents I no longer laughed. The letter was brief and almost telegraphical in style. "SONO DALLA

PADRONA," it ran, "NON MI PIACE HA RUBATO IL MIO LIBRO NON VOGLIO SUONARE PIU VOGLIO TORNARE A CASA VENGA SUBITO GUIDO." [3]

"What is it?"

I handed Elizabeth the letter. "That blasted woman's got hold of him," I said.

✦

Busts of men in Homburg hats, angels bathed in marble tears extinguishing torches, statues of little girls, cherubs, veiled figures, allegories and ruthless realisms—the strangest and most diverse idols beckoned and gesticulated as we passed. Printed indelibly on tin and embedded in the living rock, the brown photographs looked out, under glass, from the humbler crosses, headstones, and broken pillars. Dead ladies in the cubistic geometrical fashions of thirty years ago—two cones of black satin meeting point to point at the waist, and the arms: a sphere to the elbow, a polished cylinder below—smiled mournfully out of their marble frames; the smiling faces the white hands, were the only recognisably human things that emerged from the solid geometry of their clothes. Men with black moustaches, men with white beards, young clean-shaven men, stared or averted their gaze to show a Roman profile. Children in their stiff best opened wide their eyes, smiled hopefully in anticipation of the little bird that was to issue from the camera's muzzle, smiled sceptically in the knowledge that it wouldn't, smiled laboriously and obediently because they had been told to. In spiky Gothic cottages of marble the richer dead privately reposed; through grilled doors one caught a glimpse of pale Inconsolables weeping, of distraught Geniuses guarding the secret of the tomb. The less prosperous sections of the majority slept in communities, close-crowded but elegantly housed under smooth continuous marble floors, whose every flagstone was the mouth of a separate grave.

These continental cemeteries, I thought, as Carlo and I made our way among the dead, are more frightful than ours, because these people pay more attention to their dead than we do. That primordial cult of corpses, that tender solicitude for their material well-being, which led the ancients to house their dead in stone, while they themselves lived between wattles and under thatch, still lingers here; persists, I thought, more vigorously than with us. There are a hundred gesticulating statues here for every one in an English graveyard. There are more family vaults, more "luxuriously appointed" (as they say of liners and hotels) than one would find at home. And embedded in every tombstone there are photographs to remind the powdered bones within what form they will have to resume on the Day of Judgment; beside each are little hanging lamps to burn optimistically on All

[3] I am at the Padrona's—I don't like it—she has stolen my book—I don't want to play [the piano] any more—I want to return home—come quickly—Guido.

Souls' Day. To the Man who built the Pyramids they are nearer, I thought, than we.

"If I had known," Carlo kept repeating, "if only I had known." His voice came to me through my reflections as though from a distance. "At the time he didn't mind at all. How should I have known that he would take it so much to heart afterwards? And she deceived me, she lied to me."

I assured him yet once more that it wasn't his fault. Though, of course, it was, in part. It was mine too, in part; I ought to have thought of the possibility and somehow guarded against it. And he shouldn't have let the child go, even temporarily and on trial, even though the woman was bringing pressure to bear on him. And the pressure had been considerable. They had worked on the same holding for more than a hundred years, the men of Carlo's family; and now she had made the old man threaten to turn him out. It would be a dreadful thing to leave the place; and besides, another place wasn't so easy to find. It was made quite plain, however, that he could stay if he let her have the child. Only for a little to begin with; just to see how he got on. There would be no compulsion whatever on him to stay if he didn't like it. And it would be all to Guido's advantage; and to his father's, too, in the end. All that the Englishman had said about his not being such a good musician as he had thought at first was obviously untrue—mere jealousy and little-mindedness: the man wanted to take credit for Guido himself, that was all. And the boy, it was obvious, would learn nothing from him. What he needed was a real good professional master.

All the energy that, if the physicists had known their business, would have been driving dynamos, went into this campaign. It began the moment we were out of the house, intensively. She would have more chance of success, the Signora doubtless thought, if we weren't there. And besides, it was essential to take the opportunity when it offered itself and get hold of the child before we could make our bid—for it was obvious to her that we wanted Guido just as much as she did.

Day after day she renewed the assault. At the end of a week she sent her husband to complain about the state of the vines: they were in a shocking condition; he had decided, or very nearly decided, to give Carlo notice. Meekly, shamefacedly, in obedience to higher orders, the old gentleman uttered his threats. Next day Signora Bondi returned to the attack. The padrone, she declared, had been in a towering passion; but she'd do her best, her very best, to mollify him. And after a significant pause she went on to talk about Guido.

In the end Carlo gave in. The woman was too persistent and she held too many trump cards. The child could go and stay with her for a month or two on trial. After that, if he really expressed a desire to remain with her, she could formally adopt him.

At the idea of going for a holiday to the seaside—and it was to the seaside, Signora Bondi told him, that they were going—Guido was pleased and excited. He had heard a lot about the sea from Robin. "Tanta acqua!" It had sounded almost too good to be true. And now he was actually to go and see this marvel. It was very cheerfully that he parted from his family.

But after the holiday by the sea was over, and Signora Bondi had brought him back to her town house in Florence, he began to be homesick. The Signora, it was true, treated him exceedingly kindly, bought him new clothes, took him out to tea in the Via Tornabuoni and filled him up with cakes, iced strawberryade, whipped cream, and chocolates. But she made him practise the piano more than he liked, and what was worse, she took away his Euclid, on the score that he wasted too much time with it. And when he said that he wanted to go home, she put him off with promises and excuses and downright lies. She told him that she couldn't take him at once, but that next week, if he were good and worked hard at his piano meanwhile, next week . . . And when the time came she told him that his father didn't want him back. And she redoubled her petting, gave him expensive presents, and stuffed him with yet unhealthier foods. To no purpose. Guido didn't like his new life, didn't want to practise scales, pined for his book, and longed to be back with his brothers and sisters. Signora Bondi, meanwhile, continued to hope that time and chocolates would eventually make the child hers; and to keep his family at a distance, she wrote to Carlo every few days letters which still purported to come from the seaside (she took the trouble to send them to a friend, who posted them back again to Florence), and in which she painted the most charming picture of Guido's happiness.

It was then that Guido wrote his letter to me. Abandoned, as he supposed, by his family—for that they shouldn't take the trouble to come to see him when they were so near was only to be explained on the hypothesis that they really had given him up—he must have looked to me as his last and only hope. And the letter, with its fantastic address, had been nearly a fortnight on its way. A fortnight—it must have seemed hundreds of years; and as the centuries succeeded one another, gradually, no doubt, the poor child became convinced that I too had abandoned him. There was no hope left.

"Here we are," said Carlo.

I looked up and found myself confronted by an enormous monument. In a kind of grotto hollowed in the flanks of a monolith of grey sandstone, Sacred Love, in bronze, was embracing a funerary urn. And in bronze letters riveted into the stone was a long legend to the effect that the inconsolable Ernesto Bondi had raised this monument to the memory of his beloved wife, Annunziata, as a token of his undying love for one whom, snatched from him by a premature death, he hoped very soon to join beneath this stone. The first Signora Bondi had died in 1912. I thought of the old man leashed to his white dog; he must always, I reflected, have been a most uxorious husband.

"They buried him here."

We stood there for a long time in silence. I felt the tears coming into my eyes as I thought of the poor child lying there underground. I thought of those luminous grave eyes, and the curve of that beautiful forehead, the droop of the melancholy mouth, of the expression of delight which illumined his face when he learned of some new idea that pleased him, when he heard a piece of music that he liked. And this beautiful small being was dead; and the spirit that inhabited this form, the amazing spirit, that too had been destroyed almost before it had begun to exist.

And the unhappiness that must have preceded the final act, the child's despair, the conviction of his utter abandonment—those were terrible to think of, terrible.

"I think we had better come away now," I said at last, and touched Carlo on the arm. He was standing there like a blind man, his eyes shut, his face slightly lifted towards the light; from between his closed eyelids the tears welled out, hung for a moment, and trickled down his cheeks. His lips trembled and I could see that he was making an effort to keep them still. "Come away," I repeated.

The face which had been still in its sorrow, was suddenly convulsed; he opened his eyes, and through the tears they were bright with a violent anger. "I shall kill her," he said, "I shall kill her. When I think of him throwing himself out, falling through the air . . ." With his two hands he made a violent gesture, bringing them down from over his head and arresting them with a sudden jerk when they were on a level with his breast. "And then crash." He shuddered. "She's as much responsible as though she had pushed him down herself. I shall kill her." He clenched his teeth.

To be angry is easier than to be sad, less painful. It is comforting to think of revenge. "Don't talk like that," I said. "It's no good. It's stupid. And what would be the point?" He had had those fits before, when grief became too painful and he had tried to escape from it. Anger had been the easiest way of escape. I had had, before this, to persuade him back into the harder path of grief. "It's stupid to talk like that," I repeated, and I led him away through the ghastly labyrinth of tombs, where death seemed more terrible even than it is.

By the time we had left the cemetery, and were walking down from San Miniato towards the Piazzale Michelangelo below, he had become calmer. His anger had subsided again into sorrow from which it had derived all its strength and its bitterness. In the Piazzale we halted for a moment to look down at the city in the valley below us. It was a day of floating clouds—great shapes, white, golden, and grey; and between them patches of a thin, transparent blue. Its lantern level, almost, with our eyes, the dome of the cathedral revealed itself in all its grandiose lightness, its vastness and aerial strength. On the innumerable brown and rosy roofs of the city the afternoon sunlight lay softly, sumptuously, and the towers were as though varnished and enamelled with an old gold. I thought of all the Men who had lived here and left the visible traces of their spirit and conceived extraordinary things, I thought of the dead child.

Winfield Townley Scott

Winfield Townley Scott (1910-   ) was born in Massachusetts. Since his graduation from Brown University he has been a newspaperman and book reviewer, and is now editor of the book page of the Providence Sunday Journal. His poems, of which he has published four volumes, are marked by a tight intellectuality in the tradition of his friend and master, Edwin Arlington Robinson; but they have also a lyric grace which is something beyond craftsmanship. "Fine Morning" contains allusions to his own college, but the scene could be duplicated on any American campus where European teachers have found a happy refuge.

FINE MORNING

It is a fine May morning. Professor Arturo Esposito observes it shyly at 8.40
   in Providence, R. I.,
By leaving hatless for the campus and neglecting
His little twisted cigar. All this he recognizes. Or, spring is strange everywhere
So even here it is meeting with a beautiful woman, new and (perhaps)
   unattached.

Well, he is a 50-year-old exile with not enough hair and too much belly,
   he says,
Remarking on the day to his colleague, Vicquart, whom he encounters at
   the corner.
Together they go up the hill along maple-dappled brick wall and walk,
The meeting-house steeple shining below them. "Look," says Esposito:
   "even the pigeons shine."

M. Louis Vicquart, recently of Sorbonne and a discovered Jewish strain, is
   young,
Is serious, is gentle, is correct, is immaculate in morning clothes and a cane.

Esposito likes to make him laugh; Vicquart very earnestly wants to oblige;
And though the Frenchman is tense as his wing-collar, and the Italian's
    gaiety is unpressed,

Still, everything is O.K. Vicquart says always by way of applause: "That
    is O.K."
"Love moves the sun, et cetera, and only geese get moved by goose-
    step—eh?
Imagine a General marching past those lilacs on such a morning, Vicquart.
Flowers are just pretty—eh?—but why do they make so much else seem
    half-wit?"

"That is O.K.," says Vicquart. "O.K., O.K., O.K.," sing all the robins in
    international English.
The sun shines and the robins sing: and even three blocks away at the
    corner by the tulip tree,
Because old Professor Heinrich Werner, bent over his beard and pipe, pauses
Much longer than traffic requires on Angell street. "Everything smells
    good," he says aloud.

"It is not Heidelberg, but—no: It is not Heidelberg and
Everything smells good." And it does two blocks the other side of the
    campus where
Vladimir Samolkin, the round, the gleaming, the Russian mathematician,
    hums a bar
From last night's Bach, smiles blindly past wistaria as if breathing Bach
    alone.

So there they come: Esposito, Vicquart, Werner, Samolkin, into the elm-
    laved campus sun,
As the bell starts for 9-o'clocks, and students leave the paths to cross wet
    grass,
And all the dormitory windows are open, and voices loafing on the early
    breeze,
Classroom doors all open. All O.K. All on a fine May morning.

Zechariah Chafee, Jr.

Zechariah Chafee, Jr. (1885-   ), is a native of Rhode Island and a graduate of Brown University and Harvard Law School. He is a professor in the latter institution. His Free Speech in the United States *is the classic exposition of its subject: addressed to laymen, it sets forth, with a minimum of technicalities, the dangers which threaten the first of our freedoms. The essay below, originally delivered as an address to undergraduates, reveals his independent and inquiring mind. He gives vigorous expression to the idea of college as a place where we get the methods and the powers with which to meet the unsolved problems of the future.*

"GIVE YOUR MINDS SEA ROOM"

IN the fundamental conflict of academic life, stadium *v.* studium, the underdog still gives a few barks. Now and again, even in the heart of the football season, some venturesome professor affirms the belief that a college is, after all, an educational institution. Let us not be content, however, to use these words unless they possess for us a concrete and vital meaning. As Lincoln urged in beginning his House Divided speech, "If we could first know where we are, and whither we are tending, we could better judge what to do and how to do it." Otherwise, those with different views of the object of a college will easily drag us vague people along with them.

They know perfectly well what they want. One influential group wants the colleges to be a chief source of recreation for the tired business man. They want seating capacity for thousands with abundance of end runs in autumn and home runs in spring. It is an understandable wish, bound to prevail if nothing more tangible be offered. What adult has not been stirred by such sights, even though he has voted to abolish intercollegiate athletics, just as few pacifists can help marking time to a military band? And when we come to the youth who long to participate in such achievements, the most fanatical lover of learning must pause before denouncing such desires as inappropriate to the years between eighteen and twenty-two. If the scholarly critic be a historian, he will remember how baseball first became important in the Northern armies, and Wellington attributed Waterloo to the playing-fields of Eton.[1] If he rank chasing Greek roots above chasing tennis balls,

[1] However, Bertrand Russell says that "the British Empire is being lost there." *Selected Papers of Bertrand Russell* (The Modern Library), p. 166.

he will find Pindar writing almost all his poems about athletes, and Socrates preferring them as companions to the professors of his day, the Sophists. In short, the ideal of making the human body in the years of its maximum power do the best of which it is capable will never be abandoned. It may, however, be absorbed as a duly proportioned part of some broader aim which will prevent some of the vigor of the students' minds from going into their feet.[2]

A less outspoken but even larger group of persons whose view of college is much more definite than ours consists of parents who send their children to college and youth who go there, not for learning, not for sport, but, as a great legal writer used to say, "in order to maintain or improve their social status." A certain number of distasteful hours must be spent in the laboratory and the lecture hall because these are the vestibules to the University Club and the fashionable ballroom. Students dutifully associate with unpractical professors so that one day they may be among the right people at luncheon and bridge. A Boston alumnus of a small college declares that a Harvard A.B. is almost indispensable to conspicuous business success in that city. Of course, this has nothing to do with any merit in the intellectual training at Cambridge, but comes from the acquaintances formed and the lure of the label conferred on Commencement. The same result would be attained if the Harvard College Faculty were completely abolished, at a considerable saving in salaries much to be desired by modern business efficiency.

With no other ideals than these, the college is bound to go into the discard along with the medieval monasteries and other richly endowed institutions which survived their usefulness. Already, the college is getting crushed between the upper millstone of the graduate schools, which under the persuasive advice of Mr. Abraham Flexner, none the less persuasive because he is possessed of the power of the purse, are beginning, as at Johns Hopkins and in the medical schools, to dispense with the A.B. degree, and the nether millstone of the junior colleges which, perhaps, might better be called senior high schools. A harsh and unrelenting future awaits the student's ideal of "college-bred, or a four years' loaf."

And yet, when we sneer at the conception of the college rolls as an unrevised version of the society column and the Directory of Directors, or feel that it should be more than a wholesome athletic club, what alternative purpose shall we offer to justify its existence? It is not enough for this purpose to seem satisfactory to us professors and our confederates, the high-school teachers. We must offer an ideal powerful enough to blast the snobbishness of the social aspirant and awaken in the boy or girl of eighteen the same enthusiastic desire to test his or her maturing mental powers as is now

---

[2] "Sed vigor ingenii quondam velocis in alas inque pedes abiit." *Ovid, Metamorphoses,* VIII, 254, "The Flight of Daedalus."

felt with respect to physical strength and skill. Taking our own valuation of the college as an educational institution, what do we really want?

A very tempting vision pictures a college full of students obtaining from learning the same intense fascination which it gives to us professors, who are willing to devote to it our whole lives. They would thrill like Browning's Grammarian over *"hoti* and the enclitic *de,"* or spend four years happily tracing the French sources of the Arthurian legend or reading interminable correspondence between colonial governors and London officials just before the Revolution—hundreds of Arrowsmiths, all absorbed in minute research through four concentrated years—after which they would go out into banks, railroads, mail-order houses, factories, and farms.

It will not work. The enthusiasm that intensive research requires in order to be fruitful, the ability, the patience, the isolation, are peculiar to scholars, and we cannot expect to turn all our students into replicas of ourselves. It is better so, since we live in a world where not only ideas have to be mastered, but things and men as well. For that task, the main task of most college graduates, prolonged research would be of little use. And let us scholars frankly admit that some of the fascination we find in minute investigation is, in a sense, a hobby, not altogether different in nature from the appeal of chess—and cross-word puzzles. We have to be always on our guard against the lure of the unimportant, the creed that all facts are created equal. Though many of the most productive investigations have been purely theoretical at first—Pasteur is a great example—the wise investigator sooner or later, and here Pasteur may be cited again, harnesses himself to move forward the world at the same time that he gratifies his passion for research, much like the Connecticut Yankee at the Court of King Arthur, when he saw the hermit who bowed himself all day long and hitched him to a sewing-machine.

Most students will prefer other types of recreation than research. The most we professors can hope is to have them spend enough time on research to comprehend something of its method, to see why *we* love it, though they cannot share our devotion, and above all to realize its essential importance, to realize how much that amuses or serves or grips their lives was brought about by the patient, isolated, apparently useless labor of investigators. Gregor Mendel, in a monastery garden, observes the colors of sweet peas year by year. He publishes his results in an obscure periodical. Sixteen years after he is dead, scientists find out about him for the first time, and in consequence vastly improve wheat and cattle and perhaps human beings. Research is not the task of most college graduates, but if they possess an understanding of its value, theirs is often the power to make possible the material environment, the facilities for publication, the encouragement, the mental freedom, in which investigation can best flourish.

A much simpler plan to make undergraduates study would consist in convincing them that the information obtainable by hard work will be pecuniarily valuable to them in earning a livelihood. The trouble is that except for vocational subjects, like agriculture and engineering, or those needed for admission to a professional school, the college courses are obviously worth nothing in dollars and cents. All the information needed to get on in life was acquired by the student years before, when he learned to read advertisements, write business letters, and enough arithmetic not to be short-changed. Arguments that Latin and medieval history have a cash value do not deceive the wily sophomore. If he is urged to prepare himself directly for business while in college, he will turn from the useless courses offered by the Faculty to practical courses offered by student organizations in getting advertisements for a college paper or managing a great financial enterprise like a football team.

It is significant that the great benefactors of American education were not college graduates—Rockefeller, Carnegie, George F. Baker. Universities did not teach them how to make their money, only how to spend it. And indeed it is arguable that one real function of college is to teach the students how to spend money—no mean end, since economists have now emphasized unintelligent expenditure as one of the largest causes of waste, and insist that consumption must be as wisely managed in the future as production in the past. Within these walls, men and women may learn how to gain the durable satisfactions of life with their money and with what is more precious than money, their time. The great gift of modern machinery is leisure, and we hardly know what to do with it. "Getting and spending we lay waste our powers."

This, however, is but part of the real aim of college education. It will enlist the energy and enthusiasm of youth only when they realize that it possesses a direct relation to their lives, not as a preparation for money-making, but for the whole of life. Its function is to supply not so much knowledge as power, power to understand the universe and the social order in which they exist, that in which they exist now and the different social order of a quarter century hence when they will be in the lead. They must not regard the principles of today as eternal truths. Life is an adventure with new experiences and contests beyond every turn on the road. Woodrow Wilson endeavored to galvanize the colleges of his day by representing them as training-grounds for citizenship. They are this and more. The student must find here the methods and the power to enable him to be at home not only in political life, but also in more intimate human relationships, in art, scenery, and the far-flung stars, in the spiritual and religious values of his world. Here he can gain the strength and intelligence to play an efficient and understanding part in his time. Above all, he must know that his time will not be our time. He must acquire the will to march on.

And so I urge undergraduates: Give your minds sea room, pushing out into the open ocean of thought whither your teachers have longed to set your course and theirs, but all too often have been obliged instead to drag you like barges along the placid canals of knowledge where the tow-path is worn deep by their repeated journeys. And when you have finished college and gone into the outside world, keep alert against the impulse always to hug the coasts charted out by those in your own occupation, to let yourselves be hemmed in by the barriers flung up by the terrific pressure of your daily tasks. Launch out ever and again into the troubled waters of unsettled questions, into the streams of thought of men far different from yourselves, toward the western islands of philosophy and poetry and art. Expect your happiness to come from the joy of intellectual work rather than from any praise by others. President Lowell has said, "You can do a thing or you can get the credit for .it, but you can't have both." Now you look forward to great achievements which will advance the world. Later will come the realization that each man can accomplish only a little; but it is of vast importance that he should do that little with all his might. Be able to say without regret: "My dreams have all come true to other men." [3]

This conception that colleges exist to create and encourage in their students the desire to fit themselves for solving the new problems of their lives, although held by most college presidents and professors, is bound to meet opposition when they seek to put it into practice. A chief obstacle is what may be described as the hickory limb philosophy of education, because it is concisely expressed in the old poem:

> "Mother dear, may I learn to swim?"
> "Yes, my darling daughter.
> Hang your clothes on a hickory limb;
> But don't go near the water."

According to this view, those in authority are to prevent a youth from making a bad choice by protecting him from influences which they consider harmful. This philosophy results from at least three emotions. The first and strongest is fear. Men advocate the suppression of forces they think bad because they distrust the strength of the countervailing forces they think good. They want to substitute force for argument because they are afraid that their view of truth will not prevail if left to a fair fight. "It is not faith that lights the fagot, but the lurking doubt." When the choice between good and evil is to be made by a child or a youth, there exists of course a real danger that he will be too immature to reject evil if it is presented to him completely unmasked, but the advocates of censorship come to deny that anybody is sufficiently mature to be trusted to make a wise choice. High school superintendents say that open discussion of controversial questions is all very well for college students. Mr. Coolidge when Vice President expressed great

[3] Edwin Arlington Robinson, *Old Trails*.

concern in the *Delineator* at the presence of radical teachers in the women's colleges. And others have a similar fear about professional schools, while legislators endeavor to safeguard full grown citizens from communistic books and speeches. Secondly, coupled with this disbelief by the advocates of suppression in the common sense of others, is a strong belief in their own superior power to discern the truth. The books forbidden to the Roman Catholic layman by the Index Expurgatorius may be read by cardinals and bishops.[4] Trust in ourselves tends to increase with distrust of others. The belief grows, that a few men—and the speaker naturally counts himself among their number—are so much wiser than the masses that they can safely regulate their views for them. Finally, the hickory limb philosophy is based on a longing for stability, that the world shall go on unchanged from what it was in the days of our youth.

Opposed to this attitude is the philosophy of the swimming hole, that youths must be thrown into life and can best master it by struggling with it, aided by the experience handed on to them by those who have gone through the same conflict.

If the stability desired by conservatives were possible, if the world could always remain the same, perhaps it would be best to teach college students only the principles underlying the existing order. But we have seen too many changes in our own lives not to expect many more in theirs. An old Maine man declared that all the evils of his day could be traced to one fundamental mistake, the adoption of the Australian ballot. He would have stopped the clock years ago. It is just as hopeless for us to stop it now. We are fond of saying how startled our grandfathers would have been by the progressive income tax, the initiative and referendum, and votes for women, or our grandmothers by flivvers and flappers. We forget that the future may be equally shocking to us. The question is whether students shall be trained to discuss these possible changes, however distasteful in the contemplation of an older generation, and fully canvass their advantages and disadvantages, or shall be left with bandaged eyes to wander through novel situations equipped with no data for choice except a strong love for the institutions of today.

We live in a world of immense complexity. We may have developed a situation too much for our powers of control. We are like children in a speeding locomotive who do not know one lever from another and who may not be able to stop it. In four years an undergraduate cannot be furnished with the explanations of all this complexity even if they were known by his elders, but he can be supplied with the desire and the method to find out as much as possible for himself. The best that he can get in college is not information but method and the spirit of exploration, the spirit of the old monk Mendel, of Darwin in his perfect brief autobiography, of Pasteur, of

---

[4] *Codex Iuris Canonici* (1918), can. 1401.

Marshall, Hamilton, and Jefferson, men whom we admire, not because they clung tenaciously to the old, but because, faced with new conditions, they searched and planned to meet those conditions with new remedies and resources.

Not only must the student prepare for a complicated world where truth is hard to find, but for a world where the supposed truths of today may no longer hold good for tomorrow. The best kind of education I know was that received by Mark Twain and described in his *Life on the Mississippi*. After he had learned all the points and shoals from St. Louis to New Orleans, he found that many of them had changed. He had to learn them all over again and to be perpetually gathering information from which he could predict those changes.

The facts of life, tremendously uncertain in themselves, are in political, economic, and social matters made still more uncertain, because they necessarily come to us through the minds of other human beings, in newspapers and books. Consciously or unconsciously the writer is like the modern advertiser. He shapes what he says in a desired direction. For this too the student must train himself. He must learn to discount the bias of the source of any statement before assessing its value. Hence the usefulness of studying the enormous variation in two accounts of the same fact, the Pullman strike of 1894, the repeal of the Missouri Compromise, the closing days of July, 1914. And he must expect just the same sort of discrepancies in the versions presented to him of events in the future. Unless he be trained to discriminate true from false, he will either go through the world muddled, or else sink into unthinking acceptance of the editorials in the *New York Times* or the *New Republic* as the case may be.

In my statement of these needs and my vision of the far-voyaging undergraduate I cannot reckon without those who fear to let him stray beyond the well-marked channels of the past. Some alumni, some trustees, some legislators, are appalled by the dangers of freedom. The growing influence of the desire to prescribe what shall and shall not be learned, with a corresponding restriction on the inquiring mind of youth, is strikingly illustrated by two recent movements in education.

The Tennessee law punishing any teacher in a university or school supported in whole or in part by public funds who shall be found "to teach any theory that denies the story of the divine creation of man as taught in the Bible, and to teach instead that man has descended from a lower order of animals," was greeted as a mere joke when first proposed, but has been enforced in Tennessee and imitated in other states. Even if such legislation is eventually held unconstitutional under the Fourteenth Amendment, which seems doubtful since the power of a state over its educational funds is very large, this will matter little since the purpose of such laws may easily be attained through decisions by state boards that teachers with evolutionary beliefs are incompetent. The courts can accomplish little for freedom of education until the controlling officials really believe in it. Nor will the issue be settled by a demonstration satisfactory to those in authority, that evolution is not yet conclusively proved. It is not for the legislature or the regents to decide scientific truths. Where scientists find difficulties, politicians are not likely to be infallible. Whether Bryan or Darwin was right, the truth can best be found if everyone, teacher or text writer as well as preacher, be left free to present sincerely his own view and the alternative for the consideration of the student, leaving him to choose for himself. The youth brought up in blind ignorance of the evolutionary view and taught to regard every word of the Bible as unquestioned truth is all the more likely to lose his religion entirely when he is confronted, as he will be sooner or later, with the scientific evidence for the unity of all life. Much better to leave him free to arrive perhaps at the conception of organic life as the gradually unfolding creation of a Divine Thinker.

But let us not fling too many rocks at the South. We Northerners are equally ready to consider restrictions when teachers threaten our cherished principles, which happen to be in the fields of economics and politics. Far more serious than the anti-evolution statutes is the recent desire of state legislatures and patriotic organizations to regulate the teaching of American history. So far their efforts have been limited to the schools, but if they succeed there, sooner or later they will reach the colleges. The Oregon statute prohibits any text-book which "speaks slightingly of the founders of the republic, or of the men who preserved the union, or which belittles or undervalues their work." The determination of historical truth is taken away from experts and placed in the hands of government officials, who are to apply the vague tests of "slightingly" and "undervalues" to facts dependent on obscure and conflicting testimony. Indeed, the most influential of this group disavow truth as their aim, and prefer what they call patriotism though based on falsehood. "I want our children taught that our forefathers were right and the British were wrong on this subject [taxation]." And another says, "Discussion of controversial subjects has no place in a history."

There will be controversies enough in the American history of the next quarter century. Will our citizens be fitted to meet them if they are carefully excluded from any attention in the schools? They are just the subjects which should be studied as a preparation for life—not indeed by memorizing a third-rate text-book, but by reading the arguments of the best men on both sides.

The effect of an unthinking worship of past statesmen and causes is unpreparedness for the making of history, in which every citizen must take his part at the ballot box and in the continuous discussion out of which public opinion is formed. The great fact to me in our history is that the men at the helm in crises were not superhuman beings with a unanimous purpose, but men with failings who disagreed bitterly among themselves, and yet frankly faced their shortcomings and differences and overcame them so as to bring new institutions into life. So must we. To picture the past as an heroic age unlike our own will produce in the student when once in politics either disgust at the supposed decline, which will make him shrink aside, or else cynicism and willingness to play the dirty game since nothing better seems possible. In either event he is liable to ignore the opportunities for idealism which the great men of the past displayed under circumstances not much unlike those in which he lives.

The teaching of the past is of little use unless it emphasizes its similarity to the present. The time when our forefathers lived seems long ago to us, but it did not seem long ago to them, and we must judge them as living in an up-to-date world, as ignorant as we of the future. Bertrand Russell remarked that in studying about Charles I, we often forget that he lived his entire life without realizing that he lost his head. We look at the past as if it were really as simple as it is presented in the books, and we imagine that we should unhesitatingly have chosen the side which later time has shown to be right. We assume that we would have been among the first to proclaim the innocence of Dreyfus, and do not see that for the men of his time the issue was clouded by the emotions and conflicting testimony which have made it so difficult for sincere men today to decide about the innocence of Sacco and Vanzetti.

Let us have enough faith in our institutions to believe that they can safely withstand voice and paper, and enough confidence in our students to trust them in the comparative maturity of college to face all the facts frankly and choose for themselves. It is their last chance to face them under guidance. If we hide them now, they will face them later, alone, without our help.

The public should beware of limiting the freedom of the teachers of youth. In any case their task loses its freshness all too easily. An *Atlantic Monthly* article [5] comments bitterly on the tendency of us professors to fall into dry rot. Say to us, "On this point you must not exercise your mind in the class room; here you must hide what you think when you make a speech or write a book," and you deprive us of the motive for action. To direct our teaching into specified channels may occasionally strengthen the existing order by inculcating unthinking loyalties among our students. It may secure more stability, but at the expense of that freedom of thought through which alone we and they can solve the problems of the future.

Historians tell us, writes Graham Wallas, that the great periods of intellectual activity are apt to coincide with the wide extension of a sense of personal liberty. Most men can explain this from their personal experience.

[5] George Boas, "To a Young Man Bent on Entering the Professoriat," *Atlantic Monthly,* March, 1926.

There are some emotional states in which creative thought is impossible, and the chief among these is the sense of helpless humiliation and anger which is produced in a sensitive nature by the inability to oppose or avoid the "insolence of office."

Athens during the last quarter of the fifth century B.C. [he goes on] was not well governed; and if the British Empire had then existed, and if Athens had been brought within it, the administration of the city would undoubtedly have been improved in many important respects. But one does not like to imagine the effect on the intellectual output of the fifth century B.C. if even the best of Mr. Rudyard Kipling's [English] public-school [graduates] had stalked daily through the agora, snubbing as he passed that intolerable bounder, Euripides; or clearing out of his way the probably seditious group that were gathered around Socrates.[6]

The tolerance I propose involves no mushy latitudinarianism. Willingness to hear all views does not mean that we should, after hearing them, treat them all as of equal value. Like St. Paul, we must prove all things, but then, like him, hold fast that which is good. We must be slow to impose our own standards of right and wrong upon others, but rigorous in imposing them upon ourselves. That was the strength of the Puritans, the merciless steadfastness with which they held themselves to their appointed task.

Let no one think that I am advocating merely a critical and destructive attitude toward life in teacher and student and citizen. There must be constant pulling down of the old to build the new, but pulling down is useless without rebuilding. The Inquiring Mind which I urge must be joined with the Constructive Mind. In many ways the period in which we live in this country resembles that in England a century ago. Just as war and the reverberations of the Russian Revolution have shaken much that we held precious, so war and the reverberations of the French Revolution disturbed their old institutions. Some men stood aghast and inactive; others prosecuted and punished and suppressed the discontented and vociferous. Yet there were not lacking men of a different mind who realized that old ways had gone forever, and that their task was to build England anew. They were the builders—Jeremy Bentham, Sir Robert Peel, Thomas Babington Macaulay, Lord Shaftesbury, John Stuart Mill, and a host of less conspicuous helpers without whom little would have been accomplished. So in the United States, the undergraduates of today must be the builders of tomorrow.

[6] Graham Wallas, *The Great Society*, pp. 196-198.

Howard Mumford Jones

Howard Mumford Jones (1892-), Professor of English at Harvard University, pleads earnestly for the teaching of the humanities as the basis of a democratic way of life.

THE PLACE OF THE HUMANITIES IN AMERICAN EDUCATION

I HAVE entitled my remarks "The Place of the Humanities in American Education" for two excellent reasons. In the first place, this is a title sufficiently dull to be respectable in academic circles, where, I have observed, we do not believe we are being educated unless at the same time we are being a little bored. And in the second place, it is a title so vague that nobody knows what it means. Nobody knows what it means because we do not know what the humanities are, we do not know why we teach them, and we do not know what results to expect from them when they are taught.

In *The Genteel Tradition* Santayana remarks that the humanities came into being as a protest against Christianity—that is, as a protest against the restricted view of human nature into which Christian dogma had degen-erated. If this be true, time has wonderfully avenged Christianity. We con-tinue to bow ceremoniously before the humanities; but if the actions of many educators and most pupils indicate their real convictions, we now believe that the humanities offer a view of human nature so restricted that the vital parts of education are to be found almost anywhere else. The wheel has come full circle. We see without amazement the president of a great mid-western university founded by Baptists, campaigning in the twen-tieth century for a revival of neo-scholasticism, that product of medieval Catholic theology, in order to revitalize secular studies.

I have remarked that nobody knows what the humanities are, nobody knows why we teach them, and nobody knows what results we expect from our teaching. Until a few decades ago, this observation would have been nonsense. Every educated man formerly knew what was meant by a humane education. It was education in a body of material, chiefly in the classic lan-guages, supposed to comprise the wisest views of human life obtainable out-side of inspired writing. The study of this material formed the scholar and the gentleman. Men were instructed to find the model of literary excel-lence in the classics. The pattern of the historian was the Greek and Roman

79

historians. If one discussed ethics, one quoted the great moralists of the ancient world. Biography was teaching by example, and the perfect instance of such biography was Plutarch. Philosophy descended from the pagan world. A few amateurs here and there were conducting scientific experiments, as Bacon had prophesied they would, but though such experiments had penetrated certain schools, the principal scientific course was one called natural philosophy. Natural philosophy was manifestly a branch of philosophy intended to show how God had constructed the world; and though natural philosophy owed something to Christianity, it owed even more to Aristotle.

When I say that we no longer know what we mean by the humanities I do not refer to the patent fact that only a handful of Americans study Latin and Greek. Latin and Greek might diminish as Hebrew had diminished, without affecting the concept of humane education, provided that no essential change was wrought in the notion of a central body of universal knowledge. This notion, however, could not be retained. It commenced to dwindle as science became specialized and skeptical of the reasons for its own existence. Then the concept of natural philosophy broke into a hundred separate parts which not even Herbert Spencer could put together again into what he called—revealing phrase!—a synthetic philosophy.

Even this change might have been viewed as an increase in knowledge rather than a revolution in the conditions of knowledge, and the humanities and the sciences might have existed side by side as complementary portions of education, had not the humanities, forgetful of the fate of Troy, admitted a wooden horse within their walls. They permitted the concept of scientific specialization to invade their city, and it is instructive to see what followed.

For example, the idea that philosophy is a central body of wisdom was essential to the concept of humane education. But the story of philosophy has come to resemble the story of the old Austrian empire. In philosophy, as in that empire, component states have lately asserted their independence and set up for themselves. Thus psychology, formerly a branch of metaphysics, discovered it was one of the sciences. Again, Plato had discussed the state in connection with a philosophic quest for justice, but problems of government have now been transferred to a special department known as political science. Ethics was formerly moral philosophy; modern professors of ethics, catching the universal contagion, have taken to the statistical method, prove by graphs that in student opinion adultery is a more heinous offence than drunkenness, and conduct laboratory experiments in blood pressure. The process of making philosophy scientific has gone so far that the scientists have become philosophers, and the philosophers yearn to be scientists. Physicists demonstrate their faith in God, astronomers declare their belief in immortality, and biologists nowadays have turned metaphysical. As for the philosophers, I quote Viscount Samuel: "For my own part, I feel convinced that we shall find firm ground, that we shall be able to make a fresh start with any hope of success, only if philosophy, with full deliberation, accepts science as its basis."

Is literature one of the humanities? Literary study formerly meant an acquaintance with Latin and Greek and, through Latin and Greek, with the chief masterpieces of the ancient world. But the classicists in the nineteenth century also went scientific, building such admirable barricades of philological learning around their subject as successfully to defy invasion. Yet they also insisted on remaining classicists; that is, they insisted, for example, that all the Latin worth study was written before the fall of Rome; and though Latin continued as a living literary language for a thousand years, though it produced the admirable lyric poetry which John Addington Symonds and Helen Waddell have beautifully translated, the classicists would have no traffic with such modernity. Their subject therefore became known as the dead languages, and eager youth abandoned it for something more lively.

Eager youth turned to the modern languages, including English. As a result, instruction in the modern languages enormously increased. Today, in place of that extraordinary being, the professor of modern languages, who apparently taught every tongue with equal ease, expert instruction in the chief modern languages is easily available to those who want it.

Unfortunately, proportionately fewer people seem to want it. Modern languages, which were formerly required subjects, have become elective, and in some schools have almost disappeared. Part of the trouble was bad teaching. But part of the trouble was caused by that ancient enemy of liberal training, "practical" education. The theory of the assault on the modern languages in the name of practical education is one of those theories which have all the vitality of error and all the tediousness of an old friend. Of what use, it is argued, is any foreign language to American youth? Why struggle with French verbs when shorthand and typewriting may get you a job? Wide acceptance of the implied answer to these rhetorical questions has led to the abandonment in increasing degree of modern language instruction in the secondary schools, and the placing of this burden on the colleges. But when the colleges have to do elementary work, they cannot at the same time do collegiate work, and the vicious circle is thus completed: why begin the study of modern languages in college, when, after two years, you have only mastered the elements of the subject? Because the riches of foreign culture, under this extraordinary scheme of things, still seem remote, we bid fair in the matter of modern languages to become the most illiterate great nation on the face of the globe.

To offset this deficiency there has been a tendency to fall back upon English. Certainly the number of English teachers in the country has enormously increased, with the result that the National Council of Teachers of English is today one of the most powerful educational bodies in the country. But the notion that the study of the traditional English classics would compensate for the loss of Latin and Greek and the decline in the study of modern languages is also under assault, the assault coming, of all strange sources, from English teachers themselves. One of the most vocal groups in that body is not content to teach the classics; they wish to abandon the classics for contemporary literature, and some of them do not wish to teach even contemporary literature as literature—what they want to do is to teach economics, sociology, and international peace. I quote from an editorial in *The English Journal,* the official organ of the National Council:

Today there are a score of progressive schools where wide freedom to read where and when they wish from the literature of today is the program of all classes. The ghosts of the older classics still move among us, but the sturdy push of the contemporary reduces their pale ranks in every anthology and course of study that issues from the presses. Soon only those ancients "stuck fast in yesterday" and the ever-present Philistines will prescribe forced reading in a dead culture.

The spectacle of the pale ghost of Hamlet, stuck fast in the yesterday of a dead culture, escorted off the literary stage by a chorus of Philistines, in order that high school pupils may devote themselves to the novels of Mr. Faulkner, is one of those things that make the angels weep. Sturdy contemporary literature—and I note the implication that the classics are not sturdy—is, however, not to be studied, it is to be read, and read only when and how the pupils please. This is scarcely a rational concept of education; what it offers us is simply a complicated form of the "I know what I like" theory. When somebody told Whistler, "I know what I like," he responded thoughtfully, "So does a cow." And as for the theory that the principal use of literature is economic and sociological enlightenment, I shall have to refer you to the official organ of the National Council of Teachers of English for interesting reading on this topic.

Lest you think you have summoned a Harvard professor to talk to you, and got instead England's gloomy dean, I shall not discuss the ambiguous position of history, which cannot decide whether it is one of the humanities or one of the social sciences. Nor is there time to discuss the contradictory fashion in which we approach the fine arts. In college courses we expose students to masterpieces of the past; in the lower schools we insist that the so-called creative activity of the children shall never be contaminated by any knowledge of the subject. Yet, while the humanities have fallen from their high estate, the prestige of the name is such that subjects which have no possible connection with them proudly proclaim that they are as liberalizing as ever were Latin and Greek. Doubtless any subject, rightly taught, is in a sense liberalizing, but when all subjects are equally liberalizing, no one of them is relatively so; and in such a situation a phrase like "liberal education" becomes what Mr. Stuart Chase unkindly refers to as "blab words."

Why have we drifted into this curious situation? Our motives were, of course, highly honorable. Society is complex, and we wish to prepare students to take their places intelligently in that society. We want them to understand how human nature works; and biology and economics, psychology and political science, government and contemporary literature seem to be the quickest means to that end. Sociology is the key to an understanding of society. We live in an evolutionary order, and biology tells us what that order is. We live in a period of tension in domestic and social life, and perhaps the psychologist can help us. We suffer from a business depression—what more natural than to turn to the economist for instruction? We have seen revolutionary changes in the theory of government at home and abroad—cannot political science help us here? How shall we understand the confusions of our time if we do not grapple with them? The lively subjects, the thrilling subjects are not the humanities, concerned with people dead and gone these hundreds of years, but subjects which deal immediately with the problems of the citizen. Away with Shakespeare and Plato—what is the latest report from the concentration camps?

What the natural sciences and the social sciences have to tell us is both necessary and important. But the natural scientist and the social scientist are the first to warn us that wisdom will not die with them. There is a fallacy in this admirable enthusiasm of ours. The fallacy is briefly set forth in the saying which runs: "He who knows nothing about the past remains all his life a child." Select any burning issue of the day, and see how quickly it becomes both an historical and a philosophic problem.

Some of us, for example, were greatly disturbed by the attempt of Nazi Germany to swallow up Austria. From the economic point of view almost anything that would unite Austria, that head cut off from a body, by commercial and industrial relations with a country richer than itself would, in the long run, prove a good thing. A man from Mars would have great difficulty in understanding why two peoples who speak the same language and share, to some degree, a common inheritance should not be united, especially when Austrian independence was in fact a fable agreed upon. A respectable number of the Austrians are clearly of the same opinion as the man from Mars. Nevertheless, the majority of the Austrians, a proud and unhappy people, do not seem to care for the Nazis and did not desire to surrender their political independence, shadowy though it was. Why should this be so?

Unfortunately for the Nazis, the Austrians look back with fond regret upon a long, colorful, and romantic history. Anyone who has visited the empty palace of Schönbrunn in the outskirts of Vienna, populous only with

tourists and uneasy imperial ghosts—anyone who has heard an elderly Viennese woman sigh for the lost glories of the royal court, realizes that he is
face to face with imponderable values more important than finance or economics. It is not only because Vienna was formerly one of the capitals of
a powerful empire that its inhabitants do not wish to see it become a provincial town. What also counts with them is the long cultural tradition of
Vienna—that city of pleasure and regret. What memories arise at the mention of its name! What echoes of the waltzes of Strauss and the stormy
music of Beethoven, what tragic tales of the Hapsburgs, what love stories
delicately etched in the plays of the poet-dramatist Schnitzler! We remember the Congress of Vienna, where half the diplomats of Europe met to
dance and tell elaborate lies. We remember Metternich and the slim lad
who was never Napoleon II, we remember the great Napoleon and the
queenly Maria Theresa—a host of battles and intrigues, victories and defeats, pleasure, passion, melancholy, beauty, and death! Do you suppose the
Viennese have forgotten? Suppose it were economically wise, would you like
to see New England united to Quebec, its newspapers taking their cue from
Ottawa, its schools managed according to Canadian policy, its emblem the
maple leaf? Manifestly, no; but your objections, in such an imaginary case,
would arise from considerations of culture far more intangible than any
column of figures.

But if, on the other hand, we wish to understand Nazi Germany (if
anybody can), it is not sufficient to read the newspapers, hate the persecution of the Jews, or remember the Versailles treaty—the tangled thread of
history takes us back through Wagner and Nietzsche and Gobineau and
Darwin and Bismarck and Fichte and Frederick the Great and the Teutonic
Knights to the *Niebelungenlied,* and the *Germania* of Tacitus! The Prus-
sians and the Austrians are two eternal types, but it is not economics only
that has made them so. And whether we invade history along the Austrian
avenue or down the Prussian military road, at the end of the journey we
face a question of values which are eternal and not contemporary alone. Is
it better to sacrifice the individual to the state, as the Spartans believed, or
is it better to keep the state subordinate to the enriching of the individual,
as the Athenians thought? Which is the wiser legislator, Plato or Lycurgus?
Has duty or wisdom the higher imperative? Shall we say to the personified
state: Though he slay me, yet shall I trust in him, or shall we ask with the
Apostle Paul: "Why is my liberty judged of another man's conscience?"

But there is another fallacy in the theory that the paramount business
of education is only to prepare the pupil for the contemporary world. Those
who advocate this theory also insist that this is a changing world. They insist
furthermore upon the rapidity of the rate of change. Because the change is
both swift and incessant, they argue that we are more and more cut off from
the values of the past. That is why they are skeptical of traditional educa-

tional processes. Let us use the instrument of education—especially the instrument of secondary education—to prepare the next generation for an altered society. Let us accustom them as soon as may be to the dizzy pace of things. Ten years ago we were a happy and prosperous nation. Who knows what the future may bring?

But as Emerson remarked long ago of another theory, there is an optical illusion in it. If we are to educate for the future, how distant is the future we are to educate for? Is the student to be turned out fit for society as it exists at the time of his graduation, or for society as it shall be when he becomes middle-aged? When he enters the school system at the age of five or six, are we to expect that society will obligingly stand still until he is sixteen? Does my question sound casuistical? Let me remind you that a child who entered the first grade in 1910 and left the school system in 1928 was one year later plunged into the depression; and if he was socially educated according to the standards of the Coolidge regime, he was a sad misfit under Hoover. Where are the educational prophets who can predict what kind of society children now in the first grade are going to be living in by 1956, or what society is going to be like in 1983 when surviving first-graders are forty-five? When expert economists do not pretend to understand things as they are, shall we assume that professors of education and superintendents of schools have mysteriously acquired such insight into the future that they can confidently shape a curriculum which will fit adults for life half a century hence? A writer in the current [March, 1938] number of *Harper's Magazine* has amused himself by picturing the life of John Doe, an average American citizen in 1988, by which time inventions and discoveries already made may have become commonplace utilities. His sketch is as fantastic as anything by H. G. Wells, but he also points out that a hundred obstacles lie in the way of the swift acceptance of these things. We simply do not know and cannot find out what the incidence of social pressures is going to be fifty years hence.

All this does not mean that we should not pursue science and social studies or strive to be as intelligent about the contemporary world as we can. But there is a vast difference between giving the sciences and social studies an important part in the educational process, and turning our schools into ideational training camps for the supposititious society of the future. "Progressive" educators complain with considerable justice of the lock-step method which has sometimes characterized teaching in the humanities; is there no danger of the lock-step method in marching towards the so-called planned society of tomorrow? The increasing spread of requirements in social studies, civics, flag-saluting, finger-printing, intelligence testing, grading according to ability, and the like reduction of the human individual to the status of a cog in the social machine would seem to hint of this danger. That there is something to be said for each item on such a list is true, but the total impact of the cumulation of such devices may not unreasonably be expected to end in a kind of social regimentation quite as disastrous as grammar, subjects considered as "disciplines," and the necessity of learning the multiplication table were ever supposed to be.

If social education seems to me to fall from time to time into the very errors it charges against older methods, there is one point on which humanists and the progressive school of educational theorists can heartily agree. Some time ago there appeared a celebrated judicial decision concerning the condemnation of an obnoxious billboard. The owners of the billboard claimed that the state highway department had no right to destroy their property; the highway department claimed that the billboard destroyed the view and was a menace to traffic. The court upheld the state officials on the interesting doctrine that the public has a right to privacy. In a sense the object of both the progressive educator and the humanist is the public's right to privacy. They are concerned, not with the social atom, but with the individual. Differing as they do on other points, they agree on the desirability of enriching private life. They want not better citizens only, but better human beings. Society may be as perfectly adjusted as was apparently the society of ancient Peru, but it does not follow that it is an interesting society, for the simple reason that the individual members who compose it may not enjoy very interesting lives.

I think there comes a time in the careers of most men and women when the old Adam in them rebels. We cannot be citizens twenty-four hours a day. The tenth application to contribute to a worthy cause or put one's shoulder to the wheel leaves one cold. We cannot be always mourning over China, Spain, Ethiopia, Russia, and Czechoslovakia. We were born individually into the world; we became citizens only by accident and of necessity. Important as it is that we shall vote honestly, we are subject to a higher law than that of the suffrage or the courts. I am enough of a disciple of Emerson to believe that the richest and deepest life for each of us has very little relation to communism, Fascism, or the New Deal. A thousand changes have swept over the face of society, and yet the fundamental interests of the human heart remain unaltered. We fall in love without reference to politics; even in Germany mothers presumably still love their babies; and the lonely quest for a belief to live by is not satisfied with a report on the tariff. Outraged as we may be by the rank injustices of the social order, we are at long last compelled to say with Housman: "Be still, my soul, and see injustice done," or to exclaim with Augustine: "I will not say dear city of Cecrops, but rather, dear city of God!" Even in Russia sunsets are beautiful; even a Fascist may be moved by a chorus ending from Euripides. War and pestilence and disaster come and go, the form of the state perpetually changes, the sands drift over Carthage and Baalbec and

Palmyra, and at the end of the story it is all vanity and vexation of spirit except for the unconquerable vitality of the human soul.

> The world *is* too much with us; late and soon
> Getting and spending, we lay waste our powers.

Enveloping the transient economic order of our day, as it enveloped the transient economic order of yesterday and shall envelop the transient economic order of tomorrow is that vast and more perdurable order in which alone we may be said truly to live. The pale and imperfect reflection of this second world is found in those records which it is the business of the humanities to preserve and make clear to succeeding generations of men. Doubtless we teach the substance of these records badly; doubtless rosy youth, eager for the goal, cannot be tremendously excited by the life-story of the former runners. I will not say that the humanities are the most difficult subjects to teach, but I will say that no part of education demands more expert instruction, and receives less. But because the job is difficult, we are not justified in avoiding it. If the vocabulary of Shakespeare is hard to understand, we are not therefore permitted to take refuge in *The Saturday Evening Post*. I have yet to be shown why, because he is living in the twentieth century, Mr. Dale Carnegie is a more stimulating thinker than Aristotle.

Nevertheless, to many practical-minded persons these considerations seem only a noble dream. Most of our students forget the classics outside of the classroom. We do not care for poetry, since obviously we refuse to support poets. We teach the musical classics, we teach the masterpieces of painting, and the result is swing music and a healthy interest in that admirable comic strip which depicts Kayo and Moon Mullins. We advocate philosophy, and the younger generation turns on the radio and flocks to the movies. Let us therefore abandon our profitless ideal; let us directly create better taste in comic strips the movies, radio programs, and current books.

There is merit in the argument, but it cannot be pushed so far. Because tens of thousands of persons daily seek the fortune-teller, shall we abandon instruction in science? Because the Townsend plan receives wide popular support, shall we cease to teach orthodox economics? If education is to be geared to the immediate only, let us at least be consistent and change our curriculum monthly in order that it may faithfully follow the fluctuations of society. Or shall we rather remember that the good is always the enemy of the best?

But let me conclude by meeting this argument of practicality on another plane. Everyone knows, I suppose, that the error of the leaders in the French Revolution was the attempt to reshape society immediately according to an abstract intellectual formula. With the insight of genius Napoleon dubbed these men ideologues.

The ideologue is once more abroad in the world. Two great proposals for revolutionary change in society are the Marxian and the Fascist. The theoretical program of Marx derives from the philosophy of Hegel, most abstruse of German metaphysicians, and though this program has its evolutionary aspect, it tends to force the interpretation of history into a preconceived point of view, from which a plan for the reorganization of society is derived. The Fascist comes with an intellectualistic theory of the state, which, when he seizes it, he tries to reshape in the image of his ideological theory. But it would appear that society can thus be wrenched into preconceived patterns only by force, and in fact modern Caesarism, whether it be Russian, German, or Italian, exists mainly by force of arms. When, however, force is called in to implement an abstract idea, the idea presently disappears, and we have, not an era of culture, but an era of barbarism. The glorification of war which is now part of the official creed of the Fascist nations is a return to the ideas of Mohammed: slay the unbeliever with the edge of the sword. And the peculiar ferocity with which Fascist ideologues attack our inheritance from the nineteenth century arises from the instinctive consciousness that the most formidable enemy of barbarism is culture.

The rich traditional heritage of Europe is a heritage of reason. The attempt of the Fascist nations to break with the tradition is at bottom a glorification of irrationality. When Hitler states that decadent parliamentary institutions in the democratic countries no longer express the wishes of those countries, he may or may not be right; what he fails to say is why he expresses the wishes of his own country. He is Der Fuehrer; he receives his direct inspiration from some unknown and irrational source; and the duty of reasonable citizens under his control is not to question or discover, but to obey—that is, to act irrationally. When, however, millions of human beings are indoctrinated with the fanatic belief that their highest duty to the state is to surrender any notions of rational choice, we turn back the clock of history by thousands of years. When millions of human beings are indoctrinated with an equally fanatic belief that they belong to a superior race, and that the superiority of this race is such that the art, the science, the literature, the philosophy of every other race are *per se* inferior, we see a flat denial of the findings of science, the findings of history, the lessons of art, and the teachings of literature. And at long last, the only effective check upon the assumption that nations can be profitably re-made by emotion and violence is the appeal to history—to the lesson found in a study of the slow and painful progress of the so-called human race to even its present caricature of intelligence. If proof of the essential antagonism between the lesson of history and the dogma of irrationality were needed, it is to be found in the fact that the dictator nations have tried to erase the lesson of history from their books and re-write it in terms flattering to themselves. But the historical process as the humanist understands it cannot be thus falsified by fiat.

The deepest practical reason why the democracies must cling to the humanities is that it is only through the humanities that the democracies can exist. Having struggled to learn how to live peacefully together, the human race cannot successfully give up living peacefully together at this late date, if civilization is going to survive. In the long run indoctrinated hate, like indoctrinated superiority, is suicidal. I do not claim that the democracies have a monopoly of culture, though things may end by leaving them the only countries in which real culture survives; but I do claim that conciliation, tolerance, humor, and sagacity are necessary if the democracies are going to live; and I conceive it to be the practical purpose of the humanities, by examining history and the arts, philosophy and the course of religion, to inculcate these civilized attributes as widely as their share of the educational process will permit. If we, too, wish to be subject to the next ideological wind that blows, let us, by all means, abandon the study of history, of art, of philosophy, of literature; let us give ourselves over wholly to the study of the contemporary. But if the tragic lesson of recent events abroad strengthens our determination to cling to the inheritance of civilization as we rationally understand that term, let us remember that the historical point of view is the only lasting check upon ideological dogma directed toward violent shifts in society. This is, I know, not a colorful program. It is impossible to roar into the loud speakers: "Be sane"; it is impossible to march in uniformed parades in favor of common sense; it is difficult to think of popular leaders swaying the multitude by an appeal to culture. Nevertheless, only in the widest possible spread of the implications of history and of some knowledge of the significance of our cultural inheritance—only in the patient and intelligent teaching and study of the humanities may we look for effective check upon fanaticism, irrationality, violence, and despair.

Stephen Leacock

Stephen Leacock (1869-1944) was born in England but lived from early childhood in Canada. His education and his career as writer, teacher, and lecturer were divided between Canada and the United States to such an extent that he might well have called himself a citizen of North America. For many years he was head of the Department of Economics and Political Science at McGill University, Montreal. It seems to be the fate of most humorists that no one will take them seriously. Leacock was an exception. For thirty-odd years people turned to him not only for amusement but for the guidance of a laughing intelligence which was equally at home in many fields. In the following pages he entertainingly discusses the over-elaboration of modern education.

EDUCATION EATING UP LIFE

IN this discussion of education, I am addressing myself to plain people. By this I mean people who shudder at mathematics, go no further in Latin than *E Pluribus Unum* and take electricity as they find it. As opposed to these are the academic class who live in colleges, or in the shadow of them, and claim education as their province. But the plain people are of necessity interested in education because their sons and daughters go to college, or, more important, can't go to college.

Now the plain people have noticed that education is getting longer and longer. Fifty years ago people learned to read out of a spelling-book at six years old, went to high school at twelve, and taught school (for money) on a third-class certificate at sixteen. After that, two years in a saw-mill and two at a medical school made them doctors, or one year in a saw-mill and one in divinity fitted them for the church. For law they needed no college at all, just three summers on a farm and three winters in an office.

All our great men in North America got this education. Pragmatically, it worked. They began their real life still young. With the money they didn't spend they bought a wife. By the age of thirty they had got somewhere, or nowhere. It is true that for five years of married life, they carried, instead of a higher degree, bills for groceries, coal, doctors and babies' medicine. Then they broke out of the woods, into the sunlight, established men— at an age when their successors are still demonstrating, interning, or writing an advanced thesis on social impetus.

Now it is all changed. Children in school at six years old cut up paper dolls and make patterns. They are still in high school till eighteen, learning civics and social statistics—studies for old men. They enter college at about nineteen or twenty, take prerequisites and postrequisites in various faculties for nearly ten years, then become demonstrators, invigilators, researchers, or cling to a graduate scholarship like a man on a raft.

At thirty they are just beginning, ten years too late. They can't marry till it's ten years too late; they have children ten years too late, and die ten years too early. They know nothing of the early life of the man who worked in saw-mills, practiced medicine at twenty and married six months later, with no other property than a stethoscope and a horse and buggy; or of the young lawyer who married in debt, and lived happy in it ever after.

"Safety first" has put its stamp on life. Population begins to die at the top. And, all the time, education grows longer and longer. This does not deny that the average human life is now longer. It means that paternity is shorter. People do not see enough of their grandchildren—the sweetest prospect in the world. Life has all too little evening. It has all run in arrears and never catches up.

All this, you will say, is exaggerated, is overcolored, is not truth. Very likely. But a half truth in argument, like a half brick, carries better. High colors show up where neutral tints blend to nothing. Yet the main truth gets over. Education is eating up life.

In the above paragraphs I have formulated the plain man's accusations against the continued lengthening of education; or, rather, I must not say his accusation. The poor fellow hasn't the spirit to accuse. It is not an accusation that he formulates or a grievance that he voices. It is just a burden that he carries.

He carries it because of the prestige of education. Round the idea of education, as effort and opportunity, there have clustered centuries of tradition and association. These are stamped in such words and phrases as "the little red schoolhouse," "the midnight oil," "the eager student," "the kindly dominie," "the absent-minded professor." With this has grown up the notion—no doubt partly true—that the harder the path of learning the higher the achievement. "There is no royal road to learning" still cheers those who are unaware that the public road itself has become overgrown with a jungle of underbrush.

In other words, people don't complain. On the contrary, they are often proud of the burden that they carry. Parents have no regrets for the fifteen years of sacrifice that they made to give their children the education they should have had in half the time.

It is a tradition with us that education opens opportunity. To send a boy to college is an ambition that wakes to life beside a cradle. "How is your son doing at school, Mr. McGregor?" I once asked of a Scotsman of the traditional type. "Fine!" he answered. "If he keeps on as he is, we'll have to put the college to him."

Even in the clutter and failure of youth's career among the blocked avenues of our misfit world the college comes into its own as a sort of refuge. "My son," said another parent, "doesn't seem to have any particular ability, so we think we'll have to send him to college. He seems no good for anything else." The one anxiety of such parents is, "Can he get in?" Beyond that no need to look. It's like being dipped in the Jordan.

But even if the plain man were to raise his complaint against the lengthening road and the increasing burden, he would be laughed out of court by the academic class. He would be told that our education is all too short. The teachers in the high schools would say that the children come to them hopelessly unprepared and ought to stay a year longer in public school.

Every professor will tell them that the first-year students at college are simply hopeless and ought to have stayed at least a year, or call it two, at high school. The students in the second year ought never to have left the first; the third-year men haven't the proper grounding for their work; and the fourth-year are so rotten that they have to be given degrees to get rid of them. As for the graduate school, the students in it should never have been admitted; they are not yet fit for advanced work. Their minds are immature. And even when they do get out of the graduate school, by sheer lapse of time, it seems ridiculous to think of them as fit to teach, or do anything. Oh, no; they have to go to Germany for a year—anyway, to somewhere for a year—and come back with whiskers and look like something.

I once put the question of shortening the college curriculum to my old friend Dean Elderberry Foible, dean of the Faculty of Arts. You didn't know him, but there was a dean at your college just like him. "Preposterous," he said, "preposterous!" And that settled it.

If we turn from the general view to the particular subjects, the case against any attempt to shorten the curriculum becomes simply overwhelming—so much so that we are crushed and humbled in presenting it. Imagine trying to leave out mathematics—the queen of sciences; or history—the very basis for understanding our modern life; or English literature—our legacy common to England and America, dear as the very hearthstones of our homes—who dares touch that?

Or who will dare disturb Latin, the bedrock of our culture; or foreign languages, the amenity of polite life; or geology, deep as the caverns of thought; biology, life's interpretation; or the social sciences, the key to the padlock of happiness still closed. Help! Nothing but pretentious ignorance could suggest leaving out anything. As to any shortening, ask again my friend Dean Elderberry Foible and he will tell you that you can't. "My dear sir, you may wish to, but you simply can't"—with that academic finality with which professors dismiss the ideas of students.

So it appears even to ourselves on a first survey. Take mathematics. How can you shorten the subject? That stern struggle with the multiplication table, for many people not yet ended in victory, how can you make it less? Square root, as obdurate as a hardwood stump in a pasture—nothing but years of effort can extract it. You can't hurry the process.

Or pass from arithmetic to algebra: you can't shoulder your way past quadratic equations or ripple through the binomial theorem. Indeed, the other way; your feet are impeded in the tangled growth, your pace slackens, you sink and fall somewhere near the binomial theorem with the calculus in sight on the horizon. So died, for each of us, still bravely fighting, our mathematical training; except only for a set of people called "mathematicians"—born so, like crooks. Yet would we leave mathematics out? No, we hold our cross.

Latin too: do you want your son to grow up not knowing what a *sine qua non* is, and who wrote Virgil's *Aeneid*? Then he not only needs the whole present curriculum but more! At present the student learns just enough Latin not to be able to read it; he stops short of the saturation point—just gets wet with it and no more.

But why recite the entire list? The same truth holds, for the academic profession, of every one of the subjects of the school and college course. The student is not saturated, when he ought really to be soaked.

A parallel resistance blocks the pathway leading to the professions. The idea of any immediate entry into them for a young man just out of college is ridiculous. A hundred years ago a man just out of college looked as good as a coin fresh from the mint, a sickle from the whetstone. At twenty-seven he was a Member of Congress, had four or five children, owned three or four thousand dollars' worth of property in his own right—and owed five thousand dollars. But nowadays! Imagine trusting a serious case of illness to a young fellow of twenty-seven barely out of college, and till yesterday an interne in a hospital. Out of the question!

And, later, when at last his turn comes, it is but a brief acme of success, and then, all of a sudden, it seems people are saying, "He's too old for the job, losing his grip—in fact, he's nearly fifty." He's an "old doctor"—once a term of esteem and confidence but now equivalent to an "old horse."

Thus in our ill-fit world youth and age jostle and hurry one another together—too young and then too old. Those who follow gardening know that green peas are first too young to pick and then, overnight as it seems, too old to eat. So with our educated people. Homer long ago said, "As is the race of leaves, so is the race of men." Make it college graduates and garden peas and it still holds good.

How did all this come about? Our system of education arose out of the medieval Latin schools of the church. It still carries, like a fossil snake in a stone, the mark of its original structure. Not that this was the earliest kind of education. But the others were different. Greek education included music and dancing and what we call the arts. It was supposed to fit people to live.

Medieval education was supposed to fit people to die. Any school-boy of today can still feel the effect of it.

Greek education was free from the problems that have beset our own. It didn't include the teaching of languages, the Greeks despising all foreigners as barbarians. It avoided everything "practical" like the plague, and would have regarded a professor of Engineering as a child of the devil, misusing truth. Mathematics, crippled by the want of symbols, became a sort of dream—intense, difficult and proudly without purpose. Greek education carried with it no "exams" and "tests" for entry to the professions. A Greek dentist didn't have to pass in Latin. He used a hammer.

Thus philosophy, "the love of knowledge," came into its own, in talk as endless as on the porch of a Kentucky country store.

"Scholars" would deny the truth of this summary and talk of Archimedes, the world's first engineer, and Hippocrates, its earliest physician. But the proof of what I say is that Archimedes found no followers and Hippocrates waited five hundred years for Galen. Scholars always see exceptions where a plain man sees an even surface. But even a billiard ball, if you look close enough, is all covered with bumps.

Our education, then, comes down to us from the schools of the Middle Ages. These were organized by the church and the first aim was piety, not competence; the goal was the reading of the Scriptures and by that the salvation of the soul. On this basis, Alfred the Great planned schools for Saxon England. So, too, in France did Charlemagne, who couldn't read or write and felt a religious admiration for those who could—the same as an oil magnate of today feels toward a university.

So presently the monastic schools arose, and from their oriel windows came forth among the elm trees the sound of Latin chants intoned by choristers; and in the silent scriptorium the light from a stained window fell on the quiet "copyist" rewriting, letter by letter, in pigment upon parchment, "In the beginning was the Word." Thus passed monastic life in its quiet transition to Eternity.

These were the earliest schools—secluded, scholarly—born ancient like the "old-fashioned" children of aging parents. For the date, place them anywhere in the four hundred years from Alfred and Charlemagne to the days of Oxford and Paris.

These later schools—Oxford, Paris, and such—came when study no longer taught people how to die and keep out of hell, but how to live, as lawyers—two ambitions with an obvious relationship. Law hatched out under the wings of the church, as a duck hatches under a hen, later to horrify its parent.

Here again the vertebrate structure is still seen in the rock. Lincoln's Inn and Grey's Inn were originally, in a sense, works of God, the defunct Doctors Commons till its end a spirituality. Law, in England at least, struggled long before it shook off the hand of ghostly guidance. Even now the connection between law and religion remains in the quantity of oaths by which the business of the law secures its righteousness.

So there came, then, such schools as Oxford and Paris, which seem to have been at first huge random gatherings of students—medieval exaggeration puts 30,000 at Oxford in pre-record days. They had, before printing, hardly any books, and no examinations. The curriculum ran to endless discussion—more Kentucky. These "disputations" begot "tests" and awards (degrees) and brought into the world that child of sin, the written examination. A few odd people like Roger Bacon began digging into black knowledge about gunpowder, and so forth, and got put into jail for it. The lamp of learning fell only on the Kingdom of Light, with lawyers dancing in the shadow.

The curriculum of these schools, the bedrock on which ours still rests, was the famous trinity of study, the Trivium, which meant grammar, rhetoric and logic; to this was supplemented the four further studies called the Quadrivium—music, arithmetic, geometry and astronomy. All were based on the use of Latin; they comprehended the whole circuit of human knowledge, and the supreme purpose of it all was salvation. The monk Alcuin, who was Charlemagne's "specialist" in education, has described for us how he taught his students:

To some I administer the honey of the sacred writings; others I try to inebriate with the wine of the ancient classics. I begin the nourishment of some with the apples of grammatical subtlety. I strive to illuminate many by the arrangement of the stars, as from the painted roof of a lofty palace.

The whole extent of human knowledge was still within human comprehension. In our own day we meet men who think they "know it all." In the Middle Ages there were men who were sure they did. Of course, where knowledge ended superstition began, and that was infinite.

It was this curriculum which in the course of centuries has been expanded beyond recognition like the toad in Aesop that would be an ox. And still it has not burst. It drags along its huge amorphous outline, flabby as a dinosaur, over fifteen years of life.

Here is what happened to expand it. The revival of learning resuscitated Greek, a study forgotten by all but the Arabs. The rising kingdoms that replaced feudalism brought national States and set people to learning one another's languages. The English, having forgotten French, had to learn it again. Italian became "polite." Milton suggested that one ought to learn it, "in an odd hour." Modern languages were still not a part of education, but a sort of annex; so they remained till yesterday in England where all Englishmen were supposed to "know French" from a governess and a copy of Ollendorff's *Grammar* and a trip to Boulogne. But, till yesterday, Eton, Rugby and Oxford never heard of it.

Printing, once in real use, expanded both opportunity and obligation. Students henceforth had books. Contacts with the Arabs revealed a system of decimal notation that made arithmetic a reality and algebra a power. Mathematics in the time of the Stuarts, with logarithms and the calculus, ceased to be a dream. Physics converted Alcuin's wonder of the sky into classroom formulae.

But even though mathematics in the sixteen hundreds, in the days of Newton and Descartes, had become a real and intensive study—far transcending in reach and in difficulty anything within the range of the ordinary college man of today—it was still regarded rather as an annex to learning than as learning itself. The place of priority still lay with classical study, with the literature of Greece and Rome. In this America was a faithful child of England. Our earliest college education was stamped with Roman letters, and its passion for the Bible in the wilderness made it even revert somewhat to the medieval type. The rules that were promulgated in 1642 for admission to Harvard College lay down the qualification thus:—

When any scholar is able to understand Tully or such like classical Latin author *extempore,* and to make and speak true Latin in verse and prose, *suo ut aiunt Marte:* and to decline perfectly the paradigms of nouns and verbs in the Greek tongue: let him then and not before be capable of admission into the college.

For readers whose Latinity has slipped away from them, let it be explained that Tully is not Irish, but means Cicero. Earlier generations properly called Romans by their names, and not, as we have come to do, with many of them, by their nicknames. Tully was called "Cicero" (or beanhead) as one of us might be called "Shorty." Harvard Latin in 1642 was still undefiled.

On the terms indicated few of us now would get into Harvard. Fewer still would get out, since, for that, every scholar had to be

found able to read the originals of the Old and New Testaments into the Latin tongue and to resolve them logically: withal being of godly life and conversation.

On the outside edge or fringe of the classical studies, of which mathematics and logic formed an adjunct, were such things as natural philosophy, destined to vast and rapid expansion, but of which the classical doctors of divinity remained ignorant.

By the time of Queen Anne, some scholars already admitted that they didn't know everything—not many, though, or at least they qualified it by saying that what they didn't know wasn't worth knowing.

What they referred to by this last phrase was this natural philosophy, the new range of knowledge that the eighteenth century was gathering, item by item, fact by fact. These grew into the sciences of life—botany and zoology, later to get their true name of biology. Reverend classical scholars, full to the throat with declensions, set them aside as a disturbance of the Book of Genesis. But they wouldn't down.

Beside them grew, equally despised by the classicists, the electric science drawn by Franklin from the clouds, the oxygen distilled by Priestley from water, the geology of Lyell, dug up from what was once called Hades. All the world knows the story. Within another hundred years a vast series of studies known as the natural sciences—at first opposed, derided and left to mechanics and steam-engine drivers—broke at last the barriers of the schools and flooded wide over the curriculum.

But the barriers, in England at least, did not break until the waters had risen high and the pressure had become overwhelming. In the middle nineteenth century, as Professor Huxley complained, the so-called public schools had still a curriculum of the Middle Ages.

Until a few years back [he wrote in 1893], a boy might have passed through any one of the great public schools with the greatest distinction and credit and might never so much as have heard of modern geography, modern history and modern literature, of the English language as a language, or of the whole circle of the sciences, physical, moral and social; might never have heard that the earth goes round the sun; that England underwent a great revolution in 1688 and France another in 1789; that there once lived certain notable men called Chaucer, Shakespeare, Milton, Voltaire, Goethe, Schiller.

With this protest of common sense went a certain protest of spite—as against aristocratic culture by those unable to share it. Witness Herbert Spencer's diatribe against "The Education of a Gentleman."

Men dress their children's minds as they do their bodies in the prevailing fashion. As the Orinoco Indian puts on his paint before he leaves his hut . . . so a boy's drilling in Latin and Greek is insisted on, not because of their intrinsic value, but that he may not be disgraced by being found ignorant of them—that he may have the education of a gentleman.

But when at last the barriers broke, the new science came in a flood, till every high school student, in America more even than in England, turned alchemist, and every class-room sputtered with electricity. And with this, in the colleges first and spreading downwards to the schools, came a still newer set of studies—the social studies, economics and politics, the mingled brood of happiness and despair, of progress and poverty, that Mill and Spencer and such people let loose upon the world. So deeply have they spread that little children learn "civics" first and find out what it means after; and so widely that the Japanese have studied it from Europe and teach it to the Chinese.

And as if civics and social welfare were not enough for the already overburdened curriculum, a chariot creaking up the rough slope of Parnassus, "Business," in the form of schools of commerce, must needs leap on top of the load. It handed so heavy a tip to the driver that it could not be put off, and more than that it began to demand that the oldest and most respectable of the passengers be thrown out to make room for it.

So there we stand, or rather move slowly onward, the ascent of Parnassus turned into a ten years' journey during which the passengers must amuse themselves as best they may with the cards and dice of college activities.

Meantime it is only to be expected that the conditions of the journey react upon the minds of the passengers. In other words it is only natural that this vast burden of an increasing curriculum sets up a reaction in the minds of the pupil and the student. From their earliest years they become accustomed to reckon up the things that they have done and finished with. "We've finished Scripture," says a little girl in a child's school; "we had it last year." For her the mould of religious thought is all set. Don't ask her the names of the twelve Apostles. She's had them—last year. She is not responsible for the Apostles any more. So does the high school student count up his years still needed for matriculation as eagerly as a mariner measures his distance to the shore. The college student opens his career by classing himself not according to the year in which he enters but according to the year in which he hopes to get out. The class matriculating in 1940 call out in their infant breath, "Rah! Rah! Forty-four."

How strange it is, our little procession of life! The child says, "When I am a big boy." But what is that? The big boy says, "When I grow up." And then, grown up, he says, "When I get married." But to be married, what is that after all? The thought changes to "When I'm able to retire." And then, when retirement comes, he looks back over the landscape traversed; a cold wind seems to sweep over it; somehow he has missed it all, and it is gone. Life, we learn too late, is in the living, in the tissue of every day and hour. So it should be with education.

But so it is not; a false view discolours it all. For the vastly great part of it the student's one aim is to get done with it. There comes a glad time in his life when he has "finished" mathematics, a happy day when he has done philosophy, an exhilarating hour when he realizes that he is finished with "compulsory English." Then at last his four years are out, his sentence expired, and he steps out of college a free man, without a stain on his character—and not much on his mind. . . . Later on, he looks back wistfully and realizes how different it might have been.

Eve Curie

Eve Curie (1904-   ) is the daughter of two great scientists, Marie and Pierre Curie, the discoverers of radium. In her own right she has attained distinction as author of the warmly human biography of her mother, as interpreter of the French spirit to a sympathetic America in the darkest days of her nation's history, and as a personality which embodies the finest of French womanhood. In the following chapter from Madame Curie *we share the ardors and endurances of learning as "Manya" experienced them in her bare Parisian attic in 1892. Reading these pages we better understand the words of their author: "It seems to me that I have always lived near the poor student, haunted by dreams, who was Marie Sklodovska."*

FORTY RUBLES A MONTH

YES, Marie's existence had still further to be despoiled and made bare. The few months she had lived in the Rue d'Allemagne had been a stage in acclimatization. Now the girl sank slowly into solitude. The beings she rubbed elbows with existed for her no more than the walls she touched in passing, and conversation hardly cut in upon the silence in which she enveloped her hours. For more than three solid years she was to lead a life devoted to study alone: a life in conformity with her dreams, a "perfect" life in the sense in which that of the monk or the missionary is perfect.

Her life had to be of monastic simplicity in any case: for since Marie had voluntarily deprived herself of the board and lodging she had had at the Dluskis', she had to meet her own expenses herself. And her income—made up by her own savings, divided into slices, and the small sums her father could send her—resolved itself into forty rubles a month.

How could a woman, a foreigner, live decently in Paris in 1892 with forty rubles a month, *three francs* a day,[1] paying for her own room, meals, clothes, paper and books, as well as her fees at the university? Such was the problem the young student had urgently to solve. But Marie never failed to find a solution of a problem.

Manya to her brother Joseph, March 17, 1892:
You have no doubt learned from Father that I decided to live nearer to the schools, as it had become necessary for several reasons, above all for

---

[1] Forty rubles was about $20; three francs was about 60 cents.

the present quarter. The plan is now realized: I am writing to you, in fact, from my new lodging, 3 Rue Flatters. It is a little room, very suitable, and nevertheless very cheap. In a quarter of an hour I can be in the chemistry laboratory, in twenty minutes at the Sorbonne. Naturally, without the Dluskis' help I should never have been able to arrange things like this.

I am working a thousand times as hard as at the beginning of my stay: in the Rue d'Allemagne my little brother-in-law had the habit of disturbing me endlessly. He absolutely could not endure having me do anything but engage in agreeable chatter with him when I was at home. I had to declare war on him on this subject. After a few days Bronya and he began to feel badly about me, and they came to see me. We drank tea, bachelor fashion, and then we went down-stairs to see the S.'s, who also live here.

Is your wife taking care of Father, as she promised me? Let her take care, just the same, not to cut me out altogether at home! Father is beginning to speak of her a little too tenderly, and I am afraid that he will be forgetting me soon.

Marie was not the only student who lived on a hundred francs a month in the Latin Quarter: most of her Polish comrades were as poor as she was. Some lived by threes or fours in the same lodging and took their meals together; others, who lived alone, devoted several hours a day to housekeeping, cooking and sewing, and by sheer ingenuity ate as much as they wanted, shod and clothed themselves in greater or lesser elegance. This was the method adopted earlier by Bronya, whose talents as a prize cook had been celebrated among her comrades.

Marie disdained to follow such wise examples. She was too fond of her tranquillity to share her lodging with a friend or two. She was too haunted by work to bother about her own comfort. Even if she had wished to do so, for that matter, she would have been incapable of it: the girl who had been a governess in strange families at seventeen, giving seven or eight hours of lessons a day, had never found time or occasion for learning how to keep house. Everything that Bronya had learned when she was mistress of her father's house was unknown to Marie. And the report had it, in the Polish colony, that "Mademoiselle Sklodovska doesn't know what you use to make soup."

She did not know, and she did not want to know. Why should she pass a morning initiating herself into the mysteries of a broth, when she might have been learning several pages of physics, or making an interesting analysis in the laboratory?

By deliberate intention she had suppressed diversions from her schedule, as well as friendly meetings and contact with human beings. In the same way she decided that material life had no importance; that it did not exist.

And, fortified by this principle, she made for herself a Spartan existence, strange and inhuman.

Rue Flatters, Boulevard Port-Royal, Rue des Feuillantines . . . All the rooms Marie was to inhabit were alike in discomfort and cheapness of rent. The first was situated in a poorly furnished house where students, doctors, and officers of the neighboring garrison lived. Later on the girl, in search of absolute calm, was to take an attic like a servant's room at the top of a middle-class house. For fifteen or twenty francs a month she found a tiny nook which obtained light from a loophole giving directly on the slope of the roof. Through this skylight appeared a small square of sky. There was no heat, no lighting, no water.

Marie furnished this place with all the objects she possessed: an iron folding bed, the mattress she had brought from Poland, a stove, a white wooden table, a kitchen chair, a washbasin; a petroleum oil lamp, covered by a twopenny shade; a pitcher about as big as a saucer, which was to cook her meals for the next three years; two plates, a knife, a fork, a spoon, a cup, a stew-pan; and finally a kettle and three glasses into which, according to Polish custom, the student would pour tea when the Dluskis came to see her. On the occasions—very rare at present—when Marie received visitors, the rights of hospitality were asserted: the girl lighted the little stove, whose zigzag pipe described complicated angles in the room. And for a seat she pulled out of its corner the bulging brown trunk which served her as wardrobe and chest of drawers.

No service, of course: even one hour of cleaning a day would have overweighted the expense of the budget. Transportation costs were suppressed: Marie went to the Sorbonne on foot in all weathers. Coal was kept down to a minimum: one or two sacks of "lumps" for the winter, which the girl bought from the merchant on the corner and hoisted up the steep stairs herself to the sixth floor, bucketful by bucketful, stopping at each floor to breathe. Lights were at a minimum: as soon as night fell, the student took refuge in that blessed asylum called the Library of Sainte Geneviève, where the gas was lighted and it was warm. Seated at one of the big rectangular tables with her head in her hands, a poor Polish girl could work until they closed the doors at ten o'clock. From then on all that was needed was enough petroleum to keep the light going in her room until two in the morning. Then, her eyes reddened by fatigue, Marie left her books and threw herself on the bed.

The only thing she knew how to do, in the humble practical domain, was to sew—a memory of the "manual training" at the Sikorski boarding school, and of the long days in Szczuki when the governess, as she supervised the children's study, took up her sewing. . . . It would be rash to conclude from this that the exile ever, by chance, bought a bit of stuff at a low price and made herself a new blouse. She seems to have sworn, on the contrary, never to give up her Warsaw dresses, and wore them, shiny, old-fashioned and threadbare, forever. But she took great care of her clothes, cleaned them and mended them. She also condescended to wash her linen in a basin when she was too tired to work and needed relaxation.

Marie did not admit that she could be cold or hungry. In order not to buy coal—and through sheer carelessness too—she often neglected to light the little stove with the twisted pipe, and she wrote figures and equations without noticing that her fingers were getting numb and her shoulders shaking. A hot soup or a bit of meat would have comforted her; but Marie did not know how to make soup. Marie could not spend a franc and lose a half hour to cook herself a chop. She hardly ever entered the butcher's shop, and even less the restaurant: it was too dear. For weeks at a time she ate nothing but buttered bread and tea. When she wanted a feast, she went into a creamery in the Latin Quarter and ate two eggs, or else bought herself a piece of chocolate or some fruit.

On this diet the fresh, solid girl who had left Warsaw a few months before rapidly grew anaemic. Often, as she was getting up from the table, her head would go round. She had just time to get to her bed when she would lose consciousness. Coming back to herself, she would ask why she had fainted; she would think herself ill and disdain her illness as she did everything else. It never occurred to her that she was dropping with weakness and that her only disease was that of starvation.

Naturally she did not boast of this superb organization of existence to the Dluskis. Every time she went to see them she replied in monosyllables to their questions on her progress as a cook, or on her daily menus. If her brother-in-law said she did not look well, she affirmed that she was overworked—which was, in fact, in her eyes, the only reason for her fatigue. And then, dismissing such worries with a gesture of indifference, she would begin to play with her niece, Bronya's baby, for whom she had great affection.

But one day when Marie fainted in front of one of her comrades, the latter hurried to the Rue d'Allemagne to warn the pair of young doctors. Two hours later Casimir was leaping up the six flights of stairs to the attic where the girl, a little pale, was already studying tomorrow's lesson. He examined his sister-in-law. He examined even more carefully the clean plates, the empty stew-pan, and the whole room, in which he could discover only one comestible, a packet of tea. All at once he understood—and the questioning began.

"What did you eat today?"

"Today? I don't know. I lunched a while ago."

"What did you eat?" Casimir's voice took her up implacably.

"Some cherries and . . . and all sorts of things."

In the end Marie was obliged to confess: since the evening before she had nibbled at a bundle of radishes and half a pound of cherries. She had worked until three that morning and had slept four hours. Then she had gone to the Sorbonne. On her return she had finished the radishes. Then she had fainted.

The doctor made no long speeches. He was furious. Furious against Marie, whose ash-gray eyes looked at him with profound fatigue and innocent mirth. Furious at himself, for he accused himself of not watching attentively enough over "the little one" who had been confided to him by M. Sklodovski. Without listening to his sister-in-law's protests he handed her her hat and coat, and ordered her to take the books and papers she would need for the coming week. Then, silent, dissatisfied, unhappy, he carried her off to La Villette; from the threshold of the flat he hailed Bronya, who dashed for the kitchen.

Twenty minutes passed, and Marie swallowed, mouthful by mouthful, the medicines ordered for her by Casimir: an enormous underdone beefsteak and a plateful of crackling fried potatoes. As if by a miracle, the color came back to her cheeks. On the same evening Bronya herself came at eleven o'clock to put the light out in the narrow room where she had set up a bed for her sister. For several days Marie, well fed and cared for, "took the cure" and regained her strength. Then, obsessed by the approaching examinations, she returned to her attic, promising to be reasonable in the future.

And the next day she began again to live on air.

Work! . . . Work! Plunged altogether into study, intoxicated by her progress, Marie felt herself equal to learning everything mankind had ever discovered. She attended courses in mathematics, physics, and chemistry. Manual technique and the minute precision of scientific experiment became familiar to her, little by little; soon she was to have the joy of being charged by Professor Lippmann with researches of no great importance, which nevertheless permitted her to show her deftness and the originality of her mind. In the physics laboratory of the Sorbonne, a high and wide room queerly ornamented by two little staircases which led to an interior gallery, Marie Sklodovska timidly tried her strength.

She had a passionate love for that atmosphere of attention and silence, the "climate" of the laboratory, which she was to prefer to any other up to her last day. She was on her feet, always on her feet, in front of an oak table supporting precision instruments, or else in front of the chemical hood where some material in fusion bubbled away, worried at by the fierce blowpipe. She was hardly to be distinguished, in her big smock of wrinkled linen, from the thoughtful young men who bent beside her over other blowpipes and other instruments. Like them, she respected the concentration of the place. She made no noise, she pronounced no useless word.

One master's degree was not enough; Marie decided to obtain two: one in physics and one in mathematics. Her plans, once so humble, increased and grew richer so rapidly that she had not the time—and above all not the audacity—to confide them to M. Sklodovski, who, as she knew, impatiently awaited her return to Poland. As usual, the excellent man offered his help. But it could be felt that he was vaguely worried at having hatched this independent creature who had taken to flying with her own wings after so many years of submission and sacrifice.

M. Sklodovski to Bronya, March 5, 1893:
. . . Your last letter mentions for the first time that Manya intends to take her examinations for the master's. She has never spoken to me about it in her letters, even though I have questioned her on the subject. Write me exactly when these examinations will take place, at what date Manya can hope to pass them, what are the fees for them and how much the diploma will cost. I must think of all this in advance so as to be able to send some money to Manya, and on this my personal plans will depend.
. . . I intend to keep the lodging I now occupy for next year: for myself and for Manya—if she comes back—it is perfectly suitable. . . . Little by little Manya will work up a list of pupils, and in any case I am ready to share what I have with her. We shall manage without trouble. . . .

Marie, however shy she might be, could not avoid meeting human beings every day. Some of the students were cordial and friendly with her. Foreign women were highly regarded at the Sorbonne. These poor girls, generally gifted, coming from far away to the university which the Goncourts called "the nursing mother of study," inspired sympathy among young Frenchmen. The Polish girl was tamed. She discovered that her companions, who were "grinds" for the most part, esteemed her and wished to show her kindness. This kindness sometimes would have liked to become extremely kind indeed. Marie must have been very pretty: her friend, Mlle Dydynska, a charming and somewhat over-excited young woman who had appointed herself as bodyguard, one day threatened to beat off a group of too-eager admirers with her umbrella.

Allowing Mlle Dydynska to repel advances which left her indifferent, the girl drew nearer to men who did not pay court to her and with whom she could talk about her work. Between a physics lesson and a laboratory hour she would chatter with Paul Painlevé, who was already a professor; with Charles Maurain or Jean Perrin—future leaders of French science. These were distant comradeships. Marie had no time to give to friendship or to love. She loved mathematics and physics.

Her brain was so precise, her intelligence so marvelously clear, that no "Slavic" disorder intruded to corrupt her effort. She was supported by a will of iron, by a maniacal taste for perfection, and by an incredible stubbornness. Systematically, patiently, she attained each of the ends she had set for herself: she passed first in the master's examination in physics in 1893, and second in the master's in mathematics in 1894.

With her forty rubles a month she succeeded in living, and even, by depriving herself of the indispensable, achieved sometimes a certain amount of luxury: an evening at the theater, a journey to the suburbs, whence she brought back flowers picked in the woods to glow for several days on her table. The little peasant of other days was not dead; lost in the great city, she lay in wait for the birth of the leaves, and as soon as she had a little time and money she hurried to the woods.

Marie to M. Sklodovski, April 16, 1893:
The other Sunday I went to Le Raincy, near Paris, in a pretty and agreeable neighborhood. The lilacs and the fruit trees, even the apples, were in full bloom and the air was filled with the scent of flowers.

In Paris the trees get green as early as the beginning of April. Now the leaves have sprung out and the chestnuts are blooming. It is as hot as in summer: everything is green. In my room it is beginning to be torrid. Luckily in July, when I shall be working for my examinations, I shall not be here any more, for I have taken the lodging only to the eighth of July.

The nearer the examinations come, the more I am afraid of not being ready. At the worst, I shall wait until November, but that will make me lose my summer, which doesn't appeal to me. For that matter, we must wait and see. . . .

July. Fever, haste, agonizing trials, crushing mornings when, shut in with thirty students in the examination hall, Marie was so nervous that the letters danced before her eyes and she could not even read the fateful paper for several minutes, with its statement of the problem and the "questions on the course." When the composition was turned in, there came days of waiting until the solemn moment of publication of the results. Marie slipped in among the contestants and their families, crowded into the amphitheater where the names of the elect would be read aloud, in order of merit. Pushed and shoved about as she was, she waited for the entrance of the examiner. And in a sudden silence she heard him pronounce first of all her own name: *Marie Sklodovska.*

Nobody was to guess her emotion. She tore herself away from the congratulations of her comrades, escaped from the crowd and made off. The time for holidays had come now—for the departure to Poland and home.

Such homecomings among the poor Poles had their rites, which Marie scrupulously observed. She moved her furniture—bed, stove and utensils—into safety with a compatriot rich enough to keep her Paris lodging during the summer months. She took leave of her garret: before quitting it forever, she cleaned it thoroughly. She said good-by to the portress, whom she would not see again, and bought some provisions for her journey. Having counted up what she had left, she went into a big shop and did what she had not done for a year: she looked for trinkets, for scarves. . . .

It was accounted a shame to return to one's native land with money in the pocket. Grand style, supreme elegance, the law, required one to spend literally everything on presents for one's family and get into the train at the Gare du Nord without a sou. Was this not a wise course? Two thousand kilometers away, at the other end of the rails, there were M. Sklodovski and Joseph and Hela, a familiar roof to sleep under, as much food as one could eat, and a seamstress who, for a few *groszy,* could cut out and sew linen and big woollen dresses: the dresses which Marie would wear when she came back to the Sorbonne again in November.

She was to reappear there cheerful and a bit too fat, having been stuffed with food for three months in all the houses of all the Sklodovskis in Poland, indignant as they were at her thinness. And again she faced a scholastic year in which she would work, learn, prepare an examination, grow thin.

But each time the autumn returned the same anxiety assailed Marie: how could she go back to Paris? Where was she to find money? Forty rubles at a time, her savings were being exhausted; and she thought with shame of the little pleasures her father deprived himself of to come to her help. In 1893 the situation seemed desperate and the girl was on the point of giving up the journey when a miracle took place. That same Mlle Dydynska who had defended her with an umbrella the year before now extended even more opportune protection. Certain that Marie was destined to a great future, she moved heaven and earth in Warsaw to have the Alexandrovitch Scholarship assigned to her—a scholarship for students of merit who wished to pursue their efforts abroad.

Six hundred rubles! Enough to live on for fifteen months! Marie, who knew so well how to ask favors for other people, would never have thought of soliciting this help, and above all could never have had the boldness to make the necessary approaches. Dazzled and enchanted, she took flight for France.

Marie to her brother Joseph, September 15, 1893:
. . . I have already rented my room, on the sixth floor, in a clean and decent street which suits me very well. Tell Father that in that place where I was going to take a room there was nothing free, and that I am very satisfied with this room: it has a window that shuts tight, and when I have arranged it properly it should not be cold here, especially as the floor is of

wood and not tiles. Compared to my last year's room it is a veritable palace. It costs one hundred and eighty francs a year, and is therefore sixty francs cheaper than the one Father spoke to me about.

I hardly need say that I am delighted to be back in Paris. It was very hard for me to separate again from Father, but I could see that he was well, very lively, and that he could do without me—especially as you are living in Warsaw. And as for me, it is my whole life that is at stake. It seemed to me, therefore, that I could stay on here without having remorse on my conscience.

Just now I am studying mathematics unceasingly, so as to be up to date when the courses begin. I have three mornings a week taken by lessons with one of my French comrades who is preparing for the examination I have just passed. Tell Father that I am getting used to this work, that it does not tire me as much as before, and that I do not intend to abandon it.

Today I begin the installation of my little corner for this year—very poorly, but what am I to do? I have to do everything myself; otherwise it's all too dear. I must get my furniture into shape—or rather what I pompously call my furniture, for the whole thing isn't worth more than twenty francs.

I shall write soon to Joseph Boguski and ask him for information about his laboratory. My future occupation depends on this.

Marie to her brother, March 18, 1894:

. . . It is difficult for me to tell you about my life in detail; it is so monotonous and, in fact, so uninteresting. Nevertheless I have no feeling of uniformity and I regret only one thing, which is that the days are so short and that they pass so quickly. One never notices what has been done; one can only see what remains to be done, and if one didn't like the work it would be very discouraging.

I want you to pass your doctor's thesis. . . . It seems that life is not easy for any of us. But what of that? We must believe that we are gifted for something, and that this thing, at whatever cost, must be attained. Perhaps everything will turn out very well, at the moment when we least expect it. . . .

The Alexandrovitch Scholarship was providential. With passionate avarice Marie tried to string out her six hundred rubles, so as to remain a little longer in the paradise of lecture halls and laboratories. Some years later, with the same passionate avarice, she was to save six hundred rubles out of her first earnings—a technical study ordered from her by the Society for the Encouragement of National Industry—and was to take them to the secretary of the Alexandrovitch Foundation, stupefied though he was at a restitution without precedent in the annals of the committee. Marie had accepted this scholarship as testimony of confidence in her, a debt of honor. In her uncompromising soul she would have adjudged herself dishonest if she had kept for one unnecessary moment the money which now could serve as lifebuoy to another poor young girl.

Rereading a little poem of my mother's, written in Polish, on this time of her life, and remembering the accounts of it that she sometimes gave me, with many a smile and humorous remark, looking at the only portrait of herself which she dearly cherished: the small photograph of a student girl with daring eyes and determined chin, I have felt that she never ceased to prefer these hard, fervent days to all others.

> Ah, how harshly the youth of the student passes,
> While all around her, with passions ever fresh,
> Other youths search eagerly for easy pleasures!
> And yet in solitude
> She lives, obscure and blessed,
> For in her cell she finds the ardor
> That makes her heart immense.
>
> But the blessed time is effaced.
> She must leave the land of Science
> To go out and struggle for her bread
> On the grey roads of life.
> Often and often then, her weary spirit
> Returns beneath the roofs
> To the corner ever dear to her heart
> Where silent labor dwelled
> And where a world of memory has rested.

No doubt Marie knew other joys later. But even in her hours of infinite tenderness, even in the hour of her triumph and fame, the eternal student was never so content with herself, so proud, as in the poverty and fire of this integral effort. She was proud of her poverty; proud of living alone and independent in a foreign city. Working in the evening beneath the lamp in her poor room she felt that her destiny, still insignificant, mysteriously related itself to the high existences she most admired, and that she became the humble unknown companion of those great scientists of the past, who were, like her, shut into their ill-lighted cells, like her, detached from their time, and, like her, spurred their minds to pass beyond the sum of required knowledge.

Yes, these four heroic years were, not the happiest of Marie Curie's life, but the most perfect in her eyes, the nearest to those summits of the human mission toward which her gaze had been trained. When one is young and solitary and swallowed up in study, one can "not have enough to live on"—

and yet live to the fullest. An immense enthusiasm gave this girl of twenty-six the power to ignore the trials and privations she endured; to magnify her sordid existence into magic. Later on, love, maternity, the worries of a wife and mother, the complexities of crushingly hard work, were to restore the visionary to real life. But in the enchanted moment when she was poorer than she was ever to be again, she was as reckless as a child. She floated lightly in another world, that which her thought was to regard always as the only pure and true one.

Leonard Q. Ross

Leonard Q. Ross is the pseudonym of Leo Calvin Rosten (1908-   ), a research expert in the social sciences and author of authoritative studies of the Washington press corps and the Hollywood movie colony. After taking his Ph.D. at the University of Chicago he taught English in the evening classes of the University Extension. Out of this experience came the richly humorous but always kindly stories of Hyman Kaplan and his classmates. Behind the comedy of dialect and episode is a perception of the broad process of Americanization through adult education.

MR. KAPLAN AND SHAKESPEARE

IT was Miss Higby's idea in the first place. She had suggested to Mr. Parkhill that the students came to her class unaware of the *finer* side of English, of its beauty and, as she put it, "the glorious heritage of our literature." She suggested that perhaps poetry might be worked into the exercises of Mr. Parkhill's class. The beginners' grade had, after all, been subjected to almost a year of English and might be presumed to have achieved some linguistic sophistication. Poetry would make the students conscious of precise enunciation; it would make them read with greater care and an ear for sounds. Miss Higby, who had once begun a master's thesis on Coventry Patmore, *loved* poetry. And, it should be said in all justice, she argued her cause with considerable logic. Poetry *would* be excellent for the enunciation of the students, thought Mr. Parkhill.

So it was that when he faced the class the following Tuesday night, Mr. Parkhill had a volume of Shakespeare on his desk, and an eager, almost an expectant, look in his eye. The love that Miss Higby bore for poetry in general was as nothing compared to the love that Mr. Parkhill bore for Shakespeare in particular. To Mr. Parkhill, poetry meant Shakespeare. Many years ago he had played Polonius in his senior class play.

"Tonight, class," said Mr. Parkhill, "I am going to try an experiment."

The class looked up dutifully. They had come to regard Mr. Parkhill's pedagogical innovations as part of the natural order.

"I am going to introduce you to poetry—great poetry. You see—" Mr. Parkhill delivered a modest lecture on the beauty of poetry, its expression of the loftier thoughts of men, its economy of statement. He hoped it would be a relief from spelling and composition exercises to use poetry as the subject matter of the regular Recitation and Speech period. "I shall write a passage on the board and read it for you. Then, for Recitation and Speech, you will give short addresses, using the passage as the general topic, telling us what it has brought to your minds, what thoughts and ideas."

The class seemed quite pleased by the announcement. Miss Mitnick blushed happily. (This blush was different from most of Miss Mitnick's blushes; there was aspiration and idealism in it.) Mr. Norman Bloom sighed with a business-like air: you could tell that for him poetry was merely another assignment, like a speech on "What I Like to Eat Best" or a composition on "A Day at a Picnic." Mrs. Moskowitz, to whom any public performance was unpleasant, tried to look enthusiastic, without much success. And Mr. Hyman Kaplan, the heroic smile on his face as indelibly as ever, looked at Mr. Parkhill with admiration and whispered to himself: "Poyetry! Now is poyetry! My! Mus' be progriss ve makink awreddy!"

"The passage will be from Shakespeare," Mr. Parkhill announced, opening the volume.

An excited buzz ran through the class as the magic of that name fell upon them.

"Imachine!" murmured Mr. Kaplan. "Jakesbeer!"

"*Shake*speare, Mr. Kaplan!"

Mr. Parkhill took a piece of chalk and, with care and evident love, wrote the following passage on the board in large, clear letters:

> Tomorrow, and tomorrow, and tomorrow
> Creeps in this petty pace from day to day,
> To the last syllable of recorded time;
> And all our yesterdays have lighted fools
> The way to dusty death. Out, out, brief candle!
> Life's but a walking shadow, a poor player
> That struts and frets his hour upon the stage,
> And then is heard no more; it is a tale
> Told by an idiot, full of sound and fury,
> Signifying nothing.

A reverent hush filled the classroom, as eyes gazed with wonder on this passage from the Bard. Mr. Parkhill was pleased at this.

"I shall read the passage first," he said. "Listen carefully to my enunciation—and—er—let Shakespeare's thoughts sink into your minds."

Mr. Parkhill read: "'Tomorrow, and tomorrow, and tomorrow . . .'"
Mr. Parkhill read very well and this night, as if some special fire burned
in him, he read with rare eloquence. "Out, out, brief candle!" In Miss
Mitnick's eyes there was inspiration and wonder. "Life's but a walking
shadow . . ." Mrs. Moskowitz sat with a heavy frown, indicating cerebra-
tion. "It is a tale told by an idiot . . ." Mr. Kaplan's smile had taken on
something luminous; but his eyes were closed: it was not clear whether Mr.
Kaplan had surrendered to the spell of the Immortal Bard or to that of
Morpheus.

"I shall—er—read the passage again," said Mr. Parkhill, clearing his
throat vociferously until he saw Mr. Kaplan's eyes open. "'Tomorrow, and
tomorrow, and tomorrow. . . .'"

When Mr. Parkhill had read the passage for the second time, he said:
"That should be quite clear now. Are there any questions?"

There were a few questions. Mr. Scymzak wanted to know whether
"frets" was "a little kind excitement." Miss Schneiderman asked about
"struts." Mr. Kaplan wasn't sure about "cripps." Mr. Parkhill explained
the words carefully, with several illustrative uses of each word. "No more
questions? Well, I shall allow a few minutes for you all to—er—think over
the meaning of the passage. Then we shall begin Recitation and Speech."

Mr. Kaplan promptly closed his eyes again, his smile beatific. The students sank into that revery miscalled thought, searching their souls for the
symbols evoked by Shakespeare's immortal words.

"Miss Caravello, will you begin?" asked Mr. Parkhill at last.

Miss Caravello went to the front of the room. "Da poem isa gooda,"
she said slowly. "Itsa have—"

"It *has.*"

"It hasa beautiful wordsa. Itsa lak Dante, Italian poet—"

"Ha!" cried Mr. Kaplan scornfully. "Shaksbeer you metchink mit
Tante? *Shaksbeer?* Mein Gott!"

It was obvious that Mr. Kaplan had identified himself with Shakespeare and would tolerate no disparagement of his *alter ego.*

"Miss Caravello is merely expressing her own ideas," said Mr. Parkhill pacifically. (Actually, he felt completely sympathetic to Mr. Kaplan's
point of view.)

"Hau Kay," agreed Mr. Kaplan, with a generous wave of the hand.
"But to me is no comparink a high-cless man like Shaksbeer mit a Tante,
dat's all."

Miss Caravello, her poise shattered, said a few more words and sat
down.

Mrs. Yampolsky's contribution was brief. "This is full deep meanings," she said, her eyes on the floor. "Is hard for a person not so good in
English to unnistand. But I like."

"*'Like!'*" cried Mr. Kaplan with a fine impatience. "*'Like?'* Batter *love,* Yampolsky. Mit Shaksbeer mus' be *love!*"

Mr. Parkhill had to suggest that Mr. Kaplan control his esthetic passions. He did understand how Mr. Kaplan felt, however, and sensed a new bond between them. Mrs. Yampolsky staggered through several more nervous comments and retired.

Mr. Bloom was next. He gave a long declamation, ending: "So is passimistic ideas in the poem, and I am optimist. Life should be happy—so we should remember this is only a poem. Maybe is Shakespeare too passimistic."

"You wronk, Bloom!" cried Mr. Kaplan with prompt indignation. "Shaksbeer is passimist because is de *life* passimist also!"

Mr. Parkhill, impressed by this philosophical stroke, realized that Mr. Kaplan, afire with the glory of the Swan of Avon, could not be suppressed. Mr. Kaplan was the kind of man who brooked no criticism of his gods. The only solution was to call on Mr. Kaplan for his recitation at once. Mr. Parkhill was, indeed, curious about what fresh thoughts Mr. Kaplan would utter after his passionate defences of the Bard. When Mr. Parkhill had corrected certain parts of Mr. Bloom's speech, emphasizing Mr. Bloom's failure to use the indefinite article, he said: "Mr. Kaplan, will *you* speak next?"

Mr. Kaplan's face broke into a glow; his smile was like a rainbow. "Soitinly," he said, walking to the front of the room. Never had he seemed so dignified, so eager, so conscious of a great destiny.

"Er—Mr. Kaplan," added Mr. Parkhill, suddenly aware of the possibilities which the situation (Kaplan on Shakespeare) involved: "Speak *carefully.*"

"*Spacially* careful vill I be," Mr. Kaplan reassured him. He cleared his throat, adjusted his tie, and began: "Ladies an' gantleman, you hoid all kinds minninks abot dis piece poyetry, an'—"

"*Poetry.*"

"—abot dis piece *poetry.* But to me is a difference minnink altogadder. Ve mus' tink abot Julius Scissor an' how *he* falt!"

Mr. Parkhill moved nervously, puzzled.

"In dese exact voids is Julius Scissor sayink—"

"Er—Mr. Kaplan," said Mr. Parkhill once he grasped the full import of Mr. Kaplan's error. "The passage is from 'Macbeth.'"

Mr. Kaplan looked at Mr. Parkhill with injured surprise. "*Not* fromm 'Julius Scissor'?" There was pain in his voice.

"No. And it's—er—'Julius *Cae*sar.'"

Mr. Kaplan waited until the last echo of the name had permeated his soul. "Podden me, Mr. Pockheel. Isn't '*seez*or' vat you cottink somting op mit?"

"That," said Mr. Parkhill quickly, "is 'scissor.' You have used 'Caesar' for 'scissor' and 'scissor' for 'Caesar.'"

Mr. Kaplan nodded, marveling at his own virtuosity.

"But go on with your speech, please." Mr. Parkhill, to tell the truth, felt a little guilty that he had not announced at the very beginning that the passage was from "Macbeth." "Tell us *why* you thought the lines were from 'Julius Caesar.'"

"Vell," said Mr. Kaplan to the class, his smile assuming its normal serenity. "I vas positif, becawss I can *see* de whole ting." He paused, debating how to explain this cryptic remark. Then his eyes filled with a strange enchantment. "I see de whole scinn. It's in a tant, on de night bafore dey makink Julius de Kink fromm Rome. So he is axcited an' ken't slip. He is layink in bad, tinking: 'Tomorrow an' tomorrow an' tomorrow. How slow dey movink! Almost cripps! Soch a pity de pace!'"

Before Mr. Parkhill could explain that "petty pace" did not mean "Soch a pity de pace!" Mr. Kaplan had soared on.

"De days go slow, fromm day to day, like leetle tsyllables on phonograph racords fromm time."

Anxiety and bewilderment invaded Mr. Parkhill's eyes.

"'An' vat abot yestidday?' tinks Julius Scissor. Ha! 'All our yestiddays are only makink a good light for fools to die in de dost!'"

"'Dusty death' doesn't mean—" There was no interrupting Mr. Kaplan.

"An' Julius Scissor is so tired, an' he vants to fallink aslip. So he hollers, mit fillink, 'Go ot! Go ot! Short candle!' So it goes ot."

Mr. Kaplan's voice dropped to a whisper. "But he ken't slip. Now is bodderink him de idea fromm life. 'Vat is de life altogadder?' tinks Julius Scissor. An' he gives enswer, de pot I like de bast. 'Life is like a bum actor, strottink an' hollerink arond de stage for only vun hour bafore he's kicked ot. Life is a tale told by idjots, dat's all, full of fonny sonds an' phooey!'"

Mr. Parkhill could be silent no longer. "'Full of sound and fury!'" he cried desperately. But inspiration, like an irresistible force, swept Mr. Kaplan on.

"'Life is monkey business! It don' minn a ting. It signifies nottink!' An' den Julius Scissor closes his ice fest—" Mr. Kaplan demonstrated the Consul's exact ocular process in closing his "ice"—"—an' falls dad!"

The class was hushed as Mr. Kaplan stopped. In the silence, a tribute to the fertility of Mr. Kaplan's imagination and the power of his oratory, Mr. Kaplan went to his seat. But just before he sat down, as if adding a postscript, he sighed: "Dat vas mine idea. But ufcawss is all wronk, becawss Mr. Pockheel said de voids ain't abot Julius Scissor altogadder. It's all abot an Irishman by de name Macbat."

Then Mr. Kaplan sat down.

It was some time before Mr. Parkhill could bring himself to criticize

Mr. Kaplan's pronunciation, enunciation, diction, grammar, idiom, and sentence structure. For Mr. Parkhill discovered that he could not easily return to the world of reality. He was still trying to tear himself away from that tent outside Rome, where "Julius Scissor," cursed with insomnia, had thought of time and life—and philosophized himself to a strange and sudden death.

Mr. Parkhill was distinctly annoyed with Miss Higby.

II. FIRST PERSON PLURAL

LITTLE by little, the small egoist that was you grows up; that is, you become increasingly aware of other individuals and your responsible relationship toward them. *I am* has become *we are*.

The tempo quickens, the tone deepens, life takes on a new intensity. A complicated business it has become, with infinite demands for adjustment of personality to personality. Life is now something less than a perpetual playtime, and something more. There may be plenty of fun left, only you have to learn to proportion it to the rest of life. And all the time you are trying to keep the past while you eagerly run to meet the future. It is a curious time, a muddled time, a time of doubt and despair and rapture and hopefulness all rolled into one. And when these years too drop into the past you will regard them with affection as something good that was too good to last, something that could happen only once in a lifetime.

About this time, if you are fortunate, you have met the two best experiences of a lifetime, you have found a friend and you have fallen in love. Probably you have turned poet too, for these most intimate of kinships are the inevitable stuff of poetry. Whether it is the first irresponsible and delightful stirrings of romance or the steadfast faith and true intent of long devotion, whether it is a Brooklyn schoolboy mad with the spring or a shadowy hero who finds

> How soft and warm and small so proud a queen
> As this Isolt could be,

whether the lovers are English or American or Irish or Slovenian, they all speak the language of poetry no matter what form the words take on the page. This love, surely, is a constant in a shifting world. Though kingdoms and dynasties, principalities and powers, be whirled into dust and nothingness, "this will go onward the same."

"People are meant to live two by two in this world," as they say in Grover's Corners, New Hampshire. And now that one has become two, the two, by the alchemy of marriage, are made one in a new meaning. Thus we satisfy the commanding need for companionship, the urge to create a home. Thus we fulfill our deepest instincts—attachment to place and impulse for survival. In the joint enterprise of husband and wife is written the story, continued but never concluded, of humankind. The race must go on. In a world of catastrophe, the ancient traditions of home and land and family remain beautiful and unassailable.

The things of home are mostly humble, a thin purse, an old dog, a clock, a plow, a chair beside the fire. Yet these are things unspeakably dear to generation after generation of humble folk—husband and wife, father, mother, child. The relationships of home may be tender and absurd, noble and pathetic, tedious and precious, all at once. They are almost certain to bring difficulties that test the patience and challenge the quality of affection. They may even bring disaster; but the stakes are high, and few will hesitate to play. The high dramatic moments of life belong to the home—a birth, a marriage, a festival, a parting. And, for most men and women, home is the center of their lives, the first and the last of values.

Frances Frost

Frances Frost (1905-   ) is a Vermonter. Her poetry is a clear word in a time of confusion: she writes of granite mountains, of American soil, of the love of a man and a woman, always with passionate conviction of the worth of living. In the title poem of her best volume, These Acres, *she expresses ideas that are as old as the race of man: love of the land, desire for a place that is home, the urge to carry on the life cycle from harvest to harvest, from generation to generation.*

THESE ACRES

I cannot tell how long these acres will be possessed.
I cannot tell how many men will stride at dawn
Over the slopes, and fasten a horse to a plough,
Leaving behind in a white house the firm, smooth throat of a woman
Humming a song through cool rooms.

This is a morning like other April mornings,
Warm with sun and sweet with wind and filled
With a promise of grass and lilacs. This is a morning
For a man to leave a woman and go forth,
Bareheaded, into the waiting fields and take
The earth with love. Furious and clean
Is the plough in the dark loam; sure and deep
The furrows run to the hills; and there will be seeding

When the maples with their red buds cry in the afternoon,
Caught in the surging hollow of warm wind.

✦

You men who walked these fields before I came,
Was it the same?
Did your hands on plough-handles burn and harden, learning
The wrench of rock against the shining blade?

O bitter-breasted earth, do you remember them
Who came at dawn and took you for the sake
Of their undying passion? Did they break
You as they broke the flesh of women, trying
To say with harvests what could not be said?

You men who walked these fields before I came,
Was it the same?
When I am gone, will other men arise
With morning in their eyes
And leave their women for the thighs of earth?

And will they go back at dusk, as men have always gone,
To the smooth throat singing softly under rafters,
To the warm breast giving comfort to a hand
Grown hard on the earth's breast that never gathered solace
For the lonely fingers, the bended head?

✦

They will go back,
They will go back to stand in open windows,
Smelling the ploughed fields, drawing the windy Spring
Into their lungs, dreaming of grass and lilacs,
Dreaming of harvests.
They will go back to make strong children for these fields,
To say with harvests what cannot be said.

Zachary Gold

Zachary Gold was, of course, born in Brooklyn. Of course he was edu-
cated there, too. Of course he came back there from the University of
Wisconsin (where, he says, he was "very fleetingly" educated) to
marry and settle down there as a writer. He even lives on Avenue N.
Of course. That's the world for you; that's Brooklyn. In this tale of
uninhibited youth, his power of creating illusion is only exceeded by
that of his hero. Willie invents a make-believe world within the make-
believe world of the story.

SPRING OVER BROOKLYN

"HELLO, Dolly," I shouted into the telephone.
"Who is this?" Dolly said. "Where are you?"
"I'm in a phone booth." I looked out and saw the corner of a counter
and medicine bottles piled in a pyramid and a poster with shades of red
smeared on it and a sign that read: BE BEAUTIFUL. "I'm in a drugstore," I
said.
"Who is this?"
"Willie," I said. "You remember. Willie."
"Willie?"
"I live two blocks away from you. The house with the shutters."
"Willie?"
When did you see her last, Willie? I said to myself. The church bazaar?
A school dance? A family bingo game? I couldn't remember.
"Nice Willie," I said.
"Oh," said Dolly. "Crazy Willie."
"That's a fine thing to say to me. That's a fine thing to hear over a
telephone."
"What do you want, Willie?"
"Come out with me, Dolly. I looked through my little black book
today, because it's spring; and, Willie, I said, who'll you see tonight, who'll
you make happy? Come out with me, Dolly, and let me hold your hand,
because it's spring and I haven't seen you in three years."
"I'll go out with you," said Dolly.
"You won't regret it," I said and hung up.
From the drugstore to my house it's two blocks, and from my house

to Dolly's it's two blocks; and I hadn't seen Dolly in three years. That's the world for you; that's Brooklyn.

Two blocks and three years. In three years I could walk from my house to San Francisco and halfway back; but I couldn't walk two blocks.

After supper I went upstairs to get dressed. Wear a bow tie, Willie, I said to myself. Don't ask me why. Don't ask me if Dolly likes bow ties; I don't know. Wear your sport slacks, Willie. Wear your pork-pie hat with the yellow brush.

I washed and shaved and looked in the top drawer of my bureau. I had two dollars and eighty cents in the little glass. Spend it all, Willie, I said to myself; do it right. I folded the bills into my wallet and dropped the change into my pocket.

"So long, ma," I called, and closed the door easy.

"Remember you work tomorrow," ma said.

I should worry about Caesar and Company. I should worry about the shipping department. Who is Dolly, what is she? That's like a song, I thought. I walked down the street and I clipped the hedges as I passed and I banged the wires around the front lawns.

It was so clear you could see Coney Island; I swear you could see Coney Island. You could see the sky, too, all the way up; not a cloud, just blue, all blue from Avenue N to Coney Island. And from Coney Island to Sandy Hook, and from Sandy Hook to Europe, I bet. But I should worry about the color of the sky in Europe. I should worry about anything except that it was spring and the sky was blue and the lawns were fuzzy with green and the trees weren't brown any more and Dolly was only two blocks away.

When I got to the house I checked with my little black book. This is the place, Willie, I said.

"Dolly," I said, when the door opened, "Dolly, you're beautiful."

"I'm not Dolly," the girl said. "I'm her sister."

"I'm sorry," I said. "I haven't seen Dolly in three years and I forgot what she looks like."

That was a mistake, all right, but I should cry over spilt milk. I took off my hat and sat down on the porch swing. I whistled awhile and looked at my wrist watch. It was 7:38. My watch is never wrong. It is an heirloom. My brother gave it to me last year. I don't know where he got it.

This time it was Dolly. She was blond and she had a smile and she wasn't too fat and she wasn't too skinny. That was Dolly, all right. Don't ask me how I knew. I just knew.

"Let's go, Dolly," I said.

Dolly said good-by to her ma and pa, and I said hello and good-by; and I said good-by and I'm sorry to her sister, Janet, and I got Dolly into the street in five minutes.

"Dolly," I said, "you have a wonderful family. I always loved them."

"You never saw them before," Dolly said.

"Didn't I?"

"No."

"I think they're swell. I think you're swell. I've seen you before."

"At a party once," Dolly said. "You never took me out."

That's the world for you; that's Brooklyn. Three years and two blocks, and I never took her out before. Willie, I said to myself, you're slipping.

We did it right that night. Loge seats in the movies, forty cents per; sodas afterward, twenty cents per.

"Dolly," I said, "would you like a chocolate bar; would you like some candy drops, some chewing gum?"

"No, thanks."

"I have a dollar sixty to burn. What do you want to do?"

"Save it, Willie," she said. "Let's go home."

The sky was like a blot of blue-black ink.

"Home?" I said. "I don't want to go home. Let's take a walk in the park."

We got in the Ocean Avenue entrance and we walked around past the zoo and the boathouse, past the rose garden and the lily pool, under the covered bridge.

"I'm tired," I said. "Let's sit down."

Out on a point in the lake I found a bench and we sat down. "Dolly," I said, "this is the life. This reminds me of college. We used to sit on the steps of the frat house and sing songs. Those were the times. Willie, they'd say to me, tell us how you made that touchdown. Willie, did you hit that home run on a curve or a straight ball? That was a great game of basketball you played tonight, Willie. Those were the times."

"You never went to college," Dolly said.

"Be technical," I said. "It sounds nice, doesn't it? It could have been. What do you want me to say?"

"I don't know," Dolly said.

"The only reason I said it was because I wanted to get around to holding your hand. It works too. Ask me; I know."

"You can't hold my hand."

"That's a fine thing to tell me now. Why didn't you say that on the phone? Aw, come on, Dolly. It's spring and it's Willie asking."

"I'll let you hold my hand when you see a seal waiting for a trolley car," Dolly said, and laughed.

"You're not giving me a run-around?"

"No."

"Come on home, Dolly," I said.

So we walked back the way we came, past the rose garden and the lily pool and the zoo, out on to Ocean Avenue, and the first thing we saw was a trolley stalled on the tracks.

"What's the matter, bud?" I said to a fellow.

"Go look," he said. "How should I know?"

That's the world for you; that's Brooklyn.

I pushed through the crowd, and there was an animal sitting on the tracks.

"What is it?" I said to the fellow next to me.

"It's a seal," he said. "Escaped from the zoo."

"What's he doing here?" I said.

"He's waiting for a trolley car, bright boy."

"I believe you," I said.

So all the way home I held Dolly's hand.

"You're not sore at me?" I said.

"No."

I wanted to sit on the porch swing awhile, but Dolly said: "Go on home, Willie. You're not so tired that you need a rest, and it's only two blocks anyway."

When I got home I didn't feel like sleeping. Read a book, Willie, I said to myself. So I went down to the bookcase and I looked through every shelf, and I'd read them all. I looked through all the magazines, and I'd read them too. Willie, I said to myself, you read too much. So all I did was make a lettuce-and-tomato sandwich and eat it, looking out of the window, waiting for a car to pass, so I'd know I wasn't the last one in New York to go to sleep. When a car passed I got into bed.

The next morning the sun was shining. Lord, it was a beautiful day. It was a baseball day; it was a day to go swimming. It was a day for anything except work.

"Ma," I said at breakfast. "I could call up the place and tell them I was sick. I could tell them I broke my arm or something."

"You go to work, Willie," ma said.

"Why can't I tell them, ma? They'll never know."

"It's a lie," ma said.

"You don't understand about lying, ma. Sometimes you have to lie. Sometimes things aren't just right and a lie helps straighten it out. Sometimes things sound nicer when you lie. Suppose you're out with a girl. Do you have to tell the truth all the time?"

"If you're serious about the girl," ma said.

"I want you to know the truth, ma. I was out with a girl last night."

"Get out," ma said. "Go to work."

I slapped ma on the back and pulled her apron loose, and while she was still laughing I went out. On the way to the subway I stopped at the telegraph office and wrote a telegram.

MEET ME SAME PLACE STOP SAME TIME STOP URGENT
WILHELM

It cost me thirty cents. I addressed it to Dearest Dolly.

When I got to the shipping room of Caesar and Company, I felt good. "Buck," I said to the head clerk, "I'm going to ship out the whole place by myself today."

"That's fine," Buck said.

"Buck, you don't know how to say things. It's wonderful. It'll be the most stupendous thing that ever happened in Caesar and Company. Today I'm Atlas. I'm Hercules. I'm Tarzan. I'm Willie the Giant Killer."

"What's the matter with you?"

"How should I know?" I said. "How should I know?"

I worked like a demon. I tied; I packaged. I sent things out so fast the top of the shipping table burned from the friction. Don't ask me why; I don't know. Willie, I said to myself, you're terrific, you're a one-man department.

I went to the park and sat down on the bench at the point. You're sad, Willie, I said to myself; you're deep in sorrow.

By the time Dolly came, I really felt sad. I felt terrible. Nobody ever felt the way I did.

"What's the matter, Willie?" Dolly said. "Your telegram scared me."

"It's come, Dolly," I said. "It's come. Be brave."

"For heaven's sake, tell me what's the matter?"

"The company," I said. "A secret mission. I may never come back. But don't take it too hard, Dolly. I'm not worth it."

"A secret mission?" Dolly said. "You may never come back? Willie, you're not just making it up?"

"Dolly!"

"I knew it," Dolly said. "I knew it. Wilhelm. Of all the silly things."

I felt better. I didn't have to feel sad any more. "Well, it was for your sake I did it," I said.

"My sake?"

"It's spring," I said. "Let me hold your hand and hug you, because it's spring and it's Willie asking."

"You can hold my hand," Dolly said.

"Suppose I were really going away? Suppose you might never see me again?"

"You're not going away."

"What's a hug?" I said. "You talk as if it was the most important thing in the world."

"When the stars fall down," Dolly said, laughing, "I'll hug you."

"That's a fine thing to tell me," I said.

I looked up into the sky. "Look," I said. "Make a wish. It's a falling star. Make two; there's another."

They came down fizz and bang; gone.

"Dolly," I said.

"Yes."

"They fell down."

"What?"

"You said stars. You didn't say all the stars. You just said stars. Two stars are stars."

So I hugged her.

I was glad I wore my crepe-soled shoes and my hand-painted tie. I was glad I wore my tab-collar shirt. Willie, I said to myself, you look swell. Willie, I said to myself, you feel swell too.

"You're not sore?" I said to Dolly.

"No."

Walking home from Dolly's that night I met old Mr. Pranzer. "Hello, sir," I said. "It's a beautiful night."

"I have hay fever," said Mr. Pranzer.

That night I dreamt about my little black book. I dreamt I tore out all the pages. I tore out Lily's and Flo's; Jane and Jean and Helen, Phyllis, Corinne, Dorothy, Joan and Norma and Anne. The only page left was Dolly's.

As soon as I got up I looked for the book. It was there, and so were all the pages. That was close, Willie, I said to myself; be careful of the little black book.

That morning I didn't feel like working. That's how it goes. I was going to take a taxi downtown, but I only had a quarter with me. I asked the taxi driver about it and he told me I could go take a jump. I told him I'd pay him off a nickel a week.

I heard the train coming and ran for the turnstile. I just made the station as the doors were closing. A fat lady held it open for me.

"Thanks," I said to her.

"I couldn't help it," said the lady; "somebody was trying to push me off the train."

That's the world for you; that's Brooklyn.

Lunchtime I went out and had a roll and coffee. I used a nickel to call Dolly.

"This is Jay Freling Matton," I said, "counselor-at-law. We have just received word that you are the beneficiary of a large estate left by a Mr.

Dubelo, of Kansas, China. If you will meet us in front of the lions at the Public Library, we will be happy to further discuss the matter with you."

"Willie?" said Dolly. "Is that you, Willie?"

"You'll come?" I said.

"I didn't say that."

"Remember, it is to your benefit."

"The Public Library?"

"No," I said, remembering the nickel I had left. "I'll pick you up at home."

I heard Dolly say, "Willie—" just as I hung up.

"Why do you lie to me?" Dolly said. "Why do you make up all those stories?"

"It isn't lying," I said. "Why can't you have an uncle in Kansas or in China?"

"I haven't. That's all. I haven't."

"Dolly, you're wonderful. You're beautiful. Your eyes are like stars. Your mouth is a red, red ruby. Your hair is like spun gold. Your hands are like pale pieces of jade."

"Jade is green."

"There's white jade too."

"Well, my hands aren't like jade," Dolly said.

"I say they are."

"You read it in a book, Willie."

"No, I didn't. It was in a movie. The girl was in Malay and the fellow who told it to her was an international thief. It was a wonderful, wonderful scene."

"I don't like it," Dolly said.

"All right. You make up something better."

"I don't want to make up anything. I want you to tell the truth."

"I was going to tell you that your mouth was like a ripe melon. I was going to say that if I could kiss you once, just once, ah, then death would be sweet. There's a speech."

"Why didn't you just ask for a kiss?"

"You will?" I said. "Oh, Dolly!"

"I didn't say that."

"There. There you have it. I suppose if I said, 'How about it, babe?' it would have been all right?"

"No."

"That's fine," I said. "You just won't kiss me. That's fine. Aw, Dolly, it's spring and it's me, Willie, asking. Come on."

"No."

"What if I see a seal waiting for a trolley car?"

"No."

"If the stars fall down?"

"No."

"What then?"

Dolly laughed and leaned over. "Because you're such a crazy loon, Willie."

"That's a fine thing to say to me," I said.

But I kissed her.

Wonderful. Like running a strike right down the alley; like clicking off a rack in pool; like a cannon-ball ace in tennis. You're in the groove, Willie, I said to myself. You did it, Willie, you did it.

I reached down and tore off a snowball from the bush in the lawn. "Here, keep it," I said. "This is a night to remember."

"Willie—"

"What?"

"Do you love me, Willie?"

"I don't know, Dolly. It's spring; and sure I love you. Kiss me again, because it's spring and it's Willie asking."

"You better go home, Willie."

"I'm Don Juan," I said. "You're standing on a balcony and I'm serenading you. I'm singing you a love song. I'm Casanova and I'm sitting beside you whispering poetry in your ear."

"You better go home, Willie."

"Is something the matter?" I said. "Did I say something?"

"Go home, Willie." And she got up and she was crying. And before I could say anything she was in the house and the door was locked and I was standing on the porch all alone.

Willie, I said to myself, be sad; you've got a right to be sad now.

Walking home, I met Mr. Pranzer. "The trouble with you, Willie," he said, "is that you've never had hay fever. If you'd ever had hay fever you'd know how it's possible to be sad in the spring."

"Go jump in the lake, sir," I said courteously.

You do your best. You make everything nice. You think of things to say. You try to be different. You try to be romantic and glamorous. What happens?

She runs into the house crying.

You're a fool, Willie, I said to myself. You're a crazy fool. I should worry about one girl. I have a million girls. I have a choice, anyone I want. They're all mine. Brooklyn is full of girls. Look in the little black book, Willie, I said to myself.

It was no good. I looked in the little black book and I got out a number. "Hello," I said. "Is Joan home?"

"This is Joan talking."

"This is Willie. How are you?"

"Fine. And you, Willie?"

"Fine."

And then it was no good. Joan has knock-knees, I said to myself. Joan talks with a lisp.

"What is it you wanted, Willie?" Joan said.

"I'm working for the telephone company," I said. "I'm just testing the connection. Good-by, Joan," I said, and hung up.

The same with Phyllis. Ditto on Anne. Corinne has hair like wet grass. Jane always sings. Lily has a job and a boss. Flo wanted classical music.

There was something wrong with all of them.

I took out the little black book and I tore out all the pages except Dolly's. I tore them all out and scattered them in the wind. What's the good of a little black book if you don't like any of them?

Ma said I didn't sleep enough. Buck told me I looked like the devil. Every time I ran for a train I missed it. When I went out to eat lunch I wasn't hungry.

It was Dolly all right.

Dolly was the one.

A week later I wrote her a letter:

Dolly: He had your name on his lips; I who am his closest friend have undertaken the sacred duty of telling you what he said.

However, do not grieve, since I know it was his wish that we who knew him should continue to carry on in the carefree happy way he knew, despite the fact that he no longer will be with us.

But I feel that all of us must feel that something fine, something grand has disappeared now that Willie has left.

So it is with both grief and the happiness he wanted us to continue to feel that I write you this news. Be brave, my dear, be brave.

His friend,
CARTER WAINWRIGHT, JR.

P.S.: Willie asked me specially to convey to you certain matters too personal for the pages of this letter. So if you will meet me in front of the Public Library (I am sure you know the lions) I will be glad to divulge this information to you.

C. W., JR.

I went all the way up to the Bronx to mail it.

I waited three hours and ten minutes, on my brother's watch, in front of the lions, and when Dolly came, I was good and angry.

"That's it," I said to her; "keep me waiting. I don't matter at all."

"You didn't say what time to meet you in the letter," Dolly said.

"What letter? I never sent you any letter."

"Please, Willie," Dolly said. "What is it you wanted?"

"Marry me, Dolly," I said. "I'll give you a penthouse and a limousine. I'll shower you with diamonds and furs. You'll live in a house of flowers. I will be your slave. Step on me. Do as you will with me. But marry me."

"No," Dolly said.

"You let me hold your hand," I said.

"That was because of the seal."

"You let me hug you."

"The stars fell down."

"I kissed you."

"I liked your crazy talk, Willie."

"You cried over me."

"That was because I thought you didn't love me."

"I do," I said. "I do. Why won't you marry me, Dolly?"

"Willie," Dolly said. "Oh, Willie. I'll let you hold my hand and hug me because you're lucky; and I'll let you kiss me because I like you. But I won't marry you."

"I'll give you everything you want. Luxuries. Anything. Just ask for it."

"No, you won't. You know you can't do that, Willie."

So that was it. And maybe she wasn't wrong. Maybe I was wrong. Maybe, Willie, I said to myself, you're not good enough for her. I felt all washed up. I felt like the stone lions must feel in a rain.

"Dolly," I said, "you're right. I can't give you anything. I work in a shipping room and I make twenty-two-fifty a week. I haven't got any money in the bank and I'm always lying. Don't ever believe me, Dolly. All I have is myself. That's all I can give you."

"No limousine?" Dolly said.

"No."

"No furs?"

"No."

"No diamonds?"

"No."

"Just you?"

"Just me, Dolly."

"And you'd like it that way: Just you and me?"

"Oh, Dolly!" I said.

"Without lies or stories?"

"Dolly," I said, "you're breaking my heart."

"How much do you make a week, again?" Dolly said.

"Twenty-two-fifty."

"I make eighteen," Dolly said. "What do you think?"

"Dolly," I said. "Dolly!"

"Crazy Willie," Dolly said. "Who wants all those things?"

Imagine that. Furs, diamonds, limousines, penthouses—pouf, in the garbage pail; all in exchange for me—Willie. There's a girl for you.

I didn't know what to do. "Hey, lions," I yelled.

"Willie," she said. "Willie, kiss me, because it's spring and it's me, Dolly, asking."

That's the world for you; that's Brooklyn.

Dorothy Parker

Dorothy Parker (1893-   ) bears the reputation of a brilliant but mordant wit. As the following sketch from Here Lies *may show, her short stories are seldom merely funny or merely cruel. Beneath their cynical manner they are sometimes unexpectedly tender and profoundly understanding of frustrated and blundering humanity.*

THE SEXES

THE young man with the scenic cravat glanced nervously down the sofa at the girl in the fringed dress. She was examining her handkerchief; it might have been the first one of its kind she had seen, so deep was her interest in its material, form, and possibilities. The young man cleared his throat, without necessity or success, producing a small, syncopated noise.

"Want a cigarette?" he said.

"No, thank you," she said. "Thank you ever so much just the same."

"Sorry I've only got these kind," he said. "You got any of your own?"

"I really don't know," she said. "I probably have, thank you."

"Because if you haven't," he said, "it wouldn't take me a minute to go up to the corner and get you some."

"Oh, thank you, but I wouldn't have you go to all that trouble for anything," she said. "It's awfully sweet of you to think of it. Thank you ever so much."

"Will you for God's sakes stop thanking me?" he said.

"Really," she said, "I didn't know I was saying anything out of the way. I'm awfully sorry if I hurt your feelings. I know what it feels like to get your feelings hurt. I'm sure I didn't realize it was an insult to say 'thank you' to a person. I'm not exactly in the habit of having people swear at me because I say 'thank you' to them."

"I did not swear at you!" he said.

"Oh, you didn't?" she said. "I see."

"My God," he said, "all I said, I simply asked you if I couldn't go out and get you some cigarettes. Is there anything in that to get up in the air about?"

"Who's up in the air?" she said. "I'm sure I didn't know it was a criminal offense to say I wouldn't dream of giving you all that trouble. I'm afraid I must be awfully stupid, or something."

"Do you want me to go out and get you some cigarettes; or don't you?" he said.

"Goodness," she said, "if you want to go so much, please don't feel you have to stay here. I wouldn't have you feel you had to stay for anything."

"Ah, don't be that way, will you?" he said.

"Be what way?" she said. "I'm not being any way."

"What's the matter?" he said.

"Why, nothing," she said. "Why?"

"You've been funny all evening," he said. "Hardly said a word to me, ever since I came in."

"I'm terribly sorry you haven't been having a good time," she said. "For goodness' sakes, don't feel you have to stay here and be bored. I'm sure there are millions of places you could be having a lot more fun. The only thing, I'm a little bit sorry I didn't know before, that's all. When you said you were coming over tonight, I broke a lot of dates to go to the theater and everything. But it doesn't make a bit of difference. I'd much rather have you go and have a good time. It isn't very pleasant to sit here and feel you're boring a person to death."

"I'm not bored!" he said. "I don't want to go any place! Ah, honey, won't you tell me what's the matter? Ah, please."

"I haven't the faintest idea what you're talking about," she said. "There isn't a thing on earth the matter. I don't know what you mean."

"Yes, you do," he said. "There's something the trouble. Is it anything I've done, or anything?"

"Goodness," she said, "I'm sure it isn't any of my business, anything you do. I certainly wouldn't feel I had any right to criticize."

"Will you stop talking like that?" he said. "Will you, please?"

"Talking like what?" she said.

"You know," he said. "That's the way you were talking over the telephone today, too. You were so snotty when I called you up, I was afraid to talk to you."

"I beg your pardon," she said. "What did you say I was?"

"Well, I'm sorry," he said. "I didn't mean to say that. You get me so balled up."

"You see," she said, "I'm really not in the habit of hearing language like that. I've never had a thing like that said to me in my life."

"I told you I was sorry, didn't I?" he said. "Honest, honey, I didn't mean it. I don't know how I came to say a thing like that. Will you excuse me? Please?"

"Oh, certainly," she said. "Goodness, don't feel you have to apologize to me. It doesn't make any difference at all. It just seems a little bit funny to have somebody you were in the habit of thinking was a gentleman come to your home and use language like that to you, that's all. But it doesn't make the slightest bit of difference."

"I guess nothing I say makes any difference to you," he said. "You seem to be sore at me."

"I'm sore at you?" she said. "I can't understand what put that idea in your head. Why should I be sore at you?"

"That's what I'm asking you," he said. "Won't you tell me what I've done? Have I done something to hurt your feelings, honey? The way you were, over the phone, you had me worried all day. I couldn't do a lick of work."

"I certainly wouldn't like to feel," she said, "that I was interfering with your work. I know there are lots of girls that don't think anything of doing things like that, but I think it's terrible. It certainly isn't very nice to sit here and have someone tell you you interfere with his business."

"I didn't say that!" he said. "I didn't say it!"

"Oh, didn't you?" she said. "Well, that was the impression I got. It must be my stupidity."

"I guess maybe I better go," he said. "I can't get right. Everything I say seems to make you sorer and sorer. Would you rather I'd go?"

"Please do just exactly whatever you like," she said. "I'm sure the last thing I want to do is have you stay here when you'd rather be some place else. Why don't you go some place where you won't be bored? Why don't you go up to Florence Leaming's? I know she'd love to have you."

"I don't want to go up to Florence Leaming's!" he said. "What would I want to go up to Florence Leaming's for? She gives me a pain."

"Oh, really?" she said. "She didn't seem to be giving you so much of a pain at Elsie's party last night, I notice. I notice you couldn't even talk to anybody else, that's how much of a pain she gave you."

"Yeah, and you know why I was talking to her?" he said.

"Why, I suppose you think she's attractive," she said. "I suppose some people do. It's perfectly natural. Some people think she's quite pretty."

"I don't know whether she's pretty or not," he said. "I wouldn't know her if I saw her again. Why I was talking to her was you wouldn't even give me a tumble, last night. I came up and tried to talk to you, and you just said, 'Oh, how do you do'—just like that, 'Oh, how do you do'—and you turned right away and wouldn't look at me."

"I wouldn't look at you?" she said. "Oh, that's awfully funny. Oh, that's marvelous. You don't mind if I laugh, do you?"

"Go ahead and laugh your head off," he said. "But you wouldn't."

"Well, the minute you came in the room," she said, "you started making such a fuss over Florence Leaming, I thought you never wanted to see anybody else. You two seemed to be having such a wonderful time together, goodness knows I wouldn't have butted in for anything."

"My God," he said, "this what's-her-name girl came up and began talking to me before I even saw anybody else, and what could I do? I couldn't sock her in the nose, could I?"

"I certainly didn't see you try," she said.

"You saw me try to talk to you, didn't you?" he said. "And what did you do? 'Oh, how do you do.' Then this what's-her-name came up again, and there I was, stuck. Florence Leaming! I think she's terrible. Know what I think of her? I think she's a damn little fool. That's what I think of her."

"Well, of course," she said, "that's the impression she always gave me, but I don't know. I've heard people say she's pretty. Honestly I have."

"Why, she can't be pretty in the same room with you," he said.

"She has got an awfully funny nose," she said. "I really feel sorry for a girl with a nose like that."

"She's got a terrible nose," he said. "You've got a beautiful nose. Gee, you've got a pretty nose."

"Oh, I have not," she said. "You're crazy."

"And beautiful eyes," he said, "and beautiful hair and a beautiful mouth. And beautiful hands. Let me have one of the little hands. Ah, look atta little hand! Who's got the prettiest hands in the world? Who's the sweetest girl in the world?"

"I don't know," she said. "Who?"

"You don't know!" he said. "You do so, too, know."

"I do not," she said. "Who? Florence Leaming?"

"Oh, Florence Leaming, my eye!" he said. "Getting sore about Florence Leaming! And me not sleeping all last night and not doing a stroke of work all day because you wouldn't speak to me! A girl like you getting sore about a girl like Florence Leaming!"

"I think you're just perfectly crazy," she said. "I was not sore! What on earth ever made you think I was? You're simply crazy. Ow, my new pearl beads! Wait a second till I take them off. There!"

Robert Frost

Robert Frost (1875-   ) lived in San Francisco, his birthplace, until he was ten years old. Since then he has made his home in New England. After two years at Harvard he followed a variety of occupations, all with the one end: to support a growing family while he waited for recognition as a poet. Like another poet, Robert Burns, he knew at first hand the harshness of farm life. Twenty years he waited, and found a publisher only after he had gone to England to live. When the war drove him back to the United States in 1915, he at last found himself famous. He has received the Pulitzer Prize four times and many other honors. His reputation as the foremost living American poet rests on two achievements: his re-creation of New England country life in narrative poems of pungent humor and quiet understanding; and his interpretations of man and nature in lyrics of unpretentious beauty. As in so many of his poems "Two Look at Two" presents a simple experience with no need for ampler statement: the meaning is clear.

TWO LOOK AT TWO

Love and forgetting might have carried them
A little further up the mountain side
With night so near, but not much further up.
They must have halted soon in any case
With thoughts of the path back, how rough it was
With rock and washout, and unsafe in darkness;
When they were halted by a tumbled wall
With barbed-wire binding. They stood facing this,
Spending what onward impulse they still had
In one last look the way they must not go,
On up the failing path, where, if a stone
Or earthslide moved at night, it moved itself;
No footstep moved it. "This is all," they sighed,
"Good-night to woods." But not so; there was more.
A doe from round a spruce stood looking at them
Across the wall, as near the wall as they.
She saw them in their field, they her in hers.
The difficulty of seeing what stood still,
Like some up-ended boulder split in two,
Was in her clouded eyes: they saw no fear there.

She seemed to think that two thus they were safe.
Then, as if they were something that, though strange,
She could not trouble her mind with too long,
She sighed and passed unscared along the wall.
"*This,* then, is all. What more is there to ask?"
But no, not yet. A snort to bid them wait.
A buck from round the spruce stood looking at them
Across the wall as near the wall as they.
This was an antlered buck of lusty nostril,
Not the same doe come back into her place.
He viewed them quizzically with jerks of head,
As if to ask, "Why don't you make some motion?
Or give some sign of life? Because you can't.
I doubt if you're as living as you look."
Thus till he had them almost feeling dared
To stretch a proffering hand—and a spell-breaking.
Then he too passed unscared along the wall.
Two had seen two, whichever side you spoke from.
"This *must* be all." It was all. Still they stood,
A great wave from it going over them,
As if the earth in one unlooked-for favor
Had made them certain earth returned their love.

Louis Adamic

*Louis Adamic (1899-   ) is the native who returned to Carniola, now
a part of Yugoslavia, in 1933, and in* The Native's Return *(1934) told
how he rediscovered his cultural background. Since that time Adamic
has become the articulate voice of thousands of new Americans asking
for understanding and social acceptance. In its lusty gaiety and earthi-
ness "Wedding in Carniola" suggests Peter Brueghel's Wedding Feast.
This peasant life misses none of the simple joys of living.*

WEDDING IN CARNIOLA

THE wedding ceremony was set for the first Mon-
day in July, when everyone was expected to be done with haying and there
would be a lull in work.

Invitations were extended to almost everybody in the two villages and
numerous persons elsewhere in the country, but, as usual, only the young

people accepted; and those who, like myself, had not previously taken part in a Carniolan wedding were instructed how to act in the doings still to come.

Three days before the big event each of the guests sent to the bride's house a goose, a turkey, a duck, a ham, a lamb, two or three chickens, or several pigeons or rabbits, as his or her contribution to the feast, the preparation for which—baking, cooking—were in charge of a professional cook engaged for the occasion.

Late Sunday afternoon there appeared in Blato, mounted on a gaily decorated horse, a young peasant from Gatina, with flowers on his hat and jacket, and a box under his arm. With a great show of dash the "bride's messenger," as he was called, rode to Mikha's house and asked for Toné.

When the bridegroom came he said, "Toné, greetings from the bride! She sent me to you with this box, which contains flowers grown in pots on her window-sill, tended by her own hands."

Early next morning all of us "groom's people"—the *stareshina*,[1] I, the several assistant groomsmen, four musicians, and all the wedding guests, male and female, from Blato—assembled in Mikha's house (for the old man was still master of the place until Toné brought home his bride).

Most of us were in national costumes of the region. The men wore tight-fitting trousers of heavy homespun cloth or soft leather, tucked into high boots; short snug waistcoats with large round gold, brass, or silver buttons; white shirts of rough homespun linen, handsomely bordered with needlework at the wrists and neck, with bright-colored silk neckerchiefs tied beneath the collars; and narrow-rimmed green felt hats adorned with wild-rooster feathers and flowers the bride had sent the day before.

The girls were in white cotton blouses with lace trimmings and immense flowing sleeves, silk scarfs, and voluminous dark skirts, some of them accordion-pleated, with dozens of multicolored ribbons flowing from narrow waists. Some of them wore a white headgear called *hauba,* embroidered with silver or gold; nearly all wore heavy old jewelry—necklaces, earrings, brooches, and elaborate girdles, most of it of tarnished silver and gold and silver filigree.

On setting out for Gatina with the groom, the *stareshina,* and me in the first of a string of diverse vehicles, those of the young men who, unlike the groom and myself, were not required to be dignified, began to whoop and sing, and the accordion-players to play. The buggies, wagons, and horses, and several bicycles were decorated with flowers, green twigs, festoons, and bunting.

As we reached Gatina our *stareshina* commanded everyone to be well-behaved: no more whooping, singing, and music.

---

[1] *stareshina,* an elderly friend of the family who acts as a go-between.

Not a soul was visible anywhere near Galé's house. Our coming had been announced to them by the "watchman" they had stationed on the outskirts of the village; whereupon the house had been shut and everybody inside was supposed to be quiet, except the bride, for whom it is almost obligatory to sob on her mother's bosom.

Our *stareshina* knocked on the closed door. No answer. He knocked again, a little harder. Again no answer. Once more he knocked, this time with the crook of his cane. Still no answer. Then he shook the door by the knob, and all of us began to grumble, "What the devil! What kind of a house is this that they don't answer when people knock?"

Finally a voice inside, the voice of the bride's *stareshina,* called, "Who is it, and what do you want?"

"We are travelers from afar," answered our *stareshina* at the top of his lungs, so that everyone inside the house could hear him over the bride's sobbing. "We are tired and hungry. We ask to be let in, so we may rest and refresh ourselves."

"What kind of people are you?" the bride's *stareshina* asked through the closed door. "What can you say for yourselves?"

The groom's *stareshina* answered: "We don't like to boast, but since you demand to know, let me tell you we're God-fearing people. Prayer is our favorite pastime, charity our middle name. We never turn away a traveler when he knocks on our door, and we hope you, too, will turn the key and admit us."

The key turned, but the door opened only a few inches. The bride's *stareshina* looked us over, then said:

"You look to be decent people, true enough, and we believe you are pious, charitable, and hospitable; but can you say anything else for yourselves? Have you any *practical* virtues?"

Our *stareshina* said: "We don't lack practical virtues, either. We are hard-working people. Dawn never finds us in bed. We work in all kinds of weather and no form of toil frightens us. Look, our hands are calloused and chapped, and no matter how much we scrub them, we cannot make them look white, for the black soil of our fields has eaten itself into our skin. Only today, coming from afar, we are tired and hungry and appeal to your hospitality—the hospitality for which this country is famous."

The door opened, then ensued a further exchange of questions and answers between the two *stareshinas.* The rest of us outside pushed our *stareshina* from behind till we all got into the big-room and vestibule, which were full of "bride's people," most of them also in regional costumes.

The sobbing bride was in a little side-room with her mother and first bridesmaid.

The bride's *stareshina* pretended to be alarmed. "You people don't seem tired. I think this is only a trick. I trust you have no evil intentions?"

All of us "groom's people" laughed; the others looked puzzled, afraid, or indignant.

Said our *stareshina,* "No, we have no evil intentions, but you guessed right: we are neither tired nor hungry, and we did play a little trick on you folks—but with a good purpose. This young man here"—placing a hand on a shoulder of the wincing, awkward bridegroom—"is a gardener from our village. He has everything in abundance, but his heart is sad and forlorn, for he lacks a blossom which every young gardener must have. He has heard that a blossom grows in this home, and to keep him from moping around we, his fellow villagers, came with him to ask you to give him your blossom. We promise to pluck her gently and carefully plant her in his garden."

"Ah, so that's your idea!" chuckled the bride's *stareshina,* and all of the other "bride's people" laughed with him. "We have here not only one but many blossoms."

"Well, show us what you have!" said I.

The bride's *stareshina* went into an adjacent room and returned with a little eight-year-old girl dressed somewhat like a bride. "Now here's a sweet and tender blossom," he said.

"No, no!" I said. "Too tender. Transplanting would damage her. What else have you?"

Next he brought before us an elderly woman. (Custom requires that she be at least fifty, ugly, and in possession of a sense of humor and a ready tongue.) She was also rigged out like a bride, with too much finery, and tried to act coy before the bridegroom, who, panic-stricken, appealed to me to take her away, insisting she was not the blossom he had in mind, while the entire houseful of people laughed.

"Why all this laughter?" demanded the bride's *stareshina.* "Here we show you a blossom—a woman who is experienced, has most of her teeth, a nose in the middle of her face, and all the other organs and appurtenances in their proper places; a woman whose movements are as lively and graceful as one wants to see; a woman—" And as he praised her, the old woman showed her teeth and demonstrated her liveliness by dancing a jig.

But the groom's *stareshina* and I shook our heads and shoved the old woman aside. Finally, when they insisted on our taking this particular "blossom," we had to tell them why we did not want her—that she was old and cross-eyed, and looked like a half-empty sack of turnips. This, of course, provoked the "blossom" to tell us to go somewhere; she would not be transplanted to our garden, which probably was nothing but a dump, and so on, while everyone laughed, till she flicked her flouncy skirt and, pretending she was insulted, flew from the room.

"Now," I said, "we are in earnest. Show us the real blossom."

"You people are too choosy," said the bride's *stareshina*. "You all better go and leave us alone."

"Show us the blossom of blossoms," I insisted.

"We have shown you the best!"

"Well," said our *stareshina,* "if that's the case, we made a mistake. Come, people, let's go. We made a mistake."

We all turned to leave.

"Wait a minute!" cried the bride's *stareshina*. "Maybe you mean this one. *Ya, ya,* I guess you do mean this one; she *is* a blossom of blossoms!"

And so Yulka came on her father's arm, crying, her face buried in a bouquet of white flowers. Attired like the other women, but more lavishly, she wore the same bridal outfit her mother had been married in thirty-eight years before. A garland of white roses, interspersed with green leaves, encircled her elaborate *hauba*.

"*Ya, ya,* this is the one we want!" declared the bridegroom's *stareshina* and I.

The bride's *stareshina* waxed philosophical for a bit: "Well, what can we do? Nature is nature, and nature demands that the blossom be transplanted in order to bear fruit. . . . Take her. We believe you will carefully plant her in good soil and guard her from evil."

Then we all went into the orchard behind the house, where tables were set, and ate the "pre-nuptial breakfast," which consisted of cold meats, cakes, wine. There were accordion music and old wedding songs.

The "breakfast" lasted two hours. The bride's *stareshina* made a speech. He talked long in a poetic-sentimental streak, and much of what he said would sound witless in translation, for Slovenian, especially as spoken by the peasants, is a poetic language and endows sentiment with more dignity than does English.

Shortly before noon we all started for the church, but down the road a little distance came upon a mob of young men from Gatina. They had stretched a chain of twisted willow shoots and field flowers across the road, and there was a table with a white tablecloth strewn with green leaves and red and yellow blossoms, and two jugs of wine and many glasses.

This was *shranga* (the barrier).

The assistant groomsmen and I became indignant. "What the devil is this! What do you fellows mean by putting a rope across a public street?"

The leader of the Gatina boys, the biggest and handsomest of the lot, then said that Yulka was from their village and, by rights, *their* girl. "You folks come from Blato and take her. You don't expect us to like that, do you? If she wants to go to Blato, we don't mean to frustrate her wish, but we don't want the world to hear about this and say there are men in Gatina who let their girls go without saying boo. . . . Before you take her we demand you pay us *odskodnina* (recompense)."

Then our *stareshina* spoke. "We're not looking for trouble, fellows. If you think you have something coming to you, tell us your price."

"Fifty thousand dinars!"

Our side guffawed. "Your whole damn' village isn't worth that much."

For a few minutes there was a great hubbub, while I, as first groomsman, tried to console the bride, who laughed at the same time that she cried.

After a while the Gatina boys came down to five thousand.

"Don't be idiots!" said our *stareshina*. "For five thousand we can buy a good pair of oxen these days."

"Well, isn't she worth as much as a pair of oxen?"

The shouting and laughter continued. At the end the boys agreed to take five hundred ($7), which sum the *stareshina* paid them over the "barrier," to be spent by them as they saw fit; perhaps for wine or some improvement in the village's fire-fighting equipment.

Then wine was poured and the boys' leader made a speech telling Toné what a lucky dog he was, congratulating Blato on getting such a girl into one of its homes, wishing Yulka all the happiness in the world.

Whereupon the "barrier" was removed and we proceeded churchward.

The ceremony in the church was brief. When it was over the party distributed itself among the three winehouses in Gatina, to dance, talk, sing, drink, and play practical jokes on one another till five o'clock, when the cook and the bride's *stareshina* had agreed we should return to the house for the feast.

The house, meantime, had been decorated by the bride's brothers and their friends. On the road leading to it stood two Maypoles, holding a sign between them, "Greetings to the newlyweds!"

In good times wedding feasts last three or four days, never less than two, at the end of which period everybody is near exhaustion from drinking, eating, dancing, singing, and sleeplessness; now, however, because of the *kriza,*[2] the feast was scheduled to last only till midnight of the first day.

The bride, the groom, their parents, the *stareshinas,* the groomsmen, and the bridesmaids went into the big-room and took places at a large table, in the center of which was a vast cake inscribed "Happy Life!" Under the ceiling, across the entire room, were stretched chains of flowers and green twigs.

In the orchard, tables were set for the rest of the guests. When it became dark, lamps hanging on boughs were lighted.

The feast lasted for hours, and the accordion-players and other musi-

---

[2] *kriza,* crisis.

cians played almost without interruption, taking turns and time out to eat and drink.

The *stareshinas,* first one, then the other, delivered long orations on marriage, essentially alike, full of platitudes and advice, charmingly presented. I give, in part, the words of the bridegroom's *stareshina:*

"They are married now and only death can part them. Today we eat and drink and sing. But this will all be over soon. Tonight Yulka goes to her new home with her husband. It is a good home, but in the best of homes life is an earnest business. The peasant's lot is not an easy one. We pit our strength and wits against odds. Nature—the elements are not always on our side. Often we don't know what, if anything, we'll reap on the spot where we have sown. It's a fight—work from morning till night, from day to day, year to year, summer and winter, spring and autumn. There is no end to toil. That is our fate on this earth. The peasant can never get far ahead and say, 'By God, I win!' . . .

"Working on the soil, wresting a livelihood from the fields, the lot of neither man nor woman is easy. Here is Toné; he is young, at the height of his life, but before long, struggle, responsibility, and hardships of all sorts will chisel lines into his face. He will have to toil in cold and heat, and to complain will do him no good.

"And here is Yulka, our bride; her face is like a ripe apple; but in her case, too, life will soon do its work. She will have to toil; she will bear children. That is what she was born for. . . .

"What can they do? Only one thing: stick together and help each other. On his side, Toné will be harassed by one thing and another; no peasant's life is easy; and as a wanderer trudging on a hot and dusty highway seeks the shade of a tree, so will he, your Toné, come to you, Yulka, and seek calm, rest, and courage for new effort. You will be his refuge.

"And you, Toné, remember a woman is a tender thing; she is the 'blossom' we came to seek this morning. You must be to her what a wall is to the first flowers of spring. Protect her. You must be to her what a pole is to the vine. Support her. Marriage is seldom a matter of pure joy. Never for long. Storms come. When or if they come, calm them as soon as you can and close the doors and windows. Don't let those outside know of your differences. Straighten them out yourselves. Don't let anyone mix in your affairs. If you straighten out your own differences, your happiness will be so much the greater. In fact, only then will your marriage begin to gather character and depth, and the bond between you grow really strong. . . . Let us drink to the bride and the groom!"

There were other speeches by the *stareshinas.* The groom's eulogized the bride's parents, and the other way around. A toast was drunk to me because I had returned from America after nineteen years, become a writer in America, and had married an American girl, who was also a guest at the feast as companion of one of my brothers.

Thus until midnight.

At ten minutes to twelve the bridesmaids dimmed the lights in the big-room, and as many of the people outside as could came in.

The bride began to weep.

Then her *stareshina* rose and said, "We hear that in other lands *devishtvo* (purity, virginity) is a rare virtue. Among us, praise God, it still exists. Here is our bride, a jewel of this village, parish, and county. Her sun-browned brow shines under the flowers signifying *devishtvo* which entwine her head. . . . But life goes on and, like everything else, a virtue can be carried too far—"

The clock began to strike twelve. Everybody was still, only the bride sobbed, with a few of the other women joining in with her.

"It is midnight," the *stareshina* continued. "The wedding feast is over. A new day begins and with it, Yulka, your new life. The flowers must now come off your head."

The bridesmaids removed the garland from Yulka's head and placed it before Toné.

"Toné"—the *stareshina* turned to the bridegroom—"the flowers lie before you. Your bride offers them—offers herself to you. . . . My friends, let's drink once more—to the future of our newlyweds!"

Outside, the assistant groomsmen were hitching a team of horses to a wagon on which were Yulka's hope-chest and other belongings and a small coop with a chicken and a rooster—for a bride must bring something alive to her new home.

Yulka then took leave of her mother and father, brothers, bridesmaids, and friends, and, amid much feminine weeping and masculine whooping, Toné helped her onto the wagon, and they drove off—man and wife—to their home in Blato.

The rest of the party broke up soon after, but all through the rest of the night there was much whooping in the valley, the young unmarried men of Blato and Gatina answering one another, their whoops echoing against the mountains.

Sally Benson

*Sally Benson employs methods of composition which disprove the plati-
tude that genius is a capacity for taking pains. She averages from two
to two and a half hours for a story, composing a single draft (the final
one) on her typewriter. And she has never received a rejection slip!
Born in St. Louis (1900-   ), Mrs. Benson has lived since girlhood in
New York City. Her deft sketches are drawn from a quick responsiveness to the urban life about her. Her technique suggests Katherine
Mansfield's in its simple clarity, its adroit selection of detail. Here is life,
reported with convincing immediacy and not without ironic overtones.*

PEOPLE FROM OUT OF TOWN [1]

THE Marlborough Garden Apartments were a
block from Riverside Drive, far uptown, and the architect who designed
them had allowed himself to be swayed by countless desires. A vacillating
man, he wanted to make the most of the view of the river, which would be
visible if he put corner windows on the northwest side of the building, but
this would make the corresponding windows on the southwest side face on
the dreary back of another apartment, and, as his intention was to design
a group of buildings instead of one huge one, he was torn between a longing to do something homey and Elizabethan with stone, timber, and leaded
panes and a sneaking suspicion that the future tenants might want glass
bricks and plenty of light. He almost stubbornly clung to his idea of a group
of buildings in the Elizabethan manner and compromised by making the
windows larger than normal, which gave one the impression that whole
sections of the apartment had been gouged out. Carried away by a fine
enthusiasm for both atmosphere and air, he didn't bother about wall space
and recklessly slashed away at his plans. In the rare places where there were
no windows, he tucked in cunning little alcoves that gave the outside of the
buildings a charming irregularity.

When he thought of the people who would occupy the apartments, he
imagined an assemblage of childless young couples with a minimum amount
of furniture who would continue to practice a little restraint, artistically and
morally, and not clutter up the place too much. He designed a courtyard
garden with a fountain, and at the insistence of the owner, a Mr. Leibo-
witz, who had been born disillusioned, he grudgingly planned a playground

[1] By permission of *The New Yorker*. Copyright The F-R Publishing Corporation, 1943.

141

with swings, sand piles, and slides, hoping as he did so that before it ever knew the horror of the patter of tiny feet it would fall into ruins and the jungle would claim it. Completed, the apartments were advertised as having 1½, 2½, 3½, and 4½ rooms.

The architect's dream of Utopia was ended when the tenants began to move in. They seemed more like squirrels than humans and arrived with numerous odd-looking bits that obviously wouldn't fit anywhere, let alone in a place designed for the maximum amount of light, air, and beauty. The best that could be said of their furniture, which either didn't match at all or matched only too well, was that it was just a little too good to throw away. They came loaded with mementos of their sordid pasts; they hung Dutch curtains at the kitchen windows; they put cribs or painted breakfast sets in the half-rooms and radios in the bookshelves; and the garden, which was meant to look like a bit of green from another world, was noisy with the blare of music when the windows were open and smelled of cooking. Nobody entered into the spirit of the thing at all. The architect visited the place one last time. It was going full blast and a little boy was throwing dirt and grass into the fountain.

The Carters leased Apartment 210. It had three and a half rooms, which was a half-room more than they had had in the Copley Arms. It didn't take Ruth Carter long to decide what to do with the extra space. "We'll eat there," she said, "and keep Mickey's crib in the bedroom in the daytime and move it out into the living room at night, the way we've always done. It's a perfectly lovely place, and that little step going down into it just *makes* it, doesn't it?"

Roger Carter, who had been faintly repelled by the whole thing, looked at her flushed and excited face. "Well, it has more room," he admitted.

Most of the time, Roger Carter liked being married. He could even look back dispassionately and see exactly how it had happened. He had been out of college almost a year before he found a job with a large advertising agency, and by that time he was so eager to work, so tired of uncertainty that he plunged in with enthusiasm. Later he discovered that men were advanced to better positions by right of seniority and that it didn't matter at all whether you worked as hard as you could or whether you just slid along with the others. He rented a room with a kitchenette and planned to get his own meals; he sent home for his books and tried to feel self-sufficient.

When Ruth came to work at the agency he noticed her only because she was prettier, quieter, and dumber than the other girls. Although she had worked in offices since she was sixteen years old, she was never quite sure what was expected of her. One day, after she had made a particularly annoying blunder, he looked at her long enough to tell her what he thought of her. To his amazement, her eyes filled with tears. She hurried from the room and he was left feeling surprised and a little pleased. And that night he asked her to go to dinner. He had imagined that when he married he would live in a remodelled apartment somewhere in the Village with a wife who could throw together inexpensive suppers for his friends. He had even pictured her lying back on a huge sofa, drink in hand, clad becomingly and daringly in dark-red lounging pajamas. It was impossible to see Ruth in this rôle. She was small, soft, and feminine. Even when he looked at her across a table in a restaurant, she seemed to have an aura of innumerable small things about her. Not that she clanked with charm bracelets or fussed with herself; on the contrary, her pretty arms were bare and her face almost free of make-up, but he felt everything that belonged to her assumed a personal value in her eyes. "What did I do with my handkerchief?" she would ask.

And instantly the square of linen became identified. It was the white handkerchief with her initials that her Aunt Rose had given her, or it was the flowered one that she had bought to go with her blue dress. Its loss would leave a gap.

She had no interest in the things she didn't possess. And until it became obvious that he was getting pretty serious about her, she treated him with a polite, sweet respect. She was not a girl who allowed you to kiss her lightly, and she was without guile.

From the first they were a family; they were never two young people who surprisingly found themselves tied together. They had a home from the start and all the things that went with it. It worried Ruth that they had never had a dining room, and when they moved into the Marlborough Gardens she bought a shiny maple breakfast table, chairs, and a narrow sideboard. "You see," she said happily, "we gradually get everything. Maybe, when Mickey gets older, we can have an extra room for him."

She sat all afternoon in the playground while Mickey dug in the sand pile, and sometimes, in the evening, people came over for cards. On Sundays they wheeled the baby in his carriage along the Drive, because Ruth thought it would be undignified for Roger to sit in the playground in the midst of the women and children. Walking along on a clear day with the wind blowing from the river, he thought of the summers he used to spend in Connecticut and the beach there. He remembered the girls, brown and noisy, and the night that Mary Chapin got high and ran her car into a ditch. Then he would feel that there was something indecent about pushing a baby carriage, and he wondered if he looked like the other fathers, a little too neat in their good suits, as though the neglect of any small detail meant a step backward that might send them hurtling over into the chasm of complete indifference.

After these walks, Roger would sit at the shiny new maple table eating his Sunday supper. Everything in the house, from the way the furniture was arranged in the living room to the color of his neckties, was Ruth's choice. A few of his books were in the small bookshelf set between the windows, but the others lay in a box in the closet, to make room for the radio and the sets of books that Ruth liked because they looked dignified and matched. She saw to it that he lived in careful comfort, even denying herself the things she needed so that he, the house, and the baby would have what she felt was due them.

They had been living in the Marlborough Gardens for over a year when Bob Ellis and his wife came to town and asked them to dinner downtown. Bob had been one of Roger's roommates at college, and Roger was pleased at the prospect of seeing him again and elated over the idea of a party that would not consist of cream cheese and jelly or spiced-ham sandwiches. Ruth made arrangements with the Y.W.C.A. for a girl to stay with Mickey and had her hair done. There was something charming in its usual disorder and she didn't look natural with the deep ridges around her face and the tight curls at the back of her neck. Roger surveyed her critically. "Comb it out a little," he advised.

"It will fly all over," she said. "And if I leave it this way tonight, it will stay in a week."

She slipped her evening dress over her head. It was not new, and as she had put on weight, it pulled slightly across her hips and breasts. It was a shiny taffeta with puff sleeves and two artificial roses on the shoulder. Her stockings were too heavy and she walked carefully in her high-heeled evening shoes. "Is it very cold?" she asked. "Or do you think I can wear my cape?"

Without waiting for an answer, she opened the window and put her head out. "Goodness, but it's blowing!" she exclaimed. She went to the closet and got out her good coat, the one with the beaver collar.

"I think I'd better wear this," she said. "No use getting pneumonia for the sake of looks. Besides, I can check it at the coatroom when we go in."

When they left, Mickey was having his supper, enchanted with the girl from the Y.W.C.A.

It was cold waiting for the bus and the wind blew Ruth's hair loose, so that it stood out wildly around her head. With her red cheeks and the bright blue of her taffeta dress, she made Roger seem pale by comparison. In the bus she put her hand on his. "Isn't this fun?" she asked. "I can't remember *when* we've been downtown to dinner. And you look so nice. You do, really."

She smiled at him and he could see where her lipstick ended against the pale pink of her mouth. "We could have had them to dinner, I suppose," she went on. "We *should*. Maybe later in the week if they stay on. Have they any family?"

"I don't think so," Roger answered.

"Oh," she said. "That's too bad."

The bus had turned into the Drive. She looked out across the river and thought of Mickey and the nice girl from the Y.W.C.A., and remembered that they must be home by eleven. She glanced at Roger and wondered if he were enjoying himself. It was hard to tell about him at times.

The Ellises were waiting for them at a table set for four. Bob Ellis was short and plump and had a Midwestern accent, but Mrs. Ellis was as slim and sleek as a model in Bonwit Teller's window. He pumped Roger's hand and slapped him repeatedly on the back. "Roger, you old pirate!" he cried.

"Sh-h-h," Mrs. Ellis said. "Don't scream so."

She looked at Ruth and nodded. "Men are just little boys," she said.

"Oh, *aren't* they!" Ruth exclaimed. "That's what I keep telling Roger."

Ann Ellis reached for her drink. "Sit down, you two," she said.

Bob Ellis beamed at them. "This is great. This is like old times. What say we never go to bed?"

Ruth laughed. "That sounds all right to *me*," she said gaily. "But I don't know how it would sound to Mickey."

"Mickey?" Ann Ellis asked.

"Our little boy," Ruth explained. "We have someone staying with him tonight and she has to leave at eleven."

Bob Ellis stared at her curiously. "Well, the night's young. So what will it be?"

Ruth turned toward Ann Ellis. "You must see him," she said. "He's at his very cutest age. Just beginning to talk a little, and the things he says—well, you wouldn't believe the things he says."

"I'll have another Scotch," Ann told her husband.

"How about it, Roger, old boy? Scotch sound all right to you two? Waiter, four Scotch-and-sodas."

"I've been buying things and buying things all day long," Ann Ellis said. "And I'm bushed. You don't know what it's like to get to New York and see the shops, Mrs. Carter. I suppose you have some particular favorite, but I'm like a lost sheep."

Ruth frowned thoughtfully. "Well, I get the baby's things at Best's. And I usually get *my* things at Franklin Simon's. We have a charge account there."

"Oh," Ann Ellis said. "Come on, Bob, and dance with me."

Ruth watched her as she danced. The sleeves of her dress were long and the neck high. "Want to take a spin?" Roger asked.

The floor was very small and they were both glad when the orchestra started a rumba. "I guess that's that," Roger said, leading her back to their table.

They sat silently, sipping their drinks and watching the people around them.

When the Ellises returned to the table, Bob Ellis seemed subdued and nervous. His heartiness had left him and he seemed changed from a plump, jolly little man into a plump, fussy one. He finished his drink and ordered another, glancing nervously at his wife from time to time. She sat there looking around the room, not bothering to say much.

"Seen Ed Lovejoy lately?" Bob Ellis asked.

"Nope," Roger answered. "Not in over a year. What's he doing now?"

"I heard he was with the Frisbe outfit."

"Is that so?" Roger answered politely. "Well. Ever see Rip Pope?"

"Saw him in Michigan last summer," Bob Ellis said. "You remember Rip, Ann?"

"I suppose so," she said.

From their memories, the two men drew forth names and disposed of them. Ruth quietly listened to them talk, turning her head from one to the other, smiling and interested. They ordered their dinner, and when it came, Ann Ellis turned to Ruth. "What time is the floor show?" she asked.

"Oh, a floor show!" Ruth repeated. "That will be nice. I don't know what time it is, I'm sure. Roger, why don't you ask somebody for Mrs. Ellis?"

"Never mind," Ann said. "I thought you might know."

Her husband looked at her and when he spoke his voice was sharp. "Snap out of it," he told her. "You act as though you were asleep on your feet."

Ruth shook her head and laughed. "What men don't understand is how tired a lot of shopping makes you feel. Do they, Mrs. Ellis? Goodness! By the time Christmas is over I'm about dead. And to take Mickey down to get a few things! Well, it's a job, I tell you."

Roger glanced quickly at his wife. Her smile was innocent and she was eating with enjoyment. "I got much the biggest lobster," she said, "and you love them so, Roger." She picked up a claw and put it on his plate. "I really couldn't eat it. Honestly."

The men grew silent and Ruth began to talk pleasantly. Did the Ellises get to New York often? They must find time to come up and see the apartment and the baby. What shows did they plan to see? Where were they staying? And people had such a funny idea about New Yorkers, who lived exactly the same as other people. In fact, Roger and she never ate out.

It was a relief when the floor show started. When it was over and the dance music started once more, Ruth got up. "Let's dance again," she said. She picked up her bag and started toward the floor. They danced silently around the room and when they reached a far corner, Ruth fumbled with her bag. "Here," she said, slipping some bills into Roger's hand.

"What's that for?" he asked.

"I want you to pay the check," she told him.

His hand closed on the bills. "O.K.," he said, drawing her closer. In spite of the stiff waves, her hair was soft and he pressed his cheek into it.

Back at the table, she smiled down at the Ellises. "We have to run," she explained. "I had no idea it was so late. Get the check, will you, darling, and I'll get my coat."

"Here, here!" Bob Ellis blustered. "This is my party!"

"Nonsense," Ruth said. "We did so want to have you at the house for dinner, but we understand how people like to eat out when they come to New York. People from out of town."

When they got outside it had begun to snow, and Ruth buttoned the beaver collar of her coat under her chin. She took Roger's arm and unhesitatingly started toward Fifth Avenue and the bus. Roger pulled her over to the curb and held up his hand. "Taxi!" he called.

Maybe it was the way he slipped as he got in the cab, or maybe it was the relief of being alone together with the snow whirling outside that made them laugh as they started uptown.

James Thurber

For an unreliable but hilarious account of his life, James Thurber (1894-   ) has given the world My Life and Hard Times. *As a veteran contributor to* The New Yorker *Thurber is renowned for his mad distortions of life accompanied by line drawings which might have been done by a runaway planchette. Behind the perversities of his art is often a shrewd commentary on the perversities of humanity. In Walter Mitty he has exposed the soul of the little man and discovered there something comic and something pathetic, too.*

THE SECRET LIFE OF WALTER MITTY

"WE'RE going through!" The Commander's voice was like thin ice breaking. He wore his full-dress uniform, with the heavily braided white cap pulled down rakishly over one cold gray eye. "We can't make it, sir. It's spoiling for a hurricane, if you ask me." "I'm not asking you, Lieutenant Berg," said the Commander. "Throw on the power lights! Rev her up to 8,500! We're going through!" The pounding of the cylinders increased: ta-pocketa-pocketa-pocketa-*pocketa-pocketa.* The Commander stared at the ice forming on the pilot window. He walked over and twisted a row of complicated dials. "Switch on No. 8 auxiliary!" he shouted. "Switch on No. 8 auxiliary!" repeated Lieutenant Berg. "Full strength in No. 3 turret!" shouted the Commander. "Full strength in No. 3 turret!" The crew, bending to their various tasks in the huge, hurtling eight-engined Navy hydroplane, looked at each other and grinned. "The Old Man'll get us through," they said to one another. "The Old Man ain't afraid of Hell!" . . .

"Not so fast! You're driving too fast!" said Mrs. Mitty. "What are you driving so fast for?"

"Hmm?" said Walter Mitty. He looked at his wife, in the seat beside him, with shocked astonishment. She seemed grossly unfamiliar, like a strange woman who had yelled at him in a crowd. "You were up to fifty-five," she said. "You know I don't like to go more than forty. You were up to fifty-five." Walter Mitty drove on toward Waterbury in silence, the roaring of the SN202 through the worst storm in twenty years of Navy flying fading in the remote, intimate airways of his mind. "You're tensed up again," said Mrs. Mitty. "It's one of your days. I wish you'd let Dr. Renshaw look you over."

Walter Mitty stopped the car in front of the building where his wife went to have her hair done. "Remember to get those overshoes while I'm having my hair done," she said. "I don't need overshoes," said Mitty. She put her mirror back into her bag. "We've been all through that," she said, getting out of the car. "You're not a young man any longer." He raced the engine a little. "Why don't you wear your gloves? Have you lost your gloves?" Walter Mitty reached in a pocket and brought out the gloves. He put them on, but after she had turned and gone into the building and he had driven on to a red light, he took them off again. "Pick it up, brother!" snapped a cop as the light changed, and Mitty hastily pulled on his gloves and lurched ahead. He drove around the streets aimlessly for a time, and then he drove past the hospital on his way to the parking lot.

. . . "It's the millionaire banker, Wellington McMillan," said the pretty nurse. "Yes?" said Walter Mitty, removing his gloves slowly. "Who has the case?" "Dr. Renshaw and Dr. Benbow, but there are two specialists here, Dr. Remington from New York and Dr. Pritchard-Mitford from London. He flew over." A door opened down a long, cool corridor and Dr. Renshaw came out. He looked distraught and haggard. "Hello, Mitty," he said. "We're having the devil's own time with McMillan, the millionaire banker and close personal friend of Roosevelt. Obstreosis of the ductal tract. Tertiary. Wish you'd take a look at him." "Glad to," said Mitty.

In the operating room there were whispered introductions: "Dr. Remington, Dr. Mitty, Dr. Pritchard-Mitford, Dr. Mitty." "I've read your book on streptothricosis," said Pritchard-Mitford, shaking hands. "A brilliant performance, sir." "Thank you," said Walter Mitty. "Didn't know you were in the States, Mitty," grumbled Remington. "Coals to Newcastle, bringing Mitford and me up here for a tertiary." "You are very kind," said Mitty. A huge, complicated machine, connected to the operating table, with many tubes and wires, began at this moment to go pocketa-pocketa-pocketa. "The new anaesthetizer is giving way!" shouted an interne. "There is no one in the East who knows how to fix it!" "Quiet, man!" said Mitty, in a low, cool voice. He sprang to the machine, which was now going pocketa-pocketa-queep-pocketa-queep. He began fingering delicately a row of glistening dials. "Give me a fountain pen!" he snapped. Someone handed him a fountain pen. He pulled a faulty piston out of the machine and inserted the pen in its place. "That will hold for ten minutes," he said. "Get on with the operation." A nurse hurried over and whispered to Renshaw, and Mitty saw the man turn pale. "Coreopsis has set in," said Renshaw nervously. "If you would take over, Mitty?" Mitty looked at him and at the craven figure of Benbow, who drank, and at the grave, uncertain faces of the two great specialists. "If you wish," he said. They slipped a white gown on him; he adjusted a mask and drew on thin gloves; nurses handed him shining . . .

"Back it up, Mac! Look out for that Buick!" Walter Mitty jammed on the brakes. "Wrong lane, Mac," said the parking-lot attendant, looking at Mitty closely. "Gee. Yeh," muttered Mitty. He began cautiously to back out of the lane marked "Exit Only." "Leave her sit there," said the attendant. "I'll put her away." Mitty got out of the car. "Hey, better leave the key." "Oh," said Mitty, handing the man the ignition key. The attendant vaulted into the car, backed it up with insolent skill, and put it where it belonged.

They're so damn cocky, thought Walter Mitty, walking along Main Street; they think they know everything. Once he had tried to take his chains off, outside New Milford, and he had got them wound around the axles. A man had had to come out in a wrecking car and unwind them, a young, grinning garageman. Since then Mrs. Mitty always made him drive to a garage to have the chains taken off. The next time, he thought, I'll wear my right arm in a sling; they won't grin at me then. I'll have my right arm in a sling and they'll see I couldn't possibly take the chains off myself. He kicked at the slush on the sidewalk. "Overshoes," he said to himself, and he began looking for a shoe store.

When he came out into the street again, with the overshoes in a box under his arm, Walter Mitty began to wonder what the other thing was his wife had told him to get. She had told him twice before they set out from their house for Waterbury. In a way he hated these weekly trips to town—he was always getting something wrong. Kleenex, he thought, Squibb's, razor blades? No. Toothpaste, toothbrush, bicarbonate, carborundum, initiative and referendum? He gave it up. But she would remember it. "Where's the what's-its-name?" she would ask. "Don't tell me you forgot the what's-its-name." A newsboy went by shouting something about the Waterbury trial.

. . . "Perhaps this will refresh your memory." The District Attorney suddenly thrust a heavy automatic at the quiet figure on the witness stand. "Have you ever seen this before?" Walter Mitty took the gun and examined it expertly. "This is my Webley-Vickers 50.80," he said calmly. An excited buzz ran around the courtroom. The Judge rapped for order. "You are a crack shot with any sort of firearms, I believe?" said the District Attorney, insinuatingly. "Objection!" shouted Mitty's attorney. "We have shown that the defendant could not have fired the shot. We have shown that he wore his right arm in a sling on the night of the fourteenth of July." Walter Mitty raised his hand briefly and the bickering attorneys were stilled. "With any known make of gun," he said evenly, "I could have killed Gregory Fitzhurst at three hundred feet *with my left hand*." Pandemonium broke loose in the courtroom. A woman's scream rose above the bedlam and suddenly a lovely, dark-haired girl was in Walter Mitty's arms. The District Attorney struck at her savagely. Without rising from his chair, Mitty let the man have it on the point of the chin. "You miserable cur!" . . .

"Puppy biscuit," said Walter Mitty. He stopped walking and the buildings of Waterbury rose up out of the misty courtroom and surrounded him again. A woman who was passing laughed. "He said 'Puppy biscuit,'" she said to her companion. "That man said 'Puppy biscuit' to himself." Walter Mitty hurried on. He went into an A. & P., not the first one he came to but a smaller one farther up the street. "I want some biscuit for small, young dogs," he said to the clerk. "Any special brand, sir?" The greatest pistol shot in the world thought a moment. "It says 'Puppies Bark for It' on the box," said Walter Mitty.

His wife would be through at the hairdresser's in fifteen minutes, Mitty saw in looking at his watch, unless they had trouble drying it; sometimes they had trouble drying it. She didn't like to get to the hotel first; she would want him to be there waiting for her as usual. He found a big leather chair in the lobby, facing a window, and he put the overshoes and the puppy biscuit on the floor beside it. He picked up an old copy of *Liberty* and sank down into the chair. "Can Germany Conquer the World Through the Air?" Walter Mitty looked at the pictures of bombing planes and of ruined streets. . . . "The cannonading has got the wind up in young Raleigh, sir," said the sergeant. Captain Mitty looked up at him through tousled hair. "Get him to bed," he said wearily, "with the others. I'll fly alone." "But you can't, sir," said the sergeant anxiously. "It takes two men to handle that bomber and the Archies are pounding hell out of the air. Von Richtman's circus is between here and Saulier." "Somebody's got to get that ammunition dump," said Mitty. "I'm going over. Spot of brandy?" He poured a drink for the sergeant and one for himself. War thundered and whined around the dugout and battered at the door. There was a rending of wood, and splinters flew through the room. "A bit of a near thing," said Captain Mitty carelessly. "The box barrage is closing in," said the sergeant. "We only live once, Sergeant," said Mitty, with his faint, fleeting smile. "Or do we?" He poured another brandy and tossed it off. "I never see a man could hold his brandy like you, sir," said the sergeant. "Begging your pardon, sir."

Captain Mitty stood up and strapped on his huge Webley-Vickers automatic. "It's forty kilometres through hell, sir," said the sergeant. Mitty finished one last brandy. "After all," he said softly, "what isn't?" The pounding of the cannon increased; there was the rat-tat-tatting of machine guns, and from somewhere came the menacing pocketa-pocketa-pocketa of the new flame-throwers. Walter Mitty walked to the door of the dugout humming "Auprès de Ma Blonde." He turned and waved to the sergeant. "Cheerio!" he said. . . .

Something struck his shoulder. "I've been looking all over this hotel for you," said Mrs. Mitty. "Why do you have to hide in this old chair? How did you expect me to find you?" "Things close in," said Walter Mitty vaguely. "What?" Mrs. Mitty said. "Did you get the what's-its-name? The puppy biscuit? What's in that box?" "Overshoes," said Mitty. "Couldn't you have put them on in the store?" "I was thinking," said Walter Mitty. "Does it ever occur to you that I am sometimes thinking?" She looked at him. "I'm going to take your temperature when I get you home," she said.

They went out through the revolving doors that made a faintly derisive whistling sound when you pushed them. It was two blocks to the parking lot. At the drugstore on the corner she said, "Wait here for me. I forgot something. I won't be a minute." She was more than a minute. Walter Mitty lighted a cigarette. It began to rain, rain with sleet in it. He stood up against the wall of the drugstore, smoking. . . . He put his shoulders back and his heels together. "To hell with the handkerchief," said Walter Mitty scornfully. He took one last drag on his cigarette and snapped it away. Then, with that faint, fleeting smile playing about his lips, he faced the firing squad; erect and motionless, proud and disdainful, Walter Mitty the Undefeated, inscrutable to the last.

Ben Hur Lampman

Ben Hur Lampman (1886-) was born in Wisconsin. He has long been an associate editor of the Portland Oregonian, *and his name is familiar to lovers of the short story. "Blinker" is written in Hoosier dialect, but there may be some graftings from the Northwest.*

BLINKER WAS A GOOD DOG

A MAN naturally disremembers—it all happened such a while ago—a good many the yarns that used to be told up river and down about him and her, and how they was always a-jowering and a-jawing one at t'other, come day, go day, the old man and the old woman. Them as knowed them never blamed them, on account of they was so all-fired alone on the home place, with the young ones growed-up and gone, that him and her was sort of bound for to entertain theirselves, in times when there wasn't no mail in the country, and no radio.

So him and her taken to disagreeing, the whole eternal time, sort of to keep interested. All the while the old man would have give his last breath for the old woman, happen it would come in handy, and the old woman would have more'n died for the old man. Him and her was like that. Lots of folks is.

But of them times beyond reckoning when him and her was as cross as two sticks, one at t'other, in all them years at the old place on the upper river, a man recollects best of all the time the old man was plumb sot on having a regular Christian funeral for their old dog Blinker, so near as the old man could manage it. You knowed about how the old folks finally lost Blinker, him that they'd raised from a pup, on the bottle—he growed old and gray with them two, him and her—but did ever you hear tell of how Blinker was buried?

By Godfrey, that time the old man and the old woman may have been nigh to a-splittin', because the whole p'int was religion—and the old woman, she sot great store by religion; she could be hard as a niggerhead when it come to the Word. Of course the old man, he knowed this to his sorrer, but when Blinker up and died on him, and laid there in the chips in the door-yard, stiff as a poker, and the old man was recollecting how the old dog used for to grin at him, dang him if he could see any way to get out of a-burying Blinker like a Christian. For the life of him, seemed like he couldn't.

So the old man, he come into the kitchen, and he seen right away that his old woman had been a-weeping whilst at her housework—but when he taken his courage in hand, and told her what he had a mind for to do, told her as best he could manage, the old woman she give it some thought for a moment, and then she turned on him, clicking her store teeth. He knowed that for the worst sign of all. But danged if he didn't have for to admire her, like always, outfacing him like that—little and puny but bold as a bob-cat, whilst she give him a piece of her mind.

When his old woman got her dander up, seemed like she looked like the girl he fetched home from the valley. She looked like the queen on a playing card. And she give him to understand that them two had buried their own, years past, and had sorrered over them, and though the old man might be sort of minded to forget, a woman she must always recollect. She wouldn't have spoke ary word such as that—if she'd rightly knowed how it hurt. But, howsoever, when a woman gets riled— The old man, he stood there and blinked at her out of his whiskers, but he was as sot in his ways as she was in her'n, and he knowed what he allowed for to do.

"It's mighty un-Christian to bury a dog like a Christian!" the old woman says. "You want me, your own wife, for to sing a gospel hymn over Blinker, whilst you pray? God is my witness I cared full as much for old Blinker as you ever did! Who redd-up the kitchen after him, since ever he was whelped? Who seen to his platter? But I shan't have no part in mockery that's fit only for heathens. Nor shall you!" says the old woman. "It ain't fitting for Christians!"

And up come her apron whilst she cried her eyes out. She fair twisted the old man's heart—but you know how it is. There's times when a man is just bound not for to give in to them. He taken a chew of tobacco and he stomped out of the house. What was in his heart was as nigh to bitterness as ever had been there. It come to him then, like a thousand times afore, that they always got a man at a disadvantage, on account of they never lack words.

Well, sir, a man reckons that the old woman knowed she was bested, when the old man slammed the kitchen door, but first-off she dried her eyes, like women will, and put some wood in the stove against time she was going to need the oven. She clicked her store teeth, too, every once in a while—but all the time she was a-listening. She was a-listening because she knowed right well that poor Blinker wasn't more than a step from the kitchen stoop. And after a bit the old woman heard the old man say, "Whoa!" There the old fool was, with the bay mare and the stoneboat, alongside of the old dog.

She looked out and give him a look that ought to have wilted him in his tracks, but he give her a glare like ice on a duckpond, right back. "The old fool!" she was a-thinking. Might as well have taken the old dog in his two arms, and carried him to wherever it was—but, no, the old fool was sot on a Christian funeral. The tears come up to her eyes again, but still the old woman was riled as could be, and she couldn't make no allowances for him. It was so un-Christian. All she said was:—

"I declare, if you've a mind for to make an old fool of yourself, like a heathen in darkness, you might as well change your shirt! Come in here, this minute!" The old man, he taken Blinker up in his arms, and he laid the old dog down on the stoneboat, and gentle, there on the new straw, and stooped and picked off a burr, before he turned to give his old woman so much as a look. He glared at her then, like before, and breshed by into the kitchen. She might have put her hand on his arm, easy—but she couldn't bring herself to do it. She watched him stomp into their bedroom, right off the kitchen, and she seen that when he come out the old man had on a clean shirt. It wasn't the shirt she'd have chose—but at least, she seen, it was fitting. He give her never a look when he went past her and out of the kitchen door—and, a-listening, she heerd the old man say, "Giddap, Dolly! Easy, girl!" The stoneboat was a-grating on the gravel.

Soul alone in her kitchen, the old woman began for to mix a batch of lazyman's biscuit—the old man was uncommon fond of it—but all the while she knowed that her heart wasn't in it. Seemed like there come betwixt her and the dough, bat her eyes as she did, pictures of Blinker and the old man—and some of them pictures was of Blinker when he was skeercely more than a gangling pup, and of the old man when he was still so supple he could put one hand on the top fence rail and clear her.

It wasn't biscuit dough she seen, there in her kitchen on the upper fork: it was Blinker barking at the foot of the lone spruce in the meadow, whilst the old man he circled the tree—and him in his prime then, the best man on the river—with the Harpers Ferry musket cocked for a shot at a silver-gray that Blinker had treed. She seen Blinker leaping; she heerd the musket; she seen the squirrel tumbling, over and over; she seen the old man in his prime. And then she seemed to see Blinker with one flank raked open by a cougar, and still a-laughing, and the old man—he wasn't old then—with one foot on the long, lanky cat.

She seen them two a-going for the cows together, as many the time, and of a sudden her eyes they blurred till the dough wasn't there any more—and the old woman she jerked back from the table, for her mind was made up, and she taken off her apron and went straight into their bedroom. The old woman was in such a hurry a body might have suspected she had for to catch the stage at the Corners. She come out of the bedroom with her hat on, the pink roses bobbing, and she made for the kitchen door. She had a book under one arm, and when her favorite rocker got in the way she flang it clean across the kitchen. As folks used to tell it, up and down the river, the old woman was in a hurry. But she'd time for to break off one stalk of wallflower, there by the stoop.

He had stopped the bay mare back of the henhouse, where there was a considerable stand of honeysuckle, and the raw, black earth, with fish-worms in it, was throwed back in a heap. And Blinker wasn't on the stone-boat no longer, so the old woman judged that the old dog must be in his everlasting grave. Back of the henhouse and under the honeysuckle, where the old dog used for to sun himself. The old man, his eyes lifted and shut tight as could be, he seemed for to be a-praying, with his whiskers a-waggling. For the old woman heerd him say, plain enough, as she come a-hurrying up:—

"And, Lord, what You got to remember is that Blinker was a danged good dog! Dagnab me, if he wasn't! Wherefore, Lord—"

But right there his old woman shoved the old man over a ways—she had a sharp elbow—and "Amen, Lord," she says, and "You tarnation old fool!" she says, and she makes him take half of the hymn-book. She had the page open at the place. The old man opened his eyes and squinted, but he taken his half of the book, like he was used to, and she chosen the hymn mighty well, though at first she had thought of singing "Old Hundred," on account of it says to serve Him with mirth—like Blinker always done. But she changed her mind, and the place she had the book open was at "Beulah Land." So them two sang—she did, and he trailed her—the old man and the old woman, back of the henhouse, whilst the words went away across the crick and the river:

> O Beulah land, sweet Beulah land,
> As on thy highest mount I stand,
> I look away across the sea,
> Where mansions are prepared for me—

Then the old woman, she leant over and dropped in the wallflower and she seen Blinker for the last time—a-laying there on the straw at the bottom like he was sleeping. The old man, he taken up the spade and he done what he had for to do, and times he was thinking of Blinker, and times he was thinking that the old woman's voice still was like a girl's. Happened it was along toward evening, and there was a sliver of young moon in the sky. His old woman she taken a glance at the new moon, and she might have been a-thinking of times they walked in the mowing together, for what she said was, half to herself, "Yander's a hunter's moon." She meant that there'd be quite a dry spell. That there was too bad, for the old man he bridled to hear it. He tossed in the last turf and he flang down the shovel.

"Hell's fire, old woman!" the old man, he snorted. "You taken leave of your right senses? That there moon is wet as ary moon ever I see!" Then they was at it, like always, over and over, a-jowering and a-jawing again. Him and her was like that.

Sholem Asch

Sholem Asch (1880-   ) was born near Warsaw of poor parents. Today his many novels, plays, poems, and stories make him the most eminent writer in Yiddish, the German-Hebrew-Russian esperanto of the modern Jew. His greatest novel, The Nazarene, *presents Jesus as the crowning figure of Jewish history. Crowded with realistic details it is the result of thirty years' study; indeed, when he finished it, he confessed to feeling strange in "coming back" to the life of New York and the twentieth century.* The Apostle, *his story of Paul and the spread of Christianity, is scarcely second to* The Nazarene. *Its closing words are a magnificent affirmation of faith: "Rome went forth against Jerusalem with the sword, and Jerusalem went forth against Rome with the spirit. The sword conquered for a while, but the spirit conquers for ever!" As the following story shows, he is intimately familiar with the life and aspirations of the Zionists in Palestine. Aside from its special setting, "A Peculiar Gift" is the song of all pioneers everywhere who find a sure joy in the promise of the good earth.*

A PECULIAR GIFT

IN the Valley of Jezreel, within the shadow of Mount Gilboa, a Jew was following a plough pulled by two horses. The Jew guided the plough; his ten-year-old son, Solomon, whipped up the horses, one red and one black; and Sarah, his eight-year-old daughter, dropped the seed into the fresh-turned furrow.

"Drop them down straight, little one," he sang to the girl. "Right to the bottom of the furrow. God's over us, and he'll return thirty-fold, forty-fold, fifty-fold. Such returns have been and may be again. Whoa, Solomon, not so fast with the nags! Hold the red one! Hold the black one!" The Jew stopped and peered into the furrow. "Take them, good earth, and multiply them! God gave you to us, and we are back with you. Dear earth, do God's bidding, and you, little seeds, fall in good places where you will not die and rot; fall comfortably and well, so that you may sprout and feed me and my wife and my children. I have prepared a bed for you, a warm, brown bed, a bed that flows with milk and honey, as the great teacher said."

Panting as he followed the plough, the Jew kept up his breathless, ecstatic monologue. He wiped the sweat from his face. The sun blazed down on him, the wind lifted up the corners of his gaberdine and the points of his beard; it fluttered the tips of the kerchief round the little girl's head.

And all five of them, father, daughter, and son, the red horse and the black, labored joyously along the hard, sloping field, turning up the earth in the ancient Valley of Jezreel.

I, a visitor in this lonely place, sat on a stone and waited for the family to make the last furrow for that afternoon. I was worried for the Jew behind the plough; I was afraid for him. For I knew him from of old, knew the kind of man he had been. Was not this Noah the dry-goods merchant, whom I saw now after many years, Noah who had given up his business in Ekaterinoslav and who now, with son and daughter and two horses, one black and one red, was toiling along the slope of the field, disguised as a farmer? And what a farmer! A lyrical farmer such as never was on land or sea. As he came back toward me his voice was still uplifted.

"It's good, Mr. Jew," he chanted. "Do you hear me? It's good."

"It's good and hot, Reb Noah," I answered.

He halted.

"Hot? Did you say it's hot? Maybe it is. What does the Book say? 'In the summer the heat shall not burn you, and in the winter the cold shall not consume you.' What if it is hot? It's good, I tell you."

In the old days, when I had used to visit him in Ekaterinoslav, Reb Noah had been a merchant of standing, dealing with cities as wide apart as Warsaw, Kishineff, and Lodz. He was said to be worth between fifteen and twenty thousand roubles, and his credit rating was even higher, for who knew as well as Reb Noah the value of a rouble, and who guarded a coin with the same vigilance? When he came to Warsaw as a buyer, he stayed always at a third-rate inn, a rouble a day, meals and all. He welcomed a rouble with jubilation, parted with a kopeck only under duress. He always defended himself by saying that he was saving his money for Palestine; yes, some day he would close his shop, wind up his business, betake himself to the Holy Land, and become a laboring man, a tiller of the soil, which, as all the world knew, was what his ancestors and all the ancestors of the Jews had been. Of course nobody believed him, for if Reb Noah was sparing of his cash, he was most generous of his words. It was remembered, moreover, that in his boyhood Reb Noah had sung in the choir of the famous cantor of Berditchev and had become a businessman against his will; and it is a well-known fact that frustrated singers are the most talkative of mortals. But the unbelievable, or at any rate the unbelieved, came to pass. Noah the dry-goods merchant disappeared from Ekaterinoslav, in the height of the season, and the places of his business knew him no more. They waited for him in vain in the warehouses of Warsaw and Kishineff and Lodz. And soon he was forgotten, as businessmen are apt to be. Other customers took his place. Reb Noah had really gone to Palestine; and here he was, in the Valley of Jezreel, wearing, instead of the perky little bowler of the Russian Jew, the stately fez of the Turks, and talking to me as he leaned upon the plough which I had watched him guide.

"But—but—how could you really bring yourself to do it?" I asked, convinced and yet incredulous.

"I'll tell you what it is," he answered, thoughtfully. "I've always believed, deep down, that I was a gifted man, a man of peculiar gifts. My only difficulty was that I didn't know what I was gifted for. Till one day it came to me suddenly that I was *gifted for Palestine*."

"What's that?" I said. "Gifted for Palestine?"

"Why, certainly. Some Jews have a gift for this, some for that, some for the other—and some for Palestine. Take Baron Edmund Rothschild, for instance. A great man, isn't he? But who knew what he was great *for* until he discovered his peculiar gift? He had a gift for Palestine. And so did I. Not as great a one as Baron Rothschild. I'm gifted for Palestine in a smaller way. But then, I'm a smaller man, and it's all I need."

"It's a laborious talent, Reb Noah," I suggested. "A sweaty talent, if I may say so."

"Not a bit of it," he retorted, and contradicted himself by wiping a freshet of perspiration from his face. "A talent for dry-goods is a lot sweatier. You should have seen me trying to persuade a peasant woman that a length of calico was what she needed, and that she was getting it dirt cheap—which she was. Now, *that* was a sweaty job. But this? Pooh!"

"But the horses, Reb Noah? How do you get along with the horses? I knew you when you wouldn't come within a mile of a horse."

"I daresay you did. And yet—well, how was I to know? See that red nag there? He's the sweetest horse in the world, an absolute saint of a horse. Never kicked anyone in his life. Click your tongue at him, and off he goes; call 'Whoa!' and he stops. A saint, I say. The black one, I admit, was different. A lowdown horse, mean, unfriendly—an anti-Semite of a horse. A grand worker; but he loved to kick. They told me, when I bought him: 'Reb Noah, you'll never manage that horse. You'll never get round him.' 'I won't, won't I?' was all I answered, and took my horse home. And I said to myself: 'Noah, get this into your mind. The first day you handle him, he'll kick you ten times.' But did he? No, he did not. He kicked me only six times. So there I was, four kicks to the good, the very first day. The second day I counted on six, and got away with three. How's that for progress? Today he doesn't kick any more. He's learned the verse from Isaiah: 'The ox knoweth his master, and the ass his owner's crib.' I'm boss, he's servant, and we're at peace. I give him his food, he gives me his labor."

"And your wife, Yetta," I went on. "How did she take to being a peasant woman?"

"Ah, that now—that was a hard business." Reb Noah became reflective. "Things are brighter today, but the beginning—" and Reb Noah tightened his lips, drew his mouth to one side, closed one eye and nodded several times. "When we came out here, my wife and I and the little ones, the place was a wilderness. *Tohu-u-bohu.* Without form and void. Eight Jewish families in all, in this 'Arab hole' which we took over. That's what my wife called it. 'Noah, you murderer,' she cries, 'what are you doing with me and my little chicks? How do you expect us to live here?' And what could I answer? The first thing I got here was a good dose of malaria. There was no water in the place; you had to bring it by the pailful from the nearest well, miles away. The children were sick, too. And my Yetta! The things she said! And me shivering with the fever. 'Yetta,' I answer, 'don't talk that way! It's blasphemous! This is the Holy Land, of the Prophets and Kings and Priests. It's forbidden to speak evil of it. Wait,' I say, 'this "Arab hole" is a paradise. Wait till the fig trees blossom—our own fig trees now, ours. And wait till we eat the bread of our own planting. Don't you know the story of the twelve spies Moses sent into Palestine, how they brought back an evil report?' No, she knew nothing about the twelve spies. So I told her the story. And soon after that I got better, and took my two horses, and went out to the ploughing, and ploughed all day. And when I come back, she's in tears. 'What is it, Yetta?' She says she's lonely, she hankers for company, the kind she had in Ekaterinoslav. 'What have you done to me and my chicks?' she starts all over again. 'I've done nothing to your chicks,' I says. 'They've been out ploughing the fields with me. And as for your Ekaterinoslav company, a rotten fig for that. Today you're a peasant woman, and peasant women don't have company. And if you're lonely,' I say, further, 'you've only to step out of doors and take a look at our Valley of Jezreel. Look, there's Mount Gilboa, where the glory of the great King, Saul, was brought low; that's where King David pronounced his curse in olden days, no dew and no rain should fall on the hills of Gilboa. And over there is Mount Tabor, where the Prophetess Deborah sang her song of praise to the Lord, for the victory over Sisera. And way up yonder's the summit of Mount Hebron. Isn't that company enough for you? And you talk about that silly Ekaterinoslav company, which always cost money to entertain and wasn't worth a broken eggshell. Why, Yetta,' I say, 'you ought to be ashamed of yourself.' And she answers: 'Oh, you've always had plenty of words to spare. You can talk a stone into a pair of legs, and you've talked me into coming here. God help me, what's going to become of me?' What could you say to a woman like that?"

I could only echo his question: "What *could* you say?"

"Well, there's a God in heaven," he answered, elliptically. "She began to get used to the life. Bit by bit. Bit by bit. One morning I caught her standing at the door, looking out at our little field, shining with dew, and there was a smile on her face—she didn't know I saw her. And then, one evening, I see her go out into the garden, and she's murmuring to herself.

And I see her bend down and pull out a weed. And I said to myself, 'Ho, ho, it's getting you, old girl. The soil's getting you, the good mother earth.' And I went out to her and said, 'Pull 'em up, wife, pull 'em up, all the weeds. The mountain up there is still wild, and wild things grow there, and the wind carries the seed of them down, and the wild things grow in our field. But in the time to come our brothers will live up there, on the mountain, and wild things won't grow there any more. So when the wind will blow this way, and bring seed, it'll be the seed of good grain, and we won't have to tear it out.' But she didn't give in so easily, the old woman. She says: 'I wish I could tear you up by the roots, the way I'm tearing these weeds up.' But I knew she was half won over; that's why she talked that way.

"No, after that I wasn't afraid any more. The land got her. There's something in the land that gets everyone. It pulls you. And why? I'll tell you why. You come here in the beginning, and it's a howling wilderness. No people, no friends, no house, no water. Nothing! And you want to run away! You feel you won't be able to stand it twenty-four hours. But if you hold on, till the first things grow in your garden, and you've got the first loaf from your own fields, then you'll never want to leave. All land is like that. And this land of ours, the Holy Land, more than any other land in the world. Think of all the history in it, think of all the blood that's gone into it—think of—"

Reb Noah was becoming rhetorical, and that was a pity. So I interrupted him:

"And how do you get along with the Arabs, Reb Noah? They say, back there in Ekaterinoslav—"

He interrupted me in turn.

"How do I get along with my neighbors? Why, perfectly. Best of friends. When I came out here the young fellows in the neighboring colony said to me: 'Reb Noah, you've got to get yourself a revolver and a knife. If you go without them, the Arabs will find you in the middle of the field, unhitch the horses, and drive them off, leaving you there with the plough.' And what did I answer? 'My lads,' I said, 'I'm not afraid of your Arabs. See this Turkish fez? That's my revolver. And see my little boy Solomon here? That's my knife.' Because the first thing I did when I got to the Holy Land was to buy myself a fez. 'That'll show them,' I said, 'that I'm a Semite, just like them.' I went out into the field, ploughing, and my fez was on my head and my little boy by my side. I'd like to see the Arab who'd attack a father when his six-year-old boy is along with him. There is no such Arab; because the Arabs are Semites, and Semites are merciful. I'll tell you what happened once. I was out there"—he pointed to the furthest end of the field—"I was 'way out there, one day, under the hill. I was ploughing with my little Solomon, when along comes an Arab on a horse—an Arab with a gun on his shoulder and a sword by his side. When he drew alongside I passed my hand over my forehead and my breast, which is the way they greet each other here, and I said: '*Ni habik said,*' which means, 'Let your day be beautiful.' And he passed his hand over forehead and breast and answered, '*Tahbadnik,*' which means, 'Let your morning be fresh.'

"Because as soon as I came out here I learned to say 'Good morning' in Arabic. I'd like to see the murderer who's going to attack you after you've said 'Good morning' to him. Especially a Semite. Well, the Arab on the horse points to the little boy, and asks me in Arabic whose he is. So I press little Solomon to my heart, to show he's mine. Then the Arab gets off his horse and begins to finger my plough, because he'd never seen one like it before, his people still using wooden ploughs, like our ancestors ages ago. Then I touch the plough, and I point 'way over the hills, to show that in the place I come from they use iron ploughs. So he shrugs his shoulders, and smiles, and nods. And now, seeing we were good friends, I say to him, 'You, me, *achim,* brothers, Semites'; and he smiles again, showing all his teeth, and bows, and says '*Hawadji,*' which is their word for '*gospodin,*' or mister. Then he jumps on his horse and rides away. So I ask you, do I need a revolver, or a knife?"

I stared at Reb Noah, not knowing what to say now. And he, a little ashamed of his garrulity, said, "One more furrow, there and back," and turned his horses toward the field.

I stood watching him as he steered the plough; I watched the horses pulling, the children helping. It was not too straight a furrow that he drew— but it was a good one, deep and even. And I could not help thinking:

"How did this Jew find it in himself to throw away his comfortable business, his security, his ease, his Ekaterinoslav, and come out here into the wilderness? How did he throw off the habits of the city, the money curse, and take to guiding a plough under a blazing sun?"

Then I remembered what Reb Noah had just said. "I've a special gift. I'm gifted for Palestine." Undoubtedly he was; how else could he have come through? And I reflected further: "Perhaps that gift belongs not only to some Jews, but to all. Perhaps the gift for Palestine slumbers in the whole Jewish people."

James Stephens

James Stephens (1882-   ) began life as a half-starved urchin in the streets of his native Dublin. Apparently he needed no schooling to assist his Irish wit and imagination. Whether he writes in prose or in verse he is always the poet: sometimes the boisterous fun maker, sometimes the tender-hearted lover of all weak and humble things, sometimes the leprechaun at point to vanish. "The Coolin" or "darling" is a re-creation of an old Irish poem.

THE COOLIN

Come with me, under my coat,
And we will drink our fill
Of the milk of the white goat,
Or wine if it be thy will;

And we will talk until
Talk is a trouble, too,
Out on the side of the hill;
And nothing is left to do,

But an eye to look into an eye,
And a hand in a hand to slip,
And a sigh to answer a sigh,
And a lip to find out a lip.

What if the night be black
Or the air on the mountain chill,
Where the goat lies down in her track
And all but the fern is still!

Stay with me, under my coat,
And we will drink our fill
Of the milk of the white goat
Out on the side of the hill.

Archibald MacLeish

Archibald MacLeish, despairing of the power which Shakspere claimed for his fifty-fifth sonnet, has recourse to the apparently trivial but actually significant for the perpetuation of a woman's beauty.

"NOT MARBLE NOR THE GILDED MONUMENTS"

The praisers of women in their proud and beautiful poems
Naming the grave mouth and the hair and the eyes
Boasted those they loved should be forever remembered
These were lies

The words sound but the face in the Istrian sun is forgotten
The poet speaks but to her dead ears no more
The sleek throat is gone—and the breast that was troubled to listen
Shadow from door

Therefore I will not praise your knees nor your fine walking
Telling you men shall remember your name as long
As lips move or breath is spent or the iron of English
Rings from a tongue

I shall say you were young and your arms straight and your mouth scarlet
I shall say you will die and none will remember you
Your arms change and none remember the swish of your garments
Nor the click of your shoe

Not with my hand's strength not with difficult labor
Springing the obstinate words to the bones of your breast
And the stubborn line to your young stride and the breath to your breathing
And the beat to your haste
Shall I prevail on the hearts of unborn men to remember

(What is a dead girl but a shadowy ghost
Or a dead man's voice but a distant and vain affirmation
Like dream words most)

Therefore I will not speak of the undying glory of women
I will say you were young and straight and your skin fair

And you stood in the door and the sun was a shadow of leaves on your
    shoulders
And a leaf on your hair

I will not speak of the famous beauty of dead women
I will say the shape of a leaf lay once on your hair
Till the world ends and the eyes are out and the mouths broken
Look! It is there!

Edwin Arlington Robinson

*The writings of this poet (1869-1935) bear the marks of his Maine
birth: in his reticence and introspectiveness, in his fondness for understatement and indirection, he is the austere and tight-lipped down-
Easter. His Arthurian poems, however, are in large part exceptions to
this statement, for they are not wanting in color, drama, and passion.
Of the three, Merlin, Lancelot, and Tristram, the last is richest in romanticism. When Tristram appeared, in 1927, it surprised those readers
who had known Robinson only as a dexterous intellectual, but confirmed the opinion of those who had recognized him as a man of comprehensive genius. The following passage, which forms the end of
Book VII, relates the meeting of Tristram and the dark Isolt at Joyous
Gard, the castle whither Isolt has come to join her lover.*

From TRISTRAM

                        He saw dark laughter sparkling
Out of her eyes, but only until her face
Found his, and on his mouth a moving fire
Told him why there was death, and what lost song
Ulysses heard, and would have given his hands
And friends to follow and to die for. Slowly,
At last, the power of helplessness there was
In all that beauty of hers that was for him,
Breathing and burning there alone with him,
Until it was almost a part of him,
Suffused his passion with a tenderness
Attesting a sealed certainty not his
To cozen or wrench from fate, and one withheld
In waiting mercy from oblivious eyes—

His eyes and hers, that over darker water,
Where darker things than shadows would be coming,
Saw now no more than more stars in the sky.
He felt her throbbing softly in his arms,
And held her closer still—with half a fear
Returning that she might not be Isolt,
And might yet vanish where she sat with him,
Leaving him there alone, with only devils
Of hell supplanting her.

                          "Leave me the stars
A little longer," said Isolt. "In Cornwall,
So much alone there with them as I was,
One sees into their language and their story.
They must be more than fire; and if the stars
Are more than fire, what else is there for them
To be than love? I found all that myself;
For when a woman is left too much alone,
Sooner or later she begins to think;
And no man knows what then she may discover."

"Whether she be in Cornwall, or not there,
A woman driven to thinking of the stars
Too hard is in some danger," he said, sighing,
"Of being too much alone wherever she is."

Her face unseen, she smiled, hearing him sigh—
So much as if all patient chivalry
Were sighing with him. "One alone too long
In Cornwall has to think somewhat," she said,
"Or one may die. One may do worse than die.
If life that comes of love is more than death,
Love must be more than death and life together."

"Whether I know that life is more or not
Than death," he said, "I swear, with you for witness—
You and the stars—that love is more than either."

"If I should have to answer twice to that,
I should not let myself be here with you
Tonight, with all the darkness I see coming
On land and over water." Then she ceased,

And after waiting as one waits in vain
For distant voices that are silent, "Tell me!"
She cried, seizing him hard and gazing at him,
"Tell me if I should make you go away!
I'm not myself alone now• and the stars
All tell me so."

                    He plucked her clinging hands
From his arms gently, and said, holding them,
"You cannot make me go away from you,
Isolt, for I believe, with you to tell me,
All your stars say. But never mind what they say
Of shadows coming. They are always coming—
Coming and going like all things but one.
Love is the only thing that in its being
Is what it seems to be. Glory and gold,
And all the rest, are weak and hollow staves
For even the poor to lean on. We know that—
We that have been so poor while grinning hinds
And shining wenches with all crowns to laugh at,
Have envied us, know that. Yet while you see
So many things written for you in starry fire,
Somehow you fear that I may lose my vision
Not seeing them. I shall not be losing it—
Not even in seeing beyond where you have seen.
Yes, I have seen your stars. You are the stars!
You are the stars when they all sing together.
You live, you speak, and you have not yet vanished.
You are Isolt—or I suppose you are!"

He was not sure of her not vanishing
Until he felt her tears, and her warm arms
Holding him with a sudden strength of love
That would have choked him had it not been love.
Each with unyielding lips refused the other
Language unasked; and their forgotten ears
Knew only as a murmur not remembered
A measured sea that always on the sand
Unseen below them, where time's only word
Was told in foam along a lonely shore,
Poured slowly its unceasing sound of doom—
Unceasing and unheard, and still unheard,

As with an imperceptible surrender
They moved and found each other's eyes again,
Burning away the night between their faces.

"Sometimes I fear that I shall fear for you
No more," she said; and to his ears her words
Were shaken music. "Why should I fear for you,
Or you for me, where nothing of earth is left,
Nothing of earth or time, that is worth fearing?
Sometimes I wonder if we are not like leaves
That have been blown by some warm wind of heaven
Far from the tree of life, still to be living
Here between life and death."

                              "Why do those two
Vainglorious and abysmal little words
Pursue you and torment your soul?" said he.
"They are the serpents and uncertainties
That coil and rustle tonight among your fears,
Only because your fears have given to them
A shape without a substance. Life and death?
Do not believe your stars if they are saying
That any such words are in their language now.
Whenever they tell you they are made of love,
Believe it; and forget them when they tell you
Of this or that man's living a thousand years.
Why should he wish to live a thousand years?
Whether your stars are made of love or fire,
There is a love that will outshine the stars.
There will be love when there are no more stars.
Never mind what they say of darkness coming
That may come sometime, or what else they say
Of terrors hidden in words like life and death.
What do they mean? Never mind what they mean!
We have lived and we have died, and are alone
Where the world has no more a place for us,
Or time a fear for us, or death . . . Isolt!"
Her lips again had hushed him, and her name,
As when first he had found her in his arms,
Was all there was to say till he was saying
Muffled and husky words that groped and faltered,
Half silenced in a darkness of warm hair:
"Whatever it is that brings us here tonight,

Never believe—never believe again—
Your fear for me was more than love. Time lied,
If he said that. When we are done with time,
There is no time for fear. It was not fear—
It was love's other name. Say it was that!
Say to me it was only one of time's lies!
Whatever it was—never mind what it was!
There will be time enough for me to die.
Never mind death tonight. . . . Isolt! Isolt!"

Thornton Wilder

Thornton Wilder (1897-   ) was born in Madison, Wisconsin, of New England stock. Part of his childhood was spent in China. He was educated at Oberlin, Yale, Princeton, and the American Academy in Rome. For some years he was a teacher—of French at Lawrenceville, of Comparative Literature at University of Chicago. In the novel and the drama he has firmly established himself on a relatively small body of work marked by a flawless style. The Bridge of San Luis Rey, *which received the Pulitzer Prize, was one of the most widely read novels of our time.* Our Town, *which also won the Pulitzer Prize, brings together all that* Present Tense *would say about human relationships. Here in microcosm is the story of our race: birth, childhood, first love, marriage, family life, death, birth, childhood, first love, on and on, over and over, world without end. . . .*

OUR TOWN

The entire play takes place in Grover's Corners, N. H., 1901 to 1913

ACT ONE

No curtain.

No scenery.

The audience, arriving, sees an empty stage in half-light.

Presently the STAGE MANAGER, *hat on and pipe in mouth, enters and begins placing a table and several chairs down stage left, and a table and chairs down stage right.*

"Left" and "right" are from the point of view of the actor facing the audience. "Up" is towards the back wall.

As the house lights go down he has finished setting the stage and lean-

ing against the right proscenium pillar watches the late arrivals in the audience.

When the auditorium is in complete darkness he speaks:

STAGE MANAGER. This play is called "Our Town." It was written by Thornton Wilder; produced and directed by A. . . . [or: produced by A. . . . ; directed by B. . . .]. In it you will see Miss C. . . . ; Miss D. . . . ; Miss E. . . . ; and Mr. F. . . . ; Mr. G. . . . ; Mr. H. . . . ; and many others.

The name of the town is Grover's Corners, New Hampshire—just across the Massachusetts line: longitude 42 degrees 40 minutes; latitude 70 degrees 37 minutes.

The First Act shows a day in our town. The day is May 7, 1901. The time is just before dawn.

[*A rooster crows.*]

The sky is beginning to show some streaks of light over in the East there behind our mount'in.

The morning star always gets wonderful bright the minute before it has to go.

[*He stares at it for a moment, then goes up stage.*]

Well, I'd better show you how our town lies. Up here—

[*That is: parallel with the back wall.*]

is Main Street. Way back there is the railway station; tracks go that way. Polish Town's across the tracks and some Canuck families.

[*Toward the left.*]

Over there is the Congregational Church; across the street's the Presbyterian.

Methodist and Unitarian are over there.

Baptist is down in the holla' by the river.

Catholic Church is over beyond the tracks.

Here's the Town Hall and Post Office combined; jail's in the basement.

Bryan once made a speech from these steps here.

Along here's a row of stores. Hitching-posts and horse blocks in front of them. First automobile's going to come along in about five years,—belonged to Banker Cartwright, our richest citizen . . . lives in the big white house up on the hill.

Here's the grocery store and here's Mr. Morgan's drugstore. Most everybody in town manages to look into those two stores once a day.

Public School's over yonder. High School's still farther over. Quarter of nine mornings, noontimes, and three o'clock afternoons, the hull town can hear the yelling and screaming from those schoolyards.

[*He approaches the table and chairs down stage right.*]

This is our doctor's house,—Doc Gibbs'. This is the back door.

[*Two arched trellises are pushed out, one by each proscenium pillar.*]

There's some scenery for those who think they have to have scenery.

There's a garden here. Corn . . . peas . . . beans . . . hollyhocks . . . heliotrope . . . and a lot of burdock.

[*Crosses the stage.*]

In those days our newspaper come out twice a week,—The Grover's Corners *Sentinel*,—and this is Editor Webb's house.

And this is Mrs. Webb's garden.

Just like Mrs. Gibbs's, only it's got a lot of sunflowers, too.

Right here,—big butternut tree.

[*He returns to his place by the right proscenium pillar and looks at the audience for a minute.*]

Nice town, y'know what I mean?

Nobody very remarkable ever come out of it,—s'far as we know.

The earliest tombstones in the cemetery up there on the mountain say 1670-1680—they're Grovers and Cartwrights and Gibbses and Herseys— same names as are around here now.

Well, as I said: it's about dawn.

The only lights on in town are in a cottage over by the tracks where a Polish mother's just had twins. And in the Joe Crowell house, where Joe Junior's getting up so as to deliver the paper. And in the depot, where Shorty Hawkins is gettin' ready to flag the 5:45 for Boston.

[*A train whistle is heard. The* STAGE MANAGER *takes out his watch and nods.*]

Naturally, out in the country—all around—they've been lights on for some time, what with milkin's and so on. But town people sleep late.

So—another day's begun.

There's Doc Gibbs comin' down Main Street now, comin' back from that baby case. And here's his wife comin' downstairs to get breakfast.

Doc Gibbs died in 1930. The new hospital's named after him.

Mrs. Gibbs died first—long time ago in fact. She went out to visit her daughter, Rebecca, who married an insurance man in Canton, Ohio, and died there—pneumonia—but her body was brought back here. She's up in the cemetery there now—in with a whole mess of Gibbses and Herseys—she was Julia Hersey 'fore she married Doc Gibbs in the Congregational Church over there.

In our town we like to know the facts about everybody.

—That's Doc Gibbs.

And there comes Joe Crowell, Jr., delivering Mr. Webb's *Sentinel*.

[DR. GIBBS *has been coming along Main Street from the left. At the point where he would turn to approach his house, he stops, sets down his— imaginary—black bag, takes off his hat, and rubs his face with fatigue, using an enormous handkerchief.*]

[MRS. GIBBS *has entered her kitchen, gone through the motions of putting wood into a stove, lighting it, and preparing breakfast.*

[*Suddenly,* JOE CROWELL, JR., *starts down Main Street from the right, hurling imaginary newspapers into doorways.*]

JOE CROWELL, JR. Morning, Doc Gibbs.

DR. GIBBS. Morning, Joe.

JOE CROWELL, JR. Somebody been sick, Doc?

DR. GIBBS. No. Just some twins born over in Polish Town.

JOE CROWELL, JR. Do you want your paper now?

DR. GIBBS. Yes, I'll take it.—Anything serious goin' on in the world since Wednesday?

JOE CROWELL, JR. Yessir. My schoolteacher, Miss Foster, 's getting married to a fella over in Concord.

DR. GIBBS. I declare.—How do you boys feel about that?

JOE CROWELL, JR. Well, of course, it's none of my business,—but I think if a person starts out to be a teacher, she ought to stay one.

DR. GIBBS. How's your knee, Joe?

JOE CROWELL, JR. Fine, Doc, I never think about it at all. Only like you said, it always tells me when it's going to rain.

DR. GIBBS. What's it telling you today? Goin' to rain?

JOE CROWELL, JR. No, sir.

DR. GIBBS. Sure?

JOE CROWELL, JR. Yessir.

DR. GIBBS. Knee ever make a mistake?

JOE CROWELL, JR. No, sir. (JOE *goes off*. DR. GIBBS *stands reading his paper*.)

STAGE MANAGER. Here comes Howie Newsome delivering the milk.

[HOWIE NEWSOME *comes along Main Street, passes* DR. GIBBS, *comes down the center of the stage, leaves some bottles at* MRS. WEBB's *back door, and crosses the stage to* MRS. GIBBS'S.]

HOWIE NEWSOME. Git-ap, Bessie. What's the matter with you?—Morning, Doc.

DR. GIBBS. Morning, Howie.

HOWIE NEWSOME. Somebody sick?

DR. GIBBS. Pair of twins over to Mrs. Goruslawski's.

HOWIE NEWSOME. Twins, eh? This town's gettin' bigger every year.

DR. GIBBS. Going to rain, Howie?

HOWIE NEWSOME. No, no. Fine day—that'll burn through. Come on, Bessie.

DR. GIBBS. Hello, Bessie. (*He strokes her*.) How old is she, Howie?

HOWIE NEWSOME. Going on seventeen. Bessie's all mixed up about the route ever since the Lockharts stopped takin' their quart of milk every day. She wants to leave 'em a quart just the same—keeps scolding me the hull trip. (*He reaches* MRS. GIBBS's *back door. She is waiting for him*.)

MRS. GIBBS. Good morning, Howie.

HOWIE NEWSOME. Morning, Mrs. Gibbs. Doc's just comin' down the street.

MRS. GIBBS. Is he? Seems like you're late today?

HOWIE NEWSOME. Yes. Somep'n went wrong with the separator. Don't know what 'twas. (*He goes back to Main Street, clucks for Bessie and goes off right.*)

> [DR. GIBBS *reaches his home and goes in.*]

MRS. GIBBS. Everything all right?

DR. GIBBS. Yes. I declare—easy as kittens.

MRS. GIBBS. Bacon'll be ready in a minute. Set down and drink your coffee. Child-*run!* Child-*run!* Time to get up.—George! Rebecca!—You can catch a couple hours' sleep this morning, can't you?

DR. GIBBS. Hm! . . . Mrs. Wentworth's coming at eleven. Guess I know what it's about, too. Her stummick ain't what it ought to be.

MRS. GIBBS. All told, you won't get more'n three hours' sleep. Frank Gibbs, I don't know what's goin' to become of you. I do wish I could get you to go away some place and take a rest. I think it would do you good.

MRS. WEBB. Emileeee! Time to get up! Wally! Seven o'clock!

MRS. GIBBS. I declare, you got to speak to George. Seems like something's come over him lately. He's no help to me at all. I can't even get him to cut me some wood.

DR. GIBBS. Is he sassy to you?

MRS. GIBBS. No. He just whines! All he thinks about is that baseball— George! Rebecca! You'll be late for school.

DR. GIBBS. M-m-m. . . .

MRS. GIBBS. George!

DR. GIBBS. George, look sharp!

GEORGE'S VOICE. Yes, Pa!

DR. GIBBS (*as he goes off the stage*). Don't you hear your mother calling you?

MRS. WEBB. Walleee! Emileee! You'll be late for school! Walleee! You wash yourself good or I'll come up and do it myself.

REBECCA GIBBS'S VOICE. Ma! What dress shall I wear?

MRS. GIBBS. Don't make a noise. Your father's been out all night and needs his sleep. I washed and ironed the blue gingham for you special.

REBECCA. Ma, I hate that dress.

MRS. GIBBS. Oh, hush-up-with-you.

REBECCA. Every day I go to school dressed like a sick turkey.

MRS. GIBBS. Now, Rebecca, don't be impossible. You always look *very* nice.

REBECCA. Mama, George's throwing soap at me.

MRS. GIBBS. I'll come up and slap the both of you,—that's what I'll do.

[*A factory whistle sounds.*

[*The children enter and take their places at the breakfast tables:* EMILY *and* WALLY WEBB; GEORGE *and* REBECCA GIBBS.]

STAGE MANAGER. We've got a factory in our town too,—hear it? Makes blankets. Cartwrights own it and it brung 'em a fortune.

MRS. WEBB. Children! Now I won't have it. Breakfast is just as good as any other meal and I won't have you gobbling like wolves. It'll stunt your growth,—that's a fact. Put away your book, Wally.

WALLY. Aw, Ma!

MRS. WEBB. You know the rule's well as I do—no books at table. As for me, I'd rather have my children healthy than bright.

EMILY. I'm both, Mama: you know I am. I'm the brightest girl in school for my age. I have a wonderful memory.

MRS. WEBB. Eat your breakfast.

WALLY. I'm bright, too, when I'm looking at my stamp collection.

MRS. GIBBS. I'll speak to your father about it when he's rested. Seems to me twenty-five cents a week's enough for a boy your age. I declare I don't know how you spend it all.

GEORGE. Aw, Ma,—I gotta lotta things to buy.

MRS. GIBBS. Strawberry phosphates—that's what you spend it on.

GEORGE. I don't see how Rebecca comes to have so much money. She has more'n a dollar.

REBECCA (spoon in mouth, dreamily). I've been saving it up gradual.

MRS. GIBBS. Well, dear, I think it's a good thing every now and then to spend some.

REBECCA. Mama, do you know what I love most in the world—do you?—Money.

MRS. GIBBS. Eat your breakfast.

[The school bell is heard.]

THE CHILDREN. Mama, there's first bell.—I gotta hurry.—I don't want any more.

MRS. WEBB. Walk fast, but you don't have to run. Wally, pull up your pants at the knee. Stand up straight, Emily.

MRS. GIBBS. Tell Miss Foster I send her my best congratulations—can you remember that?

REBECCA. Yes, Ma.

MRS. GIBBS. You look real nice, Rebecca. Pick up your feet.

ALL. Good-by.

[The children from the two houses join at the center of the stage and go up to Main Street, then off left.

[MRS. GIBBS fills her apron with food for the chickens and comes down to the footlights.]

MRS. GIBBS. Here, chick, chick, chick.

No, go away, you. Go away.

Here, chick, chick, chick.

What's the matter with *you?* Fight, fight, fight,—that's all you do. Hm . . . *you* don't belong to me. Where'd you come from? (*She shakes her apron.*) Oh, don't be so scared. Nobody's going to hurt you.

[MRS. WEBB *is sitting by her trellis, stringing beans.*]

MRS. GIBBS. Good morning, Myrtle. How's your cold?

MRS. WEBB. Well, it's better; but I told Charles I didn't know as I'd go to choir practice tonight. Wouldn't be any use.

MRS. GIBBS. Just the same, you come to choir practice, Myrtle, and try it.

MRS. WEBB. Well, if I don't feel any worse than I do now I probably will. While I'm resting myself I thought I'd string some of these beans.

MRS. GIBBS (*rolling up her sleeves as she crosses the stage for a chat*). Let me help you. Beans have been good this year.

MRS. WEBB. I've decided to put up forty quarts if it kills me. The children say they hate 'em but I notice they're able to get 'em down all winter. (*Pause.*)

MRS. GIBBS. Now, Myrtle. I've got to tell you something, because if I don't tell somebody I'll burst.

MRS. WEBB. Why, Julia Gibbs!

MRS. GIBBS. Here, give me some more of those beans. Myrtle, did one of those second-hand furniture men from Boston come to see you last Friday?

MRS. WEBB. No-o.

MRS. GIBBS. Well, he called on me. First I thought he was a patient wantin' to see Dr. Gibbs. 'N he wormed his way into my parlor, and, Myrtle Webb, he offered me three hundred and fifty dollars for Grandmother Wentworth's highboy, as I'm sitting here!

MRS. WEBB. Why, Julia Gibbs!

MRS. GIBBS. He did! That old thing! Why, it was so big I didn't know where to put it and I almost give it to Cousin Hester Wilcox.

MRS. WEBB. Well, you're going to take it, aren't you?

MRS. GIBBS. I don't know.

MRS. WEBB. You don't know—three hundred and fifty dollars. What's come over you?

MRS. GIBBS. Well, if I could get the Doctor to take the money and go away some place on a real trip I'd sell it like that.—Myrtle, ever since I was *that* high I've had the thought that I'd like to see Paris, France. I suppose I'm crazy.

MRS. WEBB. Oh, I know what you mean.—How does the Doctor feel about it?

MRS. GIBBS. Well, I did beat about the bush a little and said that if I got a legacy—that's the way I put it—I'd make him take me somewhere.

MRS. WEBB. M-m-m. . . , What did he say?

MRS. GIBBS. You know how he is. I haven't heard a serious word out of him, ever since I've known him. No, he said, it might make him discontented with Grover's Corners to go traipsin' about Europe; better let well enough alone, he says. Every two years he makes a trip to the battlefields of the Civil War and that's enough treat for anybody, he says.

MRS. WEBB. Well, Mr. Webb just *admires* the way Doctor Gibbs knows everything about the Civil War. Mr. Webb's a good mind to give up Napoleon and move over to the Civil War, only Doctor Gibbs being one of the greatest experts in the country just makes him despair.

MRS. GIBBS. It's a fact! Doctor Gibbs is never so happy as when he's at Antietam or Gettysburg. The times I've walked over those hills, Myrtle, stopping at every bush and pacing it all out, like we was going to buy it.

MRS. WEBB. Well, if that second-hand man's really serious about buyin' it, Julia, you sell it. And then you'll get to see Paris, all right.

MRS. GIBBS. Oh, I'm sorry I mentioned it. Only it seems to me that once in your life before you die you ought to see a country where they don't talk and think in English and don't even want to.

[*The* STAGE MANAGER *returns to the center of the stage.*]

STAGE MANAGER. That'll do. That'll do. Thank you very much, ladies.

[MRS. GIBBS *and* MRS. WEBB *gather up their things, return into their homes and disappear.*]

Now we're going to skip a few hours in the day at Grover's Corners. But before we go on I want you to know some more things about the town,—all kinds of things.

So I've asked Prof. Willard of our State University to come down here and sketch in a few details of our past history,—kind of scientific account, you might say.

Is Prof. Willard here?

[PROF. WILLARD, *a rural savant, pince-nez on a wide satin ribbon, enters from the right with some notes in his hand.*]

May I introduce Prof. Willard of our University.

A few brief notes, thank you, Professor,—unfortunately our time is limited.

PROF. WILLARD. Grover's Corners . . . let me see . . . Grover's Corners lies on the old Archaeozoic granite of the Appalachian range. I may say it's some of the oldest land in the world. We're very proud of that. A shelf of Devonian basalt crosses it with vestiges of Mesozoic shale, and some sandstone outcroppings; but that's all more recent: two hundred, three hundred million years old.

Some highly interesting fossils have been found. . . . I may say: unique fossils . . . two miles out of town, in Silas Peckham's cow pasture. They can be seen at the museum in our University at any time. Did you wish the meteorological conditions?

STAGE MANAGER. Thank you. We would.

PROF. WILLARD. The mean precipitation is 40 inches. The mean annual temperature is 43 degrees, ranging between 102 degrees in the shade, and 38 degrees below zero in winter. The . . . the . . . uh . . .

STAGE MANAGER. Thank you, Professor. And have you Prof. Gruber's notes on the history of human life here?

PROF. WILLARD. Hm . . . yes . . . anthropological data: Early Amerindian stock. Cotahatchee tribes . . . no evidence before the Tenth Century of this era . . . hm . . . now entirely disappeared . . . possible traces in three families. Migration toward the end of the Seventeenth Century of English brachycephalic blue-eyed stock . . . for the most part. Since then some influx of Slav and Mediterranean types. . . .

STAGE MANAGER. And the population, Prof. Willard?

PROF. WILLARD. Within the town limits: 2,640. The postal district brings in 507 more.

Mortality and birth-rates are constant; by MacPherson's gauge: 6.032.

STAGE MANAGER. Thank you *very* much, Professor. We're all very much obliged to you, I'm sure.

PROF. WILLARD. Not at all, sir; not at all.

STAGE MANAGER. This way, Professor, and thank you again.

[*Exit* PROF. WILLARD.]

Now the political and social report: Editor Webb.—Oh, Mr. Webb?

[MRS. WEBB *appears at her back door.*]

MRS. WEBB. He'll be here in a minute. . . . He just cut his hand while he was eatin' an apple.

STAGE MANAGER. Thank you, Mrs. Webb.

MRS. WEBB. Charles! Everybody's waitin'.

[*Exit* MRS. WEBB.]

STAGE MANAGER. Mr. Webb is Publisher and Editor of The Grover's Corners *Sentinel*. That's our local paper, y'know.

[MR. WEBB *enters from his house, pulling on his coat. His finger is bound in a handkerchief.*]

MR. WEBB. Hm. . . . I don't have to tell you that we're run here by a Board of Selectmen.—All males vote at the age of 21. Women vote indirect. We're lower middle-class, sprinkling of professional men . . . 10% illiterate laborers. Politically, we're 86% Republicans; 6% Democrats; 4% Socialists; rest, indifferent.

Religiously, we're 85% Protestants; 12% Catholics; rest, indifferent.

Do you want the poverty and insanity statistics?

STAGE MANAGER. Thank you, no. Have you any comments, Mr. Webb?

MR. WEBB. Very ordinary town, if you ask me. Little better behaved than most. Probably a lot duller.

But our young people here seem to like it well enough: 90% of 'em graduating from High School settle down right here to live—even when they've been away to college.

STAGE MANAGER. Thank you, Mr. Webb. Now, is there anyone in the audience who would like to ask Editor Webb anything about the town?

WOMAN IN THE BALCONY. Is there much drinking in Grover's Corners?

MR. WEBB. Well, ma'am, I wouldn't know what you'd call *much*. Satiddy nights the farmhands meet down in Ellery Greenough's stable and holler some. Fourth of July I've been known to taste a drop myself—and Decoration Day, of course. We've got one or two town drunks, but they're always having remorses every time an evangelist comes to town. No, ma'am, I'd say likker ain't a regular thing in the home here, except in the medicine chest. Right good for snake-bite, y'know—always was.

TALL MAN AT BACK OF AUDITORIUM. Is there no one in town aware of—

STAGE MANAGER. Come forward, will you, where we can all hear you— What were you saying?

TALL MAN. Is there no one in town aware of social injustice and industrial inequality?

MR. WEBB. Oh, yes, everybody is,—somethin' terrible. Seems like they spend most of their time talking about who's rich and who's poor.

TALL MAN. Then why don't they do something about it?

MR. WEBB. Well, we're ready to listen to everybody's suggestion as to how you can see that the diligent and sensible'll rise to the top and the lazy and quarrelsome sink to the bottom. We'll listen to anybody. Meantime until that's settled, we try to take care of those that can't help themselves, and those that can we leave alone.—Are there any more questions?

LADY IN A BOX. Oh, Mr. Webb? Mr. Webb, is there any culture or love of beauty in Grover's Corners?

MR. WEBB. Well, ma'am, there ain't much—not in the sense you mean. Come to think of it, there's some girls that play the piano at High School Commencement; but they ain't happy about it. Yes, and I see where my daughter's been made to read "The Merchant of Venice" over to the school. Seems all pretty remote to 'em, y'know what I mean. No, ma'am, there isn't much culture; but maybe this is the place to tell you that we've got a lot of pleasures of a kind here: we like the sun comin' up over the mountain in the morning, and we all notice a good deal about the birds. We pay a lot of attention to them, and trees and plants. And we watch the change of the seasons: yes, everybody knows about them. But those other things—you're right, ma'am—there ain't much—"Robinson Crusoe" and the Bible; and Handel's "Largo," we all know that; and Whistler's "Mother"—those are just about as far as we go.

LADY IN A BOX. So I thought. Thank you, Mr. Webb.

STAGE MANAGER. All right! All right! Thank you, everybody.

[MR. WEBB *retires*.]

We'll go back to the town now. It's middle of the afternoon. All 2,642 have had their dinners and all the dishes have been washed.

There's an early afternoon calm in our town: a buzzin' and a hummin' from the school buildings; only a few buggies on Main Street—the horses dozing at the hitching-posts; you all remember what it's like. Doc Gibbs is in his office, tapping people and making them say "ah." Mr. Webb's cuttin' his lawn over there; one man in ten thinks it's a privilege to push his own lawn mower.

No, sir. It's later than I thought. There are the children coming home from school already.

[EMILY WEBB *comes sedately down Main Street carrying some school books. There are some signs that she is imagining herself to be a lady of striking elegance.*

[*Her father's movements to and fro with the lawn mower bring him into her vicinity.*]

EMILY. I *can't*, LOIS. I've got to go home and help my mother. I *promised*.

MR. WEBB. Emily, walk simply. Who do you think you are today?

EMILY. Papa, you're terrible. One minute you tell me to stand up straight and the next minute you call me names. I just don't listen to you. (*She gives him an abrupt kiss.*)

MR. WEBB. Golly, I never got a kiss from such a great lady before. (*He goes out of sight.* EMILY *leans over and picks some flowers by the gate of her house.* GEORGE GIBBS *comes careening down Main Street. He is throwing a ball up to dizzying heights, and waiting to catch it again. This sometimes requires his taking six steps backward.*)

GEORGE. Excuse me, Mrs. Forrest.

STAGE MANAGER (*as* MRS. FORREST). Go out and play in the fields, young man. You got no business playing baseball on Main Street.

GEORGE. Awfully sorry, Mrs. Forrest.—Hello, Emily.

EMILY. H'lo.

GEORGE. You made a fine speech in class.

EMILY. Well . . . I was really ready to make a speech about the Monroe Doctrine, but at the last minute Miss Corcoran made me talk about the Louisiana Purchase instead. I worked an awful long time on both of them.

GEORGE. Gee, it's funny, Emily. From my window up there I can just see your head nights when you're doing your homework over in your room.

EMILY. Why, can you?

GEORGE. You certainly do stick to it, Emily. I don't see how you can sit still that long. I guess you like school.

EMILY. Well, I always feel it's something you have to go through.

GEORGE. Yeah.

EMILY. I don't mind it really. It passes the time.

GEORGE. Yeah.—Emily, what do you think? We might work out a kinda telegraph from there to there; and once in a while you could give me a kinda hint or two about one of those Algebra problems. I don't mean the answers, Emily, of course not . . . just some little hint. . . .

EMILY. Oh, I think *hints* are allowed.—So-ah—if you get stuck, George, you whistle to me; and I'll give you some hints.

GEORGE. Emily, you're just naturally bright, I guess.

EMILY. I figure that it's just the way a person's born.

GEORGE. Yeah. But, you see, I want to be a farmer, and my Uncle Luke says whenever I'm ready I can come over and work on his farm and if I'm any good I can just gradually have it.

EMILY. You mean the house and everything?

[*Enter* MRS. WEBB.]

GEORGE. Yeah. Well, thanks . . . I better be getting out to the baseball field. Thanks for the talk, Emily.—Good afternoon, Mrs. Webb.

MRS. WEBB. Good afternoon, George.

GEORGE. So-long, Emily.

EMILY. So-long, George.

MRS. WEBB. Emily, come and help me string these beans for the winter. George Gibbs let himself have a real conversation, didn't he? Why, he's growing up. How old would George be?

EMILY. I don't know.

MRS. WEBB. Let's see. He must be almost sixteen.

EMILY. Mama, I made a speech in class today and I was very good.

MRS. WEBB. You must recite it to your father at supper. What was it about?

EMILY. The Louisiana Purchase. It was like silk off a spool. I'm going to make speeches all my life.—Mama, are these big enough?

MRS. WEBB. Try and get them a little bigger if you can.

EMILY. Mama, will you answer me a question, serious?

MRS. WEBB. Seriously, dear—not serious.

EMILY. Seriously,—will you?

MRS. WEBB. Of course, I will.

EMILY. Mama, am I good-looking?

MRS. WEBB. Yes, of course you are. All my children have got good features; I'd be ashamed if they hadn't.

EMILY. Oh, Mama, that's not what I mean. What I mean is: Am I *pretty*?

MRS. WEBB. I've already told you, yes. Now that's enough of that. You have a nice young pretty face. I never heard of such foolishness.

EMILY. Oh, Mama, you never tell us the truth about anything.

MRS. WEBB. I *am* telling you the truth.

EMILY. Mama, were *you* pretty?

MRS. WEBB. Yes, I was, if I do say it. I was the prettiest girl in town next to Mamie Cartwright.

EMILY. But, Mama, you've got to say *something* about me. Am I pretty enough . . . to get anybody . . . to get people interested in me?

MRS. WEBB. Emily, you make me tired. Now stop it. You're pretty enough for all normal purposes. Come along now and bring that bowl with you.

EMILY. Oh, Mama, you're no help at all.

STAGE MANAGER. Thank you. Thank you! That'll do. We'll have to interrupt again here. Thank you, Mrs. Webb; thank you, Emily.

[MRS. WEBB *and* EMILY *withdraw.*]

There are some more things we've got to explore about this town.

This time we're going to go about it in another way: we're going to look back on it from the future. I'm not going to tell you what became of these two families we're seeing most of, because the rest of the play will tell you about them.

But take some of these others:

Take Joe Crowell, Jr.:

Joe was a very bright fellow. He graduated with honors and got a scholarship to Boston Tech.,—M.I.T., that is. But the War broke out and Joe died in France. All that education for nothing.

Howie Newsome's still delivering milk at Grover's Corners. He's an old man now, has a lot of help, but he still delivers it himself. Says he gets the feel of the town that way. Carries all the accounts in his head; never has to write down a word.

Mr. Morgan's drugstore ain't the same,—it's all citified. Mr. Morgan retired and went out to live in San Diego, California, where his daughter married a real estate man, name of Kerby. Mr. Morgan died there in 1935 and was buried in a lot of palm trees. Kinda lost his religion at the end and took up New Thought or something. They read some new-fangled poetry over him and cre-mated him. The New Hampshire in him sort of broke down in him in that climate, seems like.

The Cartwrights got richer and richer. The house is closed most of the year. They're off eating big dinners in hotels now,—in Virginia Hot Springs and Miami Beach. They say the winters are cold here. I see where they've become 'Piscopalians.

The Cartwright interests have just begun building a new bank in Grover's Corners—had to go to Vermont for the marble, sorry to say. And they've asked a friend of mine what they should put in the cornerstone for people to dig up a thousand years from now. Of course, they've put in a copy of the New York *Times* and a copy of Mr. Webb's *Sentinel*. We're kind of interested in this because some scientific fellas have found a way of painting all that reading matter with a kind of glue—silicate glue—that'll make it keep a thousand—two thousand years.

We're putting in a Bible . . . and the Constitution of the United States and a copy of William Shakespeare's plays. What do you say, folks? What do you think?

Y'know—Babylon once had two million people in it, and all we know about 'em is the names of the kings and some copies of wheat contracts and . . . the sales of slaves. Yes, every night all those families sat down to supper, and the father came home from his work, and the smoke went up the chimney,—same as here. And even in Greece and Rome, all we know about the real life of the people is what we can piece together out of the joking poems and the comedies they wrote for the theater back then. So I'm going to have a copy of this play put in the cornerstone and the people a thousand years from now'll know a few simple facts about us—more than the Treaty of Versailles and the Lindbergh flight.

See what I mean?

Well, people a thousand years from now—this is the way we were in the provinces north of New York at the beginning of the Twentieth Century,—this is the way we were in our growing-up, in our marrying, in our living, and in our dying.

Now we'll return to our day in Grover's Corners.

A lot of time has gone by. It's evening. You can hear choir practice going on in the Congregational Church. All the children are at home doing their school work. The day is running down like a tired clock.

[*A choir partially concealed in the orchestra pit has begun singing, "Blessed be the tie that binds." SIMON STIMSON stands directing them.*

[*Two ladders have been pushed on to the stage; they serve as indication of the second story in the Gibbs and Webb houses. GEORGE and EMILY mount them, and apply themselves to their school work.*

[DR. GIBBS *has entered and is seated in his kitchen reading.*]

SIMON STIMSON. Now look here, everybody. Music come into the world to give pleasure.—Softer! Softer! Get it out of your heads that music's only good when it's loud. You leave loudness to the Methodists. You couldn't beat 'em, even if you wanted to. Now again. Tenors!

GEORGE. Hssst! Emily!

EMILY. Hello.

GEORGE. Hello!

EMILY. I can't work at all. The moonlight's so *terrible.*

GEORGE. Emily, did you get the third problem?

EMILY. Which?

GEORGE. The *third?*

EMILY. Why, yes, George—that's the easiest of them all.

GEORGE. I don't see it. Emily, can you give me a hint?

EMILY. I'll tell you one thing: the answer's in yards.

GEORGE. ! ! ! In yards? How do you mean?

EMILY. In *square* yards.

GEORGE. Oh . . . in square yards.

EMILY. Yes, George, don't you see?

GEORGE. Yeah.

EMILY. In square yards of *wallpaper.*

GEORGE. Wallpaper,—oh, I see. Thanks a lot, Emily.

EMILY. You're welcome. My, isn't the moonlight *terrible?* And choir prac-tice going on.—I think if you hold your breath you can hear the train all the way to Contookuck. Hear it?

GEORGE. M-m-m— What do you know!

EMILY. Well, I guess I better go back and try to work.

GEORGE. Good night, Emily. And thanks.

EMILY. Good night, George.

SIMON STIMSON. Before I forget it: How many of you will be able to come in Tuesday afternoon and sing at Fred Hersey's wedding,—show your hands. That'll be fine; that'll be right nice. We'll do the same music we did for Jane Trowbridge's last month.

—Now we'll do: "Art thou weary; art thou languid?" It's a question, ladies and gentlemen, make it talk. Ready.

DR. GIBBS. Oh, George, can you come down a minute?

GEORGE. Yes, Pa. (*He descends the ladder.*)

DR. GIBBS. Make yourself comfortable, George; I'll only keep you a minute. George, how old are you?

GEORGE. I? I'm sixteen, almost seventeen.

DR. GIBBS. What do you want to do after school's over?

GEORGE. Why, you know, Pa, I want to be a farmer on Uncle Luke's farm.

DR. GIBBS. You'll be willing, will you, to get up early and milk and feed the stock . . . and you'll be able to hoe and hay all day?

GEORGE. Sure, I will. What are you . . . what do you mean, Pa?

DR. GIBBS. Well, George, while I was in my office today I heard a funny sound . . . and what do you think it was? It was your mother chop-ping wood. There you see your mother—getting up early; cooking meals all day long; washing and ironing;—and still she has to go out in the back yard and chop wood. I suppose she just got tired of asking you. She just gave up and decided it was easier to do it herself. And you eat her meals, and put on the clothes she keeps nice for you, and you run off and play baseball,—like she's some hired girl we keep around the house but that we don't like very much. Well, I knew all I had to do was call your attention to it. Here's a handkerchief, son. George, I've decided to raise your spending money twenty-five cents a week. Not, of course, for chopping wood for your mother, because that's a present you give her, but because you're getting older—and I imagine there are lots of things you must find to do with it.

GEORGE. Thanks, Pa.

DR. GIBBS. Let's see—tomorrow's pay day. You can count on it— Hmm. Probably Rebecca'll feel she ought to have some more too. Wonder what could have happened to your mother. Choir practice never was as late as this before.

GEORGE. It's only half-past eight, Pa.

DR. GIBBS. I don't know why she's in that old choir. She hasn't any more voice than an old crow. . . . Traipsin' around the streets at this hour of the night. . . . Just about time you retired, don't you think?

GEORGE. Yes, Pa. (GEORGE *mounts to his place on the ladder.*)

[*Laughter and good nights can be heard on stage left and presently* MRS. GIBBS, MRS. SOAMES *and* MRS. WEBB *come down Main Street. When they arrive at the center of the stage they stop.*]

MRS. SOAMES. Good night, Martha. Good night, Mr. Foster.

MRS. WEBB. I'll tell Mr. Webb; I *know* he'll want to put it in the paper.

MRS. GIBBS. My, it's late!

MRS. SOAMES. Good night, Irma.

MRS. GIBBS. Real nice choir practice, wa'n't it? Myrtle Webb! Look at that moon, will you! Tsk-tsk-tsk. Potato weather, for sure.

MRS. SOAMES. Naturally I didn't want to say a word about it in front of those others, but now we're alone—really, it's the worst scandal that ever was in this town!

MRS. GIBBS. What?

MRS. SOAMES. Simon Stimson!

MRS. GIBBS. Now, Louella!

MRS. SOAMES. But, Julia! To have the organist of a church drink, and drunk year after year. You know he was drunk tonight.

MRS. GIBBS. Now, Louella! We all know about Mr. Stimson, and we all know about the troubles he's been through, and Dr. Ferguson knows too, and if Dr. Ferguson keeps him on there in his job the only thing the rest of us can do is just not to notice it.

MRS. SOAMES. Not to notice it! But it's getting worse.

MRS. WEBB. No, it isn't, Louella. It's getting better. I've been in that choir twice as long as you have. It doesn't happen anywhere near so often. . . . My, I hate to go to bed on a night like this.—I better hurry. Those children'll be sitting up till all hours. Good night, Louella. (*She hurries down stage, enters her house and disappears.*)

MRS. GIBBS. Can you get home safe, Louella?

MRS. SOAMES. It's as bright as day. I can see Mr. Soames scowling at the window now. You'd think we'd been to a dance the way the menfolk carry on.

[*Repeated good nights.* MRS. GIBBS *arrives at her home.*]

MRS. GIBBS. Well, we had a real good time.

DR. GIBBS. You're late enough.

MRS. GIBBS. Why, Frank, it ain't any later'n usual.

DR. GIBBS. And you stopping at the corner to gossip with a lot of hens.

MRS. GIBBS. Now, Frank, don't be grouchy. Come out and smell my heliotrope in the moonlight. (*They stroll out arm in arm along the footlights.*) Isn't that wonderful? What did you do all the time I was away?

DR. GIBBS. Oh, I read—as usual. What were the girls gossiping about tonight?

MRS. GIBBS. Well, believe me, Frank—there is something to gossip about.

DR. GIBBS. Hmm! Simon Stimson far gone, was he?

MRS. GIBBS. Worst I've ever seen him. How'll that end, Frank? Dr. Ferguson can't forgive him forever.

DR. GIBBS. I guess I know more about Simon Stimson's affairs than anybody in this town. Some people ain't made for small town life. I don't know how that'll end; but there's nothing we can do but just leave it alone. Come, get in.

MRS. GIBBS. No, not yet. . . . Oh, Frank, I'm worried about you.

DR. GIBBS. What are you worried about?

MRS. GIBBS. I think it's my duty to make plans for you to get a real rest and change. And if I get that legacy, well, I'm going to insist on it.

DR. GIBBS. Now, Julia, there's no sense in going over that again.

MRS. GIBBS. Frank, you're just *unreasonable!*

DR. GIBBS. Come on, Julia, it's getting late. First thing you know you'll catch cold. I gave George a piece of my mind tonight. I reckon you'll have your wood chopped for a while anyway. No, no, start getting upstairs.

MRS. GIBBS. Oh, dear. There's always so many things to pick up, seems like. You know, Frank, Mrs. Fairchild always locks her front door every night. All those people up that part of town do.

DR. GIBBS. They're all getting citified, that's the trouble with them. They haven't got nothing fit to burgle and everybody knows it.

[*They disappear.*

[REBECCA *climbs up the ladder beside* GEORGE.]

GEORGE. Get out, Rebecca. There's only room for one at this window. You're always spoiling everything.

REBECCA. Well, let me look just a minute.

GEORGE. Use your own window.

REBECCA. I did; but there's no moon there. . . . George, do you know what I think, do you? I think maybe the moon's getting nearer and nearer and there'll be a big 'splosion.

GEORGE. Rebecca, you don't know anything. If the moon were getting nearer, the guys that sit up all night with telescopes would see it first and they'd tell about it, and it'd be in all the newspapers.

REBECCA. George, is the moon shining on South America, Canada and half the whole world?

GEORGE. Well—prob'ly is.

[*The* STAGE MANAGER *strolls on.*]

STAGE MANAGER. Nine-thirty. Most of the lights are out. No, there's Constable Warren trying a few doors on Main Street. And here comes Editor Webb, after putting his newspaper to bed.

MR. WEBB. Good evening, Bill.

CONSTABLE WARREN. Evenin', Mr. Webb.

MR. WEBB. Quite a moon!

CONSTABLE WARREN. Yep.

MR. WEBB. All quiet tonight?

CONSTABLE WARREN. Simon Stimson is rollin' around a little. Just saw his wife movin' out to hunt for him so I looked the other way—there he is now.

[SIMON STIMSON *comes down Main Street from the left, only a trace of unsteadiness in his walk.*]

MR. WEBB. Good evening, Simon. . . . Town seems to have settled down for the night pretty well. . . .

[SIMON STIMSON *comes up to him and pauses a moment.*]

Good evening. . . . Yes, most of the town's settled down for the night, Simon. . . . I guess we better do the same. Can I walk along a ways with you?

[SIMON STIMSON *continues on his way without a word and disappears at the right.*]

Good night.

CONSTABLE WARREN. I don't know how that's goin' to end, Mr. Webb.

MR. WEBB. Well, he's seen a peck of trouble, one thing after another. . . . Oh, Bill . . . if you see my boy smoking cigarettes, just give him a word, will you? He thinks a lot of you, Bill.

CONSTABLE WARREN. I don't think he smokes no cigarettes, Mr. Webb. Leastways, not more'n two or three a year. He don't belong to that crowd that hangs out down by the gully.

MR. WEBB. Hm. . . . I hope not.—Well, good night, Bill.

CONSTABLE WARREN. Good night, Mr. Webb. (*Exit.*)

MR. WEBB. Who's that up there? Is that you, Myrtle?

EMILY. No, it's me, Papa.

MR. WEBB. Why aren't you in bed?

EMILY. I don't know. I just can't sleep yet, Papa. The moonlight's so *wonderful*. And the smell of Mrs. Gibbs's heliotrope. Can you smell it?

MR. WEBB. Hm. . . . Yes. Haven't any troubles on your mind, have you, Emily?

EMILY. *Troubles*, Papa. *No.*

MR. WEBB. Well, enjoy yourself, but don't let your mother catch you. Good night, Emily.

EMILY. Good night, Papa.

[MR. WEBB *crosses into the house, whistling "Blessed Be the Tie that Binds" and disappears.*]

REBECCA. I never told you about that letter Jane Crofut got from her minister when she was sick. The minister of her church in the town she was in before she came here. He wrote Jane a letter and on the envelope the address was like this: It said: Jane Crofut; The Crofut Farm; Grover's Corners; Sutton County; New Hampshire; United States of America.

GEORGE. What's funny about that?

REBECCA. But listen, it's not finished: the United States of America; Continent of North America; Western Hemisphere; the Earth; the Solar System; the Universe; the Mind of God,—that's what it said on the envelope.

GEORGE. What do you know!

REBECCA. And the postman brought it just the same.

GEORGE. What do you know!

STAGE MANAGER. That's the end of the First Act, friends. You can go and smoke now, those that smoke.

ACT TWO

The tables and chairs of the two kitchens are still on the stage. The ladders have been withdrawn.

The STAGE MANAGER *has been at his accustomed place watching the audience return to its seats.*

STAGE MANAGER. Three years have gone by.

Yes, the sun's come up over a thousand times.

Summers and winters have cracked the mountains a little bit more and the rains have brought down some of the dirt.

Some babies that weren't even born before have begun talking regular sentences already; and a number of people who thought they were right young and spry have noticed that they can't bound up a flight of stairs like they used to, without their heart fluttering a little.

Some older sons are sitting at the head of the table, and some people I know are having their meat cut up for them.—

All that can happen in a thousand days.

Nature's been pushing and contriving in other ways, too: a number of young people fell in love and got married.

Yes, the mountain got bit away a few fractions of an inch; millions of gallons of water went by the mill; and here and there a new home was set up under a roof.

Almost everybody in the world gets married,—you know what I mean? In our town there aren't hardly any exceptions. Most everybody in the world climbs into their graves married.

The First Act was called the Daily Life. This Act is called Love and Marriage. There's another Act coming after this: I reckon you can guess what that's about.

So:

It's three years later. It's 1904.

It's July 7th, just after High School Commencement. That's the time most of our young people jump up and get married. Soon as they've passed their last examinations in solid geometry and Cicero's Orations, looks like they suddenly feel themselves fit to be married.

It's early morning. Only this time it's been raining. It's been pouring and thundering.

Mrs. Gibbs's garden, and Mrs. Webb's here: drenched.

All those bean poles and pea vines: drenched.

All yesterday over there on Main Street, the rain looked like curtains being blown along.

Hm . . . it may begin again any minute.

There! You can hear the 5:45 for Boston.

And here comes Howie Newsome delivering the milk.

And there's Si Crowell delivering the papers like his brother before him.—You remember about his brother?—all that education he's going to get and that'll be wasted.

And there's Mrs. Gibbs and Mrs. Webb come down to make breakfast, just as though it were an ordinary day.

I don't have to point out to the women in my audience that those ladies they see before them, both those ladies cooked three meals a day,—one of 'em for twenty years, the other for forty,—and no summer vacation. They brought up two children apiece; washed; cleaned the house,—and never a nervous breakdown. Never thought themselves hard-used, either.

It's like what one of those Middle West poets said: You've got to love life to have life, and you've got to have life to love life. . . . It's what they call a vicious circle.

[SI CROWELL *has entered, hurling imaginary newspapers into doorways;* HOWIE NEWSOME *has come along Main Street with* BESSIE.]

HOWIE NEWSOME. Git-ap, Bessie.

SI CROWELL. Morning, Howie.

HOWIE NEWSOME. Morning, Si.—Anything in the papers I ought to know?

SI CROWELL. Nothing much, except we're losing about the best baseball pitcher Grover's Corners ever had.

HOWIE NEWSOME. Reckon he was. He's been standing off the whole of South New Hampshire single-handed, looks like.

SI CROWELL. He could hit and run bases, too.

HOWIE NEWSOME. Yep. Mighty fine ball player.—Bessie! I guess I can stop and talk if I've a mind to!

SI CROWELL. I don't see how he could give up a thing like that just to get married. Would you, Howie?

HOWIE NEWSOME. Can't tell, Si. Never had no talent that way.

[CONSTABLE WARREN *enters. They exchange mornings.*]
You're up early, Bill.

CONSTABLE WARREN. Seein' if there's anything I can do to prevent a flood. River's been risin' all night.

HOWIE NEWSOME. Si Crowell's all worked up here about George Gibbs's retiring from baseball.

CONSTABLE WARREN. Yes, sir; that's the way it goes. Back in '84 we had a player, Si,—even George Gibbs couldn't touch him. Name of Hank Todd. Went down to Maine and become a parson. Wonderful ball player.—Howie, how did the weather look to you?

HOWIE NEWSOME. No, 'tain't bad. Think maybe it'll clear up for good.

[CONSTABLE WARREN *and* SI CROWELL *continue on their way.*]

[HOWIE NEWSOME *brings the milk first to* MRS. GIBBS's *house. She meets him by the trellis.*]

MRS. GIBBS. Good morning, Howie. Do you think it's going to rain again?

HOWIE NEWSOME. Morning, Mrs. Gibbs. It rained so heavy, I think maybe it'll clear up.

MRS. GIBBS. Certainly hope it will.

HOWIE NEWSOME. How much did you want today?

MRS. GIBBS. I guess I'll need three-a-milk and two-a-cream, Howie. I'm going to have a house full of relations.

HOWIE NEWSOME. My wife says to tell you we both hope they'll be very happy, Mrs. Gibbs. Know they *will.*

MRS. GIBBS. Thanks a lot, Howie. Tell your wife I hope she gits there to the wedding.

HOWIE NEWSOME. Yes, she'll be there; she'll be there if she kin. (HOWIE NEWSOME *crosses to* MRS. WEBB's *house.*) Morning, Mrs. Webb.

MRS. WEBB. Oh, good morning, Mr. Newsome. I told you four quarts of milk, but I hope you can spare me another.

HOWIE NEWSOME. Yes'm . . . and the two of cream.

MRS. WEBB. Will it rain all day, Mr. Newsome?

HOWIE NEWSOME. No'm. Just sayin' to Mrs. Gibbs as how it may lighten up. Mrs. Newsome told me to tell you as how we hope they'll both be very happy, Mrs. Webb. Know they *will*.

MRS. WEBB. Thank you, and thank Mrs. Newsome and we hope to see you all at the wedding.

HOWIE NEWSOME. Yes, Mrs. Webb. We hope to git there. Couldn't miss that. Chck! Bessie! (*Exit* HOWIE NEWSOME.)

[DR. GIBBS *descends in shirt sleeves, and sits down at his breakfast table.*]

DR. GIBBS. Well, Ma, the day has come. You're losin' one of your chicks.

MRS. GIBBS. Frank Gibbs, don't you say another word. I feel like crying every minute. Sit down and drink your coffee.

DR. GIBBS. The groom's up shaving himself. Whistling and singing, like he's glad to leave us.—Every now and then he says "I do" to the mirror, but it don't sound convincing to me.

MRS. GIBBS. I declare I don't know how he'll get along. I've arranged his clothes and seen to it he's put warm things on,—Frank! they're too young. Emily won't think of such things. He'll catch his death of cold within a week.—Here's something I made for you.

DR. GIBBS. Why, Julia Hersey! French toast!

MRS. GIBBS. 'Tain't hard to make, and I had to do something.

DR. GIBBS. I remember my wedding morning, Julia.

MRS. GIBBS. Now don't start that, Frank Gibbs. I tell you I can't stand it.

DR. GIBBS. I was the scaredest young fella in the State of New Hampshire. I thought I'd made a mistake for sure. And when I saw you comin' down that aisle I thought you were the prettiest girl I'd ever seen, but the only trouble was that I'd never seen you before. There I was in the Congregational Church marryin' a total stranger.

MRS. GIBBS. And how do you think I felt!—Did you hear Rebecca stirring about upstairs?

DR. GIBBS. Only morning in the year she hasn't been managing everybody's business. She's shut up in her room. I got the impression that maybe she's crying.

MRS. GIBBS. Good Lord! This has got to stop.—Rebecca! Rebecca! Everything's getting cold down here.

[GEORGE *comes rattling down the stairs, very brisk.*]

GEORGE. Good morning, everybody. Only five more hours to live. (*Makes the gesture of cutting his throat.*)

MRS. GIBBS. Where are you going?

GEORGE. Just stepping across the grass to see my girl.

MRS. GIBBS. Now, George! You take an umbrella or I won't let you out of this house.

GEORGE. Aw, Ma. It's just a *step!*

MRS. GIBBS. From tomorrow on you can kill yourself in all weathers, but while you're in my house you live wisely, thank you. There are your overshoes right there in the hall. And here's an umbrella.

GEORGE. Aw, Ma!

DR. GIBBS. George, do as your mother tells you.

MRS. GIBBS. Maybe Mrs. Webb isn't used to callers at seven in the morning. Take a cup-a coffee first.

GEORGE. Be back in a minute. (*He crosses the stage, leaping over the puddles.*) Good morning, Mother Webb.

MRS. WEBB. Goodness! You frightened me!—Now, George, you can come in a minute out of the wet, but you know I can't ask you in.

GEORGE. Why not—?

MRS. WEBB. George, you know's well as I do: the groom can't see his bride on his wedding day, not until he sees her in church.

GEORGE. Aw!—that's just a superstition.

[*Enter* MR. WEBB.]

MR. WEBB. Good morning, George.

GEORGE. Mr. Webb, you don't believe in that superstition, do you?

MR. WEBB. There's a lot of common sense in some superstitions, George.

MRS. WEBB. Millions have folla'd it, George, and you don't want to be the first to fly in the face of custom.

GEORGE. How is Emily?

MRS. WEBB. She hasn't waked up yet. I haven't heard a sound out of her.

GEORGE. Emily's *asleep!!!*

MRS. WEBB. No wonder! We were up 'til all hours,—sewing and packing. I'll tell you what I'll do; you set down here a minute with Mr. Webb and drink this cup of coffee; and I'll go upstairs and see she doesn't come down and surprise you. There's some bacon, too; but don't be long about it.

[*Exit* MRS. WEBB.

[*Embarrassed silence.*]

MR. WEBB. Well, George, how are you?

GEORGE. Oh, fine. I'm fine. (*Pause.*) Mr. Webb, what sense could there be in a superstition like that?

MR. WEBB. Well, you see,—on her wedding morning a girl's head's apt to be full of . . . clothes and things like that. Don't you think that's probably it?

GEORGE. Ye-e-s. I never thought of that.

MR. WEBB. A girl's apt to be a mite nervous on her wedding day. (*Pause.*)

GEORGE. I wish a fellow could get married without all that marching up and down.

MR. WEBB. Well, every man that's ever lived has felt that way about it, George; but it hasn't done much good. It's the women that have built up weddings, my boy. From now on they have it pretty much as they like. . . . All those good women standing shoulder to shoulder making sure that the knot's tied in a mighty public way.

GEORGE. But . . . you *believe* in it, don't you, Mr. Webb?

MR. WEBB. Oh, yes; oh, yes. Don't you misunderstand me, my boy. Marriage is a wonderful thing,—wonderful thing. And don't you forget that, George.

GEORGE. No, sir.—Mr. Webb, how old were you when you got married?

MR. WEBB. Well, you see: I'd been to college and I'd taken a little time to get settled. But Mrs. Webb,—she wasn't much older than what Emily is. Oh, age hasn't much to do with it, George,—not compared to other things.

GEORGE. What were you going to say, Mr. Webb?

MR. WEBB. Oh, I don't know,—was I going to say something? (*Pause.*) George, I was thinking the other night of some advice my father gave me when I got married. Charles, he said, Charles, start out early showing who's boss, he said. Best thing to do is to give an order, even if it don't make sense; just so she'll learn to obey. And he said: if anything about your wife irritates you,—her conversation, or anything,—just get up and leave the house. That'll make it clear to her, he said. And, oh, yes! he said never, *never* let your wife know how much money you have, never.

GEORGE. Well, Mr. Webb . . . I don't think I could.

MR. WEBB. So I took the opposite of my father's advice and I've been happy ever since. And let that be a lesson to you, George, never to ask advice on personal matters.—George, are you going to raise chickens on your farm?

GEORGE. What?

MR. WEBB. Are you going to raise chickens on your farm?

GEORGE. Uncle Luke's never been much interested, but I thought—

MR. WEBB. A book came into my office the other day, George, on the Philo System of raising chickens. I want you to read it. I'm thinking of beginning in a small way in the back yard, and I'm going to put an incubator in the cellar—

[*Enter* MRS. WEBB.]

MRS. WEBB. Charles, are you talking about that old incubator again? I thought you two'd be talking about things worth while.

MR. WEBB. Well, Myrtle, if you want to give the boy some good advice, I'll go upstairs and leave you alone with him.

MRS. WEBB. Now, George, I'm sorry, but I've got to send you away so that

Emily can come down and get some breakfast. She told me to tell you that she sends you her love but that she doesn't want to lay eyes on you. So good-by, George.

[GEORGE *crosses the stage to his own home and disappears.*]

MR. WEBB. Myrtle, I guess you don't know about that older superstition.

MRS. WEBB. What do you mean, Charles?

MR. WEBB. Since the cave-men: the groom shouldn't be left alone with his father-in-law on the day of the wedding, or near it. Now don't forget that!

STAGE MANAGER. Thank you. Thank you, everybody.

Now I have to interrupt again here. You see, we want to know how all this began,—this wedding, this plan to spend a lifetime together. I'm awfully interested in how big things like that begin.

You know how it is: you're twenty-one or twenty-two and you make some decisions; then whisssh! you're seventy: you've been a lawyer for fifty years, and that white-haired lady at your side has eaten over fifty thousand meals with you.

How do such things begin?

George and Emily are going to show you now the conversation they had when they first knew that . . . that . . . as the saying goes . . . they were meant for one another. But before they do it I want you to try and remember what it was like when you were young, when you were fifteen or sixteen. For some reason it is very hard to do: those days when even the little things in life could be almost too exciting to bear.

And particularly the days when you were first in love; when you were like a person sleep-walking, and you didn't quite see the street you were in, and didn't quite hear everything that was said to you. You're just a little bit crazy. Will you remember that, please?

Now they'll be coming out of High School at three o'clock. George has just been elected President of the Junior Class, and as it's June, that means he'll be President of the Senior Class all next year. And Emily's just been elected Secretary and Treasurer.

I don't have to tell you how important that is. (*He places a board across the backs of two chairs, parallel to the footlights, and places two high stools behind it. This is the counter of* MR. MORGAN's *drugstore.*)

All ready!

[EMILY, *carrying an armful of—imaginary—school-books, comes along Main Street from the left.*]

EMILY. I can't, Louise. I've got to go home. Good-by. Oh, Earnestine! Earnestine! Can you come over tonight and do Algebra? I did the first and third in Study Hall. No, they're not hard. But, Earnestine, that Caesar's awful hard. I don't see why we have to do a thing like that.

Come over about seven. Tell your mother you *have* to. G'by.
G'by, Helen. G'by, Fred.

[GEORGE, *also carrying books, catches up with her.*]

GEORGE. Can I carry your books home for you, Emily?

EMILY (*coldly*). Thank you. (*She gives them to him.*)

GEORGE. Excuse me a minute, Emily.—Say, Bob, get everything ready. I'll be there in a quarter of an hour. If I'm a little late start practice anyway. And give Herb some long high ones. His eye needs a lot of practice. Seeya later.

EMILY. Good-by, Lizzy.

GEORGE. Good-by, Lizzy.—I'm awfully glad you were elected, too, Emily.

EMILY. Thank you. (*They have been standing on Main Street, almost against the back wall.* GEORGE *is about to take the first steps towards the audience when he stops again and says:*)

GEORGE. Emily, why are you mad at me?

EMILY. I'm not mad at you.

GEORGE. You . . . you treat me so funny.

EMILY. Well, I might as well say it right out, George. I don't like the whole change that's come over you in the last year. I'm sorry if that hurts your feelings, but I've just got to tell the truth and shame the devil.

GEORGE. I'm awfully sorry, Emily. Wha-a-what do you mean?

EMILY. Well, up to a year ago I used to like you a lot. And I used to watch you as you did everything . . . because we'd been friends so long . . . and then you began spending all your time at baseball . . . and you never even spoke to anybody any more; not even to your own family you didn't . . . and, George, it's a fact, you've got awful conceited and stuck-up, and all the girls say so. They may not say so to your face, but that's what they say about you behind your back, and it hurts me to hear them say it, but I've got to agree with them a little. I'm sorry if it hurts your feelings . . . but I can't be sorry I said it.

GEORGE. I . . . I'm glad you said it, Emily. I never thought that such a thing was happening to me. I guess it's hard for a fella not to have faults creep into his character. (*They take a step or two in silence, then stand still in misery.*)

EMILY. I always expect a man to be perfect and I think he should be.

GEORGE. Oh . . . I don't think it's possible to be perfect, Emily.

EMILY. Well, my father is, and as far as I can see your father is. There's no reason on earth why you shouldn't be, too.

GEORGE. Well, Emily . . . I feel it's the other way round. That men aren't naturally good; but girls are. Like you and your mother and my mother.

EMILY. Well, you might as well know right now that I'm not perfect. It's not as easy for a girl to be perfect as a man, because we girls are more nervous.—Now I'm sorry I said all that about you. I don't know what made me say it.

GEORGE. No, no,—I guess if it's the truth you ought to say it. You stick to it, Emily.

EMILY. I don't know if it's the truth or not. And I suddenly feel that it isn't important at all.

GEORGE. Emily, would you like an ice-cream soda, or something, before you go home?

EMILY. Well, thank you. . . . I would. (*They come into the drugstore and seat themselves on the stools.*)

STAGE MANAGER (*as* MR. MORGAN). Hello, George. Hello, Emily. What'll you have? Why, Emily Webb, what've you been crying about?

GEORGE (*he gropes for an explanation*). She . . . she just got an awful scare, Mr. Morgan. She almost got run over by that hardware store wagon. Everybody always says that Tom Huckins drives like a crazy man.

STAGE MANAGER. Here, take a drink of water, Emily. You look all shook up. There!—Now, what'll you have?

EMILY. I'll have a strawberry phosphate, thank you, Mr. Morgan.

GEORGE. No, no. You go and have an ice-cream soda with me, Emily.—Two strawberry ice-cream sodas, Mr. Morgan.

STAGE MANAGER (*working the faucets*). Yes, sir. I tell you, you've got to look both ways before you cross Main Street these days. Gets worse every year. There are a hundred and twenty-five horses in Grover's Corners this minute I'm talking to you. State Inspector was in here yesterday. And now they're bringing in these auto-mo-biles, the best thing to do is to just stay home. Why, I can remember the time when a dog could lie down all day in the middle of Main Street and nothing would come to disturb him.—Yes, Miss Ellis; be with you in a minute. Here are your sodas. Enjoy 'em. (*He goes off.*)

EMILY. They're so expensive.

GEORGE. No, no,—don't you think of that. We're celebrating. First, we're celebrating our election. And then do you know what else I'm celebrating?

EMILY. No.

GEORGE. I'm celebrating because I've got a friend who tells me all the things that ought to be told me.

EMILY. George, *please* don't think of that. I don't know why I said it. It's not true. You're—

GEORGE. No, you stick to it, Emily. I'm glad you spoke to me like you did. But you'll see: I'm going to change so quick—you bet I'm going to change. And, Emily, I want to ask you a favor.

EMILY. What?

GEORGE. Emily, if I go away to State Agriculture College next year, will you write me a letter once in a while?

EMILY. I certainly will. I certainly will, George. . . . (*Pause.*) It certainly seems like being away three years you'd get out of touch with things.

GEORGE. No, no. I mustn't do that. You see I'm not only going to be just a farmer. After a while maybe I'll run for something to get elected. So your letters'll be very important to me; you know, telling me what's going on here and everything. . . .

EMILY. Just the same, three years is a long time. Maybe letters from Grover's Corners wouldn't be so interesting after a while. Grover's Corners isn't a very important place when you think of all New Hampshire; but I think it's a very nice town.

GEORGE. The day wouldn't come when I wouldn't want to know everything that's happening here. I know *that's* true, Emily.

EMILY. Well, I'll try to make my letters interesting. (*Pause.*)

GEORGE. Y'know, Emily, whenever I meet a farmer I ask him if he thinks it's important to go to Agriculture School to be a good farmer.

EMILY. Why, George—

GEORGE. Yeah, and some of them say that it's even a waste of time. You can get all those things, anyway, out of the pamphlets the government sends out. And Uncle Luke's getting old,—he's about ready for me to start in taking over his farm tomorrow, if I could.

EMILY. My!

GEORGE. And, like you say, being gone all that time . . . in other places and meeting other people . . . If anything like that can happen I don't want to go away. I guess new people aren't any better than old ones. I'll bet they almost never are. Emily, . . . I feel that you're as good a friend as I've got. I don't need to go and meet the people in other towns.

EMILY. But, George, maybe it's very important for you to go and learn all that about cattle-judging and soils and those things. And if you're going into politics, maybe you ought to meet people from other parts of the State . . . of course, I don't know.

GEORGE (*after a pause*). Emily, I'm going to make up my mind right now. I won't go. I'll tell Pa about it tonight.

EMILY. Why, George, I don't see why you have to decide right now. It's a whole year away.

GEORGE. Emily, I'm glad you spoke to me about that . . . that fault in my character. And what you said was right; but there was *one* thing wrong in it, and that was when you said that for a year I wasn't noticing people, and . . . you, for instance. Listen, Emily . . . you say you were watching me when I did everything. . . . Why, I was doing the same about you all the time. Why, sure,—I always thought about you as one of the chief people I thought about. I always made sure where you were sitting on the bleachers, and who you were with. And we've always had lots of talks . . . and joking, in the halls; and they always meant a lot to me. Of course, they weren't as good as the talk we're having now. Lately I'd been noticing that you'd been acting kind of funny to me, and for three days I've been trying to walk home with you, but something's always got in the way. Yesterday I was standing over against the wall waiting for you, and you walked home with Miss Corcoran.

EMILY. George! . . . Life's awful funny! How could I have known that? Why, I thought—

GEORGE. Listen, Emily, I'm going to tell you why I'm not going to Agriculture School. I think that once you've found a person that you're very fond of . . . I mean a person who's fond of you, too,—at least enough to be interested in your character . . . Well, I think that's just as important as college is, and even more so. That's what I think.

EMILY. I think it's awfully important, too.

GEORGE. Emily.

EMILY. Yes, George.

GEORGE. Emily, if I improve and make a big change . . . would you be . . . I mean: *could* you be . . .

EMILY. I . . . I am now; I always have been.

GEORGE (*pause*). So I guess this is an important talk we've been having.

EMILY. Yes.

GEORGE (*takes a deep breath and straightens his back*). Wait just a minute and I'll take you home. (*He rises and goes to the* STAGE MANAGER *who appears and comes toward him.*) Mr. Morgan, I'll have to go home and get the money to pay you for this. It'll only take me a minute.

STAGE MANAGER. What's that? George Gibbs, do you mean to tell me—!

GEORGE. Yes, but I had reasons, Mr. Morgan.—Look, here's my gold watch to keep until I come back with the money.

STAGE MANAGER. That's all right. Keep your watch. I'll trust you.

GEORGE. I'll be back in five minutes.

STAGE MANAGER. I'll trust you ten years, George,—not a day more.—Got all over your shock, Emily?

EMILY. Yes, thank you, Mr. Morgan. It was nothing.

GEORGE (*taking up the books from the counter*). I'm ready. (*They walk in grave silence down the stage, turn, and pass through the trellis at the Webbs' back door and disappear.*)

STAGE MANAGER. Thank you, Emily. Thank you, George.

Now before we go on to the wedding, there are still some more things we ought to know about this—about this marriage.

I want to know some more about how the parents took it; but what

I want to know most of all is: oh, you know what I mean,—what Grover's Corners thought about marriage anyway.

You know's well as I do: people are never able to say right out what they think of money, or death, or fame, or marriage. You've got to catch it between the lines; you've got to *over*-hear it.

Oh, Doctor! Mrs. Gibbs! (*They appear at their side of the stage and exchange a glance of understanding with him. The* STAGE MANAGER *lays the same plank across two chairs that served as a drugstore counter and it has now become* MRS. GIBBS's *ironing board.* DR. GIBBS *sits down in a rocker and smokes.*)

[MRS. GIBBS *irons a moment in silence; then goes to the foot of the stairs and calls:*]

MRS. GIBBS. Rebecca! It's time you turned out your light and went to sleep. George, you'd better get some sleep, too.

REBECCA'S VOICE. Ma, I haven't finished my English.

MRS. GIBBS. What? Well, I bet you haven't been working, Rebecca. You've been reading that Sears, Roebuck catalogue, that's what you've been doing.—All right, I'll give you ten more minutes. If you haven't finished by then you'll just have to fail the course and be a disgrace to your father and me.—George, what are you doing?

GEORGE'S VOICE (*hurt*). I'm doing history.

MRS. GIBBS. Well, you'd better go to bed. You're probably sleeping at the desk as it is. (*She casts an amused eye at her husband and returns to her ironing.*)

DR. GIBBS. I had a long talk with the boy today.

MRS. GIBBS. Did you?

DR. GIBBS. I tell you, Mrs. G., there's nothing so terrifying in the world as a son. The relation of a father to a son is the damnedest, awkwardest— I always come away feeling like a soggy sponge of hypocrisy.

MRS. GIBBS. Well, a mother and a daughter's no picnic, let me tell you.

DR. GIBBS. George is set on it: he wants to marry Emily 'soon as school's out and take her right on to the farm. (*Pause.*) He says he can sit up nights and learn agriculture from government pamphlets, without going to college for it.

MRS. GIBBS. He always was crazy about farming. Gets that from my people.

DR. GIBBS. At a pinch, I guess he could start in farming;—but I swear I think he's too young to get married. Julia, he's just a green half-grown kid. He isn't ready to be a family man.

MRS. GIBBS. No, he ain't. You're right.—But he's a good boy and I wouldn't like to think of him being alone out there . . . coming into town Satiddy nights, like any old farm hand, tuckered out from work and looking for excitement. He might get into bad ways. It wouldn't be enough fun for him to come and sit by our stove,—and holding hands with Emily for a year mightn't be enough either. He might lose interest in her.

DR. GIBBS. Hm.

MRS. GIBBS. Frank, I've been watching her. George is a lucky boy when you think of all the silly girls in the world.

DR. GIBBS. But, Julia,—George *married*. That great gangling selfish nincompoop.

MRS. GIBBS. Yes, I know. (*She takes up a collar and examines it.*) Frank, what do you do to your collars? Do you gnaw 'em? I never saw such a man for collars.

DR. GIBBS. Julia, when I married you, do you know what one of my terrors was in getting married?

MRS. GIBBS. Pshaw! Go on with you!

DR. GIBBS. I was afraid we weren't going to have material for conversation more'n 'ld last us a few weeks. I was afraid we'd run out and eat our meals in silence, that's a fact. You and I've been conversing for twenty years now without any noticeable barren spells.

MRS. GIBBS. Well, good weather, bad weather, 'tain't very choice, but I always manage to find something to say. (*Pause.*)

DR. GIBBS. What do you think? What do you think, Julia? Shall we tell the boy he can go ahead and get married?

MRS. GIBBS. Seems like it's up to us to decide. Myrtle and Charles Webb are willing. They think it's a good idea to throw the young people into the sea and let'm sink or swim, as soon as they're ready.

DR. GIBBS. What does that mean? Must we decide right now? This minute?

MRS. GIBBS. There you go putting the responsibility on me!

DR. GIBBS. Here it is, almost April.—I'll go up and say a word to him right now before he goes to bed. (*He rises.*) You're sure, Julia? You've nothing more to add?

MRS. GIBBS (*stops ironing a moment*). I don't know what to say. Seems like it's too much to ask, for a big outdoor boy like that to go and get shut up in classrooms for three years. And once he's on the farm, he might just as well have a companion, seeing he's found a fine girl like Emily. . . . People are meant to live two-by-two in this world. . . . Yes, Frank, go up and tell him it's all right.

DR. GIBBS (*crosses and is about to call when—*)

MRS. GIBBS (*her hands on her cheeks, staring into the audience, in sharp alarm*). Wait a minute! Wait a minute!—(*Then resuming her ironing.*) No,—go and tell him.

DR. GIBBS. Why did you stop then, Julia?

MRS. GIBBS. Oh, you know: I thought of all those times we went through in the first years when George and Rebecca were babies,—you walking up and down with them at three in the morning; the whooping-cough;

the time George fell off the porch. You and I were twenty-five years old, and more. It's wonderful how one forgets one's troubles, like that.—Yes, Frank, go upstairs and tell him. . . . It's worth it.

DR. GIBBS. Yes, they'll have a lot of troubles, but that's none of our business. Let'm. Everybody has a right to his own troubles.—You ought to be present, Julia,—important occasion like that. I'll call him.—George! Oh, George!

GEORGE'S VOICE. Yes, Pa.

DR. GIBBS. Can you come down a minute? Your mother and I want to speak to you.

GEORGE. Yeah, sure.

MRS. GIBBS (*putting her arm through her husband's*). Lord, what a fool I am: I'm trembling all over. There's nothing to tremble about.

STAGE MANAGER. Thank you! Thank you!

Now we're ready to go on with the wedding.

[*While he talks, the actors remove the chair and tables and trellises from the Gibbs and Webb homes.*]

[*They arrange the pews for the church in the back of the stage. The congregation will sit facing the back wall. The aisle of the church is in the middle of the scene.*]

[*A small platform is placed against the back wall on which the* STAGE MANAGER *as Minister can stand.*]

There are a lot of things to be said about a wedding; there are a lot of thoughts that go on during a wedding.

We can't get them all into one wedding, naturally, and especially not into a wedding at Grover's Corners where they're awfully plain and short.

In this wedding I play the minister. That gives me the right to say a few more things about it.

For a while now, the play gets pretty serious.

Y'see, some churches say that marriage is a sacrament. I don't quite know what that means, but I can guess. Like Mrs. Gibbs said a few minutes ago: People were made to live two-by-two.

This is a good wedding, but people are so put together that even at a good wedding there's a lot of confusion way down deep in people's minds and we thought that that ought to be in our play, too.

The real hero of this scene isn't on the stage at all, and you know who that is. It's like what one of those European fellas said: every child born into the world is Nature's attempt to make a perfect human being. Well, we've seen nature pushing and contriving for some time now. We all know that nature's interested in quantity; but I think she's interested in quality, too,—that's why I'm in the ministry.—Maybe she's trying to make another good governor for New Hampshire.

And don't forget the other witnesses at this wedding,—the ancestors. Millions of them. Most of them set out to live two-by-two, also. Millions of them.

Well, that's all my sermon. 'Twan't very long, anyway.

[*The organ starts playing Handel's "Largo." The congregation streams into the church and sits in silence.*

[MRS. WEBB, *on the way to her place, turns back and speaks to the audience.*]

MRS. WEBB. I don't know why on earth I should be crying. I suppose there's nothing to cry about. It came over me at breakfast this morning; there was Emily eating her breakfast as she's done for seventeen years and now she's going off to eat it in someone else's house. I suppose that's it.

And Emily! She suddenly said: I can't eat another mouthful, and she put her head down on the table and *she* cried. (*She starts toward her seat in the church, but turns back and adds:*) Oh, I've got to say it: you know, there's something downright cruel about sending our girls out into marriage this way.

I hope some of her girl friends have told her a thing or two. It's cruel, I know, but I couldn't bring myself to say anything. I went into it blind as a bat myself.

The whole world's wrong, that's what's the matter. There they come. (*She hurries to her place in the pew.*)

[GEORGE *starts to come down the right aisle of the theater, through the audience.*

[*Suddenly three members of his baseball team appear by the right proscenium pillar and start whistling and catcalling to him. They are dressed for the ball field.*]

THE BASEBALL PLAYERS. Eh, George, George! Hsst—yaow! If things don't go right, call us in. We know what to do. Eh, fellas? Yaow! George, don't look so innocent, you old geezer. We know what you're thinking. Don't disgrace the team, big boy. Whoo-oo-oo.

STAGE MANAGER. All right! All right! That'll do. That's enough of that. (*Smiling, he pushes them off the stage. They lean back to shout a few more catcalls.*) There used to be an awful lot of that kind of thing at weddings in the old days,—Rome, and later. We're more civilized now,—so they say.

[*The choir starts singing "Love divine, all love excelling."* GEORGE *has reached the stage. He stares at the congregation a moment, then takes a few steps of withdrawal, toward the right proscenium pillar.*]

GEORGE (*darkly, to himself*). I wish I were back at school. . . . I don't want to get married.

[*His mother has left her seat and come toward him. She stops, looking at him anxiously.*]

MRS. GIBBS. George, what's the matter?

GEORGE. Ma, I don't want to grow *old*. Why's everybody pushing me so?

MRS. GIBBS. Why, George . . . you wanted it.

GEORGE. Why do I have to get married at all? Listen, Ma, for the last time I ask you—

MRS. GIBBS. No, no, George . . . you're a man now.

GEORGE. Listen, Ma, you never listen to me. All I want to do is to be a fella . . . why do—

MRS. GIBBS. George! If anyone should hear you! Now stop. Why, I'm ashamed of you!

GEORGE (*passing his hand over his forehead*). What's the matter? I've been dreaming. Where's Emily?

MRS. GIBBS. Gracious! You gave me such a turn.

GEORGE. Cheer up, Ma. What are you looking so funny for? Cheer up; I'm getting married.

MRS. GIBBS. Let me catch my breath a minute.

GEORGE. Now, Ma, you save Thursday nights. Emily and I are coming over to dinner every Thursday night . . . you'll see. Ma, what are you crying for? Come on; we've got to get ready for this.

[*In the meantime,* EMILY, *in white and wearing her wedding veil, has come through the audience and mounted on to the stage. She too draws back when she sees the congregation in the church. The choir begins: "Blessed be the tie that binds."*]

EMILY. I never felt so alone in my whole life. And George over there, looking so . . . ! I *hate* him. I wish I were dead. Papa! Papa!

MR. WEBB (*leaves his seat in the pews and comes toward her anxiously*). Emily! Emily! Now don't get upset. . . .

EMILY. But, Papa,—I don't want to get married. . . .

MR. WEBB. Sh-sh—Emily. Everything's all right.

EMILY. Why can't I stay for a while just as I am? Let's go away.

MR. WEBB. No, no, Emily. Now stop and think.

EMILY. Don't you remember that you used to say,—all the time you used to say that I was *your* girl. There must be lots of places we can go to. Let's go away. I'll work for you. I could keep house.

MR. WEBB. Sh. . . . You mustn't think of such things. You're just nervous, Emily. Now, now,—you're marrying the best young fellow in the world. George is a fine fellow.

EMILY. But, Papa,—

MR. WEBB. George! George!

[MRS. GIBBS *returns to her seat.*

[GEORGE *hears* MR. WEBB *and looks up.*

[MR. WEBB *beckons to him. They move to the center of the stage.*]

I'm giving away my daughter, George. Do you think you can take care of her?

GEORGE. Mr. Webb, I want to .·. . I want to try. Emily, I'm going to do my best. I love you, Emily. I need you.

EMILY. Well, if you love me, help me. All I want is someone to love me.

GEORGE. I will, Emily.

EMILY. If ever I'm sick or in trouble, that's what I mean.

GEORGE. Emily, I'll try. I'll try.

EMILY. And I mean for *ever*. Do you hear? For ever and ever. (*They fall into each other's arms.*)

[*The March from "Lohengrin" is heard.*]

MR. WEBB. Come, they're waiting for us. Now you know it'll be all right. Come, quick.

[GEORGE *slips away and takes his place beside the* STAGE MANAGER-CLERGYMAN.

[EMILY *proceeds up the aisle on her father's arm.*]

STAGE MANAGER. Do you, George, take this woman, Emily, to be your wedded wife, to have . . .

[MRS. SOAMES *has been sitting in the last row of the congregation.*

[*She now turns to her neighbors and in a shrill voice says:*]

MRS. SOAMES. Perfectly lovely wedding! Loveliest wedding I ever saw. Oh, I do love a good wedding, don't you? Doesn't she make a lovely bride?

GEORGE. I do.

STAGE MANAGER. Do you, Emily, take this man, George, to be your wedded husband,—

MRS. SOAMES. Don't know *when* I've seen such a lovely wedding. But I always cry. Don't know why it is, but I always cry. I just like to see young people happy, don't you? Oh, I think it's lovely.

[*The ring.*

[*The kiss.*

[*The stage is suddenly arrested into silent tableau.*

[*The* STAGE MANAGER, *his eyes on the distance, says to the audience:*]

I've married two hundred couples in my day.

Do I believe in it?

I don't know.

M. . . . marries N. . . . millions of them.

The cottage, the gocart, the Sunday afternoon drives in the Ford, the children leaving the home, the first rheumatism, the grandchildren, the second rheumatism, the deathbed, the reading of the will,— Once in a thousand times it's interesting.

Well, let's have Mendelssohn's "Wedding March"!

[*The organ picks up the March.*

[*The bride and groom come down the aisle, radiant, but trying to be very dignified.*]

MRS. SOAMES. Aren't they a lovely couple? Oh, I've never been to such a nice wedding. I'm sure they'll be happy. I always say: *happiness,* that's the great thing! The important thing is to be happy.

[*The bride and groom reach the steps leading into the audience. A bright light is thrown upon them. They descend into the auditorium and run up the aisle joyously.*]

STAGE MANAGER. That's all the Second Act. Ten minutes' intermission, folks.

ACT THREE

During the intermission the audience has seen the actors arranging the stage. On the right hand side, a little right of the center, ten or twelve ordinary chairs have been placed in three openly spaced rows facing the audience. These are graves in the cemetery.

Towards the end of the intermission the actors enter and take their places. The front row contains: toward the center of the stage, an empty chair; then MRS. GIBBS; SIMON STIMSON. *The second row contains, among others,* MRS. SOAMES. *The third row has* WALLY WEBB.

The dead sit in a quiet without stiffness, and in a patience without listlessness.

The STAGE MANAGER *takes his accustomed place and waits for the houselights to go down.*

STAGE MANAGER. This time nine years have gone by, friends—summer, 1913. Gradual changes in Grover's Corners. Horses are getting rarer. Farmers coming into town in Fords.

Chief difference is in the young people, far as I can see. They want to go to the moving pictures all the time. They want to wear clothes like they see there . . . want to be citified.

Everybody locks their house doors now at night.

Ain't been any burglars in town yet, but everybody's heard about 'em.

But you'd be surprised though—on the. whole, things don't change much at Grover's Corners.

Guess you want to know what all these chairs are here fur. Smarter ones have guessed it already. I don't know how you feel about such things; but this certainly is a beautiful place. It's on a hilltop—a windy hilltop—lots of sky, lots of clouds,—often lots of sun and moon and stars. You come up here on a fine afternoon and you can see range on range of hills—awful blue they are—up there by Lake Sunapee and Lake Winnepesaukee . . . and way up, if you've got a glass, you can see the White Mountains and Mt. Washington—where North Conway and Conway is. And, of course, our favorite mountain, Mt. Monadnock's, right here—and all around it lie these towns—Jaffrey, 'n East Jaffrey, 'n Peterborough, 'n Dublin and (*then pointing down in the audience*) there, quite a ways down is Grover's Corners. Yes, beautiful spot up here. Mountain laurel and li-lacks. I often wonder why people like to be buried in Woodlawn and Brooklyn when they might pass the same time up here in New Hampshire. Over in that corner—(*pointing to stage left*) are the old stones,—1670, 1680. Strong-minded people that come a long way to be independent. Summer people walk around there laughing at the funny words on the tombstones . . . it don't do any harm. And genealogists come up from Boston—get paid by city people for looking up their ancestors. They want to make sure they're Daughters of the American Revolution and of the *Mayflower*. . . . Well, I guess that don't do any harm, either. Wherever you come near the human race, there's layers and layers of nonsense. . . .

Over there are some Civil War veterans too. Iron flags on their graves. . . . New Hampshire boys . . . had a notion that the Union ought to be kept together, though they'd never seen more than fifty miles of it themselves. All they knew was the name, friends—the United States of America. The United States of America. And they went and died about it.

This here is the new part of the cemetery. Here's your friend, Mrs. Gibbs. 'N let me see— Here's Mr. Stimson, organist at the Congregational Church. And over there's Mrs. Soames who enjoyed the wedding so—you remember? Oh, and a lot of others. And Editor Webb's boy, Wallace, whose appendix burst while he was on a Boy Scout trip to Crawford Notch.

Yes, an awful lot of sorrow has sort of quieted down up here. People just wild with grief have brought their relatives up to this hill. We all know how it is . . . and then time . . . and sunny days . . . and rainy days . . . 'n snow . . . tz-tz-tz. We're all glad they're in a beautiful place and we're coming up here ourselves when our fit's over.

This certainly is an important part of Grover's Corners. A lot of thoughts come up here, night and day, but there's no post office.

Now I'm going to tell you some things you know already. You know'm as well as I do; but you don't take'm out and look at'm very often.

I don't care what they say with their mouths—everybody knows that *something* is eternal. And it ain't houses and it ain't names, and it ain't earth, and it ain't even the stars . . . everybody knows in their bones that *something* is eternal, and that something has to do with human beings. All the greatest people ever lived have been telling us that for five thousand years and yet you'd be surprised how people are always losing hold of it. There's something way down deep that's eternal about every human being. (*Pause.*) You know as well as I do that the dead don't stay interested in us living people for very long. Gradually, gradually, they let hold of the earth . . . and the ambitions they had . . . and the pleasures they had . . . and the things they suffered . . . and the people they loved.

They get weaned away from earth—that's the way I put it,—weaned away.

Yes, they stay here while the earth-part of 'em burns away, burns out, and all that time they slowly get indifferent to what's goin' on in Grover's Corners.

They're waitin'. They're waitin' for something that they feel is comin'. Something important and great. Aren't they waitin' for the eternal part in them to come out clear?

Some of the things they're going to say maybe'll hurt your feelings— but that's the way it is: mother 'n daughter . . . husband 'n wife . . . enemy 'n enemy . . . money 'n miser . . . all those terribly important things kind of grow pale around here. And what's left? What's left when memory's gone, and your identity, Mrs. Smith? (*He looks at the audience a minute, then turns to the stage.*) Well! There are some *living* people. There's Joe Stoddard, our undertaker, supervising a new-made grave. And here comes a Grover's Corners boy that left town to go out West.

[JOE STODDARD *has hovered about in the background.* SAM CRAIG *enters left, wiping his forehead from the exertion. He carries an umbrella and strolls front.*]

SAM CRAIG. Good afternoon, Joe Stoddard.

JOE STODDARD. Good afternoon, good afternoon. Let me see now: Do I know you?

SAM CRAIG. I'm Sam Craig.

JOE STODDARD. Gracious sakes alive! Of all people! I should'a knowed you'd be back for the funeral. You've been away a long time, Sam.

SAM CRAIG. Yes, I've been away over twelve years. I'm in business out in Buffalo now, Joe. But I was in the East when I got news of my cousin's death, so I thought I'd combine things a little and come and see the old home. You look well.

JOE STODDARD. Yes, yes, can't complain. Very sad, our journey today, Samuel.

SAM CRAIG. Yes.

JOE STODDARD. Yes, yes. I always say, I hate to supervise when a young person is taken. I see you brought your umbrella. It's going to rain and make it sadder still, seems like. They'll be here in a few minutes now. I had to come here early today—my son's supervisin' at the home.

SAM CRAIG (*reading stones*). Old Farmer McCarty, I used to do chores for him—after school. He had the lumbago.

JOE STODDARD. Yes, we brought Farmer McCarty here a number of years ago now.

SAM CRAIG (*staring at* MRS. GIBBS's *knees*). Why, this is my Aunt Julia. . . . I'd forgotten that she'd . . . of course, of course.

JOE STODDARD. Yes, Doc Gibbs lost his wife two-three years ago . . . about this time. And today's another pretty bad blow for him, too.

MRS. GIBBS (*to* SIMON STIMSON: *in an even voice*). That's my sister Carey's boy, Sam. . . . Sam Craig.

SIMON STIMSON. I'm always uncomfortable when *they're* around.

MRS. GIBBS. Simon.

SIMON STIMSON. They and their nonsense and their damned glee at being alive. . . .

MRS. GIBBS. Simon, be patient. . . .

SAM CRAIG. Do they choose their own verses much, Joe?

JOE STODDARD. No . . . not usual. Mostly the bereaved pick a verse.

SAM CRAIG. Doesn't sound like Aunt Julia. There aren't many of those Hersey sisters left now. Let me see: Where are . . . I wanted to look at my father's and mother's . . .

JOE STODDARD. Over there with the Craigs. . . . Avenue F.

SAM CRAIG. (*reading* SIMON STIMSON's *epitaph*). He was organist at church, wasn't he?—Hm, drank a lot, we used to say.

JOE STODDARD. Nobody was supposed to know about it. He'd seen a peck of trouble. Those musical fellas ain't like the rest of us, I reckon. (*Behind his hand.*) Took his own life, y'know?

SAM CRAIG. Oh, did he?

JOE STODDARD. Hung himself in the attic. They tried to hush it up, but of course it got around. His wife's just married Senator Barstow. Many a time I've seen her, eleven o'clock at night, goin' around the streets huntin' for her husband. Think o' that! Now she's married to Senator Barstow over at Manchester. He chose his own epy-taph. You can see it there. It ain't a verse exactly.

SAM CRAIG. Why, it's just some notes of music—what is it?

JOE STODDARD. Oh, I wouldn't know. It was wrote up in the Boston papers at the time.

SAM CRAIG. Joe, what did she die of?

JOE STODDARD. Who?

SAM CRAIG. My cousin.

JOE STODDARD. Oh, didn't you know? Had some trouble bringing a baby into the world. Let's see, today's Friday—'twas almost a week ago now.

SAM CRAIG (*putting up his umbrella*). Did the baby live?

JOE STODDARD (*raising his coat collar*). No. 'Twas her second, though. There's a little boy 'bout four years old.

SAM CRAIG. The grave's going to be over there?

JOE STODDARD. Yes, there ain't much more room over here among the Gibbses, so they're opening up a whole new Gibbs section over by Avenue B. You'll excuse me now. I see they're comin'.

THE DEAD (*not lugubrious; and strongly New England in accent*). Rain'll do a lot of good.—Yes, reckon things were gettin' downright parched. Don't look like it's goin' to last long, though.—Lemuel, you remember the floods of '79? Carried away all the bridges but one.

[*From left to right, at the back of the stage, comes a procession. Four men carry a coffin, invisible to us. All the rest are under umbrellas. One can vaguely see:* DR. GIBBS, GEORGE, *the* WEBBS, *etc. They gather about a grave in the back center of the stage, a little to the left of center.*]

MRS. SOAMES. Who is it, Julia?

MRS. GIBBS (*without raising her eyes*). My daughter-in-law, Emily Webb.

MRS. SOAMES (*a little surprised, but no emotion*). Well, I declare! The road up here must have been awful muddy. What did she die of, Julia?

MRS. GIBBS. In childbirth.

MRS. SOAMES. Childbirth. (*Almost with a laugh.*) I'd forgotten all about that! My, wasn't life awful—(*With a sigh.*) and wonderful.

SIMON STIMSON (*with a sideways glance*). Wonderful, was it?

MRS. GIBBS. Simon! Now, remember!

MRS. SOAMES. I remember Emily's wedding. Wasn't it a lovely wedding! And I remember her reading the class poem at Graduation Exercises. Emily was one of the brightest girls ever graduated from High School. I've heard Principal Wilkins say so time after time. I called on them at their new farm, just before I died. Perfectly beautiful farm.

A WOMAN FROM AMONG THE DEAD. It's on the same road we lived on.

A MAN AMONG THE DEAD. Yes, just near the Elks' picnic grounds. Remember, Joe? By the lake where we always used to go Fourth of July? Right smart farm.

[*They subside. The group by the grave starts singing "Blessed be the tie that binds."*]

A WOMAN AMONG THE DEAD. I always liked that hymn. I was hopin' they'd sing a hymn.

A MAN AMONG THE DEAD. My wife—my second wife—knows all the verses of about every hymn there is. It just beats the Dutch . . . she can go through them all by heart.

[*Pause. Suddenly* EMILY *appears from among the umbrellas. She is wearing a white dress. Her hair is down her back and tied by a white ribbon like a little girl. She comes slowly, gazing wonderingly at the dead, a little dazed. She stops halfway and smiles faintly.*]

EMILY. Hello.

VOICES AMONG THE DEAD. Hello, Emily. H'lo, M's. Gibbs.

EMILY. Hello, Mother Gibbs.

MRS. GIBBS. Emily.

EMILY. Hello. (*The hymn continues.* EMILY *looks back at the funeral. She says dreamily:*) It's raining.

MRS. GIBBS. Yes. . . . They'll be gone soon, dear. Just rest yourself.

[EMILY *sits down in the empty chair by* MRS. GIBBS.]

EMILY. It seems thousands and thousands of years since I . . . How stupid they all look. They don't have to look like that!

MRS. GIBBS. Don't look at them now, dear. They'll be gone soon.

EMILY. Oh, I wish I'd been here a long time. I don't like being new here.—How do you do, Mr. Stimson?

SIMON STIMSON. How do you do, Emily?

[EMILY *continues to look about her with a wan and wondering smile; but for a moment her eyes do not return to the funeral group. As though to shut out from her mind the thought of that group she starts speaking to* MRS. GIBBS *with a touch of nervousness.*]

EMILY. Mother Gibbs, George and I have made that farm into just the best place you ever saw. We thought of you all the time. We wanted to show you the new barn and a great long ce-ment drinking fountain for the stock. We bought that out of the money you left us.

MRS. GIBBS. I did?

EMILY. Don't you remember, Mother Gibbs—the legacy you left us? Why, it was over three hundred and fifty dollars.

MRS. GIBBS. Yes, yes, Emily.

EMILY. Well, there's a patent device on this drinking fountain so that it never overflows, Mother Gibbs, and it never sinks below a certain mark they have there. It's fine. (*Her voice trails off and her eyes return to the funeral group.*) It won't be the same to George without me, but it's a lovely farm. (*Suddenly she looks directly at* MRS. GIBBS.) Live people don't understand, do they?

MRS. GIBBS. No, dear—not very much.

EMILY. They're sort of shut up in little boxes, aren't they? I feel as though I knew them last a thousand years ago. . . . My boy is spending the day at Mrs. Carter's. (*She sees* MR. CARTER *among the dead.*) Oh, Mr. Carter, my little boy is spending the day at your house.

MR. CARTER. Is he?

EMILY. Yes, he loves it there.—Mother Gibbs, we have a Ford, too. Never gives any trouble. I don't drive, though. Mother Gibbs, when does this feeling go away?—Of being . . . one of *them?* How long does it . . . ?

MRS. GIBBS. Sh! dear. Just wait and be patient.

EMILY (*with a sigh*). I know.—Look, they're finished. They're going.

MRS. GIBBS. Sh—.

[*The umbrellas leave the stage.* DR. GIBBS *comes over to his wife's grave and stands before it a moment.* EMILY *looks up at his face.* MRS. GIBBS *does not raise her eyes.*]

EMILY. Look! Father Gibbs is bringing some of my flowers to you. He looks just like George, doesn't he? Oh, Mother Gibbs, I never realized before how troubled and how . . . how in the dark live persons are. From morning till night, that's all they are—troubled.

[DR. GIBBS *goes off*.]

THE DEAD. Little cooler than it was.—Yes, that rain's cooled it off a little. Those northeast winds always do the same thing, don't they? If it isn't a rain, it's a three-day blow.—Reckon it may clear up before night; often does.

[*A patient calm falls on the stage. The* STAGE MANAGER *appears at his proscenium pillar smoking.* EMILY *sits up abruptly with an idea.*]

EMILY. But, Mother Gibbs, one can go back; one can go back there again . . . into living. I feel it. I know it. Why, just then for a moment I was thinking about . . . about the farm . . . and for a minute I *was* there, and my baby was on my lap as plain as day.

MRS. GIBBS. Yes, of course you can.

EMILY. I can go back there and live all those days over again . . . why not?

MRS. GIBBS. All I can say is, Emily, don't.

EMILY (*takes a few steps toward the* STAGE MANAGER). But it's true, isn't it? I can go and live . . . back there . . . again.

STAGE MANAGER. Yes, some have tried—but they soon come back here.

MRS. GIBBS. Don't do it, Emily.

MRS. SOAMES. Emily, don't. It's not what you think it'd be.

EMILY. But I won't live over a sad day. I'll choose a happy one—I'll choose the day I first knew that I loved George. Why should that be painful?

[*They are silent. Her question turns to the* STAGE MANAGER.]

STAGE MANAGER. You not only live it; but you watch yourself living it.

EMILY. Yes?

STAGE MANAGER. And as you watch it, you see the thing that they—down there—never know. You see the future. You know what's going to happen afterwards.

EMILY. But is that—painful? Why?

MRS. GIBBS. That's not the only reason why you shouldn't do it, Emily. When you've been here longer you'll see that our life here is our hope that soon we'll forget all that, and think only of what's ahead, and be ready for what's ahead. When you've been here longer you'll understand.

EMILY (*softly*). But, Mother Gibbs, how can I ever forget that life? It's all I know. It's all I had. (MRS. GIBBS *does not answer*.) Mr. Stimson, did you go back?

SIMON STIMSON (*sharply*). No.

EMILY. Did you, Mrs. Soames?

MRS. SOAMES. Oh, Emily. It isn't wise. Really, it isn't. All we can do is just warn you. It won't be what you expect.

EMILY (*slowly*). But it's a thing I must know for myself. I'll choose a happy day, anyway.

MRS. GIBBS. No. At least, choose an unimportant day. Choose the least important day in your life. It will be important enough.

EMILY (*to the* STAGE MANAGER). Then it can't be since I was married; or since the baby was born. I can choose a birthday at least, can't I?—I choose my twelfth birthday.

STAGE MANAGER. All right. February 11th, 1899. A Tuesday.—Do you want any special time of day?

EMILY. Oh, I want the whole day.

STAGE MANAGER. We'll begin at dawn. You remember it had been snowing for several days; but it had stopped the night before, and they had begun clearing the roads. The sun's coming up.

EMILY (*with a cry*). There's Main Street . . . why, that's Mr. Morgan's drugstore before he changed it! . . . And there's the livery stable. (*She walks toward the back of the stage.*)

STAGE MANAGER. Yes, it's 1899. This is fourteen years ago.

EMILY. Oh, that's the town I knew as a little girl. And, look, there's the old white fence that used to be around our house. Oh, I'd forgotten that! Oh, I love it so! Are *they* inside?

STAGE MANAGER. Yes, your mother'll be coming downstairs in a minute to make breakfast.

EMILY (*softly*). Will she?

STAGE MANAGER. And you remember: your father had been away for several days; he came back on the early morning train.

EMILY. No . . . ?

STAGE MANAGER. He'd been back to his college to make a speech—in Western New York, at Clinton.

EMILY. *Look!* There's Howie Newsome. There's our policeman. But he's *dead;* he *died.*

[*The* STAGE MANAGER *retires to his corner. The voices of* HOWIE NEWSOME, CONSTABLE WARREN *and* JOE CROWELL, JR., *are heard at the left of the stage.*]

HOWIE NEWSOME. Whoa, Bessie!—Bessie! 'Morning, Bill.

BILL. 'Morning, Howie.

HOWIE NEWSOME. You're up early.

BILL. Been rescuin' a party; darn near froze to death, down by Polish Town thar. Got drunk and lay out in the snowdrifts. Thought he was in bed when I shook'm.

EMILY. Why, there's Joe Crowell. . . .

JOE CROWELL. Good morning, Mr. Warren. 'Morning, Howie.

[MRS. WEBB *has appeared in her kitchen, but* EMILY *does not see her until she calls.*]

MRS. WEBB. Chil-*dren!* Wally! Emily! . . . Time to get up.

EMILY. Mama, here I am! Oh! how young Mama looks! I didn't know Mama was ever that young. Oh!

MRS. WEBB. You can come and dress by the kitchen fire, if you like; but hurry.

[HOWIE NEWSOME *has entered along Main Street and brings the milk to* MRS. WEBB'S *door.*]

Good morning, Mr. Newsome. Whhhh—it's cold.

HOWIE NEWSOME. Ten below by my barn, Mrs. Webb.

MRS. WEBB. Think of it! Keep yourself wrapped up. (*She takes her bottles in, shuddering.*)

EMILY (*with an effort*). Mama, I can't find my blue hair ribbon anywhere.

MRS. WEBB. Just open your eyes, dear, that's all. I laid it out for you special—on the dresser, there. If it were a snake it would bite you.

EMILY. Yes, yes. . . . (*She puts her hand on her heart.* MR. WEBB *comes along Main Street, where he meets* CONSTABLE WARREN.)

MR. WEBB. Good morning, Bill.

BILL. Good morning, Mr. Webb. You're up early.

MR. WEBB. Yes, just been back to my old college in New York State. Been any trouble here?

BILL. Well, I was called up this mornin' to rescue a Polish fella—darn near froze to death he was.

MR. WEBB. We must get it in the paper.

BILL. 'Twa'n't much.

EMILY (*whispers*). Papa.

[MR. WEBB *shakes the snow off his feet and enters his house.*]

MR. WEBB. Good morning, Mother.

MRS. WEBB. How did it go, Charles?

MR. WEBB. Oh, fine, I guess. I told'm a few things.

MRS. WEBB. Did you sit up on the train all night?

MR. WEBB. Yes. Never could sleep on a Pullman anyway.

MRS. WEBB. Charles, seems to me—we're rich enough so that you could sleep in a train once in a while.

MR. WEBB. Everything all right here?

MRS. WEBB. Yes—can't think of anything that's happened, special. Been right cold. Howie Newsome says it's ten below over to his barn.

MR. WEBB. Yes, well, it's colder than that at Hamilton College. Students' ears are falling off. It ain't Christian.—Paper have any mistakes in it?

MRS. WEBB. None that I noticed. Coffee's ready when you want it. (*He starts upstairs.*) Charles! Don't forget; it's Emily's birthday. Did you remember to get her something?

MR. WEBB (*patting his pocket*). Yes, I've got something here.

MRS. WEBB. Goodness sakes! I hope she likes what I got for her. I hunted hard enough for it. Chil-*dren!* Hurry up! Hurry up!

MR. WEBB. Where's my girl? Where's my birthday girl? (*He goes off left.*)

MRS. WEBB. Don't interrupt her now, Charles. You can see her at breakfast. She's slow enough as it is. Hurry up, children! It's seven o'clock. Now, I don't want to call you again.

EMILY (*softly, more in wonder than in grief*). I can't bear it. They're so young and beautiful. Why did they ever have to get old? Mama, I'm here. I'm grown up. I love you all, everything.—I can't look at every-thing hard enough. There's the butternut tree. (*She wanders up Main Street.*) There's Mr. Morgan's drugstore. And there's the High School, forever and ever, and ever. And there's the Congregational Church where I got married. Oh, dear. Oh, dear. Oh, dear!

[*The* STAGE MANAGER *beckons partially to her. He points to the house. She says a breathless "yes" and goes to the house.*]

Good morning, Mama.

MRS. WEBB (*at the foot of the stairs, kissing her in a matter-of-fact way*). Well, now, dear, a very happy birthday to my girl and many happy returns. There are some surprises waiting for you on the kitchen table.

EMILY. Oh, Mama, you *shouldn't* have. (*She throws an anguished glance at the* STAGE MANAGER.) I can't—I can't.

MRS. WEBB (*facing the audience, over her stove*). But birthday, or no birth-day, I want you to eat your breakfast good and slow. I want you to grow up and be a good strong girl. (*She goes to the stairs and calls.*) Wally! Wally, wash yourself good. Everything's getting cold down here. (*She returns to the stove with her back to* EMILY. EMILY *opens her parcels.*) That in the blue paper is from your Aunt Carrie and I reckon you can guess who brought the post card album. I found it on the door-step when I brought in the milk—George Gibbs . . . must have come over in the cold pretty early . . . right nice of him.

EMILY (*to herself*). Oh, George! I'd forgotten that. . . .

MRS. WEBB. Chew that bacon slow. It'll help keep you warm on a cold day.

EMILY (*beginning softly but urgently*). Oh, Mama, just look at me one minute as though you really saw me. Mama, fourteen years have gone by. I'm dead. You're a grandmother, Mama. I married George Gibbs, Mama. Wally's dead, too. Mama, his appendix burst on a camping trip to North Conway. We felt just terrible about it—don't you remember? But just for a moment now we're all together. Mama, just for a mo-ment we're happy. Let's look at one another.

MRS. WEBB. That in the yellow paper is something I found in the attic among your grandmother's things. You're old enough to wear it now, and I thought you'd like it.

EMILY. And this is from you. Why, Mama, it's just lovely and it's just what I wanted. It's beautiful! (*She flings her arms around her mother's neck. Her mother goes on with her cooking, but is pleased.*)

MRS. WEBB. Well, I hoped you'd like it. Hunted all over. Your Aunt Norah couldn't find one in Concord, so I had to send all the way to Boston. (*Laughing.*) Wally has something for you, too. He made it at Manual Training class and he's very proud of it. Be sure you make a big fuss about it.—Your father has a surprise for you, too; don't know what it is myself. Sh—here he comes.

MR. WEBB (*off stage*). Where's my girl? Where's my birthday girl?

EMILY (*in a loud voice to the* STAGE MANAGER). I can't. I can't go on. Oh! Oh. It goes so fast. We don't have time to look at one another. (*She breaks down sobbing. At a gesture from the* STAGE MANAGER, MRS. WEBB *disappears.*) I didn't realize. So all that was going on and we never noticed. Take me back—up the hill—to my grave. But first: Wait! One more look. Good-by. Good-by, world. Good-by, Grover's Corners . . . Mama and Papa. Good-by to clocks ticking . . . and Mama's sunflowers. And food and coffee. And new-ironed dresses and hot baths . . . and sleeping and waking up. Oh, earth, you're too wonderful for anybody to realize you. (*She looks toward the* STAGE MANAGER *and asks abruptly, through her tears:*) Do any human beings ever realize life while they live it?—every, every minute?

STAGE MANAGER. No. (*Pause.*) The saints and poets, maybe—they do some.

EMILY. I'm ready to go back. (*She returns to her chair beside* MRS. GIBBS.) Mother Gibbs, I should have listened to you. Now I want to be quiet for a while.—Oh, Mother Gibbs, I saw it all. I saw your garden.

MRS. GIBBS. Did you, dear?

EMILY. That's all human beings are!—Just blind people.

MRS. GIBBS. Look, it's clearing up. The stars are coming out.

EMILY. Oh, Mr. Stimson, I should have listened to them.

SIMON STIMSON (*with mounting violence; bitingly*). Yes, now you know. Now you know! That's what it was to be alive. To move about in a cloud of ignorance; to go up and down trampling on the feelings of those . . . of those about you. To spend and waste time as though you had a million years. To be always at the mercy of one self-centered passion or another. Now you know—that's the happy existence you wanted to go back and see. Did you shout to 'em? Did you call to 'em?

EMILY. Yes, I did.

SIMON STIMSON. Now you know them as they are: in ignorance and blindness.

MRS. GIBBS (*spiritedly*). Simon Stimson, that ain't the whole truth and you know it.

[*The dead have begun to stir.*]

THE DEAD. Lemuel, wind's coming up, seems like.—Oh, dear,—I keep remembering things tonight.—It's right cold for June, ain't it?

MRS. GIBBS. Look what you've done, you and your rebellious spirit stirring us up here.—Emily, look at that star. I forget its name.

THE DEAD. I'm getting to know them all, but I don't know their names.—My boy Joel was a sailor,—knew 'em all. He'd set on the porch evenings and tell 'em all by name. Yes, sir, it was wonderful.—A star's mighty good company.—Yes, yes.—Yes, 'tis.

SIMON STIMSON. Here's one of *them* coming.

THE DEAD. That's funny. 'Tain't no time for one of them to be here.—Goodness sakes.

EMILY. Mother Gibbs, it's George.

MRS. GIBBS. Sh, dear. You just rest yourself.

EMILY. It's George.

[GEORGE *enters from the left and slowly comes toward them.*]

A MAN FROM AMONG THE DEAD. And my boy, Joel, who knew the stars—he used to say it took millions of years for that speck o' light to git to the earth. Don't seem like a body could believe it, but that's what he used to say—millions of years.

ANOTHER. That's what they say.

[GEORGE *flings himself on* EMILY's *grave.*]

THE DEAD. Goodness! That ain't no way to behave!—He ought to be home.

EMILY. Mother Gibbs?

MRS. GIBBS. Yes, Emily?

EMILY. They don't understand much, do they?

MRS. GIBBS. No, dear, not very much.

[*The* STAGE MANAGER *appears at the right, one hand on a dark curtain which he slowly draws across the scene.*]

[*In the distance a clock is heard striking the hour very faintly.*]

STAGE MANAGER. Most everybody's asleep in Grover's Corners. There are a few lights on: Shorty Hawkins, down at the depot, has just watched the Albany train go by. And at the livery stable somebody's setting up late and talking.—Yes, it's clearing up. There are the stars—doing their old, old criss-cross journeys in the sky. Scholars haven't settled the matter yet, but they seem to think there are no living beings up there. They're just chalk . . . or fire. Only this one is straining away, straining away all the time to make something of itself. The strain's so bad that every sixteen hours everybody lies down and gets a rest. (*He winds his watch.*) Hm. . . . Eleven o'clock in Grover's Corners.—You get a good rest, too. Good night.

Perrin

Chap V

Prob (1

P. 142

III. MANPOWER

WORK may be one of the major satisfactions of life. Or it may be the denial of all that life should hold. Foremost of the problems of peace is this: How shall the worker find joy in his work?

In 1819, Benjamin Wood, cooper, setting up business in a small New Hampshire town, listed for sale butter tubs, cider barrels, dippers, great wooden bowls, shaving mugs, and many other articles of wooden ware which he had manufactured. But cooperage was only a part of his busy life. He made goosequill pens, he mended boots, set axes, threshed grain, boarded yearlings, drew up notices of auction, recorded births, pulled teeth, wove bedticks, and sold catskins, candles, knitted goods, apples, cheeses, butter, veal, and turkeys.[1] Such were the activities of a single handworker in an earlier and simpler age. Perhaps Benjamin Wood was a little more versatile than his neighbors, but there were few who did not combine one or more trades with the main business of farming. From season to season, almost from day to day, a man could count on a diversity of occupation which saved him from monotony. When the harvest had been gathered in the fall, he could turn to a winter of spare-time jobs in his shop. If he felt like making or mending some tool or article of furniture he knew how to do it with whatever means he had. Some jobs took more ingenuity than expertness. But the worker who felt his way by trial and error took pride in overcoming difficulties and in using his imagination, somewhat like an artist, for a creative end. Specialization was not yet a term of dreary import. It merely meant that, besides being a farmer like everybody else, one man made the shapeliest axe-helves, another had a knack for shearing sheep, a third was a smart hand at surveying, and so on.

Keeping the home in those days was a full-time job for a woman. With the help of her daughters and sometimes a neighbor's daughter who wanted to "work out" before she married, she managed the cooking and baking, the spinning and weaving and dyeing, the washing and ironing, the soap making, candle dipping, knitting, mending, cleaning, and all the other tasks that kept a home largely self-sufficient. The life of a housewife was hard-driven, yet it was not without its tangible achievements. When her bed quilt or pumpkin pie or quince jelly or homespun tablecloth received a

[1] Marion Nicholl Rawson: *New Hampshire Borns a Town*, New York, 1942.

prize at the county fair, she too, like her husband, enjoyed the sense of accomplishment which comes from a successful creative effort.

Around the beginning of the nineteenth century men discovered how to manufacture power and apply it to machinery. This dramatic change in traditional ways of doing things was called the Industrial Revolution. Men were confident that the new age of machinery would be an age of plenty and leisure. It was simple, they said: Let one machine plus one man do the work of ten men and life must become easier for all. At a single stroke mankind would be freed of two ancient curses, drudgery and poverty. The eternal contest between man's needs and his resources would be won: there would be goods in plenty for all. The struggle to measure the body's strength against the day's work would be ended: there would be time enough for all to rest after toil. At last man would be free to build a new earth in which greed and crime and ignorance and ugliness should be no more.

But it has not worked out that way. After a hundred and fifty years these hopes are still unrealized. Gone is the satisfaction of the hand-worker in the product of his skill and inventiveness: the motions of the mechanic on the assembly-line are as standardized as the parts he handles. Gone is the independence of the craftsman who could turn his hand to a dozen different projects: the mill operative knows only a single routine. Even the promised leisure has been disappointing: a robot hardly knows what to do with free time. And as for the dreams of plenty—the poor are still with us, inadequately housed, clothed, fed; and freedom from want is perhaps the most distant of the Four Freedoms.

As for women, the Industrial Revolution has drawn them, in increasing numbers, out of the home and into industry and business, a process recently accelerated by wartime shortages of manpower. They have learned new trades and developed new abilities until the distinction between men's work and women's work has largely broken down. At the end of the war, whatever may be their "place" in theory, women will in fact stand side by side with men in most vocations and professions. The large group of trained and highly skilled women who may not choose to return to household tasks will have to be absorbed into normal employment.

The labor problem, then, with its attendant problems, is the great unfinished business of peace. The ultimate solution is neither single nor clear, but the way toward a solution may be suggested here. Obviously that way is not backward. There is no returning to the simple ways of handicraft, however attractive they seem in retrospect. We are born into an age of complexities, and they can be solved not by simplifying them but by applying to them the complex knowledge of modern science.

The way is forward, from the age of the machine into the age of the laboratory. We stand at the threshold of unforeseeable techniques. Chemistry has given us a new command over materials. Physics is annihilating time and space. Medicine has found new weapons in the fight against disease. Industry has devised standards of perfection undreamed of by rule-of-thumb. Engineering and government, working together, have undertaken such vast social experiments as TVA and proved that they can be directed for the common good. In the achievements of technology is the brightest promise for the future.

Research presents the same spur to the imagination as our ancestors found in the necessities of daily living. But where they whittled an ingenious new door-latch with their jackknife, the modern technician contrives an electronic tube which is the result of subtle and intricate calculation, and which takes its place as the indispensable servant to a million lives. Here, surely, is a new kind of creative satisfaction, restricted, however, to those who have the requisite training.

What, in conclusion, is the present relation between man and his inventions? It is foolish to say that the machine is evil, or scientific knowledge dangerous. It is equally foolish to say that man has become the slave of the machine. Rather we should consider how we can adapt society to the machine. The machine is here to stay: the question is, what shall we do with it? What shall we do with the changed conditions of life which it makes possible? If it gives us leisure, how can we make proper use of leisure? By what program of social planning can we make the machine serve our highest purposes, and distribute its benefits widely among all classes of society? How can we insure that our new techniques shall not in future be diverted to destructive purposes by unprincipled madmen? How can we, within the bounds of democracy, achieve the social controls which a complex civilization must have? How, finally, can we develop the insight, the intelligence, and the imagination to see to it that all labor in the future, of men and of women, in factory, laboratory, office, farm, or home shall render the same variety, the same creative opportunity, the same sense of achievement as the workers of former times enjoyed?

These are staggering questions. We shall not find their answers in a hurry. But answered they must be, for in their answers is the shape of the future.

Vachel Lindsay

Vachel Lindsay (1879-1931) was, as all his readers are aware, a native of Springfield, Illinois. In his insistent exaltation of Springfield he symbolized his passion for America made beautiful, democracy come true. But how his dreams were to be realized remained romantically vague; enough that he translated the American tempo into noisy and intoxicating rhythms, and that now and then, in intervals of quiet, he allowed the true singer to be heard in lyrics of delicate, haunting melody. As a youthful evangelist of beauty he tramped through the South, the Pennsylvania coal region, the Middle West, and the Rockies, carrying a pamphlet of his own poems "to be traded for bread." "Kansas" is a memory of his experiences in the wheat fields and conveys his exuberant devotion to the American way.

KANSAS

Oh, I have walked in Kansas
Through many a harvest field,
And piled the sheaves of glory there
And down the wild rows reeled:

Each sheaf a little yellow sun,
A heap of hot-rayed gold;
Each binder like Creation's hand
To mould suns, as of old.

Straight overhead the orb of noon
Beat down with brimstone breath:
The desert wind from south and west
Was blistering flame and death.

Yet it was gay in Kansas,
A-fighting that strong sun;
And I and many a fellow-tramp
Defied that wind and won.

And we felt free in Kansas
From any sort of fear,
For thirty thousand tramps like us
There harvest every year.

She stretches arms for them to come,
She roars for helpers then,
And so it is in Kansas
That tramps, one month, are men.

We sang in burning Kansas
The songs of Sabbath-school,
The "Day Star" flashing in the East,
The "Vale of Eden" cool.

We sang in splendid Kansas
"The flag that set us free"—
That march of fifty thousand men
With Sherman to the sea.

We feasted high in Kansas
And had much milk and meat.
The tables groaned to give us power
Wherewith to save the wheat.

Our beds were sweet alfalfa hay
Within the barn-loft wide.
The loft doors opened out upon
The endless wheat-field tide.

I loved to watch the windmills spin
And watch that big moon rise.
I dreamed and dreamed with lids half-shut,
The moonlight in my eyes.

For all men dream in Kansas
By noonday and by night,
By sunrise yellow, red and wild
And moonrise wild and white.

The wind would drive the glittering clouds,
The cottonwoods would croon,
And past the sheaves and through the leaves
Came whispers from the moon.

Charles Allen Smart

Charles Allen Smart (1904-   ) was for some years an editor, teacher, and writer in New York. When he inherited a farm in southern Ohio, married, and turned farmer, the story of R.F.D. began. In this plain narrative he tells about the first three years of a city-bred man on the soil, years marked by drought and flood, by blizzard and blazing sun, by hard work and long hours, by first encounters with experiences as ageless as the race of man. Through all the pages run a zest for quiet adventure, a sense of humor, and a profound appreciation of the basic satisfactions of life.

PLANTING AND HARVEST

I UNDERSTAND that every spring, in Plymouth, Massachusetts, a little procession of people, in Pilgrim costume, commemorate an event of three centuries ago by going out and planting some corn. For fertilizer, a fish is planted in each hill, with the seed. The incumbent Minister of the First Church says a prayer. Now I don't happen to go to church, or to pray. To me, all that is a confusion of fear and thought, expressed in a poetry that is too cold, respectable, and timid, and often too vulgar, in the wrong way, to be capable or worthy of expressing any real thought or real emotion about life and death. Still, every year ten million other farmers, and I, in this country, do certain profoundly strange and important things, and sometimes have strange thoughts and feelings about them, and this little ceremony in Plymouth is the only one I have heard of that recognizes, in any way, their religious significance. It's probably just as well, because all the clergymen, with the exception of this one, would doubtless try to take over this Act, too, and make it as cold, respectable, timid, and vulgar as their christenings, marriages, communions, and burials. I'm sorry I mentioned the matter at all.

The first preparatory rite is hauling out the manure, in autumn or winter or early spring. My hired man, James, and I are able to handle ours with my little truck. It is tiring, but not half as nasty as it seems. Good manure is a lot cleaner, for instance, than street refuse. Ours rots all summer.

Then the plowing, dragging, and harrowing. I have tried several times to plow, years ago as a boy, and recently, and I have never been able to do it. If I had more chance, I think I could learn, but so far, every time, the plow has gone too deep, or jumped out of the ground, or wandered all over the place, or all three, and after about five minutes I feel as though

I'd run a mile. Dragging and harrowing are easier. I don't know anything much nicer to look at than a good field all ready for seed.

We have planted corn here twice, now, in my tenure, but I do not know how to operate a corn planter. It seems to me a very strange and inefficient machine. A long wire, with pieces of metal attached to it at regular intervals, the distance between the hills of corn, is stretched across the field. The planter is driven up the wire, which releases the seeds of corn. The wire has to be moved every time a new row is begun. I should think that a catch on a wheel would do the trick, but then I'm no mechanic. It is hard to believe that these odd little machines being driven along wires in May are planting seeds that in a few weeks will be square miles of corn as faultlessly ordered as a drill at West Point, and much more exciting.

A wheat drill is larger, more complex, and more ingenious. It is used in the autumn, here, to plant wheat and other grains, and at the same time it plants timothy seed and drills in commercial fertilizer. We have had to plant rye twice, here on the hill, as a cover crop for hay, and for early pasture itself. The first time, I called up a neighbor and arranged to borrow a drill. My hired man at the time, Hubert, went and got it, with his father's team. It had been loaned to another neighbor, who had allowed fertilizer to get wet in it. Now fertilizer hardens like cement. Hubert and I spent a morning cleaning it out, and then Hubert got to work with it. I followed for a while, and everything, to my ignorant eye, seemed to be working properly. When he got through, Hubert reported no further trouble. It was only the following spring that I found that all the timothy seed (eight dollars a bushel when bought) had been dropped in a small area at one end of the field, and a band twenty feet wide, the length of the field, had not been planted in rye. I have rarely felt quite such a fool.

The following autumn, after the other field had been cleared of corn, and Hubert had departed, I got a neighbor to harrow it with a tractor, and I sowed the rye and timothy myself, by hand. I used an old seeder which is simply a gadget attached to the bottom of a sack. You fill the sack with your seed mixture, open a vent at the bottom, turn a crank that turns a disk that throws the seed many feet, and walk steadily down one corn-shock row after another. After a couple of rows, the seeder broke down, and I had to finish the job by hand. I felt certain that I could not spread that seed evenly over thirteen acres, and make it come out right, but it did. A couple of weeks later, when I happened to be in hospital, Peggy reported that the rye had come up evenly all over the field. That winter, most of it was frozen out, and it gave us only a few days of pasture, but I'd rather be beaten by twenty-two degrees below zero than by my own ignorance.

Then came the question of putting in spring grass seed. A little timothy had survived, but not much. Ordinarily, one sows clover at this time, as I had done in the other field. But I had noticed that the clover had only done well on the slope that was drained. I consulted our County Agent, and he advised a mixture of timothy, red clover, red top, lespedeza, and Kentucky blue grass. I put in about twelve pounds of the mixture to the acre, and bought enough to reseed part of the other field. I also bought a new seeder.

A couple of washtubs full of grass seed are as exciting as, say, a publisher's stock room. I plunge my arms into that cool, clean seed, and look at those mysterious, hard little grains, and I see thousands of rolling acres of grass, with roots gripping the earth, and the wind caressing the green, and great herds of cattle and sheep eating it, and lying down in it to rest and chew, and growing fat and strong. I hear the grasses murmuring, I feel them drawing up the water and the richness . . .

Then, on a clear warm day in March, without wind, when the pools of water had mostly disappeared, but the earth was still damp, I did my sowing. It's an easy job. The sack isn't heavy, and I sowed the thirteen acres and more in less than a day. The seed flies out like hard rain, and stings your hands red. You walk steadily over the earth, in the sunlight, looking up, now and then, at the hills. You imagine the grass growing. It doesn't have to be cultivated, and with any kind of soil and dampness at all, it spreads. It's good food; it's a fine, useless beauty, too. You think of Johnny Appleseed, moving west in this very country, when it was a lovely wilderness, and Abraham Lincoln's father was chopping down trees. You think of the Mongols and their herds, always moving, always looking for grass. You wonder whether, if you do something like this, the figures in your book are so terribly important after all. You remember a farmer's telling you how his father sowed grass on horseback. You think of getting your animals through the winter alive, and you know that from now on the earth is going to help you, and them, free, gratis, for nothing. You want to sing, dance, yell, get drunk, and pray. And you walk on, steadily, listening to, and watching carefully, the fall of that divine Rain.

Like most religious ecstasies, this one is followed by doubt. Is the damned stuff going to grow after all? Was that clay too wet? What about those pools of water that collected in the next few days? Then the tiny seeds begin to sprout, and take root, and you see that they are doing much better in some places than in others. And the weeds appear, too. Then it doesn't rain for three weeks, and when you wake up at night, you listen for drops on the roof. But then one day, after the stock have eaten off most of the rye, which has a different color and texture, you are walking out across the fields, with dogs, and you notice suddenly something new, a fine green fur, not the old rye, not the weeds, not moss, but grass! . . . Mine, last summer, was almost completely wiped out by a four months' drought. This year, I got a better start, but so did the weeds.

But the next spring, after another harrowing, I went out again with a sack of green mystery. I think you do this year after year, on clear, warm, windless days in March, whether it makes any money or not, whether you can afford it or not, and whether you get any breaks in weather or not. "There goes that old boy," they say, "still sowing grass." And then one fine day it's all over for you, and they take your body, like the fish at Plymouth, and put it in the earth. The process is fancy and silly, but in a short while all that, and all you, are quite forgotten. But meanwhile the roots of the trees and the grass are reaching down into the earth to the ashes, to the skull, which feeds them, and the leaves and grasses are waving in the wind and sunlight.

✦

But the real victory is in the harvest of the corn. It is on these enormous fields, drilled with such precision, kept clean with such care, with the green pennons and tassels waving all summer in the wind, and harvested with such a fight, that all of us, in this region and elsewhere, eat and live. It is these heavy ears that keep the big parade of hogs and cattle moving from pasture and barnyard to stockyards, slaughter houses, kitchens, and dining room tables. It is these yellow seeds, put carefully into good and bad ground in May, that become, in time, not only corn flakes and bacon, but also figures in checkbooks, permanent waves in hair, curtains rising in darkened theaters, and even strange ideas and emotions set down, curiously, in black and white marks on paper, and moving strangely into people's heads, like toxins and antitoxins.

When I moved out here, the meadows had to be plowed up, and so for two years even remote, uneconomic Oak Hill heard the portentous whispering of the corn in the wind. In August, depending on the weather, the stalks and leaves begin to turn yellow, at the bottom first, and the ears, if the crop is good, push upwards, outwards, and downwards towards the earth. Sometimes in midsummer we have the storms and high winds that destroyed the *Shenandoah* and her men, and that flatten the corn to the ground, so that it does not ripen properly, and is very hard to cut.

Along in September, we begin to see whether the grains are dented, and look to our corn-knives. These are formidable weapons, with straight, two-foot blades, blunt at the end. With one good blow they will cut a hill of corn (or a head, for all I know) clean off.

First, you find the four central hills in an area fourteen hills square, bend down the tops, and tie them all together. This forms a "gallus," not to be cut until the fodder is hauled in, that is the core of the shock, and provides something against which to lean the first armfuls of fodder. Then you begin to cut, hacking away with your right arm, and gathering the tall stalks, heavy with their ears, into your left arm, until you have cut so many that you can hardly carry the load. One soon learns to balance that heavy load on the hip, so that the entire weight is not on the left arm and shoulder.

It is well to tie the left cuff to the thumb, or to a glove; otherwise a few hours of cutting will rub the wrist raw. The armfuls of fodder with corn are piled into the shock, and it is very strange to me that the sound of a load moving through the corn not yet cut, and stacked against the shock, is a sound exactly, but *exactly,* like that of a wave breaking on the shore. In corn-cutting, my mind is always full of memories of the sea. When a shock is finished, you take a thing called a fodder pulley, which is merely a notched board fastened to the end of a light rope some fifteen feet long, throw it around the shock, and pull it together as tightly as you can. When you have got the pulley tight, you tie the shock together with binder twine, and then take off the pulley. Then you go on, for hour after hour, and day after day, until finally your field is no longer a West Point parade, but an even array of fortresses, with ripening pumpkins in between.

Corn-cutting, like most farm work, is hard enough. I remember well the second day of my first corn-cutting; the first day is always deceptively easy. About ten-thirty, the field began to slant and rotate. I had to sit down in the shade for a few minutes, and then with lunch, or almost instead of lunch, I had to take a stiff drink of whiskey. (In a pinch, there is nothing like it.) But corn-cutting is a good job, a constructive, satisfying release of all the sadism frustrated and stored up for a year, or years. The air is fine, with the smokiness and slight chill of early autumn, and the work itself makes one feel like Alan Breck, fighting all day with a cutlass.

Cutting is only the first step. Next comes husking, which can be postponed almost indefinitely, and stretched out through autumn and early winter, but which has to be done, sooner or later. It is rather simple, and rather dull. You untie the shock, push it over, and then rip the ears out of the husks, and throw them into a pile. Then you put the fodder back as it was, and tie it together again, to hold it from the wind until you can get it hauled in, and stacked near the barnyard, for feeding. There is a little hook, mounted on leather, that you can get and tie onto your right palm, and that makes it much easier to jerk back the husks. If cutting would be good for fighters, husking would appeal to the acquisitive. Those little piles of yellow beside the shocks, gotten there with so much effort, are literally gold. They may cost you more than they are worth, but that consideration has never yet deterred the counters.

The next thing is hauling in the fodder and corn. This job, too, can wait almost but not quite indefinitely. The winter before last was so bad that one saw piles of corn, and shocks of fodder, in the wheat fields as late as spring. Some good farmers, like Mr. Kincaid, haul their corn in right away, and their fodder as they need it, or as soon as they can. If you are in the bottoms, and don't get it in right quick, there is always a chance of its going down in a flood and landing in someone's bedroom in Memphis. If you have teams and wagons, only the worst mud can hold you back, but if you are trying to farm with an old roadster turned into a pick-up, it is another story.

Last winter, James and I labored with that corn, that fodder, and that damned (but invaluable) truck, all winter. We'd wait, apprehensively, for a hard freeze without much snow—the worst possible weather for the rye or wheat coming on—and then rush out, drive and load the truck as fast as possible, and sooner or later, get stuck. Like most city people, I had the idea that when your car got stuck, all you could do was get a team or wrecking car, but soon enough I learned what can be done with fodder, sacks, rocks, old boards, old fence posts, and the most grueling work. Several times I got Peggy into it, to drive while James and I lifted and pushed, finally got her moving, and then waited, with our hearts pounding, while Peggy drove with mad skill for the barnyard. Usually we had to unload all corn and all fodder first. James is made of iron and steel, but more than once I'd come in, plastered with mud, and chilled to the marrow, from a three-hour session of this kind, and have to lie flat on my back on the floor by the fire for a couple of hours, praising God for the Jameses of this world, and loathing my own weakness.

But we got all that corn into the crib, and all that fodder into the barnyard, and both into the bellies of the sheep and cattle, and the manure back on the earth, and there are people somewhere who had woolen socks on their feet, and ate roast beef for dinner. And spring came at last, and Peggy and I, and James, put more seeds into the earth.

Vachel Lindsay

In writing this poem Vachel Lindsay may well have had in mind these flaming words of Thomas Carlyle at the sight of industrial England of a hundred years ago: "It is not to die, or even to die of hunger, that makes a man wretched; many men have died; all men must die . . . But it is to live miserable we know not why; to work sore and yet gain nothing . . . it is to die slowly all our life long. . . . This is and remains forever intolerable to all men whom God has made."

THE LEADEN-EYED

Let not young souls be smothered out before
They do quaint deeds and fully flaunt their pride.
It is the world's one crime its babes grow dull,
Its poor are ox-like, limp and leaden-eyed.

Not that they starve, but starve so dreamlessly,
Not that they sow, but that they seldom reap,
Not that they serve, but have no gods to serve,
Not that they die but that they die like sheep.

E. B. White

*This curious essay was suggested by the experiments of a psychologist
at the University of Michigan which proved, by the reactions of rats,
that human beings suffer nervous breakdown when faced by problems
which have no apparent solution. Here is a terrifying picture of the
complexes, frustrations, and tensions of civilization. If this is the way
the world ends, we had better follow Ricardo's advice in* Conversation
at Midnight *and proceed to disintegrate "convivially imbibing the
pleasanter poisons." Or of course we can, like E. B. White, move to
the country.*

THE DOOR

EVERYTHING (he kept saying) is something
it isn't. And everybody is always somewhere else. Maybe it was the city,
being in the city, that made him feel how queer everything was and that
it was something else. Maybe (he kept thinking) it was the names of the
things. The names were tex and frequently koid. Or they were flex and oid
or they were duroid (sani) or flexsan (duro), but everything was glass (but
not quite glass) and the thing that you touched (the surface, washable,
crease-resistant) was rubber, only it wasn't quite rubber and you didn't quite
touch it but almost. The wall, which was glass but thrutex, turned out on
being approached not to be a wall, it was something else, it was an opening
or doorway—and the doorway (through which he saw himself approaching) turned out to be something else, it was a wall. And what he had eaten
not having agreed with him.

He was in a washable house, but he wasn't sure. Now about those rats,
he kept saying to himself. He meant the rats that the Professor had driven
crazy by forcing them to deal with problems which were beyond the scope
of rats, the insoluble problems. He meant the rats that had been trained to
jump at the square card with the circle in the middle, and the card (because
it was something it wasn't) would give way and let the rat into a place
where the food was, but then one day it would be a trick played on the rat,
and the card would be changed, and the rat would jump but the card
wouldn't give way, and it was an impossible situation (for a rat) and the

rat would go insane and into its eyes would come the unspeakably bright imploring look of the frustrated, and after the convulsions were over and the frantic racing around, then the passive stage would set in and the willingness to let anything be done to it, even if it was something else.

He didn't know which door (or wall) or opening in the house to jump at, to get through, because one was an opening that wasn't a door (it was a void, or koid) and the other was a wall that wasn't an opening, it was a sanitary cupboard of the same color. He caught a glimpse of his eyes staring into his eyes, in the thrutex, and in them was the expression he had seen in the picture of the rats—weary after convulsions and the frantic racing around, when they were willing and did not mind having anything done to them. More and more (he kept saying) I am confronted by a problem which is incapable of solution (for this time even if he chose the right door, there would be no food behind it) and that is what madness is, and things seeming different from what they are. He heard, in the house where he was, in the city to which he had gone (as toward a door which might, or might not, give way), a noise—not a loud noise but more of a low prefabricated humming. It came from a place in the base of the wall (or stat) where the flue carrying the filterable air was, and not far from the Minipiano, which was made of the same material nailbrushes are made of, and which was under the stairs. "This, too, has been tested," she said, pointing, but not at it, "and found viable." It wasn't a loud noise, he kept thinking, sorry that he had seen his eyes, even though it was through his own eyes that he had seen them.

First will come the convulsions (he said), then the exhaustion, then the willingness to let anything be done. "And you better believe it *will* be."

All his life he had been confronted by situations which were incapable of being solved, and there was a deliberateness behind all this, behind this changing of the card (or door), because they would always wait till you had learned to jump at the certain card (or door)—the one with the circle—and then they would change it on you. There have been so many doors changed on me, he said, in the last twenty years, but it is now becoming clear that it is an impossible situation, and the question is whether to jump again, even though they ruffle you in the rump with a blast of air—to make you jump. He wished he wasn't standing by the Minipiano. First they would teach you the prayers and the Psalms, and that would be the right door (the one with the circle), and the long sweet words with the holy sound, and that would be the one to jump at to get where the food was. Then one day you jumped and it didn't give way, so that all you got was the bump on the nose, and the first bewilderment, the first young bewilderment.

I don't know whether to tell her about the door they substituted or not, he said, the one with the equation on it and the picture of the amoeba reproducing itself by division. Or the one with the photostatic copy of the check for thirty-two dollars and fifty cents. But the jumping was so long ago, although the bump is . . . how those old wounds hurt! Being crazy this way wouldn't be so bad if only, if only. If only when you put your foot forward to take a step, the ground wouldn't come up to meet your foot the way it does. And the same way in the street (only I may never get back to the street unless I jump at the right door), the curb coming up to meet your foot, anticipating ever so delicately the weight of the body, which is some-where else. "We could take your name," she said, "and send it to you." And it wouldn't be so bad if only you could read a sentence all the way through without jumping (your eye) to something else on the same page; and then (he kept thinking) there was that man out in Jersey, the one who started to chop his trees down, one by one, the man who began talking about how he would take his house to pieces, brick by brick, because he faced a problem incapable of solution, probably, so he began to hack at the trees in the yard, began to pluck with trembling fingers at the bricks in the house. Even if a house is not washable, it is worth taking down. It is not till later that the exhaustion sets in.

But it is inevitable that they will keep changing the doors on you, he said, because that is what they are for; and the thing is to get used to it and not let it unsettle the mind. But that would mean not jumping, and you can't. Nobody cannot jump. There will be no not-jumping. Among rats, perhaps, but among people never. Everybody has to keep jumping at a door (the one with the circle on it) because that is the way everybody is, specially some people. You wouldn't want me, standing here, to tell you, would you, about my friend the poet (deceased) who said, "My heart has followed all my days something I cannot name"? (It had the circle on it.) And like many poets, although few so beloved, he is gone. It killed him, the jump-ing. First, of course, there were the preliminary bouts, the convulsions, and the calm and the willingness.

I remember the door with the picture of the girl on it (only it was spring), her arms outstretched in loveliness, her dress (it was the one with the circle on it) uncaught, beginning the slow, clear, blinding cascade—and I guess we would all like to try that door again, for it seemed like the way and for a while it was the way, the door would open and you would go through winged and exalted (like any rat) and the food would be there, the way the Professor had it arranged, everything O.K., and you had chosen the right door for the world was young. The time they changed that door on me, my nose bled for a hundred hours—how do you like that, Madam? Or would you prefer to show me further through this so strange house, or you could take my name and send it to me, for although my heart has fol-lowed all my days something I cannot name, I am tired of the jumping and

I do not know which way to go, Madam, and I am not even sure that I am not tried beyond the endurance of man (rat, if you will) and have taken leave of sanity. What are you following these days, old friend, after your recovery from the last bump? What is the name, or is it something you cannot name? The rats have a name for it by this time, perhaps, but I don't know what they call it. I call it plexikoid and it comes in sheets, something like insulating board, unattainable and ugli-proof.

And there was the man out in Jersey, because I keep thinking about his terrible necessity and the passion and trouble he had gone to all those years in the indescribable abundance of a householder's detail, building the estate and the planting of the trees and in spring the lawn-dressing and in fall the bulbs for the spring burgeoning, and the watering of the grass on the long light evenings in summer and the gravel for the driveway (all had to be thought out, planned) and the decorative borders, probably, the perennials and the bug spray, and the building of the house from plans of the architect, first the sills, then the studs, then the full corn in the ear, the floors laid on the floor timbers, smoothed, and then the carpets upon the smooth floors and the curtains and the rods therefor. And then, almost without warning, he would be jumping at the same old door and it wouldn't give: they had changed it on him, making life no longer supportable under the elms in the elm shade, under the maples in the maple shade.

"Here you have the maximum of openness in a small room."

It was impossible to say (maybe it was the city) what made him feel the way he did, and I am not the only one either, he kept thinking—ask any doctor if I am. The doctors, they know how many there are, they even know where the trouble is only they don't like to tell you about the prefrontal lobe because that means making a hole in your skull and removing the work of centuries. It took so long coming, this lobe, so many, many years. (Is it something you read in the paper, perhaps?) And now, the strain being so great, the door having been changed by the Professor once too often . . . but it only means a whiff of ether, a few deft strokes, and the higher animal becomes a little easier in his mind and more like the lower one. From now on, you see, that's the way it will be, the ones with the small prefrontal lobes will win because the other ones are hurt too much by this incessant bumping. They can stand just so much, eh, Doctor? (And what is that, pray, that you have in your hand?) Still, you never can tell, eh, Madam?

He crossed (carefully) the room, the thick carpet under him softly, and went toward the door carefully, which was glass and he could see himself in it, and which, at his approach, opened to allow him to pass through; and beyond he half expected to find one of the old doors that he had known, perhaps the one with the circle, the one with the girl her arms outstretched in loveliness and beauty before him. But he saw instead a moving stairway, and descended in light (he kept thinking) to the street below and to the other people. As he stepped off, the ground came up slightly, to meet his foot.

Vachel Lindsay

Vachel Lindsay, in lines that any child can understand, answers the man of good intentions but little courage who says: "What can one individual do to better the world?" Lao-tse, the Chinese philosopher, gave the same answer twenty-five hundred years ago: "The journey of a thousand miles begins with one step."

THE MOUSE THAT GNAWED THE OAK-TREE DOWN

The mouse that gnawed the oak-tree down
Began his task in early life.
He kept so busy with his teeth
He had no time to take a wife.

He gnawed and gnawed through sun and rain
When the ambitious fit was on,
Then rested in the sawdust till
A month of idleness had gone.

He did not move about to hunt
The coteries of mousie-men.
He was a snail-paced, stupid thing
Until he cared to gnaw again.

The mouse that gnawed the oak-tree down,
When that tough foe was at his feet—
Found in the stump no angel-cake
Nor buttered bread, nor cheese nor meat—

The forest-roof let in the sky.
"This light is worth the work," said he.
"I'll make this ancient swamp more light,"
And started on another tree.

Archibald MacLeish

Archibald MacLeish in this poem voices a thought often present in his work—that men can save themselves only by their·own efforts, that there is only the way forward, that the promises of America are only "for those who take them."

SPEECH TO A CROWD

Tell me my patient friends—awaiters of messages—
From what other shore: from what stranger:
Whence was the word to come? Who was to lesson you?

Listeners under a child's crib in a manger—
Listeners once by the oracles: now by the transoms—
Whom are you waiting for? Who do you think will explain?

Listeners thousands of years and still no answer—
Writers at night to Miss Lonely-Hearts: awkward spellers—
Open your eyes! There is only earth and the man!

There is only you: there is no one else on the telephone:
No one else is on the air to whisper:
No one else but you will push the bell.

No one knows if you don't: neither ships
Nor landing-fields decode the dark between:
You have your eyes and what your eyes see *is*.

The earth you see is really the earth you are seeing:
The sun is truly excellent: truly warm:
Women are beautiful as you have seen them—

Their breasts (believe it) like cooing of doves in a portico:
They bear at their breasts tenderness softly. Look at them!
Look at yourselves. You are strong. You are well formed.

Look at the world—the world you never took!
It is really true you may live in the world heedlessly:
Why do you wait to read it in a book then?

Write it yourselves! Write to yourselves if you need to!
Tell yourselves there is sun and the sun will rise:
Tell yourselves the earth has food to feed you:—

Let the dead men say that men must die!
Who better than you can know what death is?
How can a bone or a broken body surmise it?

Let the dead shriek with their whispering breath:
Laugh at them! Say the murdered gods may wake
But we who work have end of work together:

Tell yourselves the earth is yours to take!

Waiting for messages out of the dark you were poor.
The world was always yours: you would not take it.

Alfred North Whitehead

Alfred North Whitehead (1861-   ) is British-born and a graduate of Trinity College, Cambridge. Now in his eighties he looks back upon a distinguished career in the kindred fields of mathematics and philosophy. Since 1924 he has been a professor of philosophy, now emeritus, at Harvard University. He is a Fellow of the Royal Society, and holds honorary degrees from the world's great institutions. In the concluding pages of his Science and the Modern World *he regards without dismay the prospects of civilization, but warns against two enemies of social progress: the gospel of force and the gospel of uniformity, both, since he wrote these pages, unhappily exemplified in the history of Europe. The first, he says, can be overcome by the power of coöperation; the second must yield to the restless spirit of mankind, forever venturing into new regions of thought and experience.*

REQUISITES FOR SOCIAL PROGRESS

AT the present moment a discussion is raging as to the future of civilization in the novel circumstances of rapid scientific and technological advance. The evils of the future have been diagnosed in various ways: the loss of religious faith, the malignant use of material power, the degradation attending a differential birth-rate favouring the lower types of humanity, the suppression of esthetic creativeness. Without doubt, these are all evils, dangerous and threatening. But they are not new. From the dawn of history, mankind has always been losing its religious faith, has always suffered from the malignant use of material power, has always suffered from the infertility of its best intellectual types, has always witnessed the periodical decadence of art. In the reign of the Egyptian king, Tutankhamen, there was raging a desperate religious struggle between Modernists and Fundamentalists; the cave pictures exhibit a phase of delicate esthetic achievement as superseded by a period of comparative vulgarity; the religious leaders, the great thinkers, the great poets and authors, the whole clerical caste in the Middle Ages, have been notably infertile; finally, if we attend to what actually has happened in the past, and disregard romantic visions of democracies, aristocracies, kings, generals, armies, and merchants, material power has generally been wielded with blindness, obstinacy, and selfishness, often with brutal malignancy. And yet, mankind has progressed. Even if you take a tiny oasis of peculiar excellence, the type of modern man who would have most chance of happiness in ancient Greece at its best period is probably (as now) an average professional heavy-weight boxer, and not an average Greek scholar from Oxford or Germany. Indeed, the main use of the Oxford scholar would have been his capability of writing an ode in glorification of the boxer. Nothing does more harm in unnerving men for their duties in the present than the attention devoted to the points of excellence in the past as compared with the average failure of the present day.

. . . The watchwords of the nineteenth century have been: struggle for existence, competition, class warfare, commercial antagonism between nations, military warfare. The struggle for existence has been construed into the gospel of hate. The full conclusion to be drawn from a philosophy of evolution is fortunately of a more balanced character. Successful organisms modify their environment. Those organisms are successful which modify their environment so as to assist each other. This law is exemplified in nature on a vast scale. For example, the North American Indians accepted their environment, with the result that a scanty population barely succeeded in maintaining themselves over the whole continent. The European races when they arrived in the same continent pursued an opposite policy. They at once coöperated in modifying their environment. The result is that a population more than twenty times that of the Indian population now occupies the same territory, and the continent is not yet full. Again, there are associations of different species which mutually coöperate. This differentiation of species is exhibited in the simplest physical entities, such as the association between electrons and positive nuclei, and in the whole realm of animate nature. The trees in a Brazilian forest depend upon the association of various species of organisms, each of which is mutually dependent on the other species. A single tree by itself is dependent upon all the adverse chances of shifting circumstances. The wind stunts it: the variations in temperature check its foliage: the rains denude its soil: its leaves are blown away and are lost for the purpose of fertilization. You may obtain individual specimens of fine trees either in exceptional circumstances or where human cultivation has intervened. But in nature the normal way in which trees flourish is by their association in a forest. Each tree may lose something of its individual perfection of growth, but they mutually assist each other in preserving the conditions for survival. The soil is preserved and shaded; and the microbes necessary for its fertility are neither scorched, nor frozen, nor washed away. A forest is the triumph of the organization of mutually dependent species. Further a species of microbes which kills the forest, also exterminates itself. Again the two sexes exhibit the same advantage of differentiation. In the history of the world, the prize has not gone to those species which specialized in methods of violence or even in defensive armor. In fact, nature began with producing animals encased in hard shells for defence against the ills of life. It also experimented in size. But smaller animals, without external armor, warm-blooded, sensitive, and alert, have cleared these monsters off the face of the earth. Also, the lions and tigers are not the successful species. There is something in the ready use of force which defeats its own object. Its main defect is that it bars coöperation. Every organism requires an environment of friends, partly to shield it from violent changes and partly to supply it with its wants. The Gospel of Force is incompatible with a social life. By *force,* I mean *antagonism* in its most general sense.

Almost equally dangerous is the Gospel of Uniformity. The differences between the nations and races of mankind are required to preserve the conditions under which higher development is possible. One main factor in the upward trend of animal life has been the power of wandering. Perhaps this is why the armour-plated monsters fared badly. They could not wander. Animals wander into new conditions. They have to adapt themselves or die. Mankind has wandered from the trees to the plains, from the plains to the sea-coast, from climate to climate, from continent to continent, and from habit of life to habit of life. When man ceases to wander, he will cease to ascend in the scale of being. Physical wandering is still important, but greater still is the power of man's spiritual adventures—adventures of thought, adventures of passionate feeling, adventures of esthetic experience. A diversification among human communities is essential for the provision of the incentive and material for the Odyssey of the human spirit. Other nations, of different habits, are not enemies: they are godsends. Men require of their neighbours something sufficiently akin to be understood, something sufficiently different to provoke attention, and something great enough to command admiration. We must not expect, however, all the virtues. We should even be satisfied if there is something odd enough to be interesting.

Modern science has imposed on humanity the necessity for wandering. Its progressive thought and its progressive technology make the transition through time, from generation to generation, a true migration into uncharted seas of adventure. The very benefit of wandering is that it is dangerous and needs skill to avert evils. We must expect, therefore, that the future will disclose dangers. It is the business of the future to be dangerous; and it is among the merits of science that it equips the future for its duties. . . .

The moral of the tale [of the influence of science in the modern world] is the power of reason, its decisive influence on the life of humanity. The great conquerors, from Alexander to Caesar, and from Caesar to Napoleon, influenced profoundly the lives of subsequent generations. But the total effect of this influence shrinks to insignificance if compared to the entire transformation of human habits and human mentality produced by the long line of men of thought from Thales to the present day, men individually powerless, but ultimately the rulers of the world.

Editors of "Fortune"

The Norden bombsight contains six tiny steel balls in its tilting-control bearing. If any of these balls vary in smoothness more than one millionth of an inch, the bombardier, flying at 300 miles an hour some four or five miles above the earth, will miss his target. The miracle that insures that he shall not miss, that the steel balls shall not vary beyond an infinitesimal degree (called a tolerance), is the system of quality control described in the following case history by staff members of Fortune.

TO ONE-MILLIONTH OF AN INCH

THE management of SKF Industries, Inc., which turns out 100,000 bearings a day in some 8,000 sizes, is more like an engineering society than a group of typical executives. In part this preponderance of engineers—civil, mechanical, process, time-study, thermodynamical—reflects the sold-by-prescription character of the bearing business. In part it reflects the influence exerted by the founder of the original SKF (Svenska Kullager Fabriken, or Swedish ball-bearing factory), who was a distinguished Göteborg engineer, Sven Wingquist, and very proud of his calling. After 1907, when he perfected the bearing upon which he built a worldwide organization with fourteen factories in seven countries and 200 sales offices, Sven Wingquist invariably put a premium on engineering talent. But neither the nature of bearing production nor the weight of tradition alone accounts for the fact that the American SKF, with its four plants in the Philadelphia area, spends forty out of every hundred man-hours on quality control.

Before the war, the ratio was high but considerably less. But the onset of the defense program in 1940 changed SKF's ideas about the meaning of quality control, especially as it had to do with precision. The $\frac{1}{10,000}$-of-an-inch tolerances, so painstakingly achieved, had become too gross. Bearings for PT-boat torpedoes and anti-aircraft-gun range finders, as well as for aircraft engines and flying instruments and bombsights, were exacting a new exactitude.

Over the past three years SKF has developed a new form of ultra-precision manufacture, supported by a quality-control program where lacquer on the fingernails of a woman inspector, or powder on her nose, or a one-degree change in temperature is guarded against with a kind of breath-holding care, lest it ruin weeks of work.

While the old-fashioned "plain" bearing that slides like a hub over its axle often gets hot and burns out from this friction, the ball and roller (tapered, spherical, cylindrical) bearings of the sort made by SKF are the nearest thing to frictionless motion known to man. They roll rather than rub—the ball along a curvature, or point, contact, and the roller over a surface, or line, contact. And whether four feet in diameter, weighing 3,800 pounds, and anchoring the central shaft of an armor-plate mill, or half an inch in diameter, weighing less than .05 of an ounce, and acting as pivot for a microscope lens, ball and roller bearings have always the same fundamental function: to support a gear or shaft or wheel or other moving part in such a way as to give it freedom to rotate but not to wobble.

To turn out bearings light enough in motion, smooth enough in surface, hard enough in texture to perform their supporting role, SKF's quality control starts with the raw material, a cold-drawn alloy steel generally containing 1 per cent carbon, 1.5 per cent chrome, and .3 per cent manganese. Upon its structure depend the bearing's toughness and longevity, and to improve both is the lifework of Dr. Haakon Styri, a noted Norwegian chemist, physicist, metallurgist, who has made his home in this country for a quarter of a century as SKF's chief of research. From 1930 on, he kept at U. S. steel mills, urging them to cut down on slag inclusions (sulfides, aluminates, silicates) that sapped the strength and shortened the life of the bearing. But his recommendations met with only partial success until 1940 when war cut off Sweden as primary source for the more potent bearing steel he demanded. At that point, several U. S. steel companies got down to business with Dr. Styri and other scientists and developed a bearing steel superior to any.

Although every steel shipment is inspected by the vendor, SKF looks it over again when it arrives in bars, tubings, and coils at plant No. 2 along Tulip Street in Philadelphia. Consider the cold-drawn wire for making, say, the $\frac{3}{32}$-of-an-inch balls that go into the bearing that acts as tilting control for the Norden bombsight. As soon as this wire reaches the receiving department, ends are snipped off and sent to the laboratory, where Dr. Styri's assistants test them with Rockwell gauges for hardness and put them under microscopes that magnify 1,000 times to show up structural flaws. If the steel isn't homogeneous, if it has perhaps a certain pock, it would have the same effect on the ball as a valvular lesion on the human heart, and it is discarded.

But when the steel is approved, the creation of the ball begins. A coil of wire is fed into the automatic heading machine that shears off a $\frac{5}{32}$-of-an-inch slug, passing it into cuplike dies that mold it into a globe, squeezing out an equatorial belt called a "flash," and spewing the first rough ball into a bucket. This flash is unavoidable. No mechanism can compress a piece of cold alloy steel into complete roundness without breaking it. Hence the ball goes into the hopper of a special "flashing" device, where two cutting disks shave off the equatorial belt and the nibs at its poles. Smoother now, it is swirled around a slot between the single grinder's two wheels, which scrape off an over-all layer of steel, and do it evenly, for the ball is always changing its axis as it slips along, and every part of its surface gets a going over. Similarly, the multiple-groove grinder takes off eight more layers, as if peeling skins from an onion. Lest stray particles of steel cling to the ball's surface, it is placed inside a great metal cask, looking like a beer tun, and tumbled in a gray mixture of abrasives and water up to forty hours.

Since the ball must be heat-treated to attain its proper hardness, in this case an ability to sustain a pressure of 300,000 pounds per square inch, it is thrust into a furnace where, starting at ordinary room temperature, the ball travels along eight feet of heat gradations up to 1,500° Fahrenheit; it is then spilled into a bath of water where it is quenched to a coolness of 60°. But this is so severe a shock that, to relieve the stresses, the ball is then scooped into a bucket, which is placed in a circulatory air furnace where the temperature is kept for forty-five minutes at 240° Fahrenheit. Again the ball is cooled but this time only in factory air, tumbled, and put into a precision grinder where for thirty-nine hours it is held by a grooved grinding disk against a fine-grained grinding wheel that brings it toward its specified size of $\frac{3}{32}$ of an inch and a smoothness correct within $\frac{2}{1,000,000}$ of an inch.

Lapping, the final stage in manufacture, imparts a bright shining surface to the ball, and brings its smoothness down to $\frac{1}{1,000,000}$ of an inch, its size to within $\frac{2}{100,000}$ of an inch, and its roundness to $\frac{1}{100,000}$ of an inch, by holding it for twenty hours between two grooved plates of cast iron, the upper one stationary while the lower one rotates against it.

At the end of each operation, a process inspector who moves about among the bank of machines in his section takes a sample from the lot and goes over it with his battery of portable gauges for stains and flats, for size and roundness. He is guided by the Universal Double Sampling Plan, a supplement to the Shewhart statistical method, introduced into SKF about a year ago by Charles S. Gotwals, supervisor of Inspection and Quality Control.

Despite the aid of statistics, and the ingenuity of machines, and measuring devices almost infallible, quality control still depends upon competent inspection; and Gotwals believes that, above all, an inspector should have a Calvinist conscience. He (or she) should also be endowed with finger dexterity, a fine touch, and excellent eyesight. A fuss-budget temperament is, naturally, beyond price. At the same time, he must be able to watch out for flaws with unflagging attentiveness, day after day, without blowing his top. To allay the strain of this concentration, Gotwals shifts inspectors from one item to another as often as every two hours. He prefers the roving inspector particularly to be quiet, if not taciturn, in disposition lest he succumb to the "hoof-and-mouth disease," the impulse to start a conversation with everyone he meets on his rounds. The result may be inattention on his part, carelessness on that of the operator. He is never encouraged to broaden tolerances a fraction just over or under the line; in some cases this would do no damage, but the action could foster disregard for standards.

Unlike production workers and such indirect labor as maintenance men, inspectors no longer participate in the SKF wage incentive. It was found that the lure of the premium impaired their judgment—unconsciously for the most part, Gotwals and his colleagues believe.

At the moment, to check output, SKF needs 1,000 process or roving inspectors, and 2,100 part and assembly inspectors, who sit at benches among the machines on the factory floor or in separate inspection rooms. They are encouraged to put up a fight on the results of their work; and they do it, too, since they know that Inspection and Quality Control is an independent department with its own staff and line organization, and with Gotwals reporting directly to the factory head. The records and reports of this inspectorate provide—for forty-seven quality-control specialists who "watch the watchmen" and nineteen quality-control engineers—the data that furnish the basis for the use of the Shewhart system.

SHORT CUTS TO SAMPLING

That system at SKF consists of two parts: (1) the Shewhart "average" and "dispersion" charts, (2) the Universal Double Sampling Plan, statistical tables that show a short cut to sampling, developed by Shewhart's Bell Laboratories colleagues, Harold F. Dodge and Harry G. Romig. The Dodge-Romig tables derive from the capricious laws of probability, first discovered in games of chance and later endowed with respectability by a long line of mathematicians. In fact, this probability thesis has been invoked to validate everything from the Mendelian theory of heredity to public-opinion polls. The "expectancy" calculations, as worked out in abstruse equations by Messrs. Dodge and Romig, yield the same result as if they had actually taken, say, 970 white balls and thirty black balls, mixed them in a bowl, and drawn out any number more than thirty, counting the number of each color. This procedure, when repeated, say, 100 times, would show the black balls recurring nearly 3 per cent of the time; the more tests that are made, the nearer the average will come to the exact percentage of black balls. However, in any single draw all thirty black balls may appear, or none at all; in terms of quality control this would be the same as thirty defects or none.

By the same token, quality cannot be assessed from a single sample; in short, when a customer inspects a lot of goods (white and black balls) he cannot be sure that the lot is acceptable merely because a sample he chooses at random is without defects (as if it consisted only of white balls). In its disproportionate lack of defects, this sample reflects a probability error. But the frequency with which such errors occur can be determined by the mathematics of probability.

The risk of error for the customer will vary according to the proportion of defects (black balls) to the whole (black and white balls together). The producer is up against a similar problem since a lot is accepted upon the basis of a sample that is expected to have no more than a certain percentage of defects. But it might happen that a single sample from a particular lot would contain a preponderance of defects (much more than the 3 per cent of black balls). The lot would therefore be rejected—even though the over-all production it represented were running at a satisfactory quality level. However, over the long pull, the effect of this caprice is corrected. While the customer will get more defects in some lots, he will get less in others; so that his total purchase will not contain more than the guaranteed limit of defects. The producer, on the other hand, can always reinspect his rejected lots 100 per cent, sorting good from bad, to rectify the disproportion of defects, or black balls to white.

The Dodge-Romig tables, as used at SKF and elsewhere, guide the process inspector in choosing a sample size that will (1) provide a stipulated degree of protection, such as not permitting more than 2 per cent of defectives in the outgoing quality, and (2) do this with the smallest possible personnel. The tables have been so well worked out for the inspector that he has no more to do with the mathematical calculations behind them than a radar operator with the theory of electronics.

The process inspector who is checking Norden ³⁄₃₂-of-an-inch balls finds himself, for example, with a lot of 1,400 after lapping, just before they are to leave his section. He knows that the cost, engineering, and quality-control departments have guaranteed to the customer that the average quality will contain no more than .1 per cent defects; this is called the Average Outgoing Quality Limit (AOQL). From his daily experience he sees that the process average, or average of defects, has been running at .03 per cent. He refers to his Dodge-Romig tables, which, under these conditions, prescribe a total sample of 670 balls to be divided into two groups, the first of 430 and the second of 240. If no defects are found when he goes over the 430 group, the entire lot of 1,400 is acceptable. But if one ball out of the 430 has a defect, he has to inspect the second group of 240. If out of the total sample of 670 only one defect is discovered, he can let the lot go; but if he finds two, it is unacceptable. He reports this to the production foreman, and search for the root of the trouble, whether in the steel, or machine, or the operator, is promptly begun. (The tighter the AOQL, the larger the sample size must be. If, in the above case, the AOQL had been 2 per cent instead of .1 per cent, a sampling of only seventy balls, thirty-three in the first group and thirty-seven in the second, would have been indicated.)

Once O.K.'d by the process inspector, the 1,400 balls are coated in a film of light oil and packed in a tray swimming with heavy oil to prevent them from nicking each other. Carried like crown jewels by porters walking as in a funeral cortège, the tray is delivered to the 100 per cent ball-inspection room; for in an ultra-precision product of this kind, where extra precautions against chance-inspired defects are needed, the statistical-sampling method—despite its general dependability—is not dependable enough. Only by testing every item 100 per cent can the quality standard be maintained.

Spotless as a surgery, the ball-inspection room is air conditioned to keep out dust motes and specks, and its temperature kept constant lest balls expand or contract. Under fluorescent lamps, 140 women without make-up are seated before long tables, intent over microscopes, seeking to probe out hidden pores, scratches, or discolorations in every ball. The women wear gloves, for a bead of perspiration from a hand would corrode the ball, making it useless. As good are sorted from bad, quality-control men move from bench to bench, transcribing the record of inspections from hour to hour. Every one of the 100,000 ³⁄₃₂-of-an-inch balls that go into the Norden bombsight every month is thus 100 per cent inspected; and then inspected again before it can depart from the SKF stockroom.

IT'S IN THE GROOVE

Crucial as the ³⁄₃₂-of-an-inch ball, but infinitely more difficult to make, are the inner and outer rings between which the ball moves and has its being. While thirteen operations are required to shape the inner ring, for example, twenty-three separate inspections are needed before it can be assembled into the bearing. No other item has caused SKF quite so much trouble.

Early in 1942 Dr. Styri of SKF research reported that advances in ball-bearing steel, which he has done much to promote, made it possible to finish the inner ring's groove, or track, to a smoothness of ²⁄₁,₀₀₀,₀₀₀ of an inch. This was something that Norden very much wanted; for this inner ring, together with the balls, carries the major burden in the bearing that acts as the bombsight's tilting control. It had already been more sensitized than tumblers in a safe. But Norden wanted it to start turning if breathed on at a distance of thirty inches, because the new height in bombing, 30,000 feet, requires more accurate functioning of the sight than ever before.

Despite Dr. Styri's assurance that the new steels would allow this sensitivity, the engineering department was in a dubious mood when it prepared specifications for size and tolerance. From these it made up blueprints, passing them along to Karl Kesselring, in charge of Norden bearings as well as other SKF high-precision work. The new specifications on the inner ring were both a challenge and a routine to him. In the preceding eleven years he had held various jobs with SKF but they always added up to the same thing, the attempt to obtain better bearing performance by means of higher exactitude; and in this respect the inner ring held a special hazard.

The ring's surface was to have a hitherto unimaginable smoothness. For nine out of the thirteen stages in its manufacture, Kesselring and his aides had to design special-purpose machines, notably for lapping and grinding, and build seven of them in SKF's own tool shops, for the machine-tool fraternity was either too busy or too skeptical to take on such assignments. Sometimes he was able to buy a general-purpose machine and regrind, repolish, refit, and readjust shafts, gears, cogs, and work heads sufficiently to meet inner-ring purposes.

The grinding machine for operation No. 10 was made in this way by the hundred and is doing very well. Standing neck-high, sheathed by scrofulous black cast iron, its apron bristling with dials and gauges, this machine's interior is jammed with intricate control devices; they are like demonstrations of a physics lecture on gravitational, centrifugal, and centripetal force. Weights and counterweights, cogs, gears, and pulleys for wheels and spindles keep moving clockwise and counter-clockwise, with a stately rhythm.

But before this grinder can be used, a setup man, who at SKF must be both an instructor and a very skilled all-round mechanic, familiar with blueprints, adjusts the machine with the care of a violinist tuning for the Bach Chaconne. He makes sure that the grinding wheel is balanced on the spindle, that the mandrel, or work holder, is aligned. He then runs off fifty samples, and with his own master set of measuring instruments checks for diameter dimensions, for grooving, for wobble, for surface tears or scratches, setting down the details in his logbook. Only when his samples comply with quality-control allowances, in this case one defective ring out of every fifty, can the operator take over. As a rule the work goes serenely from this point forward, but quite often it doesn't.

Perhaps the operator is a new employee and fails to notice, after the first half hour, that the stationary gauges on which she tests the rings are warning that too many of them are not being ground to the correct finish. But she doesn't remain in ignorance for long. The process inspector, who reviews the grinder's output about every forty-five minutes, has scrutinized a dozen of her rings under his pocket magnifying glass, and some don't look right. He tells the operator to stop while he checks further. He takes a batch of twenty-five rings to his own workbench and puts them under a fifteen-power microscope. Five of them seem to show scars and chatter (steel pimples). But to be completely certain he places them, like records under a phonograph needle, below the profilometer's fine diamond point, which rides over their surfaces and transmits electrically to a dial pointer the oscillations that show ridges on the rings.

Upon this evidence, the inspector instructs the setup man to readjust the machine, and the latter fusses with sizing and other devices, but when he makes his samples they too reveal the same proportion of flaws. He notifies the foreman, who has been selected less for his administrative than for his mechanical flair and experience, and he in turn tries his hand at setting the grinder at its appropriate standard. But it still remains off the beam. The chief of the maintenance crew is summoned and he and the foreman perhaps diagnose the trouble as arising from two slides that are worn. The machine is carted off to the repair department for resynchronizing.

Meanwhile, neither the process inspector nor the foreman knows how many defectives have slipped through their *cordon sanitaire*. The entire lot is declared to be "out of control," and every ring must be inspected 100 per cent before going on to the next stage in the process. Defectives are salvaged by reoperation, or scrapped. Rings that are approved are moved along, step by step, and, when the last operation is completed, are taken to the final inspection room, where the tables are crowded with an enormous array of measuring and contour devices, to assist the inspectors to check for everything from nicks to murky appearance. There is the profile gauge, which, held to the light, will show up the slightest variation in shape. There is the visual comparator, which throws on the screen a $62\frac{1}{2}$ to 1 enlargement showing trueness of contour, and there are the master rings, with which the item is compared just before final assembly into the bearing.

By fusing statistical sampling with 100 per cent inspection, SKF has achieved a high level of quality control in certain departments, keeping rejections down to an average of 3 per cent. But in departments where quality control is not yet installed or is only partial, rejections sometimes run as high as from 7 to 20 per cent. The difference in costs for inspection and other labor, as well as for waste, is very appreciable. Upon this basis of comparison, Kesselring and Gotwals have become converted to the Shewhart system. Yet they regard it more as a valuable means of inspection, which is only a part of quality control, than as a drastic reform that has changed the entire conception of quality control from the static to the dynamic. But no one can doubt that wartime pressures have fostered a sharper recognition of quality control's value and importance and the high potentialities it affords in the post-war period for using finer materials at lower cost.

Editors of "Time"

Time likes to call itself "curt, clear, complete." To these virtues it joins certain mannerisms, amusing to some readers, irritating to others: inverted sentences, omitted connectives, audacious epithets, invented words and compounds, alliteration, all of which undoubtedly make for liveliness and emphasis and already place their impress on American style. The following biographical-scientific article represents the skilled collaboration of various editors, researchers, and other staff members of Time.

TWENTIETH CENTURY SEER

MEDICAL news last week vied with news of the days before invasion. Under the aspect of eternity, the medical news might even be more important than the military. WPB announced that the wonder drug penicillin, for three years practically a monopoly of the Army and Navy, was now being manufactured in such quantity that it can be issued to civilians. Some 1,000 hospitals will be allowed to buy generous monthly quotas for distribution to patients and other hospitals as they see fit.

For impatient sufferers (many of them dying), the good news came none too soon. Penicillin (sometimes rhymes with villain, sometimes with whistle

in) is the best treatment for all staphylococcic infections, all hemolytic strep-
tococcic infections, clostridia infections, pneumococcic infections (of the lin-
ing of skull, spinal cord, lung and heart surfaces), pneumococcic pneumonia
that sulfa drugs will not cure, all gonococcic infections (including all gonorrhea that sulfa drugs will not cure). Diseases against which penicillin is
effective but not fully tested: syphilis, actinomycosis, bacterial endocarditis.

THE SCIENTIFIC VISION

The man who made possible this incalculable alleviation of human suffering is Dr. Alexander Fleming, discoverer of the antibacterial effect of the
mold from which penicillin is made. He is a short (5 ft. 7 in.), gentle, retiring Scot with somewhat dreamy blue eyes, fierce white hair and a mulling
mind, which, when it moves, moves with the thrust of a cobra. Until time's
solvent has dissolved the human slag, it will be hard to say who the great
men of the 20th Century are. But Dr. Alexander Fleming is almost certainly one of them.

For he belongs in the tradition of the scientific seers, which includes
Galileo watching the swing of a lamp in the Cathedral of Pisa and deducing
from it the law of the pendulum, and Isaac Newton watching the fall of
an apple and deducing from it the law of gravity. For thousands of years
men looked at the cryptogamic mold called *Penicillium notatum,* but Dr.
Fleming was the first to see its cryptic meaning. His discernment, restoring
to science the creative vision which it has sometimes been held to lack, also
restored health to millions of men living and unborn.

The story of his discovery is legendary. Back in 1928 Alexander Fleming,
M.B., B.S., F.R.C.S.,[1] taught bacteriology at St. Mary's Hospital Medical
School, University of London. In his small, old-fashioned laboratory, he
grew staphylococci in petri plates (flat glass culture dishes). One day he
found that mold had spoiled one of his cultures. Staphylococcus grew on
only half of the plate. A blue-green mold spotted, but did not cover, the
other half.

He noticed that the mold had cleared a wide, bacteria-free area between
itself and the staphylococci—perhaps had killed them. He did not destroy
the moldy culture.

It was a great moment in the drama of medicine: the moment when Dr.
Faustus opens Nostradamus' secret book, comprehends in a flash the sign
of the macrocosm, and is able at last to conjure up the Earth Spirit. But that
was not the way Dr. Fleming reported his epochal perception. Said he: "I
was sufficiently interested in the antibacterial substance produced by the
mold to pursue the subject."

[1] Bachelor of Medicine, Bachelor of Surgery. Fellow of the Royal College of Surgeons. Last
year he added F.R.S. (Fellow of the Royal Society), a great honor.

THE SCIENTIFIC METHOD

Dr. Fleming stuck a loop of platinum wire into the mold colony, dipped the wire into some mold-growing liquid in a test tube. In less than a week, there was a felt-like growth at the mouth of the tube and a half-inch of cloudy liquid below it. To Dr. Fleming's amazement, the liquid in which the culture grew, even when diluted 800 times, prevented staphylococci from growing at all: "It was therefore some two or three times as strong in that respect as pure carbolic acid."

Soon Dr. Fleming had ascertained that: (1) the strange liquid did not harm fresh leucocytes (white blood corpuscles); (2) injections of the liquid did not hurt mice; (3) some bacteria (e.g., whooping cough bacillus) lived in the liquid as cozily as in a baby's throat. Modest Dr. Fleming saved the moldy plate as a souvenir, still has it.

Next year what Dr. Fleming knew about the mold's bacteria-baiting by-product appeared in the British *Journal of Experimental Pathology*. He had found out that the mold was some kind of Penicillium (from the Latin for pencil—the shape of the magnified mold). He named its by-product penicillin.

THE MAN

Alexander Fleming was born (1881) in Darvel, in Ayrshire, the son of a farmer. He went to St. Mary's Hospital Medical School, largely because it won the Rugger cup and had had a championship swimming team the year before. (Dr. Fleming still loves to swim. His other hobby is rifle shooting.) When he graduated in 1908, he took honors in physiology, pharmacology, medicine, pathology, forensic medicine and hygiene, received the University Gold Medal.

He went to work immediately in St. Mary's pathology laboratory under Sir Almroth Wright, now 83, pioneer in vaccine therapy and grand old man of British medicine. Sir Almroth whetted young Fleming's interest in the mysterious destruction of bacteria by white blood corpuscles and the problem of antiseptics. As a captain in the medical corps in France during World War I, Dr. Fleming noticed that the antiseptics then in use (chiefly Carrel-Dakin's solution) hurt the white blood corpuscles even more than they hurt bacteria. In some cases the antiseptics promoted infection by destroying the body's own defenses.

After the war, Dr. Fleming went back to the peaceful laboratory and teaching routine which he still follows. He held classes, ate his lunch in St. Mary's gloomy refectory, where diners are served soup, "cut off the joint and two veg," rice pudding, prunes, and tea for one shilling sevenpence. Sometimes at the end of the day he went across from the hospital to The Fountains, a potted-palm pub in Praed Street, for a glass of beer before going home to spend the evening with his wife and son (now a medical student in St. Mary's). Now and again he would write a scientific paper.

One idea ran through all his work: he would look for some naturally occurring bacteria-fighter (new term: antibiotic substance) that would not harm animal tissue. The first antibiotic Dr. Fleming found was lysozyme. It occurs in tears and egg white, can dissolve some bacteria, most of them harmless. That was in 1922—six years before the day when he first saw and grasped the meaning of the sterile ring around the penicillium mold.

Having made his great discovery, Dr. Fleming went on to other work. He was engaged in many other experiments—no scientist knows just which of his bottles contains the Nobel Prize. In the history of penicillin there ensued eleven years almost as sterile as the area around the penicillium.

The hiatus might not have been so long if during that period Germany's Gerhard Domagk had not discovered sulfa drugs, which began to save lives so dramatically that the experts dropped everything else to test them out. In 1933, Dr. Fleming himself lent a hand with M & B 693, also known as sulfapyridine. The sulfas almost seemed to be the dream drugs he had looked for. They stopped deadly streptococci, even cured pneumonia. But the more sulfa drugs were used, the clearer it became that they (1) sometimes delayed healing by irritating wound walls, (2) did not work well in serum or pus. When used internally, they can cause severe, sometimes fatal, toxic reactions.

THE PRACTICAL APPLICATION

By 1938, when World War II loomed, a good internal and external antiseptic was still to seek. But at Oxford's Sir William Dunn School of Pathology (53 miles from Dr. Fleming's laboratory) the man who was to make Dr. Fleming's discovery save human lives was already at work on the problem. He was Dr. Howard Walter Florey, 45, an Australia-born professor of pathology. He organized a research team to study the practical extraction of capricious penicillin. The team included experts in chemistry, bacteriology, pathology and medicine. Among them: Mrs. Florey, who is also a doctor, and Dr. Ernst Boris Chain, a brilliant half-French, half-Russian enzyme chemist who shares with Dr. Florey the honors for developing penicillin.

Under Dr. Florey's dynamic supervision, the blue-green penicillium mold began to grow again. The researchers discovered that the best growing temperature is about 75° F., that the mold needs plenty of air. At first, Dr. Florey's researchers got only about a gram of reddish-brown powder (the sodium salt of penicillin—penicillin itself is an unstable acid) from 100 liters of the mold liquid. But at last, after heroic chemical cookery, they accumulated enough penicillin to test the drug on living creatures.

OF MICE AND MEN

Then eight mice were inoculated with a deadly strain of streptococci. Says Dr. Florey: "We sat up through the night injecting penicillin every three hours into the treated group [four mice]. I must confess that it was one of the more exciting moments when we found in the morning that all the untreated mice were dead and all the penicillin-treated ones alive."

During that historic night, Dr. Fleming's vision turned into a medical reality.

From mice to men was a long, hazardous step. With practically the whole Sir William Dunn School at work, it took many months before there was enough penicillin to treat a man. Penicillin's first human guinea pig was a policeman dying of staphylococcus septicemia (blood infection). After five days on penicillin, he "felt much improved." He felt that way for ten days. Then the bacteria began to multiply again. As there was no more penicillin, he died. Case No. 2 was lost in the same way. The next cases were luckier. At the end of that first series of ten cases, Dr. Florey and his researchers had proved that:

Penicillin is effective against bacteria when injected into muscle or blood stream.

Penicillin by mouth is useless, because it is destroyed by acid stomach juices.

Penicillin works well in the presence of blood serum and pus, is therefore an ideal wound "antiseptic."

Penicillin disappears from the blood in an hour or so and about half of it is excreted in the urine. Says Dr. Florey: "Like pouring water down a basin with the plug out."

They also proved that, unlike the sulfa drugs, which cause bacteria to starve to death, penicillin prevents them from dividing and multiplying— they swell up, but for some as yet undiscovered reason, no longer divide. Penicillin does not kill bacteria—it makes them easy for the body defenses to kill. Sometimes bacteria become "penicillin-fast," *i.e.*, able to survive in the presence of penicillin. (In the presence of sulfa drugs they may also become sulfa-fast.)

Dr. Florey and his researchers also discovered that the purer they made penicillin, the paler it was and the less toxic. Since then, no patient has ever had to stop taking penicillin because of toxic reaction.

At first, U. S. manufacturers grew the mold in flasks. A few U. S. hospitals made penicillin by "kitchen culture." But through the whole winter of 1942, only enough penicillin was made in the U. S. to treat about 50 patients.

By June 1943, enough was coming through for the National Research Council's Committee on Chemotherapeutic and Other Agents, headed by

Dr. Chester J. Keefer of Boston, to begin doling penicillin out to 22 groups of doctors all over the U. S., who used it on a handful of civilian guinea pigs.

A catastrophe helped put penicillin into large-scale production. Dr. Keefer used penicillin for Boston's Coconut Grove fire victims. U. S. doctors were impressed by the results, demanded penicillin in large quantities. Priority troubles melted away. Last fall, with the help of specially loaned Army expediters, a dozen big drug and chemical manufacturers were running up $20,000,000 worth of penicillin buildings. Some manufacturers never had any pilot plants at all, performed the unheard-of feat of going into mass production right from the laboratory. Big chemical companies which had never fussed with fungus before waited patiently for the blue-green mold. Some distillers, familiar with fermentation, began growing mold in idle vats and financing experimental work in colleges. Mushroom growers around West Grove, Pa., spawned penicillium where mushrooms used to breed.

Doctors and amateurs also began to grow the mold on their own. The usual method was to let penicillium grow on gauze, then use the gauze for a bandage.

THE MIRACLE

Last year penicillin patients were still rare enough to be front-page news. First such case was two-year-old Patricia Malone of Jackson Heights, Queens. The New York *Journal-American,* which begged enough penicillin from Dr. Keefer to save her life from staphylococcic septicemia, last week won the Pulitzer Prize for the story. After that, the whole nation watched one "hopeless" case after another get well.

There were the three doctors in the California mountains last winter who saved a seven-year-old girl when gas gangrene had forced repeated amputations of her left arm up to the shoulder: "As a last resort, penicillin was given after all hope had been abandoned for a recovery, which came like a miracle." There was a doctor in Sioux Falls, S. D., who was astonished to save a man moribund with osteomyelitis and septicemia after sulfadiazine had failed: "This being the first case in which I have employed penicillin therapy, I feel that the results obtained, to say the least, were miraculous."

Doctors now know in general which diseases penicillin helps, have worked out a tentative schedule of dosage. Present consensus is that 40,000 to 120,000 units daily, given gradually by vein or intramuscular injection for about a week, should cure the average case with a systemic infection. Treatment for gonorrhea is usually much shorter; treatment for subacute bacterial endocarditis, much longer. For application to wounds, about 50,000 units in salt solution is used, varying with the size of the wound.

Penicillin seems to cure most of the bacterial diseases that the sulfa drugs cure and cures them more quickly, effectively and less dangerously. It also seems to be a quick cure of early syphilis—the first safe and effective drug to kill the spirochete. Sulfa drugs are not effective against syphilis. But penicillin will not entirely supplant sulfa drugs. The sulfa drugs are still necessary for: (1) intestinal infections (penicillin is destroyed in the digestive tract); (2) *bacillus coli* infections of the urinary tract (penicillin does not attack *b. coli*); (3) as prophylactics in epidemics of certain diseases like meningitis, pneumonia, gonorrhea (penicillin is excreted too fast to be used for this purpose).

Penicillin is already big business, yet Dr. Fleming (who discovered it) and Dr. Florey (who made it tick) have got nothing out of it but praise— doctors generally do not patent drugs. Penicillin will save more lives than war spends, but there has been no military citation. Most tangible recognition so far was the Award of Merit of the American Pharmaceutical Manufacturers' Association given to Drs. Fleming and Florey last December. Several months ago, a proposal to give Dr. Fleming a grant from the public funds was brought up in Parliament, but nothing came of it.

To Dr. Fleming, whose pioneer mind has reverted to watching and waiting, penicillin is not an end, but a beginning. He foresees that when the chemical structure of penicillin is known, chemists will make many new potent drugs out of it. And his eyes are already fixed on fungoidal infinities. For there are at least 100,000 molds and fungi, any one of which may one day supplant *Penicillium notatum,* or yield a drug with which to cure the many plagues penicillin leaves untouched. "It would be strange indeed," says Dr. Fleming, who is hard at work on other antibiotics, "if the first one described remained the best."

Anna Louise Strong

Anna Louise Strong (1885-   ) was born in Nebraska of a family which came to the United States in 1630. After undergraduate work at Bryn Mawr and Oberlin and a doctorate at University of Chicago, she entered child welfare work as an expert attached to the Children's Bureau. Since 1921, when she went to Poland to write publicity for the Quaker Relief, she has been a foreign correspondent of ability and insight. For fourteen years she interpreted Soviet Russia to American readers. She has seen revolution in Spain, China, and Mexico, and has told the story of her life in I Change Worlds *and* One Fifth of Mankind. *After twenty years she returned to the United States to study it with the objective eyes of a visitor:* My Native Land *is the account of an automobile journey across the country. Writing from a frankly liberal point of view Miss Strong describes the success of the Tennessee Valley Authority with undisguised satisfaction.*

TVA IS POWER

THE basin of the Tennessee River crosses seven state boundaries in a four-hundred-mile sweep from east to west. Down the westward slopes of the mountains of Virginia and North Carolina the waters flow to meet in a single river in the hills of Eastern Tennessee. The river curves southward to drain a corner of Georgia, crosses the northern part of Alabama, touches the edge of Mississippi, and then drives north across Tennessee again and through Kentucky to join the Ohio River and merge with it in the greater Mississippi. Half of the 26,500,000 acres in the basin are in timber or farm woodlots; the other half is in pasture and cultivated fields. Fifty-two inches of annual rainfall keep the soil forever watered. Crops range from grass and grain to cotton. Coal, potash, copper, and other minerals make possible a well-balanced civilization, including both industry and farming among these beautiful hills.

Nearly one hundred and fifty years ago Thomas Jefferson first recognized the importance of the water route from the Tennessee hills to the Gulf of Mexico. Both in the treaty which he made with Spain as Secretary of State under Washington and again in the Louisiana Purchase made when he was President, he sought to bring the entire basin of the Mississippi under American sovereignty. His great plan for internal improvements included an improved waterway down the Tennessee. It was defeated by Federalist opposition and later by the War of 1812, but still later his friend James

Monroe revived the idea and demanded—as President in 1825—a canal around Muscle Shoals as one of the three most necessary improvements for the development of America.

These far-seeing projects languished for a century. During that century everything that could be done to ruin a valley was done in the Tennessee Basin. Northern capitalism and Southern feudalism wrecked it together, first in combat and then in combination. Great battles ravaged it in the War between the States. After the war, big business of the Atlantic seaboard looted it, draining it of raw materials and preventing its industrial development by discriminatory freight rates which had the effect of a 40 per cent tariff along the northern boundary of Kentucky. Lumber companies swept through the timberlands and left them devastated. Coal companies looted the surface coal for quick profits and destroyed access to the deeper veins. Landlords, who had first despoiled the better lands by slave plantations, ruined them still further by sharecropping, which gives the soil tiller no interest in preserving the soil. Smaller free farmers, unable to compete against peon labor, fled to a poverty-stricken independence on the poor soils in the hills.

The blessing of copious rainfall became a curse under such conditions. Six thousand tons of rain fall every year upon each acre. Once it seeped slowly through luxuriant foliage and heavy undergrowth into matted humus. Now it strikes with blows on the barren or the overtilled soil. It cuts the topsoil into gullies and carries it down the slopes. From the bleeding hills the mingled soil and water rush into floods in the valleys. The direct flood destruction causes an annual loss of $1,780,000 in the Tennessee Valley alone. This loss is only the beginning. Rushing onward, the Tennessee floods pile up in the greater floods of the Mississippi, adding to their destructiveness an estimated $20,000,000 a year. Adding also the Tennessee Basin's share of precious topsoil to the acre a minute which the Father of Waters carries from American farms to the Gulf. Two million of the thirteen million acres of farmland in the Valley are permanently ruined and eight million are in less serious stages of erosion. In the Ducktown copper-mining area is a hideous man-made desert which cannot even be crossed on horseback because the unchecked water has torn it into many vertical gullies ten to twenty feet deep. This is merely one extreme example of the ravaging of the whole Tennessee Valley.

Most of the people in the Valley try to live by bending over the ground and scratching it. Despite some beautiful estates like Homer Hancock's in the Blue Grass region, the per capita wealth in the Valley is only half that of the United States as a whole. Farm families commonly have cash incomes of $100 a year. In one mountain county in 1933 the average cash income was $45 for the year—not the week or the month—and $10 of it came from relief. In another, half the farming families had no work animals, neither mule nor ox, and two out of five had neither a cow nor a pig. Two million people left the Valley to seek jobs in the Northern industrial centers during the boom years of the 1920's. After the crash of 1929 a million of them had to come back. But there was nothing to come to. There was not even a system of state relief such as the stronger Northern states support. There was only county relief from counties so bankrupt that they expected white folk to live on $3 to $5 a month, and Negroes on $1.50. They don't live long on that. Tennessee has the highest tuberculosis rate in the nation.

Such was the Valley and the human beings who received the Tennessee Valley Authority by act of Congress, May 1933. "Authority" was a new word—not "department" or "administration." It implied new powers. TVA was authorized to "maintain properties . . . in the interests of national defense, and for agricultural and industrial development, and to improve navigation on the Tennessee, and to control destructive flood waters in the Tennessee and Mississippi River Basins." Thus a whole series of tasks, usually scattered through government departments, was concentrated in a single body. This body was not a government department, supported by taxation, but a corporation which was expected to pay for itself by developing the resources of a great valley.

With TVA the whole theory of the New Deal began to come to consciousness—the view that the federal government can no longer be merely a police power and clearing-house for information between the states but must intervene actively in economic life. The words "regional planning of land and water resources" appeared for the first time in America. Yet Wall Street did not seriously attack the TVA at the beginning. You remember those tumultuous days of early 1933 when the banks were crashing all around and the whole of Wall Street finance capital was discredited, and Roosevelt called the bank holiday. The assistance he gave to the banks and the trust-encouraging policies of NRA made his intention to save the capitalists so clear from the beginning that the big private utilities naturally thought that TVA would be used for their benefit.

For ten years Wilson Dam, the first of the TVA properties, had already been used to benefit the private power companies. This dam was begun by President Wilson at Muscle Shoals to supply power for making the nitrates needed in war. When Harding came in, the war emergency was over; all work on the dam stopped until a lot of private corporations that wanted to own it allowed Congress to complete it in 1924. After this the big corporations fought for it among themselves; Ford was among the chief claimants. At one time there were a hundred and fifty-two bills before Congress, each giving the dam to somebody for a song. Senator Norris of Nebraska, that veteran fighter for public ownership, managed to keep the dam as government property, but all its power was sold wholesale to the Alabama Power Company for 2 mills per kilowatt hour. The company retailed it right on the spot for 10 cents a kilowatt hour, just fifty times what it cost them. This was what the private utility companies expected to result from the whole TVA development.

The TVA program included ten dams on the Tennessee River and its tributaries. These would make the river navigable from the Ohio to Knoxville, a distance of more than 600 miles, and would connect the Tennessee Valley with 5700 miles of inland waterways in the Mississippi Valley, thus reducing freight rates and encouraging industrial development. Floods would be prevented not only by the dam but by a system of soil-conservation work on farms and in the hills, for which the labor of local farmers and CCC boys would be employed. Not only would all floods be stopped in the Tennessee Valley, but high water on the great Mississippi would be lowered by two or three feet, a margin best appreciated by those who have laid sandbags against the fury of the floods. The dams would also supply power which would eventually reach 1,500,000 to 2,000,000 kilowatts, in an interconnected system extending along the river for almost 700 miles. The cost of the whole program was estimated at just over half a billion dollars, of which 52 per cent was allocated to power, 20 per cent to flood control, and 28 per cent to navigation. The sale of power, however, was expected in thirty years to return the whole investment, making the eventual cost for navigation and flood control zero.

When the TVA came into the Valley in 1933, it found people who had worked at lumbering and who were now sitting among the stumps of their country. It found thousands of stranded coal miners who never expected to have a chance to work in mines again. It found poverty-stricken farmers and sharecroppers on ruined lands. They were far worse off than the unemployed in Northern states, for, even if "prosperity" came back, there was no industry to reopen here. TVA bought up nearly half a million acres at an average cost of $51.82 an acre, and began removing 5002 families from the water's coming path. It began the projecting and building of dams. It arranged with the United States Forest Service and the CCC boys to build tens of thousands of tiny dams in little gullies far up in the hills, to plant seedling trees by the millions, and to supply fertilizers to farmers so that grass might again return to ruined slopes.

So far so good. But TVA did not stop with these generally applauded activities. It possessed a power plant at Wilson Dam already. It began selling power direct to municipally owned power companies and farmers' cooperatives at an average price of 7 mills per kilowatt hour, including transmission. It also fixed the retail price which these organizations might charge the ultimate consumer, beginning with 3 cents for minimum use and dropping to 4 mills for maximum use.

Then the storm broke. Families in the town of Tupelo, Mississippi, who had been paying $2.30 a month for lights in their cottage saw the bill drop to 75 cents under TVA. The big department store saw its bill for electricity go down from $65.14 to $23.69 in a single month. Everyone at once began using more electricity and buying electrical appliances. So the cost went down some more because of the larger quantity used. In a year's time the mayor of Tupelo announced that power was coming into the city at 5½ mills per kilowatt hour instead of the 17 mills of the previous year. The same thing was happening in other towns and in farmers' co-operatives. A tremendous undeveloped market of people longing for light had been opened by TVA.

At once it became clear that ownership of electric power gave authority over the Valley's whole life. The town of Florence, Alabama, situated at Wilson Dam, wanted to buy all its output and by hogging the power become the big manufacturing center, with rocketing real estate prices. "No," said TVA, "we are not building that kind of civilization. We are scattering electricity around." Half a dozen cities wanted to buy cheap electricity while maintaining the former retail price to consumers; the profits, they said, would pay all costs of city government and eliminate taxes entirely. "No," said TVA, "we aren't allowing any concealed sales tax on electricity as a basis for your city government. It wouldn't develop your city, anyway." All the time TVA was making decisions like these; it had power to determine the future movements of industry and populations, an authority greater than government, antecedent to government. This is the power that private utility companies have had since the knowledge of electricity began.

No wonder the private utility companies broke loose with fury in an attack on TVA which shook the whole United States. Court suits against the use of TVA funds for municipal plants were launched in sixty-one towns. Other suits challenged the legality of farmers' co-operatives. One suit halted the building of a municipal plant by the big city of Knoxville; another prevented the sale of TVA power to fourteen Alabama towns that had voted for it. One suit even charged the United States government with "conspiracy," presumably against the rights of private business. Two suits, which were carried as far as the Supreme Court, attacked the right of the federal government to build dams or sell power at all, though it had done so to private power companies unchallenged through three Republican administrations. In 1938, TVA estimated that forty-one suits had cost the Authority nearly six million dollars in legal expenses; they had cost the Tennessee Valley consumers seven million more through delay in securing cheap power. The aim of the suits was of course to delay the sale of TVA power, to make it expensive, to discourage those cities which had voted for TVA power and couldn't get it, and thus to make TVA so disappointing that public sentiment might turn against it.

The cost of these attacks will be forever paid for by the people of the Tennessee Valley, through the increased initial cost of TVA.

A nation-wide barrage of propaganda, of skillfully combined half-truths and lies, was launched against the TVA. Utility companies are experienced propagandists; the National Electric Light Association, their former publicity agency, spent a stupendous amount for propaganda. The manager said to members who questioned the heavy expenditure: "Don't worry about expense; the public pays it." Exposure by the Federal Trade Commission abolished that particular propaganda agency, but not the type of propaganda.

Tennessee hill farmers who had never used electricity were solemnly told that TVA power was of an inferior grade that wouldn't get over the hills. Proof was found in the light construction of poles and wires, a new invention whereby the Rural Electrification laboratories in Washington had cut transmission costs in half. "Our heavy lines," said the companies, "give 'ethyl' kilowatts." The propaganda was supplemented by direct bribes of free electric refrigerators for directors of farmers' co-operatives. Spite-lines were built to give private electricity to clusters of farms which TVA needed to strengthen a far-flung network to more distant farms. In one place the company rushed its poles into the holes of a TVA survey. Company pole-setters were so insistent that one farmer's wife in Catoosa County, Georgia, held them off her farm with a gun.

The variety of propaganda was amazing. In Southern Alabama, which gets no TVA power, the shrinkage of school funds was blamed on "TVA's non-payment of taxes" in the northern counties of the state. A bill was actually brought into the State Legislature to fine municipalities for every kilowatt of TVA power they used. But investigation showed that the decline in tax-receipts was in the southern counties, while the TVA counties were almost the only places in the United States where, owing to the boom in industry, tax-receipts had not decreased. The same kind of propaganda, however, continued on a nation-wide scale. The *Saturday Evening Post* announced: "Every time somebody switches on a light in Tupelo, each of us in Kansas City or Spokane has a little added to his taxes." Which is utter nonsense, for TVA was paid for by bonds which will be retired with interest, without adding a cent of taxes at any stage.

A favorite attack—it has kept on from the beginning—is that TVA "pays no taxes as private companies do," and hence burdens local taxpayers and lessens the income of local governments. When proof is adduced that TVA does pay taxes, the charge then shifts to the claim that it pays much less than the private companies paid. Few are the citizens who will trouble to work through the statistics until they learn that TVA possesses only the dams and big transmission lines, while the retail distributing systems—the most profitable part of the business—are owned by the municipalities and farmers' co-operatives. These also pay taxes, but their taxes are not listed as taxes of TVA. Nor do the propagandists mention the savings to the city budgets—not to mention the private consumers—on the bills for water-pumping and street lights.

TVA returned good for evil. It was an amazing paradox. All through those years of lawsuits and spite-lines and lying propaganda, TVA was helping the private utilities themselves increase their profits! Their power consumption did not decline when TVA arrived; it rose. In 1935 it passed that of the boom year 1929, and reached an all-time high in 1937 and again in 1938. The Tennessee Electric Power Company, chief TVA antagonist, solemnly stated in 1933 that a 20 per cent cut in its rates would spell ruin. The following year it cut rates 46 per cent to compete with Wilson Dam; at once its domestic sales doubled, and its sales of electric appliances tripled in a single year. It won the prize for "outstanding business growth" from the National Utilities Convention—the private companies of the whole United States meeting in Atlantic City. This was the result of the New Deal policy of forcing the capitalists to make profits, against their own tendency to stagnate.

It was a staggering revelation—for those who could understand it—of the deadening bureaucracy of these big private corporations and their incapacity to advance. Leon Jouralmon, Commissioner of Railroads and Public Utilities in Nashville, told me: "The power industry is notorious for high directors' salaries, overcapitalized plants, padded operating costs, and unconscionable profits. It is impossible to tell what their cost of production really is. . . . Attempts to regulate them are hamstrung by state legislatures and held up by courts till utility regulation is a byword for farcical futility." TVA broke through this farcical futility by forcing expansion of the market through cheap prices. It developed a market which the private companies were too lazy, too fat with monopoly profits, to develop. TVA helped them make money; yet they cursed it and tried to strangle it, for depriving them of their soft thrones of exclusive power.

After nearly six years of TVA operation, on January 20, 1939, the United States Supreme Court finally legalized the existence of TVA. At once the Commonwealth and Southern, parent corporation of a whole group of private companies in the Valley, decided to sell out to TVA. Despite their recent increase of profits, they knew they were finished in the Valley.

Katherine Anne Porter

*"My one aim is to tell a straight story and to give true testimony." In these words, Katherine Anne Porter (1894-   ) states the purpose which, steadfastly pursued, has carried her to the first rank of American writers. Her artistry is the result of self-imposed discipline and suggests, in its sheer excellence, the work of Flaubert. She has published surprisingly little—*Flowering Judas, Pale Horse, Pale Rider, The Leaning Tower—*but she will not be hurried or easily satisfied. The subtlety of her method is apparent in "A Day's Work," ostensibly a story of sordid lives but never disregardful of the fierce affections of the lowest.*

A DAY'S WORK

THE dull scrambling like a giant rat in the wall meant the dumb-waiter was on its way up, the janitress below hauling on the cable. Mrs. Halloran paused, thumped her iron on the board, and said, "There it is. Late. You could have put on your shoes and gone around the corner and brought the things an hour ago. I can't do everything."

Mr. Halloran pulled himself out of the chair, clutching the arms and heaving to his feet slowly, looking around as if he hoped to find crutches standing near. "Wearing out your socks, too," added Mrs. Halloran. "You ought either go barefoot outright or wear your shoes over your socks as God intended," she said. "Sock feet. What's the good of it, I'd like to know? Neither one thing nor the other."

She unrolled a salmon-colored chiffon nightgown with cream-colored lace and broad ribbons on it, gave it a light flirt in the air, and spread it on the board. "God's mercy, look at that indecent thing," she said. She thumped the iron again and pushed it back and forth over the rumpled cloth. "You might just set the things in the cupboard," she said, "and not leave them around on the floor. You might just."

Mr. Halloran took a sack of potatoes from the dumb-waiter and started for the cupboard in the corner next the icebox. "You might as well take a load," said Mrs. Halloran. "There's no need on earth making a half-dozen trips back and forth. I'd think the poorest sort of man could well carry more than five pounds of potatoes at one time. But maybe not."

Her voice tapped on Mr. Halloran's ears like wood on wood. "Mind your business, will you?" he asked, not speaking to her directly. He carried on the argument with himself. "Oh, I couldn't do that, Mister Honey," he answered in a dull falsetto. "Don't ever ask me to think of such a thing,

257

even. It wouldn't be right," he said, standing still with his knees bent, glaring bitterly over the potato sack at the scrawny strange woman he had never liked, that one standing there ironing clothes with a dirty look on her whole face like a suffering saint. "I may not be much good any more," he told her in his own voice, "but I still have got wits enough to take groceries off a dumb-waiter, mind you."

"That's a miracle," said Mrs. Halloran. "I'm thankful for that much."

"There's the telephone," said Mr. Halloran, sitting in the armchair again and taking his pipe out of his shirt pocket.

"I heard it as well," said Mrs. Halloran, sliding the iron up and down over the salmon-colored chiffon.

"It's for you, I've no further business in this world," said Mr. Halloran. His little greenish eyes glittered; he exposed his two sharp dogteeth in a grin.

"You could answer it. It could be the wrong number again or for somebody downstairs," said Mrs. Halloran, her flat voice going flatter, even.

"Let it go in any case," decided Mr. Halloran, "for my own part, that is." He struck a match on the arm of his chair, touched off his pipe, and drew in his first puff while the telephone went on with its nagging.

"It might be Maggie again," said Mrs. Halloran.

"Let her ring, then," said Mr. Halloran, settling back and crossing his legs.

"God help a man who won't answer the telephone when his own daughter calls up for a word," commented Mrs. Halloran to the ceiling. "And she in deep trouble, too, with her husband treating her like a dog about the money, and sitting out late nights in saloons with that crowd from the Little Tammany Association. He's getting into politics now with the McCorkery gang. No good will come of it, and I told her as much."

"She's no troubles at all, her man's a sharp fellow who will get ahead if she'll let him alone," said Mr. Halloran. "She's nothing to complain of, I could tell her. But what's a father?" Mr. Halloran cocked his head toward the window that opened on the brick-paved areaway and crowed like a rooster, "What's a father these days and who would heed his advice?"

"You needn't tell the neighbors, there's disgrace enough already," said Mrs. Halloran. She set the iron back on the gas ring and stepped out to the telephone on the first stair landing. Mr. Halloran leaned forward, his thin, red-haired hands hanging loosely between his knees, his warm pipe sending up its good decent smell right into his nose. The woman hated the pipe and the smell; she was a woman born to make any man miserable. Before the depression, while he still had a good job and prospects of a raise, before he went on relief, before she took in fancy washing and ironing, in the Good Days Before, God's pity, she didn't exactly keep her mouth shut, there wasn't a word known to man she couldn't find an answer for, but she knew which side her bread was buttered on, and put up with it. Now she was, you might say, buttering her own bread and she never forgot it for a minute. And it's her own fault we're not riding round today in a limousine with ash trays and a speaking tube and a cut-glass vase for flowers in it. It's what a man gets for marrying one of these holy women. Gerald McCorkery had told him as much, in the beginning.

"There's a girl will spend her time holding you down," Gerald had told him. "You're putting your head in a noose will strangle the life out of you. Heed the advice of one who wishes you well," said Gerald McCorkery. This was after he had barely set eyes on Lacey Mahaffy one Sunday morning in Coney Island. It was like McCorkery to see that in a flash, born judge of human nature that he was. He could look a man over, size him up, and there was an end to it. And if the man didn't pass muster, McCorkery could ease him out in a way that man would never know how it happened. It was the secret of McCorkery's success in the world.

"This is Rosie, herself," said Gerald that Sunday in Coney Island. "Meet the future Mrs. Gerald J. McCorkery." Lacey Mahaffy's narrow face had gone sour as whey under her big straw hat. She barely nodded to Rosie, who gave Mr. Halloran a look that fairly undressed him right there. Mr. Halloran had thought, too, that McCorkery was picking a strange one; she was good-looking all right, but she had the smell of a regular little Fourteenth Street hustler if Halloran knew anything about women. "Come on," said McCorkery, his arm around Rosie's waist, "let's all go on the roller coaster." But Lacey would not. She said, "No, thank you. We didn't plan to stay, and we must go now." On the way home Mr. Halloran said, "Lacey, you judge too harshly. Maybe that's a nice girl at heart; hasn't had your opportunities." Lacey had turned upon him a face ugly as an angry cat's, and said, "She's a loose, low woman, and 'twas an insult to introduce her to me." It was a good while before the pretty fresh face that Mr. Halloran had fallen in love with returned to her.

Next day in Billy's Place, after three drinks each, McCorkery said, "Watch your step, Halloran; think of your future. There's a straight good girl I don't doubt, but she's no sort of mixer. A man getting into politics needs a wife who can meet all kinds. A man needs a woman knows how to loosen her corsets and sit easy."

Mrs. Halloran's voice was going on in the hall, a steady dry rattle like old newspapers blowing on a park bench. "I told you before it's no good coming to me with your troubles now. I warned you in time but you wouldn't listen. . . . I told you just how it would be, I tried my best. . . . No, you couldn't listen, you always knew better than your mother. . . . So now all you've got to do is stand by your married vows and make the best of it. . . . Now listen to me, if you want himself to do right you have to do right first. The woman has to do right first, and then if the man won't do right in turn it's no fault of hers. You do right whether he does wrong or no, just because he does wrong is no excuse for you."

"Ah, will you hear that?" Mr. Halloran asked the areaway in an awed voice. "There's a holy terror of a saint for you."

". . . the woman has to do right first, I'm telling you," said Mrs. Halloran into the telephone, "and then if he's a devil in spite of it, why she has to do right without any help from him." Her voice rose so the neighbors could get an earful if they wanted. "I know you from old, you're just like your father. You must be doing something wrong yourself or you wouldn't be in this fix. You're doing wrong this minute, calling over the telephone when you ought to be getting your work done. I've got an iron on, working over the dirty nightgowns of a kind of woman I wouldn't soil my foot on if I'd had a man to take care of me. So now you do up your housework and dress yourself and take a walk in the fresh air. . . ."

"A little fresh air never hurt anybody," commented Mr. Halloran loudly through the open window. "It's the gas gets a man down."

"Now listen to me, Maggie, that's not the way to talk over the public wires. Now you stop that crying and go and do your duty and don't be worrying me any more. And stop saying you're going to leave your husband, because where will you go, for one thing? Do you want to walk the streets or set up a laundry in your kitchen? You can't come back here, you'll stay with your husband where you belong. Don't be a fool, Maggie. You've got your living, and that's more than many a woman better than you has got. Yes, your father's all right. No, he's just sitting here, the same. God knows what's to become of us. But you know how he is, little he cares. . . . Now remember this, Maggie, if anything goes wrong with your married life it's your own fault and you needn't come here for sympathy. . . . I can't waste any more time on it. Good-by."

Mr. Halloran, his ears standing up for fear of missing a word, thought how Gerald J. McCorkery had gone straight on up the ladder with Rosie; and for every step the McCorkerys took upward, he, Michael Halloran, had taken a step downward with Lacey Mahaffy. They had started as greenhorns with the same chances at the same time and the same friends, but McCorkery had seized all his opportunities as they came, getting in steadily with the Big Shots in ward politics, one good thing leading to another. Rosie had known how to back him up and push him onward. The McCorkerys for years had invited him and Lacey to come over to the house and be sociable with the crowd, but Lacey would not.

"You can't run with that fast set and drink and stay out nights and hold your job," said Lacey, "and you should know better than to ask your wife to associate with that woman." Mr. Halloran had got into the habit of dropping around by himself, now and again, for McCorkery still liked him, was still willing to give him a foothold in the right places, still asked him for favors at election time. There was always a good lively crowd at the Mc-Corkerys, wherever they were; for they moved ever so often to a better place, with more furniture. Rosie helped hand around the drinks, taking a few herself with a gay word for everybody. The player piano or the victrola would be going full blast, with everybody dancing, all looking like ready money and a bright future. He would get home late these evenings, back to the same little cold-water walk-up flat, because Lacey would not spend a dollar for show. It must all go into savings against old age, she said. He would be full of good food and drink, and find Lacey, in a bungalow apron, warming up the fried potatoes once more, cross and bitterly silent, hanging her head and frowning at the smell of liquor on his breath. "You might at least eat the potatoes when I've fried them and waited all this time," she would say. "Ah, eat them yourself, they're none of mine," he would snarl in his disappointment with her, and with the life she was leading him.

He had believed with all his heart for years that he would one day be manager of one of the G. and I. chain grocery stores he worked for, and when that hope gave out there was still his pension when they retired him. But two years before it was due they fired him, on account of the depression, they said. Overnight he was on the sidewalk, with no place to go with the news but home. "Jesus," said Mr. Halloran, still remembering that day after nearly seven years of idleness.

The depression hadn't touched McCorkery. He went on and on up the ladder, giving beefsteaks and beanfests and beer parties for the boys in Billy's Place, standing in with the right men and never missing a trick. At last the Gerald J. McCorkery Club chartered a whole boat for a big excursion up the river. It was a great day, with Lacey sitting at home sulking. After election Rosie had her picture in the papers, smiling at McCorkery; not fat exactly, just a fine figure of a woman with flowers pinned on her spotted fur coat, her teeth as good as ever. Oh, God, there was a girl for any man's money. Mr. Halloran saw out of his eye-corner the bony stooped back of Lacey Mahaffy, standing on one foot to rest the other like a tired old horse, leaning on her hands waiting for the iron to heat.

"That was Maggie, with her woes," she said.

"I hope you gave her some good advice," said Mr. Halloran. "I hope you told her to take up her hat and walk out on him."

Mrs. Halloran suspended the iron over a pair of pink satin panties. "I told her to do right and leave wrong-doing to the men," she said, in her voice like a phonograph record running down. "I told her to bear with the trouble God sends as her mother did before her."

Mr. Halloran gave a loud groan and knocked out his pipe on the chair arm. "You would ruin the world, woman, if you could, with your wicked soul, treating a new-married girl as if she had no home and no parents to come to. But she's no daughter of mine if she sits there peeling potatoes, letting a man run over her. No daughter of mine and I'll tell her so if she—"

"You know well she's your daughter, so hold your tongue," said Mrs. Halloran, "and if she heeded you she'd be walking the streets this minute. I brought her up an honest girl, and an honest woman she's going to be or I'll take her over my knee as I did when she was little. So there you are, Halloran."

Mr. Halloran leaned far back in his chair and felt along the shelf above his head until his fingers touched a half-dollar he had noticed there. His hand closed over it, he got up instantly and looked about for his hat.

"Keep your daughter, Lacey Mahaffy," he said, "she's none of mine but the fruits of your long sinning with the Holy Ghost. And now I'm off for a little round and a couple of beers to keep my mind from dissolving entirely."

"You can't have that dollar you just now sneaked off the shelf," said Mrs. Halloran. "So you think I'm blind besides? Put it back where you found it. That's for our daily bread."

"I'm sick of bread daily," said Mr. Halloran, "I need beer. It was not a dollar, but a half-dollar as you know well."

"Whatever it was," said Mrs. Halloran, "it stands instead of a dollar to me. So just drop it."

"You've got tomorrow's potatoes sewed up in your pocket this minute, and God knows what sums in that black box wherever you hide it, besides the life savings," said Mr. Halloran. "I earned this half-dollar on relief, and it's going to be spent properly. And I'll not be back for supper, so you'll save on that, too. So long, Lacey Mahaffy, I'm off."

"If you never come back, it will be all the same," said Mrs. Halloran, not looking up.

"If I came back with a pocket full of money, you'd be glad to see me," said Mr. Halloran.

"It would want to be a great sum," said Mrs. Halloran.

Mr. Halloran shut the door behind him with a fine slam.

He strolled out into the clear fall weather, a late afternoon sun warming his neck and brightening the old red-brick, high-stooped houses of Perry Street. He would go after all these years to Billy's Place, he might find some luck there. He took his time, though, speaking to the neighbors as he went. "Good afternoon, Mr. Halloran." "Good afternoon to you, Missis Caffery." . . . "It's fine weather for the time of year, Mr. Gogarty." "It is indeed, Mr. Halloran." Mr. Halloran thrived on these civilities, he loved to flourish his hat and give a hearty good day like a man who has nothing on his mind. Ah, there was the young man from the G. and I. store around the corner. He knew what kind of job Mr. Halloran once held there. "Good day, Mr. Halloran." "Good day to you, Mr. McInerny, how's business holding up with you?" "Good for the times, Mr. Halloran, that's the best I can say." "Things are not getting any better, Mr. McInerny." "It's the truth we are all hanging on by the teeth now, Mr. Halloran."

Soothed by this acknowledgment of man's common misfortune Mr. Halloran greeted the young cop at the corner. The cop, with his quick eyesight, was snatching a read from a newspaper on the stand across the sidewalk. "How do you do, Young O'Fallon," asked Mr. Halloran, "is your business lively these days?"

"Quiet as the tomb itself on this block," said Young O'Fallon. "But that's a sad thing about Connolly, now." His eyes motioned toward the newspaper.

"Is he dead?" asked Mr. Halloran. "I haven't been out until now, I didn't see the papers."

"Ah, not yet," said Young O'Fallon, "but the G-men are after him, it looks they'll get him surely this time."

"Connolly in bad with the G-men? Holy Jesus," said Mr. Halloran, "who will they go after next? The meddlers."

"It's that numbers racket," said the cop. "What's the harm, I'd like to know? A man must get his money from somewhere when he's in politics. They oughta give him a chance."

"Connolly's a great fellow, God bless him, I hope he gives them the slip," said Mr. Halloran, "I hope he goes right through their hands like a greased pig."

"He's smart," said the cop. "That Connolly's a smooth one. He'll come out of it."

Ah, will he though? Mr. Halloran asked himself. Who is safe if Connolly goes under? Wait till I give Lacey Mahaffy the news about Connolly, I'll like seeing her face the first time in twenty years. Lacey kept saying, "A man is a downright fool must be a crook to get rich. Plenty of the best people get rich and do no harm by it. Look at the Connollys now, good practical Catholics with nine children and more to come if God sends them, and Mass every day, and they're rolling in wealth richer than your McCorkerys with all their wickedness." So there you are, Lacey Mahaffy, wrong again, and welcome to your pious Connollys. Still and all it was Connolly who had given Gerald McCorkery his start in the world; McCorkery had been publicity man and then campaign manager for Connolly, in the days when Connolly had Tammany in the palm of his hand and the sky was the limit. And McCorkery had begun at the beginning, God knows. He was running a little basement place first, rent almost nothing, where the boys of the Connolly Club and the Little Tammany Association, just the mere fringe of the district, you might say, could drop in for quiet evenings for a game and a drink along with the talk. Nothing low, nothing but what was customary, with the house taking a cut on the winnings and a fine profit

on the liquor, and holding the crowd together. Many was the big plan
hatched there came out well for everybody. For everybody but myself, and
why was that? And when McCorkery says to me, "You can take over now
and run the place for the McCorkery Club," ah, there was my chance and
Lacey Mahaffy wouldn't hear of it, and with Maggie coming on just then
it wouldn't do to excite her.

Mr. Halloran went on, following his feet that knew the way to Billy's
Place, head down, not speaking to passers-by any more, but talking it out
with himself again, again. What a track to go over seeing clearly one by one
the crossroads where he might have taken a different turn that would have
changed all his fortunes; but no, he had gone the other way and now it
was too late. She wouldn't say a thing but "It's not right and you know it,
Halloran," so what could a man do in all? Ah, you could have gone on
with your rightful affairs like any other man, Halloran, it's not the woman's
place to decide such things; she'd have come round once she saw the money,
or a good whack on the backsides would have put her in her place. Never
had mortal woman needed a good walloping worse than Lacey Mahaffy,
but he could never find it in his heart to give it to her for her own good.
That was just another of your many mistakes, Halloran. But there was
always the life-long job with the G. and I. and peace in the house more or
less. Many a man envied me in those days I remember, and I was resting
easy on the savings and knowing with that and the pension I could finish
out my life with some little business of my own. "What came of that?" Mr.
Halloran inquired in a low voice, looking around him. Nobody answered.
You know well what came of it, Halloran. You were fired out like a delivery boy, two years before your time was out. Why did you sit there
watching the trick being played on others before you, knowing well it could
happen to you and never quite believing what you saw with your own eyes?
G. and I. gave me my start, when I was green in this country, and they were
my own kind or I thought so. Well, it's done now. Yes, it's done now, but
there was all the years you could have cashed in on the numbers game with
the best of them, helping collect the protection money and taking your cut.
You could have had a fortune by now in Lacey's name, safe in the bank.
It was good quiet profit and none the wiser. But they're wiser now, Halloran,
don't forget; still it's a lump of grief and disappointment to swallow all the
same. The game's up with Connolly, maybe; Lacey Mahaffy had said,
"Numbers is just another way of stealing from the poor, and you weren't
born to be a thief like that McCorkery." Ah, God, no, Halloran, you were
born to rot on relief and maybe that's honest enough for her. That Lacey—
A fortune in her name would have been no good to me whatever. She's
got all the savings tied up, such as they are, she'll pinch and she'll starve,
she'll wash dirty clothes first, she won't give up a penny to live on. She has
stood in my way, McCorkery, like a skeleton rattling its bones, and you were

right about her, she has been my ruin. "Ah, it's not too late yet, Halloran," said McCorkery, appearing plain as day inside Mr. Halloran's head with the same old face and way with him. "Never say die, Halloran. Elections are coming on again, it's a busy time for all, there's work to be done and you're the very man I'm looking for. Why didn't you come to me sooner, you know I never forget an old friend. You don't deserve your ill fortune, Halloran," McCorkery told him; "I said so to others and I say it now to your face, never did man deserve more of the world than you, Halloran, but the truth is, there's not always enough good luck to go round; but it's your turn now, and I've got a job for you up to your abilities at last. For a man like you, there's nothing to it at all, you can toss it off with one hand tied, Halloran, and good money in it. Organization work, just among your own neighbors, where you're known and respected for a man of your word and an old friend of Gerald McCorkery. Now look, Halloran," said Gerald McCorkery, tipping him the wink, "do I need to say more? It's voters in large numbers we're after, Halloran, and you're to bring them in, alive or dead. Keep your eye on the situation at all times and get in touch with me when necessary. And name your figure in the way of money. And come up to the house sometimes, Halloran, why don't you? Rosie has asked me a hundred times, 'Whatever went with Halloran, the life of the party?' That's the way you stand with Rosie, Halloran. We're in a two-story flat now with green velvet curtains and carpets you can sink to your shoetops in, and there's no reason at all why you shouldn't have the same kind of place if you want it. With your gifts, you were never meant to be a poor man."

Ah, but Lacey Mahaffy wouldn't have it, maybe. "Then get yourself another sort of woman, Halloran, you're a good man still, find yourself a woman like Rosie to snuggle down with at night." Yes, but McCorkery, you forget that Lacey Mahaffy had legs and hair and eyes and a complexion fit for a chorus girl. But would she do anything with them? Never. Would you believe there was a woman wouldn't take off all her clothes at once even to bathe herself? What a hateful thing she was with her evil mind thinking everything was a sin, and never giving a man a chance to show himself a man in any way. But she's faded away now, her mean soul shows out all over her, she's ugly as sin itself now, McCorkery. "It's what I told you would happen," said McCorkery, "but now with the job and the money you can go your ways and let Lacey Mahaffy go hers." I'll do it, McCorkery. "And forget about Connolly. Just remember I'm my own man and always was. Connolly's finished, but I'm not. Stronger than ever, Halloran, with Connolly out of the way. I saw this coming long ever ago, Halloran, I got clear of it. They don't catch McCorkery with his pants down, Halloran. And I almost forgot . . . Here's something for the running expenses to start. Take this for the present, and there's more to come. . . ."

Mr. Halloran stopped short, a familiar smell floated under his nose: the warm beer-and-beefsteak smell of Billy's Place, sawdust and onions, like any other bar maybe, but with something of its own besides. The talk within him stopped also as if a hand had been laid on his mind. He drew his fist out of his pocket almost expecting to find green money in it. The half-dollar was in his palm. "I'll stay while it lasts and hope McCorkery will come in."

The moment he stepped inside his eye lighted on McCorkery standing at the bar pouring his own drink from the bottle before him. Billy was mopping the bar before him idly, and his eye, swimming toward Halloran, looked like an oyster in its own juice. McCorkery saw him too. "Well, blow me down," he said, in a voice that had almost lost its old County Mayo ring, "if it ain't my old sidekick from the G. and I. Step right up, Halloran," he said, his poker-face as good as ever, no man ever saw Gerald McCorkery surprised at anything. "Step up and name your choice."

Mr. Halloran glowed suddenly with the warmth around the heart he always had at the sight of McCorkery, he couldn't put a name on it, but there was something about the man. Ah, it was Gerald all right, the same, who never forgot a friend and never seemed to care whether a man was rich or poor, with his face of granite and his eyes like blue agates in his head, a rock of a man surely. There he was, saying "Step right up," as if they had parted only yesterday; portly and solid in his expensive-looking clothes, as always; his hat a darker gray than his suit, with a devil-may-care roll to the brim, but nothing sporting, mind you. All first-rate, well made, and the right thing for him, more power to him. Mr. Halloran said, "Ah, McCorkery, you're the one man on this round earth I hoped to see today, but I says to myself, maybe he doesn't come round to Billy's Place so much nowadays."

"And why not?" asked McCorkery. "I've been coming around to Billy's Place for twenty-five years now, it's still headquarters for the old guard of the McCorkery Club, Halloran." He took in Mr. Halloran from head to foot in a flash of a glance and turned toward the bottle.

"I was going to have a beer," said Mr. Halloran, "but the smell of that whiskey changes my mind for me." McCorkery poured a second glass, they lifted the drinks with an identical crook of the elbow, a flick of the wrist at each other.

"Here's to crime," said McCorkery, and "Here's looking at you," said Mr. Halloran, merrily. Ah, to hell with it, he was back where he belonged, in good company. He put his foot on the rail and snapped down his whiskey, and no sooner was his glass on the bar than McCorkery was filling it again. "Just time for a few quick ones," he said, "before the boys get here." Mr. Halloran downed that one, too, before he noticed that McCorkery hadn't filled his own glass. "I'm ahead of you," said McCorkery, "I'll skip this one."

There was a short pause, a silence fell around them that seemed to ooze like a fog from somewhere deep in McCorkery, it was suddenly as if he had not really been there at all, or hadn't uttered a word. Then he said outright: "Well, Halloran, let's have it. What's on your mind?" And he poured two more drinks. That was McCorkery all over, reading your thoughts and coming straight to the point.

Mr. Halloran closed his hand round his glass and peered into the little pool of whiskey. "Maybe we could sit down," he said, feeling weak-kneed all at once. McCorkery took the bottle and moved over to the nearest table. He sat facing the door, his look straying there now and then, but he had a set, listening face as if he was ready to hear anything.

"You know what I've had at home all these years," began Mr. Halloran, solemnly, and paused.

"Oh, God, yes," said McCorkery with simple good-fellowship. "How is herself these days?"

"Worse than ever," said Mr. Halloran, "but that's not it."

"What is it, then, Halloran?" asked McCorkery, pouring drinks. "You know well you can speak out your mind to me. Is it a loan?"

"No," said Mr. Halloran. "It's a job."

"Now that's a different matter," said McCorkery. "What kind of a job?"

Mr. Halloran, his head sunk between his shoulders, saw McCorkery wave a hand and nod at half a dozen men who came in and ranged themselves along the bar. "Some of the boys," said McCorkery. "Go on." His face was tougher, and quieter, as if the drink gave him a firm hold on himself. Mr. Halloran said what he had planned to say, had said already on the way down, and it still sounded reasonable and right to him. McCorkery waited until he had finished, and got up, putting a hand on Mr. Halloran's shoulder. "Stay where you are, and help yourself," he said, giving the bottle a little push, "and anything else you want, Halloran, order it on me. I'll be back in a few minutes, and you know I'll help you out if I can."

Halloran understood everything but it was through a soft warm fog, and he hardly noticed when McCorkery passed him again with the men, all in that creepy quiet way like footpads on a dark street. They went into the back room, the door opened on a bright light and closed again, and Mr. Halloran reached for the bottle to help himself wait until McCorkery should come again bringing the good word. He felt comfortable and easy as if he hadn't a bone or muscle in him, but his elbow slipped off the table once or twice and he upset his drink on his sleeve. Ah, McCorkery, is it the whole family you're taking on with the jobs? For my Maggie's husband is in now with the Little Tammany Association. "There's a bright lad will go far and I've got my eye on him, Halloran," said the friendly voice of McCorkery in his mind, and the brown face, softer than he remembered it, came up clearly behind his closed eyes.

"Ah, well, it's like myself beginning all over again in him," said Mr.

Halloran, aloud, "besides my own job that I might have had all this time if I'd just come to see you sooner."

"True for you," said McCorkery in a merry County Mayo voice, inside Mr. Halloran's head, "and now let's drink to the gay future for old times' sake and be damned to Lacey Mahaffy." Mr. Halloran reached for the bottle but it skipped sideways, rolled out of reach like a creature, and exploded at his feet. When he stood up the chair fell backward from under him. He leaned on the table and it folded up under his hands like cardboard.

"Wait now, take it easy," said McCorkery, and there he was, real enough, holding Mr. Halloran braced on the one side, motioning with his hand to the boys in the back room, who came out quietly and took hold of Mr. Halloran, some of them, on the other side. Their faces were all Irish, but not an Irishman Mr. Halloran knew in the lot, and he did not like any face he saw. "Let me be," he said with dignity, "I came here to see Gerald J. McCorkery, a friend of mine from old times, and let not a thug among you lay a finger upon me."

"Come on, Big Shot," said one of the younger men, in a voice like a file grating, "come on now, it's time to go."

"That's a fine low lot you've picked to run with, McCorkery," said Mr. Halloran, bracing his heels against the slow weight they put upon him toward the door, "I wouldn't trust one of them far as I could throw him by the tail."

"All right, all right, Halloran," said McCorkery. "Come on with me. Lay off him, Finnegan." He was leaning over Mr. Halloran and pressing something into his right hand. It was money, a neat little roll of it, good smooth thick money, no other feel like it in the world, you couldn't mistake it. Ah, he'd have an argument to show Lacey Mahaffy would knock her off her feet. Honest money with a job to back it up. "You'll stand by your given word, McCorkery, as ever?" he asked, peering into the rock-colored face above him, his feet weaving a dance under him, his heart ready to break with gratitude.

"Ah, sure, sure," said McCorkery in a loud hearty voice with a kind of curse in it. "Crisakes, get on with him, do." Mr. Halloran found himself eased into a taxicab at the curb, with McCorkery speaking to the driver and giving him money. "So long, Big Shot," said one of the thug faces, and the taxicab door thumped to. Mr. Halloran bobbed about on the seat for a while, trying to think. He leaned forward and spoke to the driver. "Take me to my friend Gerald J. McCorkery's house," he said, "I've got important business. Don't pay any attention to what he said. Take me to his house."

"Yeah?" said the driver, without turning his head. "Well, here's where you get out, see? Right here." He reached back and opened the door. And sure enough, Mr. Halloran was standing on the sidewalk in front of the flat in Perry Street, alone except for the rows of garbage cans, the taxicab hoot-ing its way around the corner, and a cop coming toward him, plainly to be seen under the street light.

"You should cast your vote for McCorkery, the poor man's friend," Mr. Halloran told the cop, "McCorkery's the man who will get us all off the spot. Stands by his old friends like a maniac. Got a wife named Rosie. Vote for McCorkery," said Mr. Halloran, working hard at his job, "and you'll be Chief of the Force when Halloran says the word."

"To hell with McCorkery, that stooge," said the cop, his mouth square and sour with the things he said and the things he saw and did every night on that beat. "There you are drunk again, Halloran, shame to you, with Lacey Mahaffy working her heart out over the washboard to buy your beer."

"It wasn't beer and she didn't buy it, mind you," said Mr. Halloran, "and what do you know about Lacey Mahaffy?"

"I knew her from old when I used to run errands for St. Veronica's Altar Society," said the cop, "and she was a great one, even then. Nothing good enough."

"It's the same today," said Mr. Halloran, almost sober for a moment.

"Well, go on up now and stay up till you're fit to be seen," said the cop, censoriously.

"You're Johnny Maginnis," said Mr. Halloran, "I know you well."

"You should know me by now," said the cop.

Mr. Halloran worked his way upstairs partly on his hands and knees, but once at his own door he stood up, gave a great blow on the panel with his fist, turned the knob and surged in like a wave after the door itself, holding out the money toward Mrs. Halloran, who had finished ironing and was at her mending.

She got up very slowly, her bony hand over her mouth, her eyes starting out at what she saw. "Ah, did you steal it?" she asked. "Did you kill somebody for that?" the words grated up from her throat in a dark whisper. Mr. Halloran glared back at her in fear.

"Suffering Saints, Lacey Mahaffy," he shouted until the whole houseful could hear him, "haven't ye any mind at all that you can't see your husband has had a turn of fortune and a job and times are changed from tonight? Stealing, is it? That's for your great friends the Connollys with their religion. Connolly steals, but Halloran is an honest man with a job in the McCorkery Club, and money in pocket."

"McCorkery, is it?" said Mrs. Halloran, loudly too. "Ah, so there's the whole family, young and old, wicked and innocent, taking their bread from McCorkery, at last. Well, it's no bread of mine, I'll earn my own as I have, you can keep your dirty money to yourself, Halloran, mind you I mean it."

"Great God, woman," moaned Mr. Halloran, and he tottered from the door to the table, to the ironing board, and stood there, ready to weep with rage, "haven't you a soul even that you won't come along with your husband when he's riding to riches and glory on the Tiger's back itself, with everything for the taking and no questions asked?"

"Yes, I have a soul," cried Mrs. Halloran, clenching her fists, her hair flying. "Surely I have a soul and I'll save it yet in spite of you. . . ."

She was standing there before him in a kind of faded gingham winding sheet, with her dead hands upraised, her dead eyes blind but fixed upon him, her voice coming up hollow from the deep tomb, her throat thick with grave damp. The ghost of Lacey Mahaffy was threatening him, it came nearer, growing taller as it came, the face changing to a demon's face with a fixed glassy grin. "It's all that drink on an empty stomach," said the ghost, in a hoarse growl. Mr. Halloran fetched a yellow horror right out of his very boots, and seized the flatiron from the board. "Ah, God damn you, Lacey Mahaffy, you devil, keep away, keep away," he howled, but she advanced on air, grinning and growling. He raised the flatiron and hurled it without aiming, and the specter, whoever it was, whatever it was, sank and was gone. He did not look, but broke out of the room and was back on the sidewalk before he knew he had meant to go there. Maginnis came up at once. "Hey there now, Halloran," he said, "I mean business this time. You get back upstairs or I'll run you in. Come along now, I'll help you get there this time, and that's the last of it. On relief the way you are, and drinking your head off."

Mr. Halloran suddenly felt calm, collected; he would take Maginnis up and show him just what had happened. "I'm not on relief any more, and if you want any trouble, just call on my friend, McCorkery. He'll tell you who I am."

"McCorkery can't tell me anything about you I don't know already," said Maginnis. "Stand up there now." For Halloran wanted to go up again on his hands and knees.

"Let a man be," said Mr. Halloran, trying to sit on the cop's feet. "I killed Lacey Mahaffy at last, you'll be pleased to hear," he said, looking up into the cop's face. "It was high time and past. But I did not steal the money."

"Well, ain't that just too bad," said the cop, hauling him up under the arms. "Chees, why'n't you make a good job while you had the chance? Stand up now. Ah, hell with it, stand up or I'll sock you one."

Mr. Halloran said, "Well, you don't believe it so wait and see."

At that moment they both glanced upward and saw Mrs. Halloran coming downstairs. She was holding to the rail, and even in the speckled hall-light they could see a great lumpy clout of flesh standing out on her forehead, all colors. She stopped, and seemed not at all surprised.

"So there you are, Officer Maginnis," she said. "Bring him up."

"That's a fine welt you've got over your eye this time, Mrs. Halloran," commented Officer Maginnis, politely.

"I fell and hit my head on the ironing board," said Mrs. Halloran. "It comes of overwork and worry, day and night. A dead faint, Officer Maginnis. Watch your big feet there, you thriving, natural fool," she added to Mr. Halloran. "He's got a job now, you mightn't believe it, Officer Maginnis, but it's true. Bring him on up, and thank you."

She went ahead of them, opened the door, and led the way to the bedroom through the kitchen, turned back the covers, and Officer Maginnis dumped Mr. Halloran among the quilts and pillows. Mr. Halloran rolled over with a deep groan and shut his eyes.

"Many thanks to you, Officer Maginnis," said Mrs. Halloran.

"Don't mention it, Mrs. Halloran," said Officer Maginnis.

When the door was shut and locked, Mrs. Halloran went and dipped a large bath towel under the kitchen tap. She wrung it out and tied several good hard knots in one end and tried it out with a whack on the edge of the table. She walked in and stood over the bed and brought the knotted towel down in Mr. Halloran's face with all her might. He stirred and muttered, ill at ease. "That's for the flatiron, Halloran," she told him, in a cautious voice as if she were talking to herself, and whack, down came the towel again. "That's for the half-dollar," she said, and whack, "that's for your drunkenness—" Her arm swung around regularly, ending with a heavy thud on the face that was beginning to squirm, gasp, lift itself from the pillow and fall back again, in a puzzled kind of torment. "For your sock feet," Mrs. Halloran told him, whack, "and your laziness, and this is for missing Mass and"—here she swung half a dozen times—"that is for your daughter and your part in her. . . ."

She stood back breathless, the lump on her forehead burning in its furious colors. When Mr. Halloran attempted to rise, shielding his head with his arms, she gave him a push and he fell back again. "Stay there and don't give me a word," said Mrs. Halloran. He pulled the pillow over his face and subsided again, this time for good.

Mrs. Halloran moved about very deliberately. She tied the wet towel around her head, the knotted end hanging over her shoulder. Her hand ran into her apron pocket and came out again with the money. There was a five-dollar bill with three one-dollar bills rolled in it, and the half-dollar she had thought spent long since. "A poor start, but something," she said, and opened the cupboard door with a long key. Reaching in, she pulled a loosely fitted board out of the wall, and removed a black-painted metal box. She unlocked this, took out one five-cent piece from a welter of notes and coins. She then placed the new money in the box, locked it, put it away, replaced the board, shut the cupboard door and locked that. She went out to the telephone, dropped the nickel in the slot, asked for a number, and waited.

"Is that you, Maggie? Well, are things any better with you now? I'm glad to hear it. It's late to be calling, but there's news about your father. No, no, nothing of that kind, he's got a job. I said a *job*. Yes, at last, after all my urging him onward. . . . I've got him bedded down to sleep it off so he'll be ready for work tomorrow. . . . Yes, it's political work, toward the election time, with Gerald McCorkery. But that's no harm, getting votes and all, he'll be in the open air and it doesn't mean I'll have to associate with low people, now or ever. It's clean enough work, with good pay; if it's not just what I prayed for, still it beats nothing, Maggie. After all my trying . . . it's like a miracle. You see what can be done with patience and doing your duty, Maggie. Now mind you do as well by your own husband."

Joseph Mitchell

Joseph Mitchell (1908-   ) was born on a cotton and tobacco farm in North Carolina. After graduating from the University of North Carolina he came to New York City; there, as a newspaper reporter, he gained the curious and intimate knowledge of the metropolis which has fitted him for a staff position with The New Yorker. *He has published two collections of his writings,* My Ears Are Bent *and* McSorley's Wonderful Saloon. *The essay which follows is what* The New Yorker *calls a "profile," a form of biography based on extensive interviewing and witty character analysis. If, at first thought, Professor Sea Gull suggests less the working citizen than the lily of the field, one must at least credit him with enormous, if misguided, industry and the strenuous promotion of the more hilarious life.*

PROFESSOR SEA GULL [1]

JOE GOULD is a jaunty and emaciated little man who has been a notable in the cafeterias, diners, barrooms, and dumps of Greenwich Village for a quarter of a century. He sometimes brags rather wryly that he is the last of the bohemians. "All the others fell by the wayside," he says. "Some are in the grave, some are in the loony bin, and some are in the advertising business." Gould's life is by no means carefree; he is constantly tormented by what he calls "the three H's"—homelessness, hunger, and hangovers. He sleeps on benches in subway stations, on the floor in the studios of friends, and in quarter-a-night flophouses. Once in a while he trudges up to one of Father Divine's Extension Heavens in lower Harlem and gets a night's lodging for fifteen cents. He is five feet four and

[1] By permission of *The New Yorker*. Copyright The F-R Publishing Corporation, 1942.

he hardly ever weighs more than ninety-five pounds. Not long ago he told a friend that he hadn't eaten a square meal since June, 1936, when he bummed up to Cambridge and attended a banquet during a reunion of the Harvard class of 1911, of which he is a member. "I'm the foremost authority in the U. S. on the subject of doing without," he says. He tells people that he lives on "air, self-esteem, cigarette butts, cowboy coffee, fried-egg sandwiches, and ketchup." Cowboy coffee is black coffee without sugar. After finishing a sandwich, Gould customarily empties a bottle or two of ketchup on his plate and eats it with a spoon. The countermen in the Jefferson Diner, on Village Square, which is one of his hangouts, gather up the ketchup bottles and hide them the moment he puts his head in the door. "I don't particularly like the confounded stuff," he says, "but I make it a practice to eat all I can get. It's the only grub I know of that's free of charge."

Gould is a Yankee. His branch of the Goulds has been in New England since 1635, and he is related to the Lowell, Lawrence, Storer, and Vroom families. "There's nothing accidental about me," he once said. "I'll tell you what it took to make me what I am today. It took old Yankee blood, an overwhelming aversion to possessions, four years of Harvard, and twenty-five years of beating the living hell out of my insides with bad hooch and bad food. I'm out of joint with the rest of the human race because I don't want to own anything. If Mr. Chrysler tried to make me a present of the Chrysler Building, I'd damn near break my neck fleeing from him. I wouldn't own it; it'd own me. Back home in Massachusetts I'd be called an old Yankee crank. Here I'm called a bohemian. It's six of one, half a dozen of the other." Gould has a twangy voice and a Harvard accent. Bartenders and countermen in the Village refer to him as The Professor, Professor Bloomingdale, Professor Sea Gull, or The Mongoose. He dresses in the castoff clothes of his friends. His overcoat, suit, shirt, and even his shoes are all invariably two or three sizes too large, but he wears them with a forlorn, Chaplinlike rakishness. "Just look at me," he says. "The only thing that fits is the necktie." On bitter winter days he puts a layer of newspapers between his shirt and undershirt. "I'm snobbish," he says. "I only use the *Times*." He is fond of unusual headgear—a toboggan, a beret, or a yachting cap. One evening last summer he appeared at a party in a seersucker suit, a polo shirt, a scarlet cummerbund, sandals, and a yachting cap, all hand-me-downs. He uses a long ivory cigarette-holder, and a good deal of the time he smokes butts picked up off the sidewalks.

Bohemianism has aged Gould considerably beyond his years. He has got in the habit lately of asking people he has just met to guess his age. Their guesses range between sixty-five and seventy-five; he is fifty-three. He is never hurt by this; he looks upon it as proof of his superiority. "I get more living done in one year," he says, "than ordinary humans do in ten." He is squint-eyed and toothless, his spectacles slip down to the end of his nose a moment after he puts them on, and his lower jaw swivels from side to side when he talks; sometimes, because of these things, he distinctly resembles Mahatma Gandhi. He is aware of this. Once, in Romany Marie's, a basement bohemian gathering place in the Village, he draped a tablecloth over his shoulders and sat cross-legged on the floor for half an hour or so, gabbling all the while in a weird, made-up language. People who came in were taken aback when they caught sight of him; one woman said she had no idea Mr. Gandhi was visiting the United States.

Gould is bald on top, but the hair at the back of his head is long and frizzly, and he has a bushy, cinnamon-colored beard, which he says he trims every other Easter. He doesn't wear his spectacles on the street and without them he has the wild, unfocussed stare of an old scholar who has strained his eyes on small print. Even in the Village many people turn and look at him. He is stooped and he moves rapidly, grumbling to himself, with his head thrust forward and held to one side. Under his left arm he usually totes a bulging, greasy, brown pasteboard portfolio, and he swings his right arm aggressively. As he hurries along, he seems to be warding off an imaginary enemy. Don Freeman, the artist, a friend of his, once made a sketch of him walking. Freeman called the sketch "Joe Gould versus the Elements." Gould is as restless and footloose as an alley cat, and he takes long hikes about the city, now and then disappearing from the Village for weeks at a time and mystifying his friends; they have never been able to figure out where he goes. When he returns, always looking pleased with himself, he makes a few cryptic remarks, giggles, and then shuts up. "I went on a bird walk along the waterfront with an old countess," he said after his most recent absence. "The countess and I spent three weeks studying sea gulls."

Gould is almost never seen without his portfolio. He sits on it while he eats and he sleeps with it under his head. It usually contains a mass of manuscripts and notes, a dictionary, a bottle of ink, his extra shirts and socks, a cake of soap, a hairbrush, a paper bag of bread crumbs, and a paper bag of hard, round, dime-store candy of the type called sour balls. "I fight fatigue with sour balls," he says. The crumbs are for pigeons; like many other eccentrics, Gould is a pigeon feeder. He is devoted to a flock which makes its headquarters atop and around the statue of Garibaldi in Washington Square. These pigeons know him. When he comes up and takes a seat on the plinth of the statue, they flutter down and perch on his head and shoulders, waiting for him to bring out his bag of crumbs. He has given names to some of them. "Come here, Boss Tweed," he says. "A lady in Stewart's didn't finish her whole-wheat toast this morning and when she went out, bingo, I snatched it off her plate especially for you. Hello, Big Bosom. Hello, Popgut. Hello, Lady Astor. Hello, St. John the Baptist. Hello, Polly Adler. Hello, Fiorello, you old goat, how're you today?"

Although Gould strives to give the impression that he is a philosophical loafer, he has done an immense amount of work during his career as a bohemian. Every day, even when he is groggy as the result of hunger, he spends at least a couple of hours laboring on a formless, rather mysterious book which he calls "An Oral History of Our Time." He began this book twenty-six years ago, and it is nowhere near finished. His preoccupation with it seems to be principally responsible for the way he lives; a steady job of any kind, he says, would interfere with his thinking. Depending on the weather, he writes in parks, in doorways, in flophouse lobbies, in cafeterias, on benches on "L" platforms, in subway trains, and in public libraries. When he is in the proper mood, he writes until he is exhausted, and he gets into the mood at peculiar times. He says that one night he sat for seven hours in a booth in a Third Avenue bar and grill, listening to a beery old Hungarian woman, once a madam and once a dealer in cocaine and now a soup cook in a hospital, tell the story of her life. Three days later, around four o'clock in the morning, on a cot in the Hotel Defender, at 300 Bowery, he was awakened by the foghorns of tugs on the East River and was unable to go back to sleep because he felt that he was in the exact mood to put the old soup cook's biography in his history. He has an abnormal memory; if he is sufficiently impressed by a conversation, he can keep it in his head, even if it is lengthy and senseless, for many days, much of it word for word. He had a bad cold, but he got up, dressed under a red exit light, and, tiptoeing so as not to disturb the men sleeping on cots all around him, went downstairs to the lobby.

He wrote in the lobby from 4:15 A.M. until noon. Then he left the Defender, drank some coffee in a Bowery diner, and walked up to the Public Library. He plugged away at a table in the genealogy room, which is one of his rainy-day hangouts and which he says he prefers to the main reading room because it is gloomier, until it closed at 6 P.M. Then he moved into the main reading room and stayed there, seldom taking his eyes off his work, until the Library locked up for the night at 10 P.M. He ate a couple of egg sandwiches and a quantity of ketchup in a Times Square cafeteria. Then, not having two bits for a flophouse and being too engrossed to go to the Village and seek shelter, he hurried into the West Side subway and rode the balance of the night, scribbling ceaselessly while the train he was aboard made three round trips between the New Lots Avenue station in Brooklyn and the Van Cortlandt Park station in the Bronx. He kept his portfolio on his lap and used it as a desk. He has the endurance of the possessed. Whenever he got too sleepy to concentrate, he shook his head vigorously and then brought out his bag of sour balls and popped one in his mouth. People stared at him, and once he was interrupted by a drunk who asked him what in the name of God he was writing. Gould knows how to get rid of inquisitive drunks. He pointed at his left ear and said, "What? What's that? Deaf as a post. Can't hear a word." The drunk lost all interest in him. "Day was breaking when I left the subway," Gould says. "I was sneezing my head off, my eyes were sore, my knees were shaky, I was hungry as a bitch wolf, and I had exactly eight cents to my name. I didn't care. My history was longer by eleven thousand brand-new words, and at that moment I bet there wasn't a chairman of the board in all New York as happy as I."

Gould is haunted by the fear that he will die before he has the first draft of the Oral History finished. It is already eleven times as long as the Bible. He estimates that the manuscript contains 9,000,000 words, all in longhand. It may well be the lengthiest unpublished work in existence. Gould does his writing in nickel composition books, the kind that children use in school, and the Oral History and the notes he has made for it fill two hundred and seventy of them, all of which are tattered and grimy and stained with coffee, grease, and beer. Using a fountain pen, he covers both sides of each page, leaving no margins anywhere, and his penmanship is poor; hundreds of thousands of words are legible only to him. He has never been able to interest a publisher in the Oral History. At one time or another he has lugged armfuls of it into fourteen publishing offices. "Half of them said it was obscene and outrageous and to get it out of there as quick as I could," he says, "and the others said they couldn't read my handwriting." Experiences of this nature do not dismay Gould; he keeps telling himself that it is posterity he is writing for, anyway. In his breast pocket, sealed in a dingy envelope, he always carries a will bequeathing two-thirds of the manuscript to the Harvard Library and the other third to the Smithsonian Institution. "A couple of generations after I'm dead and gone," he likes to say, "the Ph.D.'s will start lousing through my work. Just imagine their surprise. 'Why, I be damned,' they'll say, 'this fellow was the most brilliant historian of the century.' They'll give me my due. I don't claim that all of the Oral History is first-class, but some of it will live as long as the English language." Gould used to keep his composition books in a dusty pile on the floor of a closet in a friend's photography studio in the Village. Whenever he filled a book, he would come in and toss it on the pile. Several months ago, after hearing that the Metropolitan Museum had moved its most valuable paintings to a bombproof storage place somewhere inland, he became panicky. He made a huge, oilcloth-covered bale of the Oral History and entrusted it for the duration to a woman he knows who owns a duck-and-chicken farm near Huntington, Long Island. The farmhouse has a stone cellar.

Gould puts into the Oral History only things he has seen or heard. At least half of it is made up of conversations taken down verbatim or summarized; hence the title. "What people say is history," Gould says. "What we used to think was history—all that chitty-chat about Caesar, Napoleon, treaties, inventions, big battles—is only formal history and largely false. I'll put down the informal history of the shirt-sleeved multitude—what they had to say about their jobs, love affairs, vittles, sprees, scrapes, and sorrows—or I'll perish in the attempt." The Oral History is a great hodgepodge and kitchen midden of hearsay, the fruit, according to Gould's estimate, of more than twenty thousand conversations. In it are the hopelessly incoherent biographies of hundreds of bums, accounts of the wanderings of seamen encountered in South Street barrooms, grisly descriptions of hospital and clinic experiences ("Did you ever have a painful operation or disease?" is one of the first questions that Gould, fountain pen and composition book in hand, asks a person he has just met), summaries of innumerable Union Square and Columbus Circle harangues, testimonies given by converts at Salvation Army street meetings, and the addled opinions of scores of park-bench oracles and gin-mill savants. For a time Gould haunted the all-night greasy spoons in the vicinity of Bellevue Hospital, eavesdropping on tired internes, nurses, ambulance-drivers, scrubwomen, embalming-school students, and morgue workers, and faithfully recording their talk. He scurries up and down Fifth Avenue during parades, feverishly taking notes. Gould writes with great candor, and the percentage of obscenity in the Oral History is high. He has a chapter called "Examples of the So-Called Dirty Story of Our Time," to which he makes almost daily additions. In another chapter are many rhymes and observations which he found scribbled on the walls of subway washrooms. He believes that such things are as truly historical as the strategy of General Robert E. Lee. Hundreds of thousands of words are devoted to the drunken behavior and the sexual adventures of various Greenwich Villagers in the twenties. There are hundreds of reports of ginny Village parties, including gossip about the guests and faithful reports of their arguments on such subjects as reincarnation, birth control, free love, psychoanalysis, Christian Science, Swedenborgianism, vegetarianism, alcoholism, and different political and art isms. "I have fully covered what might be termed the intellectual underworld of my time," Gould says. There are detailed descriptions of night life in the Village speakeasies, basement cabarets, and eating places which he frequented at one time or another and which are all now out of existence, such as the Little Quakeress, the Original Julius, Hubert's Cafeteria, the Troubadour Tavern, Alice McCollister's, and Eli Greifer's Last Outpost of Bohemia Tea Shoppe.

He is a night wanderer, and he has put down descriptions of dreadful things he has seen on dark New York streets—descriptions, for example, of the herds of big gray rats that come out in the hours before dawn in some neighborhoods of the lower East Side and Harlem and unconcernedly walk the sidewalks. "I sometimes believe that these rats are not rats at all," he says, "but the damned and aching souls of tenement landlords." A great deal of the Oral History is in diary form. Gould is afflicted with total recall, and now and then he painstakingly writes down everything he did for a day, a week, or a month. Sometimes he writes a chapter in which he monotonously and hideously curses some person or institution. Here and there are rambling essays on such subjects as the flophouse flea, spaghetti, the zipper as a sign of the decay of civilization, false teeth, insanity, the jury system, remorse, cafeteria cooking, and the emasculating effect of the typewriter on literature. "William Shakespeare didn't sit around pecking on a dirty, damned, ninety-five-dollar dohicky," he wrote, "and Joe Gould doesn't, either." In his essay on insanity he wrote, "I suffer from a mild form of insanity. I have delusions of grandeur. I believe myself to be Joe Gould."

The Oral History is almost as discursive as *Tristram Shandy*. In one chapter, "The Good Men Are Dying Like Flies," Gould begins a biography of a diner proprietor and horse-race gambler named Side-Bet Benny Altschuler, who stuck a rusty icepick in his hand and died of lockjaw; and skips after a few paragraphs to a story a seaman told him about seeing a group of tipsy lepers on a beach in Port-of-Spain, Trinidad; and goes from that to an anecdote about a meeting held in Boston in 1915 to protest against the showing of "The Birth of a Nation," at which he kicked a policeman; and goes from that to a description of a trip he once made through the Central Islip insane asylum, in the course of which a woman pointed at him and screamed, "There he is! Thief! Thief! There's the man that picked my geraniums and stole my mamma's mule and buggy"; and goes from that to an account an old stumblebum gave of glimpsing and feeling the blue-black flames of hell one night while sitting in a doorway on Great Jones Street and of seeing two mermaids playing in the East River just north of Fulton Fish Market later the same night; and goes from that to an explanation made by a priest of old St. Patrick's Cathedral on Mott Street of why Italian women are addicted to the wearing of black; and then returns at last to Side-Bet Benny, the lockjawed diner proprietor.

Only a few of the hundreds of people who know Gould have read any of the Oral History, and most of them take it for granted that it is gibberish. Those who make the attempt usually bog down after a couple of chapters and give up. Gould says he can count on his hands and feet those who have read enough of it to be qualified to form an opinion. One is Horace Gregory, the poet and critic. "I look upon Gould as a sort of Samuel Pepys of the Bowery," Gregory says. "I once waded through twenty-odd composition books, and most of what I saw had the quality of a competent high-school theme, but some of it was written with the clear and wonderful veracity of a child, and here and there were flashes of hardbitten Yankee wit. If someone took the trouble to go through it and separate the good from the rubbish, as editors did with Thomas Wolfe's millions of words, it might be discovered that Gould actually has written a masterpiece. I can't imagine anyone with patience enough to tackle the job. It would require months and months, maybe years." Another is E. E. Cummings, the poet, who is a close friend of Gould's. Cummings once wrote a poem about Gould, No. 261 in his "Collected Poems," which contains the following description of the history:

> . . . a myth is as good as a smile but little joe gould's quote oral
> history unquote might (publishers note) be entitled a wraith's
> progress or mainly awash while chiefly submerged or an amoral
> morality sort-of-aliveing by innumerable kind-of-deaths

Throughout the nineteen-twenties Gould haunted the office of *The Dial,* now dead, the most highbrow magazine of the time. Finally, in its April, 1929, issue, *The Dial* printed one of his shorter essays, "Civilization." In it he rambled along, referring to skyscrapers and steamships as "needless bric-a-brac," and remarking that "the auto is unnecessary. If all the perverted ingenuity which was put into making buzz-wagons had only gone into improving the breed of horses humanity would be better off." This essay had a curious effect on American literature. A copy of this issue of *The Dial* turned up three or four months later in a second-hand bookstore in Fresno, California, and was bought for a dime by William Saroyan, who then was twenty and floundering around, desperate to become a writer. He read Gould's essay and was deeply impressed and influenced by it. "It freed me from bothering about form," he says. Twelve years later, in the winter of 1941, in Don Freeman's studio on Columbus Circle, Saroyan saw some drawings Freeman had made of Gould for *Don Freeman's Newsstand,* a quarterly publication of pictures of odd New York scenes and personalities put out by the Associated American Artists. Saroyan became excited. He told Freeman about his indebtedness to Gould. "Who the hell is he, anyway?" Saroyan asked. "I've been trying to find out for years. Reading those few pages in *The Dial* was like going in the wrong direction and running into the right guy and then never seeing him again." Freeman told him about the Oral History. Saroyan sat down and wrote a commentary to accompany the drawings of Gould in *Newsstand.* "To this day," he wrote, in part, "I have not read anything else by Joe Gould. And yet to me he remains one of the few genuine and original American writers. He was easy and uncluttered, and almost all other American writing was uneasy and cluttered. It was not at home anywhere; it was trying too hard; it was miserable; it was a little sickly; it was literary; and it couldn't say anything simply. All other American writing was trying to get into one form or another, and no writer except Joe Gould seemed to understand that if the worst came to the worst you didn't need any form at all. All you had to do was say it." Not long after this issue of *Newsstand* came out, someone stopped Gould on Eighth Street and showed him Saroyan's endorsement of his work. Gould shrugged his shoulders. He had been on a spree and had lost his false teeth, and at the moment he was uninterested in literary matters. After thinking it over, however, he decided to call on Saroyan and ask him for help in getting some teeth. He found out somehow that Saroyan was living at the Hampshire House, on Central Park South. The doorman there followed Gould into the lobby and asked him what he wanted. Gould told him. "Do you know Mr. Saroyan?" the doorman asked. "Why, no," Gould said, "but that's all right. He's a disciple of mine." "What do you mean, disciple?" asked the doorman. "I mean," said Gould, "that he's a literary disciple of mine. I want to ask him to buy me some store teeth." "Come this way," said the doorman, gripping Gould's arm and ushering him to the street. Later Freeman arranged a meeting, and the pair spent several evenings together in bars. "Saroyan kept saying he wanted to hear all about the Oral History," Gould says, "but I never got a chance to tell him. He did all the talking. I couldn't get a word in edgewise."

Gould, ever since his childhood, has been perplexed by his own personality. There are scores of autobiographical essays in the Oral History, and he says that all of them are attempts to explain himself to himself. In one, "Why I Am Unable To Adjust Myself To Civilization, Such As It Is, or Do, Don't, Do, Don't, A Hell Of A Note," he came to the conclusion that his shyness was responsible for everything. "I am introvert and extrovert all rolled in one," he wrote, "a warring mixture of the recluse and the Sixth Avenue auctioneer. One foot says do, the other says don't. One foot says shut your mouth, the other says bellow like a bull. I am painfully shy, but try not to let people know it. They would take advantage of me." Gould keeps his shyness well hidden. It is evident only when he is cold sober. In that state he is silent, suspicious, and constrained, but a couple of beers or a single jigger of gin will untie his tongue and put a leer on his face. He is extraordinarily responsive to alcohol. "On a hot night," he says, "I can walk up and down in front of a gin mill for ten minutes, breathing real deep, and get a jag on."

Even though Gould requires only a few drinks, getting them is sometimes quite a task. Most evenings he prowls around the saloons and dives on the west side of the Village, on the lookout for curiosity-seeking tourists from whom he can cadge beers, sandwiches, and small sums of money. Such people are scarce nowadays. If he is unable to find anyone approachable in the tumultuous saloons around Sheridan Square, he goes over to Sixth Avenue and works north, hitting the Jericho Tavern, the Village Square Bar & Grill, the Belmar, Goody's, and the Rochambeau. He has a routine. He doesn't enter a place unless it is crowded. After he is in, he bustles over to the telephone booth and pretends to look up a number. While doing this, he scrutinizes the customers. If he sees a prospect, he goes over and says, "Let me introduce myself. The name is Joseph Ferdinand Gould, graduate of Harvard, *magna cum difficultate,* class of 1911, and chairman of the board of Weal and Woe, Incorporated. In exchange for a drink, I'll recite a poem, deliver a lecture, argue a point, or take off my shoes and imitate a sea gull. I prefer gin, but beer will do." Gould is by no means a bum. He feels that the entertainment he provides is well worth whatever he is able to cadge. He doesn't fawn, and he is never grateful. If he is turned down politely, he shrugs his shoulders and leaves the place. However, if the prospect passes a remark like "Get out of here, you bum," Gould turns on him, no matter how big he is, and gives him a frightening tongue-lashing. He is skilled in the use of the obscene epithet; he can curse for ten minutes, growing more shrill and scurrilous by the minute, without repeating himself. When aroused, he is fearless. He will drop his portfolio, put up his fists, and offer to fight men who could kill him with one halfhearted blow. If he doesn't find an audience on the trip up Sixth, he turns west on Eleventh and heads for the Village Vanguard, in a cellar on Seventh Avenue South. The Vanguard was once a sleazy rendezvous for arty people, but currently it is a thriving night club. Gould and the proprietor, a man named Max Gordon, have known each other for many years and are on fairly good terms much of the time. Gould always hits the Vanguard last. He is sure of it, and he keeps it in reserve. Since it became prosperous, the place annoys him. He goes down the stairs and says, "Hello, Max, you dirty capitalist. I want a bite to eat and a beer. If I don't get it, I'll walk right out on the dance floor and throw a fit." "Go argue with the cook," Gordon tells him. Gould goes into the kitchen, eats whatever the cook gives him, drinks a couple of beers, fills a bag with bread crumbs, and departs.

Despite his shyness, Gould has a great fondness for parties. He is acquainted with hundreds of artists, writers, sculptors, and actors in the Village, and whenever he learns that one of them is giving a party, he goes, friend or enemy, invited or not. Usually he keeps to himself for a while, uneasily smoking one cigarette after another and stiff as a board with tenseness. Sooner or later, however, impelled by a drink or two and by the desperation of the ill at ease, he begins to throw his weight around. He picks out the prettiest woman in the room, goes over, bows, and kisses her hand. He tells discreditable stories about himself. He becomes exuberant; suddenly, for no reason at all, he cackles with pleasure and jumps up and clicks his heels together. Presently he shouts, "All in favor of a one-man floor show, please say 'Aye'!" If he gets the slightest encouragement, he strips to the waist and does a hand-clapping, foot-stamping dance which he says he learned on a Chippewa reservation in North Dakota and which he calls the Joseph Ferdinand Gould Stomp. While dancing, he chants an old Salvation Army song, "There Are Flies on Me, There Are Flies on You, but There Are No Flies on Jesus." Then he imitates a sea gull. He pulls off his shoes and socks and takes awkward, headlong skips about the room, flapping his arms and letting out a piercing caw with every skip. As a child he had several pet gulls, and he still spends many Sundays on the end of a fishing pier

at Sheepshead Bay observing gulls; he claims he has such a thorough understanding of their cawing that he can translate poetry into it. "I have translated a number of Henry Wadsworth Longfellow's poems into sea gull," he
says.

Inevitably, at every party Gould goes to, he gets up on a table and delivers some lectures. His lectures are brief, but he gives them lengthy titles,
such as "Drunk as a Skunk, or How I Measured the Heads of Fifteen Hundred Indians in Zero Weather" and "The Dread Tomato Habit, or Watch
Out! Watch Out! Down with Dr. Gallup!" For a reason he has never been
able to make quite clear, statistics of any kind infuriate him. In the latter
lecture, using statistics he maintains he has found in newspaper financial
sections, he proves that the eating of tomatoes by railroad engineers was
responsible for fifty-three per cent of the train wrecks in the United States
during the last seven years. When Gould arrives at a party, people who have
never seen him before usually take one look, snicker, and edge away. Before
the evening is over, however, a few of them almost always develop a kind
of puzzled respect for him; they get him in a corner, ask him questions, and
try to determine what is wrong with him. Gould enjoys this. "When you
came over and kissed my hand," a young woman told him once, "I said to
myself, 'What a nice old gentleman.' A minute later I looked around and
you were bouncing up and down with your shirt off, imitating a wild
Indian. I was shocked. Why do you have to be such an exhibitionist?"
"Madam," Gould said, "it is the duty of the bohemian to make a spectacle
of himself. If my informality leads you to believe that I'm a rum-dumb, or
that I belong in Bellevue, hold fast to that belief, hold fast, hold fast, and
show your ignorance."

Gould is not particularly communicative about what he calls his pre-
Oral History life. "I am the most recent black sheep in a family that can
trace its ancestry right spang to William the Conqueror," he says. He is a
native of Norwood, Massachusetts, a southwestern suburb of Boston. He
comes from a family of physicians. His grandfather, Joseph Ferdinand
Gould, for whom he was named, taught in the Harvard Medical School and
had a practice in South Boston. His father, Clark Storer Gould, was a captain in the Army Medical Corps and died of blood poisoning in a camp in
Ohio during the last war. The family was well-to-do until Gould was in his
late teens, when his father invested unwisely in the stock of an Alaska land
company. Gould says he went to Harvard only because it was a family custom. "I did not want to go," he wrote in one of his autobiographical essays.
"It had been my plan to stay home and sit in a rocking chair on the back
porch and brood." He says that he was an undistinguished student. Some
of his classmates were Conrad Aiken, the poet; Howard Lindsay, the play-
wright and actor; Gluyas Williams, the cartoonist; and Richard F. Whitney,

former president of the New York Stock Exchange. His best friends were three foreign students—a Chinese, a Siamese, and an Albanian.

Gould's mother had always taken it for granted that he would become a physician, but after getting his A.B. he told her he was through with formal education. She asked him what he intended to do. "I intend to stroll and ponder," he said. He passed most of the next three years strolling and pondering on the ranch of an uncle in Canada. In 1913, in an Albanian restaurant in Boston named the Scanderbeg, whose coffee he liked, he became acquainted with Theofan S. Noli, an archimandrite of the Albanian Orthodox Church, who interested him in Balkan politics. In February, 1914, Gould startled his family by announcing that he planned to devote the rest of his life to collecting funds to free Albania. He founded an organization in Boston called the Friends of Albanian Independence, enrolled a score or so of dues-paying members, and began telegraphing and calling on bewildered newspaper editors in Boston and Manhattan, trying to persuade them to print long treatises on Albanian affairs written by Noli. After about eight months of this, Gould was sitting in the Scanderbeg one night, drinking coffee and listening to a group of Albanian factory workers argue in their native tongue about Balkan politics, when he suddenly came to the conclusion that he was about to have a nervous breakdown. "I began to twitch uncontrollably and see double," he says. From that night on his interest in Albania slackened.

After another period of strolling and pondering, Gould took up eugenics. He has forgotten exactly how this came about. In any case, he spent the summer of 1915 as a student in eugenical field work at the Eugenics Record Office at Cold Spring Harbor. This organization, endowed by the Carnegie Institution, was engaged at that time in making studies of families of hereditary defectives, paupers, and town nuisances in several highly inbred communities. Such people were too prosaic for Gould; he decided to specialize in Indians. That winter he went out to North Dakota and measured the heads of a thousand Chippewas on the Turtle Mountain Reservation and of five hundred Mandans on the Fort Berthold Reservation. Nowadays, when Gould is asked why he took these measurements, he changes the subject, saying, "The whole matter is a deep, scientific secret." He was happy in North Dakota. "It was the most rewarding period of my life," he says. "I'm a good horseman, if I do say so myself, and I like to dance and whoop, and the Indians seemed to enjoy having me around. I was afraid they'd think I was batty when I asked for permission to measure their noggins, but they didn't mind. It seemed to amuse them. Indians are the only true aristocrats I've ever known; nothing in God's world ever surprises them. They ought to run the country, and we ought to be put on the reservations." After seven months of reservation life, Gould ran out of money. He returned to Massachusetts and tried vainly to get funds for another head-measuring expedition. "At this juncture in my life," he says, "I decided to engage in literary work." He came to Manhattan and got a job as assistant Police Headquarters reporter for the *Evening Mail.* One morning in the summer of 1917, after he had been a reporter for about a year, he was basking in the sun on the back steps of Headquarters, trying to overcome a grappa hangover, when the idea for the Oral History blossomed in his mind. He promptly quit his job and began writing. "Since that fateful morning," he once said, in a moment of exaltation, "the Oral History has been my rope and my scaffold, my bed and my board, my wife and my floozy, my wound and the salt on it, my whiskey and my aspirin, and my rock and my salvation. It is the only thing that matters a damn to me. All else is dross."

Gould says that he rarely has more than a dollar at any one time, and that he doesn't particularly care. "As a rule," he says, "I despise money." However, there is a widely held belief in the Village that he is rich and that he receives an income from inherited property in New England. "Only an old millionaire could afford to go around as shabby as you," a bartender told him recently. "You're one of those fellows that die in doorways and when the cops search them their pockets are just busting with bankbooks. If you wanted to, I bet you could step over to the West Side Savings Bank right this minute and draw out twenty thousand dollars." After the death of his mother in 1939, Gould did come into some money. Close friends of his say that it was less than a thousand dollars and that he spent it in less than a month, wildly buying drinks all over the Village for people he had never seen before. "He seemed miserable with money in his pockets," Gordon, the proprietor of the Vanguard, says. "When it was all gone, it seemed to take a load off his mind." While Gould was spending his inheritance, he did one thing that satisfied him deeply. He bought a big, shiny radio and took it out on Sixth Avenue and kicked it to pieces. He has a low opinion of radio. "Five minutes of the idiot's babble that comes out of those machines," he says, "would turn the stomach of a goat."

During the twenties and the early thirties Gould occasionally interrupted his work on the Oral History to pose for classes at the Art Students' League and to do book-reviewing for newspapers and magazines. He says there were periods when he lived comfortably on the money he earned this way. Burton Rascoe, literary editor of the old *Tribune,* gave him a lot of work. In a notation in "A Bookman's Daybook," Rascoe told of an experience with Gould. "I once gave him a small book about the American Indians to review," Rascoe wrote, "and he brought me back enough manuscript to fill three complete editions of the Sunday *Tribune.* I especially honor him, because, unlike most reviewers, he has never dogged me with inquiries as to why I never ran it. He had his say, which was considerable, about the book, the author, and the subject, and there, for him, the matter ended." Gould says that he quit book-reviewing because he felt that it was beneath his dignity to compete with machines. "The Sunday *Times* and the Sunday *Herald Tribune* have machines that review books," he says. "You put a book in one of those machines and jerk down a couple of levers and a review drops out." In recent years Gould has got along on less than five dollars in actual money a week. He has a number of friends—Malcolm Cowley, the writer and editor; Aaron Siskind, the documentary photographer; Cummings, the poet; and Gordon, the night-club proprietor, are a few—who give him small sums of money regularly. No matter what they think of the Oral History, all these people greatly respect Gould's doggedness. . . .

Gould's opinion of contemporary writing other than the Oral History is low. Occasionally, at the Public Library, he takes out a recently published history and sits down with it at his favorite table in the genealogy room. Almost immediately he begins to grunt and groan and curse the author. "The hell you say," he is apt to exclaim, smacking the book with his palm and startling the other people at the table. "Who told you? It simply isn't true! Garbage, garbage, ten tons of garbage! And they saw down beautiful trees to make paper to print this stuff on! The awful waste! Oh! Oh! I just can't endure it!"

Gould's outspokenness has made him a lone wolf in the Village; he has never been allowed to join any of the art, poetry, or ism organizations. He has been trying for ten years to join the Raven Poetry Circle, which puts on the poetry exhibition in Washington Square each summer and is the most powerful organization of its kind in the Village, but he has been blackballed every time. However, the Ravens usually let him attend their readings. Francis Lambert McCrudden, a retired Telephone Company employee who is the head Raven, claims that Gould is not serious about poetry. "We serve wine at our readings, and that is the only reason Mr. Gould attends," he once said. "He sometimes insists on reading foolish poems of his own, and it gets on your nerves. At our religious-poetry night he demanded permission to recite a poem entitled 'My Religion.' I told him to go ahead, and this is what he recited:

> In winter I'm a Buddhist,
> And in summer I'm a nudist.

And at our nature-poetry night he begged to recite a poem entitled 'The Sea Gull.' I gave him permission, and he jumped out of his chair and began to wave his arms and leap about and scream, 'Scree-eek! Scree-eek!' It was upsetting. We are serious poets and we don't appreciate that sort of behavior." Last summer Gould picketed the Raven exhibition, which was held on the fence of a tennis court on Washington Square South. In one hand he carried his portfolio and in the other he held a placard on which he had printed: "JOSEPH FERDINAND GOULD, HOT SHOT POET FROM POETVILLE, A REFUGEE FROM THE RAVENS. POETS OF THE WORLD, IGNITE! YOU HAVE NOTHING TO LOSE BUT YOUR BRAINS!" Now and then, as he strutted back and forth, he would take a leap and then a skip and say to passers-by, "Would you like to hear what Joe Gould thinks of the world and all that's in it? Scree-eek! Scree-eek!"

Conrad Aiken

Conrad Aiken (1889-   ) was born in Savannah, attended school in New England, and graduated from Harvard. His life has been spent in extensive travels, and his residence has alternated between the ancient Sussex port of Rye and Cape Cod. His Selected Poems *received the Pulitzer Prize. For Aiken, poetry is akin to music. His poems use the repetition of phrase and motif, the long flow of sound, the variation of tempo and mood that suggest the symphony. Notable in the history of our century is the complexity of its social problems. But hand in hand with social wrong goes the struggle for social right. In "The Road," a poem grimly different from his typical mood, Aiken tells the story of man's long purpose to build a better world and, in spite of the pitiful slowness of the task, foresees its fulfillment.*

THE ROAD

Three then came forward out of darkness, one
An old man bearded, his old eyes red with weeping,
A peasant, with hard hands. "Come now," he said,
"And see the road, for which our people die.
Twelve miles of road we've made, a little only,
Westward winding. Of human blood and stone
We build; and in a thousand years will come
Beyond the hills to sea."
                   I went with them,
Taking a lantern, which upon their faces
Showed years and grief; and in a time we came
To the wild road which wound among wild hills
Westward; and so along this road we stooped,
Silent, thinking of all the dead men, there
Compounded with sad clay. Slowly we moved:
For they were old and weak, had given all
Their life, to build this twelve poor miles of road,

Muddy, under the rain. And in my hand
Turning the lantern, here or there, I saw
Deep holes of water where the raindrop splashed,
And rainfilled footprints in the grass, and heaps
Of broken stone, and rusted spades and picks,
And helves of axes. And the old man spoke,
Holding my wrist: "Three hundred years it took
To build these miles of road: three hundred years;
And human lives unnumbered. But the day
Will come when it is done." Then spoke another,
One not so old, but old, whose face was wrinkled:
"And when it comes, our people will all sing
For joy, passing from east to west, or west
To east, returning, with the light behind them;
All meeting in the road and singing there."
And the third said: "The road will be their life;
A heritage of blood. Grief will be in it,
And beauty out of grief. And I can see
How all the women's faces will be bright.
In that time, laughing, they will remember us.
Blow out your lantern now, for day is coming."

My lantern blown out, in a little while
We climbed in long light up a hill, where climbed
The dwindling road, and ended in a field.
Peasants were working in the field, bowed down
With unrewarded work, and grief, and years
Of pain. And as we passed them, one man fell
Into a furrow that was bright with water
And gave a cry that was half cry half song—
"The road . . . the road . . . the road . . ." And all then fell
Upon their knees and sang.
                              We four passed on
Over the hill, to westward. Then I felt
How tears ran down my face, tears without number;
And knew that all my life henceforth was weeping,
Weeping, thinking of human grief, and human
Endeavor fruitless in a world of pain.
And when I held my hands up they were old;
I knew my face would not be young again.

IV. PURSUIT OF HAPPINESS

WHERE is happiness? The Middle Ages believed that it was laid up in heaven, a promise of mystical fulfillment. The Renaissance thought it was the stuff of this world—its palaces, courts, monuments, its loves, its arts, its princes. The Puritans, in holy horror of worldly excesses, denounced the values of the Renaissance; and we today are still the uncomfortable heirs of their prejudices.

But surely the pursuit of happiness, debatable as the sole end of living, is a legitimate part of the good life. For Jefferson's phrase comprehends all those activities of mind and hand which we call the arts. And by the arts life is informed with reason and beauty. Even in an age of force, perhaps especially then, the arts need no apology.

War is inevitably force, and force is the province of the physical sciences. In time of crisis, technology is supreme. But we must not forget that the German universities, after World War I, promoted the rise of totalitarianism by their passionate confidence in technology. Technological training is a means, not an end. In warfare it serves the immediate end of military victory. But what is that, in turn, but a means to a larger end, the recovering of humane values?

Not to enjoy the good things of this earth, then, is blind ingratitude. Life can be more than day-by-day washing, dressing, eating, sleeping. To the adventurous spirit with sensibilities fully aware, living becomes an art which comprehends all arts. If we would be truly alive, we must seek out and cultivate every legitimate experience that our lives afford.

This does not mean that we must be shipwrecked in the Arctic: merely doing nothing, if assiduously pursued, has its quiet rewards. A millennial Manhattan, where the firefighters refuse to hurry to a fire but pause to dispute the number of wild geese passing overhead, will not be without its compensations. The world's largest city has never properly appreciated the advantages of idleness.

Or there is the pleasure of reducing life, Thoreau-wise, to its simplest terms. Thereby we find time to cultivate our sensitiveness to Nature through all five senses. The real "Nature-lover" does not go about talking of the beauties of Nature. He is satisfied to have experienced them, to have entered into the life of sea and mountain, of beast, bird, and flower. He knows it is useless to try to communicate his sensations in words.

Out of this heightened sensibility comes a livelier responsiveness to the fine arts—literature, music, painting, sculpture. Few are qualified to appreciate all fields equally. But all can find in the arts at one point or another some pull of the beautiful. Here or there, in this etching or that sonnet, this ballet or that symphony, an emotion is stirred, the work of art has spoken to you and you alone. Just there you touch hands with the artist. In his art you recognize some thought or feeling, some fancy, some experience, which is intimately your own. So the artist lends you his finer powers of perception that you may savor more deeply your own life.

Unless we bring to the arts an alert imagination, our pursuit of happiness is vain. Listening to music, looking at a picture, reading a poem is a partnership with the artist in which we pick up the threads of his suggestion and follow them wherever our associations lead us. Particularly in listening to music, for here we share not only the inspiration of the composer but the re-creation of his score by the performer. There is no more exhilarating pleasure than sharing, as auditor, the performance of a great piece of music by a great orchestra. And thanks to the wonders of radio and recorded music, it is a pleasure which can be approximated at will, until the melodies of the masters play themselves in our memories.

Literature is the sum of the fine arts, for it puts into the concreteness of language what music and painting convey by suggestion. Literature is the friendliest of the arts. To handle a brush or play a fiddle is an acquired skill; but we have all been on speaking terms with language since babyhood. We all know how to read, and some of us know how to write. But everyone who has struggled to lay words one after another knows that writing is an exacting process. Not words alone but the ideas which they stand for must fall into place. The medium of poetry, writes Archibald MacLeish, "is speech: most common, human, touched and worn of all materials that men have used for art. Its end is man."

Travel is the pleasantest way of learning, for every traveler can choose his own proportions of information and adventure. Both he is sure to get, whether his journey is literal or literary. War may close the well-beaten paths, but vicariously we can still journey from Greenland to Liberia, from the Andes to Palestine. Whatever the chances of fortune, nothing can deprive us of the joy of remembered places: the long light of sunset across the Roman Campagna, the first landfall of the green and white cliffs of England, the cheerful bustle of sidewalk cafés in Paris, the Vienna Woods filled with spring birdsong. These things are gone, for a while at least. Those of us who were privileged to know them once are the fortunate ones.

Finally there is the endless pleasure of play. Here we develop the muscular reactions: the grosser animal comes into his own. Far from denying such rejoicing in the body's strength, our age encourages games and sports and every manner of exercise. Out of sheer bodily fitness comes the sense of triumphing, during our best years, over the forces that would slow us down before we come home from the hunt, the playing field, or the ski-slope to sit by the fire and remember.

What does it all come to, this excursion through the arts of living? Does it not show that the things which make us happy are often the simple things? A book, a flower, a picture, a musical phrase, an open road, the feel of a baseball bat, the sound of the wind rising—these we only half know if we think that being alive is "to spend and waste time as though you had a million years." The pursuit of happiness is, on the contrary, the intensive cultivation of every small satisfaction: "night and day, brother, both sweet things; sun, moon, and stars, brother, all sweet things; there's likewise a wind on the heath."

In a civilization rocking perilously near the edge of nothingness, we will yet cling to the good things and make the most of them, even today. We will not go down to defeat while there are sports and songs, pictures and poems in the world. These things were given us to reassure us, to renew our courage and our laughter, to make conscious to all our senses

> That life, for all the woe, is worth the living
> *Even today . . .*

Robert Frost

As he is splitting wood on a spring day, Robert Frost feels himself challenged by two tramps with a logical claim to the job, and in justifying himself he discovers that working can become one with love of the work. It should be evident to any reader of Frost's poetry that he extends this principle to his writing.

TWO TRAMPS IN MUD-TIME

Out of the mud two strangers came
And caught me splitting wood in the yard.
And one of them put me off my aim
By hailing cheerily "Hit them hard!"
I knew pretty well why he dropped behind
And let the other go on a way.
I knew pretty well what he had in mind:
He wanted to take my job for pay.

Good blocks of beech it was I split,
As large around as the chopping-block;
And every piece I squarely hit
Fell splinterless as a cloven rock.
The blows that a life of self-control
Spares to strike for the common good
That day, giving a loose to my soul,
I spent on the unimportant wood.

The sun was warm but the wind was chill.
You know how it is with an April day:
When the sun is out and the wind is still,
You're one month on in the middle of May.
But if you so much as dare to speak,
A cloud comes over the sunlit arch,
A wind comes off a frozen peak,
And you're two months back in the middle of March.

A bluebird comes tenderly up to alight
And fronts the wind to unruffle a plume,
His song so pitched as not to excite
A single flower as yet to bloom.
It is snowing a flake: and he half knew
Winter was only playing possum.
Except in color he isn't blue,
But he wouldn't advise a thing to blossom.

The water for which we may have to look
In summertime with a witching-wand,
In every wheelrut's now a brook,
In every print of a hoof a pond.
Be glad of water, but don't forget
The lurking frost in the earth beneath
That will steal forth after the sun is set
And show on the water its crystal teeth.

The time when most I loved my task
These two must make me love it more
By coming with what they came to ask.
You'd think I never had felt before
The weight of an ax head poised aloft,
The grip on earth of outspread feet,
The life of muscles rocking soft
And smooth and moist in vernal heat.

Out of the woods two hulking tramps
(From sleeping God knows where last night
But not long since in the lumber camps).
They thought all chopping was theirs of right.
Men of the woods and lumber-jacks,
They judged me by their appropriate tool.
Except as a fellow handled an ax,
They had no way of knowing a fool.

Nothing on either side was said.
They knew they had but to stay their stay
And all their logic would fill my head:
As that I had no right to play
With what was another man's work for gain.
My right might be love but theirs was need.
And where the two exist in twain
Theirs was the better right—agreed.

But yield who will to their separation,
My object in life is to unite
My avocation and my vocation
As my two eyes make one in sight.
Only where love and need are one,
And the work is play for mortal stakes,
Is the deed ever really done
For Heaven and the future's sakes.

Lin Yutang

Lin Yutang (1895-) was born in China, educated at Shanghai, Harvard, and in German universities. He returned to China as a professor of English at Peking, and was active in the Revolution with brickbats as well as pamphlets. In the new China he has been an influential writer and editor. Since coming to the United States he has established his reputation as a writer in English: essays, criticism, a novel. My Country and My People *is acute interpretation of East to West;* The Importance of Living *he calls "a personal guide to enjoyment."* Between Tears and Laughter, *written under the provocation of war, discards the urbanity of the philosopher for the indignation of the political critic and lashes the Western powers for their policy toward China now and in future.*

THE IMPORTANCE OF LOAFING

CULTURE, as I understand it, is essentially a product of leisure. The art of culture is therefore essentially the art of loafing. From the Chinese point of view, the man who is wisely idle is the most cultured man. For there seems to be a philosophic contradiction between being busy and being wise. Those who are wise won't be busy, and those who are too busy can't be wise. The wisest man is therefore he who loafs most gracefully. Here I shall try to explain, not the technique and varieties of loafing as practised in China, but rather the philosophy which nourishes this divine desire for loafing in China and gives rise to that carefree, idle, happy-go-lucky—and often poetic—temperament in the Chinese scholars, and to a lesser extent, in the Chinese people in general. How did that Chinese temperament—that distrust of achievement and success and that intense love of living as such—arise?

In the first place, the Chinese theory of leisure, as expressed by a comparatively unknown author of the eighteenth century, Shu Paihsiang, who happily achieved oblivion, is as follows: time is useful because it is not being used. "Leisure in time is like unoccupied floor space in a room." Every working girl who rents a small room where every inch of space is fully utilized feels highly uncomfortable because she has no room to move about, and the moment she gets a raise in salary, she moves into a bigger room where there is a little more unused floor space, besides those strictly useful spaces occupied by her single bed, her dressing table and her two-burner gas range. It is that unoccupied space which makes a room habitable, as it is our leisure hours which make life endurable. I understand there is a rich woman living on Park Avenue, who bought up a neighboring lot to prevent anybody from erecting a skyscraper next to her house. She is paying a big sum of money in order to have space fully and perfectly made useless, and it seems to me she never spent her money more wisely.

In this connection, I might mention a personal experience. I could never see the beauty of skyscrapers in New York, and it was not until I went to Chicago that I realized that a skyscraper could be very imposing and very beautiful to look at, if it had a good frontage and at least half a mile of unused space around it. Chicago is fortunate in this respect, because it has more space than Manhattan. The tall buildings are better spaced, and there is the possibility of obtaining an unobstructed view of them from a long distance. Figuratively speaking, we, too, are so cramped in our life that we cannot enjoy a free perspective of the beauties of our spiritual life. We lack spiritual frontage. . . .

To the Chinese, therefore, with the fine philosophy that "Nothing matters to a man who says nothing matters," Americans offer a strange contrast. Is life really worth all the bother, to the extent of making our soul a slave to the body? The high spirituality of the philosophy of loafing forbids it. The most characteristic advertisement I ever saw was one by an engineering firm with the big words: "Nearly Right Is Not Enough." The desire for one hundred per cent efficiency seems almost obscene. The trouble with Americans is that when a thing is nearly right, they want to make it still better, while for a Chinese, nearly right is good enough.

The three great American vices seem to be efficiency, punctuality and the desire for achievement and success. They are the things that make the Americans so unhappy and so nervous. They steal from them their inalienable right of loafing and cheat them of many a good, idle and beautiful afternoon. One must start out with a belief that there are no catastrophes in this world, and that besides the noble art of getting things done, there is a nobler art of leaving things undone. On the whole, if one answers letters promptly, the result is about as good or as bad as if he had never answered them at all. After all, nothing happens, and while one may have missed a few good appointments, one may have also avoided a few unpleasant ones. Most of the letters are not worth answering, if you keep them in your drawer for three months; reading them three months afterwards, one might realize how utterly futile and what a waste of time it would have been to answer them all. Writing letters really can become a vice. It turns our writers into fine promotion salesmen and our college professors into good efficient business executives. In this sense, I can understand Thoreau's contempt for the American who always goes to the post office.

Our quarrel is not that efficiency gets things done and very well done, too. I always rely on American water-taps, rather than on those made in

China, because American water-taps do not leak. That is a consolation. Against the old contention, however, that we must all be useful, be efficient, become officials and have power, the old reply is that there are always enough fools left in the world who are willing to be useful, be busy and enjoy power, and so somehow the business of life can and will be carried on. The only point is who are the wise, the loafers or the hustlers? Our quarrel with efficiency is not that it gets things done, but that it is a thief of time when it leaves us no leisure to enjoy ourselves and that it frays our nerves in trying to get things done perfectly. An American editor worries his hair gray to see that no typographical mistakes appear on the pages of his magazine. The Chinese editor is wiser than that. He wants to leave his readers the supreme satisfaction of discovering a few typographical mistakes for themselves. More than that, a Chinese magazine can begin printing serial fiction and forget about it halfway. In America it might bring the roof down on the editors, but in China *it doesn't matter, simply because it doesn't matter*. American engineers in building bridges calculate so finely and exactly as to make the two ends come together within one-tenth of an inch. But when two Chinese begin to dig a tunnel from both sides of a mountain, both come out on the other side. The Chinese's firm conviction is that it doesn't matter so long as a tunnel is dug through, and if we have two instead of one, why, we have a double track to boot. Provided you are not in a hurry, two tunnels are as good as one, dug somehow, finished somehow and if the train can get through somehow. And the Chinese are extremely punctual, provided you give them plenty of time to do a thing. They always finish a thing on schedule, provided the schedule is long enough.

The tempo of modern industrial life forbids this kind of glorious and magnificent idling. But worse than that, it imposes upon us a different conception of time as measured by the clock, and eventually turns the human being into a clock himself. This sort of thing is bound to come to China, as is evident for instance in a factory of twenty thousand workers. The luxurious prospect of twenty thousand workers coming in at their own sweet pleasure at all hours is, of course, somewhat terrifying. Nevertheless, this is what makes life so hard and hectic. A man who has to be punctually at a certain place at five o'clock has the whole afternoon from one to five ruined for him already. Every American adult is arranging his time on the pattern of the schoolboy—three o'clock for this, five o'clock for that, six-thirty for change of dress; six-fifty for entering the taxi and seven o'clock for emerging into a hotel room. It just makes life not worth living.

And Americans have now come to such a sad state that they are booked up not only for the following day, or the following week, but even for the following month. An appointment three weeks ahead of time is a thing unknown in China. And when a Chinese receives an invitation card, happily he never has to say whether he is going to be present or not. He can put down on the invitation list "coming" if he accepts, or "thanks" if he declines, but in the majority of cases the invited party merely writes the word "know," which is a statement of fact that he knows of the invitation and not a statement of intention. An American or a European leaving Shanghai can tell me that he is going to attend a committee meeting in Paris on April 19, at three o'clock and that he will be arriving in Vienna on May 21 by the seven o'clock train. If an afternoon is to be condemned and executed, must we announce its execution so early? Cannot a fellow travel and be lord of himself, arriving when he likes and taking departure when he likes?

But above all, the American's inability to loaf comes directly from his desire for doing things and in his placing action above being. We should demand that there be character in our lives as we demand there be character in all great art worthy of the name. Unfortunately, character is not a thing which can be manufactured overnight. Like the quality of mellowness in wine, it is acquired by standing still and by the passage of time. The desire of American old men and women for action, trying in this way to gain their self-respect and the respect of the younger generation, is what makes them look so ridiculous to an Oriental. Too much action in an old man is like a broadcast of jazz music from a megaphone on top of an old cathedral. Is it not sufficient that the old people *are* something? Is it necessary that they must be forever *doing* something? The loss of the capacity for loafing is bad enough in men of middle age, but the same loss in old age is a crime committed against human nature.

Character is always associated with something old and takes time to grow, like the beautiful facial lines of a man in middle age, lines that are the steady imprint of the man's evolving character. It is somewhat difficult to see character in a type of life where every man is throwing away his last year's car and trading it in for the new model. As are the things we make, so are we ourselves. . . . We love old cathedrals, old furniture, old silver, old dictionaries and old prints, but we have entirely forgotten about the beauty of old men. I think an appreciation of that kind of beauty is essential to our life, for beauty, it seems to me, is what is old and mellow and well-smoked.

Sometimes a prophetic vision comes to me, a beautiful vision of a millennium when Manhattan will go slow, and when the American "go-getter" will become an Oriental loafer. American gentlemen will float in skirts and slippers and amble on the sidewalks of Broadway with their hands in their pockets, if not with both hands stuck in their sleeves in the Chinese fashion. Policemen will exchange a word of greeting with the slow-devil at the crossings, and the drivers themselves will stop and accost each other and inquire after their grandmothers' health in the midst of traffic. Someone will be brushing his teeth outside his shopfront, talking the while placidly with his neighbors, and once in a while, an absent-minded scholar will sail by with a limp volume rolled up and tucked away in his sleeve. Lunch counters will be abolished, and people will be lolling and lounging in soft, low armchairs in an Automat, while others will have learned the art of killing a whole afternoon in some café. A glass of orange juice will last half an hour, and people will learn to sip wine by slow mouthfuls, punctuated by delightful, chatty remarks, instead of swallowing it at a gulp. Registration in a hospital will be abolished, "emergency wards" will be unknown, and patients will exchange their philosophy with their doctors. Fire engines will proceed at a snail's pace, their staff stopping on the way to gaze at and dispute over the number of passing wild geese in the sky. It is too bad that there is no hope of this kind of millennium on Manhattan ever being realized. There might be so many more perfect idle afternoons.

Bertha Damon

Bertha Damon obviously is New England-born, for no one understands better the passion for high thinking and simple living which found its best expression in the great days of Emerson and Thoreau. In Grandma Griswold she presents a late survivor of a philosophy which disdained the surface goods of life for the sake of the deeper satisfactions of the spirit. If Grandma occasionally erred by excess, it was always on the right side. Mrs. Damon's memories of her austere childhood are found in Grandma Called It Carnal. *Equally entertaining accounts of her later adventures growing flowers, raising Irish cockers, and managing a husband appear in* A Sense of Humus.

GRANDMA READS THOREAU

"POOR Mrs. Parker," Grandma would say, gently shaking her corn popper over the yellow flame, while we children sat by listening to the popping kernels with the receptive expressions of young birds who hear wings flutter, "poor Mrs. Parker has had an extremely hard married life."

"Has she, Grandma?" I would inquire with hopeful curiosity.

"Yes, she has. I don't want to prejudice you against Deacon Parker, who is a good enough man in other ways as men go; but the truth is, Bertha"—her voice hushed—"after he was married to Mrs. Parker he was always wanting—wanting—Cooked Meals!"

"But, Grandma . . ."

"Yes, he was. At night he'd come home after poor Mrs. Parker had been busy all day and want a Cooked Meal, and then after she'd given him one, next morning the first thing he'd want—he'd want—another. She had a dreadfully hard time with him. So disillusioning to a woman to find out that's what a man thinks marriage is."

Cooked Meals—that phrase signified to Grandma Domestic Enemy Number One. She felt that the everlasting trouble connected with them was what was keeping her North Stonefield neighbors from the real ends of life; it was the cost of providing "Cooked Meals" that enslaved the men; the toil in preparing them that kept the women forever over the stove; the difficulty in digesting them that caused dyspepsia to fret almost every household. "Cooked Meals" in North Stonefield were indeed large, elaborate— three kinds of fancy cake and two kinds of pie at once were only a start— and repetitive, for there was little difference in size and kind between breakfast, dinner, and supper. There was little time for doing anything except to get up a Cooked Meal, clean up after it, and then get up another Cooked Meal. So Grandma had early come to the conviction that Job when he wanted to "curse God and die" wasn't so bad; to bless God and dine seemed, considering the consequences, worse.

"I have traveled a good deal in Concord," Grandma read in Thoreau, "and everywhere, in shops, in offices and in fields the inhabitants have appeared to me to be doing penance in a thousand remarkable ways. What I have heard of Brahmins hanging suspended over flames; or looking at the heavens over their shoulders until it became impossible for them to resume their natural position . . . ; or dwelling chained for life at the foot of a tree; or measuring with their bodies like caterpillars the vast breadth of empires; or standing on one leg on the tops of pillars—even these forms of conscious penance are hardly more incredible and astonishing than the scenes which I daily witness. The twelve labors of Hercules were trifling in comparison to those which my neighbors have undertaken; for they were only twelve and had an end."

Grandma likewise traveled a good deal in North Stonefield. There she saw the remarkable and incredible scenes that Thoreau had witnessed among his townsfolk. The men worked long and hard in the shops—from seven in the morning to six at night, with half an hour out for dinner; and the women worked even longer than their menfolks. The lives of almost all seemed to be a sort of tight slavery in which there was no leisure, no enjoyment, no vision. Almost all seemed to work and to get, to take care of and to hang onto, and finally to lie down in the cemetery, very tired, never having lived.

In Grandma's youth North Stonefield women had just begun to have new standards. Countless recipes for fancy dishes appeared in the new magazines. Machine production turned out cloth quickly and cheaply; so clothes had to be stylish. Machine-made furniture could be had in abundance. Competition in possessing and displaying all these things became a burden. Women in North Stonefield at about that time began to try to seem not as their mothers—housewives content in cheerful spacious kitchens which were at once dining room, living room, nursery, library, all of easy compass and easy care—but as ladies. As ladies they tried to "show off" by employing many separate rooms. For all these reasons household labor was greater than before, for adequate and sufficient "modern improvements" were not yet available, and in the nature of things there were no servants. In spite of the new freedom from spinning and soap-making, women had less time than ever.

"Perfect housekeeping" became a fetish, a cruel god that demanded and received human sacrifices. Whatever gifts of mind or body a North Stonefield woman had, if she were not a "perfect housekeeper" she had no claim to consideration. That was that. Anybody who was anybody kept her house in a state of hard, intolerable neatness. There is a neatness that is warm and lovely; it is one of the fine arts. Its origin is love for possessions that are intimate, that serve. There is a neatness that is cold; it comes out of bitter energy, lack of worthy occupation, and sometimes, not always, the desire to lay down laws for one's family, to make them miserable, and to be a martyr oneself. The love-neatness knows its place, knows it is but a means to an end, the end being a fine happiness in family life. But the hate-neatness is an end in itself. In almost every North Stonefield house some rooms were shut up and never used; some rooms had the sun entirely excluded by shades; some of even the most inhabited rooms had newspapers laid cheerlessly along the trails frequented by the menfolks.

There seemed to be no limit to the pains which women were willing to take in order to conform to that severe standard of "perfect housekeeping." "She keeps her kitchen floor so clean yer could eat yer bread 'n' milk off of it": emulation of that appetizing achievement led to endless damp drudgery on hands and knees. Miss Cole's old white mare of irreproachable character had to submit, at least once a month, to an all-over scouring with Sapolio and a thorough rinse in good dark bluing water. The reputation of being first out on the line Monday morning was zealously coveted. A triumphant bellying from the clothesline of white sails of sheets, boastful flapping of the long legs of manly underdrawers before the envious eyes of a neighbor woman just rushing out to hang up her wash was the high hope in every "perfect housekeeper's" breast. The rules of this competition were strict. To get a good head start by beginning the washing Sunday evening was a temptation, but was considered extremely irreligious: more than that, in this sport it constituted a foul. Some women were suspected of cheating, nevertheless. It was, however, allowed Sunday night after meeting, to put the clothes to soak and to get up at four in the morning and wash by kerosene lamplight. That was held to be fair enough.

Yet all the time our village and the country round was full of dawns and sunsets and starry nights; of early springs, when in the dusk thawing hylas shrilled like sleighbells and the whippoorwill insisted; of springs when by every gracious old house lilacs blossomed, and apple trees down the rocky hillsides; of summers when in all the millponds water lilies floated under flashing dragonflies; of autumns "bright as the sun . . . terrible as an army with banners," loud with katydid bands. But almost no one stopped drudging to look; almost no one turned an ear to listen.

And there were books to be read—all the thrilling books that had happened since God dictated the Old Testament until, let us say, the last poem by Browning; but almost nothing was read except *The Farmer's Almanac,* the cooking and crocheting and fashion magazines, and the doings of the villagers and their acquaintances in the *Stonefield Guardian.* There were thoughts to be wrestled with or enjoyed, but for thoughts almost everyone was too busy: men tramping the heavy treadmill of chores and of shop work; women working over "ribbons" and Cooked Meals.

But Grandma, inspired by Henry Thoreau to reduce to an irreducible minimum all household furnishings, to renounce conventional Cooked Meals and simplify to a Spartan simplicity such victuals as seemed indispensable to life, Grandma put herself and us—Alice used to say, "Thoreauly"—into the leisure class. We were never working all day long to conform to the standards of our neighbors.

We had almost all the time there was to do what we thought was worth doing. The times were frequent when Grandma—to use the words Thoreau wrote of himself—could not afford to sacrifice the bloom of the present moment to any work, whether of the head or hands. She loved a broad margin to her life. . . . She grew in those seasons like corn in the night, and they were far better than any work of the hands would have been. They were not time subtracted from her life, but so much over and above her usual allowance. She realized what the Orientals mean by contemplation and the forsaking of works. . . . This was sheer indolence to her fellow townsmen, no doubt; but if the birds and flowers had tried her by their standard, she would not have been found wanting.

Grandma was a sort of artist; hers was the art of living just the way she wanted to live. And no successful artist in any field but has had to throw his neighbors' ways aside and follow his own. It would seem that the first essential in achieving any sort of distinction is failure to conform. When Grandma stopped to think of it, Jesus and his disciples were not what seemed to most of their townsfolk desirable citizens; they were none of them doing a regular day's work. Jesus knew well this need of protecting one's time from invasion. Grandma was always delighted to recall that he rebuked

Martha who was anxious and troubled about many things (Grandma sensed that a Cooked Meal was in the offing of Martha's mind) and that he praised Mary who allowed herself calm leisure for sitting at his feet and hearing all he had to say. Our town was Martha; Grandma was Mary. Our town followed Martha's example in chiding its Mary.

"Way back when Mis' Griswold was a bride," was the town's bitter rumor, "she never used to do her dishes. She used to go roamin' round the lots with her minister husband, pickin' bouquets o' weeds, or else readin' Hebrew with him." No one not brought up in North Stonefield can know how reprehensible such conduct seemed.

But Grandma didn't care what the neighbors said, partly because she enjoyed being different, and mostly because Henry Thoreau had inquired why furniture should not be as simple as the Arab's or the Indian's instead of so elaborate as to clutter and defile our homes, and had said a good house-wife would sweep most of it into the dust hole and not leave her real morning's work undone. "Morning work! By the blushes of Aurora and the music of Memnon, what should be man's work in this world? I had three pieces of limestone on my desk, but I was terrified to find that they required to be dusted daily, when the furniture of my mind was undusted still, and I threw them out of the window in disgust."

So Grandma's house was not that conventional clutter of much furniture, draperies, tidies, bric-a-brac such as was accumulated by others in that Victorian-magpie era of decoration—not Grandma's! Unlike her neighbors, she felt no necessity of possessing Brussels carpets, lace curtains, and a Rogers group as patent of good social standing. A few hard old-fashioned chairs, a round table heaped with books, a clean rag carpet woven by Aunt Martha on the big old loom in the barn from ancestral wardrobes long past other salvage, sunlight gilding the faded walls and lying in broad sheets on the floor—for Grandma's was one of the few houses that did not keep shades down out of reverence for "property"—an open fire of logs in the winter, vases of flowers all summer, candlelight in the evenings—these are what I remember to have furnished Grandma's sitting room.

Such few needments made Grandma's housekeeping of Japanese simplicity. "A lady once offered me a mat," Grandma would quote the words of her master, "but as I had no room to spare within the house, nor any time to spare within nor without to shake it, I declined it, preferring to wipe my feet on the sod before my door. It is best to avoid the beginnings of evil." Also Grandma had a sense of order that went of itself, that dispersed disorder at its first signs.

"As Henry Thoreau says," Grandma would begin complacently, and my heart usually sank a little, and I wondered if we were going to hear another good reason why the Griswold household was not to have anything for the next meal but beans. But no— "'The cart before the horse is neither beautiful nor useful,' " she would go on; " 'before we can adorn our houses with beautiful objects the walls must be stripped, and our lives must be stripped and beautiful housekeeping and beautiful living be laid for a foundation: Now a taste for the beautiful is best cultivated out of doors, where there is no house and no housekeeping.' " That meant a long walk, and off we would go, Grandma and I, a cold lunch in our pockets, perhaps to enjoy the sight of snow melting on the edge of some swamp.

Sometimes Alice and I thought there were more exciting books in the world to read aloud than Thoreau's *Summer* or *Walden*. Sometimes we even chanted under our breath—

> By the rude bridge that arched the flood,
> His coat to April's breeze unfurled,
> Here once the bean-fed Thoreau stood . . .

But Grandma always stopped us in utter horror at our taking so revered a name in vain, so she never had the inestimable privilege of hearing how that verse was going to come out. I must confess that in my unregenerate childhood I could have done with a little less Thoreau, a little more frosting on the cake and a little less on bare tree boughs. But as I have later come to an appreciation of Thoreau's contribution to my life, through Grandma Griswold, I am glad she put so much of him in our mixture as she did.

Clifton Fadiman

Clifton Fadiman (1904-   ), whose companionable voice and engaging personality are familiar to every follower of "Information, Please," is a native of New York City and a graduate of Columbia. The essay which follows, originally part of the introduction to his Reading I've Liked, *provides a sufficient account of his earlier years. Later he became a teacher of English, a lecturer at the People's Institute, a publisher's editorial adviser, and book editor of* The New Yorker. *He edited the notable collection of personal philosophies,* I Believe, *from which Julian Huxley's essay is reprinted later in this volume. His writing has been largely confined to book reviewing, to which activity he has contributed a sane judgment, an informed intelligence, and an assured taste.*

MY LIFE IS AN OPEN BOOK

THOSE to whom reading is fated to become important generally shake hands with books early. But this is not always true. Many distinguished writers were blockheads at their letters until a comparatively advanced age. I think, however, of an undistinguished one who was a busy reader at four: me. My first book was entitled *The Overall Boys*. *The Overall Boys* was and doubtless still is a rousing tale of two devoted brothers, aged five and seven, and their monosyllabic adventures on a farm. The style was of transparent lucidity. I found *The Overall Boys* a perfect job then, and, looking back, I haven't yet been able to detect any flaws in it. I remember it in greater detail and certainly with greater pleasure than I do the 576-page novel I finished yesterday. At four I was convinced that *The Overall Boys* represented the peak of the art of narrative and sternly rejected all attempts to make me continue my reading adventures. This resistance endured for a lengthy period—about a week, I should say. Then I broke down, tried another book, and have been doing the same sort of thing ever since. But all devout readers will agree that my first literary judgment was correct. Everything after *The Overall Boys* has been anticlimax. The same new world can never be discovered twice. One's first book, kiss, home run, is always the best.

Between the ages of four and ten I read but moderately and with absolute catholicity. We had in our household the usual meaningless miscellany that accumulates if the parents are not specifically literary. Thus I read whatever lay behind the glassed-in shelves of two dreary-looking black-walnut bookcases. I devoured the standard "boys' books" scornfully discarded by my elder brother. I bored my way through at least ten volumes of an unreadable set of historical novels by some worthy named Mühlbach, I think, and got absolutely nothing from them; the same result would be achieved were I to read them now. I read an adventure story about the Belgian Congo that made an anti-imperialist out of me when I was eight; I have seen no reason to change my views since then. Something called *Buck Jones at Annapolis* similarly made me permanently skeptical of the warrior virtues.

I read an odd collection of "daring" books that many families of the period kept around the house, often hidden under lock and key: Reginald Wright Kaufman's *The House of Bondage;* something called *The Yoke,* which was on the same order; Maupassant complete, though this may not have been until I had reached the mature estate of twelve or thirteen; and similar luridness. These had no effect of any sort on me, as far as I can recollect, though I suppose a psychoanalyst could, at a price, make me tell a different story.

The child reader is an automatic selecting mechanism. What he is not emotionally ready to absorb, his mental system quietly rejects. When in later years I became a teacher of literature I could never see the point in censoring my young charges' extracurricular reading. Very often the mothers (never the fathers) of my high-school students would ask me to explain my refusal to forbid Mary or John to read James Joyce's *Ulysses*. I never offered any satisfactory explanation except to say that if John or Mary were ready to understand *Ulysses* then they were ready to understand *Ulysses,* which was a Good Thing. If they were not ready to understand it, which was apt to be the case, then *Ulysses* would at most waste their time, on which I was not prepared to set any exaggerated value. Often an anxious mother would inquire whether I didn't agree that the last chapter (Mrs. Leopold Bloom's uncorseted memories of an exuberant life) was shocking. My reply may have been frivolous, but it seems to me it contained the germ of the truth: that she found it shocking mainly because she had not had the chance to read *Ulysses* when she was seventeen, wherein Mary or John had an advantage over her. This generally closed, without settling, the controversy.

As you can see, part of my four-to-ten reading was unorthodox for a small child (I forgot to tell you that I also toddled through a volume of Ibsen, and found him impenetrable) but the unorthodoxies had no effect whatsoever. What I really liked was what any small boy or girl would like— what I was ready for. This included, of course, a moderate amount of what is called trash—the Rover Boys, Horatio Alger, Wild West yarns, Jack Harkaway, the whole conventional canon of those days.

I say trash. Actually such books are "trash" only by standards which should not be applied to children's reading. They have the incalculable value that listening to perfectly inane adult conversation holds for children: they increase the child's general awareness. They provide admittedly rough paradigms of character, motivation, life experiences. That is why it seems to me that the trash of my generation was superior to the trash of today. I submit that *The Rover Boys in the Everglades* and *Frank on a Gunboat* are preferable to Superman and his kind on two counts: they were cleanly and clearly written, and their characters were credible and not entirely un-related to the child's experience. When I was nine I could learn something interesting about life from even such highly colored affairs as the Frank Merriwell series, but I know that my son can learn nothing whatsoever of genuine interest (that is, which he can check against the expanding universe within himself) from the comics. I believe firmly that the current juvenile literature of the impossible is meretricious compared with the honest hack-work my own generation enjoyed. I also think that the kids are about ready to kick over this thriller fare in favor of something saner and more natural.

During my younger years, mainly between the ages of eight and ten, I, like my contemporaries, read a few "good" books, though they were not recommended to me as good. Such recommendations are hardly necessary. The child, if reasonably intelligent, has almost infallible good taste. Probably his good taste reaches its peak at that time. We all felt, when we encoun-tered *Tom Sawyer* or, to hit a lower level, Thomas Bailey Aldrich's *Story of a Bad Boy* or, on a still lower level, that fine New England classic *Lem* (is it still read?) that these books had something not possessed by *The Pony Rider Boys in the Ozarks.* It wasn't that they were more exciting, for sometimes they weren't, but that they were more "real." The other books were read eagerly and with joy, and then forgotten—indeed, they were read to be forgotten, to be "finished." But *Tom Sawyer* was something you caught yourself remembering a week later, and a year later. I know now, of course, the reason the child feels these books is that the authors felt them. It is as simple as that. That is why the so-called "better" juveniles that flood the bookdealers' shelves every year—the skillfully constructed, highly educational, carefully suited-to-age, morally sanitary, psychologically impeccable children's books—don't really make much of a dent on the child's consciousness. They are constructed for "the market." I don't mean the commercial market, but the market that is supposed to be the child's brain, as if that brain were a kind of transaction center in which each transaction was expressible in definite educational quanta.

The trouble with these juveniles is that their authors are greatly interested in children and not at all interested in themselves. Now, when Mark Twain wrote *Tom Sawyer* and *Huckleberry Finn* he never stopped to figure out whether his "boy psychology" was correct, or whether his story was properly adapted to a given age level. He wrote because he was passionately interested in himself, and the Mississippi River in himself, and the boy still alive in himself. Children ever since have unconsciously felt this intense reality, and that's what they've loved.

They've loved *Huckleberry Finn* even though it is over their heads, or written in old-fashioned English or dialect, or concerned with events that happened a long time ago. The machine-turned juveniles of our own day are "carefully adapted to the child's understanding," and that isn't what the child really wants. The child wants to be puzzled—not too much, but just enough. He doesn't want the characters' motivations to be automatically clear to him. He wants the satisfaction of figuring them out. As a matter of fact, the child delights as much in ambiguity as he does in clarity. *Alice in Wonderland* is still an overwhelming favorite, not because it's so funny but because it's so strange; it's a wonderful, gorgeous puzzle.

In this connection I always think of a comment my great and good friend Hendrik van Loon made to me one day. Going over, for editorial purposes, one of his manuscripts intended primarily for children, I pointed out to him the large number of long, difficult words which, as I thought, youngsters would never understand. He merely said, "I put them in on purpose." I learned later what he meant: that long words tickle the fancy of children, that they like the slight atmosphere of mystery distilled by a really bang-up polysyllable.

I think also that children—just ordinary, wholesome children, not bookworms—are more sensitive to beautiful writing than is generally supposed. They'll read reams of careless prose with great enjoyment, but when they come across the real thing, they know it. I don't know how they know it,

" *flaccid*

but they do. My own son is not overfond of books. Rather than forgo an airplane flight he would willingly see the Forty-second Street library vanish in flames. Two years ago I tried the young barbarian—he was about seven— on *The Wind in the Willows,* and he could make nothing of it. I tried him again some few months ago. He finished it with absorbed calm, clapped the book to, and said with finality, "Now, that's what I call well written!" He has never said this about any other book he's read, many of which he has "enjoyed" more. The fact is that *The Wind in the Willows* is the best-written book he has read so far, and he somehow knew it, though he had never been given any hint to affect his judgment.

The smooth confections the publishers turn out today are not well written in the sense that *The Wind in the Willows* is. They are merely correctly written. The authors in most cases have unconsciously curbed any impulse toward style, because style would express themselves, whereas they are supposed to be writing for the sake of the children. If they would forget all about the children and set down freely and lovingly the child in themselves, they might by some glorious accident produce masterpieces. *Little Women* was not written for little women or little men or little anybodies; it was the expression of a passionate memory. When Louisa May Alcott set herself to produce "juveniles," the result was often unsatisfactory, except when her native genius outwitted her conscious resolutions.

I am a firm believer in the newer methods of understanding and handling children. But it is arguable that they have made difficult the creation of a twentieth-century *Little Women* or *Alice in Wonderland*. Such books are the product not of knowledge, or even of wisdom, but of a kind of dream life, a dreaming-back to childhood on the part of the writer. That dream life and "child psychology" do not mix. That perhaps is why the modern child classics are not to be found in books at all, but in the cartoons of Walt Disney, master of an art newer, naïver, less touched by "science" than is the art of literature.

This has been a long and prosy digression, and while I'm at it, I'd like to make it a trifle longer. One of the games bibliomaniacs play in their weaker moments is the game of Century-Hencery, or literary prophecy. It's a harmless sport, the best part of it being that there can never be a loser. Here's how it works. You list the ten books you believe will be most widely read and generally admired a hundred or five hundred or a thousand years from now. Then you defend your choices. Making the unwarrantable assumption that in 2441 our civilization will still be recognizably related to that of 1941, I will now set down the ten works of literary imagination produced by the English-speaking race that I believe will be most universally alive (not merely admired in the schoolroom) five hundred years from now. Here they are, in no special order:

The Plays of William Shakespeare
Moby Dick
Gulliver's Travels
Robinson Crusoe
Alice in Wonderland
Huckleberry Finn
Little Women
Some novel of Charles Dickens, probably
    David Copperfield or *Pickwick Papers*
Treasure Island
The Mother Goose Rhymes

It is possible that in constructing this list I have been ingenious rather than ingenuous. Whether by accident or design it reflects one of my favorite theories—that the gods tend to grant immortality to those books which, in addition to being great, are loved by children. For mark well that only two books out of the ten—Shakespeare and *Moby Dick*—cannot, generally speaking, be enjoyed by youngsters. Of the remaining eight, seven are usually ranked as children's favorites. My point is simple: as the generations pass, children's tastes change more slowly than do those of grownups. They are not affected by the ukases of critics or the whims of literary fashion. Thus Shakespeare was not universally admired by the eighteenth century and again may not be (though I'd place a small bet against that possibility) by the twenty-third. But the rhymes of Mother Goose—to my mind literature, even if of a simple order—have suffered no diminution of popularity and, being unmoved by the winds of literary doctrine, are not likely to suffer any.

This is what happens. All children who read at all are introduced at a fairly early age to, let us say, *Robinson Crusoe*. Most of them like it. Later on they meet it again in school. They are told it is literature, and its hold on their minds is re-enforced. Still later, in adult life, they may encounter it again, when they are ripe to see in it qualities not apparent to them as children. Any possible resistance to accepting *Robinson Crusoe* as a great book had been broken down years ago during their childhood. Thus *Robinson Crusoe's* prestige remains undimmed. But a classic of greater artistic weight, such as *Paradise Lost,* does not enjoy the advantage of having been liked by readers as children. It is read by a small, select group of adults (college students) and so never passes into the consciousness of the generality. I do not mean that Milton will not be read five hundred years from now. I mean he will not be a casually accepted, generally enjoyed classic as I think *Little Women* or even *Treasure Island* (the most uncertain item, by the way, on my list) is apt to be. But remember, the book must be literature to begin with. Defoe's *Robinson Crusoe* will live, but A. R. Wyss' *The Swiss Family Robinson* is already dying.

We talk a great deal about the Greek classics. Yet what Greek classic has really penetrated among us? Not Plato surely, or any of the dramatists, but Homer and more particularly the simple, beautiful Greek myths that are read with pleasure by each generation of children. Similarly, I think Perrault and *The Three Musketeers* will outlast Proust and Stendhal, and Grimm's fairy tales still be widely read when Goethe is forgotten. If you wish to live long in the memory of men, perhaps you should not write for them at all. You should write what their children will enjoy. Or, to put it in another way and use a phrase that I think belongs to Lewis Mumford, a book already has one leg on immortality's trophy when "the words are for children and the meanings are for men."

May I make one or two further random comments on this list? Note that three titles—*Moby Dick, Robinson Crusoe,* and *Treasure Island*—have no women characters to speak of, and several of the others depend hardly at all on romantic interest. I do not believe that love, commonly considered one of the great staples of literature, tends as a subject to have any supreme preservative value. It is Dickens' sentiment and humor, not his lovers, that attract us. It is hardly the most romantic of Shakespeare's plays that stand highest in popular esteem. And Melville, in providing his masterpiece with an all-male cast, knew what he was doing.

Finally, if I were asked to make a wild stab at the one book likely to outlast the nine others, I would name *Alice in Wonderland*. This does not mean it is the "best" book on the list, for obviously it is not. In the end the best survives but the best of the best does not necessarily survive longest. Mankind will cling to what it admires, but even more fiercely will it cling to what it loves. And what we love perhaps above all else (as Dr. Freud pointed out in other and more dismaying connections) is ourselves as children. That is why I think it quite conceivable that Lewis Carroll will be read at some remote future time when Shakespeare is no more remembered than, let us say, Plautus and Terence are today. Twenty centuries from now Shakespeare may be entirely owned and operated by scholars. But I do not see why people should not still be laughing and exclaiming over *Alice in Wonderland*. Among the few things resistant to the tooth of time, great fantasy is one, and great fantasy is always the special possession of children.

I seem to have abandoned myself some pages back. I had just reached the age of ten. Between ten and seventeen I did the major bulk of my reading. I have never read as many books (I don't mean manuscripts) per year since, nor do I expect to in the future. Those were the splendid years, and it is my notion that they are the splendid years of most devoted readers. After seventeen (in some cases a year or two later) the books choose you, not you the books. You read within limits. Reading becomes a program. You read as part of your college curriculum, or to gain knowledge in a specific field, or to be able to bore your neighbor at dinner-table conversation. Adult reading is usually purposive. In my own case—I shall speak of this later on—it is more than purposive. I make a living by it.

Even the reading done during one's college years lacks the spontaneity, the high waywardness of one's pre-adolescent and adolescent reading. It circles around the classroom. It consists of authors recommended by authority or who you feel should be "covered." Or it has to do with books you know a good deal about in advance, one of the most effective ways to spoil one's reading pleasure. Such reading may be mentally stimulating or socially useful. It may benefit you in a dozen ways. But it is not an adventure in quite the same sense that reading in your second decade so often is.

I am not, in this random biblio-autobiography, proposing to list the books I have read. Nothing could be duller or less useful, except when he who does the listing owns a mind whose operations are really of interest to mankind, as was the case, for example, with John Stuart Mill. All I am here endeavoring to do is to outline some of the processes whereby an average person became an above-the-average reader, which is what I immodestly claim to be. To understand these processes a mere catalogue of titles is of no avail.

Yet I would like to list a few names, mainly to indicate the kind of writer that, as I recall, influenced the more bookish boys and girls of my generation. Shaw, Galsworthy, Bennett, Conrad, Merrick, Barrie, Moore, Dunsany, Yeats, Synge, Swinnerton, Chesterton, Meredith, Wilde, Hewlett, Gissing, Zangwill, and above all H. G. Wells—these, to confine the list to Englishmen only, are a few of the authors I remember devouring from my tenth to my eighteenth year, miscomprehending many, overprizing some, but getting from all an exultant sense of discovery, a peak-in-Darien thrill rarely enjoyed since.

The secret of second-decade reading, of course, is that you are not really finding out what Shaw thinks or Conrad feels, but what you think and you feel. Shaw and Conrad and the rest are but handy compasses to guide you through the fascinating jungle of your young self. When I read Wells' *Tono-Bungay* at fourteen or fifteen, I found myself saying in delight, "But that's just the way I feel!" When I now read Thomas Mann's *Joseph* story I find myself thinking how true it is to the experience of men in general. There is a difference in the quality of the emotion. The grown-up emotion may be larger and wiser (and probably more pompous), but the boyish one is unique just because it is so utterly, innocently self-centered.

During this adolescent period of my reading life I had a lucky break. My brother, five years my senior and a student at Columbia College, was at the time taking a conventional survey course that used a sound standard anthology known, I think, as *Century Readings in English Literature,* edited by Cunliffe, Pyre, and Young. For some reason, possibly a mild fraternal sadism, he made me take the course along with him—he at college, I at home. The whole thing was over my head—I was fourteen—but when I had finished my *Century Readings,* which took a year, I had at least a hazy notion of the course and development, from *Beowulf* to Stevenson, of the most magnificent, after the Greek, of all literatures. I remember writing essays, perhaps no more interminable than my subjects, on Hakluyt and Spenser. I am still unable to dislodge from my memory—which is not a good one—odd lines of verse from subminor poets like Drayton. That is all of no account. The important thing is that I got through my head at an early age a few simple truths: that the proper reading of a good writer requires energy and application; that reading is not mere "diversion"; that it is impossible to admire writing you do not understand; that understanding it does not destroy but rather enhances its beauty; that unless a writer's mind is superior to, more complicated than, your own, it is a bore to read him. (That is why I never recommend a book to a person if it is on his own mental level.)

I learned also that daydreaming and intelligent reading do not go together. There is a story told by Dr. Sandor Ferenczi, the psychoanalyst, about a Hungarian aristocrat who, while devouring a quick lunch between trains, was recognized by a boorish acquaintance.

"My dear Count! How are you?"

"Umph."

"And how is the Countess?"

"Dead."

"How shocking! It must be terrible for your daughter."

"She's dead."

"But your son—"

"Dead! Everybody's dead when I'm eating!"

During my all-out period everybody was dead when I was reading. Most children and adolescents know this magical secret of concentration, though it is not till they are older and duller that they realize it was magical.

I remember that, when I was fourteen, we lived about two miles from the nearest library. I had a choice. I could cycle there, borrow my books, and cycle back in a very few minutes—but those few minutes were lost to reading. Or, if I wished, I could walk to the library, reading the last fifty or seventy-five pages of my calculatedly unfinished book en route, make my borrowings, and walk back, reading a new volume on the way. I usually preferred the latter procedure. It is no trick at all to read while walking, to step off and onto curbs with unconscious skill, to avoid other pedestrians while your eyes are riveted to the page. There was a special pleasure in it: I had outwitted Father Time. I think Providence meant me to be an ambulant reader, for I never once even stumbled. But one afternoon when I was cycling home from the library with my wire basket full of books, I was hit from behind by a car and sent sprawling.

This absorption, this "losing yourself" in a book, though clearly quite remote from "practical life" (for children "practical life" is simply what grownups want them to do), is not daydreaming. The child does not interpose a continuous, fuzzy, wavering screen of personal desires and wishful visions between himself and the page. On the contrary, he and the page are one. The Victorian female, with whom novel reading was a disease, was the real daydreamer. For her, reading became a drug, a kind of literary marijuana, an instrumentality for the production of needed visions. The child's hearty relation to his book is devoid of this sick quality.

Well, the course my brother gave me, via that blessed trinity Cunliffe, Pyre, and Young, was calculated to make me understand that literature, beyond helping one to discover oneself, has a higher, more impersonal function. It is a challenge issued by a higher mind, the author's, to a lower mind, the reader's. Even if the challenge is not met, much pleasure may still result. But if it is met, or if a sincere attempt to meet it is made, a finer, rarer pleasure is experienced. If you read for pure diversion, well and good, but if you read for any other purpose, always read above yourself. One of the reasons for the general mental fuzziness of most "cultivated" people we know is that publishers have become too shrewd. They have learned, the cunning little fellows, just how to temper their books to the lamb-like mental innocence of their readers. The result is that every week we are deluged with books which, the publishers assure us, we can understand. It is quite true. We can understand them, all too easily. It would be much better for us if now and then we read a book just a few rungs beyond our mental capacities in their most relaxed state.

My second-decade reading—and I think this is sadly true of most of us—was in this sense educationally more valuable than any I have done since, with certain notable (and I shall note them later) exceptions. During adolescence our feeling of bewilderment and insecurity tends to be greater than at any other time. Hence the need to know, to learn, is greater. Therefore whatever reading is done is intense. It is utterly assimilated. We pay absorbed attention to it, as we would to the instructions of an expert before venturing into a trackless forest.

It seems to me that in my late teens I did more "heavy" reading and digested it more thoroughly than at any succeeding period. In this connection I recall two antithetical experiments I made extending over an interval of six months. The first was an experiment in difficult reading. The other was an experiment in nonreading.

One summer I decided to spend my evenings reading only "hard" books. I went at it with the humorless obstinacy of a sixteen-year-old—and I was more humorless and more obstinate than most. I staggered wildly through stuff like Ueberweg's *History of Philosophy,* Winwood Reade's *Martyrdom of Man,* Saintsbury's *History of English Prosody,* Taine's *History of English Literature,* Gibbon's *Decline and Fall of the Roman Empire.* It was enough for a book to seem important and forbidding—I read it at once. No novels, no light literature of any sort, no magazines for three solid months—hot months, too. Now, as I look back on this extravagant experiment, it seems like the disagreeable behavior of a young prig. Yet I was not really priggish; I didn't read for show-off purposes. I read my Ueberweg as a challenge to myself, as a test, as a deliberate gesture, if you will, of self-punishment. The boy of sixteen by overexercise will punish his body deliberately just to see how much it can take. That same boy may punish his mind in the same way. It is a kind of initiation ceremony that he performs upon himself, a queer, grotesque test of approaching manhood. Sometimes he will decide to go right through *The Encyclopaedia Britannica.*

The notable part of the experience is that just because that summer's reading came out of a powerful emotional impulse it has stuck with me, as more formal reading, particularly that done as part of my school work, has not. Also, it left me with a taste for a certain kind of "difficult" reading, a taste which, because I am a book reviewer, I rarely have an opportunity to indulge. This does not mean that I read heavy books with ease. On the contrary, I have to go through painful mental struggles to understand them, but the struggle still gives me an odd satisfaction, which I know has something to do with that lunatic summer I spent perusing nothing but huge volumes several miles above my head.

Today, for example, the books I look forward with most pleasure to reading and reviewing are books of popular science, of the Hogben-Julian Huxley-Eddington type. I am not really competent to judge them, but I like to read them, perhaps primarily because for me—I am a scientific illiterate—they present challenging difficulties. It may be an illusion, but I always feel, when I have finished a book of this sort, that I have "got" something out of it. I hardly ever get this feeling from a novel or a conventional biography.

Well, that was Experiment Number One. The second was its polar opposite. I decided to spend three months reading nothing at all, not even a daily newspaper. (The three months coincided with a long absence from school, so the conditions for the experiment were at their optimum.) Now, why did I want to do this? It was again a matter of self-testing. I felt I had grown too dependent upon other people's ideas. The only way I could perceive to cure myself of this dependence was to abjure other people's ideas completely. The mental life of the adolescent is frequently characterized by this oscillatory quality. He can find out what his real nature is only by leaping from one extreme to the other.

And so for three months I read, as nearly as I can recall, virtually nothing. It was by no means a fruitless experiment, and to those held too tightly in the grip of the reading habit I heartily recommend it. The effect is purgative. The mind disgorges a good deal of waste and clutter, it slows down, for a time it seems vacant. Then gradually it fills again, this time not with the myriad, secondhand impressions induced by nonstop reading, but with the few clear ideas and desires that reflect more accurately your true self. The experience, in addition to being cleansing, is humbling; you realize how sparse is the net content of your mind.

I have known men and women who read so voraciously and continuously that they never have the time or opportunity to discover who they really are. Indeed, I suspect it is precisely because they prefer not to make that discovery that they cling so limpetlike to books. I suppose this is better for them than alcohol or hasheesh, but it is not very different. All of us, I am sure, have noticed people who suffer from reader's fidgets. If there is a book, a magazine, any piece of print within easy reach, they will at once take it up, idly, without real intent to peruse it, but out of a kind of mechanical compulsion. They will do this while they are talking to you, while you are talking to them, while engaged in some other activity. They are victims of print. Perhaps some dim premonition that unless I watched out I too would become afflicted with reader's fidgets made me carry through with entire success my three months' literary fast.

Some years ago I helped to manage a bookstore featuring a circulating library. The main body of customers consisted of commuters. Every evening, a few minutes after five, the commuters would dash in.

"Give me a novel!"

"Any special title?"

"No, any novel will do: it's for my wife"—as if that somehow made everything clear.

These commuters' wives—there are tens of thousands of them—were not really in any active sense doing any reading at all. They were taking their daily novel in a numbed or somnambulistic state. They were using books not for purposes of entertainment, but as an anodyne, a time-killer, a life-killer. Many "great readers" are of this class. Truth to tell, they have never read a book in their lives.

Akin to these novel-addicts are the newspaper fiends who read three, four, or five papers a day and supplement them with radio news reports. There is only one Keeley cure I can recommend for this weakness, and that is for these people to save their papers for a week, and go back and read the news of seven days before. They will then see, even in the short perspective thus provided, how contradictory, foolish, ineptly stated most "spot news" is. They will perceive that, if taken in overfrequent doses, its main effect is to bewilder or even to frighten, rather than to inform. A ration of one newspaper a day ought to be enough for anyone who still prefers to retain a little mental balance.

Serious reading is an art. An art is something you have to learn. To learn an art requires a teacher. There are too few such teachers of reading in the United States, and that is one of the reasons why we are still only a semi-educated people. I, like my fellow Americans, was never taught, in elementary and high school, how to read properly. Thus, when I reached college, I was but ill-equipped to understand any really original book that was handed to me, though I found no particular difficulty in getting through the required textbooks, manuals, and other predigested matter. I do not think I would ever have learned how to read had it not been for one man and one college course.

The man was John Erskine and the course was, rather absurdly, called Honors. Erskine himself was largely responsible for the conception underlying Honors, which in turn was the only begetter of Robert Hutchins' Chicago Plan, of the St. John's College classics curriculum, and in fact of the whole return in modern education to the great tradition of Western thought. John Erskine is a man of such varied talents that his original contribution to American education is often forgotten.

It is very hard to explain why Erskine was a great teacher. He was not a character as Copeland of Harvard was. Although always genial and fair, he never attempted to make the students like him. He did not act as if he were a perennial contestant in a popularity contest. (I am convinced, by the way, that those teachers who year after year are voted Most Popular by the undergraduates are rarely educators of great value.) In his literature courses Erskine never swooned over beauty or tried to make you "feel" the lines or the paragraph.

There were two things about Erskine that may help to explain the influence he wielded over his students, even over those who didn't care greatly about literature. One was his enormous respect (not merely liking) for his subject matter. This may seem a commonplace, but it is not. Many teachers— no more surprisingly than other frustrated human beings—have a silent, gnawing contempt for what they teach. Unaware of this contempt, they often find it subtly translated into a resentment of their students. The result is vitiated teaching, teaching of a purely formal sort.

Erskine not only loved his subject but reverenced it and respected himself for teaching it. There was thus a good moral relationship between himself and his work. It may seem high-flown to say that this moral relationship was a vital aid in the production of good teaching. Yet I'm sure this was the case. He could teach his students to read because he had a large and lofty attitude toward what we were reading.

At the same time, if Erskine had been able to communicate only this attitude, he would not have been the great teacher he was. He went beyond this. To put it simply, he challenged us to understand what we were reading. He called upon us for a kind of mental exercise that is ordinarily devoted to mastering such "hard" subjects as philosophy and the sciences. (Actually, there are no "hard" or "easy" subjects. Donne is as difficult and as rewarding as Euclid.) Erskine made us work and the odd thing about it was that the more we understood, the more we liked the particular book we were reading.

The Honors Course was but a systematic extension of the Erskine educational program. For two years, under the guidance of a group of selected instructors, we read and talked about one great book a week, beginning with Homer and concluding, as I recollect, with William James. That was all there was to the course, and it was by far the most valuable one I took at college.

Pearl Buck

Pearl Buck (1892-   ), as the child of American missionaries, spent a lonely girlhood in China. Thrown upon Chinese associations she absorbed the culture of her neighbors. After graduation from Randolph-Macon College she returned to China for ten years as wife of a missionary. Her novel The Good Earth *won the Pulitzer Prize in 1932 and established her reputation as an interpreter of Oriental civilization. She is the third American to receive the Nobel Prize. The following pages reveal the wide range of Mrs. Buck's mind. No merely literary criticism, this essay unites letters and philosophy in the tradition of Matthew Arnold.*

LITERATURE AND LIFE

THE contribution of literature to life is so large a subject that to say anything definite about it is like trying to hold two large separate stars in the universe and show their cosmic relationship. What is this cosmic relationship? What, if anything, can literature contribute to the individual to enable him to know how to live in his environment?

The answer to this question depends of course on our definition of literature. Is literature what most people read, or what a few people have written? Are popular magazine stories literature? Are detective stories, romances, Wild West tales, true heart confessions, to be included in literature, and is that what we have to think of when we consider how literature contributes to life? Or are we to limit our definition of literature to a few books written by a few dead?

This we do know—most people in America know the mechanics of reading. We are not, of course, the most literate nation on earth. There are several nations where the literacy ratio is a good deal higher than ours, notably Japan. But somewhere along the way, even though formal education does not persist beyond the grades, we have been exposed, though very slightly, to what is considered great literature. We know, too, that most of us do not read very much after all,—or if we read, it is in relatively small numbers. There is, of course, the much-talked-of competition with reading— radio, motion pictures, and automobiles, all combine to keep people away from books and literature. A sort of life seems to be coming in which books could be largely eliminated and their loss scarcely noticed. Indeed, it is already here for many people.

All this is true. And yet it does not, I think, matter so much that the mass of the people are never going to read literature. The bits of Shakespeare and Browning and Tennyson—or whatever children have in school now-a-days—are not going to affect them one way or the other. No, we have to acknowledge that literature is never going to contribute to most lives at all. Most people are going to the movies, instead, not to a particular picture, but just to the movies. They will turn on the radio, not to a special program, but just turn it on. They will read newspaper headlines probably, and make a desultory choice out of the lurid array of popular magazines on the stand at the street corner or in the drugstore. If a book is talked about a great deal, as a few books a year always are in the United States, they may look into it curiously just to see what it is everybody is talking about. That is all.

I will confess this surprised me at first, since having lived so much of my life in a country where ninety per cent of the population was illiterate, I had come to value literacy and to think people would read if they knew how. I see now, after four years of watching my fellow countrymen, that knowing how to read has little to do with reading. People learn to read in order to read advertisements, bills, sports announcements, and news— although printed news does not matter so much since we are getting so many pictorial magazines. Of course in the old days of silent pictures to know how to read was necessary, because of the captions, but now we have talking pictures—and we will have talking newspapers, they tell us, before long—and the radio gives us love and crime and wisecracks.

But not all of us belong to that radio-tuning, movie-going, unthinking crowd. What concerns me is that the intelligent people—the leading people, the people who have brains and whatever we possess of culture and very often of means—they do not read; or if they do, they read too often digests of books and essays and stories rather than the works themselves.

Yet the habitual readers of digests inevitably lose the appreciation of style and grace in language, just as we would lose appreciation of food, its taste and color and texture, if we should take it in the form of chemical pellets. Our physical nourishment might be adequate, but mere physical nourishment from food is not enough. To get the plain meat out of a book or story or essay is to live on dull fare, so insidiously dull that we do not know what we are missing. So it is not enough to get the bare meaning out of a piece of music or of a painting or of a great book. "Mona Lisa" digested is nothing but a woman smiling. A digested symphony is nothing but a group of themes which can be played in five minutes. *Of Human Bondage* is a book without a plot, one which no magazine would accept as a serial, and which could be digested in a few pages of a small magazine.

When these digests are made of literature, people read them and think they know what it is all about. Yet they do not know what it is about. For they have missed that which makes literature. The blue pencil reduces everything to the dead tastelessness of a chemically prepared pellet. That graceful fleeting fancy, that individual quality which is the inherent mark of genius upon every material which it chooses to work upon is lost. People say they are so busy. *I* say, if you have only half an hour, use it not for a hurried survey of the bones of books and magazines, picked for you by someone you do not know, who may have overlooked entirely the one incident, character, or quality which would have most enriched your reading, but use that valuable half-hour for reading entire, and as it was really written, one thing—a few real pages from a book, or one actual story or essay. You will have more in the end—more real food for thought, and your literary palate will not be dulled by a succession of small dishes prepared by the same cook in the same pot and all tasting alike.

There is, of course, no harm in amusement and diversion. That is a legitimate reason for literature. What concerns me is that educated people are amused and diverted by the ephemeral passing book or story or the smart, silly patter of a columnist, and not by literature. I am not surprised or concerned when Mrs. Jones, the janitor's wife, begs the librarian for a nice book with a lot of things happening but everything turning out all right. But I am concerned when Mrs. So-and-So in Sutton Place, a graduate of the finest schools of our country and wife of one of our leading men, uses her scant leisure, after all the worthy enterprises in which she engages, from Spanish relief to a rally of Republican women, to read—what she does read. That lady once undertook to upbraid an author for writing in a certain popular magazine. Said she, "I picked up a copy of *Purple Shadows* the other day and was astonished to find a story of yours in it. How can you write for such magazines?"

Said the author, "How can you read such a magazine?"

Said she, "My dear, I only do it for relaxation."

Whereupon I began to ponder why, when she wants relaxation, she reads what even she considers trash. Why does the cheap, the ephemeral, the highly colored, the falsely romantic, relax and amuse the educated mind instead of boring it? Education, to be sure, has left this mark—it has taught people a sense of shame, so that they know they should have on their tables the great names and books of literature. But these are not what they really read. The threat to literature, the check upon its development is not from the low standards of the many ignorant, but from the low standards of the few intelligent, who more often demand of literature that it shall not be true art rather than that it shall.

There are reasons, of course, for this state of being. Foremost, perhaps, is our often boasted youth.

Culture, of course, is after all a matter of time and long, mellowing age. And collectively we are not old and individually we cling to childhood and its enjoyments. We do not want to grow up. And the reason for this is that the average person in America is not yet interested in life. That is, he is not interested in human nature and its true character. Or perhaps it would be truer to say he is interested in the activities of life, but not in its meaning or its philosophy. He is instinctively frightened of anything like a view of himself and why and how he is. And yet that view, of course, is what literature is.

What do we want when we read? We approach literature with a strange, impossible sort of expectation. We ask, on the one hand, to be supplied with unrealistic romantic ideals so earnest as to be naive, which have, it seems to me, no reality of any kind, either actual or desirable, and on the other hand, we have this childish wish to be amused, or rather to escape from the very restrictions to which we cling. We ask to be uplifted and—or—amused—if possible, a little of both at the same time. Yet literature, it seems to me, has nothing essentially to do with either of these things, except incidentally. Literature cannot have as its function the satisfaction of moralism nor the wish to escape from it if it must deal simply with life as it is.

I read modern American novels rather assiduously, as a matter of interest, and I find further evidence of what I have been trying to say in the lack of interest in life. The characters are almost universally subordinated to the incident and environment. That is, what apparently interests readers is how much characters hop, skip, and jump, and not how they feel and are. Characters are instantly recognizable types—good, bad, funny, pretty, are about all the adjectives needed to describe them. Especially in the so-called regional novels is there evident this poverty of character analysis and development—novels very properly so-called, too, for they are novels of regions—the weather of the regions, the storms, the crops, the animals, the shootings and crimes, and so forth, but never, deeply, the people. There seems in our American literature especially to be no real relationship developed between the region and its people. Yet it seems to me only when that relationship is thoroughly understood and portrayed can the result be even called regional literature.

I have recently come back from a journey through seventeen central states of our country, and as part of my preparation for this trip I read some of the regional novels. I was able to get a good idea of the landscape, of the weather and of the history of various regions, and particularly amazingly good local color, but absolutely nowhere an adequate idea of the people. In all the books the people were the least interesting part because the most slightly developed and the least understood. Yet, even in a journey, it was the people who impressed me. The landscape, for instance, of South Dakota, is in some ways the finest I have ever seen in the world—the most amazing, and the most strange, and the most beautiful. It is on such a scale and so peculiar, as well, that I cannot blame a writer for dwelling upon its shapes, its weather, and its devastations. But to me far more vivid than that terrific landscape were the people who live there—it seems to me they are the most magnificent people I ever saw, dreamers, all of them, those who are left, people held to the country in spite of abject poverty, people who live in the dream of a tomorrow, believing still in the country they cannot but love. They are not really subordinated by the landscape. They tower above it, poor as death and as triumphant. What literature lies there, unwritten—and probably never to be written, because young love is not of primary importance and there is very little action! Outwardly people seem static—they suffer and wait and dream, but what tremendous inner action there is in those three words! Not many people see the romance in a man's loving dry black soil that will not yield him food and holding to it grimly because if there were water it would yield enormously, and tomorrow it may rain. Yet there is the essence of romance in it. But the ending may not be happy.

We are afraid, we Americans, of tragedy. I mean tragedy in the deep fundamental sense of the Greeks, who understood that life is tragic in its whole course from its unexplained beginnings to its unknown end. Even comedy in that Greek sense had its foundations in tragedy—a butterfly fluttering in gaiety over a dark and bottomless river. So long as we shrink in fear from acknowledging we are what we are, beings brought into this brief consciousness which we call life, and from accepting this to proceed to the living and understanding of this life, we can have no great literature.

And yet I feel nothing is stronger in our American people than the desire to find some sort of philosophy with which to face life. The desire is inarticulate, and it expresses itself in all sorts of ways, from swing music to theosophy. There is such an earnest blind longing to know what to make of life as it is, and it is coupled at the same time with a sort of fear of knowing, so that when anything serious comes near, it is evaded by the jazz touch. And so even literature is evaded, as something too serious, though if they would only see, they would know that literature contributes to the understanding they want of what life is, and can help them to know, therefore, what their attitude toward life should be, as reasonable creatures.

It would be easy for me to do what many have done—simply shrug my shoulders at the mass of popular writing and say that it has nothing to do with literature. But I cannot. I keep going back to it—it is what most people read—then it must have its importance somewhere in relation to literature. One cannot dismiss lightly a magazine bought and read by three million people or a book bought and read even by thousands. It is important. It is a serious thing for literature if three million read—not literature, but something else which gives them greater satisfaction. I have put the blame on the people. But there is always the possibility that there is something wrong with literature. Jazz, so despised once, we have now come to think of as contributing something very especial to music. What it is we do not know, and shall not know until jazz is dead, and its vitality has become merged into the great body of permanent music. Swing—is it fad or new rhythm? Who knows or can know in our generation? It must run its course until we see it take its true place in what is past. If it has a definite value for human beings something will remain which no amount of scorn or ignoring can kill or even displace.

Perhaps it is literature which today has become devoid of philosophy—so devoid that it has no inner light, so that people, reading, have caught no real illumination of the life which most of us live so blindly from day to day. The vogue for historical novels has been, perhaps, because the novels of present day life cast no glow. Perhaps people are not afraid of tragedy, after all, if it is *their* tragedy—that is, tragedy which they recognize as beyond mere sordid living. The greatest books have always been tragedies. *Madame Bovary* is one of the most tragic books ever written. So is *Resurrection*. So is *Of Human Bondage*. So is *Vanity Fair*. The list is long, and most of these books when they first appeared were met with criticism. People did not immediately like them. It took time to get over the first revulsion against sadness and see beyond into the light. But the books that people have kept on reading are the books with that inner light which makes them have a sort of timeless rightness and accord with life which is happiness in itself, as distinguished from amusement and a mere happy ending. These are the books which give life in the full—not slantwise from the viewpoint of region or vogue. These are the books which have laid hold upon life and have had a philosophy to expound. A lesson is a glib thing—easy to teach, easy to learn and gabble off. But a philosophy is something wrought out of experience. It can be accepted or rejected but never learned by rote.

I do not need to say, I am sure, that by the word "philosophy" I mean no dry abstractions without relation to human daily lives. I mean those questions which every creature capable even of simple thought asks himself in times when he is alone—hours which he may hate and dread and from which he seeks all sorts of escapes, but which, nevertheless, exist—those hours when he asks, who am I and why was I born and what is it all for? Who are these others and what have they to do with me and what have I to do with them? To ask these questions is to seek the essentials of some sort of philosophy of life. And to answer them in one way or another, is the meaning of literature. Whenever a book, through the direct voice of poetry or through the voices of characters in a novel, recognizes these fundamental questions of the human heart, that book is read and lives on and on. And whenever a book ignores them, though it achieves a momentary popularity, it passes on and is forgotten. Light upon the deep and primitive inquiry of the human heart is the primary contribution, then, of literature to life.

It may seem a curious contradiction to say on one hand that people demand nothing but amusement from literature and then to say that literature which only amuses does not satisfy them. But such indeed is the case. The American public is peculiarly constituted and full of contradictions. With all our child-like love of a good time, we never really have a good time unless we feel we are improving ourselves, too. The moral sense is very strong in us. It may be it is only that well-known and famous puritan conscience, which it is said, is never strong enough to keep us from doing anything we want to do, but only strong enough to keep us from enjoying whatever we do do. We may be trying, in all our desire for escape, to escape not from the realities of life, but from the reality of ourselves. If so, of course escape is impossible, and yet, if it is impossible, the effort is all the more frantic. But none can escape that Hound of Heaven—his own self. And real literature has nothing to do with that attempt to escape. It has only to do with the pursuit, and it shows that the end of that pursuit is but the deeper and fuller understanding of that self.

So long as we breathe we are in this world which encloses us. Literature does offer the only real escape—but deeper into the world and not away from it. And that is what it contributes to life—more life, more understanding of that life. Any good book is like a microcosm where in a small compass we can see how life functions. In our daily experiences we are lost in the largeness of all around us. We cannot understand all that is going on. But a good book catches a part of what is going on and holds it for us, and we can see relationships there, and causes and effects which escape us in the flying by of actual time and events.

We ought when we put down a book to feel a deeper sense of completion of self, not of escape from it. We ought to understand that self better and feel in closer accord with it and more content with it. If we do, then the book is literature, and literature has made its contribution to life.

Maxwell Anderson

*Maxwell Anderson (1888-   ) was born in Pennsylvania. He gradu-
ated from the University of North Dakota and taught English for a
short time in California. From college teaching he passed to newspaper
work in San Francisco and New York, and began to write plays and
poetry.* What Price Glory?, *written in collaboration with Laurence Stall-
ings, was the most successful play of 1924 and is still regarded as a
powerful picture of life in the trenches of the First World War. In
later plays,* Elizabeth the Queen, Winterset, High Tor, Key Largo, *and
others, he began to experiment with poetic drama. Although his results
have not been uniformly satisfactory, he has gone a long way toward
bringing back poetry into the theater. In the following essay, originally
delivered as an address at Carnegie Institute, he describes the arts as
man's best way to a better destiny and the artists as the builders of that
destiny. For him the artist's faith in mankind. is the best assurance of
the continuing enlargement of the spirit of ·man.*

WHATEVER HOPE WE HAVE

THERE is always something slightly embar-
rassing about the public statements of writers and artists, for they should
be able to say whatever they have to say in their work, and let it go at that.
Moreover, the writer or artist who brings a message of any importance to
his generation will find it impossible to reduce that message to a bald statement, or even a clearly scientific statement, because the things an artist has
to communicate can be said only in symbols, in the symbols of his art. The
work of art is a hieroglyph, and the artist's endeavor is to set forth his vision
of the world in a series of picture writings which convey meanings beyond
the scope of direct statement. There is reason for believing that there is no
other way of communicating new concepts save the artist's way, no other
way save the artist's way of illuminating new pathways in the mind. Even
the mathematician leaves the solid plane of the multiplication table and
treads precariously among symbols when he advances toward ideas previously unattained.

It may be that I am trying, at this moment, to reduce to plain statement an intuitive faith of my own which cannot be justified by logic and
which may lose, even for me, some of its iridescence when examined under
a strong light by many searching eyes. For though the question I meant to
take up was only the utility of prizes for artistic excellence, I can find no

approach to that question save through a definition of the artist's faith as I see it, and no definition of that faith without an examination of the artist's place in his universe, his relation to the national culture, and the dependence of a nation on its culture for coherence and enduring significance.

Let me begin then, quite simply and honestly, even naively, with a picture of the earth as I see it. The human race, some two billion strong, finds itself embarked on a curious voyage among the stars, riding a planet which must have set out from somewhere, and must be going somewhere, but which was cut adrift so long ago that its origin is a matter of speculation and its future beyond prophecy. Our planet is of limited area, and our race is divided into rival nations and cultures that grow and press on one another, fighting for space and the products of the ground. We are ruled by men like ourselves, men of limited intelligence, with no fore-knowledge of what is to come, and hampered by the constant necessity of maintaining themselves in power by placating our immediate selfish demands. There have been men among us from time to time who had more wisdom than the majority, and who laid down precepts for the conduct of a man's brief life. Some of them claimed inspiration from beyond our earth, from spirits or forces which we cannot apprehend with our five senses. Some of them speak of gods that govern our destinies, but no one of them has had proof of his inspiration or of the existence of a god. Nevertheless there have been wise men among them, and we have taken their precepts to heart and taken their gods and their inspiration for granted.

Each man and woman among us, with a short and harried life to live, must decide for himself what attitude he will take toward the shifting patterns of government, justice, religion, business, morals, and personal conduct. We are hampered as well as helped in these decisions by every prejudice of ancestry and race, but no man's life is ready-made for him. Whether he chooses to conform or not to conform, every man's religion is his own, every man's politics is his own, every man's vice or virtue is his own, for he alone makes decisions for himself. Every other freedom in this world is restricted, but the individual mind is free according to its strength and desire. The mind has no master save the master it chooses.

And each must make his choices, now as always, without sufficient knowledge and without sufficient wisdom, without certainty of our origin, without certainty of what undiscovered forces lie beyond known scientific data, without certainty of the meaning of life, if it has a meaning, and without an inkling of our racial destiny. In matters of daily and yearly living, we have a few, often fallible, rules of thumb to guide us, but on all larger questions the darkness and silence about us is complete.

Or almost complete. Complete save for an occasional prophetic voice, an occasional gleam of scientific light, an occasional extraordinary action which may make us doubt that we are utterly alone and completely futile in this incomprehensible journey among the constellations. From the beginning of our story, men have insisted, despite the darkness and silence about them, that they had a destiny to fulfil—that they were part of a gigantic scheme which was understood somewhere, though they themselves might never understand it. There are no proofs of this. There are only indications— in the idealism of children and young men, in the sayings of such teachers as Christ and Buddha, in the vision of the world we glimpse in the hieroglyphics of the masters of the great arts, and in the discoveries of pure science, itself an art, as it pushes away the veils of fact to reveal new powers, new laws, new mysteries, new goals for the eternal dream. The dream of the race is that it may make itself better and wiser than it is, and every great philosopher or artist who has ever appeared among us has turned his face away from what man is toward whatever seems to him most godlike that man may become. Whether the steps proposed are immediate or distant, whether he speaks in the simple parables of the New Testament or the complex musical symbols of Bach and Beethoven, the message is always to the effect that men are not essentially as they are but as they imagine and as they wish to be. The geologists and anthropologists, working hand in hand, tracing our ancestry to a humble little animal with a rudimentary fore-brain which grew with use and need, reinforce the constant faith of prophet and artist. We need more intelligence and more sensitivity if ever an animal needed anything. Without them we are caught in a trap of selfish interest, international butchery, and a creed of survival that periodically sacrifices the best to the worst, and the only way out that I can see is a race with a better brain and superior inner control. The artist's faith is simply a faith in the human race and its gradual acquisition of wisdom.

Now it is always possible that he is mistaken or deluded in what he believes about his race, but I myself accept his creed as my own. I make my spiritual code out of my limited knowledge of great music, great poetry, and great plastic and graphic arts, including with these, not above them, such wisdom as the Sermon on the Mount and the last chapter of Ecclesiastes. The test of a man's inspiration for me is not whether he spoke from a temple or the stage of a theatre, from a martyr's fire or a garden in Hampstead. The test of a message is its continuing effect on the minds of men over a period of generations. The world we live in is given meaning and dignity, is made an endurable habitation, by the great spirits who have preceded us and set down their records of nobility or torture or defeat in blazons and symbols which we can understand. I accept these not only as prophecy, but as direct motivation toward some far goal of racial aspiration. He who meditates with Plato, or finds himself shaken by Lear's "fivefold never" over Cordelia, or climbs the steep and tragic stairway of symphonic music, is certain to be better, both intellectually and morally, for the experience. The nobler a man's interests the better citizen he is. And if you ask me to define nobility, I can answer only by opposites, that it is not buying and selling, or betting on the races. It might be symbolized by such a figure as a farmer boy in Western Pennsylvania plowing corn through a long afternoon and saying over and over to himself certain musical passages out of Marlowe's *Doctor Faustus*. He might plow his corn none too well, he might be full of what we used to call original sin, but he carries in his brain a catalytic agent the presence of which fosters ripening and growth. It may be an impetus that will advance him or his sons an infinitesimal step along the interminable ascent.

The ascent, if we do climb, is so slow, so gradual, so broken, that we can see little or no evidence of it between the age of Homer and our own time. The evidence we have consists in a few mountain peaks of achievement, the age of Pericles, the centuries of Dante and Michelangelo, the reign of Elizabeth in England, the century and a half of music in Germany, peaks and highlands from which the masters seem to have looked forward into the distance far beyond our plodding progress. Between these heights lie long valleys of mediocrity and desolation, and, artistically at least, we appear to be miles beneath the upper levels traversed behind us. It must be our hope as a nation that either in pure art or in pure science we may arrive at our own peak of achievement, and earn a place in human history by making one more climb above the clouds.

The individual, the nation, and the race are all involved together in this effort. Even in our disillusioned era, when fixed stars of belief fall from our sky like a rain of meteors, we find that men cling to what central verities they can rescue or manufacture, because without a core of belief neither man nor nation has courage to go on. This is no figure of speech, no sanctimonious adjuration—it is a practical, demonstrable fact which all men realize as they add to their years. We must have a personal, a national, and a racial faith, or we are dry bones in a death valley, waiting for the word that will bring us life. Mere rationalism is mere death. Mere scientific advance without purpose is an advance toward the waterless mirage and the cosmic scavengers. The doctrine of Machiavelli is a fatal disease to the citizen or the state. The national conscience is the sum of personal conscience, the national culture the sum of personal culture—and the lack of conscience is an invitation to destruction, the lack of culture an assurance that we shall not even be remembered.

No doubt I shall be accused of talking a cloudy philosophy, of mixed metaphors and fantasy, but unless I misread my history, the artist has usually been wiser even about immediate aims than the materialist or the enthusiast for sweeping political reform. The artist is aware that man is not perfect, but that he seeks perfection. The materialist sees that men are not perfect, and erects his philosophy on their desire for selfish advantage. He fails quickly always, because men refuse to live by bread alone. The utopian sees that men seek perfection and sets out to achieve it or legislate it into existence. He fails because he cannot build an unselfish state out of selfish citizens, and he who asks the impossible gets nothing. The concepts of truth and justice are variables approaching an imaginary limit which we shall never see; nevertheless those who have lost their belief in truth and justice and no longer try for them, are traitors to the race, traitors to themselves, advocates of the dust.

To my mind a love of truth and justice is bound up in men with a belief in their destiny; and the belief in their destiny is of one piece with national and international culture. The glimpse of the godlike in man occasionally vouchsafed in a work of art or prophecy is the vital spark in a world that would otherwise stand stock still or slip backward down the grade, devoid of motive power.

For national growth and unity the artist's vision is the essential lodestone without which there is no coherence. A nation is not a nation until it has a culture which deserves and receives affection and reverence from the people themselves. Our culture in this country has been largely borrowed or sectional or local; what we need now to draw us together and make us a nation is a flowering of the national arts, a flowering of the old forms in this new soil, a renaissance of our own. If we want to live, or deserve to live, as a force or in history, we must somehow encourage the artists who appear among us, and we must encourage excellence among them. How to go about it is a problem entirely unsolved. I wish I could believe that prizes or critics or governmental endowments were effective stimulants toward effort or excellence in any artistic field. They may be occasionally, but the greatest achievements have occurred in the absence of endowments or professional critics or prizes, seemingly as the result of a feverish desire for accomplishment in any single art, permeating a whole society during a period long enough to allow for more than one generation of devotees. Probably an artist can ask nothing better than a free society which likes his work and is willing to pay for it.

Looking ahead, I have no more than a hope that our nation will sometime take as great a place in the cultural history of the world as has been taken by Greece or Italy or England. So far we have, perhaps, hardly justified even the hope. But what hope there is for us lies in our nascent arts, for if we are to be remembered as more than a mass of people who lived and fought wars and died, it is for our arts that we shall be remembered. The captains and the kings depart; the great fortunes wither, leaving no trace; inherited morals dissipate as rapidly as inherited wealth; the multitudes blow away like locusts; the records and barriers go down. The rulers, too, are forgotten unless they have had the forethought to surround themselves with singers and makers, poets and artificers in things of the mind.

This is not immortality, of course. So far as I know there is no immortality. But the arts make the longest reach toward permanence, create the most enduring monuments, project the farthest, widest, deepest influence of which human prescience and effort are capable. The Greek religion is gone, but Aeschylus remains. Catholicism shrinks back toward the papal state, but the best of medieval art perishes only where its pigments were perishable. The Lutheranism of Bach retains little content for us, but his music is indispensable. And there is only one condition that makes possible a Bach, an Aeschylus, or a Michelangelo—it is a national interest in and enthusiasm for the art he practices. The supreme artist is only the apex of a pyramid; the pyramid itself must be built of artists and art-lovers, apprentices and craftsmen so deeply imbued with a love for the art they follow or practice that it has become for them a means of communication with whatever has been found highest and most admirable in the human spirit. To the young people of this country I wish to say: if you practice an art, be proud of it, and make it proud of you; if you now hesitate on the threshold of your maturity, wondering what rewards you should seek, wondering perhaps whether there are any rewards beyond the opportunity to feed and sleep and breed, turn to the art which has moved you most readily, take what part in it you can, as participant, spectator, secret practitioner, or hanger-on and waiter at the door. Make your living any way you can, but neglect no sacrifice at your chosen altar. It may break your heart, it may drive you half mad, it may betray you into unrealizable ambitions or blind you to mercantile opportunities with its wandering fires. But it will fill your heart before it breaks it; it will make you a person in your own right; it will open the temple doors to you and enable you to walk with those who have come nearest among men to what men may sometime be. If the time arrives when our young men and women lose their extravagant faith in the dollar and turn to the arts we may then become a great nation, nurturing great artists of our own, proud of our own culture and unified by that culture into a civilization worthy of our unique place on this rich and lucky continent between its protecting seas.

Malvina Hoffman

Malvina Hoffman (1887-   ) had studied painting for some years in New York before she realized the need to express herself in three-dimensional form. Color and line were not enough; she had to become a sculptor. This extract from her lively autobiography, Heads and Tales, *describes her determination to study under the great Rodin. When, by dramatic accident, she became his pupil her career had begun, a career which was to be filled with hard work, rich friendships, and romantic triumphs, and which took her later to the ends of the earth to model in bronze the hundred races of mankind for the Field Museum, Chicago.*

RODIN AND PARIS

WITHIN a year, my mother decided to give up her life in America and devote herself to helping me in my artistic studies abroad. I had worked day and night trying to collect enough funds to pay for the steamer tickets, designing covers for sheet-music and patterns for wallpapers and linoleums, and making pastel portraits of babies and young children. We sailed away with a letter of credit for one thousand dollars left to my mother in legacy by a thoughtful friend. In the good old days of 1910 we were able to travel through Italy and Switzerland, to Paris and London, establish ourselves in various studio and alcove apartments, and live in the student quarters of the *rive gauche* for fifteen months, on this thousand dollars.

To anyone who has had the good fortune of being an art student in Paris and who has been poor enough to know the joys of a Sunday lunch on the Boulevard Montparnasse, after a week of home cooking and dish-washing, when *dessert et café* were added to the menu as a real spree, it would be unnecessary to state that there were no obstacles ominous enough to dim the promise of even a distant horizon. Reading the menus from right to left during the lean years made everything edible seem precious and worth fighting for. Many were the laughs indulged in, when the inevitable *gateau de riz* would be suggested as a means of satisfying any stray hunger pangs that might still be lurking in the mind or body of a passionate young art student.

It was my determined intention to become a pupil of Rodin. While still in America I had studied his work from books and photographs, and from the varied and interesting collection of his clay studies, bronzes, and marbles owned by Mrs. John Simpson in New York.

When I had tried five times in vain to present a letter of introduction at Rodin's studio, Rue de l'Université, my hopes were almost frustrated and the situation had become pretty desperate for me. His concierge gave me little encouragement, but some last grain of hope drove me to extreme action on my fifth visit, and I said:

"Tell Monsieur Rodin that if he does not see me today I must return to America, but that I came to Paris to study with him, and that I must deliver a message to him from his friend Madame Simpson. I shall not leave, he must admit me today."

The surprised guardian seemed to sense my adamant determination, and in a few moments came back smiling.

"Well, at last I have permission to admit you," she said, and I followed her past the many studios until she knocked at Rodin's door.

I found myself in a room crowded with marbles and covered clay models on stands. There were four or five Frenchmen with black coats and red rosettes in their lapels, talking to Rodin, who looked me over with a hooded searching gaze that made me feel rooted to the spot and unable to move. He came forward slowly, and put out his hand. As I gave him the messages, in my unconjugated French, from his friend across the seas, his grip tightened and he asked me why I had not mentioned her name at my first visit. I began to feel my blood move again in my veins. "So you were determined not to leave without seeing me," he said. I nodded. "What have you under your arm in that envelope?" he asked. "Oh, just two photographs of the only sculpture I have ever done—I am just a beginner but I find I cannot escape it. Sculpture seems to have taken possession of me and my desire is to be your pupil if you will be willing to guide me and criticize my work."

"Let me see the photographs," he said. "Who are these two men?"

"Well, the marble is of my father," I replied. "He was a musician who, after a long life, was serenely meditative. The other is of a young violinist who is just making his début in America as a soloist."

Rodin looked at the photographs for some minutes, put them back into the envelope, and handed them to me. "Character seems to interest you. You have studied these men well. One is the mature artist with his life battles behind him, the other is the young dreamer with his battles ahead of him. Wait here a few moments. I am just describing this marble of mine to these gentlemen and then I am lunching with them." Rodin went back to the visitors and started to tell them that the figure represented a fallen angel that had broken his wings on a rock and that the idea had been conceived after reading a certain poem. He began reciting the lines in a deep monotone, but his memory failed him and he grew violent trying to recall the ending of the sonnet. He strode up and down before the great marble group.

By some extraordinary coincidence, I happened to know the poem, and when I saw that he could not recall the lines, I walked towards him. "Maître," I ventured, "I know that poem, shall I recite it?" He turned on me almost savagely—"What—*you* know it?—let me see if you do—recite it!" My blood was pounding, but I began the lines in a slow, quavering voice:

"J'ai perdu ma force et ma vie,
Et mes amis et ma gaîté;
J'ai perdu jusqu'à la fierté
Qui faisait croire à mon génie.

"Quand j'ai connu la Vérité,
J'ai cru que c'était une amie;
Quand je l'ai comprise et sentie,
J'en étais déjà dégoûté.

"Et pourtant elle est éternelle,
Et ceux qui se sont passés d'elle
Ici-bas ont tout ignoré.

"Dieu parle, il faut qu'on lui réponde.
Le seul bien qui me reste au monde
Est d'avoir quelquefois pleuré." [1]

I stepped back once more to my place at the door, not daring to raise my eyes.

There was a murmur of surprise from the group of men. Rodin's voice suddenly rose in a tone of almost brutal abruptness—"*Allons, au déjeuner, mes amis—il est tard.*" He showed his friends out of the door, turned towards me—"Here," he said. "This is where my keys hang," and he lifted an old rag from a nail on the wall, on which hung two keys. "You may use them to open the other studios. Uncover all the work and examine the trays

---

[1] This sonnet, entitled "Tristesse," was written by Alfred de Musset during a fit of depression in June, 1840.

I have lost my strength and my life,
My friends and my joy of living;
I have lost even the pride
Which made me believe in myself.

When I first knew Truth,
I took her for a friend;
But when I fully understood her,
I was filled with loathing.

And yet she is eternal,
And those who have done without her
Here below have missed the whole of life.

God speaks, and one must answer him.
All that is left to me now in this world
Is the tears I have sometimes shed.

of plaster studies and I will see you when I return." He went out, closed the door and locked it from the outside. I had certainly not only been admitted at last to his studio, I was locked into it—for better or worse—and I wasted no time wondering what it all meant, but started in at once to pull the linen shrouds off the marbles. A new world seemed suddenly to engulf my imagination. When I had examined one room I went to the next and then to another and finally returned to where I had started and began making drawings of the small plaster hands of which there were thirty or forty in various positions lying in wooden trays. I worked so intently that I did not notice that the fire in the stove had gone out and that the studio had grown icy cold. I did realize quite definitely, however, that I was very hungry, for I had not had anything to eat since my cup of coffee at 7:30 A.M. and I suddenly noticed that it must be well into the afternoon as the winter light had begun to fade. I re-covered all the marbles, and as I went over to try the door, hoping to be able to open it from the inside, I heard a knock. Wondering what I should do, I made no response—for if it were some visitor what would he think if I said I could not open the door? The knocking became louder and then a key turned in the lock and the door opened. Rodin came in and looked about. He caught sight of me behind one of the marble blocks. "Well," he said. "What have you done all this time? Why is everything covered over? Did you not examine the work or did you not like it, that you have covered everything again?"

I explained hastily that the sight of so many of his groups was too much for me to cope with at one time, and that although I had examined them all, I had re-covered them carefully and had concentrated my attention on the little plaster hand which seemed to be more my size. I had made a few drawings of this and he examined my sketch book. After looking through it he said, "My child, do you think these are all drawings?"

"Why, yes," I answered naively, "I *did* think so, what are they?" for I could see he was not of my opinion.

"They are sketches," he said. "Michelangelo *never* made sketches, everything he drew was a study, a real drawing. See that you never make any more sketches. Beware of the weakness of your American artists," pointing his finger at me very threateningly.

"What is their weakness?" I asked.

"*C'est leur sacrée facilité,*" he said, and then, going over to the stove, he realized how cold it had grown. The fire was out, and we were in semidarkness. He came back and felt my hands; they were cold. He took off his heavy cloth cape and wrapped it about me and went to work remaking the fire. "Why did you let it go out?" he asked, and "Why do you look so pale and tired? By the way, did you have any lunch before coming to me at noon?"

"No, I had my coffee early but did not expect to be able to stay here so long today—it has been a great feast for a hungry artist, I shall never forget it."

He sat down beside me, drawing the little stools near the stove. "You forgot the fire, my child, because of the inner fire that burns you, but you cannot neglect hunger—nature is a stern mistress, and if you play tricks with her she will punish you every time. When I locked you in today, I never thought about food, I just wanted to make sure that you would be alone with my work, and that I would find you on my return." He rubbed my hands and held them near the glowing stove. "Now you must go home and take the little hand with you and make careful drawings for a week. Every day you must go to the Louvre and study and make copies of the old masters—Leonardo Da Vinci and Michelangelo and Raphael—not to copy their technique only but to understand it, and develop a technique of your own, and each week come back here and bring me what you have done—and be sure to eat plenty of beefsteak and potatoes"—at this point he encircled my absurdly small wrist with his strong sensitive fingers—"you are too thin and sculpture needs plenty of fuel, for the fires of art burn fiercely. When you come back, I may be drawing from a model, if so you may draw with me. You know where the keys hang, from now on you may feel at home in my studio."

And so it was that my studies with Rodin began.

Irwin Edman

Irwin Edman (1896-   ) has been a teacher of philosophy at Columbia University since 1918. Gifted with the power to translate the abstractions of philosophy into sparkling realities, he has illuminated the complexities of our time with his urbane and witty essays. Philosopher's Holiday *reads like good conversation.* Candle in the Dark *shed its brave light upon the gusty days of 1939.* "Look Homeward, America!" *renounces our immemorial practice of turning to Europe for leadership in the arts and finds at home our finest incentive to creative work. Here, or nowhere, is the land of cultural opportunity.*

LOOK HOMEWARD, AMERICA!

AMONG the things that would have seemed incredible as late as ten years ago is the vanishing of Europe as a combination Nirvana and happy hunting ground for educated or semi-educated Americans. The peculiar part Europe has played in the lives and imaginations of the more literate Americans is permanently ended. For Europe as Nirvana is over. Europe once meant liberation, it once meant escape. It provided at once a moral holiday and a spiritual tonic. The angles and crudities of the workaday American world, all business and all Philistinism, were left behind. One went abroad to live in the past and in a present steeped in a past. It was an excursion into a cultural paradise.

There were the artistic monuments of the dead and the urbanities of the living. It is difficult to say which gave the more acute thrill to the visiting American, the cathedral of Chartres or the apéritif drunk in the café in its shadow; Racine heard at the Comédie Française, or the French spoken by the hotel porter; Westminster Abbey or the Cockney wit of the London policeman, and the charm of a house-party in Sussex.

It hardly needs to be said just now that all that is over. Europe will not for a long time, possibly never again, offer the kind of escape into history and charm in which the irritating present can be forgotten. For a genera-tion the agony of living will be too urgently visible in the poverty, disease, and disorganization of a post-war and post-Hitler continent. Nor will Europe be a happy hunting ground either. Even if many of the monuments of the past survive the bombs, the sense of the past will be seriously dulled by the acute intrusions of the present. The sense of leisure, tea on an English lawn, or dinner on a French *terrasse,* lunch in the storied corner of a London club, all the haunts of Americans acting as transient beneficiaries of a long tradition of cultured leisure, will hardly have the same flavor. Cultured leisure may be unknown in post-war Europe, even to the class—much smaller than visiting Americans realized—who ever knew it in Europe at all. . . . What Americans looked for in Europe they will have to find—as they had of late, even before the outbreak of this second world war, been seeking it—at home.

The long-continued trek of the American imagination to Europe began over a century ago. It brought Emerson to England and Henry James, Sr., too, who thought, among other things, that he could not find proper schools for his children (Henry and William James) in America. The hegira was continued until the late nineteen-thirties by students, writers, cultivated ladies, all restless refugees (how ironic it seems to use the term in this sense now) from America. What drove them abroad was in the first place what amounted to almost a national inferiority complex, a sense of the colonialism and provincialism of America. "Who reads an American book?" a famous English critic asked contemptuously as late as the middle of the nineteenth century. A great many Americans did not do so, not when they could lay hold of an English one. Even in the Golden Day of New England many of the shining figures of that day turned eastward, Emerson to Carlyle and to the Germans, Longfellow to Dante and the Italian past, Hawthorne to

Italy and Greece. A multitude of lesser Americans followed them in their spiritual pilgrimages and, when they could afford to, turned their spiritual longings into physical visits. Baedeker in hand, they could be found rapt before all the monuments next to whose name Baedeker had placed two stars. The stars, it should be noted, were not shifted to newer monuments in successive editions.

As the nineteenth century moved on, Americans with a taste for ideas and beautiful things in letters or art had an increasing sense, as their colonial past receded, of their still colonial dependence on Europe in cultural matters. At home the Golden Age was succeeded by the Gilded one. The opulent vulgarities of Newport succeeded the high austerities of Concord. The American mind—that is, the American intelligence (for contemplation was at a discount)—went into the building and the economic exploitation of the country. "Culture" was an effeminate minority voice in the land. Cultivated persons, especially men, had to go abroad to cease to be, or to feel, exotic, and to find a society where the things of the spirit and of the refined senses did not seem shadowy and illicit.

Among the comfortable classes business was the concern of the men, culture of the ladies; and through the eighties many American men, lovers of the arts and ideas, could not help feeling that in the general opinion there was something trivial and unimportant about the ideas and arts they cherished. They felt, sadly, that ideas and *belles-lettres* and music and painting were not the preoccupations of the influential classes, or of anyone else, in American society. Furthermore, those things on which the mind and the imagination fed were to be found, so educated Americans came to feel, chiefly in Europe. At college, literature meant chiefly English literature; even in childhood young Americans were brought up on Dickens and Scott and Thackeray, and pictures of English country houses and cathedrals. When people built fine houses were they not ambitiously imitative? Were not churches Gothic, and banks Greek? Why should it not seem natural to go to Europe to find their originals and to drink deep from the fountain whence the original inspiration of these things came? Henry Adams may have protested later that he got no education from England and Italy or Germany, though he confessed he did get Beethoven by accident in a German beer garden. But for many others a sense that the cherishable past was European was combined with a conviction that nothing worth cherishing was being thought or felt in expanding industrial America. All the young men of the genteel tradition (and their mothers and sisters too) went to Europe—their fathers were too busy making money for its own sake and too busy paying for the trip.

But it was not only for the past that culture-loving Americans crossed the Atlantic. Echoes reached America that the new too, the materials of sensibility and talent, were to be found chiefly in Europe. From Dickens to the visiting English and French lecturer of today, from the youthful Paderewski to young Serkin, from Wagner to Hindemith, from Monet to Dali, the striking, the original, the distinguished, it was believed, were not to be found in a country whose talent all went into gadgets and skyscrapers. For the *dernier cri* in living culture as well as for the tradition of the past, Americans had to go abroad.

Even the last war did not disenchant them. With the wave of disillusion, with the lapse of the idealistic rhetoric of the Wilsonian period, America seemed culturally more insular than ever. Realistic American fiction portrayed the stupidity of the Babbitts, and the mean streets of the slum cities, and the mean hovels of the rural poor. America was the twentieth century incarnate, bleak and angular, without nuance or overtone. One fled the four-lane highways and skyscrapers and country clubs for the café terraces, the winding roads, the shadowed cathedral closes of England, the châteaux of France, the hills of Fiesole overlooking Florence, where a whole colony of writers and art critics lived, or to Rome where lived the Pope— and Santayana. One went to bask in past beauties or to have a look at that ferment of new artistic and intellectual movements current in Europe after the last war, not least in Germany and Austria. Some went to see the new Expressionist movements in the theater in Berlin, some to study the co-operative movement in Denmark, or Sweden's model Middle Way, or the socialist housing schemes of Vienna, or the brilliant and humane housing schemes for working people in Amsterdam.

To mention these things now is to speak a bitter obituary. Even before the outbreak of the war in 1939 most of these experiments were over and their inventors or moving spirits were dead or in concentration camps or in exile in America; Europe had become considerably less agreeable or psychologically satisfactory or intellectually tenable as an escape or as a tonic. Germany and Austria, for a brief period so fashionable among the literate (Salzburg was briefly a musical Mecca), were rubbed off their pilgrim's map. The brilliant circle of liberal intelligence led once by young Papini had long ago vanished in Italy. And when one was in Europe, everywhere the shadow of war and the sense of a dark future, or none at all, made it clear to even the most sentimental idealizing American that Europe was no longer a museum or a spiritual haven. The American went to England for its past and found Englishmen ready to turn to America for their future. The monuments of culture were still there, *pro tem,* but there was nothing for the contemporary imagination to feed on. And then the war came, and even those who during the rise of Fascism and the descent of poverty still fled to Europe for escape, could do so no longer. Even the Europe that one could see in America was ceasing to arrive, or to mean as much, or anything. The Russian Ballet was a ghost of a vanished culture; the Russian Art Theater was no more. German theater directors were in

Hollywood and German novelists in Princeton. The literates now must not only stay at home; they must look within the American landscape, physical and imaginative, for their stimulus and their liberation. It is perhaps one of the few healthy consequences of our tragic time that this should be so. The Innocent Abroad has been for too long a familiar figure. Heaven knows for how long American thinking and creative impulse have been semi-paralyzed by a superstitious respect for Europe, and a sentimental confusing of the patrimony of the past with the Europe of the present. Americans were still visiting the Goethe house in Weimar while the Brown House was already in sinister existence in Munich.

It would be a silly exaggeration to say that because Europe is now going through the agony of possibly complete collapse, Americans were foolish in turning to Europe for certain beauties of the past and charms of the present. Europe, whatever happens, still remains the source of our own past in science, in letters, and in art. Whatever be said of that unhappy continent, whatever the political stupidities and barbarities, it is the world from which Western culture derives, and Europe in ruins, or in Nazi conquest, would carry with it much of what has formed the mind and imagination of every civilized American.

Nor were Americans ill advised in enjoying the delicious surface of current but long-established ways of life, the pleasant incidentals of the bourgeois social tradition. It would be dishonest not to admit that in the delightful smaller arts of life, in delicious food cooked and served with art, in gracious holiday spots, in the courtesies of casual intercourse, Americans found across the Atlantic what they did not find in Kansas or Ohio or, for that matter, in Boston or New York.

But no culture ever survived or grew by being derivative and colonial. No artistic vision is steady or clear when it wears only distance glasses. Americans, looking across the Atlantic, missed seeing with accuracy or vividness what lay before them at their feet.

It is just as well that Americans look homeward for their culture. It may well be that, for the long present, not only because of the economic and political insecurity in Europe, but because of the concerted Nazi-Fascist antipathy to ideas and art, this country may be the only vehicle of free cultural expression, of thought and feeling and perception, for a long time to come. If the light goes out here it may not be lighted anywhere else. The Europe that cultivated Americans cared about, so far as it is the past, can in some measure be found at home. This is suggested by the revival of the humanistic tradition in American colleges, the passion for the classics being nurtured, if only in translation, among young people of college age, the widespread enjoyment, on radio and records, of the tradition of European music, painting enjoyed both in museums and in reproductions as it has never been enjoyed before. The Europe that Americans feel must not die, cannot die so long as music, art, and literature flourish as studies and enthusiasms in America.

But obviously a culture purely receptive is dead or decadent. It would be foolish spiritual isolationism to turn our backs on the European past or on what can be saved of its present. It would be, and is, simply honest vitality to find our present in ourselves. For it is clear that when Americans fled to Europe, not for its past, but for its present, they were fleeing largely to what was really illusory or, as events have proved, insecure. What they were really seeking was largely an escape that came not so much from the actual conditions of European life as Europeans lived it, as from the surface delights of European leisure, as enjoyed by Americans on a holiday, an interlude often prolonged for years by well-to-do expatriates. This escape was largely infertile as Henry James, the most gifted of the refugees from American life, confessed in his later years. The creative or the merely connoisseur American living abroad lived largely in a synthetic and reconstructed past or an alien present seen from the outside. He was not at home nor did he know America in his own time; he did not intimately know any other world, nor was he at home anywhere else. He was a spectator, not a dramatist; a collector of bric-a-brac, not an artist.

Only lately have Americans begun to examine the materials of American culture in terms both of their own patrimony and their own present. There are various surface symptoms. There is, in the first place, the flood of historical novels and of regional ones. In the former, American writers (and their readers) are waking to the drama, the color, and the human meaning of facts they had not remembered save as dull sentences in schoolbooks. The history of America has begun to come alive in terms of literary art, and the very familiarity of the events and materials used gives works that use them an accent and overtone that speak with added poignancy to the native heart. Again there have been all the class and regional studies, some fictional, some scientific. Among the latter may be mentioned *Middletown,* that analytic portrait of the middle class in the Middlewest; Howard Odum's *Rainbow Round My Shoulder,* the Negro brought to light without halo or without nonsense in his setting in the South as he lives. There are Jonathan Daniels' books in which a Southerner discovers New England and the South. There began, in the twenties, the "realistic" novels, some tender and compassionate and confused like Sherwood Anderson's *Winesburg, Ohio;* some bitter and satirical like *Babbitt* and *Main Street.* There was the fading New England type presented with irony and pity in Marquand's *The Late George Apley* and by Santayana in *The Last Puritan.* There are Van Wyck Brooks' careful documentary studies of the dwindling light of New England culture.

But there is something further and more important. It is not the discovery of the American past or even of the American present in terms of broad sociological patterns or social types. It is the finding of the American present, not in terms at all, but in images; in those things that are the present as it stirs us to specific emotions and perceptions and thoughts: the present as specific qualities and specific promises in our own here and now. It hardly needed the catastrophe of a world war to make Americans, especially writers and artists, aware with delight and with hope, of colors and intimations of the civilization they were living in and which, as a nation, they were creating. America might be (as some foreign observers like Georges Duhamel have shudderingly observed) the twentieth century incarnate. Americans had already begun to discover that they had a past, a short one, but crowded with interest, even by the most fastidious standards of art and thought; but they began now to take up the challenge that America typified the present and suggested the direction of the future. That present was starred through all its failures and uncertainties with beauties, some new to the world, many inalienably beautiful, and all full of promise.

Americans found they did not have to go to the châteaux of the Loire or the Renaissance palaces of Italy to have something for the imagination to feed upon. New York began to be beautiful when it began doing business in towers. Architects learned to turn the conditions of contemporary work and play and the materials at their disposal into soaring loveliness in steel and glass. An American visiting in Europe used to look only at the old; the foreign visitor to the United States and the American himself know that the striking man-made beauties in this country are new: the great vaulting bridges at New York and San Francisco, the parkways all over the country, the streamlined trains, the airports. These are enchanting for their beauty and impressive for their power. But they are exhilarating for another reason. To any flexible mind they carry with them a hint and a challenge as to what the American imagination, inventive and disciplined, can make out of our own conditions and our own resources in our own day for our own future. In one city, New York, under one municipal administration, the city has achieved a new and quite singular beauty, borrowing nothing from a European yesterday, portending everything for an American tomorrow.

Nor is architecture the only art in which the American future is taking beautiful shape and finding expressive voice. Painters too are discovering in native types and in native scenes and—after long aping of the. French—in a native technic, a way of speaking to us visually of what our own experience may be in color and design. A cornfield in Iowa is no less artistic material than a valley in France, and a Middlewestern painter may find it a theme to embody, more truly and spontaneously than a Mediterranean landscape, what is in his heart; and his audience may see and feel more in it too. Poets, tired of imitating the French imagists or the genteel English tradition of hawthorn and hedges may, like Robert Frost, speak with an incorrigible and unduplicable native accent. (And they may, incidentally, like Robert Frost, be first recognized in England.) Novelists ceased, even before the war, to flee to Europe to write about a continent to which they were strangers or about other Americans who were equally strangers there, or from a disdainful distance about an America with which they had lost touch. They write like John Steinbeck about the migrants in California, about little people at home in little places, or, if they write about the sophisticated mind and heart, those hearts are exhibited beating in their native setting in Ohio or New Orleans or Mississippi or in apartments in Chicago or New York.

The most expert historians of literature and the arts assure us that even so delicate a thing as style, where it is distinctive and genuine, is the fruit of a culture, the function of a social pattern. Even so soaring a spirit as Plato was a characteristic product of the Athens in which he lived, and Shelley's skylark rose from an English earth. If genius is to flourish in America it will be our own characteristic flowering, as were Emerson and Thoreau and Whitman, and Pennsylvania barns and New England churches.

One of the fears the cultivated American used to have, a fear still operative in certain quarters today, was that culture was destined to be killed by the fact of democracy. In the present state of Europe the old argument of the esthetes and intellectuals already seems quaint. It ran substantially as follows: Democracy was synonymous with mediocrity, a leveling down of distinction to and by the mass; our society, in its scale of values, was getting to be a regimented five-and-ten-cent store. Only in a society still imaginatively dominated by aristocratic traditions could culture survive. There are two growing classes of fact that have made this thesis almost fantastic. In Europe at present the arts and philosophy are paralyzed, and even before the outbreak of war, political and economic instability made impossible the concentration necessary to art and thought. Now, in addition, the power reigning over a large part of Europe is the avowed enemy of free creation, of the intellect, of art.

The war, we have been told repeatedly, is a revolution. It is such in many senses, and one of them is that it is a war against the West, a war against the traditional elements and motives of Western culture as we have known it in art, in thought, and in religion. There is significance for America and possibly for world culture in the fact that the leaders in European science, art, and scholarship have come, in some cases by necessity, in some by choice, to this country. It can no longer be said by anyone who reads the daily papers that the arts and sciences as free inquiries and creations are flourishing in Europe. And unless these enterprises are free they cease to be at all. One may parallel now the scornful comment of the nineteenth-century English critic: "Who now reads a German or Italian book?" Or ask, "Who writes them?" . . .

Meanwhile the old fear that a democratic society cannot nourish American culture is proving curiously ill-founded. For it is not only by virtue of European conditions that America is emerging as a world center of the arts and sciences, not simply because artists and scientists, and experimentally observed rats as well, are being shipped to America. But the native arts and the native mind are beginning to have an audience in this country and a widespread popular participation that a generation ago one might have believed impossible. There is importance in the epidemic interest in music—several million people, for instance, listen to Toscanini on Saturday night. It is significant that literally hundreds of thousands came to see, within a few weeks' time, the exhibition of Italian masterpieces and of Picasso at the Museum of Modern Art in New York. There is something arresting in the fact that even automobile designers and manufacturers of kitchen utensils and railroad trains are concerned with the grace and design of their products because they know their public suddenly has come to care about them. The importance of these things is not simply that beauty is being widely enjoyed, that America has come of age in appreciation. Their larger significance is suggested by the line of Walt Whitman's, "To have great poets there must be great audiences too." One of the things that drove Americans abroad as spiritual waifs was the sense that at home no one could understand them, no one would listen to them. There is now almost a pathetic eagerness for the best and a widespread attempt to create it too. The spiritual refugee used to feel not only that no one would listen to him, but that nobody was "speaking his language." Many are speaking the musician's language now; there are literally thousands of high school orchestras, and even college glee clubs sing Palestrina and Bach. Much of the radio is still tripe, but poets are heard over it too.

It would be absurd to turn one's back on that European tradition of which America is, in the largest perspective, a variation and an extension. Isolationism, autarchy in the arts, is as absurd and unworkable in art as it is in the realm of economics and politics. In the contemporary timetable of distances, it is one world, all of it, and Europe is not a different planet; and in all times the arts have been trans-local. But it is also true that the arts have always flourished in their own soil and out of their own roots. In each instance they have been nourished by the sun that lighted other soils and by winds that blew from a "world elsewhere." But they have always grown where they grew in their own way and in their own climate. The climate is becoming more salubrious to the arts in America, and the flowers are being more lovingly and more expertly tended.

There is, moreover, at this dubious moment in Europe's destiny, a special reason, not unconnected with the nature of democratic life, why Americans should look homeward. There is, oddly enough, a political condition for the fine arts which both passionate democrats and passionate artists and connoisseurs forget. That is the condition of freedom, of spontaneous choice. Artists in uniform are not artists at all. The very essence of a work of art, in so far as it is more than a mere physical object or an ingenious contraption, is its uniqueness, its freshness, its personal signature. The very character of intellectual work is its individuality and integrity. The artist must say what he sees and speak what he is. The thinker must follow scrupulously the lead of his subject, and the standards imposed by his technic. Where the habits of freedom, individuality, and integrity are at a discount, as they are in totalitarian societies, the arts and sciences, except as slavish routines, are ended. There are many reasons why American democracy is worth defending if it should be imperiled. Not the least important is that it looks very much as if only in America is there, for the long present, a chance for the survival of those conditions of individual variation and spontaneous play of mind and heart which are essential to the arts.

Political freedom is the prerequisite of artistic invention, as the sterility of art and literature and thought under contemporary totalitarian rule proves. While this freedom endures, the opportunities for a native American culture are nothing short of thrilling. Here is a great people of many stocks, enriched of late by the sad accidents of European destiny, by the best of European minds and creative art. Here are stories crying to be told, pictures to be painted, feelings to be transmuted into the "potable gold" of poetry. Here are audiences too, larger, more eager, and more discriminating than they have ever been. Here is a future, possibly the only future for culture or creation in the Western world. Americans may still go to Europe after the war, as they go to the ruins of Rome at Baalbek, or of Greece at Epidauris and Delphi, beautiful cemeteries of the spirit of man. But for the future of their own imagination and thinking, for the possible survival of art and thought at all, Americans will have to look to their own land and lives for incitement and materials. It would be arrogant to believe that the will to create or widening audiences or maturing talents will produce, of themselves, anything comparable in stature to the great monuments of European genius of the past two thousand years. It would be shocking not to be shocked that a long tradition of genius may be coming to an end. But the spirit bloweth where it listeth; today the conditions for creation are ours, and our works will at least not be poorer because they are honestly and natively our own.

Edna St. Vincent Millay

Edna St. Vincent Millay (1892-   ) was born and grew up on the
Maine coast. Her first important poem, "Renascence," was a triumph for
the Vassar undergraduate of nineteen. From those early ecstasies to the
bitterness of her later verse she has come a long and reluctant journey.
Always in love with life, she cherishes its beauty and resents its brevity.
In music she finds temporary escape. Compare her sonnet with these
words of the music critic, Lucien Price: "A symphony requires from
half to three-quarters of an hour to perform. In that brief space is con-
centrated and poured into the receptive listener the combined energy of
one-hundred-and-one lives, plus that of the composer, all brought to
focus and projected into my consciousness or yours. It is a charge of
spiritual electricity the like of which is obtainable in but few other
places."

ON HEARING A SYMPHONY OF BEETHOVEN

Sweet sounds, oh, beautiful music, do not cease!
Reject me not into the world again.
With you alone is excellence and peace,
Mankind made plausible, his purpose plain.
Enchanted in your air benign and shrewd,
With limbs a-sprawl and empty faces pale,
The spiteful and the stingy and the rude
Sleep like the scullions in the fairy-tale.
This moment is the best the world can give:
The tranquil blossom on the tortured stem.
Reject me not, sweet sounds! oh, let me live,
Till Doom espy my towers and scatter them,
A city spell-bound under the aging sun.
Music my rampart, and my only one.

David L. Cohn

David L. Cohn (1896-   ), who obviously comes from the Deep South, understands the Negro almost as well as his friend Roark Bradford. In this "strictly personal" tale, which may or may not be true, he tells what it feels like to be a white man disastrously misunderstood by his colored neighbors. Cohn's God Shakes Creation *is a study of Negro life and customs.*

ROARK BRADFORD'S REVENGE

ROARK BRADFORD, the author of distinguished novels and books of short stories including "Ol' Man Adam an' His Chillun" from which "The Green Pastures" was made, is a man of many talents. As an orator in the Negro pulpits around Plain Dealing, Louisiana, he rivals the famous Reverend Childress, the Albino Preacher. As the owner of Little Bee Bend Plantation in Bossier Parish he can, when the spell is upon him, take a middle-buster [1] and make it sing as it plows through the gumbo. He can pick a guitar, moan the blues, and read a mule's mind. But, above all, he is a catfishing man out'n the book who can do more with a cane pole and a dime's worth of hooks and string than most folk could do with all the tackle in Abercrombie & Fitch.

Mistah Royce (as the colored folk call him) is a slow-and-easy man, as kind and gentle as his own Angel Gabriel who passed out ten-cent seegars to de Lawd. Yet this is the story of how he wreaked an awful vengeance for a wrong I had done him.

It all began one day when we went fishing along the banks of Deer Creek in Mississippi. Brad and I are skilled fishermen who go out to hook fish by fair means or foul with the coarse intention of having something to put in the pan, and we are not at all interested in the considerations of sportsmanship which move the more effete. On this occasion we were especially anxious to catch an elusive catfish of giant size known to the countryside as "Ole Tom." We baited our hooks with meat; spit on 'em for luck; the heavy sinkers took them near the bottom where we suspected Ole Tom was likely to be, and then we sat back to talk as we watched our floaters.

My fishing skill and piety are far less than Brad's, but just before that evening sun went down, I caught Ole Tom who weighed nearly five pounds,

---

[1] a lister, or double-moldboard plow.

and as he flopped upon the bank Brad gazed unhappily on my prize. Then he said: "Boy, I'm going to get revenge on you for doing me bad."

That night Ole Tom was served up golden brown with a bait of mustard greens, hot biscuits, country butter, sorghum molasses, and cold buttermilk. We ate heartily and, while I boasted of my prowess to the assembled company, Mistah Royce kept his peace and thought his awful thoughts. If I had known what was in store for me, I'd have left the country—as I was eventually compelled to do.

A day or two later, we went to Greenville, the Mississippi Delta town where I was born, to spend a few days with our mutual friend, William Alexander Percy, who was then writing "Lanterns on the Levee." From him we learned that the Old Jerusalem Baptist Church was dedicating its new building that evening and naturally we felt that we had to go. This was of course a great occasion. The church was filled to overflowing with the pious, while you could hardly see the pulpit for the pastors who had come from everywhere to rejoice with the people that they had forged a new weapon with which to fight Ole Satan. We were received with great courtesy, were given a place in the front row, and were soon hearing the Reverend Perkins deliver his stirring sermon, "No Boll Weevil in Heaven." He was followed by a number of visiting pastors until finally, at midnight, the pastor of the local church stood up, and said, "Won't one of the white gentlemen say a few words?"

Naturally I wanted to talk myself but, since I was among a people who have natively good manners and therefore had to be manne'ble myself, I arose and said that my distinguished friend, Mr. Bradford, would speak for us.

Much surprised, Mistah Royce got up and, walking slowly backward and forward in front of the pulpit, began to talk about what a fine thing it is to worship the Lawd in a beautiful building; about King Solomon's temple, and columns of porphyry and onyx and ceilings of gold and marble. He continued in this vein for some minutes and then he abruptly changed the tenor of his talk.

"Friends," he said, "I just want to tell y'all that there's an old Greenville boy in this congregation tonight, Mr. David Cohn. (Congregation: Do tell!) He grew up in this town, hunted rabbits on the protection levee, graduated from that high school down there by the Leavenworth sawmill, and could have got him a job right here in town. But, oh, no. The town wasn't big enough for *him!* So he went down to New Awleens where he got so rich that he bought out the biggest bank in town!" (Congregation: Well, suh!)

As I beamed on the congregation and they beamed on me, Brad went on:

"But Mr. Dave is a man that's hard to please. So one day he got on that Panama Express train, went clean up to Chicago, Illinois, got him a taxi, and told the man to take him out to Sears and Roebuck. There he saw Mr. Julius Rosenwald, the boss man. 'Mr. Julius, how much do you want for this business?' asked Mr. Dave. 'Two million dollars,' said Mr. Julius just like that. So Mr. Dave reached in his pocket, handed him two thousand one-thousand dollar bills and said, 'I'm the boss man from here out.'"

This caused an immense stir in the church. Folks shuffled their feet, said, "Well, Lawd," and indulged in exclamations of delightful surprise because they all knew Sears, Roebuck and here was a boy born and brought up right there in Greenville who had risen to such eminence that he could just walk in and buy out its boss man. I was myself pleased by my vicarious rise to greatness. Again the congregation and I beamed on one another and we were, so to speak, lapped in warm waves of adulation that flowed back and forth. While I revelled in my rise to fame and riches, Brad continued:

"But even that didn't satisfy Mr. Dave," he said. "Next thing he did was to go up to New York City where he got on one of those steamboats that cross the Atlantic Ocean and he got off in Paris, France. There he bought a house with a hundred rooms. And he had him a lady and a case of drinking whiskey in every room!"

The sensation caused by this announcement was so great that it was some minutes before quiet was restored. The men laughed aloud in delight. The ladies fluttered their palmetto fans with Finlay's Drug Store advertisement stencilled on the back, modestly hung their heads, and said "Lawd, he'p us"; everybody was pleased that a Greenville boy had gone out and conquered the world. While the church was still filled with the warm murmurings of the congregation, I wondered to what heights of magnificence Brad could take me now that I seemed to be at the peak. He continued:

"Well, there he was with all those ladies and all that whiskey when, one night, he looked up on the wall and there it was in letters of fire ten feet tall: 'Minny, Minny, Tikel, Tikel.' Then he heard a Voice coming from the ceiling. It said: 'You are doing the wrong thing. You are wasting your substance in sin and losing your chances of glory up yonder. You ought to go back to the town where you were born and give all your time and *all your money* to the church.'" Brad suddenly stopped— "And that's what Mr. Dave is doing here tonight!"

He sat down. The congregation whispered excitedly. The forty visiting preachers on the pulpit looked at one another significantly. Brad smiled a smile of deep satisfaction. He knew what was coming and so did I as I slumped in my seat.

Then the Reverend Arbuckle, a pastor of engaging charm, arose, put his hand on the Book and gazing benignly at me said: "Mistah Dave, I'm coming aroun' to see you fust thing in the mawnin and I know I'm gonna write you' name behin' a hundred dollar bill."

Now Brad looked at me as I had looked at him the day I had caught the catfish. No one knew better than he that long before the services were over that night the glad news would have spread by the grapevine all over the Mississippi Delta that the Lawd had told a rich man to come home from sinning and give all his money to the church. There is indeed no day in that area when preachers, deacons, and plain pulpit-hands are not out asking their white friends to give them something to help repair the church or reduce the mortgage. And here was a rich man who would spend his time handing out folding money to the folks who were doing the Lawd's work. I would become the target of hundreds of pastors, whether ordained or jackleg, from Rolling Fork to Rena Laura, from Itta Bena to Hushpuckana, and as far away as Lake Village, Arkansas. I would never again be able to tread the ground of my beloved hometown in peace.

My course was plain. Common decency required that I give $100 to the Reverend Arbuckle. But self-protection demanded that I flee the region at once. I put my check in an envelope and asked The Queenly Woman, Mr. Will's cook, to give it to the pastor. Then I arose early and was up and away in Brad's car bound for New Orleans with him, he grinning all the while like a catfish stealing bait. As we drove through the sleepy towns and hamlets, I saw dozens of rickety churches whose pastors even now were dreaming of shining new tin roofs and gallons of paint bought as emblems of my repentance of a life of sin.

To this day I have never been able to revisit my home town except under cover of night. And that old pulpit orator Roark Bradford often reminds me: "What doth it profit a man to gain the whole world, if he hooks the catfish of a friend?"

W. E. Burghardt Du Bois

W. E. Burghardt Du Bois (1868-   ) at seventy-two sat down to write the story of his life, the story of a lifetime devotion to the cause of the Negro in America. Born in New England of French, Dutch, and African blood, he received the degree of Doctor of Philosophy from Harvard, studied in Europe, became Professor of Economics and History at Atlanta University, a director of the National Association for the Advancement of Colored People, and editor of Crisis. *He is the first Negro to be named to the National Institute of Arts and Letters. In the selection which follows, he tells how President Coolidge sent him as his representative at the inauguration of the President of Liberia. There is a note of homecoming in this experience, but the surroundings are strange enough to make it exotic adventure.*

"WHAT IS AFRICA TO ME?"

WHEN shall I forget the night I first set foot on African soil? I am the sixth generation in descent from forefathers who left this land. The moon was at the full and the waters of the Atlantic lay like a lake. All the long slow afternoon as the sun robed herself in her western scarlet with veils of misty cloud, I had seen Africa afar. Cape Mount—that mighty headland with its twin curves, northern sentinel of the realm of Liberia—gathered itself out of the cloud at half past three and then darkened and grew clear. On beyond flowed the dark low undulating land quaint with palm and breaking sea. The world grew black. Africa faded away, the stars stood forth curiously twisted—Orion in the zenith—the Little Bear asleep and the Southern Cross rising behind the horizon. Then afar, ahead, a lone light shone, straight at the ship's fore. Twinkling lights appeared below, around, and rising shadows. "Monrovia," said the Captain.

Suddenly we swerved to our left. The long arms of the bay enveloped us and then to the right rose the twinkling hill of Monrovia, with its crowning star. Lights flashed on the shore—here, there. Then we sensed a darker shading in the shadows; it lay very still. "It's a boat," one said. "It's two boats!" Then the shadow drifted in pieces and as the anchor roared into the deep, five boats outlined themselves on the waters—great ten-oared barges with men swung into line and glided toward us.

It was nine at night—above, the shadows, there the town, here the sweeping boats. One forged ahead with the flag—stripes and a lone star flaming behind, the ensign of the customs floating wide; and bending to the long oars, the white caps of ten black sailors. Up the stairway clambered a soldier in khaki, aide-de-camp of the President of the Republic, a custom-house official, the clerk of the American legation—and after them sixty-five lithe, lean black stevedores with whom the steamer would work down to Portuguese Angola and back. A few moments of formalities, greetings and good-bys and I was in the great long boat with the President's aide—a brown major in brown khaki. On the other side, the young clerk and at the back, the black barelegged pilot. Before us on the high thwarts were the rowers: men, boys, black, thin, trained in muscle and sinew, little larger than the oars in thickness, they bent their strength to them and swung upon them.

One in the center gave curious little cackling cries to keep up the rhythm, and for the spurts and the stroke, a call a bit thicker and sturdier; he gave a low guttural command now and then; the boat, alive, quivering, danced beneath the moon, swept a great curve to the bar to breast its narrow teeth of foam—"t'chick-a-tickity, t'chick-a-tickity," sang the boys, and we glided and raced, now between boats, now near the landing—now cast aloft at the dock. And lo! I was in Africa.

Christmas Eve, and Africa is singing in Monrovia. They are Krus and Fanti—men, women and children, and all the night they march and sing. The music was once the music of mission revival hymns. But it is that music now transformed and the silly words hidden in an unknown tongue—liquid and sonorous. It is tricked out and expounded with cadence and turn. And this is that same rhythm I heard first in Tennessee forty years ago: the air is raised and carried by men's strong voices, while floating above in ob-bligato, come the high mellow voices of women—it is the ancient African art of part singing, so curiously and insistently different.

So they come, gay appareled, lit by transparency. They enter the gate and flow over the high steps and sing and sing and sing. They saunter round the house, pick flowers, drink water and sing and sing and sing. The warm dark heat of the night steams up to meet the moon. And the night is song.

On Christmas Day, 1923, we walk down to the narrow, crooked wharves of Monrovia, by houses old and gray and step-like streets of stone. Before is the wide St. Paul River, double-mouthed, and beyond, the sea, white, curling on the sand. Before us is the isle—the tiny isle, hut-covered and guarded by a cotton tree, where the pioneers lived in 1821. We board the boat, then circle round—then up the river. Great bowing trees, festoons of flowers, golden blossoms, star-faced palms and thatched huts; tall spreading trees lifting themselves like vast umbrellas, low shrubbery with gray and laced and knotted roots—the broad, black, murmuring river. Here a tree holds wide fingers out and stretches them over the water in vast incantation; bananas throw their wide green fingers to the sun. Iron villages, scarred clearings with gray, sheet-iron homes staring, grim and bare, at the ancient tropical flood of green.

The river sweeps wide and the shrubs bow low. Behind, Monrovia rises in clear, calm beauty. Gone are the wharves, the low and clustered houses of the port, the tight-throated business village, and up sweep the villas and the low wall, brown and cream and white, with great mango and cotton trees, with lighthouse and spire, with porch and pillar and the color of shrubbery and blossom.

We climbed the upright shore to a senator's home and received his wide and kindly hospitality—curious blend of feudal lord and modern farmer—sandwiches, cake, and champagne. Again we glided up the drowsy river—five, ten, twenty miles—and came to our hostess, a mansion of five generations with a compound of endless native servants and cows under the palm thatches. The daughters of the family wore, on the beautiful black skin of their necks, the exquisite pale gold chains of the Liberian artisan and the slim, black little granddaughter of the house had a wide pink ribbon on the thick curls of her dark hair, that lay like sudden sunlight on the shadows. Double porches, one above the other, welcomed us to ease. A native man, gay with Christmas and a dash of gin, sang and danced in the road. Children ran and played in the blazing sun. We sat at a long broad table and ate duck, chicken, beef, rice, plantain, collards, cake, tea, water and Madeira wine. Then we went and looked at the heavens, the uptwisted sky—Orion and Cassiopeia at zenith; the Little Bear beneath the horizon, now unfamiliar sights in the Milky Way—all awry, a-living—sun for snow at Christmas, and happiness and cheer.

The shores were lined with old sugar plantations, the buildings rotting and falling. I looked upon the desolation with a certain pain. What had happened, I asked? The owners and planters had deserted these homes and come down to Monrovia, but why? After all, Monrovia had not much to offer in the way of income and occupation. Was this African laziness and inefficiency? No, it was a specimen of the way in which the waves of modern industry broke over the shores of far-off Africa. Here during our Civil War, men hastened to raise sugar and supply New York. They built their own boats and filled the river and sailed the sea. But afterwards, Louisiana came back into the Union, colored Rillieux invented the vacuum pan; the sugar plantations began to spread in Cuba and the Sugar Trust monopoly of refining machinery, together with the new beet sugar industry, drove Liberia quickly from the market. What all this did not do, the freight rates finished. So sugar did not pay in Liberia and other crops rose and fell in the same way.

As I look back and recall the days, which I have called great—the occasions in which I have taken part and which have had for me and others the widest significance, I can remember none like the first of January, 1924. Once I took my bachelor's degree before a governor, a great college president, and a bishop of New England. But that was rather personal in its memory than in any way epochal. Once before the assembled races of the world I was called to speak in London in place of the suddenly sick Sir Harry Johnston. It was a great hour. But it was not greater than the day when I was presented to the President of the Negro Republic of Liberia.

Liberia had been resting under the shock of world war into which the Allies forced her. She had asked and been promised a loan by the United States to bolster and replace her stricken trade. She had conformed to every preliminary requirement and waited when waiting was almost fatal. It was not simply money, it was world prestige and protection at a time when the little republic was sorely beset by creditors and greedy imperial powers. At the last moment, an insurgent Senate peremptorily and finally refused the request and strong recommendation of President Wilson and his advisers, and the loan was refused. The Department of State made no statement to the world, and Liberia stood naked, not only well-nigh bankrupt, but peculiarly defenseless amid scowling and unbelieving powers.

It was then that the United States made a gesture of courtesy; a little thing, and merely a gesture, but one so unusual that it was epochal. President Coolidge, at the suggestion of William H. Lewis, a leading colored lawyer of Boston, named me, an American Negro traveler, Envoy Extraordinary and Minister Plenipotentiary to Liberia—the highest rank ever given by any country to a diplomatic agent in black Africa. And it named this Envoy the special representative of the President of the United States to the President of Liberia, on the occasion of his inauguration, charging the Envoy with a personal word of encouragement and moral support. It was a significant action. It had in it nothing personal. Another appointee would have been equally significant. But Liberia recognized the meaning. She showered upon the Envoy every mark of appreciation and thanks. The Commander of the Liberian Frontier Force was made his special aide, and a sergeant, his orderly. At ten A.M. New Year's morning, 1924, a company of the Frontier Force, in red fez and khaki, presented arms before the American Legation and escorted Solomon Porter Hood, the American Minister Resident, and myself as Envoy Extraordinary and my aide to the Presidential Mansion—a beautiful, white, verandaed house, waving with palms and fronting a grassy street.

Ceremonials are old and to some antiquated and yet this was done with such simplicity, grace and seriousness that none could escape its spell. The Secretary of State met us at the door, as the band played the impressive Liberian national hymn, and soldiers saluted:

> All hail! Liberia, hail!
> In union strong, success is sure.

We cannot fail.
With God above,
Our rights to prove,
We will the world assail.

We mounted a broad stairway and into a great room that stretched across the house. Here in semi-circle were ranged the foreign consuls and the cabinet—the former in white, gilt with orders and swords; the latter in solemn black. Present were England, France, Germany, Spain, Belgium, Holland, and Panama, to be presented to me in order of seniority by the small brown Secretary of State with his perfect poise and ease. The President entered—frock-coated with the star and ribbon of a Spanish order on his breast. The American Minister introduced me, and I said:

"The President of the United States has done me the great honor of designating me as his personal representative on the occasion of your inauguration. In so doing, he has had, I am sure, two things in mind. First, he wished publicly and unmistakably to express before the world the interest and solicitude which the hundred million inhabitants of the United States of America have for Liberia. Liberia is a child of the United States, and a sister Republic. Its progress and success is the progress and success of democracy everywhere and for all men; and the United States would view with sorrow and alarm any misfortune which might happen to this Republic and any obstacle that was placed in her path."

And now a word about the African himself—about this primitive black man. I began to notice a truth as I entered southern France. I formulated it in Portugal. I knew it as a great truth one Sunday in Liberia. And the Great Truth was this: efficiency and happiness do not go together in modern culture. Going south from London, as the world darkens it gets happier. Portugal is deliciously dark. Many leading citizens would have difficulty keeping off a Georgia "Jim Crow" car. But, oh, how lovely a land and how happy a people! And so leisurely. Little use of trying to shop seriously in Lisbon before eleven. It isn't done. Nor at noon; the world is lunching or lolling in the sun. Even after four P.M. one takes chances, for the world is in the Rocio. And the banks are so careless and the hotels so leisurely. How delightfully angry Englishmen get at the "damned, lazy" Portuguese!

But if this of Portugal, what of Africa? Here darkness descends and rests on lovely skins until brown seems luscious and natural. There is sunlight in great gold globules and soft, heavy-scented heat that wraps you like a garment. And laziness; divine, eternal languor is right and good and true. I remember the morning; it was Sunday, and the night before we heard the leopards crying down there. Today beneath the streaming sun we went down into the gold-green forest. It was silence—silence the more mysterious because life abundant and palpitating pulsed all about us and held us drowsy captives to the day. Ahead the gaunt missionary strode, alert, afire, with his gun. He apologized for the gun, but he did not need to, for I saw the print of a leopard's hind foot. A monkey sentinel screamed, and I heard the whir of the horde as they ran.

Then we came to the village; how can I describe it? Neither London, nor Paris, nor New York has anything of its delicate, precious beauty. It was a town of the Veys and done in cream and pale purple—still, clean, restrained, tiny, complete. It was no selfish place, but the central abode of fire and hospitality, clean-swept for wayfarers, and best seats were bare. They quite expected visitors, morning, noon, and night; and they gave our hands a quick, soft grasp and talked easily. Their manners were better than those of Park Lane or Park Avenue. Oh, much better and more natural. They showed breeding. The chief's son—tall and slight and speaking good English—had served under the late Colonel Young. He made a little speech of welcome. Long is the history of the Veys and comes down from the Eastern Roman Empire, the great struggle of Islam and the black empires of the Sudan.

We went on to other villages—dun-colored, not so beautiful, but neat and hospitable. In one sat a visiting chief of perhaps fifty years in a derby hat and a robe, and beside him stood a shy young wife done in ebony and soft brown, whose liquid eyes would not meet ours. The chief was taciturn until we spoke of schools. Then he woke suddenly—he had children to "give" to a school.

I see the last village fading away; they are plastering the wall of a home, leisurely and carefully. They smiled a good-by—not effusively, with no eagerness, with a simple friendship, as we glided under the cocoa trees and into the silent forest, the gold and silent forest.

Louis Golding

Louis Golding (1895-   ), novelist, essayist, traveler, lecturer, is an English Jew who writes with quiet fervor of travels in the homeland of his race. His visit to the Zionist colony of Ain Charod, like Sholem Asch's story, "A Peculiar Gift," shares the adventure of pioneers upon the frontier of an ancient culture reborn.

BY THE WATERS OF GIDEON

THE colony of Ain Charod[1] in Esdraelon was the first Jewish colony I alighted upon in Palestine. Whatsoever stage it had attained, whatever its character might be, it was something more than a collection of wooden shacks or stone houses, flanked by outhouses, topped by cisterns and grain-elevators. Obviously a traveller may meet settlements like these, more comfortable or less, in the backwoods and waste places of any new country between Australia and Alaska. But Palestine is not a new country. It is an ancient, an exhausted country. The backwoodsman on the Gold Coast has a simple enough proposition to tackle. He must make his holding work. Sometimes the actual physical job he has set himself is more desperate than anything the Palestinian has to tackle (though it is possible that certain of the tasks undertaken by the Jews in malarial marshes and upon salty dunes are actually as formidable as any in the lands of virgin colonization). If the backwoodsman does not make his holding work, he is either ruined or will pack up his traps and trek further.

But if the Jewish colonist whom the traveller comes upon in Palestine is ruined—I take him generically for the moment—then the greatest opportunity is ruined which history has afforded his race. I would not care to speculate what the effect would be of this failure upon the race itself. The race seems impervious to ruin. But it seems arguable that the consummation which Tiglath-Pileser and Haman, Titus and Torquemada[2] failed to achieve, in which the captain of them all, Adolf Hitler, will be frustrated, might follow upon a blow aimed by the race itself at its own heart. It is possible that the conditions under which the experiment is being initiated, and will be for a time continued, are of such a nature that the experiment is doomed to failure—those conditions external to the race, I mean, such as the complex of political relationships in which the Jewish experiment is noth-

[1] *ain*, a well or spring (Hebrew).
[2] Assyrian, Persian, Roman and Spanish enemies of the Jewish people.

ing more than one of the hundred constituent elements. I mean also the domestic problem involved by the established existence in this country of a large population with entirely different instincts and standards. Such conditions as these may doom the experiment to failure—or the essential character of the Jewish race, which may, during the two thousand years in which it has not occupied this country, have totally unfitted itself for such an occupation a second time.

Whatever the cause of failure might be, it might be questioned whether the race itself could survive it with the ancient vitality, or even survive at all for long. Acute diplomacy and hard manual labour, united with every sort of moral and spiritual fervour, would all have been exercised and all have proved fruitless. A nucleus of piety might persist for a time, believing as of old in the personal intervention of Jehovah and the physical appearance of a Messiah, but this, too, would slowly bleed to death. Or it would petrify into a curiosity, like the Joanna Southcott Christians or the Samaritans of Nablus. It would not have the intellectual and spiritual prestige which would hold together the elements scattered throughout every city in every country. During a certain century or the century after, there would be no Jews. It would not be relevant here to decide whether this might be fortunate or unfortunate. I cannot help feeling it would be very dull.

It was with some such consciousness that I found myself with certain friends approaching the colony of Ain Charod, which is a *kvutzah,* a communal group, in the Valley of Esdraelon. The toneless sun of *khamsin* [3] lay upon the morose crags; the sparse olives held out their leaves stiffly, like metal sculpture. The accidents of the landscape were eliminated in that unifying air. They had no contours which were not majestic. On the projecting branch of a holm-oak perched a black and white stork, solitary, the genius of that evening, presenting impartially the Yea or Nay, the Life or Death, which it is for them who plough the thin furrows of Esdraelon to choose, affirm, and establish.

We had descended from the last low hills of Samaria. We lurched over a region of no tracks. The arid unfructified earth humped itself into a mound of uneven desolation. So lamentable it seemed that the mean beasts of the desert, jackal and hyena and the hatchet-jawed lizard, might have spurned it, sooner seeking out for themselves rifts in solid rock, which is earth's own proud substance, rather than permit their homes to be in a dump of mud, so lousy and forlorn.

But the lights in the colony of Ain Charod shone imperturbably, blocked out against the hill-side of Gilboa. So we lurched and stumbled over the barrenness, recognizing in these lights not merely a beacon to us benighted wanderers in Esdraelon, but a beacon to wanderers in the tortuous ghettos, a beacon that outshone for jaded eyes the blind lights of Broadway.

---

[3] *khamsin,* a hot and sultry wind from the Sahara (Arabic).

And of a sudden woods were about us, and the coolness that is in woods even upon the days of *khamsin*. There was the sound of water also, and this was the Well of Charod where Gideon was encamped over against the Midianites, and, bidding his troops drink, chose out of them those that drank decently and alertly.[4]

Two young men came forward to meet us, seeing our lights and hearing our engines, as we swung out of the eucalyptus-grove. One of these limped, for he had a wooden leg. He had lost his own fighting in the Jewish Legion, in Palestine here, against the Turks. It seemed to me appropriate and touching that it should be upon Jewish land that he must henceforth stump on his wooden leg, in the country where he had himself suffered grievous loss, and his brother had his head shot from his shoulders. It was Jewish land in Palestine for the purchase of which the pennies of little sempstresses no less than the thousands of rich merchants had been contributed. It was a purchase effected under the sanction of England, with the assembled nations agreed upon that sanction. The young soldier of the Jews had been luckier than others. They had removed his leg from the groin, but Fate had afforded him great consolation. His companion came forward, blinking through spectacles, and with more than a hint of bent back and stooping shoulders. Though he follow the plough another score or twoscore years his shoulders will never be quite straightened. Once, for days and nights, almost without pause, he studied physics and chemistry in his small attic. He passed his degrees with gold medals. But he heard Gideon's water calling under the flank of Gilboa and he swept his papers aside and came over to be one of the new warriors. His shoulders will never be straight; but I saw his small boy in the kindergarten next day, and heaven knows that all the nurseries of Eton house no small child with straighter limbs.

In the dining-hall of that colony of Ain Charod, there was a collection of the world's vastest tea-pots. When the last mouthful of tea had been drained through the last cube of sugar the colonists, and I amongst them, arose to wander among the groves of the colony in the cool of the evening. As we followed the course of the stream coming down from Gideon's grotto, we heard no noise at all but the water whispering and the branches of the eucalyptus shaking in the misty moonlight. And it was only when we sat down by the small bridge which leads over into the deeper wood, that we became aware that a third sound was added to these, where a group of young people were gathered together in a small clearing beyond the bank. The moonlight striking through the branches diapered them curiously with light and shade, and they looked more like a flat abstract pattern than a living group. It took some moments to resolve them into a company of young men in black blouses and girls in white frocks gathered about the

[4] *Judges* vii.

knees of an older man, whose voice, likewise, did not immediately detach itself from the consonance of leaves and water. He spoke unhurriedly like those, and in Hebrew. Only slowly the drift of his exposition became clear to our friend from Galicia, who thereon whispered to me what its burden was. He was expounding the Republic of Plato, the correct meaning of justice and injustice, and their reference to practical living not merely in the ideal state of Socrates, but in a community, for instance, like this of Ain Charod.

I do not recall many experiences so beautiful as that group and that moonlit moment, nor any so pregnant with philosophy. It seemed to me that those young folk had transcended both Plato and Lenin; they had tempered the feverish Russian empiricism into a Greek graciousness. They had condensed the mists of Platonic idealism into a concrete and living organism. They were a thousand years ahead of, and a thousand years behind, all contemporary politics. But as between Russia and Athens, they seemed to me nearer to Athens. Who else governed this sodality of theirs but their philosophers? It certainly was not he who had the brawniest arms, nor he who had most wealth, for none of them had any wealth which did not belong to all. It was not an academic philosophy that ruled their destinies, but a natural wisdom. I could not but recall Plato's earlier symposium as I listened to that level voice in the clearing of the eucalyptus-wood. This was not Esdraelon, but Piraeus, whither Socrates had repaired for the festival, with Glaucon, his friend. There was talk of a further festival that same evening, and I could not determine whether the Jewish lads and girls were to carry pitchers with candles in them or the young Greeks were to race on horseback, handing their torches to each other.

"None the less," said Polimarchus, who was born in Prague, "we can go out and watch it after dinner, and many of the young men here will join our party and we shall talk."

So Socrates stayed, and the young people gathered about him. "And what do you consider," asked Socrates, "to be the greatest advantage in the possession of riches?" For they have no possessions in Ain Charod, and they do not seem unhappy on that account. And Socrates himself, who was born in Ekaterinoslav, took up the reply. And the language he spoke in was not Greek, but Hebrew, that evening of misty moonlight by Gideon's stream in Esdraelon.

Anne Morrow Lindbergh

Foreseeing that the day would come when pioneering in the air would be a thing of the past, Anne Morrow Lindbergh (1907-), daughter of Dwight Morrow and wife of Charles A. Lindbergh, has set down in her books, North to the Orient *and* Listen! the Wind, *a first-hand report of her sensations. In a foreword to the latter book her husband has written, "As time passes, the perfection of machinery tends to insulate man from contact with the elements in which he lives." But in these books, day and night, air and water, and above all, wind are keenly realized and enjoyed. The following chapter is part of the story of a trans-Atlantic flight from Africa to Brazil in December, 1933. In Mrs. Lindbergh's deft and delicate art the scientific age is changed to poetry.*

"LISTEN! THE WIND IS RISING"

> Listen! the wind is rising,
> and the air is wild with leaves—

I WAS lying on my bed in Government House, in the middle of the afternoon, learning poetry. There was nothing else to do. Everything was done. My husband was asleep. The plane was in shape. We were packed up, ready to go. And I was resting. We needed the rest for we were going to try again tonight, our last attempt to fly to South America from Bathurst.

"Could we take off tomorrow night?" I had asked my husband in the morning.

"Yes," he had said, doubtfully, "but that's about the last."

"Well, you could still take off at daybreak, couldn't you?" I had pursued.

"No—you see the moon rises later every night. There wouldn't be any moon at all when we reached South America."

I hesitated—that last question, "Could you get off now with *no* wind?"

"Almost!" he had said.

It was tonight, then, or—well, better not think about it. Rest; sleep; learn poetry. I opened my pocket scrapbook.

> Listen! the wind is rising,
> and the air is wild with leaves—

I had copied those lines as we left England, in October; when the last of the dahlias hung clumsy golden heads above their blackened stalks; when leaves rose in gusty flames into the sky, lifting a whole tree before your eyes, bodily, it seemed, into the air. Elm and oak and beech—to think of them here gave me some of the peace of England.

we have had our summer evenings—

(Like long English meadows, rolling out to the sky. There was strength in having them behind your back.)

now for October eves!

It might help, too. Poetry did, sometimes, filling up the mind. I might need it tonight, bobbing up and down under the stars, or even plunging ahead through the dark sky, over the dark ocean—if we got off—

The great beech-trees lean forward,
and strip like a diver—

(Bright copper leaves, turned up this way and that, burning like coals, under foot.)

and strip like a diver. We—

That was enough, really. The rest was not for us.

. . . We
had better turn to the fire,
and shut our minds to the sea—

We couldn't do that—not yet, anyway. We still had work to do.

where the ships of youth are running
close-hauled on the edge of the wind—

Oh—if only we had a wind like that! A wind you could bite into, a wind you could pull hard against, as you could in a boat, heeled over, the sail taut, bowed to the water; the tiller hard against your aching arm; your feet braced on the leeward seat; your cheeks in the wind, warm and tingling underneath but firm and chilled on the surface—like fruit. And the sound of water, rushing, gurgling, racing, tearing under you.

where the ships of youth are running
close-hauled on the edge of the wind,
with all adventure before them . . .[1]

Yes, but that was the Maine coast I was thinking of. And this was Africa. There was the mosquito net over my head. Here was the white airless room. It was time for tea. And after tea, a drive to the Cape, and after that, supper, and after that—

Listen! the wind is rising—

[1] Humbert Wolfe, "Autumn Resignation."

I got up and dressed. I had tea. My husband went down to the bay.

"Is there anything to do?" I asked.

"No," he said. "But I think I'll just go down and look over the plane." I knew how he felt—anything to fill up the afternoon.

The Governor's wife was taking me for a drive to the gardens where we were the other night. (There, at least, there will be a wind!) We got out and walked in the dusty shade of trees. ("The great beech-trees lean forward—") But these were not beech. They were Casuarina, with long whip-like branches spraying above our heads. They were spiny palm and strange gray-leaved trees whose name I did not know. The dry turf crackled under our feet. Spikes of cactus speared the sunshine. There was not a breath of wind, even here. The tangled creepers dripped their yellow flowers, motionless in the still air. Insects rasped out their songs like sawdust. And small metallic-colored birds flicked brightly from one shrub of oleander to another, the only sign of life in that lifeless garden.

I could hardly look at the birds, at the lancet-leaved oleanders, at the trees, strangled with ropes of vine. Like someone in love, all sights, all objects, led back to one thing in my mind. As one might say, "But he is not here to see them," I could only think, "But there is no wind, even here." I could only see that the vines hung listless from their branches. There was not a tremor in the ferns.

We climbed into the car and started back to Government House. Even the artificial breeze from our speed was a relief, although one could tell nothing from that, of course. Out of the window I watched the tops of palms against the sky, and, as we crossed a river, the small boats ("close-hauled on the edge of the wind—"). But they were not close-hauled. Their sails were slack and dimpled untidily, making no headway. There was no wind. The dust on the road, the smoke from distant huts, the ripples in a marsh—everything, I watched. And finally I was looking at the limp flag, wrapped around the pole outside of Government House. We were back again.

I spoke at last, like a sick person who can no longer control his obsession. "I am afraid there is very little wind this evening," I said, dry-mouthed.

"Oh, you can't tell from here," said the Governor's wife, anxiously, "we'll go down to the pier and look."

We hurried across the road and walked out over the water. It felt cooler there but the bay was glassy. I held up my hand.

"No, there isn't a breath of wind," I said.

"There is a *little*," said the Governor's wife, "but I can't tell from where." She turned to face the harbor mouth.

I pulled out my handkerchief. "We can see," I said, "if there is any—" The handkerchief hung down limply, swinging slightly from my hand.

"No, there isn't enough to lift a handkerchief." And to myself I thought, what a heavy thing a handkerchief is!

We walked back across the road.

"You see, it's our last chance tonight," I said, "tomorrow the moon won't be bright enough. If we can't get off tonight—well, we'll just have to change our plans."

"But you can't tell yet," urged the Governor's wife kindly, "the wind may come up after sunset."

"Yes, of course," I said, but I did not feel hopeful. I went up to my room and tried to write, to read, to rest.

> Listen! the wind is rising,
> and the air—

But it wasn't rising. It was completely dead. Why did I learn that poem? I couldn't get it out of my head now. It would taunt me the rest of the evening. It would go on singing inanely in my head no matter what happened. Calm yourself. Learn something else, something quieting. Get out the little scrapbook.

> Brave flowers—that I could gallant it like you,
>   And be as little vain!
> You come abroad, and make a harmless show—[2]

No, that was too difficult. It would never come to you in a crisis. Only the first line rolled out like a banner:

> Brave flowers—that I could gallant it like you—

Fifteen minutes, a half-hour, three-quarters passed. It was after sunset. I could stay in no longer. I would go out to the pier again. You couldn't tell, sometimes everything changed in a second and started rolling the right way. It might be happening right now. This might be the very second, the knife edge, when the wind changed. It would do no harm to go and see.

I slipped out of my room quietly and walked in a firm taut step down the stairs and through the halls—the kind of step you used in a dream when you wished to hurry from the person behind, but it would be fatal to run. Down the steps of Government House, out of the driveway. Not in a hurry at all, just a nice brisk walk. Once out in the road, I could clip along faster; it was dark. And when I reached the pier, I was running, my feet clumping down the boardwalk. Yes, it was cooler, definitely cooler, but— ("Sister Anne, Sister Anne, do you see anyone coming?" Old fairy tales, old rhymes, raced through my mind. "Flounder, Flounder, in the sea!") was there a wind? I took out my handkerchief, crumpled whiteness in the dark. It hung from my hand; it swayed; it fluttered; it pulled gently away from me.

---

[2] Henry King, "A Contemplation upon Flowers."

It leaned upon a breath of air. Yes, yes, it had changed! Oh—"Listen! the wind is rising, and the air—"

I ran back to Government House and burst into the room. My husband had just come back from the bay.

"The wind has changed," I panted, out of breath, "I've just been down to the pier. There's enough to lift a handkerchief!"

"Good," he said, "I'll go down with you and see."

We walked down side by side, across the road again, I pushing my steps ahead to keep up with his long ones. Yes, there was a wind. Two handkerchiefs fluttered from the pier. It occurred to me, an aftermath to my excitement, that a wind that could lift a handkerchief might not be able to lift a plane. Still, it was a good sign. There was definitely a change. And there might be more when the moon came up.

We went back to dinner. The Governor toasted our success. I wondered—for the third time—if that would be the last. We said good-by.

"We'll probably see you at breakfast, though," we laughed in bravado.

The Governor's wife squeezed both my hands.

"Send us a cable, will you, when you get there?" said the Governor. (Casual, taking it for granted. How British—how grand of him!)

"Yes, we will, good-by, thank you."

We walked out to the pier again. The moon was up, low and reddish on the horizon, and terribly squashed in, since last night. It looked lopsided and bruised, like a misshapen pear. I was shocked. How fast it changed. This was certainly the last night we could use it. But the wind was a little stronger. That helped.

We went back to the house. There was nothing more to do. Our things, a small handful only, were rolled into the bottom of the white canvas sack. The rest of our clothes lay on the pile of discarded equipment. My husband took only the suit he was wearing. I had, besides my flying clothes, one silk dress, a pair of stockings and a linen hat, wound up in a roll. Altogether we had about twelve ounces in the bottom of the white sack. It was tucked away now. We were ready to go.

But we could not leave until the moon was high; we needed all the light we could get for our take-off. We lay down and waited for the minutes to pass. The house was still. Everyone else had settled for the night. It had not started for us—not yet. Wait, wait, wait—my heart hammered in my throat:

> with all adventure before them—
> with all adventure . . .

At ten-twenty the tall house-boy, Samiker, knocked on the door for our luggage. Luggage? We had none. Only the half-empty white sack, my radio bag, an extra shirt and sweater, and the helmets. He shouldered the limp bag silently and went out. The small open car was at the door. We climbed in the back quietly. Samiker jumped in after us. It wasn't necessary for him to come, but I was glad because I felt he cared. And it was nice to have around you people who cared, even if they said nothing. We started off. Radio bag? Helmets? Lunch? Yes. Samiker sat in front with the white sack. We bumped through the dimly lighted streets. People were closing up for the night. Someone pushed open a shutter above our heads, as we passed, and leaned down out of a lighted window to see what it was. Oh, I thought—looking up for one flashing second at the bright window, at the dark hand stretched out carelessly to draw back the shutters—oh, if only it were as casual as that to us!

The car sighed to a stop in front of the closed gates. The sleepy guard came out and let us through. ("Listen! the wind is rising—" There was not a breath, not a breath on shore.) We climbed into the leaky rowboat. Samiker sat down behind us with the white sack. The water sucked and slopped around our feet. ("—and the air is wild with leaves"—no wind—no wind.) The boy at the oars coughed painfully. We pushed slowly ahead toward the indistinct form of the plane.

There was a fair light from the moon. I could see the captain of the port sitting in a small rowboat near us. There was more wind out here. I turned my head to let it blow back my hair.

"There's as much wind as the morning we tried before, Charles," I said as we touched the side of the plane.

"But not as much as the night?" He climbed out of the boat.

"No—I had on my sweater that night."

We started to arrange the cockpits, to pump out the pontoons, those endless small jobs we had done so many times before. But tonight, it was the last time, they took on an incredible importance. They were lit with an intensity of feeling and stood out like the smallest branches of trees at night in a bright crack of lightning. I knelt on the nose of the pontoon and held the flashlight while my husband pumped. The water sloshed out in regular gasps. "All right, now, the anchor box." Words, too, seemed weighted beyond their usual freight of feeling. He took some putty and worked it with his fingers along the edges of the hatch. "That ought to keep the water out." The circle of light followed his fingers as they moved, deftly and swiftly up and down.

It was very still. I drummed with my fingernails on the light metal under me. *First* in *war—First* in *peace—First* in the *hearts* of his *count*ree *men:*" my fingernails beat out the rhythm in the stillness. Ping, ping, ping; ping, ping, ping. Was there no other sound? Listen, listen, listen—listen, the wind is rising—

My husband looked up from his work. "There's about a five-mile wind right now," he called across the water.

The captain of the port held up his hand in the dim moonlight. "You air-folk must look at it differently," he drawled back good-naturedly.

"Why? What would you call it?" We stopped bolt still, and listened. ("—and the air is wild with leaves—")

"Almost a dead calm!"

We laughed and bent over the pontoons again. Ping, ping, ping. Ping, ping, ping, *"First* in the *hearts* of his *count*ree *men."*

But there *was* more wind, I thought, as I climbed into the cockpit. There was enough for me to put my sweater on. "Charles, there's enough wind for me to put my sweater on!" But he could not hear. He was untying the lantern, now the bridle.

"If we come back, we'll want these," he said, "otherwise—" The end of his sentence was lost in the moonlight, like the shores, like the trees.

He stood up to say good-by. "Well, we'll have another try."

He swung up into the cockpit. He started the engine.

I felt under my feet for obstructions; saw that the control wires were free; sat on my extra shirt, stuffed the lunch in the aluminum case; put the radio bag in the seat beside me. There now, fasten the belt. Ready.

We pushed out into the bay. It was not such a strange world tonight. We had been here before. I greeted old landmarks. There were the lights of the town. There was the path of the moon.

(—where the ships of youth are running
close-hauled on the edge of the wind—)

If only there were a wind. There was more out in the bay, but it was not as rough as the other night. Still, we were about two hundred pounds lighter. We taxied over our take-off stretch. We tried out the engine; we throttled down; we swung into the wind. That pause for breath. The last look out: the palms outlined dimly above the town; the moon, a bright path ahead; and the wind—the wind was rising—

"All set?"

"All right."

Here we go. Hold on. The roar, the spray over the wings. Look at your watch. Won't be more than two minutes. Then you'll know. You can stand two minutes. Look at your watch. That's your job. Listen—listen—the spray has stopped. We are spanking along. We are up on the step—faster, faster— oh, much faster than before. Sparks from the exhaust. We're going to get off! But how long it takes. Spank, spank—we're off? Not yet—spank— almost. Splutter, choke—the engine? My God—it's coming then—death. He's going on just the same. We're off—no more spanks. Splutter—splutter. What is wrong? Will he turn? Will we land? The wobble pump? Gas? Mixture? Never mind, your job, the watch. Just two, Greenwich. Yes— we're off—we're rising. But why start off with an engine like that?

But it smooths out now, like a long sigh, like a person breathing easily, freely. Like someone singing ecstatically, climbing, soaring—sustained note of power and joy. We turn from the lights of the city; we pivot on a dark wing; we roar over the earth. The plane seems exultant now, even arrogant. We did it, we did it! We're up, above you. We were dependent on you just now, River, prisoners fawning on you for favors, for wind and light. But now, we are free. We are up; we are off. We can toss you aside, you there, way below us, a few lights in the great dark silent world that is ours—for we are above it.

Hudson Strode

In an age when travel by airplane has become a commonplace, it is still permitted to thrill to the accounts of those travelers for whom nothing is commonplace. Such a traveler is Hudson Strode (1893-   ), Professor of English at the University of Alabama, whose South by Thunderbird *dramatizes the airways of South America.*

WINGS ACROSS THE ANDES

A TELEPHONE'S buzzing waked Norbourne. It was the alarum bell to a longed-for adventure. The weather was propitious. The voice said the plane would fly over the Andes this morning. In a moving picture he had once watched airplanes sailing through the icy corridors of an Andean pass. As the tips of their wings sometimes seemed to brush the glistening palisades, he had got gooseflesh from a combination of the excitement and beauty. Then and there he had set his heart on experiencing the thrill in the flesh. And now, as he dressed hurriedly and ate the breakfast brought to his room, it seemed that all he had seen and heard in the past thirty-odd days of travel was like the prelude of a love affair, the climax of which would be reached this morning.

Since two planes were flying today with capacity loads of fourteen passengers each, two buses were used to convey the passengers to the airport. Because of treacherous weather in the mountains, the Tuesday plane's flight had been postponed once and then again on Wednesday. Except where the street lamps cast a glow it was still quite dark. Here and there, out of the darkness, singly and in groups, peasants, muffled to the nose and bearing baskets of blossoms, rushed to secure the best stalls at the open-air flower market. Mme. Thibaud in the front seat hunched her shoulders and shrunk her face down into the upturned collar of her fur coat. The temperature stood just at freezing point. It was as cold as Santiago gets. Moiseiwitsch sat beside her in heavy-eyed silence. He had never flown before, and he was not comfortable in his mind. Besides he was sleepy, for he had been up all night playing cards.

Thibaud was in high spirits. He told Norbourne about Mischa Elman's crossing the Andes when scheduled for a series of performances in Santiago after an engagement in Buenos Aires. It was midwinter and there were, of course, no trains. Nothing would induce Elman to fly. No statistics of safe performances could convince him. So in Mendoza they arranged a mule train to transport him and his luggage over the mountains. The journey was far more hazardous than Hannibal had made by elephant over the Alps. Three mules gave up the ghost en route. After prolonged days of hardship, the battered Elman and what was left of his entourage turned up in Santiago. In the meantime Heifetz had hopped a plane in Buenos Aires, flown across the continent and over the Cordilleras in five hours, and received an ovation in the capital.

"In the same number of the *Musical Courier*"—Mme. Thibaud raised her head out of her furs—"appeared a picture of Heifetz jauntily boarding the airplane and one of dear Elman uncertainly mounting his ass."

At the airport coffee and biscuit were served, while the pilots checked their papers and the radio operator got the final report from the lookout man on the mountain heights. The activity in the office was expeditious, smoothly expert, exact, confidence-inspiring. A clerk reassured Moiseiwitsch. "Pan American Grace planes have crossed the Andes 1,899 times with only one fatal accident, and that happened in the pioneering days four years ago, and was due to lack of knowledge of weather conditions. But now the weatherman in The Pass keeps the pilot on the ground unless the conditions are completely favorable."

Norbourne looked over the personnel, those who remained on the ground and those who flew. Here, too, they were all youngish. Captain Disher, the pilot of the *Santa Lucia,* the plane Norbourne was to go in, was in the early thirties. Captain Parks, the other pilot, was only twenty-four. "The handsomest in the service," said Purser Elliott to an inquiring American lady with a twelve-year-old boy. "He's very skillful—and married," he added, noting her vague wistfulness as she stared at the dark young man with the amiable, adventurous eyes. Norbourne was delighted to find that by chance Elliott was again to be his steward. He knew he could get wide-awake answers to his questions.

"I'll warn you when we come to the Christ," Elliott said. "It's very interesting. In 1904 at the conclusion of a series of peace pacts and boundary agreements between Argentina and Chile, the symbolic figure was placed on the boundary between the two countries. The statue was shipped 750 miles over the mountains by mule back. It's twenty-six feet tall, and rests on a granite hemisphere five feet high, with the western continents marked in bronze bas-relief. In the unveiling of the monument, the presiding bishop proclaimed, 'Sooner shall these mountains crumble into dust than Argentinians and Chileans break the peace sworn at the feet of Christ the Redeemer.' "

"I want to know about the radio man who lives up there in the mountains."

"Ah, Nemsoff. He's a rare one. A husky young giant. His full name is Gregorio Nemsoff. He's an Argentino born in Russia. You'll see his hut not far from the statue. It is built on Argentinian territory forty feet from Chilean soil. It's two miles from the nearest railway station, which is deserted in winter. This was the first radio station in the Cordilleras of the Andes to communicate with airplanes in flight. From February, 1933, until June, 1934, Nemsoff lived entirely alone, sending messages to Santiago and Buenos Aires and keeping in touch with flyers en route. Sometimes at night hungry mountain lions would surround his retreat, attracted by the smell of meat kept in the open air for its preservation. Nemsoff says shooting stealthy lions in pitch darkness is not exactly fun. If a plane was scheduled to fly next morning, he would spend half the night clinging perilously to his ropes along the ledges of precipices, noting the direction and intensity of the wind. Excuse me—" Elliott was away in a flash on some routine duty.

Floodlights played on the landing field. Like silver dragon flies just alighted on a green pool, the two great Douglases were lined up one behind the other, their twin propellers twirling, their motors making harmonious thunder. The chief mechanic announced to Captain Parks that his plane was ready. After the second bell, the Thibauds and Moiseiwitsch and eleven others followed the captain and co-pilot up the flight of portable steps. The field manager lowered his red flag. The plane taxied down the field and turned to get into the wind. The white flag was lifted. Skimming the turf lightly, kissing it three farewell kisses, the thunderbird plunged joyously up into the air like a lark scenting the sunrise.

Ten minutes later the *Santa Lucia's* passengers chose their seats. Before and behind Norbourne sat young Doctors of Philosophy, one a lecturer at Columbia University, the other a professor at Copenhagen. They had their laps full of tubes and pumps and charts and diagrams. (Along with eight others from world famous universities, they had been sent by some international scientific organization to study the effect of altitude on human physiology. The others had remained in the mountains of Bolivia.) These gentlemen asked Norbourne to serve as their guinea pig. He consented on the promise that when they reached The Pass he would not be encumbered with rubber bands on his arms or intelligence tests on his mind.

He settled back in his seat and touched the little oxygen tube dangling out of the blue enameled wood work under the window frame. It was rare that any passenger ever needed oxygen, but sometimes they took a sniff just for the fun of it or to prevent a headache. Before he realized it, they were in the air, headed for Aconcagua. With astounding celerity they climbed until they reached an altitude of 15,000 feet. At the scientists' request, Norbourne removed his coat. Outside the weather was zero, but the air-conditioned temperature within was 72°. The professors bound the blood pressure pad about his arm, and pumped, and took the record.

A quarter of an hour after leaving the field, the *Santa Lucia* passed high over the foothills of the Cordilleras. At some exact mechanical demarcation she swerved to the right as naturally as if turning down a hedged country lane. In another minute they had entered the stupendous gap in the mountains known as The Pass. Norbourne demanded to be unstrapped. He walked up the aisle to the front seat on the left, the only one vacant.

The glory of Aconcagua to the left seemed as close as a New York skyscraper seen from the Battery. Norbourne stood transfixed with enchantment. Everywhere was eternal whiteness—the blue-tinctured whiteness of ice and diamonds, an intensely clean whiteness with subtle shadows of aquamarine and sapphire that shifted enchantingly before the vast crystal alcoves. A few thousand feet beneath, the gallery's pavement was the purplish color of wet violets.

Purser Elliott pointed out peaks and promontories, called them by name, enumerated their respective altitudes. It was as if one applied geography to a mystical vision of Blake. The Indians say that only on the crest of the Andes can one talk with God. This corridor of carved crystal through which they tore like the west wind might have been the approach to heaven's throne. On either side chalky pencils of cathedral spires wrote Andean choruses on the fresh morning's azure slate. And directly in front of them the youthful sun god, hurling gold-feathered darts of light, rose to meet the thunderbird.

Though they could not see the other plane which had taken off just before they did, the captain knew exactly where it was. "When there are two planes in The Pass, the respective radio operators keep in constant touch with each other, giving their exact position by squares on the map of the charted territory." Purser Elliott showed Norbourne on the map the spot where the other plane was at the moment. "Most people have the idea that The Pass is a narrow way," he said. "As you see, it's miles wide."

But to Norbourne it looked like a tunnel. Once he involuntarily tensed all his muscles. "Aren't they going to hit that left bank there?" he cautioned.

Elliott smiled. "It's a good three miles away."

Norbourne looked down on land where no man had set foot, where so small a proportion of the world's people would ever set eye. It was exciting to be breathing in such an age when the most ordinary of mortals had the privilege of acting a part that only a few of the greatest of the ancient seers played in their most extravagant dreams.

Elliott touched his arm and he went back to his seat for a better view of the famous Christ they were approaching. Beneath, like a figurine in ivory, stood a gigantic statue of the Lord, the right hand raised in benediction, the left clasping a cross that extended high above the head. In the shadow of the lonely Christ stood the diminutive stone hut of Nemsoff. There, companioned only by howling pumas and the shadow of the silent Christ with cyclonic winds thundering out mad symphonies, the young giant lived in Olympian isolation, controlling—with his finger tips and his voice—the trans-continental movements of mail and men.

Disher kindly circled about the statue and the station once again for the passengers' better view. "Whenever possible," Elliott said to Norbourne, as they looked down through the frosty windows, "magazines and bundles of newspapers are thrown from the planes to Gregorio to enlighten his monotonous routine. Sometimes we can see him dashing down the mountain side like a wild goat in his eagerness to get them. In the summer he once brought back two women from an Argentine village to cheer his loneliness. But it proved unsatisfactory. The women couldn't adjust themselves to harem ways and fought for his sole affections at the very feet of the Peacemaker. So he got rid of them both, and on good days when no planes were scheduled to fly he would radio that he was signing off to go to the village to get a haircut. The operators in Mendoza and Santiago would smile and call out into the office: 'Nemsoff has gone for a haircut.' Everybody knew what it meant."

"What is that other house?" Norbourne asked, noticing another simple structure alongside the first.

"That's the new meteorological station the Argentinian Government constructed. Gregorio [1] is no longer entirely alone."

Norbourne strained his eyes, hoping to catch a glimpse of that modern messenger of the gods, whose advice pilots in two countries heeded like the word of deity. But nothing stirred except the thunderbird's shadow which passed like a phantom over the invisible boundary out of Chile.

These hanging gardens of crystal, these blue canyons and white promontories were no different in quality from the others. But on the maps they proclaimed allegiance to Argentina.

Norbourne, leaning back, recalled how Melville had believed that the quality of whiteness enhanced beauty in natural objects like japonicas, marble, pearls, because the "quality of whiteness is emblematic of something most worthy of reverence and has for man innumerable beautiful and kindly associations." Here where the landscape was covered with snow

---

[1] Since the above was written, Gregorio Nemsoff on vacation met his death on the civilized streets of Mendoza, when his automobile skidded over some weeping willow branches that lay across the road after a heavy rain.

whiter than samite, he could feel the supernatural implications Hudson described.

The pilot touched the controls lightly and the thunderbird obeyed his silent commands, as if it were a live and intelligent thing. The great snow-covered peaks and ridges might have been some white monster that had lain there challenging man for generations, as Moby Dick had challenged super-stitious seafarers. But now it had been outwitted. The thunderbird flew among its tempting treacheries as serenely as a dragonfly passing over a clump of white pitcher plants growing by a meadow brook. The wind was still now. All nature looked hushed, as if having no ear except for the scien-tific sounds emitted from the thunderbird's great vocal cords. "Man is nor-mally scientific and loves to get at the bottom of all mysteries, and yet at the same time his older, deeper, primitive, still persistent nature is non-scientific and mystical." Following Hudson's speculations, Norbourne won-dered anew at the change wrought by this miraculous manifestation of in-telligent life and power, while the primitive in him remained spellbound at the quintessence of whiteness.

"In a few minutes we begin the descent," the purser said. Norbourne would have restrained them if it had been reasonable and in his power. He was loath to return so quickly to the world of pavements, politics, statistics, to bargaining and aimless babble. He would have liked to stay in the air all day flying among those immaculate pinnacles and thrilling precipices.

But the thunderbird knew its business and had no notion of lingering in the region of enchantment longer than was necessary. There was inter-national mail to be delivered; business men to whom time was money to be got to their destinations. The fashionable restaurants of Buenos Aires were impatient for the lobsters from Robinson Crusoe's Island. A lady in Buenos Aires whose ship was about to sail for New York was frantic for fear her set of false teeth made by a Santiago dentist would not arrive in time and she would be condemned to a seventeen days' milk diet and an agony of humiliated vanity.

The thunderbird tore away from the white draperies of The Pass out over a savage undulating plain with tight dry bushes and cactus growing in rocky aridity. Rusty condors flapped wide wings above granite boulders. Below lay Uspallata where San Martín and his liberty-seeking men began their historic climb over a way twice as steep and perilous as that Napoleon had negotiated in the Alps.

Norbourne took one last look back at the majesty of Aconcagua, now forty miles away. It lay serene against the blue silk of the sky like an exhibi-tion jewel in a show case. Then it vanished from sight like a conjurer's trick, and the thunderbird dropped completely away from the mystery and glory, and sailed out over a "meaningless confusion of piled rocks."

In a state of semi-intoxication Norbourne returned to his seat. The

Columbia Ph.D. and the Copenhagen Ph.D. put him to doing some sort of quick co-ordination tests, made him mark horizontal and vertical lines in white checkerboard spaces on specimen paper within an allotted time to test the effect of the altitude on his brain functioning.

When he looked out again, they were passing over the dry foothills with their stunted trees and shrubs. Almost immediately they were hovering over the city of Mendoza that reposed like a summerhouse in the midst of illimitable irrigated vineyards, twenty-five hundred feet above the level of the sea. The plane descended slowly so that the ear drums of the passengers would suffer no discomfort. It was a quarter of an hour after they were in sight of Mendoza before the pilot made his imperceptibly smooth landing. The whole trip had consumed only one hour of time. As Norbourne set foot on earth he knew that never in all his life would any hour of travel hold so much.

Rockwell Kent

If the name of Rockwell Kent (1882-   ) suggests only drawings and paintings, one should take note of these words of the artist-writer: "I have always loved adventure, and reflecting on it. As a result I have needed to paint and, because painting alone was inadequate, to write. The arts all seem to me much alike in the character that should distinguish them." Certainly there is little difference between the bold rugged black-and-white of Kent's Arctic scenes and the clarity and strength of Wilderness, Voyaging, or N. by E. Whatever this man touches bears the imprint of his energy and zest for experience. In "Shipwreck" he tells of the loss of the small boat in which he suffered disaster on the coast of Greenland.

SHIPWRECK

THE motion woke me. Where was I? I remembered. Daylight came but faintly through the fo'castle ports, shadowed as they were by the dinghy. My clock showed ten-thirty. How I had slept!

We were rolling violently; a sudden roll, a lurch to starboard. I heard steps on deck, voices, the sound of hawser paying out. Oh, well, we're at anchor; and no one has called. I braced my knees against the side board of the bunk; I had need to.

Suddenly we were careened so far that I was almost catapulted onto the floor. I got out, dressed hastily and opened the door into the cabin. It was broad daylight there. The skipper was in bed.

"She's drifting with both anchors," called the mate from deck.

"Give 'em more rope," answered the skipper.

I reached the ladder. At that moment something rolled us over, far, far down, and held us there; and the green sea came pouring in as if to fill the ship.

"Damn it!" I cried, "and I'd made everything so neat!"

On deck a hurricane; I'd never felt such wind before. The sea was beaten flat, with every wave crest shorn and whipped to smoke; cold spray and stinging rain drove over us.

I helped the mate. "We'll need the third anchor," I said, and started aft.

The skipper appeared. "Good, get it out," he said as I passed him. I went below for the last time.

The spare anchor was knocked down and stowed under the coal sacks and provisions in the after hold; it was not easy to come at. Removing the companion ladder I set to work. Hard work it was cramped in that narrow space on hands and knees. As I dragged the hundred pound sacks out onto the cabin floor—always, strangely, careful not to damage anything—I'd look up and see the gray sky through the opening above my head. Then one time glancing up I saw the brow of the mountain; and always after that more mountain showed and less sky. And at last the mountain side itself seemed to have moved against the ship and to be towering over it.

I had laid a lighted cigarette carefully upon the chart table; this, as I worked, was always in my mind—that it should not be left to burn the wood. And so, from time to time, I'd move it just a bit. We were so careful of our boat, to mar it in no way!

But all the while I had been shifting goods and moving sacks of coal; so that at last I came to the anchor. It was a large anchor and very heavy. I dragged it out into the cabin.

"Come," I called to the mate, "and help me get this thing on deck." And as I looked up I saw the mate in his yellow oilskins, bright against the near dark mountain side.

"Not much use now," said the mate; but he came down.

It was hard work to lift that anchor up, and we seemed not to be very strong. "I lose my strength from excitement," said the mate. I thought that I did too—but I didn't say so.

We lifted the cumbersome affair head high and tumbled it out into the cockpit. As I started to follow, a great sea lifted us and rolled us over; I hung on, half out of the cabin. And I stared straight at an oncoming wall of rock so near astern it seemed about to crush us. The sea rose high against it, and broke and became churned water that seethed around us. It cradled us and lowered us gently; and the dark land drew quietly away.

Then came another sea that hurled us and the land together. "Now for the crash!" I thought—and I gripped hard and braced myself against it, and watched the moment—thrilled by its impending horror.

There was no crash—that time. Ever so gently, just as we seemed to draw away again, our stern post touched the ledge; so lightly touched it that it made no sound, only a little tremor. And the tremor ran through the iron keel and the oak, and through the ribs and planking, and through every bolt and nail, through every fibre of the boat and us. Maybe we had not known that the end had come; now, as if God whispered it, we knew.

So for a third time we were floated back.

Then, as if the furies of the sea and wind were freed at last to end their coquetry, they lifted us—high, high above the ledge—and dropped us there. And the impact of that shock was only less than those that followed for that half an hour until *Direction* sank.

That half an hour! We lay, caught in the angle of a giant step of rock, keel on the tread and starboard side against the riser; held there by wind and sea; held there to lift and pound; to lift so buoyantly on every wave; to drop—crashing our thirteen iron-shod tons on granite. Lift and pound! There the perfection of our ship revealed itself; only, that having struck just once, she ever lived, a ship, to lift and strike again.

A giant sledge hammer striking a granite mountain; a hollow hammer; and within it a man. Picture yourself the man. I stayed below, and was.

See me as Adam; set full blown into that pandemonium of force, his world—of wind, storm, snow, rain, hail, lightning and thunder, earthquake and flood, hunger and cold, and the huge terrifying presence of the un-known—using his little wit toward self-containedness against the too-much of immensity; and quietly—for Adam lived—doing the little first-at-hands one on another in their natural course, thinking but little and reflecting less. Adam and Man; and me in that compacted miniature of man's universe, the cabin of the yacht *Direction* on the rocks of Greenland.

We live less by imagination than despite it.

Matches: They're in the fo'castle cupboard. I get out a lot. Next: Keep 'em dry. A big tin on the shelf. Lentils! I pour them out on the floor;—no, not all; we don't need all that room for matches. Pack in matches, put on the cover. Good. Now something to put the tin into. Sam's little bag lying there; the very thing! Good neckties and white collars! Out with them!

Put in the tin of matches; add odds and ends of food; close it; that's done.

Kerosene: Five-gallon tin too big to get ashore. The one-gallon. Buried under stores.

Over the coal sacks into the after storage space. God what a mess! Dig in the stores; dig—and find it. Good!

Alcohol for priming: find it—a small bottle.

And the Primus stove? Crushed on the floor.

There's another in my pack-sack with pup tent, nest of pots, etc. Under the starboard fo'castle bunk. Smothered under spare sails, spare rope, spare clothes, painting supplies. Out with everything. Ha! the sack!

Flour, rice, butter, beans, dried soups, coffee, bacon, chocolate, cigarettes: fill up the sack with them. Done.

Chronometers, the beauties! I take them from their boxes and wrap them carefully in layer on layer of clothes. I partly fill a duffle bag with blankets; put in watches; add the sextant, my silver flute, my movie camera, more blankets.

And this and all the rest, plus now and then a garment or a blanket, I pass on deck to the mate.

"Enough!" I think, with pride.

"Come out of there," calls the mate for the fourth time, peering down into the havoc of that hold.

Havoc! It's no-man's land; a mass of wreckage: doors, drawers, shelves, sheathing, stove lids, pots and pans and crockery, springs, mattresses, tools, beans and butter and books,—torn, splintered, crashed and mashed, lifted and churned and hurled again with every shivering impact of the ship.

Over my writing table in the fo'castle, nailed to a timber, was my sweetheart's picture. I had not forgotten it. I will take that picture, I had thought, tuck it for safety next my skin; and carry it, last thing, ashore with me. Then on my return I'll say, "Look, darling, what I have brought home!" And I'll take the picture from over my heart and show it to her. And with not so much modesty as to hide my valor I'll tell how in that hour of confusion and terror I had thought of her. And what a fine fellow I shall be!

So I now clambered, somehow, back to the fo'castle; found her image looking out serenely over the carnage; took her down and tucked her next to me; put an envelope containing my money, my passport and my permit to land in Greenland next to me too; and—wading, climbing, dodging, holding on for dear life—made my way out and to the deck.

The mate, working like ten stevedores, was getting things to shore. It was not far: a jump from deck to rocks, jump on a rising sea and scramble out of it and up before that step of rock was flooded. Hurling a sack, he'd follow it; clutch it and drag it to the safety of a higher ledge.

The sack containing the chronometers rolled back into the water. It was retrieved intact. Some things, washed from the rocks, were lost. The tide was littered with our gear and goods.

The thrashing of the main boom added confusion to the deck. Only the too stout standing rigging saved the mast.

The skipper was on shore desperately struggling to secure a mast-head line to a great boulder. Finished on board I leaped to help him. The yawing mast-head tore the line away from us each time we'd nearly made it fast. But once as the mast leant far down toward us we got two turns of line around the rock; we braced ourselves and held. The three-inch cable snapped like grocer's twine!

Direction's end was near. Quickly undoing the sack I got out the movie camera. Listen! Even above the noise of sea and wind and rain I hear for a short minute its small whirring like the beating of a heart. And by that sound, what happened there, in Karajak Fiord in Greenland, at eleven in the morning of July 15, 1929, achieved soundless immortality.

William Faulkner

William Faulkner (1897-   ) was born in Mississippi of a once wealthy and prominent family that had been ruined by the Civil War. His early career, interrupted by flying experience in World War I, was desultory and aimless. His first novel was written to raise money, but he suddenly discovered his capacities as a writer and was quick to develop a powerful and imaginative style. In his novels and short stories social disintegration and decay, perversion and cruelty, are subjectively experienced. In "The Bear" he departs from the morbid to shape again, in terms of back-woods adventure, the truth which Keats discovered in a Grecian urn.

THE BEAR

HE was ten. But it had already begun, long before that day when at last he wrote his age in two figures and he saw for the first time the camp where his father and Major de Spain and old General Compson and the others spent two weeks each November and two weeks again each June. He had already inherited then, without ever having seen it, the tremendous bear with one trap-ruined foot which, in an area almost a hundred miles deep, had earned for itself a name, a definite designation like a living man.

He had listened to it for years: the long legend of corncribs rifled, of shotes and grown pigs and even calves carried bodily into the woods and devoured, of traps and deadfalls overthrown and dogs mangled and slain, and shotgun and even rifle charges delivered at point-blank range and with no more effect than so many peas blown through a tube by a boy—a corridor of wreckage and destruction beginning back before he was born, through which sped, not fast but rather with the ruthless and irresistible deliberation of a locomotive, the shaggy tremendous shape.

It ran in his knowledge before he ever saw it. It looked and towered in his dreams before he even saw the unaxed woods where it left its crooked print, shaggy, huge, red-eyed, not malevolent but just big—too big for the dogs which tried to bay it, for the horses which tried to ride it down, for the men and the bullets they fired into it, too big for the very country which was its constricting scope. He seemed to see it entire with a child's complete divination before he ever laid eyes on either—the doomed wilderness whose edges were being constantly and punily gnawed at by men with axes and plows who feared it because it was wilderness, men myriad and nameless even to one another in the land where the old bear had earned a name, through which ran not even a mortal animal but an anachronism, indomitable and invincible, out of an old dead time, a phantom, epitome and apotheosis of the old wild life at which the puny humans swarmed and hacked in a fury of abhorrence and fear, like pygmies about the ankles of a drowsing elephant; the old bear solitary, indomitable and alone, widowered, childless and absolved of mortality—old Priam reft of his old wife and having outlived all his sons.

Until he was ten, each November he would watch the wagon containing the dogs and the bedding and food and guns and his father and Tennie's Jim, the Negro, and Sam Fathers, the Indian, son of a slave woman and a Chickasaw chief, depart on the road to town, to Jefferson, where Major de Spain and the others would join them. To the boy, at seven and eight and nine, they were not going into the Big Bottom to hunt bear and deer, but to keep yearly rendezvous with the bear which they did not even intend to kill. Two weeks later they would return, with no trophy, no head and skin. He had not expected it. He had not even been afraid it would be in the wagon. He believed that even after he was ten and his father would let him go too, for those two November weeks, he would merely make another one, along with his father and Major de Spain and General Compson and the others, the dogs which feared to bay it and the rifles and shotguns which failed even to bleed it, in the yearly pageant of the old bear's furious immortality.

Then he heard the dogs. It was in the second week of his first time in the camp. He stood with Sam Fathers against a big oak beside the faint crossing where they had stood each dawn for nine days now, hearing the dogs. He had heard them once before, one morning last week—a murmur, sourceless, echoing through the wet woods, swelling presently into separate voices which he could recognize and call by name. He had raised and cocked the gun as Sam told him and stood motionless again while the uproar, the invisible course, swept up and past and faded; it seemed to him that he could actually see the deer, the buck, blond, smoke-colored, elongated with speed, fleeing, vanishing, the woods, the gray solitude, still ringing even when the cries of the dogs had died away.

"Now let the hammers down," Sam said.

"You knew they were not coming here too," he said.

"Yes," Sam said. "I want you to learn how to do when you didn't shoot. It's after the chance for the bear or the deer has done already come and gone that men and dogs get killed."

"Anyway," he said, "it was just a deer."

Then on the tenth morning he heard the dogs again. And he readied the too-long, too-heavy gun as Sam had taught him, before Sam even spoke. But this time it was no deer, no ringing chorus of dogs running strong on a free scent, but a moiling yapping an octave too high, with something more than indecision and even abjectness in it, not even moving very fast, taking a long time to pass completely out of hearing, leaving even then somewhere in the air that echo, thin, slightly hysterical, abject, almost grieving, with no sense of a fleeing, unseen, smoke-colored, grass-eating shape ahead of it, and Sam, who had taught him first of all to cock the gun and take position where he could see everywhere and then never move again, had himself moved up beside him; he could hear Sam breathing at his shoulder and he could see the arched curve of the old man's inhaling nostrils.

"Hah," Sam said. "Not even running. Walking."

"Old Ben!" the boy said. "But up here!" he cried. "Way up here!"

"He do it every year," Sam said. "Once. Maybe to see who in camp this time, if he can shoot or not. Whether we got the dog yet that can bay and hold him. He'll take them to the river, then he'll send them back home. We may as well go back, too; see how they look when they come back to camp."

When they reached the camp the hounds were already there, ten of them crouching back under the kitchen, the boy and Sam squatting to peer back into the obscurity where they huddled, quiet, the eyes luminous, glowing at them and vanishing, and no sound, only that effluvium of something more than dog, stronger than dog and not just animal, just beast, because still there had been nothing in front of that abject and almost painful yapping save the solitude, the wilderness, so that when the eleventh hound came in at noon and with all the others watching—even old Uncle Ash, who called himself first a cook—Sam daubed the tattered ear and the raked shoulder with turpentine and axle grease, to the boy it was still no living creature, but the wilderness which, leaning for the moment down, had patted lightly once the hound's temerity.

"Just like a man," Sam said. "Just like folks. Put off as long as she could having to be brave, knowing all the time that sooner or later she would have to be brave once to keep on living with herself, and knowing all the time beforehand what was going to happen to her when she done it."

That afternoon, himself on the one-eyed wagon mule which did not mind the smell of blood nor, as they told him, of bear, and with Sam on the other one, they rode for more than three hours through the rapid, shortening winter day. They followed no path, no trail even that he could see; almost at once they were in a country which he had never seen before. Then he knew why Sam had made him ride the mule which would not spook. The sound one stopped short and tried to whirl and bolt even as Sam got down, blowing its breath, jerking and wrenching at the rein while Sam held it, coaxing it forward with his voice, since he could not risk tying it, drawing it forward while the boy got down from the marred one.

Then, standing beside Sam in the gloom of the dying afternoon, he looked down at the rotted overturned log, gutted and scored with claw marks and, in the wet earth beside it, the print of the enormous warped two-toed foot. He knew now what he had smelled when he peered under the kitchen where the dogs huddled. He realized for the first time that the bear which had run in his listening and loomed in his dreams since before he could remember to the contrary, and which, therefore, must have existed in the listening and dreams of his father and Major de Spain and even old General Compson, too, before they began to remember in their turn, was a mortal animal, and that if they had departed for the camp each November without any actual hope of bringing its trophy back, it was not because it could not be slain, but because so far they had had no actual hope to.

"Tomorrow," he said.

"We'll try tomorrow," Sam said. "We ain't got the dog yet."

"We've got eleven. They ran him this morning."

"It won't need but one," Sam said. "He ain't here. Maybe he ain't nowhere. The only other way will be for him to run by accident over somebody that has a gun."

"That wouldn't be me," the boy said. "It will be Walter or Major or—"

"It might," Sam said. "You watch close in the morning. Because he's smart. That's how come he has lived this long. If he gets hemmed up and has to pick out somebody to run over, he will pick out you."

"How?" the boy said. "How will he know—" He ceased. "You mean he already knows me, that I ain't never been here before, ain't had time to find out yet whether I—" He ceased again, looking at Sam, the old man whose face revealed nothing until it smiled. He said humbly, not even amazed, "It was me he was watching. I don't reckon he did need to come but once."

The next morning they left the camp three hours before daylight. They rode this time because it was too far to walk, even the dogs in the wagon; again the first gray light found him in a place which he had never seen before, where Sam had placed him and told him to stay and then departed. With the gun which was too big for him, which did not even belong to him, but to Major de Spain, and which he had fired only once—at a stump on the first day, to learn the recoil and how to reload it—he stood against a gum tree beside a little bayou whose black still water crept without movement out of a canebrake and crossed a small clearing and into cane again, where, invisible, a bird—the big woodpecker called Lord-to-God by Negroes—clattered at a dead limb.

It was a stand like any other, dissimilar only in incidentals to the one where he had stood each morning for ten days; a territory new to him, yet no less familiar than that other one which, after almost two weeks, he had come to believe he knew a little—the same solitude, the same loneliness through which human beings had merely passed without altering it, leaving no mark, no scar, which looked exactly as it must have looked when the first ancestor of Sam Fathers' Chickasaw predecessors crept into it and looked about, club or stone ax or bone arrow drawn and poised; different only because, squatting at the edge of the kitchen, he smelled the hounds huddled and cringing beneath it and saw the raked ear and shoulder of the one who, Sam said, had had to be brave once in order to live with herself, and saw yesterday in the earth beside the gutted log the print of the living foot.

He heard no dogs at all. He never did hear them. He only heard the drumming of the woodpecker stop short off and knew that the bear was looking at him. He never saw it. He did not know whether it was in front of him or behind him. He did not move, holding the useless gun, which he had not even had warning to cock and which even now he did not cock, tasting in his saliva that taint as of brass which he knew now because he had smelled it when he peered under the kitchen at the huddled dogs.

Then it was gone. As abruptly as it had ceased, the woodpecker's dry, monotonous clatter set up again, and after a while he even believed he could hear the dogs—a murmur, scarce a sound even, which he had probably been hearing for some time before he even remarked it, drifting into hearing and then out again, dying away. They came nowhere near him. If it was a bear they ran, it was another bear. It was Sam himself who came out of the cane and crossed the bayou, followed by the injured bitch of yesterday. She was almost at heel, like a bird dog, making no sound. She came and crouched against his leg, trembling, staring off into the cane.

"I didn't see him," he said. "I didn't, Sam!"

"I know it," Sam said. "He done the looking. You didn't hear him neither, did you?"

"No," the boy said. "I—"

"He's smart," Sam said. "Too smart." He looked down at the hound, trembling faintly and steadily against the boy's knee. From the raked shoulder a few drops of fresh blood oozed and clung. "Too big. We ain't got the dog yet. But maybe someday. Maybe not next time. But someday."

So I must see him, he thought. I must look at him. Otherwise, it seemed to him that it would go on like this forever, as it had gone on with his father and Major de Spain, who was older than his father, and even with old General Compson, who had been old enough to be a brigade commander in 1865. Otherwise, it would go on so forever, next time and next time, after and after and after. It seemed to him that he could see the two of them, himself and the bear, shadowy in the limbo from which time emerged, becoming time; the old bear absolved of mortality and himself partaking, sharing a little of it, enough of it. And he knew now what he had smelled in the huddled dogs and tasted in his saliva. He recognized fear. *So I will have to see him,* he thought, without dread or even hope. *I will have to look at him.*

It was in June of the next year. He was eleven. They were in camp again, celebrating Major de Spain's and General Compson's birthdays. Although the one had been born in September and the other in the depth of winter and in another decade, they had met for two weeks to fish and shoot squirrels and turkey and run coons and wildcats with the dogs at night. That is, he and Boon Hoggenbeck and the Negroes fished and shot squirrels and ran the coons and cats, because the proved hunters, not only Major de Spain and old General Compson, who spent those two weeks sitting in a rocking chair before a tremendous iron pot of Brunswick stew, stirring and tasting, with old Ash to quarrel with about how he was making it and Tennie's Jim to pour whisky from the demijohn into the tin dipper from which he drank it, but even the boy's father and Walter Ewell, who were still young enough, scorned such, other than shooting the wild gobblers with pistols for wagers on their marksmanship.

Or, that is, his father and the others believed he was hunting squirrels. Until the third day he thought that Sam Fathers believed that too. Each morning he would leave the camp right after breakfast. He had his own gun now, a Christmas present. He went back to the tree beside the little bayou where he had stood that morning. Using the compass which old General Compson had given him, he ranged from that point; he was teaching himself to be a better-than-fair woodsman without knowing he was doing it. On the second day he even found the gutted log where he had first seen the crooked print. It was almost completely crumbled now, healing with unbelievable speed, a passionate and almost visible relinquishment, back into the earth from which the tree had grown.

He ranged the summer woods now, green with gloom; if anything, actually dimmer than in November's gray dissolution, where, even at noon, the sun fell only in intermittent dappling upon the earth, which never completely dried out and which crawled with snakes—moccasins and water snakes and rattlers, themselves the color of the dappled gloom, so that he would not always see them until they moved, returning later and later, first day, second day, passing in the twilight of the third evening the little log pen enclosing the log stable where Sam was putting up the horses for the night.

"You ain't looked right yet," Sam said.

He stopped. For a moment he didn't answer. Then he said peacefully, in a peaceful rushing burst as when a boy's miniature dam in a little brook gives way, "All right. But how? I went to the bayou. I even found that log again. I—"

"I reckon that was all right. Likely he's been watching you. You never saw his foot?"

"I," the boy said—"I didn't—I never thought—"

"It's the gun," Sam said. He stood beside the fence, motionless—the old man, the Indian, in the battered faded overalls and the frayed five-cent straw hat which in the Negro's race had been the badge of his enslavement and was now the regalia of his freedom. The camp—the clearing, the house, the barn and its tiny lot with which Major de Spain in his turn had scratched punily and evanescently at the wilderness—faded in the dusk, back into the immemorial darkness of the woods. *The gun,* the boy thought. *The gun.*

"Be scared," Sam said. "You can't help that. But don't be afraid. Ain't nothing in the woods going to hurt you unless you corner it, or it smells that you are afraid. A bear or a deer, too, has got to be scared of a coward the same as a brave man has got to be."

The gun, the boy thought.

"You will have to choose," Sam said.

He left the camp before daylight, long before Uncle Ash would wake in his quilts on the kitchen floor and start the fire for breakfast. He had only the compass and a stick for snakes. He could go almost a mile before he would begin to need the compass. He sat on a log, the invisible compass in his invisible hand, while the secret night sounds, fallen still at his movements, scurried again and then ceased for good, and the owls ceased and gave over to the waking of day birds, and he could see the compass. Then he went fast yet still quietly; he was becoming better and better as a woodsman, still without having yet realized it.

He jumped a doe and a fawn at sunrise, walked them out of the bed, close enough to see them—the crash of undergrowth, the white scut, the fawn scudding behind her faster than he had believed it could run. He was hunting right, upwind, as Sam had taught him; not that it mattered now. He had left the gun; of his own will and relinquishment he had accepted not a gambit, not a choice, but a condition in which not only the bear's heretofore inviolable anonymity but all the old rules and balances of hunter and hunted had been abrogated. He would not even be afraid, not even in the moment when the fear would take him completely—blood, skin, bowels, bones, memory from the long time before it became his memory—all save that thin, clear, quenchless, immortal lucidity which alone differed him from this bear and from all the other bear and deer he would ever kill in the humility and pride of his skill and endurance, to which Sam had spoken when he leaned in the twilight on the lot fence yesterday.

By noon he was far beyond the little bayou, farther into the new and alien country than he had ever been. He was traveling now not only by the compass but by the old, heavy, biscuit-thick silver watch which had belonged to his grandfather. When he stopped at last, it was for the first time since he had risen from the log at dawn when he could see the compass. It was far enough. He had left the camp nine hours ago; nine hours from now, dark would have already been an hour old. But he didn't think that. He thought, *All right. Yes. But what?* and stood for a moment, alien and small in the green and topless solitude, answering his own question before it had formed and ceased. It was the watch, the compass, the stick—the three life-less mechanicals with which for nine hours he had fended the wilderness off; he hung the watch and compass carefully on a bush and leaned the stick beside them and relinquished completely to it.

He had not been going very fast for the last two or three hours. He went no faster now, since distance would not matter even if he could have gone fast. And he was trying to keep a bearing on the tree where he had left the compass, trying to complete a circle which would bring him back to it or at least intersect itself, since direction would not matter now either. But the tree was not there, and he did as Sam had schooled him—made the next circle in the opposite direction, so that the two patterns would bisect somewhere, but crossing no print of his own feet, finding the tree at last, but in the wrong place—no bush, no compass, no watch—and the tree not even the tree, because there was a down log beside it and he did what Sam Fathers had told him was the next thing and the last.

As he sat down on the log he saw the crooked print—the warped, tre-mendous, two-toed indentation which, even as he watched it, filled with water. As he looked up, the wilderness coalesced, solidified—the glade, the tree he sought, the bush, the watch and the compass glinting where a ray of sunlight touched them. Then he saw the bear. It did not emerge, appear; it was just there, immobile, solid, fixed in the hot dappling of the green and windless noon, not as big as he had dreamed it, but as big as he had expected it, bigger, dimensionless against the dappled obscurity, looking at him where he sat quietly on the log and looked back at it.

Then it moved. It made no sound. It did not hurry. It crossed the glade, walking for an instant into the full glare of the sun; when it reached the other side it stopped again and looked back at him across one shoulder while his quiet breathing inhaled and exhaled three times.

Then it was gone. It didn't walk into the woods, the undergrowth. It faded, sank back into the wilderness as he had watched a fish, a huge old bass, sink and vanish back into the dark depths of its pool without even any movement of its fins.

He thought, *It will be next fall.* But it was not next fall, nor the next nor the next. He was fourteen then. He had killed his buck, and Sam Fathers had marked his face with the hot blood, and in the next year he killed a bear. But even before that accolade he had become as competent in the woods as many grown men with the same experience; by his fourteenth year he was a better woodsman than most grown men with more. There was no territory within thirty miles of the camp that he did not know— bayou, ridge, brake, landmark tree and path. He could have led anyone to any point in it without deviation, and brought them out again. He knew game trails that even Sam Fathers did not know; in his thirteenth year he found a buck's bedding place, and unbeknown to his father he borrowed Walter Ewell's rifle and lay in wait at dawn and killed the buck when it walked back to the bed, as Sam had told him how the old Chickasaw fathers did.

But not the old bear, although by now he knew its footprint better than he did his own, and not only the crooked one. He could see any one of the three sound ones and distinguish it from any other, and not only by its size. There were other bears within those thirty miles which left tracks almost as large, but this was more than that. If Sam Fathers had been his mentor and the back-yard rabbits and squirrels at home his kindergarten, then the wilderness the old bear ran was his college, the old male bear itself, so long unwifed and childless as to have become its own ungendered progenitor, was his alma mater. But he never saw it.

He could find the crooked print now almost whenever he liked, fifteen or ten or five miles, or sometimes nearer the camp than that. Twice while on stand during the three years he heard the dogs strike its trail by accident; on the second time they jumped it seemingly, the voices high, abject, almost human in hysteria, as on that first morning two years ago. But not the bear itself. He would remember that noon three years ago, the glade, himself and the bear fixed during that moment in the windless and dappled blaze, and it would seem to him that it had never happened, that he had dreamed that too. But it had happened. They had looked at each other, they had emerged from the wilderness old as earth, synchronized to that instant by something more than the blood that moved the flesh and bones which bore them, and touched, pledged something, affirmed something more lasting than the frail web of bones and flesh which any accident could obliterate.

Then he saw it again. Because of the very fact that he thought of nothing else, he had forgotten to look for it. He was still-hunting with Walter

Ewell's rifle. He saw it cross the end of a long blow-down, a corridor where a tornado had swept, rushing through rather than over the tangle of trunks and branches as a locomotive would have, faster than he had ever believed it could move, almost as fast as a deer even, because a deer would have spent most of that time in the air, faster than he could bring the rifle sights up to it, so that he believed the reason he never let off the shot was that he was still behind it, had never caught up with it. And now he knew what had been wrong during all the three years. He sat on a log, shaking and trembling as if he had never seen the woods before nor anything that ran them, wondering with incredulous amazement how he could have forgotten the very thing which Sam Fathers had told him and which the bear itself had proved the next day and had now returned after three years to reaffirm.

And he now knew what Sam Fathers had meant about the right dog, a dog in which size would mean less than nothing. So when he returned alone in April—school was out then, so that the sons of farmers could help with the land's planting, and at last his father had granted him permission, on his promise to be back in four days—he had the dog. It was his own, a mongrel of the sort called by Negroes a fyce, a ratter, itself not much bigger than a rat and possessing that bravery which had long since stopped being courage and had become foolhardiness.

It did not take four days. Alone again, he found the trail on the first morning. It was not a stalk; it was an ambush. He timed the meeting almost as if it were an appointment with a human being. Himself holding the fyce muffled in a feed sack and Sam Fathers with two of the hounds on a piece of plowline rope, they lay down wind of the trail at dawn of the second morning. They were so close that the bear turned without even running, as if in surprised amazement at the shrill and frantic uproar of the released fyce, turning at bay against the trunk of a tree, on its hind feet; it seemed to the boy that it would never stop rising, taller and taller, and even the two hounds seemed to take a sort of desperate and despairing courage from the fyce, following it as it went in.

Then he realized that the fyce was actually not going to stop. He flung, threw the gun away, and ran; when he overtook and grasped the frantically pinwheeling little dog, it seemed to him that he was directly under the bear.

He could smell it, strong and hot and rank. Sprawling, he looked up to where it loomed and towered over him like a cloudburst and colored like a thunderclap, quite familiar, peacefully and even lucidly familiar, until he remembered: This was the way he had used to dream about it. Then it was gone. He didn't see it go. He knelt, holding the frantic fyce with both hands, hearing the abased wailing of the hounds drawing farther and farther away, until Sam came up. He carried the gun. He laid it down quietly beside the boy and stood looking down at him.

"You've done seed him twice now with a gun in your hands," he said. "This time you couldn't have missed him."

The boy rose. He still held the fyce. Even in his arms and clear of the ground, it yapped frantically, straining and surging after the fading uproar of the two hounds like a tangle of wire springs. He was panting a little, but he was neither shaking nor trembling now.

"Neither could you!" he said. "You had the gun! Neither did you!"

"And you didn't shoot," his father said. "How close were you?"

"I don't know, sir," he said. "There was a big wood tick inside his right hind leg. I saw that. But I didn't have the gun then."

"But you didn't shoot when you had the gun," his father said. "Why?"

But he didn't answer, and his father didn't wait for him to, rising and crossing the room, across the pelt of the bear which the boy had killed two years ago and the larger one which his father had killed before he was born, to the bookcase beneath the mounted head of the boy's first buck. It was the room which his father called the office, from which all the plantation business was transacted; in it for the fourteen years of his life he had heard the best of all talking. Major de Spain would be there and sometimes old General Compson, and Walter Ewell and Boon Hoggenbeck and Sam Fathers and Tennie's Jim, too, because they, too, were hunters, knew the woods and what ran them.

He would hear it, not talking himself but listening—the wilderness, the big woods, bigger and older than any recorded document of white man fatuous enough to believe he had bought any fragment of it or Indian ruthless enough to pretend that any fragment of it had been his to convey. It was of the men, not white nor black nor red, but men, hunters with the will and hardihood to endure and the humility and skill to survive, and the dogs and the bear and deer juxtaposed and reliefed against it, ordered and compelled by and within the wilderness in the ancient and unremitting contest by the ancient and immitigable rules which voided all regrets and brooked no quarter, the voices quiet and weighty and deliberate for retrospection and recollection and exact remembering, while he squatted in the blazing firelight as Tennie's Jim squatted, who stirred only to put more wood on the fire and to pass the bottle from one glass to another. Because the bottle was always present, so that after a while it seemed to him that those fierce instants of heart and brain and courage and wiliness and speed were concentrated and distilled into that brown liquor which not women, not boys and children, but only hunters drank, drinking not of the blood they had spilled but some condensation of the wild immortal spirit, drinking it moderately, humbly even, not with the pagan's base hope of acquiring thereby the virtues of cunning and strength and speed, but in salute to them.

His father returned with the book and sat down again and opened it.

"Listen," he said. He read the five stanzas aloud, his voice quiet and deliberate in the room where there was no fire now because it was already spring. Then he looked up. The boy watched him. "All right," his father said. "Listen." He read again, but only the second stanza this time, to the end of it, the last two lines, and closed the book and put it on the table beside him. "'She cannot fade, though thou hast not thy bliss, for ever wilt thou love, and she be fair,'" he said.

"He's talking about a girl," the boy said.

"He had to talk about something," his father said. Then he said, "He was talking about truth. Truth doesn't change. Truth is one thing. It covers all things which touch the heart—honor and pride and pity and justice and courage and love. Do you see now?"

He didn't know. Somehow it was simpler than that. There was an old bear, fierce and ruthless, not merely just to stay alive, but with the fierce pride of liberty and freedom, proud enough of that liberty and freedom to see it threatened without fear or even alarm; nay, who at times even seemed deliberately to put that freedom and liberty in jeopardy in order to savor them, to remind his old strong bones and flesh to keep supple and quick to defend and preserve them. There was an old man, son of a Negro slave and an Indian king, inheritor on the one side of the long chronicle of a people who had learned humility through suffering, and pride through the endurance which survived the suffering and injustice, and on the other side, the chronicle of a people even longer in the land than the first, yet who no longer existed in the land at all save in the solitary brotherhood of an old Negro's alien blood and the wild and invincible spirit of an old bear. There was a boy who wished to learn humility and pride in order to become skillful and worthy in the woods, who suddenly found himself becoming so skillful so rapidly that he feared he would never become worthy because he had not learned humility and pride, although he had tried to, until one day and as suddenly he discovered that an old man who could not have defined either had led him, as though by the hand, to that point where an old bear and a little mongrel dog showed him that, by possessing one thing other, he would possess them both.

And a little dog, nameless and mongrel and many-fathered, grown, yet weighing less than six pounds, saying as if to itself, "I can't be dangerous, because there's nothing much smaller than I am; I can't be fierce, because they would call it just noise; I can't be humble, because I'm already too close to the ground to genuflect; I can't be proud, because I wouldn't be near enough to it for anyone to know who was casting that shadow, and I don't even know that I'm not going to heaven, because they have already decided that I don't possess an immortal soul. So all I can be is brave. But it's all right. I can be that, even if they still call it just noise."

That was all. It was simple, much simpler than somebody talking in a book about a youth and a girl he would never need to grieve over, because he could never approach any nearer her and would never have to get any farther away. He had heard about a bear, and finally got big enough to trail it, and he trailed it four years and at last met it with a gun in his hands and he didn't shoot. Because a little dog— But he could have shot long before the little dog covered the twenty yards to where the bear waited, and Sam Fathers could have shot at any time during that interminable minute while Old Ben stood on his hind feet over them. He stopped. His father was watching him gravely across the spring-rife twilight of the room; when he spoke, his words were as quiet as the twilight, too, not loud, because they did not need to be, because they would last: "Courage, and honor, and pride," his father said, "and pity, and love of justice and of liberty. They all touch the heart, and what the heart holds to becomes truth, as far as we know truth. Do you see now?"

Sam, and Old Ben, and Nip, he thought. And himself too. He had been all right too. His father had said so. "Yes, sir," he said.

Paul Gallico

Paul Gallico (1897-   ) was born in New York and attended Columbia University. For thirteen years he was a sports writer and columnist on the New York Daily News. *When he resigned this position in 1936 to become a free lance fiction writer, he wrote his valedictory in* Farewell to Sport, *the volume from which is reprinted the following chapter, a tribute to the least-written-about of the five senses.*

THE FEEL

A CHILD wandering through a department store with its mother, is admonished over and over again not to touch things. Mother is convinced that the child only does it to annoy or because it is a child, and usually hasn't the vaguest inkling of the fact that Junior is "touching" because he is a little blotter soaking up information and knowledge, and "feel" is an important adjunct to seeing. Adults are exactly the same, in a measure, as you may ascertain when some new gadget or article is produced for inspection. The average person says: "Here, let me see that," and holds out his hand. He doesn't mean "see," because he is already seeing it. What he means is that he wants to get it into his hands and feel it so as to become better acquainted.

I do not insist that a curiosity and capacity for feeling sports is necessary to be a successful writer, but it is fairly obvious that a man who has been tapped on the chin with five fingers wrapped up in a leather boxing glove and propelled by the arm of an expert knows more about that particular sensation than one who has not, always provided he has the gift of expressing himself. I once inquired of a heavyweight prizefighter by the name of King Levinsky, in a radio interview, what it felt like to be hit on the chin by Joe Louis, the King having just acquired that experience with rather disastrous results. Levinsky considered the matter for a moment and then reported: "It don't feel like nuttin'," but added that for a long while afterwards he felt as though he were "in a transom."

I was always a child who touched things and I have always had a tremendous curiosity with regard to sensation. If I knew what playing a game felt like, particularly against or in the company of experts, I was better equipped to write about the playing of it and the problems of the men and women who took part in it. And so, at one time or another, I have tried them all, football, baseball, boxing, riding, shooting, swimming, squash, handball, fencing, driving, flying, both land and sea planes, rowing, canoeing, skiing, riding a bicycle, ice-skating, roller-skating, tennis, golf, archery, basketball, running, both the hundred-yard dash and the mile, the high jump and shot put, badminton, angling, deep-sea, stream-, and surf-casting, billiards and bowling, motorboating and wrestling, besides riding as a passenger with the fastest men on land and water and in the air, to see what it felt like. Most of them I dabbled in as a youngster going through school and college, and others, like piloting a plane, squash, fencing, and skiing, I took up after I was old enough to know better, purely to get the feeling of what they were like.

None of these things can I do well, but I never cared about becoming an expert, and besides, there wasn't time. But there is only one way to find out accurately human sensations in a ship two or three thousand feet up when the motor quits, and that is actually to experience that gone feeling at the pit of the stomach and the sharp tingling of the skin from head to foot, followed by a sudden amazing sharpness of vision, clear-sightedness, and coolness that you never knew you possessed as you find the question of life or death completely in your own hands. It is not the "you" that you know, but somebody else, a stranger, who noses the ship down, circles, fastens upon the one best spot to sit down, pushes or pulls buttons to try to get her started again, and finally drops her in, safe and sound. And it is only by such experience that you learn likewise of the sudden weakness that hits you right at the back of the knees after you have climbed out and started to walk around her and that comes close to knocking you flat as for the first time since the engine quit its soothing drone you think of destruction and sudden death.

Often my courage has failed me and I have funked completely, such as

the time I went up to the top of the thirty-foot Olympic diving-tower at
Jones Beach, Long Island, during the competitions, to see what it was like
to dive from that height, and wound up crawling away from the edge on
hands and knees, dizzy, scared, and a little sick, but with a wholesome respect for the boys and girls who hurled themselves through the air and down
through the tough skin of the water from that awful height. At other times
sheer ignorance of what I was getting into has led me into tight spots such
as the time I came down the Olympic ski run from the top of the Kreuzeck,
six thousand feet above Garmisch-Partenkirchen, after having been on skis
but once before in snow and for the rest had no more than a dozen lessons
on an indoor artificial slide in a New York department store. At one point
my legs, untrained, got so tired that I couldn't stem (brake) any more, and
I lost control and went full tilt and all out, down a three-foot twisting path
cut out of the side of the mountain, with a two-thousand-foot abyss on the
left and the mountain itself on the right. That was probably the most scared
I have ever been, and I scare fast and often. I remember giving myself up
for lost and wondering how long it would take them to retrieve my body
and whether I should be still alive. In the meantime the speed of the descent
was increasing. Somehow I was keeping my feet and negotiating turns, how
I will never know, until suddenly the narrow patch opened out into a wide,
steep stretch of slope with a rise at the other end, and *that* part of the journey
was over.

By some miracle I got to the bottom of the run uninjured, having made
most of the trip down the icy, perpendicular slopes on the flat of my back. It
was the thrill and scare of a lifetime, and to date no one has been able to persuade me to try a jump. I know when to stop. After all, I am entitled to rely
upon my imagination for something. But when it was all over and I found
myself still whole, it was also distinctly worth while to have learned what is
required of a ski runner in the breakneck *Abfahrt* or downhill race, or the
difficult *slalom*. Five days later, when I climbed laboriously (still on skis)
halfway up that Alp and watched the Olympic downhill racers hurtling
down the perilous, ice-covered, and nearly perpendicular *Steilhang,* I knew
that I was looking at a great group of athletes who, for one thing, did not
know the meaning of the word "fear." The slope was studded with small
pine trees and rocks, but half of the field gained precious seconds by hitting
that slope all out, with complete contempt for disaster rushing up at them
at a speed often better than sixty miles an hour. And when an unfortunate
Czech skidded off the course at the bottom of the slope and into a pile of
rope and got himself snarled up as helpless as a fly in a spider's web, it was
a story that I could write from the heart. I had spent ten minutes getting
myself untangled after a fall, *without* any rope to add to the difficulties. It
seems that I couldn't find where my left leg ended and one more ski than

I had originally donned seemed to be involved somehow. Only a person who has been on those fiendish runners knows the sensation.

It all began back in 1922 when I was a cub sports-writer and consumed with more curiosity than was good for my health. I had seen my first professional prizefights and wondered at the curious behavior of men under the stress of blows, the sudden checking and the beginning of a little fall forward after a hard punch, the glazing of the eyes and the loss of locomotor control, the strange actions of men on the canvas after a knockdown as they struggled to regain their senses and arise on legs that seemed to have turned into rubber. I had never been in any bad fist fights as a youngster, though I had taken a little physical punishment in football, but it was not enough to complete the picture. Could one think under those conditions?

I had been assigned to my first training-camp coverage, Dempsey's at Saratoga Springs, where he was preparing for his famous fight with Luis Firpo. For days I watched him sag a spar boy with what seemed to be no more than a light cuff on the neck, or pat his face with what looked like no more than a caressing stroke of his arm, and the fellow would come all apart at the seams and collapse in a useless heap, grinning vacuously or twitching strangely. My burning curiosity got the better of prudence and a certain reluctance to expose myself to physical pain. I asked Dempsey to permit me to box a round with him. I had never boxed before, but I was in good physical shape, having just completed a four-year stretch as a galley slave in the Columbia eight-oared shell.

When it was over and I escaped through the ropes, shaking, bleeding a little from the mouth, with rosin dust on my pants and a vicious throbbing in my head, I knew all that there was to know about being hit in the prize-ring. It seems that I had gone to an expert for tuition. I knew the sensation of being stalked and pursued by a relentless, truculent professional destroyer whose trade and business it was to injure men. I saw the quick flash of the brown forearm that precedes the stunning shock as a bony, leather-bound fist lands on cheek or mouth. I learned more (partly from photographs of the lesson, viewed afterwards, one of which shows me ducked under a vicious left hook, an act of which I never had the slightest recollection) about instinctive ducking and blocking than I could have in ten years of looking at prizefights, and I learned, too, that as the soldier never hears the bullet that kills him, so does the fighter rarely, if ever, see the punch that tumbles blackness over him like a mantle, with a tearing rip as though the roof of his skull were exploding, and robs him of his senses.

There was just that—a ripping in my head and then sudden blackness, and the next thing I knew, I was sitting on the canvas covering of the ring floor with my legs collapsed under me, grinning idiotically. How often since have I seen that same silly, goofy look on the faces of dropped fighters—and understood it. I held onto the floor with both hands, because the ring and the audience outside were making a complete clockwise revolution, came to a stop, and then went back again counter-clockwise. When I struggled to my feet, Jack Kearns, Dempsey's manager, was counting over me, but I neither saw nor heard him and was only conscious that I was in a ridiculous position and that the thing to do was to get up and try to fight back. The floor swayed and rocked beneath me like a fishing dory in an off-shore swell, and it was a welcome respite when Dempsey rushed into a clinch, held me up, and whispered into my ear: "Wrestle around a bit, son, until your head clears." And then it was that I learned what those little love-taps to the back of the neck and the short digs to the ribs can mean to the groggy pugilist more than half knocked out. It is a murderous game, and the fighter who can escape after having been felled by a lethal blow has my admiration. And there, too, I learned that there can be no sweeter sound than the bell that calls a halt to hostilities.

From that afternoon on, also, dated my antipathy for the spectator at prizefights who yells: "Come on, you bum, get up and fight! Oh, you big quitter! Yah yellow, yah yellow!" Yellow, eh? It is all a man can do to get up after being stunned by a blow, much less fight back. But they do it. And how a man is able to muster any further interest in a combat after being floored with a blow to the pit of the stomach will always remain to me a miracle of what the human animal is capable of under stress.

Further experiments were less painful, but equally illuminating. A couple of sets of tennis with Vinnie Richards taught me more about what is required of a top-flight tournament tennis-player than I could have got out of a dozen books or years of reporting tennis matches. It is one thing to sit in a press box and write caustically that Brown played uninspired tennis, or Black's court covering was faulty and that his frequent errors cost him the set. It is quite another to stand across the net at the back of a service court and try to get your racket on a service that is so fast that the ear can hardly detect the interval between the sound of the server's bat hitting the ball and the ball striking the court. Tournament tennis is a different game from week-end tennis. For one thing, in average tennis, after the first hard service has gone into the net or out, you breathe a sigh of relief, move up closer and wait for the cripple to come floating over. In big-time tennis second service is practically as hard as the first, with an additional twist on the ball.

It is impossible to judge or know anything about the speed of a forehand drive hit by a champion until you have had one fired at you, or, rather, away from you, and you have made an attempt to return it. It is then that you first realize that tennis is played more with the head than with the arms and the legs. The fastest player in the world cannot get to a drive to return it if he hasn't thought correctly, guessed its direction, and anticipated it by a fraction of a second.

There was golf with Bob Jones and Gene Sarazen and Tommy Armour, little Cruickshank and Johnny Farrell, and Diegel and other professionals; and experiments at trying to keep up in the water with Johnny Weissmuller, Helene Madison, and Eleanor Holm, attempts to catch football passes thrown by Benny Friedman. Nobody actually plays golf until he has acquired the technical perfection to be able to hit the ball accurately, high, low, hooked or faded and placed. And nobody knows what real golf is like until he has played around with a professional and seen him play, not the ball, but the course, the roll of the land, the hazards, the wind, and the texture of the greens and the fairways. It looks like showmanship when a top-flight golfer plucks a handful of grass and lets it flutter in the air, or abandons his drive to march two hundred yards down to the green and look over the situation. It isn't. It's golf. The average player never knows or cares whether he is putting with or across the grain of a green. The professional *always* knows. The same average player standing on the tee is concentrated on getting the ball somewhere on the fairway, two hundred yards out. The professional when preparing to drive is actually to all intents and purposes playing his *second* shot. He means to place his drive so as to open up the green for his approach. But you don't find that out until you have played around with them when they are relaxed and not competing, and listen to them talk and plan attacks on holes.

Major-league baseball is one of the most difficult and precise of all games, but you would never know it unless you went down on the field and got close to it and tried it yourself. For instance, the distance between pitcher and catcher is a matter of twenty paces, but it doesn't seem like enough when you don a catcher's mitt and try to hold a pitcher with the speed of Dizzy Dean or Dazzy Vance. Not even the sponge that catchers wear in the palm of the hand when working with fast-ball pitchers, and the bulky mitt are sufficient to rob the ball of shock and sting that lames your hand unless you know how to ride with the throw and kill some of its speed. The pitcher, standing on his little elevated mound, looms up enormously over you at that short distance, and when he ties himself into a coiled spring preparatory to letting fly, it requires all your self-control not to break and run for safety. And as for the things they can do with a baseball, those major-league pitchers . . . ! One way of finding out is to wander down on the field an hour or so before game-time when there is no pressure on them, pull on the catcher's glove, and try to hold them.

I still remember my complete surprise the first time I tried catching for a real curve-ball pitcher. He was a slim, spidery left-hander of the New York Yankees, many years ago, by the name of Herb Pennock. He called that he was going to throw a fast breaking curve and warned me to expect the ball at least two feet outside the plate. Then he wound up and let it go, and that ball came whistling right down the groove for the center of the plate.

A novice, I chose to believe what I saw and not what I heard, and prepared to catch it where it was headed for, a spot which of course it never reached, because just in front of the rubber, it swerved sharply to the right and passed nearly a yard from my glove. I never had a chance to catch it. That way, you learn about the mysterious drop, the ball that sails down the alley chest high but which you must be prepared to catch around your ankles because of the sudden dip it takes at the end of its passage as though someone were pulling it down with a string. Also you find out about the queer fade-away, the slow curve, the fast in- and out-shoots that seem to be timed almost as delicately as shrapnel, to burst, or rather break, just when they will do the most harm—namely, at the moment when the batter is swinging.

Facing a big-league pitcher with a bat on your shoulder and trying to hit his delivery is another vital experience in gaining an understanding of the game about which you are trying to write vividly. It is one thing to sit in the stands and scream at a batsman: "Oh, you bum!" for striking out in a pinch, and another to stand twenty yards from that big pitcher and try to make up your mind in a hundredth of a second whether to hit at the offering or not, where to swing and when, not to mention worrying about protecting yourself from the consequences of being struck by the ball that seems to be heading straight for your skull at an appalling rate of speed. Because, if you are a big-league player, you cannot very well afford to be gun-shy and duck away in panic from a ball that swerves in the last moment and breaks perfectly over the plate, while the umpire calls: "Strike!" and the fans jeer. Nor can you afford to take a crack on the temple from the ball. Men have died from that. It calls for undreamed-of niceties of nerve and judgment, but you don't find that out until you have stepped to the plate cold a few times during batting practice or in training quarters, with nothing at stake but the acquisition of experience, and see what a fine case of the jumping jitters you get. Later on, when you are writing your story, your imagination, backed by the experience, will be able to supply a picture of what the batter is going through as he stands at the plate in the closing innings of an important game, with two or three men on base, two out, and his team behind in the scoring, and fifty thousand people screaming at him.

The catching and holding of a forward pass for a winning touchdown on a cold, wet day always make a good yarn, but you might get an even better one out of it if you happen to know from experience about the elusive qualities of a hard, soggy, mud-slimed football rifled through the air, as well as something about the exquisite timing, speed, and courage it takes to catch it on a dead run, with two or three 190-pound men reaching for it at the same time or waiting to crash you as soon as your fingers touch it.

Any football coach during a light practice will let you go down the field and try to catch punts, the long, fifty-yard spirals and the tricky, tumbling end-over-enders. Unless you have had some previous experience, you won't hang on to one out of ten, besides knocking your fingers out of joint. But if you have any imagination, thereafter you will know that it calls for more than negligible nerve to judge and hold that ball and even plan to run with it, when there are two husky ends bearing down at full speed, preparing for a head-on tackle.

In 1932 I covered my first set of National Air Races, in Cleveland, and immediately decided that I had to learn how to fly to find out what that felt like. Riding as a passenger isn't flying. Being up there all alone at the controls of a ship is. And at the same time began a series of investigations into the "feel" of the mechanized sports to see what they were all about and the qualities of mentality, nerve, and physique they called for from their participants. These included a ride with Gar Wood in his latest and fastest speedboat, *Miss America X,* in which for the first time he pulled the throttle wide open on the Detroit River straightaway; a trip with the Indianapolis Speedway driver Cliff Bergere, around the famous brick raceway; and a flip with Lieutenant Al Williams, one time U. S. Schneider Cup race pilot.

I was scared with Wood, who drove me at 127 miles an hour, jounced, shaken, vibrated, choked with fumes from the exhausts, behind which I sat hanging on desperately to the throttle bar, which after a while got too hot to hold. I was on a plank between Wood and his mechanic, Johnson, and thought that my last moment had come. I was still more scared when Cliff Bergere hit 126 on the Indianapolis straightaways in the tiny racing car in which I was hopelessly wedged, and after the first couple of rounds quite resigned to die and convinced that I should. But I think the most scared I have ever been while moving fast was during a ride I took in the cab of a locomotive on the straight, level stretch between Fort Wayne, Indiana, and Chicago, where for a time we hit 90 miles per hour, which of course is no speed at all. But nobody who rides in the comfortable Pullman coaches has any idea of the didoes cut up by a locomotive in a hurry, or the thrill of pelting through a small town, all out and wide open, including the crossing of some thirty or forty frogs and switches, all of which must be set right. But that wasn't sport. That was just plain excitement.

I have never regretted these researches. Now that they are over, there isn't enough money to make me do them again. But they paid me dividends, I figured. During the great Thompson Speed Trophy race for land planes at Cleveland in 1935, Captain Roscoe Turner was some eight or nine miles in the lead in his big golden, low-wing, speed monoplane. Suddenly, coming into the straightaway in front of the grandstands, buzzing along at 280 miles an hour like an angry hornet, a streamer of thick, black smoke burst from the engine cowling and trailed back behind the ship. Turner pulled up immediately, using his forward speed to gain all the altitude possible, turned and got back to the edge of the field, still pouring out that evil black smoke. Then he cut his switch, dipped her nose down, landed with a bounce and a bump, and rolled up to the line in a perfect stop. The crowd gave him a great cheer as he climbed out of the oil-spattered machine, but it was a cheer of sympathy because he had lost the race after having been so far in the lead that had he continued he could not possibly have been overtaken.

There was that story, but there was a better one too. Only the pilots on the field, all of them white around the lips and wiping from their faces a sweat not due to the oppressive summer heat, knew that they were looking at a man who from that time on, to use their own expression, was living on borrowed time. It isn't often when a Thompson Trophy racer with a landing speed of around eighty to ninety miles an hour goes haywire in the air, that the pilot is able to climb out of the cockpit and walk away from his machine. From the time of that first burst of smoke until the wheels touched the ground and stayed there, he was a hundred-to-one shot to live. To the initiated, those dreadful moments were laden with suspense and horror. Inside that contraption was a human being who any moment might be burned to a horrible, twisted cinder, or smashed into the ground beyond all recognition, a human being who was cool, gallant, and fighting desperately. Every man and woman on the field who had ever been in trouble in the air was living those awful seconds with him in terror and suspense. I, too, was able to experience it. That is what makes getting the "feel" of things distinctly worth while.

David J. Bradley

Since his graduation from Dartmouth in 1938, David J. Bradley (1916-) has left his ski tracks over widely separated parts of the earth's surface: Norway, Switzerland, Austria, and Finland, and during the summers Australia, New Zealand, and Chile. For a year he attended Cambridge University and then, after covering the Russo-Finnish war as a reporter, returned to study medicine at Harvard. He received his M.D. in 1944. In the unassuming style of a diary or a personal letter, he writes of his experiences in Norway during the last winter before the storm of war broke over Europe. As we read his words in the light of after events they gain the poignance of all good things resigned but unforgotten.

EUROPEAN SAGA

I'M writing from the top of some peak in the middle of the Jotunheim, Norway, the home of Giants, the hideout of Loki. I don't know the name of this pinnacle, and I couldn't pronounce it if I did, but here I sit on a pair of good old hickory slabs, on whose scratched surface the snow has melted to glistening drops, like perspiration from some worthy exercise. And so it is: we have made many a mile of tracks during the past five days.

What time of the year is it? I don't know. The beginning of April I guess. It must be a new spring in Hanover, with the roads drying in the middle, and the dogs more playful, and the bells more lighthearted than before. What is all that spring doing without me? I can almost hear the duck boards splashing on the campus, the paddles on the river, and the ski boots sloshing through the mud of the Sherburn Trail.

But here it is still mid-winter. The powder snow takes no notice of the sun in its horizontal path in the south—though our faces do. This Jotunheim is a lot like Tuckerman and the cone of Washington, only on a bigger scale and in unlimited variety. It is all so good that had I not already had five days of it I should never be stopping here to write this. I don't wonder they have to have a midnight sun in Norway. Twenty-four hours of daylight would not be too much.

But let me try to make you a sketch: I am sitting a little back from the eaves of a cornice; at my back is a precipice of black rock, vertical to a pocket glacier below—oh, nothing much, perhaps eight hundred feet down. In front of me the snow falls away in a smooth white slope which flattens out imperceptibly into an enormous glacier. From here it all looks as even as a well-made bed. Between my boots I can see a tiny ring of people—the rest of the expedition—camped for lunch on the glacier. Half a mile down; half a minute away. I think if I kicked loose a big snow ball it would roll into the middle of them.

They are sitting on their skis or packs, eating bread and goat cheese and chocolate. I can hear them laughing. Someone is waxing his skis; another seems to be smearing his face with cream—which reminds me that I must do the same. Five days on these snowfields have left glorious tan all honeycombed with blisters. A real breeze would blow away my complexion like large sheets of newspaper.

But nothing stirs—not a cloud, not a cool impulse in the air. I have seen no ptarmigan or ermine today; not even an eagle.

They are unpretentious, these mountains: not all precipice and cataracts of ice, like the Alps. Once they may have been, but the ice age came, covering all but the highest peaks, grinding off the alpine fierceness into rounding contours and great open valleys. What did remain above the ice was chipped and chiselled into all sorts of strange, angular formations. The result is the finest country for ski mountaineering I know, unspoiled by funiculars and ski schools, belonging just now wholly to us—a small dark ring in the middle of some glacier.

They look pretty insignificant down there—our expedition—surrounded on all sides to the very horizon by snow and rock, but they are the only sign of life in the Jotunheim. Who are they? A motley group: seven English boys, three English girls, a Scotch lass, three Norskis, a Swede, a Swiss, a Czech, a Canadian, and myself—a Dartmouth man. Nearly all the important countries in the world. Our leader is a husky sun-faced Norwegian of thirty, game to climb anything, game to schuss anything, game to drink anything. They say that Otto is a big man in the shipping business when he is in Oslo, but out here in the mountains he is a far bigger man, the last of the descendants of Hemming, great skier among the Gods of Asgard.

From the camp down there I can follow our tracks as they meander in a careless happy way across the glacier. There on the other side is the overhanging cornice where we spent an hour getting down. Using our skis as axes we cut through the cornice at its lowest point, and then, placing a pair across the notch as a horizontal bar, we could drop a matter of some fifteen feet to the snowfield below.

Fortunately in this well-ordered country they have no avalanches. Slopes, which, anywhere else, an alpine goat would not dare to bleat at, here can be skied down in leisurely turns. I cannot say why, perhaps it is because the sun is so far in the south. At any rate nothing ever seems to— Hold on! What's that hissing? By Jove, there is a little snow slide on a peak across the way. Just a surface slip, pried loose by the warm afternoon sun. It is stopping already, before it reaches the glacier. That is the first avalanche I have seen—or rather the second.

The first happened on the roof of our cabin last night, when the snow was no longer able to stand the way we were singing "Alouette." Noldi Kaech, the Swiss boy, the philosopher who, after a winter in America, decided that the earth was composed of three essential elements: snow, blondes and apple pie à la mode, well, this same Noldi led us in an "Alouette" which would have shamed the Don Cossack chorus.

That was an especially good evening. We sat around the great stone fireplace, which stood, as they all do, a little out from the corner to allow the circulation of air and the drying of wood, and there we were until midnight, in spite of the miles behind and the miles to come, singing. "Old Black Joe" and "Suwanee River" have become very popular, and ever since I initiated the chorus to "I'm Oola ski yumper from Norvay," and "Ja ja vi skal ha, lutefisk og lefse," these two songs have become almost the national anthem.

Beyond the valley where we spent last night I can just make out the general route we took through the mountains—here and there a peak we climbed or a glacier we slid down; a valley where we stayed overnight— here the place where we nearly broke up a stove during a free for all wrestling match; there the night we skied under the northern lights.

And finally, on the very sky-line is the gleaming blade of Mt. Fanaroken. Our second night was spent in a little cabin at the top. Five hours of climbing in an "eight foot blizzard" of blowing particles of ice, and our last steps lit by a flaming sunset. The cabin was scarcely more than a chimneyed drift; and supper a battle of cave men for bread, cheese, and frozen sardines. It was here that our party was augmented by one Erich—two weeks ago he was a Czech. Now he is a *Jude*.

Somehow the minutes seem to get away from us. There is an eagle now, swinging in slow arcs above the glacier, and the camp below is getting under way again. Time to be tightening my boots. I can pick out most of our route: first a climb to a low col, and then down over another glacier—six kilometers, all in one piece!—down to the last valley, grimming already with shadow. Tomorrow we must follow the course of a rebellious stream down to spring, to the mud and meadow-larks of spring.

Old skis, do you remember the many battering races we had in New England, Sun Valley, Switzerland?—they were our adolescent passions. But "this is the end for which we twain are met"—this is the honeymoon of a life of ski mountaineering together, and my feet are impatient for the embrace of the Kandahar. . . .

✦

Bad weather! Some fifty of us standing among the rocks at Keilhaustopp waiting for the start of the Galdhopiggen race. Good Friday—snowing just enough to obliterate the great glaciated valley below us. Oh, it will ever be so as long as skiers insist upon matching madness.

Somewhere down there in that amorphous grey the *Damen* were already racing. Laila Schou Nielsen had taken a bad fall and the race belonged to the Swedish champion, May Nilsson of the auburn hair.

The *Damen* started from Skarret, a narrow gap where the gentler snow fields above pitch off suddenly into the valley proper. It was a mile and a quarter from Keilhaustopp—a mile and a half of two beautifully graded schusses. As I stood on the rocks, chewing chocolate, I frequently and involuntarily recalled a vivid picture of Geoffery and Rolly on the day before rattling down over that field, passing me with the sound of a couple of racing cars, and seeming to take off at Skarret in one long jump for the bottom of the valley. That would be all invisible during the race. Geoffery was down at the finish now, reconciled by the weather and by a French Mademoiselle to his sprained ankle.

Who were we at Keilhaustopp? There was Hans Hansson, the defending champion. He stood with his Swedish teammates discussing some difficulty of the course. I had seen him in action only once—on a clear day, when he was training over the section from Skarret down to Blue Ice. There the course, controlled by a number of flags, weaves in and out between islands of rocks. Skiing here is the nearest thing to flying I know, nearer even than jumping, for a jump is an instantaneous experience, and presumably in a straight line. But here the snow is as soft as air underfoot, and one wheels on the shoulders and skims through the gullies as easily as an eagle rides on the air currents above a cliff. Hansson had run this section like an army engineer planning how to straighten out the corners.

Then there were three *enfants de la Patrie:* Agnel paraffining his skis; Besson, fifteen years old, relacing his boots; and the world champion James Couttet peeling an orange and staring vacantly out over that invisible valley. Perhaps he was quizzing himself, as most of us were, on the last half mile plunge from Blue Ice down: the V-shaped gully lined with soft snow where three people had already twisted their legs; the four controls; the narrow trail through the brush—that was our path to the finish.

There were many others, too. Olaf Raabe was standing apart, exhaling smoke and bits of yodelling simultaneously. He felt certain of being in the first five, but did not know that he would beat our Agnel by one tenth of a second for fourth place. And Olaf's buddy, Nils Eie—a hard fall, like a tight wire stretched across his path, was waiting for him just before the finish. And Bob Ferguson—an hour later he was on a toboggan, wondering if his ankle were broken. And Mike Angus—he did not know that a sprained knee and a slight concussion were impending. No, he was asking if anyone had some paraffin.

Soon Einer Bergsland, the popular dictator of the Galdhopirennet, set off down the groove to clear the course. He dissolved quickly in the cloud—in four minutes he would be warning the timers three thousand feet below.

12:29! "Fem . . . fir . . . tre . . . to . . . en . . . GO! No. 2, No. 3, get ready please." No. 4 was Noldi Kaech.

"Two bottles," I warned him. He grinned.

"Well, Otto wants to come in the bet too. . . ."

"Make it three, then."

". . . And he suggested champagne, so I said that was Ho Kay. I like champagne better, you know."

I have given this rather full account of the start of the Galdhopiggen downhill race because once started I saw nothing at all of the course. True, I had an impression of moving rapidly through space, and there was a disturbing jarring sensation in the feet, but only the control flags, the familiar rocks, and an occasional shouting figure, which came and went in an instant, guided my skis to the valley floor.

And there was Noldi chewing on a cigarette.

"Salut," he said, "how did it go?"

"Oh, not so bad—pretty lucky."

"But why did you fall just up there? We could see it from here."

"Ha! The ice in that gully piped me out the bottom like water out of a fire hose. And you?"

"Oooh, I stemmed the whole thing down—but halt! Here comes Couttet!"

Sure enough. Crouching low and going very fast, Couttet cleared Blue Ice. We could just see him on the sky-line. He disappeared for many seconds in the gully—then out, through the controls, well done, into the brush. There was a great pot-hole next! He sprang from the rim, landing in a christie, steady as a cat, and flashed down the last slope to the finish.

Click! A dozen private stop watches started. Hansson next! Couttet had made 3 min. 8 sec., four seconds faster than his teammate Besson. The hands of the watches fairly crawled. Ten seconds. An average speed of 45 mph. All eyes were on the sky-line. Twenty seconds. The French trainer sighed heavily. Twenty-five. The Swedes were getting anxious. Thirty! Where was Hansson? Then a shout from Blue Ice, and we saw Hansson where we had just seen Couttet, coming like a meteor. Out of sight in the gully. Forty. Into the controls. No hesitation; no slip yet. Fifty. In the brush. *Fifty!* Through the brush. FIFTY! The same jump into the pot-hole. Were the watches frozen? The Frenchman had not breathed since Hansson appeared, and with a great gasp he saw the second hand speed across the finish line two seconds ahead of the Swede.

There was another little drama, an anticlimax, which few people knew about. It concerned only three of us. Noldi and I finished tenth and ninth, two seconds apart, but Otto, wild Otto, was sixth.

The duelling, however, was only half done. The slalom remained, and two seconds in a hundred and ninety is not much of an advantage, particularly when the long slalom course was made more hazardous by patches of ice and soft snow. Nevertheless Couttet and Hansson finished their first runs in identical times—and Noldi was $^2/_{10}$ of a second up on the next bottle of champagne.

Then in the second run the Swedish champion went for the combined in earnest. That polished style wiped away four seconds. It was Couttet's turn to race the second hand. The championship depended utterly on this last run.

There was something more than *sang-froid* in the way he looked down over the forest of flags and waited for the signal: "Clar . . . GO!" And Couttet went—like a sparrow through a cane brake—but once he tripped! nearly fell, recovering on his pole. It was enough. Hansson won the slalom and Couttet barely salvaged the combined. Norway had to be content with Raabe's third, and console itself with Laila's triumph in the ladies' slalom.

As for me—well, the last flush was set in a 40° slope, and I only managed to get at it after stalking it from below. Then Noldi came, and I could hear the popping of champagne corks every time he made a gate. But where I fell he also fell and hurt his ankle so that Otto won again.

The Galdhopirennet closed with the last run of Second Lieutenant Peter Wrenford. For the first time I realized what is meant by the old saying that: "the army moves on its stomach." As he chinned himself through the last flush he was heard to say those now immortal words: "Well, I give it bloody up!"

The last supper at Galdhopiggen was a riot. We sang (not entirely together; indeed, frequently not even the same song) during the courses and shouted for more food in between. Everyone wanted to make a speech; some were not satisfied with two or three speeches. One of the French girls gave a charming oration in what was alleged to be Norwegian, and then Einer Bergsland retaliated in the French of some unknown Chinese dialect. Most memorable of all, though, were a few words from Noldi. He began with: "Well, since, unlike Mademoiselle, I do not speak such good Norwegian, I must try to say what I want to say, like Einer, in English . . . (Cries of "No, no, that was French!" from Einer's table, and "Hear, hear!" from the British Isles.) . . . Some of you might wonder that I don't speak in German, but I tell you that I speak 'Schweitzer Deutsch,' and that is quite another thing. . . ." It was five minutes before the echoes permitted him to continue. He finished by saying: "So, I lift my glass to the friendship which is always between skiers when they come together in the mountains, no matter where they come from, and of which we have all found so much here at Galdhopiggen."

Two days later we were in Oslo. We learned for the first time that Italy had invaded Albania three days before, on Good Friday, while we were climbing to Keilhaustopp in the shadow of an approaching snow storm.

That evening our ship sailed for England. And when the vessel began to glide away from the wharf, and more and more of the twilight mingled with the darker eddies of the Oslofjord, we could still hear "Ja, ja, vi skal ha," and "I'm Oola, ski yumper from Norvay. . . ."

Geoffrey Winthrop Young

*Geoffrey Winthrop Young (1876-   ) was born in London, educated
at Cambridge University, traveled widely, and had a distinguished career
as commander of Friends' Ambulance Units in France and Italy during
World War I. But the passion of his life since the age of 15 has been
mountaineering. Undaunted by his years he is still, as President of the
Alpine Club, preaching the sanative discipline of the mountains and the
moral values of the outdoor life. "The motive of my life, if any," he
writes, "has been to attempt to recover something of the Greek balance
between the activity of the body and of the mind; to pursue adventurous
living, open-air discipline, natural human intercourse; and to attempt to
express the rhythms achieved in movement or perceived in nature by
means of the rhythm of words." The latter purpose is realized in his*
Mountain Craft, On High Hills, *and several volumes of verse. "Mountain Speed" is remarkable both for its ingenious technique and for its
stirring athleticism.*

MOUNTAIN SPEED

Oh, the winter joy of the flying of feet over snow-clad hill,
the rush and the snow-leap vying with the flight of our will;
the hiss of our ski, and the sighing of speed that frost cannot still!

The race of the strong thrust urging the froth of the turn,
the pace of the snow-blast purging with clean heart-burn,
the face of the valley up-surging to meet our sweep of return!

Oh, the sunshine glory of lying a-dream on the steep,
above restless forests defying their burden of sleep,
with the whisper of white worlds dying, lulling our hearts from the deep!

As the swoop of the swift keen-shrilling in twilight of May,
as the stoop of the hawk to the killing from visionless gray,
as the plunge of the rainbow filling the haggard spaces of day—

Like the pouring of glacier on ocean, in fiords of the sea,
like the flood of a people's devotion, in arms to be free,
is our soaring of passionate motion o'er mountains, the swirl of our ski!

Though the way be uphill and long winding, with irksome sleet,
and a slabbery snow-broth binding our lift and beat,

there'll be day o'er the pass, and the blinding of wind, and all heaven in
   our feet!

Spurn the crest fierce-driven from falling fountain of snow;
Earn the rest that is given to all whom the mountains know;
Learn the best of all living from height, and the glory of speed, and the
   glow!

V. AMERICAN HERITAGE

SO far we have been looking at the individual life in its single growth and its more intimate relationships. To these we have added some note of special satisfactions to be found in work, play, the arts. Now we must place the individual against a larger background than that of home and community. As a citizen, he plays his part in the world of our time, especially the United States.

. . . Especially the United States. How many Americans were really aware of their country as an object of devotion before that Sunday afternoon when they listened, in pain and horror, to the story of Pearl Harbor? In the swift crescendo of war their country became their dearest concern, to understand, to justify, to defend at any cost.

The motorized march of events has thrust upon the United States a sudden leadership in world affairs and in world thought. Only yesterday, "Look homeward, America!" meant an incitement to develop our own cultural resources. Today it becomes a command which touches every concern of national life. No longer can we look to Europe for guidance, cultural, political, economic, or social. The sources from which we came are either destroyed or forever changed. From now on we must blaze our own trail.

But the trail goes forward under Western skies of promise. Whatever the fate of the older countries, we are still at the beginning of American history. It is our privilege to write a chapter of that history, a chapter big with events, a chapter of tension and suspense. Are we prepared—not only in arms but in ideas—to keep its pages fresh and true? Do we know the faiths for which men die? Or are we tragic marchers in the dark, gropers in a black-out of the understanding?

These pages attempt to bring together some of our faiths. We must be prepared to examine all the threads of our tangled present and patiently tie them into the fabric of the future. Our inquiry must include the failures as well as the triumphs of democracy: indeed we realize that the world has come to its present pass because we were so slow in seeing clearly the forces that were eating away our civilization. Only by bringing these forces, too, into the light can we expect to overcome them and so make the world again a place where men and women gladly live.

We begin with familiar things, the well-loved features of these States. This is the back-drop against which the action will be played. It is a noble setting, regarded merely in geographical terms. In its vastness and its variety, its power and its beauty, it is the most imposing setting in history. From the green hills of New England to the great gorge of the Columbia, across the infinite reach of the prairies and down the greatest river in the world, from the high snows of the Rockies to the warm sands of the Gulf, it is a fit background for a diverse and dynamic people. The United States is scenery, first of all: but how much can be implied in scenery, how it can stir the heart with pride, how it can itself be a factor in the currents of American history!

For the American Scene is inseparable from the American Heritage: the men and women in the covered wagons and the mountains marching like dim giants across the edge of the grasslands; the battlefield of Gettysburg and Lincoln speaking; the farmsteads of the colonists and the dust of forgotten roads. Scenery and history melt into one, and we call it love of country, "roots in the region." Our roots are the roots of the first settlers and they strike deep into this land—how deep some of us are just beginning to understand.

The American Heritage is something more than words. We gain little by talking of the virtues of dead pioneers however heroic. We have a job to do; we are pioneers in our own right. We have to generate out of ourselves the conviction, the courage, and the devotion which will build a better America in a better world. Truly it is a task for the strong.

But we must be certain of our way at home if we hope to give effective leadership abroad. Out of the self-criticism which is a by-product of the war we have come face to face with some of the maladjustments of our society. What of our industrial system? Are we living up to the sort of individualism which accords every citizen an equal chance? or are we interpreting individualism as merely freedom for one's self and one's class to exploit other human beings? Problems of race, which exist even in America, are the most conspicuous examples of the disparity between our humanistic ideals and their working out. Here there is little to quicken our pride in being Americans. The denial of the dignity of the individual is a rejection of fundamental democracy. But if there is cause for misgiving in our fumbling of social issues, there is the promise of moral adventure in the solving of them. And solved they must be, whatever the present diversion of our powers to the overmastering necessities of war. Ours will be a hollow victory over fascism abroad if we allow our exploited groups to lose confidence in democracy and so take the fatal short cut of fascism at home. Now, as never before in this country, we must dedicate ourselves to the "long labor of liberty."

Archibald MacLeish

Ever since Archibald MacLeish, exploring a Paris library, came upon the record of Spanish conquest in the New World from which grew his Conquistador, *his poetry has been deeply conscious of the westward movement of man across the earth: "the journey westward from the sea into the unknown and dangerous country beyond which lies the rich and lovely city for which men hope."*

THE WESTERN SKY

Stand stand against the rising night
O freedom's land, O freedom's air:
Stand steep and keep the fading light
That eastward darkens everywhere.

Hold hold the golden light and lift
Hill after hill-top, one by one—
Lift up America O lift
Green freedom to the evening sun.

Lift up your hills till conquered men
Look westward to their blazing height:
Lift freedom till its fire again
Kindles the countries of the night.

Be proud America to bear
The endless labor of the free—
To strike for freedom everywhere
And everywhere bear liberty.

Lift up O land O land lift clear
The lovely signal of your skies.
If freedom darkens eastward here
Here on the west let freedom rise.

Thomas Wolfe

Thomas Wolfe (1900-1938) was born in Asheville, North Carolina. He graduated from the University of North Carolina, received the degree of A.M. at Harvard, and studied abroad as a Guggenheim Fellow. For six years he taught English at Washington Square College, New York University. His first book, Look Homeward, Angel, *is an uninhibited picture of his native city and his own family, a pattern which was to repeat itself in subsequent novels.* Of Time and the River, *most widely discussed of his works, is a vast and undisciplined flood of words, prodigious in its energy, Whitmanesque in its lyric intensity, romantic in its transformation of the commonplace. The adjective most often applied to Wolfe was "unpredictable"; it was still applicable to his eventual rank when he died at thirty-eight. In the lusty vitality and headlong drive of the following passage, Thomas Wolfe and his United States are fused in a single tremendous assertion.*

AMERICAN LANDSCAPE

AMERICA has a thousand lights and weathers and we walk the streets, we walk the streets forever, we walk the streets of life alone.

It is the place of the howling winds, the hurrying of the leaves in old October, the hard clean falling to the earth of acorns. The place of the storm-tossed moaning of the wintry mountainside, where the young men cry out in their throats and feel the savage vigor, the rude strong energies; the place also where the trains cross rivers.

It is a fabulous country, the only fabulous country; it is the one place where miracles not only happen, but where they happen all the time.

It is the place of exultancy and strong joy, the place of the darkened brooding air, the smell of snow; it is the place of all the fierce, the bitten colors in October, when all of the wild, sweet woods flame up; it is also the place of the cider press and the last brown oozings of the York Imperials. . . .

It is the place where great boats are baying at the harbor's mouth, where great ships are putting out to sea; it is the place where great boats are blowing in the gulf of night, and where the river, the dark and secret river, full of strange time, is forever flowing by us to the sea. . . .

It is the place of autumnal moons hung low and orange at the frosty edges of the pines; it is the place of frost and silence; of the clean dry shocks and the opulence of enormous pumpkins that yellow on hard clotted earth; it is the place of the stir and feathery stumble of the hens upon their roost, the frosty, broken barking of the dogs, the great barn-shapes and solid shadows in the running sweep of the moon-whited countryside, the wailing whistle of the fast express. It is the place of flares and steamings on the tracks, and the swing and bob and tottering dance of lanterns in the yards; it is the place of dings and knellings and the sudden glare of mighty engines over sleeping faces in the night; it is the place of the terrific web and spread and smouldering, the distant glare of Philadelphia and the solid rumble of the sleepers; it is also the place where the Transcontinental Limited is stroking eighty miles an hour across the continent and the small dark towns whip by like bullets, and there is only the fanlike stroke of the secret, immense and lonely earth again. . . .

It is the place of the wild and exultant winter's morning and the wind, with the powdery snow, that has been howling all night long; it is the place of solitude and the branches of the spruce and hemlock piled with snow; it is the place where the Fall River boats are tethered to the wharf, and the wild gray snow of furious, secret, and storm-whited morning whips across them. It is the place of the lodge by the frozen lake and the sweet breath and amorous flesh of sinful woman; it is the place of the tragic and lonely beauty of New England; it is the place of the red barn and the sound of the stabled hooves and of bright tatters of old circus posters; it is the place of the immense and pungent smell of breakfast, the country sausages and the ham and eggs, the smoking wheat cakes and the fragrant coffee, and of lonely hunters in the frosty thickets who whistle to their lop-eared hounds. . . .

It is the place of the crack athletes and of the runners who limber up in March; it is the place of the ten-second men and the great jumpers and vaulters; it is the place where spring comes, and the young birch trees have white and tender barks, of the thaw of the earth, and the feathery smoke of the trees; it is the place of the burst of grass and bud, the wild and sudden tenderness of the wilderness, and of the crews out on the river and the coaches coming down behind them in the motor-boats, the surges rolling out behind when they are gone with heavy sudden wash. . . .

It is the place where they like to win always, and boast about their victories; it is the place of quick money and sudden loss; it is the place of the mile-long freights with their strong, solid, clanking, heavy loneliness at night, and of the silent freight of cars that curve away among raw piney desolations with their promise of new lands and unknown distances—the huge attentive gape of emptiness. It is the place where the bums come singly from the woods at sunset, the huge stillness of the water-tower, the fading light, the rails, secret and alive, and trembling with the oncoming train; it is the place of the great tramps, Oklahoma Red, Fargo Pete, and the Jersey Dutchman, who grab fast rattlers for the Western shore; it is the place of old blown bums who come up in October skirls of dust and wind and crumpled newspapers and beg, with canned heat on their breaths: "Help Old McGuire: McGuire's a good guy, kid. You're not so tough, kid: McGuire's your pal, kid: How about McGuire, McGuire—?"

. . . It is the place of the immense and lonely earth, the place of fat ears and abundance where they grow cotton, corn, and wheat, the wine-red apples of October, and the good tobacco. . . .

It is the place where you come up through Virginia on the great trains in the night-time, and rumble slowly across the wide Potomac and see the morning sunlight on the nation's dome at Washington, and where the fat man shaving in the Pullman washroom grunts, "What's this? What's this we're coming to—Washington?"—And the thin man glancing out the window says, "Yep, this is Washington. That's what it is, all right. You gettin' off here?"—And where the fat man grunts, "Who—me? Naw—I'm goin' on to Baltimore." It is the place where you get off at Baltimore and find your brother waiting. . . .

It is the place of the fast approach, the hot blind smoky passage, the tragic lonely beauty of New England, and the web of Boston; the place of the mighty station there, and engines passive as great cats, the straight dense plumes of engine smoke, the acrid and exciting smell of trains and stations, and of the man-swarm passing ever in its million-footed weft, the smell of the sea in harbors and the thought of voyages—and the place of the goat-cry, the strong joy of our youth, the magic city, when we knew the most fortunate life on earth would certainly be ours, that we were twenty and could never die.

And always America is the place of the deathless and enraptured moments, the eye that looked, the mouth that smiled and vanished, and the word; the stone, the leaf, the door we never found and never have forgotten. And these are the things that we remember of America, for we have known all her thousand lights and weathers, and we walk the streets, we walk the streets forever, we walk the streets of life alone.

Editors of "Fortune"

To analyze and summarize the complex pattern—topographic, economic, and social—of these United States would seem to require a good-sized volume: the editors of Fortune *have achieved this task within the limits of a single article. Starting from the contradictions in the American character, they turn to the single undoubted fact about America—its integration. They then break down their subject into seven economic "shadow nations," only to show that the intertwining interests of the several regions re-emphasize their essential oneness. Here is a new kind of geography, in which information is imaginatively vitalized. In the organization of material, the use of data, and the definiteness of conclusions, the article may well stand as a model research paper. Since 1940, when this article was written, war has altered some details, but the basic features of American life as here described are unchanged.*

THE U. S. A.

LESS by definition than by achievement, the United States is the greatest nation on earth. Everybody knows it, everybody believes it, everybody says it—usually without quite knowing why. It isn't the greatest nation in size. Its continental area of 3,026,789 square miles is less than half the size of the Soviet Union, and smaller than Canada or Brazil. It is almost once and a half the size of Europe without the Soviet Union, but with all possessions it occupies only 7 per cent of the total land area of the world, whereas the British Empire sprawls across a third of the globe, Soviet Russia's chunk equals 14 per cent, and the French reservation another 8 per cent. The U. S. isn't the greatest nation by nose count. Its population of 130,085,000 is small compared to 450,000,000 Chinese, 353,000,000 Indians, and 170,000,000 Russians. Per square mile it has only forty-three inhabitants, and is more sparsely settled than any of the major nations with the exception of Soviet Russia; in contrast the 742 persons per square mile in England seems almost fantastic. Nor is the U. S. by any means the fastest-growing nation. Its birth rate has declined from 23.7 per thousand in 1920 to 17.9 per thousand estimated for 1938, and in a couple of decades at this rate persons of fifty or over will constitute the dominant population bloc.

In spite of an unparalleled industrial civilization, the U. S. is not predominantly a manufacturing nation. Manufacturing accounts for less than a fifth of the country's total realized income, whereas in the United Kingdom and Japan over 30 per cent of national income is derived from factory trades; in Sweden 40 per cent. The U. S. has built the world's most fabulous cities, but it is not the most urbanized nation, even though the population of citified New York exceeds that of either Canada or Argentina, and though Pennsylvania has more inhabitants than Belgium or Hungary, citified Illinois more than Finland and Denmark together. But less than 30 per cent of U. S. citizens live in big cities. In England nearly 45 per cent of the people dwell in cities of 100,000 or more, and in Germany over 30 per cent. The U. S. is still predominantly small-town and rural; not metropolitan.

Commonly presumed to be wealthier in natural resources than any other nation, the U. S. in some respects is probably equaled and in others exceeded by the British Empire and the Soviet Union, and its reserves may someday be equaled by those awaiting exploitation or discovery in South Africa, South America, and the hinterland of Asia. Furthermore, the U. S. has certain vital deficiencies. It consumes more than half the world's rubber crop, grows none. It drinks half the world's coffee, and again grows none. It uses three-fourths of the world's raw silk without cultivating any silkworms to speak of. It brings in (mainly from Argentina) 15 per cent of its hides. Its production of sugar, taken with that supplied by U. S. island possessions, is about 12 per cent of the world's total, but it consumes 20 per cent, and that 8 per cent difference amounts to 2,770,000 tons. It has virtually no tin, or platinum, or chromite, or antimony; precious little manganese, quicksilver, tungsten, and nickel. Granted that the superb U. S. technology could stop some of these gaps if war or other *force majeure* cut off imports, the fact remains that in a number of categories the U. S. is far from being independent of the outside world.

But in spite of all lacks and unfavorable comparisons the U. S. *is* the greatest nation on earth. It might be great simply on account of its 3,026,789 square miles. It might again be great on account of its 130,085,000 people. It might be great because of its tremendous agriculture. It might be great because of its vast industrialization. It might be great on account of basic mineral and energy resources. It might have greatness of a sort because of its political system. But its actual greatness rests not on these single assets, but on their combination. The greatness of the U. S. is the sum of a vast land area; a great, resourceful population of diverse origins and talents; a great agriculture of such richness that it embarrasses; a universal industry of cosmic dimensions; an enormous treasury of resources; a form of government that has stimulated the optimum development of all the components of the economy. It is the compounding of all these sources of greatness that makes the U. S. great.

And it is this compounding that has resulted in the creation of an American superman. For in a civilization based on energy and productivity the meaning and the effectiveness of every U. S. citizen are magnified and extended. Each has the largest per capita share of the world's coal and corn and iron ore and wheat and electricity and automobiles and bathtubs and radios and telephones and machines in general. It is as a nation of industrialized individuals who are in effect supermen that the U. S. has attained wealth, productivity, and strength far beyond comparison with any other nation, or, for that matter, most combinations of nations.

Just as the greatness of the U. S. is a source of wonder and envy to the rest of the world, so the character of the U. S. people has always been a tantalizing enigma. The English are "great colonizers" and "shopkeepers." The French are "a gay nation, fond of light wines and dancing." The Russians invariably are "mad," the Orientals "inscrutable," the Germans "thorough," the Italians "sentimental." Doubtless these epithets are highly inaccurate, but no handle has ever been fitted to the American character, and in spite of numerous attempts the psychoanalysis of the race is yet to be made. The world's statesmen have spent a century and a half trying to understand Americans, and countless European commentators have swarmed across the U. S. The commentators have gone everywhere, seen everything, talked with everyone, taken mountains of notes, and gone home to write searching books about the U. S., which invariably turn out to be no more than delightful commentaries on the commentators. The U. S. has been called "Uncle Shylock," the "Land of Greed," the "Land of Dollar Grabbers," but let a famine develop in Asia or a war break out in Africa or an earthquake level a city in South America and at once Americans rush to the rescue with fleets of supplies, or money, or ambulances, or anything else that would come in handy.

The U. S. is the world's greatest democracy, but its fundamental law was written mainly by aristocrats and conservatives who feared the people. The U. S. is the world's most tireless advocate of the principles of freedom, equality, tolerance, and due process of law. Yet it is peculiarly susceptible to wholly undemocratic outbursts of mob violence resulting in lynchings, repression, and vigilantism; and every so often it produces a Ku Klux Klan or a Black Legion, and it supports a fair share of indigenous fascist movements. The U. S. is a law-abiding nation, which recorded 1,400,000 major crimes in 1937 and has a hard time finding jail space to house the criminals. It has a divine faith in the power of legislation. It spends more money on making laws and governing itself than any other country, outside of the U.S.S.R., and it takes a peculiar satisfaction in circumventing or ignoring its own laws. The U. S. is the arch-enemy of injustice throughout the world, and sounds off at frequent intervals on the iniquities of foreign governments, foreign philosophies, and foreign methods based on persecution, imperialism, and force; yet it tolerates the most brutal exploitation of certain classes of its own people and shrugs nonchalantly at the organized persecution of unpopular characters. So close to the frontier that many a living man has filed notches in his gun, the U. S. has canonized its most colorful banditti—Jesse James and Billy the Kid are typical heroes—and exhibits a thinly disguised admiration for its Dillingers and Baby Face Nelsons.

The U. S. has over 30,000,000 students enrolled in schools and colleges. But over 4 per cent of the population is illiterate, a rate comparing unfavorably with the averages of most European countries. The U. S. is a religious nation, with 64,000,000 churchgoers who occasionally visit 248,000 churches to worship and play bingo. It is a nation of home and family lovers, and its divorce rate of sixteen per hundred marriages is next to the highest in the world.

INTEGRATION OF A UNIVERSE

But if Americans are altogether too paradoxical for any compact description, at least they can be measured in terms of their major achievement. That achievement has been the integration within the boundaries of a single, unified nation of the infinite variety of racial, cultural, economic, and geographic components of the U. S. scene.

In the beginning there were pioneers who created pioneer colonies based on the pioneer ideal of self-sufficiency. Although they achieved a loose political unity when they were leagued under the Articles of Confederation, for all practical purposes they remained separate nations. Even under the Constitution the states placed their individual interests above the national interest, and this selfishness—becoming sectional—led to the Civil War. But a nation had been created, the frontier was pushed westward, and industry became a strong integrating force. A northern factory might employ southern labor and sell to the West; and the transcontinental railroads helped bind the nation together with their long steel tracks. For industry was essentially national rather than sectional or regional. It prospered in the expanding free-trade area.

See the sweep, the magnitude of the achievement. On the map this gigantic slab of earth confronts the mind, the eye, and the imagination like a cake too big to eat. There is a thumb thrust toward the warm Caribbean, and here a fist reaching for icebergs in the North Atlantic. Here is the gentle loveliness of velvet lawns and flaming autumn hillsides in New England, and here the parched, harsh desolation of the prairies on a snowless day in winter. Here is East Texas as flat as a frozen lake, and here the high Sierras with their snowy crests floating like swans in the tall blue sky. Here is the Boston Common calf-deep in mud on a dim November afternoon, and here on the same afternoon is a black-shadowed date grove in Phoenix under a sun that burns like mustard plaster, in air so dry it stings. Here is the moss-hung lushness of palms tossing in the moonlight on the Louisiana shore, and here the austere march of evergreens up the western slopes of the Cascades.

Here is New York at night, hell-red with neon and fogged by the factories in Hoboken, and here is a lone rider herding sheep on an empty Wyoming plateau. Here is the whole land, laid lavishly across the belly of a continent, washed by three seas, warmed by a dozen suns, breathing a hundred airs, so vast its horizons exhaust the eye, so turbulent with beauty, ugliness, terror, and hope that it wears a thousand faces and speaks with ten thousand tongues. All this has been integrated.

Or consider the history and derivation of the people. At first there are the Latins, here for plunder for the galleons of Spain, or land and furs for Paris. Then there are the English, coming for freedom, or what they then considered freedom; finding it, losing it, and fighting to have it again. Narrow, stern, hard-muscled, tough-minded English yeomen in the North, and English Cavaliers of a quite different breed in the South. The Englishmen pushing westward out of curiosity, or because the land along the coast was thin, or because they hated the sight of the neighbors' chimneys, or because they wanted less government. Some of them dropped like seeds into pockets of the Appalachians, but always there were some who could not stop. By 1810 they had traversed most of the West, and by 1850 had settled most of it—in spots. All this is very new. The battle of the Little Bighorn was fought in 1876, and as late as 1890 Pershing was campaigning against the Sioux in Dakota. A hundred years ago the state of Texas was a full-fledged republic with heroic traditions and a promising future. The Latter-day Saints under Brigham Young not only created an independent nation beside the Great Salt Lake but established a moral code that made New England puritans shudder. Only seventy-five years ago we were "engaged in a great civil war, testing whether that nation or any nation so conceived and so dedicated can long endure." Only twenty-eight years ago the U. S. flag had forty-six stars, before New Mexico and Arizona were admitted to the union. All this has been integrated.

And culturally and racially the country is still in the process of integration. The tidal wave of immigration that started around 1820 had brought some 40,000,000 new Americans to the U. S. by 1938. The mass immigration ended in 1929, when a strict quota law went into effect, and in the next decade the net population gain from abroad was a mere 150,000. Still, over 10 per cent of the total population—some 14,500,000 people—is foreign-born, and the melting pot has not yet produced the ultimate American man. Granted that Americans are a mongrel race, they are perhaps the one people with the energy, the vision, the guts, the greed, and the divine impatience to subdue so quickly the fecund, terrifying land and to create the historic phenomenon called the United States. All that is being integrated.

THE REGIONS

But of course the overshadowing achievement of the American people—the achievement that is the foundation of the nation's greatness—has been the integration of the divergent economies of the U. S. Externally the nation looks like a compact, single economic unit, but a familiar inspection reveals that it is scarcely that. Indeed, it is a union composed of countless units, each with its own economy based upon its own sources of wealth, dominated by self-interest, and competing with every other unit. To take a *reductio ad absurdum,* each citizen is a complete unit, and essentially every worker is in competition with every other worker for the job he has, or a better one. At the other end of the scale there are certain vast and vague areas that have been traditionally divided against each other: the North versus the South, the East versus the West. The passions aroused by the conflicting interests of those areas have at times been intense. In politics these passions are known collectively as sectionalism.

Indeed there are any number of ways of dividing the U. S., and concerning few of them do scholars agree. But they are most nearly in agreement on the relatively modern doctrine of regionalism, which is distinguished from sectionalism on a number of counts, but chiefly in the fact that, whereas the basis of sectionalism is often emotional and political, the basis of regionalism is truly economic, cultural, and social. In any event, a division of the U. S. into its regions provides the best opening to an understanding of its fundamental achievement.

Even regionally, however, there are a great number of ways of dividing the U. S. Few regions are crystallized; few correspond exactly to state borders. Yet for statistical purposes the regions must be built of whole states. *Fortune* has arbitrarily chosen the division: the Northeast, the Southeast, the Middle States, the Mountain and Plains States, the Southwest, the Pacific Northwest, and the Far West. While each of these regions contains sub-regions, this division would seem to be the most realistic one, on most counts, that students have devised.

THE NORTHEAST

Closest to Europe, and more nearly European than any other U. S. region, the Northeast has three tiers—New England; New York, New Jersey, Pennsylvania; Delaware, Maryland, West Virginia. Almost any snap characterization of this group of states is certain to be wrong. It has thirty-four cities of more than 100,000. Therefore it is a metropolitan region. Yet there is nothing so truly rural in the U. S. as the New England villages off the big highways radiating north from New York, where farming is still largely unmechanized and milch cows with bells around their necks are prodded down Main Street by towheaded youngsters, and sheep crop the green plots around the monuments to those who died at Cold Harbor and Bull Run. It is a metropolitan region with a population of over forty million occupying about 7 per cent of the nation's area. It is a highly civilized, highly educated, ultrasophisticated region, yet witchcraft flourishes in parts of southeastern Pennsylvania, where barns and houses wear cabalistic symbols designed to ward away the dreaded hex, and the pious Amish folk refuse to have their pictures taken. It is a calm, orderly, and settled region, but feuds still smolder and occasionally blaze among the mountain clans of West Virginia.

Economically the Northeast stands in relation to the U. S. about the way England stands in relation to the British Empire. The region is dependent on the rest of the country for its wheat and flour, and for a large part of its fresh meats, fruits, vegetables, and canned goods. It likewise is a heavy importer of lumber and allied products, newsprint, cotton, petroleum, although it supplies most of its own iron and coal.

To the U. S. the Northeast sells heavy machinery, coal, steel, railway equipment, paints, varnishes, glass, clothing and New England textiles, leather goods and shoes, paper, and tools. Again like England, the Northeast is the great concentration point of finance, ownership, and control. Of the national income the region draws nearly 40 per cent, and has 41 per cent of the nation's wealth. The value of its manufactures is 39 per cent of the nation's total; half the foreign imports of the U. S. clear through its ports.

Thus the Northeast draws financial tribute from every part of the U. S., and intellectual tribute as well. A common complaint throughout the country is, "All our smartest young people go east." They are drawn east, principally to New York and principally by the legendary glamour of the city that is the country's main source of information and entertainment. On a rock beside a river that is still one of the loveliest in the world the metropolis perches and its skyscrapers "lift their foggy plumes of stranded smoke out of a stony mouth." It is a phenomenon, but a typically American phenomenon. "Here, world, is a city," it seems to say. "Where but in America could you expect to find the like?"

From Pennsylvania on the south to New England on the north is a jump from a concentrated heavy-industry state to a section wherein industry is a small-scale, specialized operation. Only 2 per cent of the industrial plants in New England employ more than 500 workers, while in 88 per cent of the factories there are fewer than 100. The New England economy is a craft economy, reflecting the section's original isolation and its remoteness from the raw materials that make possible a mass-production economy. But the New Englander who first launched the craft economy had a native ingenuity that poverty sharpened. He put his eggs in as many baskets as possible, with the result that there are 200-odd different lines of manufacture in New England today, or about two-thirds of all the lines in the U. S. The section thus is virtually a "little nation" existing within the Northeast regional nation; economically indeed it is comparable to Switzerland. Its people are its chief asset, and its crafts its chief *raison d'être* in the U. S. economy. New England is preoccupied with its own problems, and they are sufficient to keep the New England mind firmly centered on New England. There is probably no more insular city on earth than Boston, and a perfect commentary on the Boston attitude is contained in the little anecdote about the Bostonian who planned to drive to California, and when asked which route he intended to take replied that he was "going by way of West Newton."

THE SOUTHEAST

The Southeast—Virginia, Kentucky, Tennessee, the Carolinas, Georgia, Alabama, Mississippi, Louisiana, Arkansas (which most Southerners consider more western than southern and pretty no-account anyway), and Florida (a freakish national phenomenon having little in common with the rest of the region)—has just entered the twentieth century. In a loose way it resembles the Northeast of the early days of the industrial revolution. The South begins in the Washington airport terminal where the signs on the two doors read "MEN (White Only)" and "WOMEN (White Only)." Across the Potomac lie Virginia's red-clay fields; to the southwest, the laurel-tangled mountains humping through Tennessee, Kentucky, and North Carolina; southward, the flatlands and thinly rooted pines of Georgia and South Carolina, the treeless, hard-baked vistas of Alabama and Mississippi, and the near-jungles of Florida and the lands along the Gulf. Down near latticed Charleston the Gullahs speak a primitive, liquid tongue, and bastard French is a useful language in the south Louisiana parishes. Mobile by night is hauntingly lovely, and Paris, Algiers, and Marseille converge beneath the wrought-iron balconies of New Orleans. To the west across the Huey Long Bridge the country is like a Rousseau painting, with pink flamingos toe-dancing across the black, green-scummed bayous. In this romantic imagery, and indeed in almost every respect, the Southeast is the precise opposite of the Northeast. It has more than twice as much land as the Northeast but only two-thirds as many people. Of these 70 per cent are rural, and their per capita income is less than half that of the Northeast. Whereas the Northeast contains well over half of the 13,000,000 foreign-born U. S. white population, the Southeast has less than 2 per cent. Therefore it lays claim to being "the most American region," even though 30 per cent of its people are black and unassimilable.

There is no occasion here to trace the history of the Southeast through feudal beginnings to the Civil War and the later Reconstruction, which failed to reconstruct. Slaves and cotton built the South, and the descendants of the slaves are today its greatest problem, and cotton its greatest curse. Among the U. S. regions it is the *enfant terrible*. Unlike New England, it is naturally rich, and if it is retarded the blame rests squarely on the shoulders of the inhabitants, whose character, economy, and attitude are so different from New England's, and who thus far have displayed little of the Yankee's ingenuity in squeezing the best out of the land, and in developing appropriate regional industries.

However, precisely because it has been retarded the industrial South appears to have the greatest growth potential of any region in the U. S. Today the value of southern manufactures is 10 per cent of the U. S. total, and almost four times the value of the agricultural production of the region. It has 40 per cent of the U. S. forest land, accounts for 40 per cent of the total timber cut in the U. S., and has an investment of $225,000,000 in its pulp and paper industry. There is bauxite in Arkansas; there are oil, natural gas, and sulfur in Louisiana; phosphates in Florida, Tennessee, and South Carolina; marble, high-grade clays, and vast quantities of limestone. Around Birmingham coal crops up close to important iron deposits, and years ago the late Henry C. Frick predicted that by 1940 Birmingham would be a bigger steel city than Pittsburgh. It isn't—its capacity is only 3.4 per cent of the total U. S. steel capacity. But it could be.

The trouble with Birmingham—as the South sees it—is that it is owned by the North and, economically, that is the trouble with most southern industry. And as a tributary region this one is saddled with not only absentee industrialism, but also absentee farming, and northern hands take the dollars out of its pockets almost as rapidly as it puts them in. Thus its chronic depression will not be solved automatically by further industrialization by the North. And while dreamily contemplating the ivy twining higher around the crumbling white columns of a gracious, vanished southern past, the rest of the U. S. would do well to remember that if the per capita income of each Southerner were raised from its present $285 to the national average of $485 the nation would have captured a new market half again as big as the entire export trade, and be richer by billions.

THE MIDDLE STATES

If Hitler had captured the Russian Ukraine and annexed it to the industrial Reich, the combination would have produced an economy and a territory similar in many respects to the Middle States region, taking in Ohio, Indiana, Michigan, Illinois, Wisconsin, Minnesota, Iowa, and Missouri. Of all the regions, this one is most nearly independent of the others, could most easily drop out of the Union and survive as a separate nation. One of the world's greatest agricultural sections, it also ranks second only to the Northeast as an industrial region. It has few imports—coal, oil, lumber, and such—many exports, and its economy has been developed to a point where it processes its own raw materials and sells both commodities and finished goods. Since it has no reason for being jealous of any other region it has few conflicts. And the conflicts that exist are chiefly social and political and cultural, rather than economic.

Settled originally by New Englanders and Southerners, followed by Germans and Scandinavians, the Middle States have a population of 35,000,000 dwelling on 15 per cent of the U. S. land. About two and a half millions of the people are farmers, and there are over four million workers in the industrial cities—those cities strung like beads of stone around the southern shores of the Lakes. The chief cities are not merely the national but the world headquarters of an industry—Detroit, Akron, Cleveland. Manufacture ranges from beer and soap and cash registers to steel and the heaviest of heavy machinery, and brings an income of four billion dollars to the middle-western economy.

The region is also second to the Northeast in the extent of urbanization. Yet it cannot by any stretch of imagination be called "urban." The urban Middle West is an arc from Cleveland to Milwaukee—close to the docks of the long, flat-topped freighters that carry through Sault Ste. Marie locks more tonnage than clears the Suez or the Panama. Behind the cities of the Lakes lies a farming checkerboard, waving with yellow corn, black with plowed earth, and dotted loosely with fat red silos, magnificent barns, indifferent homes. Here—in addition to some 60 per cent of the nation's corn and a good 20 per cent of its wheat—are half the hogs and the greatest number of purebred, registered cattle in the U. S., producing (chiefly in Minnesota and Wisconsin) half of all the creamery butter, 70 per cent of the factory cheese, more than 40 per cent of the milk. Here are also more than a third of the chickens laying nearly 40 per cent of the eggs.

In such lavish country a fundamental optimism is natural and infectious. The Middle West sees no confining horizons, is confident, boastful, scornful of penny pinching. Chicago is BIG—biggest hotel, biggest trading center, biggest crooks, biggest recreational waterfront. Detroit too is big—biggest American flag (in a department store) and biggest crucifix (at Father Coughlin's shrine)—but Detroit is a renegade that constantly strives to have itself grouped with eastern rather than midwestern cities. And Cleveland has forgotten about bigness and pays more attention to cultural and intellectual niceties.

Outside of the cities the population is introspective rather than exuberant. Your typical farmer of the region is an individualist who will not be bossed, yet nowhere will you find a man more eager to be taught or more willing to make sacrifices for co-operative ventures. He knows soil chemistry, avidly follows the experimentation going on at his state agricultural

college, and sits on his county agent's doorstep waiting for advice. He is
rarely isolated, and almost never hidebound. The big cities he dislikes not
so much on principle but because they represent—the eastern cities especially—the forces that are always trying to deprive him of political relief for
the "farm problem"—i.e., the glut resulting from the application of his
superior agricultural technology to his extraordinarily fertile land. No
humble peasant, he has successfully used his political power time and again.
He flocked to the Progressive party in Wisconsin, the Bull Moose standard
back in 1912, created the Farmer-Labor party in Minnesota; and in Iowa
and elsewhere oiled his shotgun and halted the wave of mortgage foreclosures in 1932 by the simple expedient of preventing bidding on fore-
closed farms. He is probably the most completely democratic individual in
the entire U. S., and he knows how to make democracy work for him.

THE MOUNTAINS AND THE PLAINS

West of the Mississippi you begin to find your pockets cluttered with
round bits of white metal—mill pieces to pay the sales taxes—and west of
the states bordering the river the last few vertebrae are ironed out of the
land and the roads shoot westward like black arrows. To say that it is flat
means nothing because flatness is only one dimension and here the sky
closes in around your upraised hand, and the idea that the earth is round
seems preposterous. Between the western Mississippi states and the foothills
of the Rockies the only considerable break in the flatness occurs in the Black
Hills of Wyoming and South Dakota, which loom up like a great island in
a sea and then subside again in flatness. You drive across the plains at sixty,
seventy, eighty—any speed. The ditches beside the road are dry and seamed
like gingerbread, and a rime of dust settles on your lips and on your wind-
shield. Wheat stretches to the right of the road and to the left, and behind
and ahead, and a few miles across the lonely flatness you see the combines
spouting chaff. That treetop standing like a semaphore ten miles beyond
your radiator cap means a farmhouse, and that gray smudge ten miles beyond the tree, a town. And when the wind blows hard, as it so often does,
the tan dust eddies up above the tossing wheat and an iridescent curtain
dims the sun.

There is no part of the American land that the men living on it do not
love, but by all conventional standards the Northwest Plains states—Kansas,
Nebraska, North and South Dakota—are the least attractive in the U. S.
The plains run into the eastern halves of Wyoming, Montana, and Colo-
rado, with the Rockies beyond running through Utah. These eight states
cover 750,000 square miles—almost a quarter of the nation—and support a
twentieth of the U. S. people. They were settled long after the Pacific states,
in large part by a backwash of the Oregon and California migrations, and

lately the settling process has been coming to a halt. The reason is simply that in spite of its great area the region is not productive enough to provide a living for its inhabitants. If the Middle West is an almost perfectly balanced economy this region is entirely off balance, and it is certainly the least independent U. S. region. It is almost wholly agricultural, with only about 8 per cent of its $3,000,000,000 income coming from manufacturing, and it must import virtually all its finished goods, as well as many raw commodities. The region possesses enormous mineral resources—but these are largely low grade and unexploited, and the existing mining industry is controlled in large part by "foreign," i.e., eastern, capital, which draws the profits out of the region as fast as they are created.

Thus the region's most important resource is the land itself, and owing to a combination of factors the land is of diminishing value. Plowed up and mined for wheat during the years of the War wheat boom, the Plains states contain 165,000,000 acres of the most seriously eroded land in the U. S., and hardly a section in the area fails to show signs of damage by wind or water. By 1930 the region was growing half the U. S. wheat and had become the third biggest corn producer, the largest sheep raiser, and ranked second in horses and cattle. But its cows give less milk than other cows, and its horses and chickens are valued lower at the market—in all, the realized agricultural income amounts to $530,000,000. Always arid, the Plains have been experiencing a chronic drought for nearly ten years, and farmers have stopped hoping for more than the present average annual rainfall of 18.7 inches. Wheat has sucked the subsurface moisture from the earth, the rain no longer flattens the dust, and a considerable fraction of the population can sit on their front porches and watch their livelihoods blowing away into the sky. As farmers go bankrupt, land reverts to the government by default of taxes, and much of it is returned to its original grass. Timothy and alfalfa replace wheat on thousands of acres, and the agronomists work ceaselessly to discover new crops suitable for the parched soil, new ways of utilizing the last drops of the scanty rain that falls.

It would be hard to say that these states conflict with other regions in view of the dominant conflict of the region versus nature. It resembles the South in that its main resource is apparently declining, yet it lacks the South's opportunities for expansion in other directions. Except for the $25,000,000 sugar beet crop, mining, oil, and range land, scenery and national parks are the chief assets of Utah, Colorado, Wyoming, and Montana, and tourists are their main source of cash.

THE SOUTHWEST

Historically the oldest, politically the youngest of the regions, the Southwest is a colonial economy exporting vast quantities of raw materials, importing most fabricated goods, and having more than a superficial resemblance to Brazil, Argentina, Venezuela, and Peru. It exports cotton for British, southern, and New England mills; cattle for the Chicago abattoirs; oil and minerals for the world. The region consists of Texas—where most of the developed resources are located and where the industrial dawn is breaking in the sparkling new cities of the eastern plains—Oklahoma and empty New Mexico and Arizona.

Texas is a thing apart; too big, too rich, too varied, too prophetic to be lumped in any general regional description, or synthesized in a paragraph or two. Bigger than any European nation except the U.S.S.R. and Germany, its widest points are more than 800 miles apart, and it has close to a tenth of the U. S. land area with a population of only 6,200,000—smaller than Greater New York. Texas grows more than a fourth of U. S. cotton and claims that it could supply the entire world. It furnishes close to 40 per cent of U. S. crude oil. On the coastal ranges it supports seven million head of cattle. Thanks to a $100,000,000 investment in irrigation ditches, the lower Rio Grande valley has already become a large producer of oranges, lemons, and grapefruit, and a distinct worry to the California citrus growers.

Nearly all of this fabulous wealth and growth are in East and Central Texas. West of Big Spring, Texas blends into the New Mexico-Arizona Southwest, with "centers" (*not* cities) separated by scores of miles of empty desert, incredible conformations of the land, always the hot sun, the high, dry air, the giant, theatrical, green cacti standing like sentries against the sky. New Mexico is Santa Fe, Roswell, and Albuquerque set down in 123,000 square miles with 422,000 inhabitants. Arizona is another 114,000 square miles, another 412,000 people, and Phoenix and Tucson, eternally bickering over each other's attractions. Phoenix is a spectacular working model of what other parts of the region may someday hope to be—a road or a fence separating cactus desert from lushly blooming irrigated fields of lettuce, orange groves, and every fruit and vegetable. Here is an American machine-conscious culture, rather than machine culture, built upon deep strata of ancient Indian and Mexican civilizations, and achieving a wholly pleasant compromise. In addition to the $77,500,000 annual copper output, tourists constitute a main source of income in Arizona and New Mexico, approximately $48,000,000 being spent by visitors. Arizona in particular visualizes itself as a tourist center and is often tempted to make a good thing better by legalizing gambling and relaxing the divorce laws to steal Nevada's lure.

THE FAR WEST

Nevada and California combine to form an almost indescribable region, with the infinite variety of California on one side of the mountains and the wild Nevada desert on the other. California is the second biggest state in area and, with 6,154,000 people, is sixth in population; Nevada has only 101,000 inhabitants and is forty-eighth in population, but sixth in area. Along with per capita income of $717, California has the fourth highest total income in the U. S., whereas Nevada keeps herself going mainly by virtue of spinning roulette wheels, blinking red lights, the eastern cartwheels dropping into slot machines, and the complacent magistrates handing down three thousand six-week divorces per year in Reno, "The Biggest Little City in the World." There is also a mining industry (chiefly copper) bringing in $14,000,000 annually; and there are minor livestock and farming activities in the infrequent irrigated portions of the state.

The great Golden State is a good deal like the amazing elephant encountered by the blind men. The coast line measures a thousand miles, runs from Oregon to Mexico. The northern quarter of California has some of the wildest forest and mountain terrain in North America; the southern quarter has an empty and dangerous desert—Death Valley. According to some experts the finest ski country in the U. S. lies along the slopes of the Sierra Nevada; a few hours away the Pacific rolls onto golden beaches under palms and a semitropical sun. The contrast between the state's two great cities is as sharp as any—San Francisco a cosmopolitan, compactly built, sophisticated place, probably more completely unionized than any other U. S. city; gusty, vital Los Angeles, the booster and cheesecake capital of the world, attempting to become a city but still nothing but a garbled town sprawling across 450 square miles. "L. A." stands as immortal reproach to the subdividing realtors. It is bitterly anti-union, bitterly clear in its remembrance of the bombing of the *Times* by the NcNamara brothers back in 1910. Just as sharp as the contrast between Los Angeles and San Francisco is the contrast between the state's intellectual centers and the southern California crackpot preserve, where new grocery stores are inaugurated with floodlight displays.

Since Sutter's Mill in '48, California has produced something like $2,000,000,000 in gold, and its gold production is still worth more than $40,000,000 a year—including the driblets panned by thousands of prospectors working the streams and earning from a quarter to $5 a day. But more important than the gold is the agriculture, which accounts for a good 11 per cent of the state's income. California produces everything from avocados and citrus fruits in the South to the wine grapes of the San Joaquin. Virtually no crop refuses to grow in California, and practically no crops are overlooked, although citrus is the leading one. On the state borders fruit-inspection stations have been established for the ostensible purpose of preventing the importation of insects or fruit diseases, but in effect they form a barrier against fruit imports—diseased or otherwise.

A major part of California's industry consists of canning, packing, bottling, and other functions subsidiary to its agriculture. Although southern

California is the chief center of the U. S. aircraft industry, and although more and more automobile-assembly plants have been erected by eastern companies, the state has comparatively few large factories. Its economy is in transition between the raw-material exporting economy of the Southwest and the agricultural-industrial economy of the Middle West.

THE PACIFIC NORTHWEST

Just as the Far West appears to be the least integrated of the regions, so the 250,000 square miles of Washington, Oregon, and Idaho are perhaps more closely unified than any other part of the U. S. Although the Pacific Northwest was explored by Lewis and Clark around 1805, its intensive settlement did not begin until the Northern Pacific linked Chicago with Seattle in 1883. Today it is closer to the frontier—topographically and economically—than the rest of the West, and, as of the census of 1930, less than half the population was native to the region.

The population today amounts to 3,200,000, or 2.5 per cent of the nation's total, whereas the Pacific Northwest has 8.3 per cent of the U. S. land, with a high ratio of resources to population. It has, for example, about 40 per cent of all U. S. potential waterpower, mostly accounted for by the Columbia River system. Yet this power is for the most part incidental to irrigation and water-conservation projects, because about 60 per cent of the region lies to the east of the Cascades, which block the rains from the Pacific. The mountains make for fogs and forests on the western slope, but semi-arid areas inland. Thus the whole economy of the Pacific Northwest revolves around the problem of bringing water to the land, and it is laced together by the branches of the Columbia, the main source of water. Today only a quarter of the 160,000,000 acres is in farms, and almost two-thirds of this land is suitable only for grazing. Here, and throughout the West generally, a good deal of the soil is potentially arable provided it can be watered, and the region looks forward to a conservative increase in productive farm acreage as the existing water supply is put to use. Grand Coulee alone will provide water for more than a million acres.

On the land that it currently farms the region grows over a fifth of the nation's apples, a quarter of the cherries, nearly a third of the pears, a tenth or more of the potatoes, onions, strawberries, green peas, and dry beans. It also accounts for close to an eighth of the wheat, over 10 per cent of the wool, and a slightly lower percentage of sheep and lambs. Mineral resources thus far have been scarcely touched, but even so the region mines large amounts of zinc, lead, and silver. However, its greatest source of wealth is the forest that covers the western slopes of the Cascades, representing about half the standing saw timber in the U. S. and producing roughly 40 per cent of the nation's output of softwood lumber. Over 50 per cent of all wage earners in Pacific Northwest manufacturing are employed in lumber industries. Currently the annual cut of slightly under ten billion board feet runs ahead of the new growth by two or two and a half to one, and the region is becoming pocked with stranded communities decaying in the devastated cutover areas similar to those in northern Wisconsin, Minnesota, and Michigan. There is much talk of bringing the cut and the growth into balance, but so far few effective steps have been taken. Safe from destruction are 70,000-odd square miles of forest standing in three great national parks and on other U. S. Government land—land that amounts to a phenomenal 48 per cent of the region's total and an incredible 58 per cent of the area of Idaho.

The region is in competition with practically every part of the country. Its lumber competes with southeastern lumber; its wheat with the Middle West and Plains states; its orchards with those of the Northeast; its potatoes with Maine; its sheep and wool with the Southwest; and so on. Virtually its only noncompetitive export is the Columbia River salmon catch—and even that has Alaskan competition.

Meanwhile, with manufacturing accounting for only 16 per cent of its income, the Pacific Northwest must import nearly all finished goods, as well as oil, sugar, and other commodities. Ostensibly the heavy raw-material exports would balance the imports for an over-all profit, but a catch exists in the form of freight rates. The region's markets are thousands of miles away—the fruit is shipped to New York, for example—and freight eats up from a quarter to a half of the farmer's wholesale price in the East, whereas the local growers have no such handicap. The result is that the Washington farmer, to compete with the Easterner, must be content to receive far less in net cash. When middle-western wheat growers were complaining about fifty-four-cent wheat, Pacific Northwest farmers growing the same wheat were realizing only thirty cents per bushel for their crop.

Conversely, the region is squeezed when it buys eastern manufactured goods. An Allis-Chalmers tractor delivered in Spokane would cost between 20 and 30 per cent more than the same tractor unloaded in Ohio. In effect the Pacific Northwest produces raw materials, pays a stiff price to get them out of the region, pays again to bring in its manufactured goods. Consequently, next to irrigation and power development, the freight-rate squeeze is the region's chief preoccupation, and few conversations go on very long without the subject's coming up and without the city of Chicago's being mentioned with infinite loathing.

However, these are familiar troubles in a pioneer economy, and the region will unquestionably outgrow them. For it has plenty of room, abundant resources, tremendous power, and perhaps more usable land. Cheap power is certain to lead to the creation of regional industries, and already Portland has begun an expansion that may make it the leading industrial city of the north coast. Seattle is a little San Francisco, economically and in spirit, with shipping and lumber to sustain it and Alaska acknowledging it as an "unofficial capital." Posters in the state of Washington announce that such-and-such is the "fastest-selling" article of its kind in "the Pacific Northwest and Alaska." The northern U. S. outpost, which seems so remote to the rest of the country, comes close to being a part of the Pacific Northwest region.

"E PLURIBUS UNUM"

From this hasty tour of 3,026,789 square and fabulous miles the secret of U. S. power emerges clearly. The U. S. is not great by nature or by accident. It is great by the act of man. The purpose of the political system invented by the founders of the republic was the political integration of sovereign states. But this political integration resulted in an economic integration far beyond anything man had ever attempted before. The economic interests of the states burst the boundaries of the states; they intertwined, merged, became compounded one with another. The result, as we have seen, has been the formation of shadow nations within a nation—seven of them by this count, fewer or more by others. The boundaries of these shadow nations are economic rather than geographical; they do not necessarily coincide with political sovereignties. The northern part of California seems to belong to the Pacific Northwest instead of to the Far West, and so does western Montana, though it is included in the Mountain States. The eastern half of the state of Texas goes with the old South, the western half with the Southwest. And so forth. The economic forces cut across political forces, check them, merge with political forces elsewhere, bind two into one. The action is like that within a huge retort in which dissimilar substances mix and compound, to create a new substance of a higher power. That new substance is what we know as the U. S. A.

This new entity is greater than the sum of its own parts. If the shadow nations were real nations, if the political boundaries coincided with the economic boundaries, then the area now known as the U. S. would be far less potent, far less rich than it is. Then New England would be struggling for food, and in the Northwest an automobile would be as rare as in other agricultural countries that have difficulty accumulating foreign exchange. It is when the Aluminum Co. of America contracts for waterpower in Oregon that the U. S. is created. It is when the rich coupon clippers on Manhattan are taxed to help build highways in empty Nevada that the U. S. lives. Every time a freight train crosses a state line, every time a purchasing department makes up its mind to buy an out-of-state commodity, every time an order clerk receives an out-of-state demand, the U. S. grows greater. For in these events, as in thousands of others, one is working for all, and all for one.

This—and not nature or accident—is why the U. S. has become the greatest agricultural nation on earth, ranking first, second, or third in most of the basic commodities. This is why the U. S. produces a third of the world's coal and a third of the world's iron ore; makes 27 per cent of the steel. This is why it produces more than 60 per cent of the oil—and 62 per cent of the automobiles. This is why it makes a quarter of the wood pulp, generates almost a third of the electric power, produces 72 per cent of the sulfur, 20 per cent of the lead, almost 30 per cent of the zinc, more than a quarter of the phosphates. It is true that the U. S. has abundant supplies to start with, but so have other people who fail to produce them. That almost incredible—though fragmentary—record is more descriptive than words or statistics of what it means for 30,000,000 families to share some $322,000,000,000 worth of wealth, and about $62,450,000,000 ($2.082 per family) of national income.

John Buchan

John Buchan, Lord Tweedsmuir (1875-1940) was born in Scotland and educated at Glasgow and Oxford. Trained for the law he early turned to literature and, throughout a life crowded with action, found time to write over fifty books—war correspondence, history, biography, and, above all, romances. He entered Parliament in his fifties; in 1935 he was raised to the peerage and was made Governor General of Canada. Characteristically he threw himself into his new work, traveling all over the Dominion in order to know it at first hand. His devotion to his office and his happy personality made him the most popular Governor in Canada's history. That he had an equally remarkable understanding of the United States is shown in the following chapter from his beautifully told autobiography, Pilgrim's Way.

MY AMERICA

THE title of this chapter exactly defines its contents. It presents the American scene as it appears to one observer—a point of view which does not claim to be that mysterious thing, objective truth. There will be no attempt to portray the "typical" American, for I have never known one. I have met a multitude of individuals, but I should not dare to take any one of them as representing his country—as being that other mysterious thing, the average man. You can point to certain qualities which are more widely distributed in America than elsewhere, but you will scarcely find human beings who possess all these qualities. One good American will have most of them; another, equally good and not less representative, may have few or none. So I shall eschew generalities. If you cannot indict a nation, no more can you label it like a museum piece.

Half the misunderstandings between Britain and America are due to the fact that neither will regard the other as what it is—in an important sense of the word—a foreign country. Each thinks of the other as a part of itself which has somehow gone off the lines. An Englishman is always inclined to resent the unfamiliar when it is found under conditions for which he thinks he has some responsibility. He can appreciate complete and utter strangeness, and indeed show himself highly sympathetic towards it; but for variations upon his own ways—divergencies in speech, food, clothes, social habits—he has little tolerance. He is not very happy even in his own colonies and dominions, and in America he can be uncommonly ill at ease.

On a higher level, when it comes to assessing spiritual values, he often shows the same mixture of surprise and disappointment. America has lapsed from the family tradition; what would have been pardonable and even commendable in a foreigner is blameworthy in a cousin. Matthew Arnold, for example, was critical of certain American traits, not on their merits, but because they were out of tune with that essential European tradition of which he considered himself the guardian. The American critic can be not less intolerant, and for much the same reason. His expositions of England are often like sermons preached in a Home for Fallen Women, the point being that she has fallen, that her defects are a discredit to her relations, that she has let down her kin, and suffered the old home to fall into disrepute. This fretfulness can only be cured, I think, by a frank recognition of the real foreignness of the two peoples. No doubt they had a common ancestor, but he is of little avail against the passage of time and the estranging seas.

2

I first discovered America through books. Not the tales of Indians and the Wild West which entranced my boyhood; those seemed to belong to no particular quarter of the globe, but to an indefinable land of romance, and I was not cognisant of any nation behind them. But when I became interested in literature I came strongly under the spell of New England. Its culture seemed to me to include what was best in Europe's, winnowed and clarified. Perhaps it was especially fitted to attract youth, for it was not too difficult or too recondite, but followed the "main march of the human affections," and it had the morning freshness of a young people. Its cheerfulness atoned for its occasional bleakness and anaemia. Lowell was the kind of critic I wanted, learned, rational, never freakish, always intelligible. Emerson's gnomic wisdom was a sound manual for adolescence, and of Thoreau

I became—and for long remained—an ardent disciple. To a Scot of my up-bringing there was something congenial in the simplicity, the mild austerity, and the girded discipline of the New England tradition. I felt that it had been derived from the same sources as our own.

Then, while I was at Oxford, I read Colonel Henderson's *Stonewall Jackson* and became a student of the American Civil War. I cannot say what especially attracted me to that campaign: partly, no doubt, the romance of it, the chivalry and the supreme heroism; partly its extraordinary technical interest, both military and political; but chiefly, I think, because I fell in love with the protagonists. I had found the kind of man that I could whole-heartedly admire. Since those days my study of the Civil War has continued, I have visited most of its battlefields, I have followed the trail of its great marches, I have read widely in its literature; indeed, my memory has be-come so stored with its details that I have often found myself able to tell the descendants of its leaders facts about their forbears of which they had never heard.

My interest soon extended from the soldiers to the civilians, and I ac-quired a new admiration for Abraham Lincoln. Then it was enlarged to include the rest of America's history—the first settlements, the crossing of the Appalachians, the Revolution, the building of the West. Soon America, instead of being the unstoried land which it appears to most English trav-ellers, became for me the home of a long tradition and studded with sacred places. I dare to say that no American was ever more thrilled by the prospect of seeing Westminster Abbey and the Tower, Winchester and Oxford, than I was by the thought of Valley Forge and the Shenandoah and the Wilder-ness.

I came first into the United States by way of Canada—a good way to enter, for English eyes are already habituated to the shagginess of the land-scape and can begin to realize its beauties. My first reflection was that no one had told me how lovely the country was. I mean *lovely,* not vast and magnificent. I am not thinking of the Grand Canyon and the Yosemite and the Pacific coast, but of the ordinary rural landscape. There is much of the land which I have not seen, but in the East and the South and the North-west I have collected a gallery of delectable pictures. I think of the farms which are clearings in the Vermont and New Hampshire hills, the flowery summer meadows, the lush cow-pastures with an occasional stump to re-mind one that it is old forest land, the quiet lakes and the singing streams, the friendly accessible mountains; the little country towns of Massachusetts and Connecticut with their village greens and elms and two-century-old churches and courthouses; the secret glens of the Adirondacks and the mountain meadows of the Blue Ridge; the long-settled champaign of Mary-land and Pennsylvania; Virginian manors more Old-England perhaps than anything we have at home; the exquisite links with the past like much of

Boston and Charleston and all of Annapolis; the sunburnt aromatic ranges of Montana and Wyoming; the Pacific shores where from snow mountains fishable streams descend through some of the noblest timber on earth to an enchanted sea.

It is a country most of which I feel to be in a special sense "habitable," designed for homes, adapted to human uses, a friendly land. I like, too, the way in which the nomenclature reflects its history, its racial varieties, its odd cultural mixtures, the grandiose and the homespun rubbing shoulders. That is how places should be named. I have no objection to Mechanicsville and Higginsville and Utica and Syracuse. They are a legitimate part of the record. And behind are the hoar-ancient memorials of the first dwellers, names like symphonies—Susquehanna, Ticonderoga, Shenandoah, Wyoming.

3

"Ah, my cabbages!" Henry Adams wrote, "when will you ever fathom the American? Never in your sweet lives." He proceeds in his genial way to make epigrams about his own New Englanders: "Improvised Europeans we were and—Lord God!—how thin!"—"Thank God I never was cheerful. I come from the happy stock of the Mathers, who, as you remember, passed sweet mornings reflecting on the goodness of God and the damnation of infants." Where an Adams scrupled to tread it is not for a stranger to rush in. But I would humbly suggest a correction to one reading which, I think, has the authority of Robert Louis Stevenson. America is, no doubt, a vast country, though it can be comfortably put inside Canada. But it is not in every part a country of wide horizons. Dwellers on the Blue Ridge, on the prairies, and on the western ranges may indeed live habitually with huge spaces of land and sky, but most of America, and some of its most famous parts, is pockety, snug and cosy, a sanctuary rather than a watch-tower. To people so domiciled its vastness must be like the mathematician's space-time, a concept apprehended by the mind and not a percept of the eye. "The largeness of Nature and of this nation were monstrous without a corresponding largeness and generosity of the spirit of the citizen." That is one of Walt Whitman's best-known sayings, but let us remember that the bigness of their country is for most Americans something to be learned and imaginatively understood, and not a natural deduction from cohabiting with physical immensities.

Racially they are the most variegated people on earth. The preponderance of the Anglo-Saxon stock disappeared in the Civil War. Look today at any list of names in a society or a profession and you will find that, except in the Navy, the bulk are from the continent of Europe. In his day Matthew Arnold thought that the chief source of the strength of the American people lay in their homogeneity and the absence of sharply defined classes, which made revolution unthinkable. Other observers, like Henry James, have deplored the lack of such homogeneity and wished for their country the "close and complete consciousness of the Scots." (I pause to note that I cannot imagine a more nightmare conception. What would happen to the world if a hundred and thirty million Scotsmen, with their tight, compact nationalism, were living in the same country?) I am inclined to query the alleged absence of classes, for I have never been in any part of the United States where class distinctions did not hold. There is an easy friendliness of manner which conceals a strong class pride, and the basis of that pride is not always, or oftenest, plutocratic. Apart from the social snobbery of the big cities, there seems to be everywhere an innocent love of grades and distinctions which is enough to make a Communist weep. I have known places in the South where there was a magnificent aristocratic egalitarianism. Inside a charmed circle all were equal. The village postmistress, having had the right kind of great-great-grandmother, was an honoured member of society, while the immigrant millionaire, who had built himself a palace, might as well have been dead. And this is true not only of the New England F.F.M.'s and the Virginian F.F.V.'s, the districts with long traditions, but of the raw little townships in the Middle West. They, too, have their "best" people who had ancestors, though the family tree may only have sprouted for two generations.

No country can show such a wide range of type and character, and I am so constituted that in nearly all I find something to interest and attract me. This is more than a temperamental bias, for I am very ready to give reasons for my liking. I am as much alive as anyone to the weak and ugly things in American life: areas, both urban and rural, where the human economy has gone rotten; the melting-pot which does not always melt; the eternal coloured problem; a constitutional machine which I cannot think adequately represents the efficient good sense of the American people; a brand of journalism which fatigues with its ruthless snappiness and uses a speech so disintegrated that it is incapable of expressing any serious thought or emotion; the imbecile patter of high-pressure salesmanship; an academic jargon, used chiefly by psychologists and sociologists, which is hideous and almost meaningless. Honest Americans do not deny these blemishes; indeed they are apt to exaggerate them, for they are by far the sternest critics of their own country. For myself, I would make a double plea in extenuation. These are defects from which today no nation is exempt, for they are the fruits of a mechanical civilisation, which perhaps are more patent in America, since everything there is on a large scale. Again, you can set an achievement very much the same in kind against nearly every failure. If her historic apparatus of government is cranky, she is capable of meeting the "instant need of things" with brilliant improvisations. Against economic plague-spots she can set great experiments in charity; against journalistic baby-talk a standard of popular writing in her best papers which is a model of idiom and perspicuity; against catch-penny trade methods many solidly founded, perfectly organised commercial enterprises; against the jargon of the half-educated professor much noble English prose in the great tradition. That is why it is so foolish to generalise about America. You no sooner construct a rule than it is shattered by the exceptions.

As I have said, I have a liking for almost every kind of American (except the kind who decry their country). I have even a sneaking fondness for George Babbitt, which I fancy is shared by his creator. But there are two types which I value especially, and which I have never met elsewhere in quite the same form. One is the pioneer. No doubt the physical frontier of the United States is now closed, but the pioneer still lives, though the day of the covered wagon is over. I have met him in the New England hills, where he is grave, sardonic, deliberate in speech; in the South, where he has a ready smile and a soft, caressing way of talking; in the ranges of the West, the cowpuncher with his gentle voice and his clear, friendly eyes which have not been dulled by reading print—the real thing, far removed from the vulgarities of film and fiction. At his best, I think, I have found him as a newcomer in Canada, where he is pushing north into districts like the Peace River, pioneering in the old sense. By what signs is he to be known? Principally by the fact that he is wholly secure, that he possesses his soul, that he is the true philosopher. He is one of the few aristocrats left in the world. He has a right sense of the values of life, because his cosmos embraces both nature and man. I think he is the most steadfast human being now alive.

The other type is at the opposite end of the social scale, the creature of a complex society who at the same time is not dominated by it, but, while reaping its benefits, stands a little aloof. In the older countries culture, as a rule, leaves some irregularity like an excrescence in a shapely tree-trunk, some irrational bias, some petulance or prejudice. You have to go to America, I think, for the wholly civilised man who has not lost his natural vigour or agreeable idiosyncrasies, but who sees life in its true proportions and has a fine balance of mind and spirit. It is a character hard to define, but anyone with a wide American acquaintance will know what I mean. They are people in whom education has not stunted any natural growth or fostered any abnormality. They are Greek in their justness of outlook, but Northern in their gusto. Their eyes are shrewd and candid, but always friendly. As examples I would cite, among friends who are dead, the names of Robert Bacon, Walter Page, Newton Baker, and Dwight Morrow.

But I am less concerned with special types than with the American people as a whole. Let me try to set down certain qualities which seem to me to flourish more lustily in the United States than elsewhere. Again, let me repeat, I speak of America only as I know it; an observer with a different experience might not agree with my conclusions.

First I would select what, for want of a better word, I should call homeliness. It is significant that the ordinary dwelling, though it be only a shack in the woods, is called not a house, but a home. This means that the family, the ultimate social unit, is given its proper status as the foundation of society. Even among the richer classes I seem to find a certain pleasing domesticity. English people of the same rank are separated by layers of servants from the basic work of the household, and know very little about it. In America the kitchen is not too far away from the drawing-room, and it is recognised, as Heraclitus said, that the gods may dwell there. But I am thinking chiefly of the ordinary folk, especially those of narrow means. It is often said that Americans are a nomad race, and it is true that they are very ready to shift their camp; but the camp, however bare, is always a home.[1] The cohesion of the family is close, even when its members are scattered. This is due partly to the tradition of the first settlers, a handful in an unknown land; partly to the history of the frontier, where the hearth-fire burnt brighter when all around was cold and darkness. The later immigrants from Europe, feeling at last secure, were able for the first time to establish a family base, and they cherished it zealously. This ardent domesticity has had its bad effects on American literature, inducing a sentimentality which makes a too crude frontal attack on the emotions, and which has produced as a reaction a not less sentimental "toughness." But as a social cement it is beyond price. There have been many to laugh at the dullness and pettiness of the "small town." From what I know of small-town life elsewhere, I suspect obtuseness in the satirists.

Second, I would choose the sincere and widespread friendliness of the people. Americans are interested in the human race, and in each other. Deriving doubtless from the old frontier days, there is a general helpfulness which I have not found in the same degree elsewhere. A homesteader in Dakota will accompany a traveller for miles to set him on the right road. The neighbours will rally round one of their number in distress with the loyalty of a Highland clan. This friendliness is not a self-conscious duty so much as an instinct. A squatter in a cabin will share his scanty provender and never dream that he is doing anything unusual.

American hospitality, long as I have enjoyed it, still leaves me breathless. The lavishness with which a busy man will give up precious time to entertain a stranger to whom he is in no way bound remains for me one of the wonders of the world. No doubt this friendliness, since it is an established custom, has its fake side. The endless brotherhoods and sodalities into

[1] In the Civil War homesickness was so serious a malady that the "printed forms for medical reports contained an entry for nostalgia precisely as for pneumonia."—Douglas Freeman, *The South to Posterity*, p. 4.

which people brigade themselves encourage a geniality which is more a mannerism than an index of character, a tiresome, noisy, backslapping heartiness. But that is the exception, not the rule. Americans like company, but though they are gregarious they do not lose themselves in the crowd. Waves of mass emotion may sweep the country, but they are transient things and do not submerge for long the stubborn rock of individualism. That is to say, people can be led, but they will not be driven. Their love of human companionship is based not on self-distrust, but on a genuine liking for their kind. With them the sense of a common humanity is a warm and constant instinct and not a doctrine of the schools or a slogan of the hustings.

Lastly—and this may seem a paradox—I maintain that they are fundamentally modest. Their interest in others is a proof of it; the Aristotelian Magnificent Man was interested in nobody but himself. As a nation they are said to be sensitive to criticism; that surely is modesty, for the truly arrogant care nothing for the opinion of other people. Above all they can laugh at themselves, which is not possible for the immodest. They are their own shrewdest and most ribald critics. It is charged against them that they are inclined to boast unduly about those achievements and about the greatness of their country, but a smug glorying in them is found only in the American of the caricaturist. They rejoice in showing their marvels to a visitor with the gusto of children exhibiting their toys to a stranger, an innocent desire, without any unfriendly gloating, to make others partakers in their satisfaction. If now and then they are guilty of bombast, it is surely a venial fault. The excited American talks of his land very much, I suspect, as the Elizabethans in their cups talked of England. The foreigner who strayed into the Mermaid Tavern must often have listened to heroics which upset his temper.

The native genius, in humour, and in many of the public and private relations of life, is for overstatement, a high-coloured, imaginative, paradoxical extravagance. The British gift is for understatement. Both are legitimate figures of speech. They serve the same purpose, for they call attention to a fact by startling the hearer, since manifestly they are not the plain truth. Personally I delight in both mannerisms and would not for the world have their possessors reject them. They serve the same purpose in another and a subtler sense, for they can be used to bring novel and terrible things within the pale of homely experience. I remember on the Western Front in 1918 that two divisions, British and American, aligned side by side, suffered a heavy shelling. An American sergeant described it in racy and imaginative speech which would have been appropriate to the Day of Judgment. A British sergeant merely observed that "Kaiser 'ad been a bit 'asty." Each had a twinkle in his eye; each in his national idiom was making frightfulness endurable by domesticating it.

4

The United States is the richest, and, both actually and potentially, the most powerful state on the globe. She has much, I believe, to give to the world; indeed, to her hands is chiefly entrusted the shaping of the future. If democracy in the broadest and truest sense is to survive, it will be mainly because of her guardianship. For, with all her imperfections, she has a clearer view than any other people of the democratic fundamentals.

She starts from the right basis, for she combines a firm grip on the past with a quick sense of present needs and a bold outlook on the future. This she owes to her history; the combination of the British tradition with the necessities of a new land; the New England township and the Virginian manor *plus* the frontier. Much of that tradition was relinquished as irrelevant to her needs, but much remains: a talent for law which is not incompatible with a lawless practice; respect for a certain type of excellence in character which has made her great men uncommonly like our own; a disposition to compromise, but only after a good deal of arguing; an intense dislike of dictation. To these instincts the long frontier struggles added courage in the face of novelties, adaptability, enterprise, a doggedness which was never lumpish, but alert and expectant.

That is the historic basis of America's democracy, and today she is the chief exponent of a creed which I believe on the whole to be the best in this imperfect world. She is the chief exponent for two reasons. The first is her size; she exhibits its technique in large type, so that he who runs may read. More important, she exhibits it in its most intelligible form, so that its constituents are obvious. Democracy has become with many an unpleasing parrot-cry, and, as I have urged elsewhere in this book, it is well to be clear what it means. It is primarily a spiritual testament, from which certain political and economic orders naturally follow. But the essence is the testament; the orders may change while the testament stands. This testament, this ideal of citizenship, she owes to no one teacher. There was a time when I fervently admired Alexander Hamilton and could not away with Jefferson; the latter only began to interest me, I think, after I had seen the University of Virginia, which he created. But I deprecate partisanship in those ultimate matters. The democratic testament derives from Hamilton as well as from Jefferson.

It has two main characteristics. The first is that the ordinary man believes in himself and in his ability, along with his fellows, to govern his country. It is when a people loses its self-confidence that it surrenders its soul to a dictator or an oligarchy. In Mr. Walter Lippmann's tremendous metaphor, it welcomes manacles to prevent its hands shaking. The second is the belief, which is fundamental also in Christianity, of the worth of every human soul—the worth, not the equality. This is partly an honest emotion, and partly a reasoned principle—that something may be made out of any-body, and that there is something likeable about everybody if you look for it—or, in canonical words, that ultimately there is nothing common or unclean.

The democratic testament is one lesson that America has to teach the world. A second is a new reading of nationalism. Some day and somehow the peoples must discover a way to brigade themselves for peace. Now, there are on the globe only two proven large-scale organisations of social units, the United States and the British Empire. The latter is not for export, and could not be duplicated; its strength depends upon a thousand-year-old monarchy and a store of unformulated traditions. But the United States was the conscious work of men's hands, and a task which has once been per-formed can be performed again. She is the supreme example of a federation in being, a federation which recognises the rights and individuality of the parts, but accepts the overriding interests of the whole. To achieve this com-promise she fought a desperate war. If the world is ever to have prosperity and peace, there must be some kind of federation—I will not say of democ-racies, but of states which accept the reign of Law. In such a task she seems to me to be the predestined leader. Vigorous as her patriotism is, she has escaped the jealous, barricadoed nationalism of the Old World. Disraeli, so often a prophet in spite of himself, in 1863, at a critical moment of the Civil War, spoke memorable words:

There is a grave misapprehension, both in the ranks of Her Majesty's Gov-ernment and of Her Majesty's Opposition, as to what constitutes the true mean-ing of the American democracy. The American democracy is not made up of the scum of the great industrial cities of the United States, nor of an exhausted middle class that speculates in stocks and calls that progress. The American democracy is made up of something far more stable, that may ultimately decide the fate of the two Americas and of "Europe."

For forty years I have regarded America not only with a student's in-terest in a fascinating problem, but with the affection of one to whom she has become almost a second motherland. Among her citizens I count many of my closest friends; I have known all her presidents, save one, since Theo-dore Roosevelt, and all her ambassadors to the Court of Saint James's since John Hay; for five years I have been her neighbour in Canada. But I am not blind to the grave problems which confront her. Democracy, after all, is a negative thing. It provides a fair field for the Good Life, but it is not in itself the Good Life. In these days when lovers of freedom may have to fight for their cause, the hope is that the ideal of the Good Life, in which alone freedom has any meaning, will acquire a stronger potency. It is the task of civilisation to raise every citizen above want, but in so doing to permit a free development and avoid the slavery of the beehive and the ant-heap. A humane economic policy must not be allowed to diminish the stature of man's spirit. It is because I believe that in the American people the two impulses are of equal strength that I see her in the vanguard of that slow upward trend, undulant or spiral, which today is our modest definition of progress. Her major prophet is still Whitman. "Everything comes out of the dirt—everything; everything comes out of the people, everyday people, the people as you find them and leave them; people, people, just people!"

It is only out of the dirt that things grow.

Gaetano Salvemini

To a reporter seeking biographical information Dr. Salvemini, a voluble Latin, exclaimed: "No, no, no. I don't even talk about myself to myself. What do you think I am, a Hollywood actress? You are wasting your time. Go, go, go." However, it is a matter of record that Gaetano Salvemini (1873-), a native of Italy, was Professor of Modern History in the University of Florence when, for his fearless denunciation of Fascism, he was arrested and later went into exile. Since 1934 he has been a Lecturer in the History of Italian Civilization at Harvard and became an American citizen in 1940. He is part author of What to Do with Italy, *a blueprint for a future Italy based on democratic principles. The following essay furnishes a clear-headed exposition of what democracy is and what it is not.*

WHAT IS FREEDOM?

A FREE régime consists of three different groups of institutions. One group aims at assuring the personal rights of the citizen: the rights of habeas corpus and of freedom of thought, of worship, of education, of locomotion, and of work. Another set of institutions guarantees the citizen his political liberties: freedom of speech, of the press, and of association, and the right to participate in assemblies. Finally, there are those institutions which entitle the citizen, if he so desires, to change the party in power by means of elections. Those citizens who do not share the opinions of the party in power are entitled to expound publicly their reasons for dissent and to form opposition parties whose aim is the overthrow of the party in power.

The existence of competing parties is an essential feature of a free constitution. Liberty is fundamentally the right of the citizen to dissent from the party that is in power, and from this right spring all the other rights of the citizen.

Personal rights, political liberties, and representative institutions are indissolubly bound together. If we admit freedom of thought as a personal right of the citizen, we cannot contest his right to express his thoughts in speech or through the press, or to join his fellow citizens in associations for the propagation of their thoughts. Thus a constitution which recognizes the personal rights of the citizen cannot suppress his political liberties. Similarly, if we recognize the political liberties of the citizen—that is to say, his right to oppose the party in power—we must also recognize his right to substitute for the party in power an opposition party, when the latter has won the supporting faith of the majority of the citizens.

If the citizen had the right to criticize the party in power but not the right to change it by means of lawful elections, either the exercise of the right of opposition would be reduced to fruitless slander, or freedom of speech, of the press, and of association, and the right to assemble would burst out into the violence of revolution. On the other hand, a constitution which entitled the citizens to choose the men who were to control their government would be a sham if the government were entitled to violate the habeas corpus of the citizens or to suppress their political liberties whenever they tried to oppose the party in power.

As a consequence, we cannot have personal rights and political liberties without having representative institutions, and we cannot suppress representative institutions without suppressing, or at least deeply curtailing, political liberties and personal rights.

DEMOCRACY

A free régime is not necessarily a democratic régime. The English constitution before the Reform Act of 1832 was free but not democratic. Personal rights, political liberties, and the franchise were the privileges of an upper-class oligarchy. During the last century the English constitution has been democratized by the gradual extension of these privileges to all classes. The characteristic feature of a free but oligarchical constitution is a restricted franchise. The characteristic feature of a free constitution which has become democratic is universal suffrage.

In Europe at the close of World War I, all the formerly oligarchical constitutions became democratic. Freedom and democracy became interchangeable terms. The rise of dictatorships in recent years on the ruins of democratic régimes has drawn still more closely together the ideas of liberty and democracy. In the countries in which universal suffrage has been either abolished or reduced to a sham, personal rights and political liberties have also been abolished. One party only—the party in power—is allowed to exist;

opposition parties are criminal organizations; an opponent of the government is an outlaw.

Under free and democratic institutions, you may curse freedom and democracy and, if you like, invoke a dictatorship. Under a dictatorship, you are allowed only to sing the praises of the dictator and the benefits he has bestowed upon your country. And the more unhappy your country becomes, the louder your praises of the dictator must be.

WEAK SPOTS IN DEMOCRACY

One may be a convinced liberal and yet not feel oneself obliged to regard all free and democratic institutions as sacrosanct.

When electoral institutions were created, they were based on the assumption that the electorate would choose the best among themselves as representatives, and that those who were chosen would legislate and supervise the work of the executive in the interests of the community. Experience has shown that the electorate rarely choose the best. In fact, they as a rule choose the mediocre, and sometimes they even choose the worst men in the community. This is the first weak spot in free and democratic institutions.

Secondly, the task of the legislative power has been rendered more and more difficult by changing economic and social conditions. In the first half of the nineteenth century the government was not obliged to take cognizance of many matters which during the past half-century have gradually passed from the sphere of private initiative into that of public law. In those days a member of a legislative assembly could give a conscientious examination to the bills which he was called upon to sanction. Today, where can you find a man with the technical knowledge necessary to an intelligent evaluation of all the measures on which a congressman or a senator must vote? Even a man with a technical equipment above the average would not have time enough to master the enormous volume of business which claims his consideration.

The third weak point in present-day democracy is the daily press. A century ago, when freedom of the press was one of the principal demands of liberals everywhere, any group of men with talent and a small sum of money could start a newspaper and acquire an influence in the country proportionate to their ability. This was a period of free competition between small daily papers. But during the past half-century the daily newspaper has become a great capitalist enterprise requiring millions of dollars for its establishment. Hence, whoever has the necessary millions is in a position to flood the country daily with tons of printed matter, although his genius may consist solely in knowing how to find out what particular brand of crime and type of feminine legs most appeal to the sensibilities of the less educated section of the population. Many of these papers are the property of capitalist concerns or are subservient to personal vanities which too often do not promote the welfare of the community. The publisher of one of these newspapers can poison the mind of a whole country with mendacious stories or by the suppression of news. He is a despot who is not responsible to anyone for the manner in which he exercises his authority; he has liberty without responsibility.

The press is now a dictatorship of a unique kind. Planted in the midst of free institutions, it insidiously disturbs and perverts them. The division of powers on which free government was originally based has disappeared, and the Fourth Estate, the great daily press, having overcome all the other powers—the executive, the legislative, and the judicial—reigns supreme in their stead. The omnipotence of the press is perhaps the most dangerous disease which infects free institutions today. If the daily press were not so corrupt and stupid (probably more often stupid than corrupt), even the vote-catching system would not work so badly; and congressmen directed by an intelligent and honest press would be able to cut a better figure.

I am not so presumptuous as to try to suggest solutions for these problems in a few minutes. I confine myself to pointing out that one may approach these problems from two different points of view. A liberal approaches them with the desire and the purpose to heal free and democratic institutions of their present sickness and to make them more sincere and more efficient through free discussion and the free coöperation of the citizens; he refuses to give up to one man and his party the right to work their will in a country of deaf-mutes and slaves. A Fascist or a Communist, on the contrary, approaches these problems with the ulterior motive of taking advantage of the deficiencies of certain democratic institutions in order to destroy all of them.

FALLACIES ABOUT DEMOCRACY

Even the strictest dictatorship is not incompatible with a certain amount of liberty. No other man is so free as a dictator, for no opposition hampers him. And those who are faithful to the dictator remain in full enjoyment of freedom of speech, of the press, and of association. In fact, they enjoy a more complete measure of freedom than they would under a free government, because their rights are not limited by the rights of their opponents.

Neither can dictatorship suppress all the personal rights of the subject. For example, in May 1927 Mussolini issued orders that Italian women were to have more children. Nine months after the issue of these orders the Italian birth rate was found to have dropped precipitously, and it continues to drop. There is a certain residue of personal right which no dictator can check or suppress.

On the other hand, there is no free constitution in existence which does not authorize the government to use some compulsion against its opponents. The latter have the right to criticize the laws made by the party in power, but they must obey those laws until they are abolished by legal means. Revolt against those laws is punishable by imprisonment. Thus, even the most liberal form of democracy does not allow absolute liberty.

The difference lies in the proportion of liberty to compulsion. Freedom and democracy begin when there is more liberty than compulsion for the opposition. Dictatorship begins when there is more compulsion than liberty. Neither pure dictatorship nor pure freedom is to be found anywhere.

From this fact a fallacy easily arises: the mistake of concluding that there is no difference between a free and a dictatorial régime. Both Fascists and Communists make a wide use of such a fallacy. For example, if a daily paper is sentenced for libel in England, they say: "You see, freedom of the press does not exist even in England. Why then do you object to the fact that there is no freedom of the press in Russia, or in Germany, or in Italy?" The fallacy is based on the trick of giving the word "freedom" one meaning in the first sentence and a quite different meaning in the second. If we eliminate this trick, the argument becomes as follows: "You see, *unrestrained* liberty does not exist even in England. Why then do you object to the fact that there is no freedom *for any opposition party* in Russia, or in Germany, or in Italy?"

In an address at Columbia University in December 1933, the German Ambassador to the United States, Dr. Luther, proclaimed that the German Nazi Constitution was democratic. Germany, Dr. Luther admitted, is not a nation in which parliament rules, but "the democratic idea appears in Chancellor Hitler's submission to the vote of the people and his promise to submit himself to their vote in four years." I surmise that while Dr. Luther was preparing his address he remembered Oscar Wilde's remark that many people were rendered stupid by education, and hoped that this law applied to President Butler's students. Undoubtedly democracy means submission to the vote of the people. But the vote of the people must be free. It is not free when the right to oppose the party in power leads to a concentration camp. One is entitled to assert that autocracy is preferable to democracy. What not even an ambassador should allow himself to do is to try to fool his audience by describing an autocratic constitution as a democratic constitution.

I was listening not long ago to a lecture on European dictatorships. During the question period the speaker, although himself a liberal, admitted that for the time being the majority of the German people had confidence in Hitler. Hereupon a voice in the audience made the following comment: "Then Nazism is democracy." Underlying this comment was the idea that rule by the consent of the majority is democracy.

This also is a mistake. The most absolute tyrant will always maintain that he is ruling in behalf of the majority of the people—nay, more, in behalf of all the people and by their consent. Similarly, under a democratic régime all the parties in power maintain that the majority of the people are on their side. The essential difference between dictatorship and democracy lies in the fact that under a despotic régime those who challenge that statement go to jail, while under a democratic régime anyone has the right to make such a challenge and may publicly attempt to prove the falsity of the statement in question.

Democracy means not only that the right to rule is vested in the majority, but also that the right to criticize the rule of the majority is vested in the opposition.

POLITICAL AND ECONOMIC LIBERTY

Wider powers concentrated in the executive in a period of emergency should not be termed dictatorship. In time of war or other emergency, even the most sincere believer in democracy may advocate a greater concentration of authority as a temporary measure to meet exceptional difficulties. As Mr. Walter Lippmann aptly puts it, a democracy which freely grants extraordinary powers to the executive but retains the authority to recall them at will, is still a democracy. The dictator, on the contrary, holds his power by his own right, and remains in power until he is overthrown by force or his armed organization disintegrates from within.

The opposition is not between democracy and emergency powers, but between democracy, which to meet an emergency may provisionally grant wider powers to the executive, and dictatorship, in which absolute authority is permanently vested in one man and his party without the coexistence of a check in the hands of a legislative body.

Another fallacy to be avoided is that of confusing political liberty with economic liberty, and therefore of calling any intervention in economic life dictatorship or Fascism. This error is often made in this country in connection with discussions of the economic policy of President Roosevelt. President Roosevelt is often called a dictator because he intervenes in the processes of production and distribution. Italian Fascists also regard Mr. Roosevelt as one of Mussolini's disciples, though not so big and so heroic as the master. They say: "Either you stick to laissez faire, or you have the state intervene in the production and distribution of wealth. If government intervention takes the form of complete operation of the machinery of production and distribution, then you have communism. If the government does not destroy private enterprise, but only obliges it to fit itself into the framework of a governmental program, then you have Fascism."

This fallacy is disproved if one remembers that every government, be it democratic or oligarchical, free or despotic, is obliged, in greater or less degree, to intervene in economic life. Even a government which adhered most fanatically to the doctrine of laissez faire must enforce respect for the penal, civil, and commercial codes, must issue paper currency, and must have a tariff system. Yet what are these if not examples of governmental intervention in business? England, which in the nineteenth century was the classic country of laissez faire, gave the first examples of social legislation, which is governmental interference with business. A policy of absolute disinterestedness towards economic problems on the part of the government is impossible, and no such policy is known to have been practiced in the world's history. There has always been more or less governmental interference in business.

Such interference becomes a dictatorship only when it is coupled with the abolition of the political rights of the citizen. President Roosevelt would be a Fascist dictator if, besides intervening in economic life, he suppressed personal rights, political liberties, and representative institutions; if the citizens of the United States were no longer allowed to read whatever news papers they liked; if they could not assemble freely in their associations and parties; if those who opposed President Roosevelt were interned on the Philippine Islands without trial, or bludgeoned or killed, while their assailants went unpunished. This would be Fascism. It is an entirely different thing from the intervention of the government in the process of production and distribution of wealth. . . .

DEMOCRACY AND COMMUNISM

This leads us to detect another fallacy which is circulated by Communists when they speak of Soviet Russia. The Ambassador of Soviet Russia to the United States, when he was speaking in Cincinnati in 1934, said: "We believe that we already have full democracy." If somebody had asked him whether Trotsky's living in exile was a proof that Soviet Russia already had "full democracy," the Ambassador would probably have answered that by "full democracy" he meant a régime which proposes to grant economic equality to all its subjects—not one which grants the right to dissent from the views and policies of Stalin and the other leaders of the Communist Party. He who deprives a word of its traditional meaning and uses it in a new sense which he does not define, seeks to deceive his listeners not by the lie direct, but by persuading them to deceive themselves. An ambassador— "a gentleman sent to lie abroad for his country"—must make continual use of this device.

In actual fact, democracy is a system of political institutions, whereas Communism is a system of economic institutions. They are neither the same thing nor opposite things. They are different things. According to many Communists, they do not go together in Russia today, but they will go together when a new generation comes to the front which has been completely imbued with the Communist faith. Then there will be no more reason for suppressing liberty, that is, the right to disagree with the party in power, since there will be no disagreement. Political liberty, in other words, will rise again when it has become useless. Then, and then only, will a Soviet Ambassador be entitled to state that Russia "already has full democracy."

It is likely that an economy supervised by the government has become more necessary in modern society than in former periods of history. Just how far the government should intervene in economic life—and whether it should go so far as to abolish private enterprise entirely or almost entirely, as the Bolshevists did in Russia—is a tremendous problem. But the more intense the intervention of the government becomes, the more we need to keep alive and active free institutions, that is to say, personal rights, political liberties, and the right of representation. The more governmental activities multiply, the more necessary becomes free discussion of the aims, the methods, and the results of those activities. The government becomes an appalling tyranny if the authority intrusted to it in the economic field degenerates into a political dictatorship—if, besides controlling the economic life of the citizen, it can forbid him to express his content or discontent by the normal means available under free rule.

What, then, is the difference between a Fascist constitution, like those of Italy and Germany, a free and democratic constitution, like those of England and the United States, and a Communist constitution, like that of Soviet Russia? A Fascist constitution does away with personal rights, political liberties, and representative institutions, but maintains private property, under more or less strict governmental supervision. A free and democratic constitution grants the citizens personal rights, political liberties, and representative institutions, and either maintains private property, although under a system of more or less strict governmental supervision, or suppresses it altogether. Communism does away with political freedom and private property at the same time. The leaders of the party in power—the Communist Party—are endowed with dictatorial powers, and through these powers they directly control and operate the whole economic machinery of the country.

TWO CONFLICTING PHILOSOPHIES

Freedom and democracy are based on the assumption that nobody is infallible and that no one person possesses the secret of good government.

There is no social science in existence that is as exact as the physical sciences. The phenomena of social life are infinitely more complicated than those of the physical world. Furthermore, the numerous and complex forces which keep the social machine working cannot be measured by objective standards as can those of the physical world. Finally, hypotheses about social facts cannot, as in the physical sciences, be verified by experiment. The more complex society grows, the more difficult it becomes to foresee its future, and the more intricate becomes the art of government. No one, for instance, can tell in advance what repercussions a change in the American tariff system will have on the rest of the world and on the United States itself. A law like prohibition, promoted with the highest moral intentions, may produce disastrous moral effects. Vice versa, a banking law promoted by men concerned only for their own profit at the expense of the country at large may end by producing results that are highly beneficial to the country.

Since no one has infallibility, there is no other method of facing problems than to try out the various possible methods one after the other. The citizens organize themselves into parties and confide the government to that party whose leaders for the time being inspire the most confidence. If this party fails to justify the confidence placed in it, another one is put in its place. By trial and error—"muddling through" as the English say—a way out is found.

Dictatorship is based on the assumption that humanity is divided into two unequal parts: the mass, the "common herd," which knows and understands nothing; and a minority, "the chosen few," who alone know the secret which will solve all problems. Now, "the chosen few," by definition, must be chosen by someone. This is the business of the dictator. "Authority comes from above."

The leader of a free and democratic régime says to his adversaries: "I think I am right, but I may be wrong; let me try and see what are the practical results of my actions. If they are bad, then you will have your chance to do otherwise."

The dictator says: "I am right, and the results of my activity will always be good"; "every man is either for me or against me"; "everything within the state, nothing outside the state, nothing against the state"; "I am the state."

Despotism is easier to conceive and to practice than liberty. Nothing is harder than to respect in our opponents the human dignity common to us both, to tolerate contradiction, to accept competition on equal terms, to trust to the good sense and moral sanity of our countrymen, to face with fortitude the struggle of today which is preparing a broader and more stable coöperation for tomorrow. It is easier to crack the skull of an opponent than to convince him. As the great Italian liberal, Count Cavour, was wont to say: "Any idiot can rule a country by martial law."

Charles A. Beard

Charles A. Beard (1874-   ) was born in Indiana, and holds degrees from DePauw, Oxford, Cornell, and Columbia Universities. His early career was spent in England, where he was associated with the Labor Movement and co-operative groups. From 1907 to 1917 he taught politics at Columbia, resigning in protest against encroachments upon academic freedom. Now a free-lance writer, with some 200 magazine articles and many books to his credit, he makes history live for his readers as formerly he made it live for his students. His central thesis, declared in The Rise of American Civilization *and elsewhere, is his faith in the promise of American life. The following essay vigorously rejects the facile identification of democracy and capitalism and shows how the democratic process is adaptable to change and growth.*

THE RISE OF THE DEMOCRATIC IDEA IN THE UNITED STATES

IS IT TRUE that democracy is only a mask for capitalism, that it contains no humane values forever defensible in themselves, that it offers no methods for the solution of grave problems of state and for the continuous adjustments so necessary for social living? Surely no other question is more fundamental, more worthy of our consideration. It is not academic. Our lives and welfare hang upon the answer to this question and upon our willingness to defend and develop democratic institutions by every sacrifice of fortune and comfort that may be required.

The true answer to this question is not to be found in the fogs of metaphysical and dialectic debate. It lies written in the history of the centuries and in the plain experience of the hour. Whoever runs and reads may find it in the papers and documents that record the past and in the practices of legislatures, executives, and courts now open to general observation.

Is democracy merely a mask for capitalism? Is it true that capitalists originally conceived the idea of democracy in western civilization, that they put it forward in America, that they championed it, fought for it, and embodied it in constitutions and institutions—all for the purpose of providing a mask for their system? If it is true, then the records of history should disclose the supporting facts. What do the records reveal?

At the outset two preliminary definitions are necessary, unless we are to grope in the dark. If by capitalism is meant the mere private ownership of land and other instruments of production, then capitalism is far older than

445

anything that may be correctly called democracy and has existed under many forms of government. But capitalism is not to be identified with private property as such; nor is it one and the same thing in all times and places. It is only to be identified with the use of property for the prime purpose of making profits out of it, as distinguished from its use for the prime purpose of securing a livelihood. Moreover, capitalism is a matter of origins, growth, degree, and change. Certainly in the Middle Ages the great majority of the people and the major part of the instruments of production were employed primarily in the production of commodities for use, not for the profit of the owners in any exact sense of the term profit.

It was only during three centuries of change that the production of wealth for profit became what may be called a major concern of economy in western nations. The degree of that concern varied from nation to nation. If we take 1850 as an arbitrary date we may say that the degree was higher in England than in Germany or Italy or France. It was about this time that the value of manufacturing enterprises, railways, ships, and urban property generally in the United States rose above the value of the land and capital employed in agriculture where production was extensively carried on for domestic use. It is fairly accurate to say that the general triumph of capitalism in western civilization came in the closing decades of the nineteenth century. In human matters the exactness of mathematics and physics cannot be attained, but the weight of historical evidence supports this broad conclusion. If an arbitrary date must be chosen we may venture the judgment that capitalism did not become the dominant mode of production in the United States until after 1865, the year that marked the downfall of the planting class.

Now let us define democracy provisionally as a government resting on a popular base and controlled directly or indirectly by all adults without distinction of property. Certainly that is a justifiable definition of democracy in the political sense of the term even though the social implications of democracy are as broad as life.

Here too we find matters of growth and degree. The steps by which this system of government was approximated may be traced in the records of history as positively as the story of the earth in the findings of geology.

Leaving antiquity and the Middle Ages out of account, for lack of time, we may open the record of democracy in England in the seventeenth century. There were rumblings and grumblings long before that period, but it is in the seventeenth century that we encounter on a large scale systematic demands for "natural rights" and for the right of all men to share in government. Were these demands put forward, approved, or fought for by the property owners and incipient capitalists of that century? The record is plain. They were not. These demands were advanced by obscure, humble persons called "levellers" who were thoroughly despised by the possessing classes of the time. The system of political democracy was attained in England by repeated struggles extending over three centuries, culminating in the suffrage acts of our own day. In these struggles we do not find either capitalists or landlords as a class looking with favor on universal suffrage. They were ready to demand the ballot for themselves, but their philanthropy was limited. Individual capitalists and landlords, sometimes for the purpose of partisan triumph, aided in the movement. But to say that the capitalist owners of property gave the vote to the propertyless for the sake of protecting property—as a mask for capitalism—is to falsify the facts of English history.

The generalization also applies to American history. The property owners who voted under the British system in colonial times did not give the ballot to the propertyless when they threw off the British yoke in 1776. On the contrary the first state constitutions adopted after the revolution began, kept generally property qualifications on voting and office-holding, for the clear purpose of keeping government in the hands of property. It was only through innumerable local struggles that the suffrage was widened to include substantially all adult white males. That state of affairs was practically, but not completely, achieved by 1835, years before the triumph of capitalism in the United States.

And who led in these struggles to democratize our American government? Did capitalists as a class originate them, approve them, and carry them to triumph, all for the purpose of providing a mask for capitalism? Here too the records of American history are clear. In the main the movement for democracy in America received its impetus from mechanics, industrial workers and farmers, who can scarcely be called capitalists by any stretch of the imagination. Leaders in this suffrage battle, men and women alike, derived some aid and comfort from individuals who may be called capitalists, but the establishment of democracy in the United States was not the work of capitalists.

Apart from the cold historical facts, a glance at the theory makes it absurd on its face. Property owners and capitalists, it maintains, turned the government over to the propertyless majority for the sake of protecting their property, providing a mask for capitalism. Common sense logic makes the idea preposterous, while the facts of history demonstrate its falsity. The rise of capitalism coincided roughly with the rise of democracy in some respects; but capitalism did not originate the democratic idea, deliberately promote the realization of the idea, or welcome its triumph. All through the long struggle for democracy, spokesmen of great wealth warned members of their class that democracy was incompatible with the prevailing concentration of property. If outstanding examples need be cited, Lord Macaulay and Daniel Webster may be chosen to illustrate the proposition.

No, the rise of democracy represented a movement of humane forces deeper than capitalism, deeper than the accumulation of profits. Yet the idea of democracy has never been entirely disassociated from the forms and distribution of wealth. Thomas Jefferson did not choose the label "democrat" for himself or the party he founded, but he may be called, with some justification, the leading promoter of the democratic idea in the early days of the American republic. And Jefferson associated popular government with a wide distribution of property. He believed that the true basis of such a government was an agricultural population, composed of freeholders and their families—not capitalists, but tillers of the soil who looked to the labor of their own hands—not to profits—for their sustenance, and thus possessed liberty and independence necessary for popular government. Jefferson thought that the safety of the republic was assured as long as there was an abundance of land for occupation, and that when Americans were piled upon one another in cities, as in Europe, they would start to eating one another up, as in Europe. This is what President Franklin D. Roosevelt must have meant when he quoted the old saying that necessitous men are not freemen.

So today American democracy, in seeking to preserve its institutions, does not offer itself as a mere foil or mask for capitalism and the poverty and degradation that have accompanied its triumph. It is not true that democracy originated or is identical with the creed and practice of laissez-faire which capitalism and its professors have sought to impose upon the people as public policy. Raw and unregulated capitalism was far advanced before the mass of the people were allowed to vote in Great Britain and the United States. Adam Smith, Ricardo, Nassau Senior, and Herbert Spencer had elaborated the doctrine of capitalist anarchy plus the police constable for labor before democracy was well launched upon its career; and the impetus to social legislation mitigating the evils of capitalism and subjecting it to conceptions of common welfare came from the same sources as the impetus to democracy—from leaders in the democratic movement. If capitalism has succeeded in delaying and beating off such legislation, it has been generally *against* the forces of democracy, not with the sanction of its thought and policy.

At this very hour in the United States it is the spokesmen of democracy, not the spokesmen of capitalism, who inquire into the present concentration of wealth, demand security for all, enact social legislation, seek to prevent additional concentration of capitalist power, and strive to effect a more equitable distribution of wealth. To be sure, enlightened capitalists recognize the justice and necessity of such demands, but the center of gravity of capitalism is not on the side of this emphasis in contemporary democracy. It is democracy that now tears the mask of economic theory and legal fiction from the face of historic capitalism and proposes to state the terms on which it may continue to exist and operate. The resolve of democracy to do this is largely responsible for the tensions of the time, for the criticism of democracy in respectable circles, and for the demand that fascist dictatorship be substituted.

No less significant for humanity than the democratic ideal and its economic aspects is the *method* which democracy offers for making the political and economic adjustments required by change in the production of wealth, the advance of knowledge, and the eternal urge of the human spirit. Democracy proclaims that these changes are to be effected by the processes of inquiry, discussion, deliberation, popular decision, and continuous appraisals of results. It offers a way of enlightenment and peace under rules of law, and thus stands in eternal contradiction to government created by force, maintained by force, and unchangeable save by force. It asserts for the human mind freedom of inquiry, without which knowledge cannot be advanced. It upholds freedom of the press and communications, without which intelligence is crippled and discussion is a sham and a farce. It throws about the individual the protection of civil tribunals. It allows no leader hoisted into power by sheer force to imprison or shoot down citizens without trial, without a hearing, without the right to have the truth sifted by witnesses and judicial scrutiny. Its law and custom are yet far from perfect; in practice ignorance and bigotry pervert their purpose; and their principles are often violated. Yet with all the shortcomings, delays, and confusions duly admitted, the ideals and achievements of these institutions stand in flat and eternal contrast to the institutions and practices of governments founded on sheer force.

The very substance of all discussion under this head turns upon the relation of government to change. Certainly the very essence of history is change. Men and women die. New generations arise. The sickle of time cuts down dictators as well as their victims. Ideas appear and exfoliate. Material and spiritual interests alter. Old values are discarded. New values are created and cherished. Neither Hitler nor Mussolini nor Stalin is immortal. No government is fireproof against change. If confirmation be sought, look at the wrecks of states, empires, kingdoms, principalities, dictatorships scattered along the path of more than seventy centuries. Those that do not bend, adjust, or adapt, surely perish. Even despotisms are tempered by assassinations.

All despotisms, under whatever name they masquerade, are efforts to freeze history, to stop change, to solidify the human spirit. There is only one way by which a despotism can be altered; that is, by revolution, by the kind of violence employed in its establishment. Such government may last many years. Cromwell created one; it passed. Napoleon I established one; it passed. Napoleon III established one; it passed. Diaz established one; it lasted longer than Napoleon I's; but it too passed. It may be that none of us assembled here will live to see the passing of the new dictators now preening themselves for their brief period on the earthly stage. But history is merciless. The more they strut, the more they proclaim the eternity of their systems, the more certain we may be of their decay and doom. If there is not a Brutus for every Caesar, there is an old man lying in wait for him.

The institutions of democracy, on the other hand, provide for change and depend not upon the life of any person or self-constituted group of persons. They do not form a closed system of economy or culture. They are devised to cope with the rise, flow, and alteration of social and economic systems, with the creation, modification, and adaptation of systems. They rest upon human ideals, interests and judgments more eternal than systems. They do not deny the role of leadership in history; nor prevent masses of people from rallying around leaders. Indeed they are designed to facilitate this process through discussion, deliberation and matured decisions.

All this the founders of the American republic understood. They were familiar with the history of despotism in the Old World. Between 1780 and 1787 hundreds of Americans believed a republic impossible and popular government of any kind a chimera. In 1782 a colonel in the American army wrote to General George Washington: "The war must have shown to all, but to the military in particular, the weakness of republics." He then proposed that an immense territory be set apart as a distinct state to be governed under such a mode as the military men who moved to it might decide upon. In reply to this letter, Washington wrote a stinging rebuke which will forever stand among the landmarks in the history of American institutions.

No, the founders of popular government in the United States and the leaders among the men and women who have sought to extend democracy in every direction have not been ignorant of history, of the nature and fate of despotism and dictatorships. Nor have they been unaware of the difficulties, risks, and perils of self-government. After independence was declared the way was opened for a military dictatorship and there were many who would have walked therein; but that choice was deliberately rejected and the other course was deliberately taken. With these traditions and these instructions imbedded in the very substance of their civilization, Americans may be pardoned for refusing to accept at face value the old maxims of new upstarts and for renewing their determination to preserve the democratic processes of government. In so doing they need not undertake to give Europe or the Orient any gratuitous lessons, save insofar as tending their own garden may seem instructive.

Herbert Agar

"There is nothing worth fighting for except an idea, for it alone can last, can provide a basis for the developing future." In World War II Agar has put his words into action by directing, from London, a radio forum for United States soldiers in Europe. By experience as well as conviction he was well fitted to help the Army understand what it was fighting for. Herbert Agar (1897-   ) was born in the state of New York; he graduated from Columbia and earned a Ph.D. at Princeton. For five years London correspondent of the Louisville Courier, *he was later its editor. He was an early and forceful advocate of American intervention in the European war. In* Land of the Free, Pursuit of Happiness, *and* A Time for Greatness *he urges no change of the American system but the recovery of our original faith in democracy. If the spiritual convictions at the base of democracy are forgotten, or if the economic rights of men are violated, all the machinery of politics is—machinery. America requires more of us than votes.*

DEMOCRACY IN THE MAKING

DEMOCRACY cannot be understood if it is pictured solely as a political or economic system. Underlying all else, democracy must be a moral code, or it will not be effective. The concept of democracy has never been well defined; perhaps it eludes definition. . . .

There are three parts to the democratic ideal: the spiritual affirmation on which it rests, the economic order which it demands, and the political machinery which puts it into effect. I have stated the three parts in the order of their importance. The third is the least important part of democracy, and it is the only part which exists fully in a place like New York City. It is a mere tool, capable of implementing democracy, if democracy should exist. But if democracy does not exist, the tool cannot bring it into being. The tool will merely be used for other purposes.

As a spiritual affirmation, democracy says that all men have certain minimum rights and requirements which must not be denied—the right to look after themselves and their families in decency without being forced into a slave relationship toward a master or toward the State, the right to a chance to do as well for themselves as their endowments permit, the right to the great basic freedoms which go with the name of civil liberties, the right to a recognition that in a true sense (perhaps best stated by the phrase, "in the eyes of God") all men are equal.

451

These phrases have become smooth and soothing through much use. But if they be taken seriously, they are fighting words. They are almost as revolutionary as Christianity. . . . We must decide whether to take the phrases seriously, or whether to abandon them once and for all. We can no longer afford to use them merely as magic spells to keep our consciences quiet. . . .

On the economic side democracy demands that society be so ordered that the spiritual affirmation has a chance to come true. It demands that men shall not be chattel slaves or wage slaves. It demands that there shall not be such differences in economic opportunity and in chances for self-betterment, that people at the bottom are denied hope.

This, too, is revolutionary; but it is a necessary deduction from the first point. It is dishonest to pretend to accept an ideal if we are unwilling to arrange the physical facts of life in such a way as to give the ideal a chance to come true. Over large areas of Jimmy Hines's [1] New York, in much of our farming country, in many of our mine and textile towns, it is ironic to talk about a man's "right" to look after himself and his family in decency. The time has come to give up pretending to believe in that right, or else to give up pretending that conditions in many parts of our country can be endured.

On the political side democracy demands such machinery of government as will enable the free man, the citizen who is neither spiritually nor economically enslaved, to express his will, to have his way when he is in a majority, to seek to persuade his fellow-citizens when he is in a minority. This political machinery exists in America. It is the only aspect of democracy which we have fully attained. By itself, however, the political machinery means little. If we forget the spiritual demand of democracy, if we let ourselves be persuaded that the economic demand is so difficult that it is impractical and may therefore be ignored, there is no use flattering ourselves that we are a democratic state, merely because we have met the third and easiest of the demands. Political democracy alone, without spiritual and economic democracy behind it, is a fraud. And because it is a fraud, it breeds corruption.

We give the vote, for example, to every adult in Jimmy Hines's district. But we do not give those people economic freedom, or even that minimum of economic safety which helps a man be true to his better nature. And we do not give them the feeling that we really believe all men have a right to self-respect and freedom, or that all men in the eyes of heaven are equal. So what do they do with their vote? They sell it to Jimmy Hines for "a pair of shoes, a scuttle of coal, a parole, a job, or a bottle of milk." But suppose our citizens could have these commodities without graft? Suppose America, the

---

[1] James J. Hines, Tammany boss and dispenser of patronage, convicted in 1939 of selling protection to the policy racket.

richest country in the world, had as little grinding poverty as Sweden, as much equality of opportunity as Denmark? Jimmy Hines would go out of business.

Another field in which we can see the machinery of political democracy breaking down under the absence of real democracy is the field of policy-making. If our democracy were vital, the major policies of government would be formed by a process of public argument. "Such an argument," as the National Policy Committee has pointed out, "is the very essence of the democratic process. In a country where democratic procedure prevails, the Executive does what he finds to be politically possible after an open argument has run its course, instead of merely doing what his experts tell him is best for the country. It does not make much difference who starts the argument. The Executive may start it, or the Legislature, or some group of private citizens. The important thing is that, prior to the enactment of legislation, or the initiation of administrative action, an argument should be started and carried on—citizens arguing with each other and with the government until the issue is defined and the alternatives are understood."

In the absence of such creative argument, the Executive is forced to formulate policy, on expert advice, and to push the appropriate laws through the Legislature by means of party discipline. But these policies may be inadequate, or actively unpopular to that large part of the public which has had no hand in their formulation. The Executive may then be driven to popularize his policies by the use of propaganda. Or some demagogue may take advantage of the public's bewilderment, may use the modern machinery of propaganda to foist off ready-made answers upon a public which has not faced the questions, has not argued them at home, has not heard them debated in public.

In these ways the democratic machinery is step by step perverted into the machinery for a dictatorship. The essence of modern dictatorships is that the leader first initiates policy and the people are then propagandized into voting "Yes" by overwhelming majorities. The essence of democracy is that the people first discuss and argue over policy, lengthily and inefficiently, and the Executive then "does what he finds to be politically possible after an open argument has run its course."

An important point to notice, and a hopeful point, is that the size of America does not defeat this process of open argument. For purposes of argument and public debate, America is smaller today than she was in the days of Jefferson and Jackson. For these purposes, America is smaller today than was the state of Virginia in the days of Jefferson and Jackson. Public policy-making is not defeated by geography or by Fate. It is defeated by our neglect of the two prime aspects of democracy—the spiritual ideal and the economic order. President Roosevelt says that a third of our people are "ill-clothed, ill-housed, and ill-fed." The statement is probably optimistic. And every report, public and private, on our system of popular education reveals a deplorable mediocrity. Can we expect these people to play a vital part in democratic policy-making? Can we expect such a response from people who know we do not mean what we are saying when we talk of equality, and who know furthermore that we are not doing our best to provide a larger chance of equality for their children?

Modern means of communication can help support a true democracy, or they can help turn a fraudulent democracy into a tyrant State. But no machinery can do either of these things by itself. The result depends on the moral purpose of the citizens.

We shall never reform our society merely through trying, from time to time, to tinker with the political machine—passing direct primary laws, or laws to secure an "honest count," etc. The result of "reform" has always been disappointing—and for a good reason. For even if the political machinery should at last be made perfect, there would still be no true democracy in America until we had faced the other two demands. . . . No political reform can save us until we accept the moral and economic obligations of our ideal. . . .

I have not raised the question, "What has gone wrong?" in order to impose my own answer. I have raised it because I hope, by tracing the history of the Democracy, to make the question come alive, so that more and more Americans will insist on facing it, insist on finding the answer that seems to them true.

One man's answer to this question is more than likely to be wrong. But the question itself is not wrong. The question is a great fact. Life has flung the question at us. If we face it wisely and explore its meaning, we are probably good enough to find, through argument and experiment, a working answer. But if we deny the question, turning a foolish face of optimism on the problems which assail us, we shall not deserve success and neither shall we attain it.

One moral, I think, can be drawn . . . The Episcopal prayer book has a phrase about "God, in whose service is perfect freedom." And John Milton wrote, "None can love freedom heartily but good men." If America is to become a free nation, she must find her freedom in the service of a high ideal. Freedom for its own sake, mere absence of restraint, is bound to mean freedom for the powerful to oppress the poor. It is bound to mean anarchy like that of the robber-baron period, when the foundations were laid for our present national plight.

If democracy is taken with full seriousness, it means immense sacrifice, immense self-discipline on the part of society. It means a noble moral and economic code; it means no compromise with the forces that make for plutocracy. A society seeing democracy in these terms, and truly desiring it, truly submitting to the restraints imposed by the quest for it, might attain the freedom which the theologian finds in the service of God. But if democracy is pictured solely in terms of votes for everybody and the least possible restraint on enterprise, then democracy becomes the disorderly self-indulgence which the dictators say it is.

If democracy means the slack assertion that every man is as good as every other (which in worldly terms is obviously a lie), if it means that the prejudices of an ignorant or a misled majority are to be accepted as the last word, then democracy has become the degradation of a noble ideal. As such, it cannot be defended. It is open to all the popular attacks which are leveled against it today.

"All men are created equal" can be interpreted in this shoddy way. It can be made into an excuse for spiritual sloth and for tolerating the second-rate. It can also be made into a demand for nobility and devotion.

Let us imagine an America trying with self-sacrifice to live in steady consciousness of the affirmation that in some high sense men are equal. Our life would not then exhibit that vulgarization of democracy which the dictators deride. On the part of the privileged members of our world there would be a sense of *noblesse oblige,* a driving desire to create in more and more detail the physical circumstances which would make it possible for more and more men to experience equality. We should not be saying that "everybody ought to be equally rich"; but each year fewer of us would care whether we were rich or not. We should not be saying that "one man's notion is intrinsically as good as another's"; but each year more of us would be in a position to make a wise contribution to our common life. Even so, we should never build a democracy. We should never reach our goal, with nothing further to do but stay there. Yet so long as we remained keyed to this effort we should be attempting something noble. And in the process we should make America a great nation. . . .

I have seen a real democracy in the making. I have seen a community that believes in the democratic life as strongly as the western counties of Virginia believed in it when they elected Jefferson President. Having seen this it is not possible to be content with fake democracy or with none at all.

The citizens of northeastern Nova Scotia—fishermen and farmers, miners and storekeepers, priests, teachers, and business men—have for twenty years been building a democratic society through adult education and co-operative enterprise. They have contrived no paradise; but they have lifted themselves out of poverty, ignorance, despair. And while improving their worldly state they have learned the excitement and the sense of goodness that comes to people who work with their fellows disinterestedly for the common well-being. This rare excitement is shared by most of the community; it is not the privilege of a few superior people.

The movement, which started in one corner of Nova Scotia, has reached a point where it is an inspiration over the whole of the Maritime Provinces and out to the island of Newfoundland. If it continues to prosper it will not be long before all those Provinces see a demonstration of what can be meant, in this world, by the brotherhood of man.

The movement may fail; but so far it has gone steadily ahead. If any American has forgotten what democracy feels like, he can learn his own heritage by visiting northeastern Nova Scotia. He will discover good men making a new world—unfrightened men who do not hate the enemy in a personal sense. It is not a class war these men are making. It is a war against institutions and against the sort of physical conditions that deprive men of hope. It is also a war of reason and liberation against the antisocial elements in man. And it is not a fanatical war; it is a war in which the soldiers dare to have fun.

I do not think that any social and political ideal except democracy could produce this result among men. Democracy, as practiced by those Nova Scotians, could be the answer to the strife and hatreds which appear to be destroying Western civilization. Statesmen and philosophers have for generations been looking for the "moral equivalent to war." Democracy, if taken with high seriousness, could be the answer to that long search.

Anyone who has seen the ease with which all people can be roused to fight must know that war gratifies some important part of human nature. Much as we hate war there is a part of each one of us which loves it also. It is that part which betrays us to the propagandists when the war-drums are beaten. And the most attractive feature of war is that it gives men a superb chance to work together, side by side in the same ditch and with the same fate before them. In a lonely and divided world, war breeds a comradeship which most men want and which all men need. Democracy can breed that same comradeship—but only if we serve it honestly and with our hearts. For example, if we really should seek to practice the phrases of the Declaration of Independence we could build a good America without the use of guns or tear-gas or Siberias. We could even enjoy ourselves while we did it.

The "if" may seem fantastic to many readers. I can only repeat that I have seen the thing happening. I do not think that Nova Scotia is the only corner of our continent where men can rise to moral passion.

Bruce Bliven

*Bruce Bliven (1889-   ) was born in Iowa. He is a graduate of Stan-
ford University. For several years he served on the editorial staff of the
New York Globe; since 1923 he has been editor-in-chief of The New
Republic. The following "notes" do not pretend to integration or com-
pleteness, but they do suggest several approaches to a definition of that
elusive and paradoxical myth, the average American citizen.*

NOTES ON THE AMERICAN CHARACTER

THE last four decades in American life have been
a period of extraordinarily complete disillusionment. The preceding forty
years had been a time of widening horizons in science, of amazing progress
in invention and discovery, a time when it seemed certain that things would
go on getting better and better forevermore. Yet at about the turn of the
century, doubts began to be heard. The reservations regarding the benefi-
cence of the evolutionary process which Tennyson had uttered so far ahead
of his time in "Locksley Hall," began to sink into the general consciousness. A few years later Freud knocked the props from under the false com-
placency with which the average man had viewed the purity of his own
character and the disinterestedness of his motives. The Great War shattered
violently the dreams of a generation which supposed that force had been
ruled out of a world dominated by sweetness of life. For a variety of reasons
too complicated to discuss here, the autocratic character of the home, with
the father as autocrat, crumbled away. The process of painful adjustment to
reality reached its climax in the 1930's when the totalitarian states completed
the ruin of the Victorian ideal. Nazism in particular gloried in cruelty, denied the existence of objective truth, repudiated the very core of the nineteenth-century code, which held that the human personality is sacred and
central, that the state exists for man, and not the contrary.

For millions of human beings, there was one particular disillusionment
harder to bear than any other. For nearly a hundred years, the belief had
been growing and spreading that many of the ills of our society could be
traced to its wrong economic basis. The argument had for all these people
been conclusive that if the injustice could be removed from the arrangements
by which man's worldly goods are produced, cruelty and greed would disappear as poverty was vanquished. To be sure, the followers were always
more innocently Utopian than their leaders; but it is the followers I am

talking about. When a group of men who accepted the Marxian analysis became the heirs, by default, of the Tsar's empire, millions of persons throughout the world pinned their hopes for a new society to what was happening in Russia. They of course overestimated the possibilities and underestimated the difficulties. As the years passed and Russia looked little more like Utopia than it had two decades earlier, as the promised civil liberties still remained largely on paper, as a dictator emerged for whom Marxian theory certainly had not provided, in the minds of millions of too innocent and trusting souls, the disheartenment was great.

The series of disillusionments referred to here have of course been worldwide; but for special reasons due to our peculiar position they have been less strong in America than elsewhere. The "American Dream," inconsistent as it is with many of the known facts of today's life, still exercises a compelling force upon vast numbers of our people.

A common delusion on both sides of the Atlantic is that the Americans and the English are very much alike. This is an error based on the similarity of language and the fact that so many Americans are descended from British, Welsh, Scotch or Irish ancestors. Actually, however, the American is singularly unlike the Briton. The rhythm of his thought is different; his general outlook on life is wholly dissimilar; his preferences in literature, the theatre, recreation and everything else tend to diverge, with the area of difference usually larger than the area of resemblance. Comparisons between nationalities are always dangerous, but if one felt compelled to find a resemblance it would be between the American and the French or the Russians. The Americans are quick, like the French; they also come much closer to the cynical-seeming realism of the French than they do to what someone has called England's strangulated sentimentality. There are strong resemblances between the Americans and the Russians.

Despite the interesting work of Ellsworth Huntington and others, far too little attention has thus far been paid to the influence of climate on character. Take mountain types from New Hampshire or Switzerland—tall, angular, taciturn and rather morose—and settle them on the level plains of the Upper Mississippi Valley: within a couple of generations, the children reveal all the attributes of the plain-dwelling inhabitants of the new home, volubility, optimism, good nature. It is no accident that nearly all the inhabitants of Southern California come to exhibit the same mental and physical pattern in an astonishingly brief number of years. The cartoonists' Uncle Sam, faithfully copied for three-quarters of a century, is a Vermont type no longer typical of the country as a whole.

A hundred years hence, the anthropologists (if there are any left) may attach a good deal of importance to the year 1924, when the new immigration restrictions went into effect. This law confirmed the stoppage of the immigrant flood which had taken place not long before the World War.

Since 1924, partly because of the depression, and partly because of restrictions on emigration by European countries, we have in most years lost more aliens than we have received. The immigration quotas, based upon the make-up of our population a quarter of a century earlier, were nicely calculated to permit the largest number of immigrants from the countries where the smallest number wanted to come, and vice versa.

The stoppage of the immigration is already being reflected in many ways. In some industries such as steel and coal, machines at last take the place of men, since greenhorns are no longer so plentiful, or so capable of being malignantly exploited, as in the past. The foreign sections of our great cities, reservoirs of immigrants who formerly lived in the new world the life of the old, in costume, speech and social custom, are being drained off into the general population as their children go to our schools, learn American ways and are vocally bitter about the failure of the older generation to "talk United States."

At the turn of the century it really seemed possible that the American character might finally be dominated by the vast hordes of East Europeans who came clumping through Ellis Island, a million a year. Not only were their numbers formidable, in relation to an America a good deal smaller than at present, but their birth rate was substantially higher than that of the older American stock. But the fears based upon the second of these phenomena have proved as chimerical as those which sprang from the first. Today the birth rate of the country districts (especially in the South) is higher than that of the cities, where immigrants and the sons of immigrants mostly dwell. It is higher among the poor than among the rich, for obvious reasons of ignorance and lack of money; but in the city there is no appreciable difference between the situation of the foreign-born and the native of the same station.

The American type which seems destined to survive and to dominate is therefore that of the older American, the Anglo-Saxon Protestant stock which is found most characteristically in the small towns of the Middle West. What sort of man is he? This is an extraordinarily variegated country; generalizations are always dangerous and are subject to numerous exceptions. Within the limits of these restrictions, however, there are a few things that can be said.

The American talks a great deal about democracy but his libertarianism is full of contradictions and inconsistencies in practice. He is willing to let you disagree with him, but only within fairly narrow limits. If he is a Methodist, he doesn't much mind your being a Baptist, but he objects strongly to atheism. Translated into political terms this means that a Republican tolerates a Democrat easily but a Socialist or Communist with difficulty if at all.

Many Americans, certainly a majority in numerous communities and perhaps in the country as a whole, don't see very much point in protecting civil liberties for persons whose views differ widely from their own. (Hitler has been the best press agent democracy ever had. His repressions in Germany have been so obnoxious that people who have quite an impulse in the same direction are repelled into a considerably stronger affection for tolerance.) Vigilantism, the tendency toward lynch law, which springs up so readily in many parts of the country, is not solely an immediate economic phenomenon, the well-to-do inciting the poor to oppress the trouble-maker, or one section of the poor acting against another section which is its competitor in the labor market. It is also an expression of several rather profound American traits: the violent lashing out at those who disturb the accustomed mores, the lack of veneration for such established machinery as courts and juries, the determination to have one's own way which is essentially infantile and is a powerful part of the American character.

No doubt for generations to come people will continue to talk about the continuing influence of the frontier on American institutions. That it has had an influence, no one can deny, any more than it is possible to fix a date in the past or predict one in the future which marks the termination of frontier psychology. The field in which generalization seems most safe is that of American optimism, the psychology of an expanding economy. Even today, when so many of the fundamental theses are clearly outmoded and in spite of the disillusionments noted above, most Americans continue to think in terms of an assumption that everything is going to get bigger and better. No business man can imagine an existence in which his volume, even if not his profits, did not expand from year to year. The sudden sharp contraction in a period of depression is regarded as a temporary unavoidable misfortune, like spending a few days in bed with a cold. When the population really does turn downward, when the proportion of the aged is markedly increased and of the young diminished, this easy faith is going to have a head-on collision with some hard and unpleasant facts; but up to now, the iron has entered our collective soul only to a limited extent. . . .

One American characteristic that comes near to being unique is our passion for individual self-improvement. The English tend to feel they are doing quite well as they are, thank you; the Frenchman naturally assumes that France and its inhabitants are perfect; the German, at least in his present incarnation, looks forward only to more blood and bigger monuments; the Russian ideal is improvement for the whole mass, at the pace of the most laggard (although genius is encouraged and, if not recalcitrant, given room to work in). Only the American is obsessed with the idea that he as an individual must become a paragon, and if possible, overnight. He buys rowing machines by the million, to be tried for three days and then hidden in a hall closet. He, or more probably she, takes a multitude of nostrums to reduce weight and produce glowing health, neither of which things ever happens. He is forever buying encyclopedias of all human knowledge, which he expects to read in his spare time during the winter, only to discover too late that he hasn't any such time and that the encyclopedias bore him. He rubs paste on his hair until he is completely bald; he attends an incredible quantity of lectures. On the whole, the passion for self-improvement, for a desire to speak French, have good-looking hair, play the saxophone, be brilliant in repartee and a convincing after-dinner speaker, is part of the American myth that evolution means improvement, that the world is getting more and more wonderful all the time and that each individual owes it to God and the American flag to help along the process as best he can.

While the typical American is not very much interested in liberty, one must not overlook the existence of a large minority which is keenly concerned about the struggle for the preservation of civil rights. In part, this group is found within the ranks of organized labor (although there are also many unionists whose outlook is precisely that of the conservative middle class). In part, it consists of people who have no immediate axe to grind but recognize the importance of keeping the channels of communication open even for unpopular doctrines. These are the people who support the American Civil Liberties Union, read the progressive weeklies, sign petitions and give financial aid to victims of oppression throughout the country, attend mass meetings for causes unpopular with the majority. They constitute, it seems to me, the most healthy single force within our body politic. As long as they continue to exist and to function, no one can say that pessimism about our future is wholly justified.

The statement is often made that the American mind has been standardized in the past decades by the tremendous influences making for uniformity: syndicated newspaper features appearing simultaneously all over the country; movies that play in the course of a few weeks in every town from Florida to Oregon; nationwide radio programs with their audiences of thirty or forty millions. How far this is true it is impossible to say conclusively. I suspect, however, that the importance of these things is exaggerated. Americans were pretty much alike in the fundamentals before these devices came along, and I can't see that they are any more so today than they were in my boyhood. Certainly, the radio has not succeeded in standardizing American speech. It is still easy to identify on first hearing the accents of Virginia, Georgia, Iowa and Maine.

The important change of the past generation has been the great decrease in parochialism. There are still plenty of backwaters—in the South for instance—where the current civilization of movies, radio and automobiles has made little impression; but they are now the uncharacteristic exceptions. Today, all over the country even in remote farm areas the young people (and the older ones too) listen to Charlie McCarthy on Sunday night, follow their favorite movie stars in the county-seat picture house, know all about Oldsmobile's new fluid clutch. Whether they get their clothes from a Chicago mail-order house or from the town an hour's ride away over an amazingly good road, their styles are pretty much those to be seen on Park Avenue or Wall Street. This ability to participate in the national procession goes amazingly far down the economic scale, though of course the poorest group are cut off from participation and are isolated in the prison of their poverty.

The country districts and the small towns are no longer parochial about foreign affairs (I suspect they were never so aloof as their detractors maintained). A short-wave radio set works as well or better in Wyoming as in Connecticut; no one on the Atlantic seaboard could follow world events any more closely than do the inhabitants of the Mississippi Valley, the intermountain states and the Pacific slope. If these regions seem somewhat cooler in their judgments, more detached in their viewpoints than does the East, it is perfectly possible that they are right, and that their perspective is improved by their lack of the large masses of undigested foreigners who still, though their numbers are dwindling, bring European affairs vividly and immediately and with bitter partisanship to many communities in the northeastern quarter of the country. . . .

All this, at any rate, for the older generation. The younger is changing in ways that haven't yet got into any textbook, ways that make tomorrow difficult to predict. The hallmarks of the older America were its inhibitions and a sort of sublimated infantilism that went with them. The younger generation seems to be losing these inhibitions with dizzying speed. Drop into any little country dance hall on a Saturday night, being careful to avoid the places where city people go, and watch the dancing not merely of the jitterbugs but of the whole group, or see them while they listen to a swing band that is really in the groove. You will see a simple open pleasure in living and in rhythmic movement for its own sake that is new and very strange—at least, to the last generation.

This new freedom extends into many fields. With the authority of the home destroyed, with the stern parent of the past a discarded image and the new-type father and mother pathetically straining to be just good pals, responsibility rests with the young for their own behavior, and is on a basis nobody would dare to put into any book. In every part of the country, whether in theoretically dry states or those that have now returned to the open sale of alcoholic beverages, young men and women are facing and solving the problem of holding their liquor. With contraceptives on sale not only in every drug store but, in some parts of the country, in every filling station, sexual behavior is no longer dictated by fear of disastrous consequences any more than it is by the moral strictures of the past generation. A good many people are no doubt surprised and secretly a little regretful to find that even under these circumstances the vast majority of the rising generation is "good," even in the strictest interpretation of the word, and has the same ambitions that preceding generations did—a job, a home, children, health and security.

It is obvious that the American character holds dangerous tendencies. We have a long tradition of violence, of overriding established legal forms, of reluctance to listen carefully or long to the other man. It is easy to say— and a great many people are saying it—that we are in danger of a native brand of fascism. If you use this term loosely enough, it may be true; but if you are thinking of anything like what now exists in Germany or Italy, I would enter a strong exception. It has often been noted that fascism has never yet obtained control of any country where the people had enjoyed democratic political institutions for any length of time. The Americans are proud and stubborn, individually, as the Germans and Italians have never been. I find it impossible to imagine Madison Square Garden or the San Francisco Municipal Auditorium full of people shouting the American equivalent of "Duce!" or "Sieg Heil!" The very fact that the American home long ago discarded parental tyranny gives us a safeguard that was lacking in those countries. Our people do not feel the need of a substitute father image as do Europeans brought up in homes that were little oligarchies.

To be sure, a triumph of fascism in Europe would have dangerous repercussions here; but far more dangerous would be a continuance of conditions under which some 30,000,000 people are half starving on public charity, millions of skilled workers can find nothing to do, sharecroppers in the South get shelter worse than that of the cattle on a prosperous Iowa farm. Enough desperation, long enough continued, produces an explosion. To prevent it, we need all possible encouragement of democratic forces here and abroad. I see nothing in the American character to cause discouragement for democrats. I see only a reason to emphasize the ancient warning that eternal vigilance is the price of liberty.

Frances Frost

New Englanders especially will recognize the subject of Frances Frost's poem: forgotten ghosts of roads lost in the second growth which is covering up the earlier stages of our history, reminders of the first settlers who came and saw and conquered. The builders of these roads were creators of the American heritage.

LOST ROAD

The feet which wore this earth to a twisted road
Between two mountains, are halted now and gone
Under the mountains where restless feet are still.
The small green things with blossoms have come back:
Year by year the tangled woods push down
And thicken the shadows above the wagon-track
And cover with fires of blossoming the brown
Wander of dust.

The russet ghosts of lilac-bloom are summer
About a door long opened to the rain.
A locust in a brazen, husky stammer
Stretches tight a yellow afternoon;
And sun and rain fall deeply on this road
Where men with wide, burned shoulders and steady breath
Went, through the ache of days and nights, toward death.

The walls men made in woods . . . beneath the moon
Of summer run forever . . . and by these
Men outlive the hour wherein they die.
Under a sky
Of boughs, the way is lost by which a child
Went laughing from one white house to another,
Scuffling beneath the mounting, golden day.

A road is a message many men wrote down
In dust, of love that listened for the sound
Of footsteps coming home. A road is where
Women, at evening, before the light was gone,

Walked with children living in their flesh
And dreamed of other roads on other mountains
To be carved by strong sons born to wilderness.

A road is a chronicle of loves and years.
A road remembers until the green things take
With blossoms the last faint trace of footsteps going
Between a beginning and an end.
                                        O bitter
Growing of woods and sumac, of thorns and fern,
Possess at last
This road which is a word
Spoken from darkness, uttered from the years
Abandoned long ago. O wildness, burn
With deep green shadow, the memory of those
Who left this sign between tall grass and grass
As they went past.

Lewis Mumford

*Lewis Mumford (1895-   ) was born on Long Island, spent his boy-
hood in New York City, and attended the College of the City of New
York and other institutions. With a universal range and a power of synthesis that suggest Ruskin he writes of the social problems of our modern
civilization in terms of culture. Like Ruskin he points out, in* Technics
and Civilization, The Culture of Cities, *and* The Condition of Man *the
relation between architecture, especially city architecture, and a richer,
freer life for all classes. In "Roots in the Region" he describes the loss
and the return of regional loyalties in the United States. With a burning
vision of the society which might be, he challenges youth to build the
solid regional cultures which are the first requisite for the new America,
the America where every man and woman will be firmly rooted in his
home soil.*

ROOTS IN THE REGION

MEN are attached to places as they are attached
to families and friends. When these loyalties come together, one has the
most tenacious cement possible for human society.

One of the great effects of the age of discovery and the age of invention
that followed it was the worldwide displacement of millions of people. In

Europe, they left lands that their families had occupied for hundreds of years, sometimes a good thousand at least. They dropped their old associations, with this river, with that mountain, with a castle hanging over a crag or a group of church towers pricking the sky over mist-hung marsh; they left the earth that had molded them to find a place for themselves in the new lands. First they trickled into the New World, trading and fighting and shrewdly seeking profits; then the trickle, in the nineteenth century, became a spring flood of people carrying in its turbid course not merely human bodies but the very silt and detritus of their cultures.

Millions came to America: particularly, perhaps, those with shallow roots, or those whose rootlets had been killed by political despotism and economic oppression. Some of them struck root; from Massachusetts to Georgia there are families that stayed put from scratch: groups that identified themselves with a particular spot of soil and sky and water, and bear its marks on speech and skin. Others moved on, settled, became restless, kept moving: sometimes they turned their backs to the soil and found themselves a place in the new cities.

The will to move was there; so were the vehicles; people came by ocean steamship, and moved on by wagon and railroad. Mere ease in locomotion aided this transplanting of individuals and groups; the open land, so plentiful and so cheap, tempted them, too. Like a child confronted with too many toys at one time, they grabbed everything, stuck to nothing, and kept on changing over.

A certain uniformity in superficial things abetted this movement in the United States: a common system of government that by mid-century covered a good part of the continent: laws and canned goods and sheet-iron roofs and transport vehicles and plumbing, being all uniform, kept the restless pioneers from feeling any shock when they slipped from one environment to another. Underneath, regional differences continued to exist; but, after 1850, national fashions and a national market began to minimize them.

Quickly enough these new immigrants became patriotic; but, unlike the older families and regions, the patriotism of the newcomers was attached to institutions rather than to places. It had to do with the machinery for voting, making laws, imposing taxes. Hence patriotism became entangled in a quite abstract conception: political uniformity and national unity. After the War between the States, it was finally established that laws that are passed by the Congress of the United States must apply uniformly to all citizens, without regard to local conditions and regional characteristics. This either put the burden for local legislation on the separate states, which often had no geographic or social identity, or made it necessary to recognize differences within the national pattern by subterfuge and hypocrisy. Local politics became shabby and down at the heels; only national government mattered.

Another result of this thinning out of a community's natural loyalties to the land, was the fact that patriotism tended to identify itself with the reactionary and the old-fashioned: a little like religion, it reserved its ceremonies for occasional use; piously permitting the wealth of the country to be hastily extracted by those who had an eye on the main chance. Even today, at the hint of a national emergency, the first instinct of many selfish people is to suggest an immediate abandonment in the name of patriotism of any laws or acts that restrain the privileges or emoluments of their group.

Surely there is not the least reason why patriotism should be monopolized by reactionaries. Neither is there any reason why the only kind of patriotism that should be recognized is that which is identified with the sovereign national state. On this point, one feels that the Southern regions lost a war in fighting for a poor cause that one might well have wished them to win had they been fighting solely for the right to retain their individualities as communities. Sectionalism became a word of reproach after the Civil War. People tried to forget Hawthorne's wise dictum, to the effect that New England was as large a spot of earth as he could love. As a result our politics lacked love: love of country was honored by words of praise on the Fourth of July, not by actions every day in the year.

Now patriotism is a universal attribute of normal people. It is grounded in space and time; that is, in the actual soil and landscape of a region, and in the experience of life that, in retrospect, constitutes its people's history. The deepest source of this love of country is neither law nor property, although they play a part in qualifying it: the ultimate source is the land as land, the sky as sky, the people as people.

—The red soil of the Shenandoahs in Virginia, with the apple trees whose boughs skirt the ground; the granite hills of Vermont with their white churches, stiff against the north winds, honest and unyielding as only fanatics are honest and unyielding; the undulating meadow land of Iowa, with curves as delicate as a pea's tendrils; or the hard primeval clarity and the enveloping loneliness of the desert, from the white alkali of Utah to the red canyons of Arizona.

These are samples of our regions: samples of backgrounds, to be filled out with the stories that are told and the pictures painted, by the houses that are fabricated, by all that the hand of man has added. All that—and the people themselves, speaking an English speech that now glides over the tongue and now clogs it, that halts at the nose or escapes half formed through soft and lazy lips. The plow and the lariat; the yoke that holds the maple bucket; the dusty threshing machine; the filling station and the relentless assembly line; the steel mill and skyscraper that is itself a gigantic filing case, holding other filing cases. The things that men love because they are easy, and those they love because they are hard and the men can take it—the hayfield at 110 degrees or the rolling mill at 120.

These are the sights and experiences and places and ways and tools that make the indelible reality of our American patriotism. But in its best sense, patriotism is always narrow and intense: close to one's family, one's village or city and·the land around. Regional sentiments spring out of a settled way of life: deep roots in the ·soil itself.

In the restless movings about of the last two centuries, this essential relation between the human spirit and· its background was derided, underestimated, sometimes overlooked. Had it been acknowledged for what it was worth, it might have stayed the pioneer in his very act of pulling up stakes and moving away. The land itself was looted and mined because men did not yet love it sufficiently; nor did they heed what sort of life they would leave for those who came after them. What had posterity done for them? Where men shifted so easily no cultural humus formed; no human tradition thickened. Did the farmers who became rich in Iowa after World War I stay in their state, and devote their leisure and their savings to its common life? By report, just the opposite happened: they uprooted themselves from their lovely landscape, to become a herd of flighty, money-obsessed people in California.

But now the period of terrestrial exploration is over. All over the world men are beginning to settle down and take root. Or rather, that was what was happening before the new fascist barbarians began to tear men away from their dear lands. In America the process of settlement reached its first apogee along the Eastern seaboard between 1800 and 1850: the period of the Golden Day. Now it is beginning over again; and what happened in New England in the period of Hawthorne's and Emerson's youth, when every village had its history and its lovers of tradition, is at last starting to happen in every part of the country.

The reason is plain. Great continental states or empires are too big to be in intimate relations with men's daily needs and desires; great financial corporations and administrative organizations are likewise too impersonal by nature and cover too small a fragment of life, even when their intentions are humane. But there must be a focus for communal attachment, bigger than the family or the city, smaller than the country or all mankind; and the surest source of that sustaining kind of patriotism is the region.

The conscious recovery of regional roots has been going on in the world for almost a hundred years: indeed, if one counts in New England, where the roots had not been severed, it goes back longer than this. This movement is sometimes confused with nationalism; but it has a more local and concentrated objective, except in places where the regional and the national boundaries coincide, as in Ireland. Actually, the conscious re-establishment of the local and historical tradition first was the work of a group of Provençal poets in France; the Félibrigistes. But what happened in France, once the most centralized of modern states, has been happening everywhere else.

To create a balanced life in each region has become a contribution to local self-respect and to world-culture. We must concentrate our loyalties before we can expand them; we must have the practice of dressing and keeping the land, and embodying our love for it in the very way we fashion the buildings that we build. Regionalism, then, grows out of an immediate fondness for a soil and a way of life: for the language and the cultural products of a group of people, intimately connected with a particular landscape. As it develops, regionalism embraces more and more the political and economic aspects of a community. When a people, like the Jews, lacks a regional home it restores its loss through dreams and utopias, like that of Zion. At the first opportunity it returns, even under hardships and handicaps, to its land. The alternative to regionalism is not nationalism, but dispersion.

In America, regionalism has two sides to it; one, the conservation movement, connects with the use of resources, with the balance of nature, with the intelligent exploitation of water power, minerals, forests, and the like. The other side is the cultural and sentimental side. Each of these movements lacks something that the other supplies; for a sentimental regionalism, that dreams dreams without putting a foundation under them, must finally lose its own self-respect and be pushed over by more aggressive economic and political interests originating outside the region, sometimes hostile to it, sometimes simply callous. The conservation of resources, on the other hand, is hardly a program to stir men's blood: one might as well intone the *World Almanac* for inspiration. Politics is always a battleground of interests; and a low, anti-social interest can be combated only by another interest that shows a higher human potential.

Conservation, it is true, has had many modest triumphs in America, ever since the first National Parks were set aside as public domains. Yet it is hard to imagine any considerable body of our youth being willing to die for the ideal of conservation. At times, where the imagination is kindled by a visible threat, the need for conservation may persuade a university town, like Eugene, Oregon, to buy up a neighboring mountain to keep the forest on it from being cut down completely. But one does no injustice to the conservation program to say that, admirable as it is, it has not awakened anything like a universal sense of obligation.

The same observation applies in part to the valuable studies of the National Resources Committee and the various co-operating State Boards. They have every indispensable characteristic, many of these studies, except the breadth of imagination, the human sentiment, and the co-operative understanding that would bring them to life.

The regionalist movement, at the same time, has shown a characteristic weakness, which was not lacking in the earliest stages and has not yet been completely sloughed off. This is visible in the South and in New England— the tendency to hark back too fondly to its image in the past. In New England this makes the local patriots think highly of their Puritan or Georgian architecture, but to forget the noble-looking factories of Fall River and Lowell, and to ignore the freshest contributions of all before the twentieth century, the cottage architecture of Richardson. It makes the regionalist think that old iron forges were indeed worthy of another generation, but new steel mills are just the horrid present. It even makes people take pride in local warts, because they are local, and forget the unblemished face, because it is universal.

Sometimes, then, the regional patriot tries to isolate the local unit itself from the great stream of history, which carried it along, and gave it its larger meaning. The historical basis of development, which should serve as a point of departure, becomes a resting place, a trap that lures the regionalist into attempting to return to a past that has ceased to exist. Under this delusion history becomes a utopia; the good days are always behind; and instead of his undertaking the perpetual reconquest of the environment, in terms of all man's accumulating inventions, purposes, and desires, the regionalist contents himself with a dream of archaic reconstruction—as if life could be lived in a museum.

Even on the purely practical side, regionalism tends often unconsciously to misdirect its aims to an obsolete past. Witness the attempt on the part of individual states to erect trade barriers against other states. What is this but a blind chaotic effort to go back to a past when natural obstacles created a narrow, self-sufficient economy? The means which would serve to create a balanced region demand quite a different kind of planning: planning which would embrace a continental or a global area, and would not merely provide for an intensive, many-sided development of resources and industries within the local area, but would at the same time provide a planetary organization of markets, for the orderly interchange of surpluses, specialties, and highly localized resources. This not merely means cultivating all that one has; it also means reaching out for all the things that the region lacks. That principle applies on both the economic and the cultural levels.

We in America have often taken the view, to use Carlyle's brutal words about Whitman, that we must be a great people because we live in a large country. We have acted as if the mere abundance of natural resources and raw materials was any guarantee that we would utilize them in a rational, purposeful fashion. Similarly we have created units of local government and administration, our states and counties, without worrying in the least whether the land enclosed by their legal boundaries constitutes any sort of organic unit, in history and geography, to which men's natural loyalties and affections would cling. Hence we have river valleys like the Connecticut, the Ohio, the Mississippi, and the Columbia, in which the very unity that is promoted by a river system is destroyed by the mapmaker's ingenious nonsense of calling a river a boundary line because the black line that represents it on the map looks like one.

Our belief that resources by themselves make us great has another serious defect. It gives but feeble counsel to those parts of the country that nature has endowed sparingly with wealth, as in our grand desert regions, or in those parts which war and human erosion have left blighted, as in certain regions of the South.

In renewing our relations with the land we must not be deceived by the specious belief that abundance is the sole guarantee of culture. Dearth and poverty are sometimes more effective challenges to human powers than is wealth; witness the case of Holland, which lacked, so to say, ground to stand on. Out of their poverty the Netherlanders won from the sea and reclaimed for agriculture one of the richest and most thriftily used soils in Europe; and as a by-product they achieved a skill in hydraulic engineering and building that gave them pre-eminence in the seventeenth century, both in technics and science. Thanks to their original poverty, they created a garden where four hundred years before a handful of fishermen kept a bare hold on a spit of sand. The same is true of our salt desert, Utah; which provided the stimulus for the most provident and politically adroit piece of colonization that the country can boast.

At best, resources are capital reserves. It is well to have rich land, a plentiful water supply, a heavy forest cover, an abundance of metals and minerals. But none of these things is indispensable; and the mere quantity of resources does not determine the purposes and ends of a regional culture. Purpose rather determines the quantity that shall be used. Where money purposes have been consistently uppermost, resources that should have lasted half a millennium have been gutted out in twenty years. Without vision, therefore, both resources and people perish.

The Grand Coulee Dam, for example, is a piece of imaginative planning of genuine value, on the level of technics: it promises potentially to transform a region of difficulty into a region of increment; and it does this with a breath-taking adroitness in commanding natural possibilities. Thanks to the dam and its hydro-electric works and its coming irrigation system, there is the opportunity of creating a desert culture that will offer far higher possibilities for the life abundant than the half-arid, thinly settled region that now exists.

But is anything like the same quality of imagination available as yet on the human and communal level? To ask that question is to make the answer ludicrous. The new resources that will be created in eastern Washington by the new dam demand an heroic order of public service, a generation disciplined to creative thinking and co-operative public action, a corps of architects, educators, poets and philosophers, no less than farmers, agricultural experts, and engineers. Do they exist in the Pacific Northwest except in minute samples? No. Do they exist even in the United States? Only a handful.

We are not handicapped by lack of opportunity to exploit our regional resources; we are burked by lack of creative purposes. Our love for the land is a lazy one. Our civilization as a whole is partly parasitic on both the machine and nature; it has yet to create a pattern for regional living and the means that would make that pattern effective.

Meanwhile our young people are starving for lack of real tasks and vital opportunities. Many of them live like sleepwalkers, apparently in contact with their environment, but actually dead to everything but the print of the newspapers, the blare of the radio, or the flickering shadows on the screen. . . .

Work alone is no answer to this frustration; not even part of an answer. Work at good wages, with social security and an ultimate pension, seems a promise of paradise only to a starved, anxiety-ridden body. For the very nature of the work itself, its impersonality, its automatism, its imperviousness to human requirements, makes it almost as much the cause of frustration as unrelieved idleness.

But the young will care for their regional home if they have a part in creating it. They will live an effective and responsible life if once they have an opportunity to see and feel and touch and listen to all those activities that belong to their native scene. Why should the young people not have their first experience of public service on work that serves for local improvement? They should help clear the slums, as well as study housing; they should help plant the forests as well as study conservation; it is our school children, and not the dreary and defeated Joads, who should have a turn at camping and picking the peaches and apples—on terms that will wipe out every last vestige of economic despotism in places like the Imperial Valley. It is our youngsters nearing military age who should be toughened off in lumber camps, on fishing boats, behind the hay-wagon and the threshing machine, on the road gang and in the quarry.

Such regional experiences—and inter-regional experiences—are the very basis of communal health. They begin and end with a loving awareness of one's environment, comradely intercourse with and participation in the lives of one's fellows: a role in the regional drama, and a part, if only a super's part, in regional history.

The Civilian Conservation Corps and the various activities of the National Youth Administration have made a brave start here. But the chief defect of both these organizations is that they deal only with those who are unemployed: a segregated class. We need a Civilian Conservation Corps that will enlist, at least for a year's service, every girl and boy in the country. This corps should be organized on a regional basis; but there should be special opportunities, for those most adventurous and capable, of taking on work in other parts of the country. This would be a true circulation of the élite.

Such a corps will become the very backbone of our new democracy. By mixing classes and groups, it will undermine the dreary caste system that now pushes its snobberies and impertinences right into many of our public high schools, and has already left dead areas of social isolation throughout our once largely democratic country. The work of this larger CCC will eventually include far more than reforestation: the Quaker work camps, for example, have pointed the way to wider social efforts.

These youngsters will not merely reforest our barren slopes and fight insect pests; they will plant trees along bare roads, for shade and beauty, pushing the trail of Johnny Appleseed beyond the Alleghenies; they will keep up our otherwise too costly parkways and help extend them further; they will clear out the rural slums, trim up the rundown edges of our landscape, and bring music, art, and personal beauty into parts of the country that are now ugly, infamous, and unfit for human habitation.

Such universal service was advocated earnestly a generation ago by one of the stoutest exponents of American individualism and self-reliance, Liberty Hyde Bailey: a name that every American with a rural background must respect to the point of reverence. Without such a collective instrument of democratic service as this Civilian Corps, our young people must remain at loose ends, tied to petty tasks, cramped by lack of a horizon, never quickened to the opportunities for comradeship and bold pioneering that our country offers—offers and *demands* if we are to create a worthier civilization.

All the new tasks of regional improvement claim more than routine service; and the performance of them in youth will be a discipline in public duties that our democracy has long lacked. Those who have camped together, traveled together, worked together, and exchanged ideas and matched beliefs while scrubbing their clothes or jawing over a campfire, will have a new stake in their country and a new confidence in themselves. The hardships they will encounter in the service, the lack of domestic comforts, the lean days of backbreaking, sometimes ugly work, the individual's occasional loneliness far from his own roof—all this will breed a toughness that no other mode of education, short of war, can produce, except under conditions that permanently stultify the spirit.

And mark this: to be able to stand routine and hardship is an absolute necessity of personal development. All play and no work is as debilitating a prescription for education as all work and no play is for life itself. Every citizen should have, as a condition of his holding the full privileges of citizenship, a spell of disciplined collective work: bread-work, earth-work, man-work: work devoted to improving the face of the land, to combating the destructive natural forces that are in action, to salvaging and redeeming for civilization those families and communities that are near to relapsing into barbarism, out of their poverty and isolation.

That way lies a democracy of comrades, as staunch in peace as in war; and that way, too, lies the intimate knowledge of our human background that will guide effectively our efforts to make the community itself a high work of art.

On his weekend walks over the Boston hinterland the planner, Charles Eliot, Jr., when only a schoolboy, laid out in his mind the great Metropolitan Parks System of Boston: an outstanding feat of the imagination. When such deliberate first-hand contact with nature and man becomes a common element in American citizenship and education, there will be no lack of opportunities for our youth. If their elders falter, youth will have the discipline and insight and experience that will fit them to deal with political realities. They will be ready for more vital changes in our institutions than the copybook communism that is now offered to them can suggest.

In short, education begins at home; and one of the outstanding advantages of identifying oneself with one's regional home, native or adopted, lies in the land's capacity to provide the materials for an effective education. Regional survey and regional service—these are the chief ingredients for a responsible citizenship; and laboring *on* the land, laboring *with* the land, laboring *for* the land, should be the first initiation of every boy and girl in their duties toward the whole community.

Before we Americans can effectively enter in a wider partnership on the basis of a worldwide civilization—and that after all is one of the prime meanings of a long religious and scientific development—we must first of all strike root. It is by regional cultivation, not by the legal tokens of citizenship, that patriotism in the deepest sense, now vitiated by all manner of cynicism, will come back to us. Without it, the ideas of democracy can have no body.

Already we have made a serious start here. That love for the sea and the soil that made Ryder, Homer, and Fuller the very breath of New England has spread outward over the country. Up and down the land young men and women are looking at their country and painting it. They have gone forth with kodaks and motion picture cameras, showing its woes, proclaiming its beauties: they have floated down the Mississippi and followed the Plow That Broke the Plains. There has been a stir during these last ten years: more vital culture has come out of the sobering poverty of the depression than ever came out of the riotous period of so-called prosperity in the twenties.

Above all, our WPA projects in music, drama, literature, and the graphic and plastic arts—and not least the great series of state and regional guidebooks—have shown what new energies these regional interests can unleash, even in their first bare beginnings. Out of this will grow a pride of life, an eagerness, a deep and intimate knowledge, and a sentiment of possession: qualities that will bring within the realm of practical operation a multitude of projects that now lack understanding and backing. And partly out of this new knowledge and pride, many half-baked or irregional projects, like sky-line drives and National Parks developed as primeval Coney Islands, will be passionately rejected.

In this mood, one can repeat again, with an even more solemn sense of obligation, Thoreau's question:

Who would not rise to meet the expectation of the land?

A new generation is already at hand, eager to answer this question. They have tasted their native soil and found it good; and they have dreams for it that gallop far ahead of any politician's promise. They will write for their region a platform no politician would dare to stand on yet: the restoration of the land to the people and the people once more to the land.

If old property lines and mortgages and franchises and vested interests get in the way, these firm young hands will give the tractor a little more gas and push over such ancient snags. This solid partnership, with loving knowledge to guide it, will cultivate the entire countryside and rebuild and rearrange the cities. That will be only a beginning. Our regions—from the heights of Mt. Hood, where the moccasin flower blows, to the swampy Everglades of Florida—expect more than this of us Americans; and we will not be loath to rise still higher, once we get a start.

Carl Sandburg

Carl Sandburg (1878-   ) was born in Illinois, the son of poor but sturdy Swedish immigrants. Although he grew up with little schooling and much hard work, he managed to enter Lombard College and rapidly asserted his powers as a writer. For some years he was a newspaper man. Chicago Poems *(1916) established him as a "red-blooded" interpreter of the American city. Later volumes have shown a mellowing lyricism, though* The People, Yes *is a return to the social assertion of his earlier poetry. Section 47 of this pageant of democracy is a poet's distillation of the tall stories about Paul Bunyan, most typical of American folk heroes.*

WHO MADE PAUL BUNYAN?

Who made Paul Bunyan, who gave him birth as a myth, who joked him into life as the Master Lumberjack, who fashioned him forth as an apparition easing the hours of men amid axes and trees, saws and lumber? The people, the bookless people, they made Paul and had him alive long before he got into the books for those who read. He grew up in shanties, around the hot stoves of winter, among socks and mittens drying, in the smell of tobacco smoke and the roar of laughter mocking the outside weather. And some of Paul came overseas in wooden bunks below decks in sailing vessels. And some of Paul is old as the hills, young as the alphabet.

The Pacific Ocean froze over in the winter of the Blue Snow and Paul Bunyan had long teams of oxen hauling regular white snow over from China. This was the winter Paul gave a party to the Seven Axmen. Paul fixed a granite floor sunk two hundred feet deep for them to dance on. Still, it tipped and tilted as the dance went on. And because the Seven Axmen refused to take off their hob-nailed boots, the sparks from the nails of their dancing feet lit up the place so that Paul didn't light the kerosene lamps. No woman being on the Big Onion river at that time the Seven Axmen had to dance with each other, the one left over in each set taking Paul as a partner. The commotion of the dancing that night brought on an earthquake and the Big Onion river moved over three counties to the east.

One year when it rained from St. Patrick's Day till the Fourth of July, Paul Bunyan got disgusted because his celebration on the Fourth was spoiled. He dived into Lake Superior and swam to where a solid pillar of water was coming down. He dived under this pillar, swam up into it and climbed with powerful swimming strokes, was gone about an hour, came splashing down, and as the rain stopped, he explained, "I turned the dam thing off." This is told in the Big North Woods and on the Great Lakes, with many particulars.

Two mosquitoes lighted on one of Paul Bunyan's oxen, killed it, ate it, cleaned the bones, and sat on a grub shanty picking their teeth as Paul came along. Paul sent to Australia for two special bumble bees to kill these mosquitoes. But the bees and the mosquitoes intermarried; their children had stingers on both ends. And things kept getting worse till Paul brought a big boatload of sorghum up from Louisiana and while all the bee-mosquitoes were eating at the sweet sorghum he floated them down to the Gulf of Mexico. They got so fat that it was easy to drown them all between New Orleans and Galveston.

Paul logged on the Little Gimlet in Oregon one winter. The cook stove at that camp covered an acre of ground. They fastened the side of a hog on each snowshoe and four men used to skate on the griddle while the cook flipped the pancakes. The eating table was three miles long; elevators carried the cakes to the ends of the table where boys on bicycles rode back and forth on a path down the center of the table dropping the cakes where called for.

Benny, the Little Blue Ox of Paul Bunyan, grew two feet every time Paul looked at him, when a youngster. The barn was gone one morning and they found it on Benny's back; he grew out of it in a night. One night he kept pawing and bellowing for more pancakes, till there were two hundred men at the cook shanty stove trying to keep him fed. About breakfast time Benny broke loose, tore down the cook shanty, ate all the pancakes piled up for the loggers' breakfast. And after that Benny made his mistake; he ate the red hot stove; and that finished him. This is only one of the hot stove stories told in the North Woods.

Louis Zara

Louis Zara (1910-   ) was born in New York, educated at the University of Chicago, and makes his home in Chicago. Before turning to literature he followed a variety of occupations; as a writer he is a versatile producer of short stories, novels, and movie and radio scripts. In This Land Is Ours *he has written a novel of American history. "The Citizner" tells a story that has been repeated thousands of times in our great cities, yet no other author has written it down to bring out, with such understanding, the dignity of citizenship in the humblest individual.*

THE CITIZNER

MAMA KRAMER waited for the sun to come up: she had not been able to sleep at all. She was too excited to stay in bed. She put on her old quilted robe and watched for the dawn through the window. The night was so long a person could fall asleep waiting for it to end. But soon the stars were fading, the night was lifting, and the golden shadow of the sun was advancing from the east. She looked out gratefully. Such a lovely morning!

She could eat no breakfast; she had no appetite. She bustled about nervously and glanced every few minutes at the kitchen clock. This morning passed reluctantly. At last she dressed. She spent nearly two hours over her clothes, running from the clock to the mirror and from the mirror to the clock.

She was a gray-haired woman, short and plump, her hands roughened from housework, her body from childbearing. There were furrows in her cheeks, deep lines in her forehead, and suffering in the set of her jaw. She was often sad, even morose. But this morning she was transformed. Her dark eyes lit up; her mouth became broad with such love of life she felt young again. Today she would go again to the Court House and—if God were willing and the questions not too hard—she would become a citizner of the United States!

Her heart pounded. If the questions were not too hard! A flood of harsh interrogations swept her mind and chilled her. She flew to her purse. She took the booklet with the Constitution in English and in Yiddish. She fumbled for her spectacles and sat down at the window. In the morning light she went over the articles, the sections, and the clauses. It was all wonderful, even if the phrases did make her head swim.

A President must be thirty-five years old, not less. A President is four years elected, then if they like him he has another chance. A Senator is thirty, a Representative is only twenty-five. It bothered her that the Representatives should be such young fellows, but the Constitution said so, black on white.

Now the Supreme Court has nine men, and not a word about how old *they* should be. *A Senator has a job for six years, a Representative for two years, the President for four years, and the Supreme Court judges for life.* The difference puzzled Mama Kramer, but the Constitution said so. *On the Fourth of July was Independence. George Washington was the first President and today is F. D. R., Franklin D. Roosevelt. The capital city was New York,—no, Washington: the same as the first President. Abraham Lincoln freed the slaves.*

She rocked back and forth as she studied, her lips moving, her eyelids fluttering. What a shame it was that Ezra Kramer—may he rest in peace!— had not thought to take out "second papers" before they changed the law. Then she would have been a citizner without these endless sections and clauses and questions. But Ezra had been neglectful. The man—may he forgive us!—was always like that, good to a fault but neglectful. A man who never dunned a debtor, who gave his charities without adding his name and descent, who was more interested in his children's education than in the size of his fortune—how should such a man remember? An easy-going man, who had been in America forty years or more, but had not got all his papers until his oldest son insisted on it, so that his father might vote in the Presidential election of 1928.

It was her own fault, too. After all, a woman who had lived in a land forty years, who had raised four children and had seen one go off to war in 1917 and never return, who had a grandson now in an aviation school in New York, such a woman should know better herself. It was when she had to register as an alien that her heart ached so that she resolved to have "papers," too. Why should they fingerprint her and ask her so many questions and give her a passport and call her "alien"? She had children and grandchildren and nephews and nieces, all born in America, all citizners. And she loved America!

She had not consulted the children. Her only daughter lived in the city, but Hadassah had troubles enough of her own with little Edgar learning a whole concert to play at a recital in Kimball Hall. And the other children were scattered and had their own problems. Secretly Mama Kramer hoped to accomplish this all by herself. The children lived their lives and she lived hers.

What is the Bill of Rights? Why was it called a "bill"? Maybe it meant it was something the Government *owed* the citizner. *Freedom of the speech, of the press, of meetings, of praying to anybody you like, a trial by jury.* . . . She swayed as she studied and wondered whether her Ezra—may he rest in peace!—had known every jot and tittle. Were they making it harder for people to become citizners, or easier? Would she get a strict judge or an easy one? Would she be deported if she failed on the questions? She had answered them once safely. Would they be harder in this final examination?

Outside a horn tooted. She ran to the window. A long black limousine was waiting.

"Krakauer, don't go away!" she shouted and completed her preparations feverishly. "Hurry, hurry!" she panted. The witnesses were down there waiting. Witnesses should not be kept waiting. "Quickly, Goldie!"

For six months she had had ready two witnesses—Slemo Marcus, the butcher, and Abraham Loeb, the fish man. She had been buying her meats and fish from them for twenty-odd years. But the first summons to come to the Naturalization Court had appointed a Tuesday, and Tuesday is no small day at the fish market. So Abraham Loeb had had to excuse himself. Desperately Mama Kramer had looked about for another witness. Her oldest friends were all dead or removed to distant quarters. The younger people worked during the day and could not leave their jobs. In that moment of trial she had happened to pass a group of mourners near Perez's Chapel and met her old *landsman,* Jake Krakauer. This was the Jacob Krakauer who had from a peddler of fruits and vegetables become very wealthy. He now owned the Krakauer Krown Food Stores and lived in a suburb. His house, they said, was the size of a small hotel.

Gray, weary-looking, he studied her. "Mama Kramer!"

"You still haven't forgotten your own people, Jacob! At least you come to their funerals."

Krakauer shrugged. "I am a plain man, Mama Kramer. If you could look inside my heart, you would see that I am still a democrat. The Angel of Death is also a democrat. He does not look at the income tax. When our time comes, he takes all."

She smiled. "Jacob," she asked, fixing her dark eyes on him, "when my times comes, would you do it for me, too? Would you come to my services?"

He blinked solemnly. "That I promise you, Mama."

"Ah, you'll help the dead but not the living!" she exulted.

A look of pain came into his face. "Who ever said that of Jacob Krakauer?"

"Then be for me a witness so that I can die a citizner."

"Be a citizner, Mama Kramer, and live to a hundred and twenty!" He wrenched out a smile. And this morning, here he was again, as he had promised faithfully, waiting for her in his big black limousine.

She bustled down the stairs and across the walk, a new flowered hat on her head, her purse under her arm, and an envelope of documents clutched to her heart. "A good morning, Krakauer!"

The chauffeur leaped out.

Krakauer offered his hand to help her in. "Good morning, Mama Kramer! All ready, *nu?*"

She sighed and settled into the upholstery. "All ready is right. So what are we waiting for, Jake?"

The car floated down to Twelfth Street and stopped at Slemo Marcus's butcher shop. Slemo, a little man with a tuft of a gray beard and a hunted look in his brown eyes, came out wearing his black derby and his Sabbath coat.

After the greetings, he sat on one side of Mama Kramer, Jacob Krakauer on the other. He uttered hardly a word on the long ride to the Naturalization Court. Sitting in that limousine, he could find no words. But Mama Kramer talked; she was very fond of Slemo. He had taught her to write her own name in English.

When the first summons had come, she had marched into his meat market and slipped behind the counter.

"Slemo, show me how to write the name." She pushed the pencil and paper at him. "Write: 'Goldie Kramer'!"

"Goldie . . . Kramer," he wrote out laboriously. "Goldie! I don't like that Goldie."

"What's a matter with Goldie?"

Slemo tweaked his beard. "Now is a chance. Change into something fancy. Could be Gertrude or Gladys. Make it Gladys."

She frowned. "Make it nothing. Gladys Kramer!" Her shoulders jerked up. "I am not a Yankee. I am Goldie," she prodded him. "I was born Goldie, Goldie I lived, Goldie I'll die. Write Goldie!"

He shrugged and wrote Goldie and let her toil over it. The pencil was nearly hidden in her large work-roughened hands. Her lips moved, her eyebrows twisted, her breath labored: she moved the pencil slowly and spelled the letters. She showed Slemo her first effort. He lifted his eyes to heaven. She wrote a third and a fourth, a fifth and a sixth. She covered one sheet and another. She paused only when her fingers cramped and her arm ached.

She applied herself again the next day and the next. Sympathetically, her fingers and eyes spelled it out—invisibly—when she washed dishes, when she made the bed, when she kneaded bread, when she scrubbed the floor, when she chopped meat or fish, and even when she lay down to sleep. "Goldie Kramer . . . Dzshee aw ell dee eye ee—" She wished she had a shorter name, but soon she had learned to write it. She was so pleased she wrote it on the mailbox. She wrote out slips to put in the pockets of her dresses and in her coat. It was so wonderful to be able to write: "Goldie Kramer . . . Dzshee aw ell—"

As she rode in Krakauer's limousine, Mama Kramer spelled her name in the air. *How many men on the Supreme Court?* If it were only over!

In the old Court House the halls were broad and gray. People wound out of this room and into that, and weary policemen herded them along. "So many people!" thought Mama Kramer. When she went up in the elevator, she held on to her witnesses. The cage was packed; she might lose them. On the sixth floor they worked into a line toward a large painted sign which read "Naturalization Court." Krakauer went ahead and held Mama Kramer's hand; Slemo Marcus tagged behind.

"So many people!" muttered Mama Kramer to herself. "And all not citizners!" She looked at them closely.

There were other Jewish women like herself and many Jewish men, but there were also people who looked like "Yankees," English or Irish or perhaps Scottish, and Mexicans, Poles, Greeks, Italians, Armenians, Bohemians, Norwegians, and so many others that neither she nor Slemo Marcus could hazard what they were.

Jacob Krakauer smiled loftily. "What difference what they are today?" he asked. "Tomorrow they are United States citizners."

A child began to weep and Mama Kramer patted it. When she looked up at the mother, she thought the other must be German. For a moment she shuddered, but the woman's face was drawn and worried. Soon Mama Kramer was holding the child in her own arms.

The line moved on slowly. Mama Kramer reviewed the questions in her mind and grumbled, "If they made so much trouble for Columbus, he would never have come to America!"

Krakauer chortled. "Columbus had troubles, too, Mama. *Plenty!*"

At last they were in the courtroom. It was like a big schoolroom, and the teacher was the Judge, a white-haired smooth-shaven man in a black robe, who sat behind a high bench. When he rapped his gavel, people rose, others sat down. Hands shot into the air. People mumbled words. Then he looked at his papers, rapped his gavel again. People tiptoed out. Some sat down; others got up.

"Goldie Kramer!"

Neither Mama Kramer nor Jacob Krakauer nor Slemo Marcus heard it the first time. The third call she shook herself. "Is it me, Krakauer?"

"You, you!"

Slemo trembled. "Go first, Mama!"

But she was frightened, too. "You go first, Krakauer."

"Ladies first!" he said.

All eyes were on her—she was sure of it—as she went down the aisle, her purse in one hand, her documents in the other. Her witnesses shuffled behind her.

"Goldie Kramer!" the Judge read from his papers.

"Here I am, Judge!" She stood before the high bench.

He looked down at her while a clerk pushed more papers toward him. "You are Goldie Kramer?"

"Of course, Judge."

"Goldie Kramer, are you ready to be a citizen?"

She smiled. "What do you think, Your Honor? What did I come for but to—"

"Are you ready to be a citizen of the United States of America?" His voice was suddenly stern.

She became rigid. "Sure, sure, Judge!" Her hand jerked. "Of course, I want to be a citizner." Tears welled in her eyes.

"Do you understand what is meant by the Constitution?"

Fear blanched her face. *Constitution!* She wanted to talk but couldn't.

He looked at her keenly. "Constitution. Do you know what that means?"

Her eyes wandered from his face to the flag, to the clerk, to the bailiff. Where was Krakauer? Where was Slemo Marcus? She looked at the pictures of Washington and Lincoln on the wall behind the bench. "Ye-ye-yeah!" she stuttered.

She saw the clerk smiling and she remembered. "Oh, Constitution!" she cried. "Constitution! Judge, I'm surprised! Constitution is the laws of the land. 'We, the People of the United States because we want to make a perfect government—' We have Congress, is Senators, two to a State, and Representatives, lots of them, and a President, a Supreme Court—" She tittered. "Oh, Judge, I been studying the Constitution. Ask me anything, Judge!"

He brushed at his mouth and chin. "So you know the Constitution, Goldie Kramer? Good. Now tell me what is the capital of the United States?"

Again she was horror-stricken. She heard Jacob Krakauer harumphing at her side. "Vashington," she replied nervously. Her fingers knit together and her lips quivered to pronounce the name: "Washington."

"Who makes the laws? Do you know that?"

Her tongue was thick and her knees were trembling. "Congress makes the laws."

"What does the Supreme Court do?"

"You want," she began timidly, "I should say the truth?"

He nodded. His eyes crinkled.

"Then, Judge, if it's the truth—the Supreme Court they say if the law that Congress makes is any good."

The gavel rapped as an audible chuckling rattled about the bench. "Goldie Kramer, what do you know about the President?"

She beamed. "Oh, the President is thirty-five years old. At least. He has a job four years. Maybe more if the people want him. He works hard, Judge. Then he becomes an ex-President."

Gravely the Judge studied his papers. He spoke briefly to the witnesses. "That's all, Goldie Kramer."

She frowned. "That is all you are going to ask me, Judge?"

"That's all."

"But I learned so much, Judge!" She gestured excitedly. Krakauer and Marcus nudged her, but she ran on. "For three months now I studied and you don't ask me—"

The Judge pulled at his ear. "Very good, Goldie Kramer. One more question. Do you love this country?"

She smiled. "Oh, Judge, what a question! Do I love it? Who wouldn't love such a country? Forty years I been here. My oldest boy he died in France. My grandson will fly an airplane soon for the Army." Her dark eyes flashed. "Judge, even if you gave me some other countries, *gave* them to me free—just like that—I wouldn't take them. But America, Judge—America is for me—and me, I'm for America!"

The courtroom applauded. The Judge smiled. Again he rapped his gavel. "It is a pleasure," he declared, "to say, 'Welcome, Goldie Kramer, to our free commonwealth of citizens!'"

She listened, bewildered, but he sounded nice. She wanted to say something, but Krakauer nudged her.

"Clerk, will you administer the oath?"

She looked straight at the Judge as she raised her right hand and listened to the oath of allegiance. "I do!" she responded clearly.

It was all over. Before she knew what had happened, she was in the hall and Krakauer and Marcus were shaking her hand.

A flood of tears poured from her eyes. Krakauer offered her his handkerchief; Marcus wrung his hands. Then she dried her eyes, blew her nose, and cleared her throat. The men gazed at her in astonishment.

"What for did you cry, Mama?" Krakauer asked.

"You are not a judge to ask questions," she said. "I wanted to cry, so I cried."

"But Mama Kramer, you should be happy!"

She gave him a look of scorn. "Slemo, who said I wasn't happy?"

Slemo shrugged his shoulders and pursed his lips.

They went down in the elevator and walked across the lobby.

She stood on the walk and looked up at the sky.

"A beautiful day!" she sighed happily and began to cry again.

Margaret Walker

Margaret Walker (1915-   ), a native of Alabama, is the first Negro poet to win the annual competition of the Yale Series of Younger Poets. Passionately conscious of the gulf between black and white she urges, with dignity and simplicity, a common ground of interracial good will and co-operation:

> *"This is a journey from the me to you*
> *This is a journey from the you to me.*
> *A union of the two strange worlds must be."*

FOR MY PEOPLE

For my people everywhere singing their slave songs repeatedly: their dirges and their ditties and their blues and jubilees, praying their prayers nightly to an unknown god, bending their knees humbly to an unseen power;

For my people lending their strength to the years, to the gone years and the now years and the maybe years, washing ironing cooking scrubbing sewing mending hoeing plowing digging planting pruning patching dragging along never gaining never reaping never knowing and never understanding;

For my playmates in the clay and dust and sand of Alabama backyards playing baptizing and preaching and doctor and jail and soldier and school and mama and cooking and playhouse and concert and store and hair and Miss Choomby and company;

For the cramped bewildered years we went to school to learn to know the reasons why and the answers to and the people who and the places where and the days when, in memory of the bitter hours when we discovered we were black and poor and small and different and nobody cared and nobody wondered and nobody understood;

For the boys and girls who grew in spite of these things to be man and woman, to laugh and dance and sing and play and drink their wine and religion and success, to marry their playmates and bear children and then die of consumption and anemia and lynching;

For my people thronging 47th Street in Chicago and Lenox Avenue in New York and Rampart Street in New Orleans, lost disinherited dispossessed and happy people filling the cabarets and taverns and other people's pockets needing bread and shoes and milk and land and money and something—something all our own;

For my people walking blindly spreading joy, losing time being lazy, sleeping when hungry, shouting when burdened, drinking when hopeless, tied and shackled and tangled among ourselves by the unseen creatures who tower over us omnisciently and laugh;

For my people blundering and groping and floundering in the dark of churches and schools and clubs and societies, associations and councils and committees and conventions, distressed and disturbed and deceived and devoured by money-hungry glory-craving leeches, preyed on by facile force of state and fad and novelty, by false prophet and holy believer;

For my people standing staring trying to fashion a better way from confusion, from hypocrisy and misunderstanding, trying to fashion a world that will hold all the people, all the faces, all the adams and eves and their countless generations;

Let a new earth rise. Let another world be born. Let a bloody peace be written in the sky. Let a second generation full of courage issue forth; let a people loving freedom come to growth. Let a beauty full of healing and a strength of final clenching be the pulsing in our spirits and our blood. Let the martial songs be written, let the dirges disappear. Let a race of men now rise and take control.

Langston Hughes

Langston Hughes (1902-   ) was born in Missouri, the son of a lawyer. After various humble jobs in New York, at sea, and in Paris, he got his opportunity in a Washington hotel where he was working as a bus-boy. He left three of his poems beside Vachel Lindsay's plate and the famous poet read them to his next audience. When others became interested in the young man he found a publisher for his The Weary Blues *and was enabled to attend Lincoln University. Since his graduation he has become a leading writer on Negro life in the United States. He went to Spain during the Civil War as a correspondent sympathetic with the Loyalist cause. His poetry shows the influence of Sandburg and Whitman, still more of the blues singers. But it is above all proudly race-conscious: "I, too, am America."*

THE NEGRO SPEAKS OF RIVERS

I've known rivers:
I've known rivers ancient as the world and older than the flow of human
    blood in human veins.

My soul has grown deep like the rivers.

I bathed in the Euphrates when dawns were young.
I built my hut near the Congo and it lulled me to sleep.
I looked upon the Nile and raised the pyramids above it.
I heard the singing of the Mississippi when Abe Lincoln went down to New
    Orleans, and I've seen its muddy bosom turn all golden in the sunset.

I've known rivers:
Ancient, dusky rivers.

My soul has grown deep like the rivers.

Alexander Woollcott

Alexander Woollcott (1887-1943) needs no introduction to those who have seen The Man Who Came to Dinner. *Even allowing for farcical exaggeration, the portrait is "all Woollcott and a yard wide." For some twenty years he contributed his highly personalized theater reviews to various New York newspapers. Later, as a literary critic, he commanded a huge radio following. His free-lance writings were distinguished by their excessive elegance, their urbane and gossipy wit, their audacious combination of sophistication and sentimentalism.*

COLOSSAL BRONZE

LATE on the first night of 1933, I started back to London from the country house in Kent where I had been spending the week-end to see the New Year in—started back in a hired Daimler which moved majestically through the fog and was about the size and shape of a small house boat. Clutched in one hand was a spray of priceless orchids from the nursery on the place, and in the other was a forty-inch cutlass of sinister appearance.

My host had heard me innocently admiring them, and to my genuine surprise had pressed them into my hands at parting. As I drove off into the night, I made a note to remember that on my next visit I must be overheard expressing my enthusiasm for several paintings there by Augustus John and the late Mr. Sargent, for a small bronze head by Epstein, for the avenue of immemorial yews which glorifies the drive, for the bride of the younger son of the house, and for a small black spaniel bitch named, if memory serves, Tiny.

But as my car trundled along in the midnight fog my thoughts shifted to the music we had plucked from the air after dinner, and, with that as a start, I found myself from there on reviewing, as one might a parade, the long procession of my acquaintance with one who was a groping and per-plexed youth when first I met him, and is today a colossus bestriding the world—the wide, wide world which is his home. You see, we had tuned in that evening on the Hilversum station which broadcasts from the Neth-erlands, and we were the more amused to stumble on someone singing no quaint old Dutch tune at all, but a melody as unmistakably American as *Huckleberry Finn,* corn pone, or the late Calvin Coolidge.

> "He don't plant 'taters,
> He don't plant cotton,
> An' dem dat plants 'em is soon forgotten . . ."

This, mind you, from Holland, on New Year's Night. It was "Ol' Man River," and we realized too that it was being sung with a voice of such ripe, rich, moving beauty that it could belong only to him for whose uses that song originally was written.

Wherefore, I fell to thinking of all the times my path had crossed Paul Robeson's in years past, and if Sherlock Holmes had been sharing the car with me and could see in the dark, he might have read the sequence of my recollections just from the way I sighed, chuckled, groaned, snorted, scowled, and hummed my way to London. For Paul Robeson and I are old friends and neighbors—neighbors in a sense possible only to those of us whose tent is usually pitched at one or another of the great crossroads of the world. Such a one is a species of innkeeper, and can count the times when this or that person has dropped out of the caravan for a moment and rested under his roof.

Thus Paul Robeson has come my way a dozen times. Often a year or two will go by without my seeing him or having a word from him, and then, unannounced, his great, dusky bulk will fill my doorway and my heart rejoices, for of the countless people I have known in my wanderings over the world, he is one of the few of whom I would say that they have greatness. I do not mean greatness as a football player or as an actor or as a singer. I am not, I think, confusing his personal quality with his heroic stature. I do not even have in mind what is, I suppose, the indisputable fact, that he is the finest musical instrument wrought by nature in our time. I mean greatness as a person.

In his case I despair of ever putting into convincing words my notion of this quality in him. I can say only that by what he does, thinks and is, by his unassailable dignity, and his serene, incorruptible simplicity, Paul Robeson strikes me as having been made out of the original stuff of the world. In this sense is he coeval with Adam and the redwood trees of California. He is a fresh act, a fresh gesture, a fresh effort of creation. I am proud of belonging to his race. For, of course, we both are members of the one sometimes fulsomely described as human.

"Ol' Man River!" I remembered a day in 1926 when Jerome Kern telephoned me in what seemed a state of considerable excitement. That inexhaustible mind of melody had just read a story which he thought would provide him with the libretto for which he had been waiting all his life. It was called *Show Boat*. Had I read it? I had. And did I know this Edna Ferber? I did, indeed. Well, then, would I give him a note of introduction to her? This was too much.

"If you were to call her up and say you were Jerome Kern and tell her you wanted to write a score for that story of hers," I said bitingly, "I suppose she would slam down the receiver and barricade the door."

But he wanted a note, so I did as I was bid. And posted it to him. It so happened that that very night I went to the theater with Miss Ferber and that in the lobby between the acts none other than the shrinking Kern drifted in our direction. I assumed, of course, he had done so to scrape an acquaintance with his favorite authoress, and scarcely bothered to introduce them. It was only a chance word which identified her for him.

"You mean this *is* Edna Ferber?" he cried, and metaphorically fell into her arms. From then on, neither of them remembered that I was there.

But even then the exit speech had not yet been written for my own modest role. Two weeks later, he was on the wire again. This time he was in too fine a frenzy of creation to bother with mere introductions. That morning he had written a song called "Ol' Man River" and please did I have Paul Robeson's telephone number? A half-hour later he was climbing the steps to Paul Robeson's flat in Harlem.

Afterwards I heard all about that first meeting. The song was sung for the first time from a rough manuscript, with Kern himself at the piano and Mrs. Robeson as audience. Then the composer was possessed that Robeson should come right downtown with him and sing it for young Oscar Hammerstein, who had written the words.

Paul did not mind, but turned for funds to Mrs. Robeson. She is a flashing, resourceful woman, far lighter in color than her husband, being of mixed Negro and Jewish blood. Hers is the custody of the privy purse. He wanted two dollars for taxi fare. But Kern was going to drive them down. She knew he would need only fare for the ride back. One dollar would be plenty.

"Aw, go on," he said; "be all nigger and give me two."

Yet because the production of *Show Boat* was delayed and delayed, when finally its first curtain rose, Robeson had been booked for a concert tour and was not free to join the cast and sing his song. He did not become available until a London cast was assembled to duplicate *Show Boat* in Drury Lane. Thus it happened that New York never heard or saw Paul Robeson in this role until after an interval of two years. After only two years it was revived at the Casino in New York in the spring of 1932.

Against the recklessness of such revival after so short a time, Miss Ferber protested vehemently. It was, she said, about as bad an example of showmanship as she had ever known. No one, she said, would come to see it. And when she was voted down, she could at least refuse to attend the opening. Her family might go, and did, but, for her own part, she announced loftily that nothing would drag her there.

As they left for the theater she called out after them, "I am not one to enjoy seeing something I love killed before my eyes." But let me quote from the letter she wrote me about it afterwards:

So at ten minutes to nine I put on my hat and coat and took a walk enjoying the fine spring night and thinking about Life and one thing and another and imagine my surprise to find myself in front of the Casino Theater. There was what appeared to be a mild riot going on outside and I immediately decided that infuriated ticket-purchasers were already demanding their money back. Sure enough, as I fought my way inside there was a line in front of the box office, though the play had begun. They were milling around and thrusting their hands forward toward the man in the box office. He was saying, over and over, in a firm, monotonous chant, "Nomoreseatsnomoreseatsnomoreseatsnomoreseats." I trampled down women and children and pressed my white little face up against the bars and said, "I want to buy a seat." He said, "I'm sorry, Miss Foibah, nomoreseatsnomoreseatsnomore—"

"I'll stand up."

The Casino doesn't allow standing room because there's no place to stand. The last row is smack up against a wall, and that settles it. I went in, leaned against the door and looked at the audience and the stage at the very moment when Paul Robeson came on to sing "Ol' Man River."

In all my years of going to the theater—and that dates way back to the Ottumwa, Iowa, Opera House, when I judiciously regarded the drama from the cushioned comfort of Mrs. Julia Ferber's lap—I never have seen an ovation like that given any figure of the stage, the concert hall, or the opera. It was completely spontaneous, whole-hearted, and thrilling. The audience was what is known as a fashionable one—"carriage trade." Motor cars, evening clothes, warm May night, and a revival ordinarily would make a combination to cause any lover of the theater to rush sobbing into the night. That audience stood up and howled. They applauded and shouted and stamped. Since then I have seen it exceeded but once, and that was when Robeson, a few minutes later, finished singing "Ol' Man River." The show stopped. He sang it again. The show stopped. They called him back again and again. Other actors came out and made motions and their lips moved, but the bravos of the audience drowned all other sounds.

And here, in the last hours of that same year, he had been singing it from Holland—singing it to all Europe, to the islands thereto adjacent, and to ships at sea. As I rode on through the fog, I fell to thinking of the first time I met him. That was in 1922, when he came around to see me in a small flat I had in the gas-house district of New York.

He was twenty-four then, having been born in Princeton, New Jersey, in 1898, the son of a Negro preacher who, through some skulduggery on the part of two scheming divinity students, was ousted from his pulpit when Paul was a little boy. Instead of leaving town under a cloud, old Mr. Robeson got him a wheelbarrow and a rake and went right to work in Princeton as a free-lance gardener, standing his ground until the truth prevailed. He lived long enough to see his son triumphant at Rutgers—a Phi Beta Kappa man and not only an All-American football player in 1918, but pretty generally recognized as one of the greatest players the game had ever known.

Even while he was studying law at Columbia and setting up his bride in a Harlem flat, he would slip out of town for the autumn week-ends to finance his studies and his new household with a few bouts of professional football. There had been a rather nasty ruckus on the field in Milwaukee one afternoon in the preceding fall. Paul's team was playing against the team from Marion, where Mr. Harding came from. It was a team of Indians, and one of them was a real bad boy. He had, Paul was warned, a mean trick of sticking his fingers into the eyes of the player opposite.

In the middle of one play that afternoon, Paul saw those fingers headed for his own eyes. He also saw red, and promptly knocked the brave unconscious. At that, the opposing eleven fell upon him as one Indian. Out of the corner of his eye, Paul could see his own one-hundred-per-cent Anglo-Saxon team-mates discreetly leaving the scene. It looked as if he might have to beat up all those Indians single-handed. Before intervention became effective, he had entered upon this chore with such a genuine pleasure and such concentrated destructiveness that the story of his quality as a fighter spread over the country before nightfall. Drooping fight-promoters were galvanized into sudden action. Within a week, more than a million dollars had been confidentially pledged to back him as the prospective heavyweight champion of the world. I think he must have shown considerable promise for, as Frank Lloyd Wright once scornfully remarked, there is nothing so timid as a million dollars.

But Robeson would have none of them. He was uncertain what he wanted to be, but he was quite sure it wasn't a prize fighter. No, nor a lawyer, either. He would finish the law course because he had started it, but a Negro lawyer's chances are slim, and anyway, he felt he was meant to be something quite different. An actor, perhaps. He had already tried himself out as an actor in a small-scale revival of *The Emperor Jones*. I was skeptical, because the number of available Negro roles was even smaller then than now.

Well, then, he might do something with his voice. He told me shyly that he had just discovered (which is more than the Rutgers Glee Club ever did) that he had a pretty good voice. He would come around some evening, he said, and roar a few spirituals at me. With which promise, he pulled his vast bulk together and roamed off through the gas-house district.

Perhaps I am only being wise after the event, but I think I felt at the time that I had just crossed the path of someone touched by destiny. He was a young man on his way. He did not know where he was going, but I never in my life saw anyone so quietly sure, by some inner knowledge, that he was going somewhere.

When I ran into him in London ten years later—it was the week before Christmas of the year just past—it was plain that he had not only traveled quite a distance, but now saw the rest of his road stretching clear and inviting before him. In those ten years, he had become famous as a singer of spirituals, had, with increasing skill played many roles both in New York and London, and had set for himself the goal of becoming a jongleur of such equipment that he could forget the frontiers which crib, cabin, and confine the rest of us.

More than any other artist in the world, save, perhaps, their own lost Chaliapin, the Russians are eager to have Paul Robeson come to them, and he is even now getting ready the songs he wants to sing there and the plays he dearly wants to play. For he has found, in the homemade speech of Pushkin and in the rugged music of Moussorgsky, the one medium that really delights him.

My Russian friends tell me he already speaks their language without a trace of accent, and if that surprises you as much as it did me, I can explain it only by saying that Paul Robeson has such extraordinary powers of concentration that he can sit rapt at a Linguaphone twelve hours a day, leaving it only long enough to go to the ice box for an occasional glass of milk, but never leaving it at all to answer the persistent telephone. Offers of vast sums for movie and vaudeville work arrive by mail and remain blandly unanswered. Only when word comes from Mrs. Robeson that the rent is due on their flat in the Strand, or from Switzerland that his small son in school there needs a new pair of skis—that husky kid who adores his father but is pretty patronizing about the latter's imperfect German—only then does the old man emerge and sing or play for a week or two to establish a little balance in the bank. Then back he goes into the luxurious seclusion of the work which he now at last enjoys as much as he once enjoyed football.

As an economist, Robeson reminds me of the darky in a story I used to tell with some condescension and great success. A householder, whose lawn needed cutting, saw Mose scuffling along the dusty road and called out, "Hey, Mose! Want to make a quarter?" Mose paused only long enough to reply, "No, suh, Ah got one." Which used to seem to us more bee-like economists an amusingly childish reply. Of late I have had rather less success with this once dependable anecdote. Perhaps there has begun to dawn on more and more people an uneasy suspicion that Mose had the right idea. Anyway, it is Paul Robeson's idea.

In those ten years he has jogged on his way unperturbed by the most head-turning experiences. On my way back from Kent, I fell to thinking of the time when he played Othello in London. I did not see that performance, but Rebecca West and Aldous Huxley tell me they never saw better Shakespearean acting in all their days. . . .

Then I remembered how confidently, but how inaccurately, the tabloids had prophesied the Robeson divorce during the preceding summer. And the agitation in London when Lady Mountbatten could scotch a preposterous rumor linking her name with Robeson's only by bringing a libel action against the deluded newspaper which had done some baseless hinting. And

I recalled, with malicious pleasure, Robeson's little exchange of discourtesies with Lady Astor, whose visit to his dressing room in Drury Lane brought such a rush of southern blood to her head that she seemed to think she was benevolently visiting one of the cabins on the old family plantation.

Indeed, I was just thinking that I would some day do a story about that encounter and call it "Paul and Virginia" when the aforesaid Daimler turned into the Haymarket and drew up at the curb in front of the Carlton. One New Year's Eve reveler, insufficiently recovered from his celebrations, was seemingly impressed with the vehicle and yelled out, for obscure reasons of his own, "Make way for Lord Kitchener!"

This clarion call naturally drew quite a little crowd, which was considerably surprised when there emerged from the car, not the ghost of Kitchener of Khartoum at all, but merely a well-nourished American in a camel's-hide coat with a spray of orchids in one hand and a dangerous weapon in the other. Surprised, and, I think, faintly alarmed. At least, the block emptied in what is technically known as a twinkling.

Since then Robeson has made a screen version of *The Emperor Jones* in Haiti and for three weeks he played Eugene O'Neill's *All God's Chillun* in London with an extraordinary new-risen actress named Flora Robson.

I have seldom read such tributes as that revival wrung from the usually comatose critics of the English press. The *Manchester Guardian* was delirious, and even the old *London Times* picked up her bombazine skirts and did a fandango in the streets. The phrase "great acting" was tossed about like confetti. These two were compared to John Philip Kemble and Mrs. Siddons. Robeson sent me the clippings with a brief message—my favorite among the epistles of Paul. He merely said: "How'm I doin'?"

Gunnar Myrdal

Gunnar Myrdal (1899-   ) is a prominent Swedish social-economist, a Professor in the University of Stockholm, and a member of the Swedish Senate. Seeking a scholar untrammeled by American preconceptions, the Carnegie Corporation engaged him to make an objective study of our Negro problem. An American Dilemma, *in two volumes, was the result of five years' research. The dilemma referred to in the title is the conflict between our good intentions, which we like to call the American Creed, and our actual practices, our local interests, personal jealousies, group prejudices and so forth, which keep us from realizing our ideal of democracy. In the final analysis Dr. Myrdal stresses the problem of* white *Americans, for it is their failure to live up to their high principles which creates the problem of black Americans.*

AMERICAN IDEALS AND THE AMERICAN CONSCIENCE

IT is a commonplace to point out the heterogeneity of the American nation and the swift succession of all sorts of changes in all its component parts and, as it often seems, in every conceivable direction. America is truly a shock to the stranger. The bewildering impression it gives of dissimilarity throughout and of chaotic unrest is indicated by the fact that few outside observers—and, indeed, few native Americans—have been able to avoid the intellectual escape of speaking about America as "paradoxical."

Still there is evidently a strong unity in this nation and a basic homogeneity and stability in its valuations. Americans of all national origins, classes, regions, creeds, and colors have something in common: a social *ethos,* a political creed. It is difficult to avoid the judgment that this "American Creed" is the cement in the structure of this great and disparate nation.

When the American Creed is once detected, the cacophony becomes a melody. The further observation then becomes apparent: that America, compared to every other country in Western civilization, large or small, has the *most explicitly expressed* system of general ideals in reference to human interrelations. This body of ideals is more widely understood and appreciated than similar ideals are anywhere else. The American Creed is not merely—as in some other countries—the implicit background of the nation's political and judicial order as it functions. To be sure, the political creed of America is not very satisfactorily effectuated in actual social life.

But as principles which *ought* to rule, the Creed has been made conscious to everyone in American society.

Sometimes one even gets the impression that there is a relation between the intense apprehension of high and uncompromising ideals and the spotty reality. One feels that it is, perhaps, the difficulty of giving reality to the *ethos* in this young and still somewhat unorganized nation—that it is the prevalence of "wrongs" in America, "wrongs" judged by the high standards of the national Creed—which helps make the ideals stand out so clearly. America is continuously struggling for its soul. These principles of social ethics have been hammered into easily remembered formulas. All means of intellectual communication are utilized to stamp them into everybody's mind. The schools teach them, the churches preach them. The courts pronounce their judicial decisions in their terms. They permeate editorials with a pattern of idealism so ingrained that the writers could scarcely free themselves from it even if they tried. They have fixed a custom of indulging in high-sounding generalities in all written or spoken addresses to the American public, otherwise so splendidly gifted for the matter-of-fact approach to things and problems. Even the stranger, when he has to appear before an American audience, feels this, if he is sensitive at all, and finds himself espousing the national Creed, as this is the only means by which a speaker can obtain human response from the people to whom he talks.

The Negro people in America are no exception to the national pattern. "It was a revelation to me to hear Negroes sometimes indulge in a glorification of American democracy in the same uncritical way as unsophisticated whites often do," relates the Dutch observer, Bertram Schrieke. A Negro political scientist, Ralph Bunche, observes:

> Every man in the street, white, black, red or yellow, knows that this is "the land of the free," the "land of opportunity," the "cradle of liberty," the "home of democracy," that the American flag symbolizes the "equality of all men" and guarantees to us all "the protection of life, liberty and property," freedom of speech, freedom of religion and racial tolerance.

The present writer has made the same observation. The American Negroes know that they are a subordinated group experiencing, more than anybody else in the nation, the consequences of the fact that the Creed is not lived up to in America. Yet their faith in the Creed is not simply a means of pleading their unfulfilled rights. They, like the whites, are under the spell of the great national suggestion. With one part of themselves they actually believe, as do the whites, that the Creed is ruling America.

These ideals of the essential dignity of the individual human being, of the fundamental equality of all men, and of certain inalienable rights to freedom, justice, and a fair opportunity represent to the American people the essential meaning of the nation's early struggle for independence. In the clarity and intellectual boldness of the Enlightenment period these tenets were written into the Declaration of Independence, the Preamble of the Constitution, the Bill of Rights and into the constitutions of the several states. The ideals of the American Creed have thus become the highest law of the land. The Supreme Court pays its reverence to these general principles when it declares what is constitutional and what is not. They have been elaborated upon by all national leaders, thinkers and statesmen. America has had, throughout its history, a continuous discussion of the principles and implications of democracy, a discussion which, in every epoch, measured by any standard, remained high, not only quantitatively but also qualitatively. The flow of learned treatises and popular tracts on the subject has not ebbed, nor is it likely to do so. In all wars, including World War II, the American Creed has been the ideological foundation of national morale.

AMERICAN NATIONALISM

The American Creed is identified with America's peculiar brand of nationalism, and it gives the common American his feeling of the historical mission of America in the world—a fact which just now becomes of global importance but which is also of highest significance for the particular problem studied in this book. The great national historian of the middle nineteenth century, George Bancroft, expressed this national feeling of pride and responsibility:

In the fulness of time a republic rose in the wilderness of America. Thousands of years had passed away before this child of the ages could be born. From whatever there was of good in the systems of the former centuries she drew her nourishment; the wrecks of the past were her warnings . . . The fame of this only daughter of freedom went out into all the lands of the earth; from her the human race drew hope.

And Frederick J. Turner, who injected the naturalistic explanation into history that American democracy was a native-born product of the Western frontier, early in this century wrote in a similar vein:

Other nations have been rich and prosperous and powerful. But the United States has believed that it had an original contribution to make to the history of society by the production of a self-determining, self-restrained, intelligent democracy.

Wilson's fourteen points and Roosevelt's four freedoms have more recently expressed to the world the boundless idealistic aspirations of this American Creed. For a century and more before the present epoch, when the oceans gave reality to the Monroe Doctrine, America at least applauded heartily every uprising of the people in any corner of the world. This was a tradition from America's own Revolution. The political revolutionaries of foreign countries were approved even by the conservatives in America. And America wanted generously to share its precious ideals and its happiness in enjoying a society ruled by its own people with all who would come here. James Truslow Adams tells us:

The American dream that has lured tens of millions of all nations to our shores in the past century has not been a dream of merely material plenty, though that has doubtless counted heavily. It has been much more than that. It has been a dream of being able to grow to fullest development as man and woman, unhampered by the barriers which had slowly been erected in older civilizations, unrepressed by social orders which had developed for the benefit of classes rather than for the simple human being of any and every class. And that dream has been realized more fully in actual life here than anywhere else, though very imperfectly even among ourselves.

This is what the Western frontier country could say to the "East." And even the skeptic cannot help feeling that, perhaps, this youthful exuberant America has the destiny to do for the whole Old World what the frontier did to the old colonies. *American nationalism is permeated by the American Creed,* and therefore becomes international in its essence.

SOME HISTORICAL REFLECTIONS

It is remarkable that a vast democracy with so many cultural disparities has been able to reach this unanimity of ideals and to elevate them supremely over the threshold of popular perception. Totalitarian fascism and nazism have not in their own countries—at least not in the short range of their present rule—succeeded in accomplishing a similar result, in spite of the fact that those governments, after having subdued the principal precepts most akin to the American Creed, have attempted to coerce the minds of their people by means of a centrally controlled, ruthless, and scientifically contrived apparatus of propaganda and violence.

There are more things to be wondered about. The disparity of national origin, language, religion, and culture, during the long era of mass immigration into the United States, has been closely correlated with income differences and social class distinctions. Successive vintages of "Old Americans" have owned the country and held the dominant political power; they have often despised and exploited "the foreigners." To this extent conditions in America must be said to have been particularly favorable to the stratification of a rigid class society.

But it has not come to be. On the question of why the trend took the other course, the historians, from Turner on, point to the free land and the boundless resources. The persistent drive from the Western frontier—

now and then swelling into great tides as in the Jeffersonian movement around 1800, the Jacksonian movement a generation later, and the successive third-party movements and breaks in the traditional parties—could, however, reach its historical potency only because of the fact that America, from the Revolution onward, had an equalitarian creed as a going national *ethos*. The economic determinants and the force of the ideals can be shown to be interrelated. But the latter should not be relegated to merely a dependent variable. Vernon L. Parrington, the great historian of the development of the American mind, writes thus:

The humanitarian idealism of the Declaration [of Independence] has always echoed as a battle-cry in the hearts of those who dream of an America dedicated to democratic ends. It cannot be long ignored or repudiated, for sooner or later it returns to plague the council of practical politics. It is constantly breaking out in fresh revolt. . . . Without its freshening influence our political history would have been much more sordid and materialistic.

Indeed, the new republic began its career with a reaction. Charles Beard, in *An Economic Interpretation of the Constitution of the United States,* and a group of modern historians, throwing aside the much cherished national mythology which had blurred the difference in spirit between the Declaration of Independence and the Constitution, have shown that the latter was conceived in considerable suspicion against democracy and fear of "the people." It was dominated by property consciousness and designed as a defense against the democratic spirit let loose during the Revolution.

But, admitting all this, the Constitution which actually emerged out of the compromises in the drafting convention provided for the most democratic state structure in existence anywhere in the world at that time. And many of the safeguards so skillfully thought out by the conservatives to protect "the rich, the wellborn, and the capable" against majority rule melted when the new order began to function. Other conservative safeguards have fastened themselves into the political pattern. And "in the ceaseless conflict between the man and the dollar, between democracy and property"—again to quote Parrington—property has for long periods triumphed and blocked the will of the people. And there are today large geographical regions and fields of human life which, particularly when measured by the high goals of the American Creed, are conspicuously lagging. But taking the broad historical view, the American Creed has triumphed. It has given the main direction to change in this country. America has had gifted conservative statesmen and national leaders, and they have often determined the course of public affairs. But with few exceptions, only the liberals have gone down in history as national heroes. America is, as we shall point out, conservative in fundamental principles, and in much more than that, though hopefully experimentalistic in regard to much of the practical arrangements in society. But *the principles conserved are liberal* and some, indeed, are radical.

America got this dynamic Creed much as a political convenience and a device of strategy during the long struggle with the English Crown, the London Parliament and the various British powerholders in the colonies. It served as the rallying center for the growing national unity that was needed. Later it was a necessary device for building up a national morale in order to enlist and sustain the people in the Revolutionary War. In this spirit the famous declarations were resolved, the glorious speeches made, the inciting pamphlets written and spread. "The appeal to arms would seem to have been brought about by a minority of the American people, directed by a small group of skillful leaders, who, like Indian scouts, covered their tracks so cleverly, that only the keenest trailers can now follow their course and understand their strategy."

But the Creed, once set forth and disseminated among the American people, became so strongly entrenched in their hearts, and the circumstances have since then been so relatively favorable, that it has succeeded in keeping itself very much alive for more than a century and a half.

THE ROOTS OF THE AMERICAN CREED IN THE PHILOSOPHY OF ENLIGHTENMENT

The American Creed is a humanistic liberalism developing out of the epoch of Enlightenment when America received its national consciousness and its political structure. The Revolution did not stop short of anything less than the heroic desire for the "emancipation of human nature." The enticing flavor of the eighteenth century, so dear to every intellectual and rationalist, has not been lost on the long journey up to the present time. Let us quote a contemporary exegesis:

Democracy is a form of political association in which the general control and direction of the commonwealth is habitually determined by the bulk of the community in accordance with understandings and procedures providing for popular participation and consent. Its postulates are:

1. The essential dignity of man, the importance of protecting and cultivating his personality on a fraternal rather than upon a differential basis, of reconciling the needs of the personality within the frame-work of the common good in a formula of liberty, justice, welfare.
2. The perfectibility of man; confidence in the possibilities of the human personality, as over against the doctrines of caste, class, and slavery.
3. That the gains of commonwealths are essentially mass gains rather than the efforts of the few and should be diffused as promptly as possible throughout the community without too great delay or too wide a spread in differentials.
4. Confidence in the value of the consent of the governed expressed in institutions, understandings and practices as a basis of order, liberty, justice.

5. The value of decisions arrived at by common counsel rather than by violence and brutality.

These postulates rest upon (1) reason in regarding the essential nature of the political man, upon (2) observation, experience and inference, and (3) the fulfillment of the democratic ideal is strengthened by a faith in the final triumph of ideals of human behavior in general and of political behavior in particular.

For practical purposes the main norms of the American Creed as usually pronounced are centered in the belief in equality and in the rights to liberty. In the Declaration of Independence—as in the earlier Virginia Bill of Rights —equality was given the supreme rank and the rights to liberty are posited as derived from equality. This logic was even more clearly expressed in Jefferson's original formulation of the first of the "self-evident truths": "All men are created equal *and from that equal creation* they derive rights inherent and unalienable, among which are the preservation of life and liberty and the pursuit of happiness."

Liberty, in a sense, was easiest to reach. It is a vague ideal: everything turns around *whose* liberty is preserved, to *what extent* and *in what direction*. In society liberty for one may mean the suppression of liberty for others. The result of competition will be determined by who got a head start and who is handicapped. In America as everywhere else—and sometimes, perhaps, on the average, a little more ruthlessly—liberty often provided an opportunity for the stronger to rob the weaker. Against this, the equalitarianism in the Creed has been persistently revolting. The struggle is far from ended. The reason why American liberty was not more dangerous to equality was, of course, the open frontier and the free land. When opportunity became bounded in the last generation, the inherent conflict between equality and liberty flared up. Equality is slowly winning. The New Deal during the 'thirties was a landslide.[1]

THE ROOTS IN CHRISTIANITY

If the European philosophy of Enlightenment was one of the ideological roots of the American Creed, another equally important one was Christianity, particularly as it took the form in the colonies of various lower class Protestant sects, split off from the Anglican Church.[2] "Democracy was envisaged in religious terms long before it assumed a political terminology."

[1] New Dealers, like most American liberals today, pronounce liberty before equality. But they do so in the eighteenth century Jeffersonian sense, not in the American businessman's sense. The "four freedoms" of Franklin D. Roosevelt are liberties, but they are liberties to get equality, not liberties of the stronger to infringe on the weaker. In this sense, equality is logically derivable from liberty, just as liberty is from equality: if there is real liberty for all there will be equal opportunity and equal justice for all, and there will even be social equality limited only by minor biological inequalities.

[2] While the Protestant sects emphasized the elements of the American Creed, it should not be forgotten that there was an older trait of humanitarianism and equalitarianism in the creed of the Medieval Church.

It is true that modern history has relegated to the category of the pious patriotic myths the popular belief that *all* the colonies had been founded to get religious liberty, which could not be had in the Old World. Some of the colonies were commercial adventures and the settlers came to them, and even to the religious colonies later, to improve their economic status. It is also true that the churches in the early colonial times did not always exactly represent the idea of democratic government in America but most often a harsher tyranny over people's souls and behavior than either King or Parliament ever cared to wield.

But the myth itself is a social reality with important effects. It was strong already in the period of the Revolution and continued to grow. A small proportion of new immigrants throughout the nineteenth century came for religious reasons, or partly so, and a great many more wanted to rationalize their uprooting and transplantation in such terms. So religion itself in America took on a spirit of fight for liberty. The Bible is full of support for such a spirit. It consists to a large extent of the tales of oppression and redemption from oppression: in the Old Testament of the Jewish people and in the New Testament of the early Christians. The rich and mighty are most often the wrongdoers, while the poor and lowly are the followers of God and Christ.

The basic teaching of Protestant Christianity is democratic. We are all poor sinners and have the same heavenly father. The concept of natural rights in the philosophy of Enlightenment corresponded rather closely with the idea of moral law in the Christian faith:

The doctrine of the free individual, postulating the gradual escape of men from external political control, as they learned to obey the moral law, had its counterpart in the emphasis of evangelicism upon the freedom of the regenerated man from the terrors of the Old Testament code framed for the curbing of unruly and sinful generations. The philosophy of progress was similar to the Utopian hopes of the millennarians. The mission of American democracy to save the world from the oppression of autocrats was a secular version of the destiny of Christianity to save the world from the governance of Satan.

But apart from the historical problem of the extent to which church and religion in America actually inspired the American Creed, they became a powerful container and preserver of the Creed when it was once in existence. This was true from the beginning. While in Europe after the Napoleonic Wars the increasing power of the churches everywhere spelled a period of reaction, the great revivals beginning around 1800 in America were a sort of religious continuation of the Revolution.

In this way great numbers whom the more-or-less involved theory of natural rights had escaped came under the leveling influence of a religious doctrine which held that all men were equal in the sight of God. Throughout the Revival period the upper classes looked upon the movement as "a religious distemper" which spread like a contagious disease, and they pointed out that it made its greatest appeal to "those of weak intellect and unstable emotions, women, adolescents, and Negroes." But to the poor farmer who had helped to win the Revolution only to find himself oppressed as much by the American ruling classes as he had ever been by Crown officials, the movement was "the greatest stir of Religion since the day of Pentecost."

Religion is still a potent force in American life. "They are a religious people," observed Lord Bryce about Americans a half a century ago, with great understanding for the importance of this fact for their national ideology. American scientific observers are likely to get their attentions fixed upon the process of progressive secularization to the extent that they do not see this main fact, that America probably is still the most religious country in the Western world. Political leaders are continuously deducing the American Creed out of the Bible. Vice-President Henry Wallace, in his historic speech [3] of May 8, 1942, to the Free World Association, where he declared the present war to be "a fight between a slave world and a free world" and declared himself for "a people's peace" to inaugurate "the century of the common man," spoke thus:

The idea of freedom—the freedom that we in the United States know and love so well—is derived from the Bible with its extraordinary emphasis on the dignity of the individual. Democracy is the only true political expression of Christianity.

The prophets of the Old Testament were the first to preach social justice. But that which was sensed by the prophets many centuries before Christ was not given complete and powerful political expression until our Nation was formed as a Federal Union a century and a half ago.

Ministers have often been reactionaries in America. They have often tried to stifle free speech; they have organized persecution of unpopular dissenters and have even, in some regions, been active as the organizers of the Ku Klux Klan and similar "un-American" (in terms of the American Creed) movements. But, on the whole, church and religion in America are a force strengthening the American Creed. The fundamental tenets of Christianity press for expression even in the most bigoted setting. And, again on the whole, American religion is not particularly bigoted, but on the contrary, rather open-minded. The mere fact that there are many denominations, and that there is competition between them, forces American churches to a greater tolerance and ecumenical understanding and to a greater humanism and interest in social problems than the people in the churches would otherwise call for.

I also believe that American churches and their teachings have contrib-

[3] See page 521.

uted something essential to the emotional temper of the Creed and, indeed, of the American people. Competent and sympathetic foreign observers have always noted the generosity and helpfulness of Americans. This and the equally conspicuous formal democracy in human contacts have undoubtedly had much to do with the predominantly lower class origin of the American people, and even more perhaps, with the mobility and the opportunities—what de Tocqueville called the "equality of condition"—in the nation when it was in its formative stage. But I cannot help feeling that the Christian neighborliness of the common American reflects, also, an influence from the churches. Apart from its origin, this temper of the Americans is part and parcel of the American Creed. It shows up in the Americans' readiness to make financial sacrifices for charitable purposes. No country has so many cheerful givers as America. It was not only "rugged individualism," nor a relatively continuous prosperity, that made it possible for America to get along without a publicly organized welfare policy almost up to the Great Depression in the 'thirties, but it was also the world's most generous private charity.

THE ROOTS IN ENGLISH LAW

The third main ideological influence behind the American Creed is English law. The indebtedness of American civilization to the culture of the mother country is nowhere else as great as in respect to the democratic concept of law and order, which it inherited almost without noticing it. It is the glory of England that, after many generations of hard struggle, it established the principles of justice, equity, and equality before the law even in an age when the rest of Europe (except for the cultural islands of Switzerland, Iceland, and Scandinavia) based personal security on the arbitrary police and on *lettres de cachet*.

This concept of a government "of laws and not of men" contained certain fundamentals of both equality and liberty. It will be a part of our task to study how these elemental demands are not nearly realized even in present-day America. But in the American Creed they have never been questioned. And it is no exaggeration to state that the philosophical ideas of human equality and the inalienable rights to life, liberty, and property, hastily sowed on American ground in a period of revolution when they were opportune—even allowing ever so much credit to the influences from the free life on the Western frontier—would not have struck root as they did if the soil had not already been cultivated by English law.

Law and order represent such a crucial element both in the American Creed and in the spotty American reality that, at a later stage of our argument in this chapter, we shall have to devote some further remarks to this particular set of ideological roots.

AMERICAN CONSERVATISM

These ideological forces—the Christian religion and the English law—also explain why America through all its adventures has so doggedly stuck to its high ideals: why it has been so conservative in keeping to liberalism as a national creed even if not as its actual way of life. This conservatism, in fundamental principles, has, to a great extent, been perverted into a nearly fetishistic cult of the Constitution. This is unfortunate since the Constitution of 1789 is in many respects impractical and ill-suited for modern conditions and since, furthermore, the drafters of the document made it technically difficult to change even if there were no popular feeling against change.

The worship of the Constitution also is a most flagrant violation of the American Creed which, as far as the technical arrangements for executing the power of the people are concerned, is strongly opposed to stiff formulas. Jefferson actually referred to the American form of government as an experiment. The young Walt Whitman, among many other liberals before and after him, expressed the spirit of the American Revolution more faithfully when he demanded "continual additions to our great experiment of how much liberty society will bear." Modern historical studies of how the Constitution came to be as it is reveal that the Constitutional Convention was nearly a plot against the common people. Until recently, the Constitution has been used to block the popular will: the Fourteenth Amendment inserted after the Civil War to protect the civil rights of the poor freedmen has, for instance, been used more to protect business corporations against public control.

But when all this is said, it does not give more than one side of the cult of the Constitution. The common American is not informed on the technicalities and has never thought of any great difference in spirit between the Declaration of Independence and the Constitution. When he worships the Constitution, it is an act of American nationalism, and in this the American Creed is inextricably blended. The liberal Creed, even in its dynamic formulation by Jefferson, is adhered to by every American. The unanimity around, and the explicitness of, this Creed is the great wonder of America. The "Old Americans," all those who have thoroughly come to identify themselves with the nation—which are many more than the Sons and Daughters of the Revolution—adhere to the Creed as the faith of their ancestors. The others—the Negroes, the new immigrants, the Jews, and other disadvantaged and unpopular groups—could not possibly have invented a system of political ideals which better corresponded to their interests. So, by the logic of the unique American history, it has developed that the rich and secure, out of pride and conservatism, and the poor and insecure, out of dire need, have come to profess the identical social ideals. The reflecting observer comes to feel that this spiritual convergence, more than America's strategic position behind the oceans and its immense material resources, is what makes the nation great and what promises it a still greater future. Behind it all is the historical reality which makes it possible for the President to appeal to all in the nation in this way: "Let us not forget that we are all descendants from revolutionaries and immigrants." . . .

"LIP-SERVICE"

The conflict in the American concept of law and order is only one side of the "moral overstrain" of the nation. America believes in and aspires to something much higher than its plane of actual life. The subordinate position of Negroes is perhaps the most glaring conflict in the American conscience and the greatest unsolved task for American democracy. But it is by no means the only one. Donald Young complains:

In our more introspective moments, nearly all of us Americans will admit that our government contains imperfections and anachronisms. We who have been born and brought up under the evils of gang rule, graft, political incompetence, inadequate representation, and some of the other weaknesses of democracy, American plan, have developed mental calluses and are no longer sensitive to them.

The *popular* explanation of the disparity in America between ideals and actual behavior is that Americans do not have the slightest intention of living up to the ideals which they talk about and put into their Constitution and laws. Many Americans are accustomed to talk loosely and disparagingly about adherence to the American Creed as "lip-service" and even "hypocrisy." Foreigners are even more prone to make such a characterization.

This explanation is too superficial. To begin with, the true hypocrite sins in secret; he conceals his faults. The American, on the contrary, is strongly and sincerely "against sin," even, and not least, his own sins. He investigates his faults, puts them on record, and shouts them from the housetops, adding the most severe recriminations against himself, including the accusation of hypocrisy. If all the world is well informed about the political corruption, organized crime, and faltering system of justice in America, it is primarily not due to its malice but to American publicity about its own imperfections. America's handling of the Negro problem has been criticized most emphatically by white Americans since long before the Revolution, and the criticism has steadily gone on and will not stop until America has completely reformed itself.

Bryce observed: "They know, and are content that all the world should know, the worst as well as the best of themselves. They have a boundless faith in free inquiry and full discussion. They admit the possibility of any number of temporary errors and delusions." The present author remembers, from his first visit to this country as an inexperienced social scientist at the end of the 'twenties, how confused he often felt when Americans in all walks of life were trustingly asking him to tell them what was "wrong with this country." It is true that this open-mindedness, particularly against the outside world, may have decreased considerably since then on account of the depression, and that the present War might work in the same direction, though this is not certain; and it is true also that the opposite tendency always had its strong representation in America. But, by and large, America has been and will remain, in all probability, a society which is eager to indulge in self-scrutiny and to welcome criticism.

This American eagerness to get on record one's sins and their causes is illustrated in the often quoted letter by Patrick Henry (1772), where he confessed that he had slaves because he was "drawn along by the general inconvenience of living here without them."

> I will not, I cannot, justify it. However culpable my conduct, I will so far pay my *devoir* to virtue as to own the excellence and rectitude of her precepts, and lament my want of conformity to them.

American rationalism and moralism spoke through Patrick Henry. America as a nation is like its courageous and eloquent son of the Revolution. It is continuously paying its *devoir* to virtue; it is repeating its allegiance to the full American Creed by lamenting its want of conformity to it. The strength and security of the nation helped this puritan tradition to continue. No weak nation anxious for its future could ever have done it. Americans believe in their own ability and in progress. They are at bottom moral optimists.

In a great nation there is, of course, division of labor. Some Americans do most of the sinning, but most do some of it. Some specialize in muckraking, preaching, and lamentation; but there is a little of the muckraker and preacher in all Americans. On the other hand, superficially viewed, Americans often appear cynical. Their social science has lately developed along a deterministic track of amoralistic nonconcernedness; but this is itself easily seen to be a moralistic reaction. As a matter of fact, this young nation is the least cynical of all nations. It is not hypocritical in the usual sense of the word, but labors persistently with its moral problems. It is taking its Creed very seriously indeed, and this is the reason why the ideals are not only continuously discussed but also represent a social force—why they receive more than "lip-service" in the collective life of the nation. The cultural unity of the nation is this common sharing in both the consciousness of sins and the devotion to high ideals.

John Steinbeck

John Steinbeck (1902-　) was born in California. He attended Stanford University as a special student but left to pursue a writing career in New York. Failing in this purpose he returned to California where, in 1935, he achieved his first success, Tortilla Flat. *Since then the growth of his reputation has been phenomenal: first in the novel and play,* Of Mice and Men, *then in the novel,* The Grapes of Wrath. *Steinbeck is endowed with a powerful and individual style, to which he joins a lively social conscience.* The Grapes of Wrath *made the whole United States suddenly conscious of what had been a local problem, the dispossessed Okies. From* The Grapes of Wrath *is selected one of the chapters in which the scope of the novel is widened for the purpose of panoramic social commentary.*

TWO FOR A PENNY

ALONG 66 the hamburger stands—Al & Susy's Place—Carl's Lunch—Joe & Minnie—Will's Eats. Board-and-bat shacks. Two gasoline pumps in front, a screen door, a long bar, stools, and a foot rail. Near the door three slot machines, showing through glass the wealth in nickels three bars will bring. And beside them, the nickel phonograph with records piled up like pies, ready to swing out to the turntable and play dance music, "Ti-pi-ti-pi-tin," "Thanks for the Memory," Bing Crosby, Benny Goodman. At one end of the counter a covered case; candy cough drops, caffeine sulphate called sleepless, No-Doze; candy, cigarettes, razor blades, aspirin, Bromo-Seltzer, Alka-Seltzer. The walls decorated with posters, bathing girls, blondes with big breasts and slender hips and waxen faces, in white bathing suits, and holding a bottle of Coca-Cola and smiling—see what you get with a Coca-Cola. Long bar, and salts, peppers, mustard pots, and paper napkins. Beer taps behind the counter, and in back the coffee urns, shiny and steaming, with glass gauges showing the coffee level. And pies in wire cages and oranges in pyramids of four. And little piles of Post Toasties, corn flakes, stacked up in designs.

The signs on cards, picked out with shining mica: Pies Like Mother Used to Make. Credit Makes Enemies, Let's Be Friends. Ladies May Smoke But Be Careful Where You Lay Your Butts. Eat Here and Keep Your Wife for a Pet.

Down at one end the cooking plates, pots of stew, potatoes, pot roast, roast beef, gray roast pork waiting to be sliced.

Minnie or Susy or Mae, middle-aging behind the counter, hair curled and rouge and powder on a sweating face. Taking orders in a soft low voice, calling them to the cook with a screech like a peacock. Mopping the counter with circular strokes, polishing the big shining coffee urns. The cook is Joe or Carl or Al, hot in a white coat and apron, beady sweat on white forehead, below the white cook's cap; moody, rarely speaking, looking up for a moment at each new entry. Wiping the griddle, slapping down the hamburger. He repeats Mae's orders gently, scrapes the griddle, wipes it down with burlap. Moody and silent.

Mae is the contact, smiling, irritated, near to outbreak; smiling while her eyes look on past—unless for truck drivers. There's the backbone of the joint. Where the trucks stop, that's where the customers come. Can't fool truck drivers, they know. They bring the custom. They know. Give 'em a stale cup a coffee an' they're off the joint. Treat 'em right an' they come back. Mae really smiles with all her might at truck drivers. She bridles a little, fixes her back hair so that her breasts will lift with her raised arms, passes the time of day and indicates great things, great times, great jokes. Al never speaks. He is no contact. Sometimes he smiles a little at a joke, but he never laughs. Sometimes he looks up at the vivaciousness in Mae's voice, and then he scrapes the griddle with a spatula, scrapes the grease into an iron trough around the plate. He presses down a hissing hamburger with his spatula. He lays the split buns on the plate to toast and heat. He gathers up stray onions from the plate and heaps them on the meat and presses them in with the spatula. He puts half the bun on top of the meat, paints the other half with melted butter, with thin pickle relish. Holding the bun on the meat, he slips the spatula under the thin pad of meat, flips it over, lays the buttered half on top, and drops the hamburger on a small plate. Quarter of a dill pickle, two black olives beside the sandwich. Al skims the plate down the counter like a quoit. And he scrapes his griddle with the spatula and looks moodily at the stew kettle.

Cars whisking by on 66. License plates. Mass., Tenn., R.I., N.Y., Vt., Ohio. Going west. Fine cars, cruising at sixty-five.

There goes one of them Cords. Looks like a coffin on wheels.

But, Jesus, how they travel!

See that La Salle? Me for that. I ain't a hog. I go for a La Salle.

'F ya goin' big, what's a matter with a Cad'? Jus' a little bigger, little faster.

I'd take a Zephyr myself. You ain't ridin' no fortune, but you got class an' speed. Give me a Zephyr.

Well, sir, you may get a laugh outa this—I'll take a Buick-Puick. That's good enough.

But, hell, that costs in the Zephyr class an' it ain't got the sap.

I don' care. I don' want nothin' to do with nothin' of Henry Ford's.

I don' like 'im. Never did. Got a brother worked in the plant. Oughta hear him tell.

Well, a Zephyr got sap.

The big cars on the highway . . . The big car cruising along at sixty. I want a cold drink.

Well, there's something up ahead. Want to stop?

Do you think it would be clean?

Clean as you're going to find in this God-forsaken country.

Well, maybe the bottled soda will be all right.

The great car squeals and pulls to a stop. The fat worried man helps his wife out.

Mae looks at and past them as they enter. Al looks up from his griddle, and down again. Mae knows. They'll drink a five-cent soda and crab that it ain't cold enough. The woman will use six paper napkins and drop them on the floor. The man will choke and try to put the blame on Mae. The woman will sniff as though she smelled rotting meat and they will go out again and tell forever afterward that the people in the West are sullen.

Truck drivers. That's the stuff.

Here's a big transport comin'. Hope they stop; take away the taste of them—. When I worked in that hotel in Albuquerque, Al, the way they steal—ever' darn thing. An' the bigger the car they got, the more they steal—towels, silver, soap dishes. I can't figger it.

And Al, morosely, Where ya think they get them big cars and stuff? Born with 'em? You won't never have nothin'.

The transport truck, a driver and relief. How 'bout stoppin' for a cup a Java? I know this dump.

How's the schedule?

Oh, we're ahead!

Pull up, then. They's a ol' war horse in here that's a kick. Good Java, too.

The truck pulls up. Two men in khaki riding trousers, boots, short jackets, and shiny-visored military caps. Screen door—slam.

H'ya, Mae?

Well, if it ain't Big Bill the Rat! When'd you get back on this run?

Week ago.

The other man puts a nickel in the phonograph, watches the disk slip free and the turntable rise up under it. Bing Crosby's voice—golden. "Thanks for the memory, of sunburn at the shore— You might have been a headache, but you never were a bore—" And the truck driver sings for Mae's ears, you might have been a haddock but you never was a whore—

Mae laughs. Who's ya frien', Bill? New on this run, ain't he?

The other puts a nickel in the slot machine, wins four slugs, and puts them back. Walks to the counter.

Well, what's it gonna be?

Oh, cup a Java. Kinda pie ya got?

Banana cream, pineapple cream, chocolate cream—an' apple.

Make it apple. Wait— Kind is that big thick one?

Mae lifts it out and sniffs it. Banana cream.

Cut off a hunk; make it a big hunk.

Man at the slot machine says, Two all around.

Two it is. . . .

Al, slicing onions carefully on a board, looks up and smiles, and then looks down again. Truck drivers, that's the stuff. Gonna leave a quarter each for Mae. Fifteen cents for pie an' coffee an' a dime for Mae. . . .

Sitting together on the stools, spoons sticking up out of the coffee mugs. Passing the time of day. And Al, rubbing down his griddle, listening but making no comment. Bing Crosby's voice stops. The turntable drops down and the record swings into its place in the pile. The purple light goes off. The nickel, which has caused all this mechanism to work, has caused Crosby to sing and an orchestra to play—this nickel drops from between the contact points into the box where the profits go. This nickel, unlike most money, has actually done a job of work, has been physically responsible for a reaction.

Steam spurts from the valve of the coffee urn. The compressor of the ice machine chugs softly for a time and then stops. The electric fan in the corner waves its head slowly back and forth, sweeping the room with a warm breeze. On the highway, on 66, the cars whiz by.

They was a Massachusetts car stopped a while ago, said Mae.

Big Bill grasped his cup around the top so that the spoon stuck up between his first and second fingers. He drew in a snort of air with the coffee, to cool it. "You ought to be out on 66. Cars from all over the country. All headin' west. Never seen so many before. Sure some honeys on the road."

"We seen a wreck this mornin'," his companion said. "Big car. Big Cad', a special job and a honey, low, cream-color, special job. Hit a truck. Folded the radiator right back into the driver. Must a been doin' ninety. Steerin' wheel went right on through the guy an' lef' him a-wigglin' like a frog on a hook. Peach of a car. A honey. You can have her for peanuts now. Drivin' alone, the guy was."

Al looked up from his work. "Hurt the truck?"

"Oh, Jesus Christ! Wasn't a truck. One of them cut-down cars full a stoves an' pans an' mattresses an' kids an' chickens. Goin' west, you know. This guy come by us doin' ninety—r'ared up on two wheels just to pass us, an' a car's comin' so he cuts in an' whangs this here truck. Drove

like he's blin' drunk. Jesus, the air was full a bed clothes an' chickens an'
kids. Killed one kid. Never seen such a mess. We pulled up. Ol' man that's
drivin' the truck, he jus' stan's there lookin' at that dead kid. Can't get a
word out of 'im. Jus' rum-dumb. God Almighty, the road is full a them
families goin' west. Never seen so many. Gets worse all a time. Wonder
where the hell they all come from?"

"Wonder where they all go to," said Mae. "Come here for gas sometimes, but they don't hardly never buy nothin' else. People say they steal.
We ain't got nothin' layin' around. They never stole nothin' from us."

Big Bill, munching his pie, looked up the road through the screened
window. "Better tie your stuff down. I think you got some of 'em comin'
now."

A 1926 Nash sedan pulled wearily off the highway. The back seat
was piled nearly to the ceiling with sacks, with pots and pans, and
on the very top, right up against the ceiling, two boys rode. On the top of
the car, a mattress and a folded tent; tent poles tied along the running
board. The car pulled up to the gas pumps. A dark-haired, hatchet-faced
man got slowly out. And the two boys slid down from the load and hit the
ground.

Mae walked around the counter and stood in the door. The man was
dressed in gray wool trousers and a blue shirt, dark blue with sweat on the
back and under the arms. The boys in overalls and nothing else, ragged
patched overalls. Their hair was light, and it stood up evenly all over their
heads, for it had been roached. Their faces were streaked with dust. They
went directly to the mud puddle under the hose and dug their toes into the
mud.

The man asked, "Can we git some water, ma'am?"

A look of annoyance crossed Mae's face. "Sure, go ahead." She said
softly over her shoulder, "I'll keep my eye on the hose." She watched while
the man slowly unscrewed the radiator cap and ran the hose in.

A woman in the car, a flaxen-haired woman, said, "See if you can't git
it here."

The man turned off the hose and screwed on the cap again. The little
boys took the hose from him and they upended it and drank thirstily. The
man took off his dark, stained hat and stood with a curious humility in
front of the screen. "Could you see your way to sell us a loaf of bread,
ma'am?"

Mae said, "This ain't a grocery store. We got bread to make san'widges."

"I know, ma'am." His humility was insistent. "We need bread and
there ain't nothin' for quite a piece, they say."

" 'F we sell bread we gonna run out." Mae's tone was faltering.

"We're hungry," the man said.

"Whyn't you buy a san'widge? We got nice san'widges, hamburgs."

"We'd sure admire to do that, ma'am. But we can't. We got to make a dime do all of us." And he said embarrassedly, "We ain't got but a little."

Mae said, "You can't get no loaf a bread for a dime. We only got fifteen-cent loafs."

From behind her Al growled, "God Almighty, Mae, give 'em bread."

"We'll run out 'fore the bread truck comes."

"Run out, then, goddamn it," said Al. And he looked sullenly down at the potato salad he was mixing.

Mae shrugged her plump shoulders and looked to the truck drivers to show them what she was up against.

She held the screen door open and the man came in, bringing a smell of sweat with him. The boys edged in behind him and they went immediately to the candy case and stared in—not with craving or with hope or even with desire, but just with a kind of wonder that such things could be. They were alike in size and their faces were alike. One scratched his dusty ankle with the toe nails of his other foot. The other whispered some soft message and then they straightened their arms so that their clenched fists in the overall pockets showed through the thin blue cloth.

Mae opened a drawer and took out a long waxpaper-wrapped loaf. "This here is a fifteen-cent loaf."

The man put his hat back on his head. He answered with inflexible humility, "Won't you—can't you see your way to cut off ten cents' worth?"

Al said snarlingly, "Goddamn it, Mae. Give 'em the loaf."

The man turned toward Al. "No, we want ta buy ten cents' worth of it. We got it figgered awful close, mister, to get to California."

Mae said resignedly, "You can have this for ten cents."

"That'd be robbin' you, ma'am."

"Go ahead—Al says to take it." She pushed the waxpapered loaf across the counter. The man took a deep leather pouch from his rear pocket, untied the strings, and spread it open. It was heavy with silver and with greasy bills.

"May soun' funny to be so tight," he apologized. "We got a thousan' miles to go, an' we don' know if we'll make it." He dug in the pouch with a forefinger, located a dime, and pinched in for it. When he put it down on the counter he had a penny with it. He was about to drop the penny back into the pouch when his eye fell on the boys frozen before the candy counter. He moved slowly down to them. He pointed in the case at big long sticks of striped peppermint. "Is them penny candy, ma'am?"

Mae moved down and looked in. "Which ones?"

"There, them stripy ones."

The little boys raised their eyes to her face and they stopped breathing; their mouths were partly open, their half-naked bodies were rigid.

"Oh—them. Well, no—them's two for a penny."

"Well, gimme two then, ma'am." He placed the copper cent carefully on the counter. The boys expelled their held breath softly. Mae held the big sticks out.

"Take 'em," said the man.

They reached timidly, each took a stick, and they held them down at their sides and did not look at them. But they looked at each other, and their mouth corners smiled rigidly with embarrassment.

"Thank you, ma'am." The man picked up the bread and went out the door, and the little boys marched stiffly behind him, the red-striped sticks held tightly against their legs. They leaped like chipmunks over the front seat and onto the top of the load, and they burrowed back out of sight like chipmunks.

The man got in and started his car, and with a roaring motor and a cloud of blue oily smoke the ancient Nash climbed up on the highway and went on its way to the west.

From inside the restaurant the truck drivers and Mae and Al stared after them.

Big Bill wheeled back. "Them wasn't two-for-a-cent candy," he said.

"What's that to you?" Mae said fiercely.

"Them was nickel apiece candy," said Bill.

"We got to get goin'," said the other man. "We're droppin' time." They reached in their pockets. Bill put a coin on the counter and the other man looked at it and reached again and put down a coin. They swung around and walked to the door.

"So long," said Bill.

Mae called, "Hey! Wait a minute. You got change."

"You go to hell," said Bill, and the screen door slammed.

Mae watched them get into the great truck, watched it lumber off in low gear, and heard the shift up the whining gears to cruising ratio. "Al—" she said softly.

He looked up from the hamburger he was patting thin and stacking between waxed papers. "What ya want?"

"Look there." She pointed at the coins beside the cups—two half-dollars. Al walked near and looked, and then he went back to his work.

"Truck drivers," Mae said reverently . . .

Flies struck the screen with little bumps and droned away. The compressor chugged for a time and then stopped. On 66 the traffic whizzed by, trucks and fine streamlined cars and jalopies; and they went by with a vicious whiz. Mae took down the plates and scraped the pie crusts into a bucket. She found her damp cloth and wiped the counter with circular sweeps. And her eyes were on the highway, where life whizzed by.

Al wiped his hands on his apron. He looked at a paper pinned to the wall over the griddle. Three lines of marks in columns on the paper. Al counted the longest line. He walked along the counter to the cash register, rang "No Sale," and took out a handful of nickels.

"What ya doin'?" Mae asked.

"Number three's ready to pay off," said Al. He went to the third slot machine and played his nickels in, and on the fifth spin of the wheels the three bars came up and the jack pot dumped out into the cup. Al gathered up the big handful of coins and went back of the counter. He dropped them in the drawer and slammed the cash register. Then he went back to his place and crossed out the line of dots. "Number three gets more play'n the others," he said. "Maybe I ought to shift 'em around." He lifted a lid and stirred the slowly simmering stew.

"I wonder what they'll do in California?" said Mae.

"Who?"

"Them folks that was just in."

"Christ knows," said Al.

"S'pose they'll get work?"

"How the hell would I know?" said Al.

She stared eastward along the highway. "Here comes a transport, double. Wonder if they stop? Hope they do." And as the huge truck came heavily down from the highway and parked, Mae seized her cloth and wiped the whole length of the counter. And she took a few swipes at the gleaming coffee urn too, and turned up the bottle-gas under the urn. Al brought out a handful of little turnips and started to peel them. Mae's face was gay when the door opened and the two uniformed truck drivers entered.

"Hi, sister!"

"I won't be a sister to no man," said Mae. They laughed and Mae laughed. "What'll it be, boys?"

"Oh, a cup a Java. What kinda pie ya got?"

"Pineapple cream an' banana cream an' chocolate cream an' apple."

"Give me apple. No, wait—what's that big thick one?"

Mae picked up the pie and smelled it. "Pineapple cream," she said.

"Well, chop out a hunk a that."

The cars whizzed viciously by on 66.

VI. PORTRAIT OF A WORLD

ONCE upon a time a man could dwell in a cozy world which centered in his own back yard, a familiar world of village, town, and native land, no more than a patch of yellow, green, or pink on the pages of a geography book. Today the children of the air age inhabit the whole earth. The patch on the map has become a spinning globe. Today the world is our neighborhood.

Thus, while it is true, in terms of time, that the world has grown smaller, that "No spot on earth is more than sixty hours' flying time from your local airport," it is also true, in terms of space, that the world is as big as ever; and in terms of the individual's relation to it, far bigger than ever before.

And so the citizen of the United States is entering upon a global extension of his interests and sympathies. The measure of his citizenship grows with the growing prestige of his country in international affairs. Whether he likes it or not, he is forced out of his comfortable isolation. He assumes new responsibilities, ventures into new areas of thought. When the world is our neighborhood, the peoples of the world are our neighbors. In a world ravaged by two great wars, there is no lack of constructive work to occupy our hands. We shall do it the better if we seek to understand our neighbors—not so much to look for differences as to find points of common likeness.

As Dwight Morrow once said at Mexico City: "When it comes to the profound experiences of life, the men and women of this small earth are not very different. When it comes to the death of parents or the birth of children, or the straining of eager eyes for needed rain, or the rising and standing uncovered of great groups of people when a national anthem is played—the men and women and children of this earth behave in much the same way."

Thus the great business of the foreseeable future is to bring about, through understanding among peoples, those things for which we have been fighting in a great war. What those things may be is variously interpreted, but one great objective all agree upon: a real peace. Only in a world at peace can we have security or freedom, love or charity, justice or happiness, beauty or culture or any other good thing. But it must be a real peace, not merely the absence of war or even the crushing of militarism—a positive and active force working ever toward justice, democracy, and stability. Those are "great and marching words" and they raise many questions not to be answered without the help of the best minds of our time.

What is a just peace? Is it the fulfillment of the Four Freedoms? How sincerely do we believe in the Four Freedoms as a practical world program?

What is a democratic peace? Are we in earnest when we subscribe to the ideals of democracy—for all men everywhere? Can we achieve a democratic peace if we merely repair the political and economic machinery of the world but neglect the crowding problems of social change?

What is a stable peace? How can we be sure of keeping the gains which men have bought with blood? How can we make free speech, free press, and free education so effective that public opinion shall be aware of every danger which may threaten peace henceforth? How can we make certain that, as time passes and the stark outlines of war grow dim, we shall not again relax the fierce necessity of watchfulness?

How shall we begin to reconstruct civilization after the storm of war? Which comes first, a workable organization to guarantee the world against new aggression? or a stronger and more self-reliant democracy at home? What of the Four Freedoms in the land of the free? What of equal opportunity in the land of opportunity? What of racial justice in the land of justice? Where do we begin?

In the ensuing pages various thinkers, writing from different points of view, comment on the same fundamental conflict at the heart of modern society: economic *laissez-faire* versus social planning—muddling versus meddling, if you like. Of course the issue is not so simple as that. There is no such thing as absolute non-interference or complete planning. But if there is a tendency one way or the other, is it not better to go forward to meet change than to wait until it comes upon us, perhaps by force? It is too late to turn back; but it is not too soon to say what kind of world we want in the future.

And, in any case, we shall have much to say about it. In the march of the nations toward a just and lasting peace, toward an intelligently directed social order, toward a broader democracy, the United States must lead. As Richard Hovey wrote of another time when destiny knocked at our gates:

> I do not know beneath what sky
> Nor on what seas shall be thy fate;
> I only know it shall be high,
> I only know it shall be great.

Christopher La Farge

Christopher La Farge (1897-   ) was born in New York of distinguished ancestry which includes Benjamin Franklin, Commodore Oliver Hazard Perry, and John La Farge, the painter. He is a brother of Oliver La Farge, whose novels interpret the American Indian. His youth was fortunate in its cultivated home background. He graduated from Groton and Harvard and became an architect. When the depression ended the demand for his services, he turned without hesitation to literature and began to experiment with the difficult form of the verse-novel. After a qualified success in Hoxsie Sells His Acres, *he achieved his purpose in the brilliant poem of married life,* Each to the Other.

THE GREAT AND MARCHING WORDS

These are the great words marching with high proud steps
Over the valleys of effort, pain, and war:
Liberty, Democracy, Sacrifice,
Freedom to worship God, Freedom to speak,
Freedom to seek the heights.
                These are huge words
Dwarfing our selves to littleness, our lives
Condensed from the single love into the collective
Passion of nationhood.
                These are lofty words
That are to the eye of the grounded man like planes
Tilting against imponderable heaven,
Swift atoms against the blue of the day's far
And unapproachable robe, too high,
No ceiling to valor.
                Yet in the end,
You must bring Freedom in to your hearth to burn
Like a cut hickory log, you must put on
Democracy like a patched and friendly coat,
You must bring Sacrifice down to street-level
And sweep with it, like a cloud-broom made usual,
You must pour Liberty warm into the bottle
Your infant's suckled at.

It is not easy, this. I know it. War breeds the need;
War's a great needer, hungry for our souls

Before it eats our bodies. It inflicts
Vision upon us when our comfort lies
In the soft darkness of the used, the well-rubbed way
Our fingers found for us.
                              We shall not grow
Wings to our passion until these over-tall,
These too-resounding and too-often-mouthed words
Draw to a hunger in us, and we feed
On simple knowing.
                        As for this—
It must have ceased to fret you. You must become one
Who in all good humility can see
God comforting in the dog curled before your fire,
Can hear Christ speak in the latch that opens wide
To let children run into the fields for mischief,
Taste freedom in the movements of your hand,
See all your country in one poor small drawing,
Know the good scarred face
Of all democracy because a friend
Tells you good morning on a city street,
Know sacrifice because a woman joins
Her life to yours and helps you as you build
Smaller, from less materials, in effort,
To make life better though it be less life.
                                        You see—
Thus do the answers come.
                            Or, to be true,
Thus they begin, for still such stuff is general,
Being like air, like clouds,
You may not quite wrap up in it, but breathe it
Since you must breathe. Democracy's still too big
In a friend's face; a woman is love, and marriage
Is a first loving and its privilege
Has sacrifice for essence; children are keys to Christ,
Yet leave unchristian residue; the whole
Of this diversity of many-colored acres we call
America is beyond the grasping mind no matter
How it may clutch at it. One touches
The general only when the particular
Has come to hand and been rubbed smooth and dear—
Lest it be lost.
                    These matters move, they move,
But seem like air that floats over the water

Barren of power to ripple it, while we long
For the tempest, crave the storm, want hurricanes
To force our bodies into a sense of force.
                                        I tell you,
The big vast words that seem so difficult,
Lie in the hand's palm, beneath the daily glance,
Beyond the doorsill but two little steps,
And are for each as near, for each as strangely
Different as the conception of death's use
To old and young.
                        You must first have named
The sleeping dog, a name become familiar
In comfort to you as you have comforted, tending
The wire's cut on the shank of the leg, the burrs
Plucked from the matted hair, you must have seen
The eyes that rolled up
In love to your least movement.
                                You must own
Anguish in the child's fall, pride in the growth,
Companionship in the small words of life lived
In the river of days, and there must be a fear
In the called name that echoes over empty green fields
At evening for a tardiness, and a lift
To the heart as the thin wind of the dusk brings answer
To love re-owned.
                    You must make actual
The scarred face, give it a name, say Rappaport,
Or MacNamara, or Anderson, Green or Schmidt,
Seen not in image-city, greeted but in the mind, no.
But here, here, on Third Avenue, where the sun
Lies marked as a tiger hot on the barred street and loses
Stripes to the fleeting shadow of a great cloud
Of fierce sound rolling on steel above you, you must cry out
The name from the heart, to the friend real and there
In the real place.
                    You must reach out your hand
To your own woman's hand, touch it, and feel it warm, and know
That love flows out of the fingers and says Love
In the silence of speech no longer wholly needed,
As you say Wife in your heart and know your heart
Echoes to Husband—that it is all as true
As time, not fleeting as the dog's life is mortgaged
To brevity, as children's childhood waits only on the slipping

Of the clock's hand forward, as greetings
Under the steel thunder are for the friendship held
In a moment's haste more dearly because the haste
Hardly abated—but yours, and never less than yours
Beyond all thievery of the larcenous clock,
Because you made it yours in the you that holds
Time's flesh a hostage.

                    Then you may surely feel
Your own about you, then
You can conceive God's goodness as lost with the same cutting
Pain as the lost dog breeds, an image of all fidelity
Wandering, looking, yet not finding—
Because you let him go; then you can place
Your heart in the child's heart weeping for a lost marble
That somehow rolled into the high jungle
Of fern fronds; then can imagine in bitterest clarity
Your woman absent, cutting the cords of love
With the sharp knife of an old wrong; then you can conceive
The friend as vanished, the greetings gone, unhoped for,
Since wild explosive lightnings that wings flung down,
Blasted familiar streets.

                    Oh, in that day, those big words,
Liberty, Freedom and Sacrifice, Democracy,
Will march above you and beyond you no longer,
But will blaze warm on your hearth, cover your body,
Move in affection under your loving, just hands,
Come to your call at evening as though you came
Clothed in their spring and youth,
Lie by your side in comfort
In the dark and hard nights, greet you and call you
Friend in the sunlight of the new morning.

Henry A. Wallace

Henry A. Wallace (1888-   ) is Iowa-born and a graduate of Iowa State College. For more than twenty years, as associate editor and editor of Wallace's Farmer, *he had been accumulating the broad knowledge of farm conditions which fitted him to fill the office of Secretary of Agriculture in the first and second administrations of Franklin D. Roosevelt. He became Vice President in 1941, Secretary of Commerce in 1945. In* New Frontiers, Statesmanship and Religion, *and* America Must Choose *he wrote the gospel of the New Deal and put himself on record as an intelligent idealist. In* Whose Constitution? *Wallace recognizes the crucial importance of the economic factor in modern government and argues for national planning to replace the easy-going theory of laissez-faire. "The Price of Free World Victory" is one of the great documents of the war. This speech, made before the Free World Association on May 8, 1942, answers Sandburg's question: "The people march: 'Where to? what next?'"*

THE PRICE OF FREE WORLD VICTORY

WE, who in a formal or an informal way represent most of the free peoples of the world, are met here tonight in the interests of the millions in all the nations who have freedom in their souls. To my mind this meeting has just one purpose—to let those millions in other countries know that here in the United States are 130 million men, women and children who are in this war to the finish. Our American people are utterly resolved to go on until they can strike the relentless blows that will assure a complete victory, and with it win a new day for the lovers of freedom, everywhere on this earth.

This is a fight between a slave world and a free world. Just as the United States in 1862 could not remain half slave and half free, so today the world must make its decision for a complete victory one way or the other.

As we begin the final stages of this fight to the death between the free world and the slave world, it is worth while to refresh our minds about the march of freedom for the common man. The idea of freedom—the freedom that we in the United States know and love so well—is derived from the Bible with its extraordinary emphasis on the dignity of the individual. Democracy is the only true political expression of Christianity.

The prophets of the Old Testament were the first to preach social justice. But that which was sensed by the prophets many centuries before Christ was not given complete and powerful political expression until our nation was formed as a Federal Union a century and a half ago. Even then, the march of the common people had just begun. Most of them did not yet know how to read and write. There were no public schools to which all children could go. Men and women cannot be really free until they have plenty to eat, and time and ability to read and think and talk things over. Down the years, the people of the United States have moved steadily forward in the practice of democracy. Through universal education, they now can read and write and form opinions of their own. They have learned, and are still learning, the art of production—that is, how to make a living. They have learned, and are still learning, the art of self-government.

If we were to measure freedom by standards of nutrition, education and self-government, we might rank the United States and certain nations of Western Europe very high. But this would not be fair to other nations where education has become widespread only in the last 20 years. In many nations, a generation ago, 9 out of 10 of the people could not read or write. Russia, for example, was changed from an illiterate to a literate nation within one generation and, in the process, Russia's appreciation of freedom was enormously enhanced. In China, the increase during the past 30 years in the ability of the people to read and write has been matched by their increased interest in real liberty.

Everywhere, reading and writing are accompanied by industrial progress, and industrial progress sooner or later inevitably brings a strong labor movement. From a long-time and fundamental point of view, there are no backward peoples which are lacking in mechanical sense. Russians, Chinese, and the Indians both of India and the Americas all learn to read and write and operate machines just as well as your children and my children. Everywhere the common people are on the march. Thousands of them are learning to read and write, learning to think together, learning to use tools. These people are learning to think and work together in labor movements, some of which may be extreme or impractical at first, but which eventually will settle down to serve effectively the interests of the common man.

When the freedom-loving people march—when the farmers have an opportunity to buy land at reasonable prices and to sell the produce of their land through their own organizations, when workers have the opportunity to form unions and bargain through them collectively, and when the children of all the people have an opportunity to attend schools which teach them truths of the real world in which they live—when these opportunities are open to everyone, then the world moves straight ahead.

But in countries where the ability to read and write has been recently acquired or where the people have had no long experience in governing themselves on the basis of their own thinking, it is easy for demagogues to arise and prostitute the mind of the common man to their own base ends. Such a demagogue may get financial help from some person of wealth who is unaware of what the end result will be. With this backing, the demagogue may dominate the minds of the people, and, from whatever degree of freedom they have, lead them backward into slavery. Herr Thyssen, the wealthy German steel man, little realized what he was doing when he gave Hitler enough money to enable him to play on the minds of the German people. The demagogue is the curse of the modern world, and of all the demagogues, the worst are those financed by well-meaning wealthy men who sincerely believe that their wealth is likely to be safer if they can hire men with political "it" to change the sign posts and lure the people back into slavery of the most degraded kind. Unfortunately for the wealthy men who finance movements of this sort, as well as for the people themselves, the successful demagogue is a powerful genie who, when once let out of his bottle, refuses to obey anyone's command. As long as his spell holds, he defies God Himself, and Satan is turned loose upon the world.

Through the leaders of the Nazi revolution, Satan now is trying to lead the common man of the whole world back into slavery and darkness. For the stark truth is that the violence preached by the Nazis is the devil's own religion of darkness. So also is the doctrine that one race or one class is by heredity superior and that all other races or classes are supposed to be slaves. The belief in one Satan-inspired Fuehrer, with his Quislings, his Lavals, and his Mussolinis—his "gauleiters" in every nation in the world—is the last and ultimate darkness. Is there any hell hotter than that of being a Quisling, unless it is that of being a Laval or a Mussolini?

In a twisted sense, there is something almost great in the figure of the Supreme Devil operating through a human form, in a Hitler who has the daring to spit straight into the eye of God and man. But the Nazi system has a heroic position for only one leader. By definition only one person is allowed to retain full sovereignty over his own soul. All the rest are stooges—they are stooges who have been mentally and politically degraded, and who feel that they can get square with the world only by mentally and politically degrading other people. These stooges are really psychopathic cases. Satan has turned loose upon us the insane.

The march of freedom of the past 150 years has been a long-drawn-out people's revolution. In this Great Revolution of the people, there were the American Revolution of 1775, the French Revolution of 1792, the Latin-American revolutions of the Bolivarian era, the German revolution of 1848, and the Russian Revolution of 1918. Each spoke for the common man in terms of blood on the battlefield. Some went to excess. But the significant thing is that the people groped their way to the light. More of them learned to think and work together.

The people's revolution aims at peace and not at violence, but if the rights of the common man are attacked, it unleashes the ferocity of a she-bear who has lost a cub. When the Nazi psychologists tell their master Hitler that we in the United States may be able to produce hundreds of thousands of planes, but that we have no will to fight, they are only fooling themselves and him. The truth is that when the rights of the American people are transgressed, as those rights have been transgressed, the American people will fight with a relentless fury which will drive the ancient Teutonic gods back cowering into their caves. The Götterdämmerung has come for Odin and his crew.

The people are on the march toward even fuller freedom than the most fortunate peoples of the earth have hitherto enjoyed. No Nazi counter-revolution will stop it. The common man will smoke the Hitler stooges out into the open in the United States, in Latin America, and in India. He will destroy their influence. No Lavals, no Mussolinis will be tolerated in a Free World.

The people, in their millennial and revolutionary march toward manifesting here on earth the dignity that is in every human soul, hold as their credo the Four Freedoms enunciated by President Roosevelt in his message to Congress on January 6, 1941. These four freedoms are the very core of the revolution for which the United Nations have taken their stand. We who live in the United States may think there is nothing very revolutionary about freedom of religion, freedom of expression, and freedom from the fear of secret police. But when we begin to think about the significance of freedom from want for the average man, then we know that the revolution of the past 150 years has not been completed, either here in the United States or in any other nation in the world. We know that this revolution cannot stop until freedom from want has actually been attained.

And now, as we move forward toward realizing the Four Freedoms of this people's revolution, I would like to speak about four duties. It is my belief that every freedom, every right, every privilege has its price, its corresponding duty without which it cannot be enjoyed. The four duties of the people's revolution, as I see them today, are these:

1. The duty to produce to the limit.
2. The duty to transport as rapidly as possible to the field of battle.
3. The duty to fight with all that is in us.
4. The duty to build a peace—just, charitable and enduring.

The fourth duty is that which inspires the other three.

We failed in our job after World War No. 1. We did not know how to go about it to build an enduring world-wide peace. We did not have the nerve to follow through and prevent Germany from rearming. We did not insist that she "learn war no more." We did not build a peace treaty on the fundamental doctrine of the people's revolution. We did not strive whole-heartedly to create a world where there could be freedom from want for all the peoples. But by our very errors we learned much, and after this war we shall be in position to utilize our knowledge in building a world which is economically, politically and, I hope, spiritually sound.

Modern science, which is a by-product and an essential part of the people's revolution, has made it technologically possible to see that all of the people of the world get enough to eat. Half in fun and half seriously, I said the other day to Madame Litvinoff: "The object of this war is to make sure that everybody in the world has the privilege of drinking a quart of milk a day." She replied: "Yes, even half a pint." The peace must mean a better standard of living for the common man, not merely in the United States and England, but also in India, Russia, China and Latin America—not merely in the United Nations, but also in Germany and Italy and Japan.

Some have spoken of the "American Century." I say that the century on which we are entering—the century which will come out of this war—can be and must be the century of the common man. Perhaps it will be America's opportunity to suggest the freedoms and duties by which the common man must live. Everywhere the common man must learn to build his own industries with his own hands in a practical fashion. Everywhere the common man must learn to increase his productivity so that he and his children can eventually pay to the world community all that they have received. No nation will have the God-given right to exploit other nations. Older nations will have the privilege to help younger nations get started on the path to industrialization, but there must be neither military nor economic imperialism. The methods of the nineteenth century will not work in the people's century which is now about to begin. India, China, and Latin America have a tremendous stake in the people's century. As their masses learn to read and write, and as they become productive mechanics, their standard of living will double and treble. Modern science, when devoted whole-heartedly to the general welfare, has in it potentialities of which we do not yet dream.

And modern science must be released from German slavery. International cartels that serve American greed and the German will to power must go. Cartels in the peace to come must be subjected to international control for the common man, as well as being under adequate control by the respective home governments. In this way, we can prevent the Germans from again building a war machine while we sleep. With international monopoly pools under control, it will be possible for inventions to serve all the people instead of only the few.

Yes, and when the time of peace comes, the citizen will again have a duty, the supreme duty of sacrificing the lesser interest for the greater interest of the general welfare. Those who write the peace must think of the whole world. There can be no privileged peoples. We ourselves in the United States are no more a master race than the Nazis. And we cannot perpetuate economic warfare without planting the seeds of military warfare. We must use our power at the peace table to build an economic peace that is just, charitable and enduring.

If we really believe that we are fighting for a people's peace, all the rest becomes easy. Production, yes—it will be easy to get production without either strikes or sabotage; production with the whole-hearted cooperation between willing arms and keen brains; enthusiasm, zip, energy geared to the tempo of keeping at it everlastingly day after day. . . .

And then there is the task of transportation to the line of battle by truck, by railroad car, by ship. We shall joyously deny ourselves so that our transportation system is improved by at least 30 per cent.

I need say little about the duty to fight. Some people declare, and Hitler believes, that the American people have grown soft in the last generation. Hitler agents continually preach in South America that we are cowards, unable to use, like the "brave" German soldiers, the weapons of modern war. It is true that American youth hates war with a holy hatred. But because of that fact and because Hitler and the German people stand as the very symbol of war, we shall fight with a tireless enthusiasm until war and the possibility of war have been removed from this planet. We shall cleanse the plague spot of Europe, which is Hitler's Germany, and with it the hell-hole of Asia—Japan.

The American people have always had guts and always will have. You know the story of Bomber Pilot Dixon and Radioman Gene Aldrich and Ordnanceman Tony Pastula—the story which Americans will be telling their children for generations to illustrate man's ability to master any fate. These men lived for 34 days on the open sea in a rubber life raft, eight feet by four feet, with no food but that which they took from the sea and the air with one pocket knife and a pistol. And yet they lived it through and came at last to the beach of an island they did not know. In spite of their suffering and weakness, they stood like men, with no weapon left to protect themselves, and no shoes on their feet or clothes on their backs, and walked in military file because, they said, "if there were Japs, we didn't want to be crawling."

. . . As we nerve ourselves for the supreme effort in this hemisphere we must not forget the sublime heroism of the oppressed in Europe and Asia, whether it be in the mountains of Yugoslavia, the factories of Czechoslovakia and France, the farms of Poland, Denmark, Holland and Belgium, among the seamen of Norway, or in the occupied areas of China and the Dutch East Indies. Everywhere the soul of man is letting the tyrant know that slavery of the body does not end resistance.

There can be no half measures. North, South, East, West and Middle-west—the will of the American people is for complete victory.

No compromise with Satan is possible. We shall not rest until all the victims under the Nazi yoke are freed. We shall fight for a complete peace as well as a complete victory.

The people's revolution is on the march, and the devil and all his angels cannot prevail against it. They cannot prevail, for on the side of the people is the Lord.

He giveth power to the faint; to them that have no might He increaseth strength . . .

They that wait upon the Lord shall mount up with wings as eagles; they shall run, and not be weary; they shall walk, and not be faint.

Strong in the strength of the Lord, we who fight in the people's cause will never stop until that cause is won.

Julian Huxley

Julian Huxley (1887-   ) is a grandson of Thomas Huxley and a grand-nephew of Matthew Arnold. He was educated at Oxford, and has had a busy career as a professor and research scholar in zoölogy. But he does not confine• himself to a single field of knowledge. Indeed, in the catholicity of his interests he exemplifies his scientific humanism which makes the most of this life without requiring the consolations of mysticism. In the following essay he discusses, with a clarity worthy of his famous grandfather, the nature of the revolution in which we find ourselves, and directs our thought to the only alternatives within our choice: whether the revolution shall be totalitarian or whether it shall be truly democratic.

ON LIVING IN A REVOLUTION

THE world's most important fact is not that we are in a war, but that we are in a revolution. It is perhaps a pity that the word *revolution* has two senses—one an insurrection, a bloody uprising against constituted authority, the other a drastic and major change in the ideas and institutions which constitute the framework of human existence; yet so it is. If we like, we can use *rebellion* for the first, *historical transformation* for the second; but I prefer the word *revolution,* and shall continue to use it in what follows, with the express warning that I do not thereby mean merely barricades or bolshevism. If we once accept that statement and all its implications, we find ourselves committed to the most far-reaching conclusions concerning both immediate action and future policy.

From a combination of brute fact and human reason an argument emerges, proceeding as inexorably to its conclusion as a proposition of Euclid.

Let me anticipate my detailed discussion by setting down the proposition as baldly as possible. This is the sequence of its steps:

First. The war is the symptom of a world revolution, which, in some form or another, is inescapable.

Second. There are certain trends of the revolution which are inevitable. Within nations, they are toward the subordination of economic to non-economic motives; toward more planning and central control; and toward greater social integration and cultural unity and a more conscious social purpose. Between nations, they are toward a higher degree of international organization and a fuller utilization of the resources of backward countries.

Third. During the present war both military efficiency and national morale are positively correlated with the degree to which the inevitable trends of the revolution have been carried through.

Fourth. There are alternative forms which the revolution may assume. The chief alternatives depend on whether the revolution is effected in a democratic or a totalitarian way.

Fifth. The democratic alternative of achieving the revolution is the more desirable and the more permanent; the purely totalitarian method is self-defeating in the long run.

Sixth. The only universal criterion of democracy and the democratic method is the satisfaction of the needs of human individuals, their welfare, development, and active participation in social processes. A further democratic criterion, applicable in the immediate future, is equal co-operation in international organization, including the treatment of backward peoples as potential equals.

Seventh. The revolution, like the war, must be consciously accepted and deliberately entered upon. Formally, this can be accomplished by proclaiming war aims or peace aims which include the achieving of the revolution. This releases the latent dynamism of the nation and the social system.

Eighth and last. This again can be done on a democratic as well as on a totalitarian basis. By deliberately entering on the revolution in a fully democratic way it is possible to arrive at satisfactory and detailed war or peace aims which will release the powerful forces latent in the democracies, shorten the war, and, if implemented, produce a stable peace.

There is our proposition of political Euclid in skeleton form. Let us now take its bare bones and clothe them with convincing flesh and blood.

2

Point Number One was that the war is a symptom of a world revolution. Clearly the first thing to do about a revolution is to recognize it as a fact. Surprisingly enough, however, it is quite possible to ignore its existence. Just as Monsieur Jourdain in Molière's *Bourgeois Gentilhomme* discovered that he had been speaking prose all his life without knowing it, so many people today are beginning to discover that they have been living in a revolution without knowing it, and many others have still to discover this surprising phenomenon.

This is possible, partly because a world revolution is so vast in scope and, even though it proceeds at a rate far faster than that of history in its more normal phases, so gradual compared with the happenings of everyday life. The ordinary man sees his taxes raised, or unemployment go up, or banks crash down, or the central government extend its control, or war break out in some remote part of the globe; and he is concerned with each incident as an event in itself, not as a symptom of a larger process. It is also partly because most of us dislike radical change; after all, it is a somewhat dubious privilege to be living in anything so drastic as a revolution. Because we dislike it, we unconsciously push it away from us, begin to treat the danger as if we were ostriches, and are temporarily enabled to believe that the nasty revolution doesn't really exist.

It is worth remembering that it took us democracies a long time to recognize the existence even of the war. It is and always has been a world war, ever since its first beginnings in Manchukuo. But we refused, most of us, to admit the fact. German rearmament and the occupation of the Ruhr; Italy's attack on Abyssinia; the fighting in Spain; Munich: though some were bloodless, all were parts of a rapidly ripening world conflict. Both the fact that a world war existed and the ostrichism of our reactions to it were most obvious in the case of Spain. Here we had Franco's revolution, aided and abetted by the Axis; then Italy and Germany actively intervening, partly to secure the triumph of their side and partly to enjoy a little practice for the major struggle that they knew was to come; the Axis intervention providing counter-intervention by the Russians and the Volunteer Brigades, and undercover help from France. And yet the democratic Great Powers persisted in building up the fiction that it was nothing but a local civil war. I remember a cartoon in a left-wing French paper—an official of the Non-Intervention Committee saying to an attendant, "Put the non-carafe on the non-table." Non-Intervention was England and France saying to each other, "Let us take non-sides in the non-war." It was the political expression of a psychological refusal to recognize an unpleasant fact—the fact that a world conflict existed. Hitler's marching into Czechoslovakia at last made Britain as a nation realize that the world war existed. I suppose it was not till his invasion of Poland that the full realization came to the United States.

It was even later that the democracies began to recognize the existence of a world revolution. This is a surprising fact, considering that it had been going on for much longer than the war. The old tribal and feudal Japan had always been totalitarian in the sense that the individual was entirely subordinated to society. The new Japan merely translated this into modern terms, with the addition of an aggressive foreign policy (in the process anticipating many of the ideas of the Nazis); but the transformation was drastic and had obvious immediate consequences. The Russian Revolution of 1917, the Turkish Revolution, the Fascist Revolution in Italy, the social and industrial transformation in Britain and other Western European democracies, the New Deal in America, the Nazi Revolution in Germany, the establishment of a dictatorship in Portugal, the revolution and counter-revolution in Spain—these, among other events, were all manifestations, sometimes total and drastic, sometimes partial and hesitant, of the world transformation that is in progress.

The Russians long ago recognized its existence, and so, in their fashion, did the Fascists, the Nazis, and the Japanese expansionists. Britain as a nation did not recognize it until much later, but when it came the recognition was explicit enough. A distinguished Swedish woman economist who spent some weeks in England in 1941 on her way to the U.S.A. told me how one night in the Savoy Hotel she found herself sitting next to a young officer in one of the Guards regiments, a typical English aristocrat. "You know," he said, "we're living in a Social Revolution here: very interesting, what?" Very interesting indeed to a representative of a class which was likely to suffer considerably as a result! The remark was a symptom. Toward the end of 1940 the adjustments of people and Government alike to the threat of invasion and to the Nazi air bombardment, together with the writings and radio talks of men like Priestley, had brought an acceptance of the fact which was both general and, on the whole, remarkably good-natured.

France had to accept the revolution, in the guise of Pétain's pale imitation of Fascism. The United States is the only great Power which has not generally recognized its existence as an inescapable fact. The proportion of its people who still imagine that after the war they can go back to the old social and international system—with a few minor differences no doubt, but essentially the same—is still high. When I was there in the winter of 1941-42 I would have said at least eighty per cent; many American friends to whom I talked said ninety or more. Thanks to events and the writings of men like Wendell Willkie and Walter Lippmann, the proportion has been much reduced; but it is still high enough, especially as regards social and economic affairs, to prevent the emergence of a common consciousness. The most important single thing for the Americans to do now is to recognize that they, like the rest of the world, are living in a revolution, and that in some form or other it will achieve itself inevitably, whether they like it or not.

3

The next step after recognizing the existence of the revolution is to understand its nature and probable results. This can best be done by studying the trends already manifested by the revolution as it has operated in various countries, discovering what they have in common, and projecting them forward to their logical conclusion. At the outset let us be quite clear in our minds that the revolution can achieve itself in a democratic or a totalitarian way (or a mixture of the two), but that in all cases it manifests certain common tendencies. We thus can and must distinguish sharply between the inevitable aspects of the revolution and its alternative possibilities.

The inevitable aspects of the revolution are those trends which are being produced by economic and social forces entirely beyond our control. It is they that constitute the "wave of the future." But it is a plain error to equate this revolutionary "wave of the future" with Nazism or any other brand of totalitarianism. The character of the wave depends on which of the alternative methods we adopt to achieve the revolution—or, perhaps we had better say, to guide the revolution as it inevitably achieves itself. Thus dictatorship and forcible regimentation are not inevitable aspects of the revolution. Neither, we may add, is greater concern for the Common Man.

The revolution is a result of the breakdown of the nineteenth-century system, and especially of economic *laisser-faire* and political nationalism. Peter Drucker documented this in an exciting and stimulating book called *The End of Economic Man*. But he made no attempt to characterize the new system that is destined to emerge from the transformation of the old. If one must have a summary phrase, I would say that the new phase of history should be styled the Age of Social Man. Let us consider the trends of the revolution so far as it has taken place, to justify this assertion.

Within nations, in the first place, purely economic motives, though naturally they continue to be important, are being relegated to second place in favour of non-economic motives which may broadly be called social, since they concern the national society as a whole, or else the welfare of the individual considered in his relation to the society of which he forms a part.

In Nazi Germany the primary motive has been national power and prestige, to be realized through war. The complete subordination of purely economic motives can be measured by the criticisms levelled by orthodox economists against the methods adopted by Dr. Schacht. Since then the democratic countries have had to do the same sort of thing. The extent of the change can be realized when we find the May Committee reporting, only eight years before the outbreak of this war, that "democracy was in danger of suffering shipwreck on the hard rock of finance," because Britain was confronted with a budget deficit of 120 million pounds—not much more than a week of its war expenditure in 1942. Today finance has come to be generally regarded merely as a necessary part of the machinery for realizing our aims. People are no longer asking, "How shall we pay for the war?" Instead, they are beginning to say, "If we can finance the war in this way, why can't we apply similar methods on a similar scale to realizing social and cultural aims in peace?"

In Russia the subordination of the ordinary profit motive to social ends has been even more obvious. The deliberate encouragement of heavy industry under the Five Year Plan, at the expense of all other kinds of enterprise which would have flourished in a *laisser-faire* economy, is the most clear-cut example. In general, though economic efficiency is naturally insisted upon, the primary criterion for an enterprise is not whether it shall show a profit in its balance sheet, but whether it is desirable from the broad national point of view summed up in the current plan. A particular example of some interest is the expenditure on scientific research. As Bernal has pointed out in his book *The Social Function of Science,* the U.S.S.R., in spite of its low *per capita* wealth, was already before the war expending one per cent of its national income on scientific research. Under the system of competitive private enterprise this does not "pay"; and we find that Britain (before the war) expended only one-tenth of one per cent of its national income on science, and even the U.S.A. only six-tenths of one per cent.

In many other aspects of life in totalitarian countries the economic motive has been relegated to the background. I will mention only the concern with recreation. In Italy the *Dopo Lavoro* organization and in Germany the *Kraft durch freude* or "Strength through Enjoyment" did give the common man an outlet and a sense that the community was interested in him and his personal needs for a richer life: economic considerations were entirely subordinated to this. In Russia the elaborate system of rest-houses and holiday centres and the equally elaborate arrangements for holiday transport achieved the same end.

It is especially significant that similar trends have been at work in democratic countries, even when there has been no recognition of the existence of a revolution. One of the most telling examples is that of housing in Britain. It is impossible to provide the lower-income group with decent housing which shall give an economic return. Accordingly, the State has stepped in, and has given subsidies toward the building of no fewer than one and a quarter million houses or apartments in England and Wales alone during the inter-war period. The economic motive of profit has been overridden by the social motive of providing adequate living accommodation.

Nutrition offers in some ways a still more interesting example because of the progressive change to be seen. In the nineteenth century charity did its best to alleviate obvious distress. The new outlook was first expressed in Britain by the recognition that badly undernourished children could not possibly profit by education, and the consequent provision of cheap or free school meals for them. Today the provision of free meals has been considerably extended and has been combined with the scheme for providing cheap dinners to a steadily increasing proportion of all children in State-aided schools. Free or undercost milk for children and for all expectant and nursing mothers is also being provided on a much more generous scale than before the war.

In general, the motives that have become dominant or are tending to do so are those of social security, health and housing, education and culture, recreation and amenity, and national prestige and military power; in special cases economic considerations have been overridden for almost mythological considerations, as in the Nazi persecution of the Jews as an inferior and enemy race, and the expulsion from Germany of some of the best German brains, in the interests of uncritical acceptance of orthodox Nazi doctrine.

Other apparently inevitable trends are those toward more planning and toward a greater degree of social unity or self-consciousness. The trend toward planning is so universal and obvious that little need be said on the subject. It is inevitable because, with the end of the era of primary industrial expansion, *laisser-faire* was defeating itself and unregulated private and sectional interests were coming into disastrous conflict with one another and with the common good. The trend is not merely toward more extensive planning in more fields; it is also toward a greater initiative and authority at the centre. Here again the totalitarian countries have gone farther; but the U.S.A. contains some remarkably developed examples of planning, such as the Tennessee Valley Authority, and the war has forced a planned economy on every belligerent country.

Social unity and self-consciousness perhaps demand a little more discussion. The Nazi doctrine of "Aryan" and Germanic superiority and Jewish inferiority and evil is a myth encouraging permanent and super-patriotic unity. In all totalitarian nations, and in the U.S.A. as well, the Government has encouraged art and other cultural activities on a large scale until they provide a much fuller and more intensive expression of society's awareness of itself and its ideals than in other countries. In Britain the war has produced C.E.M.A.[1] to fill the cultural gap. In the U.S.S.R. the subsidiary nationalities have been deliberately encouraged to develop their own traditional cultures. The organized youth and health movements of the totalitarian countries and of pre-war Czechoslovakia, the fostering of the belief in a peculiar "German science," the great prestige and publicity given in Russia to scientific and geographical achievement are also symptoms of the same

[1] Council for Encouragement of Music and the Arts.

trend, as is the tendency to see in education not merely an intellectual, a moral, or a practical function, but a social one—the function of projecting the character, the ideals, the needs, and, in general, the social consciousness of the nation into the next generation.

In international affairs one inevitable trend is toward a higher degree of international organization. This has gone much farther in totalitarian countries—largely theoretically in Japan's "East Asia Co-Prosperity Sphere," very practically in the unification of Europe in Hitler's iron "new order." In the democratic countries it is beginning to appear under the stress of war. Lend-Lease, the leasing and sharing of strategic bases, organizations like the Middle East Supply Council, the various organizations for unified strategy and supply—these are important beginnings.

The second international trend is the greater concern with the organized exploitation of the resources, both material and human, of backward areas. This, like the first, is an inevitable outcome of that shrinking of the world to which Mr. H. G. Wells has so forcibly drawn attention. The world has become a unit, its frontiers and empty spaces are filling up.

The exploitation may be exploitation in the bad sense, like that of occupied and dominated Europe by Germany at the present moment, or like that of the mineral resources of helpless or dependent peoples by powerful foreign financial interests. Or it may be exploitation in the good sense, like the encouragement given by the United States to the political development of the Filipinos, or certain aspects of native development in British colonies like Uganda or the Gold Coast. Another symptom of the trend is the widespread talk about the need for investing very large sums in the development of backward regions, even if this be uneconomic in the short-range terms of private finance.

The logical conclusion of these various inevitable trends is a world where nations or federations put non-economic aims into first place, and exhibit a high degree of central planning, extending to every main activity of life, and a high degree of social integration in education, cultural expression, and social self-consciousness; but also a world where nations are getting tied together more closely in international organizations, and where the resources of backward areas are being more consciously exploited and developed.

4

The third step in our proposition was that the degree to which the revolution had been achieved was in some way related to military efficiency in the war. The correlation is striking though by no means complete, and the relation appears to be a causal one, in the sense that planning, social integration, and the deliberate relegation of economic motives to second place are all essential to the successful waging of modern total war.

Here again the totalitarian countries provide the most obvious examples. Germany and Japan have been able to score their spectacular military successes because they have for years been planning for war, and because they have carried out the most drastic revolutions of their economy and social structure in the interests of that plan. The same is true of Russia: the military and technical efficiency which has surprised the world is the fruit of a deliberate and truly revolutionary plan. The lesser military efficiency of Italy has many reasons; but it is a fact that the Fascist revolution was not so thoroughgoing or so wholehearted as the Nazi revolution in Germany or the Communist revolution in Russia, and this fact is undoubtedly one of the causes for Italy's military failure in this war.

In other countries failure to embark upon the revolution has demonstrably impeded military efficiency. The most conspicuous example was France, where conflict as to the form the revolution should take was so acute that no agreed action was possible, and the result was disunity, disintegration of morale and national feeling, unpreparedness, and inefficiency. The inadequacy of British production and planning during the Chamberlain "phony war" period is another illustration. So is the unfortunate effect of Britain's slowness in changing her official attitude toward so-called inferior races, whether subject peoples or allies. American readers will be able to provide plenty of examples from their own country during the early months after Pearl Harbor. From an earlier period, the shipment of oil and scrap iron to Japan, the behaviour of Standard Oil and other big companies with regard to synthetic rubber and other new technical advances, and the huge output of pleasure automobiles during 1941 provide further examples of how failure to abandon the ideas of an earlier age may interfere with military efficiency when the revolutionary war eventually blasts its way in.

There will be more to say on this subject in relation to war and peace aims. Meanwhile the fact that there is a definite connection between the extent to which a country has progressed in achieving the inevitable trends of the revolution and that country's efficiency in the war, is a solemn warning to those who persist in proclaiming that the war is no time for social experiments. On the contrary, the war itself calls for the most drastic social experimentation, so drastic as to merit the term revolutionary. The only question at issue is the form which the social experiment is to take.

5

This brings us to the most interesting step in the argument, for it is here that alternatives present themselves and that the outcome may be determined by our conscious choice and deliberate effort. The revolution itself is inescapable. Even if we struggle against it we merely make the inevitable process longer, more painful, perhaps more bloody. But its form and character are not: it can be achieved in different ways, of which the alternative extremes may be described as the democratic way and the totalitarian way.

So our fifth point concerns the desirability and the efficiency of the two alternatives. We in the democracies know the undesirability of the totalitarian way. It is the way of force and domination. Inside the nation, it is employed to secure power for a small gang. It operates by means of armed force, secret police, concentration camps, the building up of irrational mass enthusiasm, the suppression of freedom of discussion, thought, and inquiry, and the persecution of contrary opinion and of scapegoat minorities. It demands disciplined uniformity and regimentation. Internationally, it imposes the domination of a chosen people or a master race, who will shoulder the burden of directing the international organization required; in return, other peoples are expected to acquiesce in remaining at a lower level of development and prosperity. In both cases, power is the primary aim, force is the primary method, and domination of the less powerful by the more powerful is the primary object.

The totalitarian method of achieving the revolution may be undesirable, but it is certainly capable of producing extreme efficiency, as the enemies of Nazi Germany have found to their cost. However, there is every reason to believe that this advantage is not lasting, and that the method is essentially a self-defeating one. It is self-defeating just because it holds its power by sheer force and can maintain itself only by constantly extending that power. But the more it extends its power the more resistance it generates both from the inside and from the outside. The question is thus not whether it will fail in the long run, but how long that run will be, and how much of civilization it will destroy in the process.

What of the democratic way? To be clear on this, the sixth step in our proposition of political Euclid, requires some hard mental effort. We may be sure in principle that it is preferable, and that it does not contain the necessary seeds of its own defeat within itself. But we must be quite sure of what we mean by democracy, sure that we are not misapplying the term or merely talking platitudes. Democracy requires rethinking in relation to the changing world. A great deal of what we have taken for granted as being of the essence of democracy turns out to be applicable only to a partial aspect of democracy or only in the particular period from which we are now escaping.

Thus it is entirely wrong to equate democracy with a system of free individual enterprise. That was the form taken by democracy, in its economic aspects, during the period initiated by the industrial revolution. In those conditions that aspect of democratic freedom worked efficiently in many ways, but also generated contradictions—for instance, by creating economic unfreedom for large masses of the lower-paid workers. For a different reason, it is entirely wrong to equate democracy with representative government. That is one aspect only of democracy, the political aspect: democracy must extend into the economic and social and all other aspects of life if it is to be complete.

Our first problem is, then, to find a criterion or a principle of democracy which is universal and is applicable in every period of history, under any conceivable set of conditions. So far as I can see, there is only one such criterion—the individual human being, his needs and his development. The yardstick by which we can measure democratic achievement is the satisfaction of the needs of human individuals, and the yardstick by which we can measure democratic method is their active and voluntary participation in all kinds of activities. The two are in reality not separate, for participation is itself a human need to be satisfied, but for some purposes the distinction is useful.

Under the satisfaction of needs there is to be included not merely the provision of a reasonable standard of security and welfare, including adequate nutrition and health, but also equal opportunity for education, for recreation, for freedom, and for self-development and self-expression. Looked at from another angle, every human being born into the world has in the eyes of true democracy a certain individual birthright—a birthright of health, strength, intelligence, varied enjoyment, and free interest, which must not be denied or stunted if the society into which he is born lays claim to being democratic.

Under participation there is to be included participation in national politics and in local government and community affairs, by discussion, through the ballot box, and by actual service; but there is also freedom of participation in group organizations, whether to protect particular interests (like trade unions), or to give outlet to a shared enthusiasm (like choral societies or natural history clubs); and there is also the opportunity of participation in cultural life and in organizations for service. The technique adopted in planning schemes like the TVA or the Columbia Basin projects is demonstrating how the general public can participate in a bold central plan.

Throughout, the basic criterion is that the individual and his ultimate welfare and fullest development shall be paramount; not the State, nor national power or wealth, nor maximum profits, nor even the cultural achievements of a society in art or science or literature. And this implies the maximum amount of freedom, the fullest equality of opportunity for development, and the maximum degree of co-operation. The freedom must not be freedom at the expense of others, the opportunity must not impair the possibilities of co-operation.

The individual is the ultimate yardstick; but he cannot develop fully or freely except in an organized society. Nor is any one individual the yardstick: his freedom and opportunities must obviously be limited by the need for guaranteeing freedom from interference to his fellow-individuals.

6

So much for the universal criterion of democracy. What remains is to
find those special applications of democracy which will be necessary in the
new phase upon which the world is now entering. Liberty, Equality, Fraternity—these will always constitute democracy's triple crown; but, to change
the metaphor, their edges have grown blunted by use, so that they need re-
defining in new terms; and their particular expressions must be to a large
extent determined by the social and economic conditions of the time.

The outstanding characteristic of the early nineteenth century was that
it was an expanding and an industrial world. In that world democratic freedom was inevitably concerned with throwing off the shackles of the semi-
feudal past, and with the rights and duties of free individual enterprise to
exploit the resources of nature to the fullest possible degree; democratic
equality was largely limited to political equality for the middle classes; and
democratic fraternity was still largely confined to the concepts of charity and
noblesse oblige. The outstanding characteristic of the world we are now
entering upon is that it is a closed world, still organized in the form of
independent nation-states, but with those states brought into constant contact and constant friction. What application of democratic principle will
these conditions bring out and emphasize?

Nationalist self-determination leads, in this closed world, to competition and war; but cultural self-determination (as practised, for instance,
to a notable extent in the U.S.S.R., where regional cultures are encouraged
to develop fully and freely) is perhaps the best expression of Liberty in
tomorrow's internationalism. The principle of Fraternity may be broadly
translated as co-operation: co-operation for defense, for trade, for increased
general consumption. This at once rules out punitive tariffs, purely national armies, and imperialist domination, and suggests the lines for new
world-scale economic and political organizations, both international, trans-
national, and supernational.

In the new international sphere the most difficult of the three democratic principles to translate into the relevant concrete terms is Equality,
since at the present time the world is composed of peoples at such manifestly
unequal levels of cultural and economic development. However, we find
a general principle to hand in that of Potential Equality. Our aim with
backward peoples will then be to raise them to a position where they can
take their international place on a footing of actual equality. This does not
imply that all peoples are potentially identical culturally or that there may
not be real differences in innate temperament or capacity. Cultural diversity
is as desirable as individual diversity. As with individuals, peoples and nations contain vast reservoirs of untapped potentiality, and the democratic

approach demands in both cases that they should be provided with equality of opportunity to develop that potentiality.

We are beginning to realize the implications of these ideas in relation to China: the Chinese people must be treated on a footing of equality if the war is to be won and if we are to have a stable peace in the Far East. The same realization is dawning with regard to India. In the case of politically dependent peoples, the United States adopted the principle of potential equality in its encouragement of the Filipino's development toward independence. This was in strong contrast with the British attitude in Malaya—with appropriate results in the military sphere.

The general implications of this principle are twofold. First, a redefinition of the status of colonies and dependent peoples, with a formal pronouncement to the effect that the goal of colonial administration is preparation for self-government at the earliest possible moment. And second, a policy of large-scale development for all peoples or regions who are backward in the sense of being below standard in any aspect of life. This would not "pay" in the short-range terms of *laisser-faire* finance, but will certainly do so in the long run if our other two principles of co-operation and of freedom for cultural development are borne in mind.

7

The final step in our argument remains—the need for entering upon our revolution consciously and of set purpose, deliberately guiding its course instead of allowing its blind forces to push and buffet our unplanned lives. The war is not merely a symptom of the world revolution; it is also one of the agencies for its accomplishment. The two are bound up together.

Our best method for achieving the revolution deliberately is through the proclamation of comprehensive war or peace aims which include the achieving of the revolution. Our enemies have long ago done this. Hitler, for instance, has included in his aims the establishment of a "new order" in Europe, with the establishment of Germany in a dominant position as a "Master Race," and with the crushing both of bolshevism and democracy in favour of National Socialism. Japan has done the same with its slogan of Asia for the Asiatics, and its project of the "East Asia Co-Prosperity Sphere," with Japan in a similar dominant position as divinely appointed leader.

The war and peace aims of the United Nations are beginning to take more definite shape. But they could and should become both more comprehensive and more precise. For this it is not necessary that we should refer explicitly to the revolution nor envisage its complete fulfilment. But it is necessary that we take it and its implications into account.

If the revolution in some form is inevitable, and if we agree that the democratic way of carrying it out is the better way, that is the first step. The next is to make sure that we understand the inevitable trends of the revolution, and also learn how to translate the standards and methods of democracy into the new terms that the changing world demands. Then we shall have not only a body of principles to act as a touchstone, but a set of general aims to give us our direction. Our concrete schemes can then be framed in relation to those aims and checked in detail against that touchstone.

It is surprising how much assistance such a coherent body of aims and principles can give—on social security, on our treatment of subject peoples, on the role of art in the community, on international trade, and a hundred other subjects. They can also be important in warning us against possible mistakes—against a disregard of the trends of history, against every kind of undemocratic short cut to apparent efficiency, against the possible imposition of plans, however admirable, without the interest and the participation of the plannees (if I may coin a term), against every kind of narrow exploitation and racial arrogance.

It may be suggested that the best method of setting about this business is to draw up and proclaim a series of Charters, extending the general principles of the Atlantic Charter into greater detail and into various special fields. Once these were formally proclaimed by as many as possible of the United Nations there could be no going back on them; and meanwhile the experts behind the scenes could be charged with working out the practical schemes through which they would take effect. There has already been considerable talk in Britain of a Colonial Charter. A Pacific Charter might be useful to formulate the democratic point of view on the relations between the Asiatic and the white nations. A Charter of Welfare and Service would formulate the rights and duties of the individual and be in effect the charter of the common man; a Charter of Security would be the banner under which nations would be invited to co-operate in the prevention of war and aggression; and one might add a Charter of Prosperity to cover international economic co-operation, and a Charter of Peaceful Change as the first step toward the setting up of new international machinery for political adjustment.

Meanwhile it is imperative that we should be clear in our own minds as to the inescapable nature of our proposition of political Euclid. Only when we have accepted the logic of its earlier steps and fearlessly worked out their implications, can we hope to write Q.E.D. at its close by drawing the final conclusion of a set of aims which shall shorten the war, revivify the democratic nations, and lay solid foundations for peace.

James P. Warburg

James P. Warburg (1896-   ) is best known as a businessman, with important positions in banking, railroads, and other corporations. He has written various technical books in the fields of finance and industry, and was financial adviser to the World Economic Conference at London. When the war came he entered the Office of War Information and organized its London office. Yet he also finds time to write for the general reader on political and economic subjects and has even published verse. In Foreign Policy Begins at Home, from which the following chapter is reprinted, he realistically examines the injustices within the American system with a view to correcting them before we shall presume to establish justice throughout the world.

DOMESTIC PREREQUISITES TO PEACE

BEFORE we proceed to the consideration of some of the problems involved in the post-war relation of this country to the rest of the world, let us summarize briefly what would appear to be the domestic prerequisites of successful co-operation with other nations in the interests of lasting peace.

Montesquieu once said, "The sentiment of justice was created in man before reason itself." And it remains true today that in the face of reason, which tells us that war is a senseless abomination, the "sentiment of justice," older than reason, bids us nevertheless to fight when justice, as we see it, is sufficiently outraged.

Peace cannot long endure when justice is not firmly established.

Mere peace, even the peace of slavery, cannot be enforced forever. Man's sense of justice cannot be suppressed by force, and men will fight, so long as they are men, whenever sufficient violence is done to their sense of justice. Hence the foundations of peace must be something more than the mere machinery for the suppression of attempts to change the status quo by violence.

The foundations of peace must rest upon the establishment of justice and the maintenance of an order so permeated with justice that the majority of men will not be moved to violence.

Justice is not static. The arrangement which seemed fair and just to us last year often seems less so today. Circumstances have arisen which change the assumptions upon which that arrangement was made. The agreement we make today may seem equally unfair a year from now. We must conclude, then, that the order for which we are groping must provide the means for constant adjustment to changing circumstances, if it is to be so permeated with justice that the majority of men will not be moved to violence.

This is true not only *among* nations but *within* nations.

We, the people of America, cannot help to establish such an order among nations unless justice is firmly established here at home among ourselves.

With all our faults we are still looked upon today by the oppressed peoples of other nations as the haven of justice and the citadel of freedom. They will not long so regard us unless we continue to move forward. Already they are beginning to suspect that all is not well from the manner in which we behave abroad. They are hoping and waiting for a sign.

But the enemies of freedom in other countries, the selfish despoilers of democracy abroad, know every chink in our armor—every crack and crevice in our social structure. They and their conscious and unconscious helpers in this country are busy night and day widening each chink into a cleavage. Sectional disputes or jealousies, economic conflicts and labor troubles, racial discrimination and religious prejudice all are grist to their mill. Wherever there is conflict they will be found nourishing it, often by furnishing arguments to both sides.

Our job is to work toward the removal of those factors in our society which originally created the cleavages.

The most important of these factors are economic. Our failure to understand and regulate modern capitalism in the interests of society as a whole has tended to divide us one from the other in special interest groups, has kept the fear of unemployment hanging over us, and has created widespread insecurity and a sense of injustice. At the same time, the tradition of unregulated "free enterprise" has got into our blood to such an extent that it inhibits us from being willing to undertake the necessary cure.

We have much to do. We must harness "free enterprise" to economic democracy.

If we wish to preserve an economic order based upon the profit incentive, we must make that order distribute most of the profit in the form of purchasing power directly into the hands of those who would be consumers if they *had* purchasing power. This does not mean simply taxing estates and high incomes; to do this merely transfers the problem from the economic to the political system. It means recognizing the broad principle that those who use the tools of production (labor) are partners rather than the hirelings of those who own the tools (capital); and that both the owners and the users of the tools have a responsibility to society as a whole (the consumer).

This is not "production for use instead of profit," which is state-socialism.

It is production for profit by those who will spend the profit—as opposed to production for profit by those whose immediate demands are more or less satisfied and who will merely accumulate more capital.

Nearly everyone is agreed that our economic order must be made to provide full employment. "Free enterprise" can provide full employment only if there is full production. There can be full production only if there is full consumption. And there can be full consumption only if the would-be consumers have the necessary purchasing power.

Government—that is, society as a whole—can take up the slack by providing employment in temporary periods of adjustment by increased public works. But, unless government takes over the means of production (socialism), it cannot do more than this.

There is no way of creating purchasing power except by production.

If "free enterprise" is to do the job assisted by government—instead of government doing it altogether—then our basic concept of property rights will have to be redefined. Our present-day laws recognize and protect the ownership of physical property, which, broadly speaking, means the owner-ship of the plant, machinery and tools of production. But our laws have only begun to recognize the rights of those whose labor makes the tools of pro-duction productive. Recent labor and social-security legislation was badly needed to counteract some of the evils of our present system, but it did not and could not go to the root of the matter. It was designed merely to pro-tect the workers against long hours, low wages, unhealthy working condi-tions, and, to a certain extent, against the hazards of old age, sickness, and unemployment. This protection is absolutely necessary and must be main-tained until the evil is eradicated, but it does not cure—it merely palliates.

The basic question is not one of humanitarianism, it is one of justice. Labor should not need to be paternally protected. The social and economic order should in itself provide justice and security.

The necessary change in the concept of property rights would, of course, involve a change in the attitude of both the present owners and non-owners. The owners would have to accept labor as a full partner in "free enterprise," and labor would have to be ready to assume the full responsibilities and some of the risks of partnership. Both parties would share in the determina-tion of business policy and in the profits of the enterprise. Management would have to become the joint trustee of the interests of capital *and* labor and no longer regard itself merely as the trustee of capital. Labor would have to realize that it would no longer be the stepchild of the economic family with a special and neglected interest to protect against the rest of the community, but a full-fledged partner in "free enterprise" with a respon-sibility to the community.[1]

Some of this change in attitude on both sides has already occurred. The labor-management councils in many industries are already working in this direction. Management is in many cases no longer solely the trustee of capital; and labor is in many cases already accepting some of the responsi-bilities of partnership. But until we revise our concept of property rights and the distribution of profits, a real partnership cannot be established.

Another thing, which we need to do in overhauling our present system, is to re-examine carefully the device of the corporation, and to find out how to curb its tendency to become a monopolistic octopus. This will require a redefinition of the rights, immunities, and obligations of corporate enter-prise, and a revision of some of the legal concepts which were developed for the protection of the individual before the corporate device was invented.

We shall have to make up our minds either to abolish monopoly alto-gether, or else to allow certain monopolies to exist under government con-trol, or even perhaps under government ownership.[2]

In the same way we shall have to re-examine our present attitude toward natural resources, and even toward new inventions, when such inventions affect the public interest. It would seem that the harnessing of "free enterprise" to the interests of society would require the recognition that the country's natural resources belong to the people as a whole, rather than to those individuals or groups of individuals who happen to discover them. It would seem reasonable that the reward of discovery should be the right to develop and exploit for reasonable profit, but not the right either to waste or to withhold.

The same principle would apply to inventions which have an impor-tant bearing on the welfare of society as a whole. The explorer of natural resources and the explorer of the resources of science should certainly be entitled to a profit which compensates them for their discovery and for

---

[1] If a true labor-capital partnership is established, and management becomes the trustee for the interests of both—and if monopoly and monopolistic practices are abolished—the commu-nity as a whole, that is, the consumer, ought not to require any additional protection or repre-sentation. Free competition and the wider distribution of profits should protect the consumer's interest. It may, nevertheless, be found desirable in some cases to provide for direct consumer representation on the board of managers. But the difficulty about such representation is that it is hard to evolve a formula of selection, unless perhaps there should be new officials of local government elected for this specific purpose.

[2] There are no doubt certain sectors in our economy in which it will be impossible to abolish monopoly without making certain essential goods and services much more expensive to the consumer than they are now. This is true especially of some of the so-called public service corporations, which require heavy investment in plant and machinery. In these limited sectors the author favors "socialization" of such monopolies as may be permitted to continue their existence—either by transference to state ownership, or by state regulation, or by state-controlled "yardstick" competition. But this should be the exception and not the rule. We should under-take such "socialization" only where it is in the public interest not to follow the rule, which would be to abolish monopoly altogether.

the risk of development, which often requires substantial capital. They should even be granted limited monopoly (patent rights) for a time; but they should not be allowed to squander the country's resources, nor to withhold benefits from society. Under our present patent laws monopolies and international cartels do precisely this.

The same principles of justice and equal opportunity must be applied to remedy the unhappy state of a large part of our agricultural population.

Basically the whole agricultural population suffers from a lack of balance between industrial and agricultural production. We have failed to achieve this balance for many reasons, but chiefly because our foreign trade policy has been the result of pressure-group horse-trading rather than of planning for a balanced economy.

The log-rolling procedure of tariff legislation has tended to raise the costs of manufactured articles (which the farmer must buy) while at the same time, it tended to destroy the foreign markets for his surplus farm products. To protect himself against the industrial pressure groups, which fostered this process, the farmer organized pressure groups of his own, which sought subsidies and price controls. Worse than that, some of these pressure groups worked against the interest of the small farmer and sought only to benefit certain big agricultural interests.

As a result, we still have the disgrace of the share-cropper, the poverty-ridden small farmer, and the disinherited agricultural nomad, while corporate industrialized agriculture flourishes on special privilege. In our agricultural society we have both the relics of feudalism and the evils of pressure-group industrial capitalism.

The further development of true co-operatives—not pressure groups—suggests a partial remedy. But basically our agricultural problem will never be solved until we regulate "free enterprise" as a whole in the public interest, and then plan our foreign trade policies to achieve domestic balance between industry and agriculture. This, in turn, we shall never do so long as we have invisible government by economic pressure groups.

If we proceed to reorganize our society along the lines thus sketchily indicated—with the ideals of justice, equal opportunity, and the interests of society as a whole always before our eyes—we shall be able to do our share toward establishing peace and justice throughout the world. We shall find ourselves marching in step with all the peoples of the world, though not necessarily with some of their present governments.

If we move in this direction we shall be able to meet our own immediate post-war problem. We shall be able to retrain and re-employ the ten to eleven million men and women now working in our war industries. We shall be able to get our house in order to receive the eleven million men and women who will be returning home from the armed forces. We shall be able to receive them into a society which welcomes them as badly needed productive workers instead of once more giving them apples to sell on the streets.[3]

In a recent article in the *Atlantic Monthly*, President James B. Conant of Harvard University said: "The demobilization of our armed forces is a God-given moment for reintroducing the American concept of a fluid society. If it is handled properly we can ensure a healthy body politic for at least a generation. Handle it improperly and we may well sow the seeds of a civil war within a decade."

There can be no "fluid society" unless "free enterprise" is made to shake off the shackles of runaway greed as expressed by the artificial rigidities imposed by runaway capitalism.

There can be no "fluid society" unless we emancipate ourselves from the way of thinking which has produced runaway capitalism.

We have a choice to make, as citizens of this country, which cannot be long postponed: either we must accept the class conflict engendered by modern society as inevitable, and enlist in it on one side or the other; or else we must all make up our minds to abolish the injustice which causes the class conflict to exist.

If we accept the conflict as inevitable, sooner or later the vast majority of American citizens will realize that they are disinherited by our economic order and that they have the political power to assert their rights. This would in all probability mean a mass trend toward state-controlled socialism. Such a trend would in turn almost certainly evoke a counter-trend toward fascism on the part of those who had enlisted on the other side of the struggle to preserve their capitalistic privileges. We should then have "the seeds of civil war" of which President Conant speaks. The result might be a violent and successful socialist revolution. Given our long tradition of runaway capitalism, it is far more likely that the revolution would be aborted into some form of fascist dictatorship.

If, on the other hand, we refuse to accept the inevitability of the class conflict—if all of us enlist together to abolish it from our society by eliminating its causes—then we need fear neither revolution nor fascism.

We cannot overnight remove the injustices which cause the class con-

[3] Carl A. Gray of Plainsville, Connecticut, a forward-looking industrial leader and author of *The Gray Plan for Post-War Reemployment*, says, in stating the general principles of his proposal:

"Because, with the coming of peace, the flow of manpower is reversed, it is the basic concept of this plan that the entire manpower machinery be also reversed. This implies as much planning, technical skill, expenditure of time, money and patience, in readjusting men to jobs, as are now being used in placing men in military positions."

In conclusion Mr. Gray says: "This is our first job when the war is won. We can win the war and still lose our country if we are not willing to face the facts and do something about it. American boys who are fighting all over the globe love their country as they never have before. We must justify this love by making their return to that country a reception, not a rebuff."

The most comprehensive study of the world problem of post-war employment has been made by the International Labor Office. The reader will find its report on *Organization of Employment in the Transition from War to Peace* well worth careful attention.

flict. We cannot overnight emancipate ourselves from the habits of selfish thinking and prejudice.

But we can overnight get started in the right direction.

We did get started with Theodore Roosevelt's Square Deal, and again with Woodrow Wilson's New Freedom, and again more recently under the New Deal of Franklin D. Roosevelt. But unhappily on each of the latter occasions the preoccupation of war coincided with the swing of the pendulum and combined to make us lose our momentum.

We must recapture our momentum if America is to be a dynamic force for democracy in a world which already contains the dynamic force of Soviet Russia.

Our perfection as a democracy—or the lack of it—counts less at this moment of history than the direction in which we are moving. What we are counts less than what we intend to be. The important thing is that the world—and we ourselves—must know for certain that here at home we are moving forward.

At present we appear to be standing still. But there is no such thing as standing still in the world today. Unless we feel on our faces the keen wind of our own forward progress, we shall know that we are drifting back.

Do we dare drift backward and betray the very cause for which we are fighting?

Do we dare drift backward and thus help to betray another peace?

Carl J. Friedrich

Carl J. Friedrich (1901-   ) came to the United States from Germany in 1922. He has become an American citizen. He is a Professor of Government at Harvard and, during the war, Director of the School for Overseas Administration in Cambridge. The following chapter from his suggestive book, The New Belief in the Common Man, *is an honest facing of the questions which arise out of world-wide extension of the Four Freedoms.*

PAN-HUMANISM

EACH passing day makes it more abundantly clear that the world of the past is dead and gone, that we are moving on into a new world. If it is not to be Hitler's, it will be ours. What do we want it to be? Unless we want to take on Hitler's job and become the world's masters, imposing on it our own conceptions of life, liberty, and the pursuit of happiness, we are confronted with a gigantic problem. Upon what common ground can mankind meet? What principles, values, standards are common to a majority of mankind? A majority! For it would plainly be absurd to ask for unanimity. But even a majority presents us with a problem of the first magnitude.

THE FOUR FREEDOMS

We want to live in a world where law and order reign. Right. But upon what common ground are such law and order to be erected? When speaking of our own constitution, we used to use the language of the eighteenth century. We talked of a "Bill of Rights." It was the right of a man to his *property* that loomed large in those words. In more recent years, *civil liberties* have taken the place of those rights. It has been the liberty of the *person* that has seemed most important in the age of individualism. Now comes a further step. On January 6, 1941, President Roosevelt proclaimed four *freedoms* as essential to a democratic world. Freedom of speech, freedom of religion, freedom from want, and freedom from fear—these four freedoms he insisted upon as essential.

They were meant as a challenge and they are a challenge. Whom were they meant to challenge? Americans heard the message with a brief flurry of enthusiasm, but they were perplexed. "Those are fine words," they seemed to say, "but what do they mean?" "Are we going to make the world safe for democracy once more?" sneered the men who disliked the President's foreign policy. There were many others, men and women firmly convinced of the urgency of defeating Hitlerism, who also were left wondering. The words seemed to echo an old battle cry—they stirred up uneasy memories of a crusade that had left them stranded.

Why this anxious questioning, this uncertainty about the meaning of these freedoms?

It cannot be a question of words, for the words are clear. Under the two freedoms of speech and of religion are comprised all those rights associated with a man's personal self-expression. Free press and free, peaceful assembly, and latterly the freedom of peaceful association, are covered by the first of these freedoms. Freedom of conscience and all that goes with it are taken care of by the second. We here in America find little difficulty in understanding the imperatives which these two freedoms of speech and of religion embody. What bothers us is the suspicion that we are far from having realized these aspirations.

OUR OWN SHORTCOMINGS

Any reader of literature on civil liberties will hesitate to consider freedom of expression a reality even in America. Only the thoughtless will forget the man who was put in jail for several years because he ventured to discuss peace problems in 1918. To speak of these high aspirations in the face of the treatment meted out to our colored people makes most of us feel ill at ease. Have we been able to make these freedoms secure to our own citizens? Yet after all is said and done, an impressive residue of really achieved freedom is left, as any refugee from Hitler will gladly testify.

Is there any immediate prospect of eliminating want from America, let alone from wide areas of the earth's surface? Freedom from want means first and foremost freedom from unemployment. Yet unemployment remains an unsolved problem right here in America. Want is, of course, a flexible term, but an equal standard of living should be the ultimate goal, although the President did not make it clear to what extent he meant to imply an equalizing of living standards throughout the world. Surely we do not wish to hide under a different set of words what Hitler brutally proclaims as his aim: to make the Nazi master race benefit from the toil of the rest of the world. At the same time, how can we hope even to approximate freedom from want? How many of our people are willing to share their real income with other peoples? How many of our people have been willing to admit that the equalizing of living standards even within the United States is necessary?

Probably the most important single item in the whole creed is freedom from fear. The right of *habeas corpus,* secured through centuries of hard struggle, is the freedom from arbitrary arrest. Its lack is the most bitterly felt loss of all those who have fallen under the domination of the Nazis. The terror of the totalitarian tyranny is quintessentially opposed to this freedom. Almost equally important nowadays is some kind of provision for protection against mob violence. Have we been able to provide it? Even on paper, we have not succeeded in outlawing lynchings. How is such freedom, then, to be brought to the suffering millions of poor bloody humanity?

WORLD PROBLEMS

It does not seem sensible for us to proclaim as a goal for the whole world what we have not been prepared to attempt at home. How can we become the pioneers of a new world order, a free co-operative world order, unless we seek to bring these high-sounding phrases down to earth? But even assuming that we have to some extent succeeded, how are we to secure adherence to all these freedoms on the part of other people?

Eighty million Germans, a hundred and fifty million Russians, tens of millions of other Slavic peoples, well over two hundred million Indians, between four and five hundred million Chinese and Japanese, not to speak of the numerous other peoples in the Near and the Far East, in all probably three fourths of the earth's population, have been living under social and political conditions where freedom of speech, of the press, and of assembly are almost meaningless phrases.

And as for freedom of religion—and of education? Do not many of these people acknowledge faith in a religion which dogmatically denies the desirability of tolerating other creeds? Can we force them to accept toleration? The British troubles in India furnish a striking object lesson; Mohammedan and Hindu have persecuted each other with relentless ferocity. The profound sympathy which any free man must feel for Indian demands is badly shattered by the discovery that, like the New England Puritans, they often seem to seek freedom the better to suppress their dissenting neighbors.

President Wilson was unable to secure adoption of an article guaranteeing the freedom of religious worship into the Covenant of the League of Nations. The Japanese dislike for such an article was intense; but in order to bring home their view they adopted the very telling device of suggesting that the Covenant contain an article guaranteeing all peoples under the Covenant against discrimination. The Australians, as hostile as America toward Japanese immigration, secured the rejection of this proposal, and so religious freedom was also abandoned. It is such conflicts that the advocate of a democratic world has to face; a readiness to make compromises upon one's own fundamental premises seems to be required at the very outset. Yet, to what extent can such a readiness be expected in others? This is in many respects a pure question of fact, but one with regard to which we lack the most elementary knowledge.

It was wise and helpful of the President to have the long and involved Bill of Rights of our constitution thus made more compact. It was bold and imaginative to bring the idea of the pursuit of happiness face to face with a twentieth-century reality: unemployment. And yet I know people of real ability and insight who are filled with enthusiasm for the world order, but who would not be the least happy over a tax increase that would help to banish want from our own country, to say nothing of China.

THE PUBLIC'S REACTION

Shall we then do nothing? Shall we allow things to drift? This also seems impossible. The four freedoms *are* the great symbols we are fighting for. But neither here nor abroad has the declaration of the four freedoms met with the enthusiasm to which its high idealism entitled it. Why? Wherein does it fail to rouse us—and more particularly the younger generation? Obviously a vast educational crusade is called for. Extensive conversations with all kinds of people, students and workers, farmers and businessmen, doctors and preachers, housewives and schoolboys, will convince anyone that the statement of these freedoms lacks that peculiar something which gives to an idea its representative, its symbolic value.

The spirit of the common man in America is practical and realistic. Though deeply attached to ideals, he wants to see them meaningfully related to what he knows about the world. He feels himself freer and more nearly in possession of what the four freedoms proclaim than most other people are. Yet he knows that we are far from any realization of these freedoms. He wants to know what is to be done about them.

Can we say that Americans in the mass are behind these four freedoms, not only for themselves but for China or Poland? Or do they look upon the idea of freeing the majority of mankind from want and fear as utterly chimeric? A survey has convinced me that the general feeling is one of great uncertainty. "How do I know what's good for China?" "I never met a Hindu, so I can't tell whether they would go along." The plain fact of the matter is that we have little or no idea, most of us, of what are the basic beliefs, values, standards of the majority of mankind. Here is the greatest stumbling-block to that "new world" which we seek to achieve.

THE WORLD CITIZEN

There can be no democratic world order without a democratic world citizen, any more than there can be a democratic American order without a democratic American citizen. What is more, we cannot be the protagonists of such a democratic world order if we are not prepared to be such world citizens ourselves. This will involve very great efforts and sacrifices on our own part. These sacrifices are part of establishing the world order we want to live in. The only basis on which we can ask other people to share the four freedoms and to be willing to accept their guarantees through effective world government is our own use of them. This means that our own policies and commitments must be such as to help other people to prosper. Carl Schurz once said: "If you want to be free, there is but one way: it is to guarantee an equally full measure of liberty to all your neighbors. There is no other."

We cannot hope to go forward by ourselves, either materially or spiritually, on this planet. And when we say this, we are not thinking of this year or next year, but of the generation now in the making. The citizen of the past was a national citizen. It was a question of turning folks from many lands into Americans. The citizen of the future will be a world citizen, or there will be no democratic world order. Frankly, I believe that this building of world citizenship has to begin right here in America.

Undoubtedly there will be great difficulties in establishing this world consciousness abroad, especially where totalitarianism has been rampant. On the other hand there may be a violent reaction against totalitarianism after it collapses. That is what happened last time, and such a reaction may well be even more far-reaching this time. Quite a few of those who have lived for years under Hitler know more about the beauty of freedom than we do. From the little countries that have been overwhelmed by the Nazi war machine come persistent voices that proclaim the end of national sovereignty. Out of Germany come demands of a similar nature.

We have indulged ourselves in much self-criticism. I feel that there has been too much talk about the purely organizational side of things, about the League and whether it would all have been different if we had gone in—or had we never espoused it in the first place. Every thoughtful American is agreed that that must not happen again. Americans are afraid of the ideals which inspired them then, because they found themselves confronted with tasks from which they recoiled. Why did they? Primarily, it seems to me, because Americans had assumed that making the world safe for democracy required nothing of them but to defeat the Kaiser. They did not realize that they, too, had to become something new, something almost unheard of—world citizens. Not quite unheard of, though. For at the very beginning of our democracy, there were a few world citizens: Tom Paine, Thomas Jefferson, Benjamin Franklin, Lafayette.

It was admittedly this failure of ours to mold ourselves in the spirit of our own professed idealism which left us stranded. We do not want to be so stranded again. Can we escape the job then of looking beyond our immediate responsibilities? Of facing the task of becoming ready for world citizenship ourselves? Obviously not. Well, what does that imply?

MANKIND'S COMMON GROUND

Our most intensive efforts must be shaped to meet this challenge in the years to come. Blueprints of world organization, economic programs, and social institutions are important, to be sure, but among the things to come, the most basic is the new man. Democratically speaking, we cannot have a new world without him. Yet this is no call for Utopia, no demand for changing basic human nature. But in a changed environment human nature can be brought to respond to different ideals and different needs. There will be balanced men and reckless adventurers, brilliant minds and reliable souls of pedestrian imagination, honest men and crooks—but unless their strivings and doings can be given a world orientation, America cannot assume leadership in world government.

There are such basic human facts—experiences which provide a starting point for understanding. Women of all nations can talk with each other about childbirth and children, no matter how diverse their background. These are feelings and interests common to all of them. Almost all mankind seems to be agreed that the mother has first claim on her infant. All of the questions large and small which grow out of this basic right are readily understood by women the world over. It is from simple facts such as these that we can start.

I do not feel at all ready myself to be dogmatic in formulating fundamental human rights on a cosmopolitan civilization. I do not feel that I have much to work with that would give me sympathetic understanding of the ethical aspirations of mankind. We have read a little Confucius, and we have a very vague idea of Buddhism and Mohammedanism, but our grasp of the ethical implications of their teachings leaves us uncertain. What *behavior* do we have in common with them? The group of writers known as "the Humanists," notably Irving Babbitt and Walter Lippmann, strove toward such a broad base, but their efforts were in the prefatory mood. They were too concerned with pointing out the shallowness of their contemporaries to make an attempt at being practical. "And so the mature man would take the world as it comes, and within himself remain quite unperturbed," Lippmann wrote in the *Preface to Morals*. It appears that he has lately—and quite rightly—ceased to be such a mature man and has become quite perturbed once more. It is right and proper that this should be so. It is just as true of the rest of us. The moralist, that old-fashioned creature who takes ideals seriously, is turning to and becoming practical. In doing so, let's start at home.

AN EDUCATIONAL TASK

For if we ourselves are in no sense ready to become citizens of a new world order, neither are our children. Whether they go to bad schools or to good schools, they are brought up to think of themselves as American citizens. All schools have gone in for civics, but civics in the past has tended toward a shallow nationalism. Cheap patrioteering has found more of a place in courses of this kind than any good educator could accept. The mere fact that America has been a democracy longer than any other large country seems to foster smugness. Fortunately, educators are more and more aware of this pitfall. Recent programs, such as that set forth in *The Education of Free Men in American Democracy,* candidly insist that American democracy is far from fulfilling its ideal. While a knowledge of the resources, achievements, and promise of American democracy is considered essential, an understanding of our weaknesses is declared to be equally so by this program.

But this self-critical attitude is not enough. There is need for a generous reaching out towards others. The democratic creed contains the seeds for a broader flowering. Our insistence upon tolerance is being broadened into respect and appreciation for peoples with a different culture from our own. But to date, we have thought too much in terms of minorities, racial, cultural and religious. In the emerging world order it is not merely a matter of minorities, but of the majority of mankind. Let us become familiar with the long struggle to liberate the human mind and civilize the human heart.

It was one of the strong points of humanist education that it conveyed a real feeling for another culture and its concrete aspirations. It provided a window out into another world. I shall never forget the glowing enthusiasm with which I wrote my graduation essay: "What the Greeks Mean to Us Today," even though I have long lost that sense of intimacy with Homer and Sophocles which inspired it.

The realistic trend of recent education, while admirable in its insistence upon making the teaching meaningful for the present, has tended toward a "spiritual provincialism." Our children may learn much about history, they may acquire wider knowledge of the broad sweep of civilization and yet fail to reach down to the core of understanding, for this can only be achieved through wrestling intensely with different conceptions of what is good and what is beautiful. The value judgments upon which culture rests are the decisive understanding of their inner springs. For it is in terms of these that they unfolded their colorful creative detail.

If this is a task too difficult for the school perhaps it should be attempted in the home. But how equipped are we, as parents, to handle this task? Suppose your eight-year-old girl comes to you, as mine did recently, and wants to know: "Are the Russians on our side?" How ready are you to help her to understand the broader issue of democracy versus Communism? I found it extremely difficult to get across to her the reasons why we must help the Russian people against the Nazis, and yet must also work for a more democratic union. I told her that they are not exactly on our side, but that we have a common enemy; still, I found myself handicapped by a sense of failure, an inability to present the ethical issue simply and clearly.

Education for free men in a democracy is confronted, then, with a new task of far-reaching consequences. If this is true at home, it is even more true at school. Out of a realistic approach to the problems of democracy, we are faced with the need for what may be an entirely new curriculum. It's not a matter of going back to the old literary humanism. To that the realist might well retort that such acquaintance lacked vital relationship to our own problems. One of their number, referring to Walter Lippmann's comments in a column entitled "On Being Too Current," recently exclaimed: "Seriously, does Mr. Lippmann think that young people of 1941 can be insulated, sterilized, wrapped in cotton batting, fed only on what was written and what happened before 1800, and at the age of twenty-one spring full-armed from the brain of Jove as responsible citizens of the world's greatest democracy?" I greatly sympathize with the protest, but I should like to add that probably no single educational task is of greater importance today than to ensure that these youngsters shall become ready for a citizenship wider than that of American democracy.

COMMON ETHICAL ASPIRATIONS

The new ethical realism, closely tied as it is to a realistic conception of the common man, provides the general approach. Rather than just proclaiming the principles of tolerance, an attempt should be made to bring clearly into focus the common ethical aspirations of mankind, to show that certain basic patterns of behavior are common to the vast majority of mankind, whether they be Christians or Buddhists, Mohammedans or Jews, Confucians or secular humanists. The elimination of special religious instruction from our schools, in keeping with the separation of church and state, has removed from the classroom the most essential of all subjects— namely, the ethical aspirations of man. In this our age of maturity it should be possible to return to it in the spirit of a new fellowship of man. That is the prime educational task, and it certainly is not an easy one. But if we don't start this effort, who will?

Beyond this educational task lies a political one. Politics in a democracy is adult education, at least half of the time. We may not think of it that way, but the educational value of a free discussion of public affairs is nevertheless one of the most important arguments in favor of democracy. John Stuart Mill put it very well in his *Representative Government*. Arguing against the Greek philosophers, especially Plato, he pointed out that the notion of an ideal king is bad, because the more benevolent his rule, the more enervating its effect in the long run. "Their minds are formed by, and consenting to, this abdication of their own energies." It is this active participation which makes of democratic politics a school for adults. How can this participation be elicited? How can we rouse ourselves to facing the same issues which the schools are groping toward in their work with our children?

A CONCRETE PROPOSAL

What might be done to give us a democratic basis for proceeding with the task that the presidential declaration opened up? Might we not gather forthwith, under either governmental or civic auspices, a world convention of men and women of thought rather than action, who could represent *a majority of mankind*? These representatives should not scatter before they have agreed to a more specific formulation of the ideals of the four freedoms in conformity with the great religions which mankind professes. It need not be a vast group of men; a gathering the size of our original

Constitutional Convention would probably be quite adequate. One for each 75,000,000-150,000,000 population among the peoples should be sufficient.

It is probably foolhardy to guess as to some of their conclusions, but it may serve to arouse disagreement and thereby promote discussion.

In spite of vast differences in theology, all the great religions have in common, first of all, what we have already been implying: a belief in ethics as such. In practice, this means the recognition of personal responsibility. It means that elemental realm of freedom which in our culture is institutionally protected by the freedom of religious worship. But it is this device of a written constitution, rather than the idea itself, which is peculiar to our own ways. In the Mohammedan world, as well as in China and elsewhere, a considerable measure of this freedom has been accepted for a long time. The Turkish Empire was the marvel of Europe in this respect in the sixteenth century. While the bitter religious wars were raging in England, France and Germany, men pleading for toleration time and again pointed to the Turks' willingness to live and let live so far as the realm of conscience was concerned.

Where a measure of religious freedom has been denied, it has usually been denied in the name of religion. It remained for the totalitarians of our own day to deny religious freedom out of a nihilistic denial of all religion. To be sure, they proclaimed their own, anti-ethical doctrines in pseudo-religious terms, but that does not alter the fact that they denied freedom of conscience to all but those who agreed with their particular version of determinism and materialism. In doing this, they attacked the *human* core of civilization. Human beings were asked to become something worse than slaves: robots. For the human being who is deprived of a belief in his responsibilities becomes an automaton executing the irresistible commands of social forces, biological drives, and the rest.

The universal recognition, then, of a belief in ethics and personal responsibility would be the first freedom that the pan-humanist congress would, I believe, agree upon.

An interesting confirmation comes from Professor Toynbee, whose comparative interpretation of world civilizations entitles him to great respect in a matter of this kind. "There can be no international ethos without a religious basis," he wrote, pointing out at the same time that this basis need not be necessarily Christian, and that religious elements in Islam, Hinduism, Buddhism and other religions offer hope of reaching such an ethos.

Freedom of conscience and of religious worship depends, in the world of hard facts, upon the right to one's physical person. In our own culture, in the English-speaking countries, this has found institutional expression in the right of *habeas corpus*. It has been discussed before. Protection against arbitrary searches and seizures, against being detained without being charged with a legally determinate crime, would be a first and foremost function of world government. Any local authorities unable to guarantee this protection to the inhabitants of their territory would forfeit the right to continue in office; it would be prima-facie evidence that that territory was not yet ready to govern itself. Such a condition may well be found in many parts of Europe after the collapse of the Nazis' rule of terror. If so, the other nations will find themselves saddled with the job of administering such countries for a transition period. For it is my second guess that a pan-humanist congress would agree upon what corresponds to the right of *habeas corpus* as the second universal imperative. It embodies the quintessence of freedom from fear. Without it, the common man as we understand him cannot come into action on a world-wide basis any more than he can on a national one. Even his collective judgment, fallible as it is, cannot come into play if the common man is terrorized.

PAN-HUMANISM

Is all this Utopia? Or is it the shape of things to come? All that mortals can do is to embrace the future with faith in the creative possibilities of mankind. What I hope I have shown is that a solid foundation for a free world is to be found only in a universal common man, a world public. The four freedoms, or indeed any other constitutional guarantees, are of little avail unless they give us that universal common man.

A French skeptic, looking at America in the early nineteenth century, wrote:—

It is immensely difficult to create a country out of states without any community of religion and interests, states which have been peopled by different stocks, and are living on varied soils and under diverse climates. What link is there between a Frenchman of Louisiana, a Spaniard of Florida, a German of New York, an Englishman of New England, Carolina, Georgia—all considered Americans? . . . How many centuries will be needed to make these elements homogeneous?

What Chateaubriand overlooked was that they were all *men,* common men united in the allegiance to those freedoms which they had come to live under. After their escape from the despotism, benevolent and otherwise, which they left behind them in Europe, they had become primarily human rather than English, French, German or Spanish. They came first, and the collectivity lived only in and through them.

We have had Pan-Slavism and Pan-Germanism, Pan-Europeanism and Pan-Americanism. All these are expressions of a dying nationalism. Pan-Europa and Pan-America are lame attempts to rescue this moribund force by putting it on a continental basis. The belief in the common man, tempered and restrained by modern knowledge of man and society, gives rise to Pan-Humanism. It is the banner of the future.

The proclamation of the four freedoms has opened a great debate: What are the common patterns of conduct that will enable the world's common men to join forces in solving their common problems? Is there a basis for a world community?

On the answer to this question hinges the future of peace and of a democratic world order.

Corliss Lamont

Corliss Lamont (1902-   ), though the son of a partner of J. P. Morgan, is a Socialist who regards the Soviet experiment with "critical sympathy." He graduated from Harvard, studied at Oxford, and received the degree of Ph.D. from Columbia. For five years he taught philosophy at Columbia; since 1933 he has been a writer on political and economic subjects. In the following essay he shows how politics and economics can be integrated through state planning. Here is one of the possible blueprints for the future, one of the alternatives to be accepted or rejected in the inevitable course of social evolution.

THE PRINCIPLES OF PLANNING

THE fundamental principle that lies behind planning is fairly simple and one which we encounter in some form in many different realms of human behavior. It consists of co-ordinating our activities in the light of our capacities and of the objective external environment, especially its economic aspects. As individuals we all plan to some extent, whether it be for a day or a month, a year or a decade, always keeping a weather eye on the state of our finances.

If we have a family, then planning becomes more complex and essential. The intelligent family looks into the future so far as is possible and plans, according to its resources, for the needs of its various members. If it is wise and has any sort of dependable income, it will make an annual budget, allocating definite sums to food, housing, clothing, recreation, baby carriages and the like. It will also probably try to set aside certain amounts as savings; and the most prudent heads of families will plan years and years ahead for the particular needs and vicissitudes of old age. Thoughtful people will take an even further step and, through the process of wills, lay careful plans for friends and family long after they are dead.

Coming to purely economic units, we find that every kind of business concern, no matter what its size and nature, must plan. The larger and more complex it is, the more attention it has to pay to planning. Any big corporation, for instance, with its many different departments, must have central planning in order to co-ordinate its various activities and to function successfully as a business. This is true whether the U. S. Steel Corporation or General Motors is concerned, whether R. H. Macy and Company or American Telephone and Telegraph, whether Standard Oil of New York or the Pennsylvania Railroad. The planning necessary for the efficient management of huge businesses like these reaches out to all parts of America and in some degree abroad as well. And in certain fields where big business has come to be overwhelmingly predominant, the planning of a few large trusts or even of a single monopoly may extend over well-nigh a whole industry.

The purpose of planning in all capitalist enterprise is, of course, to make money. And this means that each business, in the process of continually establishing and re-establishing its own superiority, must plan *against* its rivals and win away from them more and more customers. Trusts in the same industry have to plan against each other and also, in order to capture a larger and larger share of the general consumer's income, against trusts in other industries. Thus, in enterprise both large and small, the plans of individual businesses and businessmen tend to cancel one another out to a considerable extent. The capitalist theory is that the most efficient and intelligently managed concerns come out on top. Undeniably this is frequently true; just as often, however, it is ruthlessness and lack of moral scruple that turn the trick, as has been amply illustrated in the lives of our "robber barons." But whether efficiency or ruthlessness or perhaps both together are operative in any particular case, the result for the community is in the end economic chaos.

In order to mitigate or prevent the disastrous results of anarchic Capitalism in some important field, capitalist governments sometimes put into effect a species of planning for an entire industry. In most European countries the telephone and telegraph are publicly owned and operated, and in several the railways as well. Then, too, there are public planning schemes in existence over particular localities. A good example of this is the Tennessee Valley Authority (TVA), which is exploiting the power resources of the Tennessee basin on behalf of the population of the vicinity, much to the chagrin of the private utility companies. These types of piecemeal planning, however, no matter how well they may work in the sectors allotted to them, cannot go far in solving the economic problems of a country as a whole.

It is characteristic that the most far-reaching schemes of public planning under Capitalism should be for profit, or for profit *and* war. The so-called planning of the New Deal during President Roosevelt's first term was directed, especially in agriculture, toward *decreasing* production in order to bring back profits by making goods scarcer and prices higher. While the Great Depression was still ravaging the United States, the NRA (National Recovery Administration) and the AAA (Agricultural Adjustment Administration) nobly co-operated, through planned destruction, with the usual haphazard destruction for profit by individual capitalists. Those were the days when almost over-night a fourth of the cotton crop was ploughed under, the wheat acreage reduced by 20 per cent, and five million pigs destroyed. The AAA, doing its best under the circumstances to rescue the American farmer by boosting the price level, actually paid bonuses to all the producers who participated in this wholesale sacrifice to the capricious gods of capitalist economics.

During World War I, America, and more than half the nations of the earth as well, carried out planned destruction on an even larger scale. Not only did this war planning entail the shooting away into nothingness of billions and billions of dollars' worth of goods in the form of munitions; even the food, clothing and other supplies for the military and naval forces were for the purpose of enabling millions of men to engage in the entirely unproductive function of fighting to the death millions of other men. In order to wage war more efficiently, the American Government proceeded to co-ordinate in some measure the economic life of the United States by setting up the War Industries Board, the War Trade Board, the Shipping Board, the Fuel Administration, the Food Administration and the Railroad Administration. Since the railroads under private management could not stand the added strain of war conditions, the Government took them over entirely and administered them on a unified basis.

Unhappily, today again, the bulk of the planning that is going on in capitalist countries is for belligerent purposes. This is especially true of the Fascist Powers—Germany, Italy and Japan—in each of which the whole economy has for a number of years been on a war basis. As these Fascist states push farther and farther their present aggressions and prepare for new ones, they are forcing the democratic Capitalisms to introduce ever more extensive planning for the object of armed self-defense.

This brief review of the limited planning that takes place under Capitalism shows how far removed it is in aim and scope from Socialist planning. Planning under Socialism is for *use,* not profit, for *increasing* production, not decreasing it, for *peace,* not war. And it demands as an absolute prerequisite the socialization of production and distribution. For as long as private capitalists retain possession of a country's natural resources and transportation facilities, of factories, farms, banks and all the rest, they have the power to throw out of gear the best-laid of Plans. It is common knowledge that even with the minor public controls established under Roosevelt's NRA, the American capitalists, long before the law was declared unconstitutional, constantly sabotaged, dodged and defied the Act.

But Socialist planning puts a finish to that unending tug of war, so characteristic of Capitalism, between the Government, supposedly representing the public in general, and various business interests jockeying for control of it and determined to carry out whatever profit-promising policies seem most advantageous. Under Socialism, politics and economics are thoroughly integrated.

The socialization of economic activity which I have in mind, however, does not necessarily entail either nationalization by the federal government or ownership by state or city governments. Many industries under Socialism the national government will certainly take over; many other economic concerns, less far-reaching in their ramifications, state or city governments will own and operate. But besides all this, there will be a broad sector of enterprise which is socialized yet not governmental. It will be advisable to run some industries through the instrumentality of Public Corporations, which will be subject to control by the government planning authorities, but largely independent in their administrative work. In the non-governmental class will also be collective farms and fisheries, and indeed almost the whole of agriculture; co-operative societies for production and distribution; and much of journalism, art and culture in general.

This means that there will be a sizable number, running into several millions, of independent individuals not on the pay-roll of any governmental concern. These will include a large proportion of the handicraftsmen, farmers, fishermen, inventors, teachers, authors, journalists, actors, artists and intellectuals. They will make their living by working in such organizations as I have just mentioned; or by selling their products or services to such organizations, to public agencies or to other individuals. So, in the Socialist state there will be plenty of room for free-lance workers of every type.

Socialist planning differs from any sort of capitalist planning, lastly, in that it is not confined to special localities, industries or periods of time, but is *continuous* and *nation-wide*. A genuinely planned economy demands not only that all individual businesses in one industry, whether it be concerned with hats, shoes, sugar, coal or anything else, be consciously coordinated, but that each industry as a whole, including the prices of its products and the wages and working hours of its employees, be co-ordinated with every other industry as a whole. Think of the increase in efficiency and the decrease in waste that would result from planned co-ordination among America's big energy-producing industries: coal, gas, oil and electric power. Such co-ordination, however, could reach its high point only when there was complete co-ordination also among the industries to be served.

For only when we know how much energy is required throughout the whole country, and where and when, can we accurately gauge how much coal, how much gas, how much oil and how much electric power should be made available in a given period and in a particular locality.

Again, it is obvious that there is so much overlapping in the field of transportation—among railways, boats, buses, trucks and airplanes—that the situation cries out for unified planning. But it is not possible to separate transportation from the things to be transported. A plan for co-ordinated transportation implies a plan for coal and steel, farm products and finished goods, just as a plan for all these things definitely implies a plan for transportation.

And of course all of agriculture must be carefully correlated with all of manufacture. The flow of foodstuffs to the cities must be co-ordinated with the flow of manufactured goods from them. The needs of the farmers must be estimated. Our steel plan, for example, must take into consideration the demand for tractors, combines and other agricultural machinery; and our agricultural plan the particular food requirements of the heavily laboring steel workers.

Likewise there must be a well-worked-out plan for wholesale and retail trade, linking up these two main branches of distribution all along the line with industry, transportation and agriculture. The shops in town and city, the restaurants, the warehouses, the gasoline stations and other such distributive units all come into the planning picture here.

Since the planning I envisage covers the entire socio-economic scene, it naturally extends into the fields of health and recreation, of education and culture. Socialism is particularly concerned to bountifully provide all the different activities and services in these realms with the necessary equipment and other economic prerequisites. The educational plan of the country, moreover, must be always closely interrelated with the economic plan, so that there may never be a lack of the needed technicians, scientists and other experts nor a deficiency of suitable employment opportunities for graduating students.

Finally, the entire economic and cultural life of the country must be carefully correlated with finance under one vast, unitary budget that takes in all branches of industry and agriculture, of commerce and trade and extra-economic endeavor.

This completes, in outline form, the picture of the great National Plan which Socialism sets in motion, a Plan which brings into the economic and social affairs of any country that adopts it a closely knit unity, a smoothly functioning team-work, among all the myriad enterprises and individuals involved, making each one count for infinitely more and lifting the collective achievement to new and unheard-of heights.

Because of its controls over production and distribution, currency and capital investment, prices and wages and hours, Socialist planning is able to overcome totally and permanently the central capitalist difficulty of lack of purchasing power. As more and more goods come out of the factories, wages go up throughout the land or prices decrease or the working day grows shorter. To take care of the increased turnover in commodities, currency may, depending on its velocity of circulation, be expanded. Since there are no capitalists to appropriate a large proportion of the value which the people produce, the full instead of only the partial value of their labor returns to them in one form or another. Thus, the unceasing abundance of goods is matched by an unceasing abundance of purchasing power. And this results in that depression-defeating, prosperity-ensuring balance between production and consumption, supply and demand, which every orthodox economist and capitalist has fondly dreamed of seeing Capitalism itself attain.

The United States and other capitalist nations are only as rich as the amount of goods that can be sold for a profit during any given period. But Socialist planning makes a country exactly as rich as its entire productive capacity during any period. This is why I say without hesitation that Socialism, in terms of sheer economic efficiency, is sure to far outstrip Capitalism.

Since finance is the most important single element in Socialist planning and more crucial, if anything, than in a capitalist economy—a fact which ought to give some slight consolation to capitalist bankers—I want to discuss the subject in more detail. In a Socialist state the banking system operates under and administers an all-embracing Financial Plan for the nation as a whole. This Financial Plan is the counterpart of the Material Plan and translates all the production and distribution schedules of the latter into dollar units. The dollar is the common denominator in which the various aspects of the National Plan can be accurately expressed and clearly related to one another. The Financial Plan and the Material Plan are, in effect, two versions of the National Plan and each serves as a check on the other.

The Government Treasury Department, together with the State Bank and its numerous branches, acts as a great central pool for the national income. This it does not only through taxation of Socialist business concerns and of individuals, but also through receiving a substantial share of whatever surpluses the different businesses, including those involved in foreign trade, succeed in accumulating. A considerable portion of such surpluses, however, are retained locally by the factory or other unit earning them and are used collectively for expansion, improvements or social benefits connected with the same enterprise. The Government also raises a certain amount of capital through savings banks and through the flotation of public loans, which continue to be necessary during the first stages of Socialism.

The surpluses or "profits" which economic enterprises build up under Socialism have a very different status and play a very different role from what we have been accustomed to expect under Capitalism. They are, in fact, mainly a book-keeping device. Socialist business is run, as I have said, not for the sake of making profits, but in order to provide goods and services to the community. The most convenient process of accounting and of distribution, however, demands the mechanism of buying and selling, of money and prices. Furthermore, identifiable "profits" are necessary so that our Socialist planners can set aside a certain proportion of the nation's income in order to meet depreciation and obsolescence and, above all, in order to expand the means of production. Soviet Russia, for instance, put into social savings for such purposes an annual average of one-third its total income during the first two Five-Year Plans, a feat which stands out all the more owing to the fact that capitalist economists have always argued that a Socialist government would act like a reckless spendthrift and could not possibly exercise the foresight and intelligence to accumulate capital.

Whereas under Capitalism money and prices control the output of goods, under Socialism it is the output of goods that controls money and prices. Money is on a goods standard, not a gold standard. No real need exists for the latter unless to make the initial transition from Capitalism psychologically easier in the minds of the people. There can be no such thing, as financial bankruptcy unless the supply of commodities proves inadequate; the value of the currency does not depend on any gold reserve, but on the quantity and quality of goods that nation-wide planning has made available. Money ceases to be a commodity in itself, as under the capitalist system. It simply serves as the recognized unit of economic measurement and exchange, a function that some medium will have to perform in any future stage of society.

The most obvious advantage of a Socialist financial system is that it enables the public authorities to distribute and re-distribute the nation's capital resources according to the needs of the entire economy. The surpluses acquired in one sector of business can be transferred to other less developed and less lucrative branches of economic activity. This is analogous, on a national scale, to the various allocations within the huge budgets of some of the bigger capitalist corporations. Under Socialism a number of enterprises, particularly in the sphere of education and social services, will continue to show financial loss, perhaps permanently. And there will also be deficits in the industrial field, especially when some great new project is getting under way.

Socialist financial planning requires that there be an ordered flow of capital investment all along the line in place of the slap-dash, haphazard methods prevalent in capitalist countries today. Instead of over-investment in some directions and under-investment in others, with crisis-causing disproportions as the certain result, Socialist planning ensures a balanced and even distribution of capital resources, that is, social savings, in the directions most useful and important. It would be inconceivable, for example, for vast quantities of capital to go into the building of palatial homes, yachts and other super-luxuries for a small class of the economically privileged while millions of families lived in houses beneath even a minimum standard of decency.

It would also be inconceivable for socialized capital to go into the production of things clearly harmful to health and well-being—such as noxious drugs, patent medicines and deleterious foodstuffs—for which there might be unintelligent and perverse demand. It would be impossible, too, for capital to create manufacturing plants and services that would be continually duplicating one another, ruining one another through cut-throat competition, spending huge fortunes in misleading advertising, and inundating a locality or even the entire country with a bewildering flow of practically identical goods. The huge sums of money and the very large personnel involved in speculative activities in commodities, in land, and in stocks and bonds would also become a thing of the past. And, alas for the gamblers of high finance, that symbol of Capitalism at its worst, the stock market, would be no more.

The perfect synchronization between savings and capital investment that Socialist planning makes possible is one of the weightiest arguments in its favor. Since the decision of how much and where and when to save and the decision of how much and where and when to invest rests in the hands of the Planning Commission and the Government, there is no danger that these important decisions will be at odds with each other as they so often are under Capitalism. The unplanned capitalist method means that two sets of different people, frequently with conflicting interests, save and invest as they see fit, with the result that the relations between saving and investment are always becoming maladjusted. Either savings cannot find an outlet in profitable investment or needed investment cannot find sufficient savings to put it across. In either case economic troubles are the outcome.

Under the financial system I have been outlining, every producing and distributing unit in the country has an account in the central State Bank or one of its branches. And it is the duty of each bank to check up on the use of the credits, long-term, short-term or emergency, which it issues at any time. It must make certain that the automobile factory, for instance, to which it has advanced a certain amount of credit, actually produces the motorcars called for by the Plan and supposedly made possible by the credit. The factory has the obligation of giving the bank definite reports on definite dates showing how it is fulfilling its program. If the bank discovers that the credit is being wasted or used inefficiently, it will at once stop further credits until the matter is cleared up, even instituting a special investigation if necessary.

Thus, under Socialist planning, the banks become the watchdogs of the whole economy by carrying on what amounts to a constant audit of all business enterprises. They act as the vital link between the various sets of plans drawn up on paper and the fulfillment of these plans in terms of concrete goods and services. Their vigilance means that there can be no let-down on the part of either management or workers in a concern without the whole personnel being called to task. In this function the banks are aided by a system of accounting which penetrates into every nook and cranny of economic activity. Socialist accounting, organized on the strictest basis, aims to cut production costs and to attain the greatest possible results for the least possible expenditure. Book profits enter again into the picture here as a partial test of whether or not a plant is being operated efficiently. So the idea sometimes advanced that, under Socialism, extravagant executives will fling away heedlessly and without restraint the financial resources of the community is merely a caricature.

Furthermore, besides the checks and balances inherent in the technical set-up of Socialist planning, there is always the control exercised by the people themselves through regular democratic procedures. At established intervals they can approve or disapprove of the planning schemes in effect or proposed by electing representatives and officials committed to carrying out the popular will. And at all times they can bring pressure to bear by criticisms and suggestions through public meetings, the organs of opinion, individual or organized lobbying, and other such processes of democracy. Of paramount importance in this connection will be the role of the trade unions, to which virtually all working persons will presumably belong. There is nothing, then, in the nature of Socialist planning which prevents it from being administered in a thoroughly democratic manner.

One can easily imagine some of the big public issues which are almost certain to emerge in the natural course of collective economic planning. Since the standard of living under Socialism goes steadily up, the question will arise as to how the people can most benefit from the increasing wealth. Shall our planners put the emphasis on raising wages continually or on providing more and better free services like libraries, parks and public concerts? How much of the national income shall be saved for the purpose of new capital construction? And in this connection will the time come when the population will prefer to stabilize the standard of living at a certain point and concentrate on enjoying the consumers' goods producible at that level rather than to continue with vast expansion programs? For under

Socialist planning there is no categorical imperative, as under Capitalism, for an economy to keep on expanding indefinitely.

This particular issue might well develop in relation to the matter of the average annual working time. In order that more leisure be secured, one political party might advocate reducing the work-day by a third or augmenting the number of holidays or cutting the age of retirement to fifty; another party might call for the maintenance of existing work-time schedules and for a mighty increase in production which would lift the standard of living to even greater heights. Or another burning issue might come to the fore, once the necessities of life had been provided for everyone, over whether to stress the provision of cultural as distinct from material goods and services.

The exact planning techniques which I have been describing will certainly not be used in all stages of Socialism nor in all countries adopting the new system. For it is crystal clear that each nation will use somewhat different methods, adapting Socialism to its characteristic traditions, political institutions and degree of economic development. It would be foolish to imagine that if central planning were introduced in China at the same time as in the United States, it could be put into effect by precisely the same measures or at the same rate. Indeed, there will be plenty of differences even between two countries both as highly evolved industrially as America and Great Britain, one obvious reason being that the latter is in so many ways economically dependent on the outside world. But just as the general principles of the capitalist system were potentially applicable in every quarter of the globe, so the general principles of Socialist planning are applicable to the United States and all other nations.

Carl Becker

Carl Becker (1873-1945) had a long and distinguished career as teacher of history at Dartmouth, University of Kansas, University of Minnesota, and, since 1917, at Cornell. Gifted with a relentlessly logical mind and a hard-hitting style, he asks disconcerting questions about the dreams of post-war planners in his solid little book, How New Will the Better World Be? *The upshot of his inquiry is that the "better" world of the future will not be conspicuously different from the world of the past. In the following chapter, for example, without turning New Dealer he argues the inevitability of social-economic controls in the coming era.*

WHAT KIND OF COLLECTIVISM DO WE WANT?

MOST people in the United States would probably answer this question by saying: "We do not want any kind of collectivism at all." The word "collectivism" is apt to suggest the word "socialism," and Socialism is for most people the same thing as Communism. This mistake leads to a great deal of useless confusion in thinking about such matters. First of all, therefore, I wish to make perfectly clear what I mean by collectivism. By collectivism I mean no more than the governmental regulation or control of the economic life of a community. Such regulation or control may be more or less complete, so that there are different kinds of collectivism, depending on the extent to which the regulation or control is carried out and the methods by which it is achieved. To say that we do not want any kind of collectivism is merely to express a pious wish. It is not a question of what we should like if it were possible to have it, but a question of what we must accept under conditions as they exist. We already have a certain amount of collectivism, a certain amount of governmental regulation of economic life; and it is about as clearly on the cards as anything can be that we must have still more of it.

But why must we have more of it? Why can't we have what we want? This raises the interesting question which philosophers have discussed from time out of mind: Do men make their own history, or is it made for them by some power over which they have no control? The proper answer is that neither part of the question can be answered wholly in the affirmative. Men make their own history in part, and in part it is made for them by certain conditions which they cannot change, or cannot altogether change.

One of these conditions is physiographic—conditions of geography, soil, climate, and the like. Men can raise rice and bananas, but it would be a waste of effort to try to raise them in Labrador or New England. The other condition is historic—the pattern of habits and customs and institutions that exists at any time and place as the result of a long process of historical development. Men living in New England today can have all the rice and bananas they want, because these foods can now be so easily and cheaply brought to New England from the places where they are raised. But modern methods of transportation are part of the complex pattern of habit and institutions which has been historically created; and this complex pattern of habit and institutions is itself a limitation which determines in part the power of men to make their own history. It has been said that we should be better off if there were no steam engines, automobiles, or airplanes. Maybe we should. But the fact is that we have these things. We cannot get rid of them by wishing; and we can make our own history from now on only within the limits set by the existence and use of steam engines, automobiles, and airplanes, and the kind of society which these and a thousand and one other technological devices make necessary.

The pattern of thought and behavior, of customs and institutions that exist at any time can be changed by men, but not easily or all at once; and the way in which it can be changed, and the direction which the change must take, are as much determined by what has occurred and what exists as they are by men's will and desire. During the last century social and political institutions, and men's ways of thinking about them, have been changing, at times pretty rapidly; but they have been changing in a certain direction. This direction, the historical trend of our time, has been steadily away from unrestrained "private economic enterprise" and towards governmental regulation of private economic enterprise—that is to say, towards some form of what I have defined as collectivism.

Four different forms of collectivism have in fact been proposed or adopted—Socialism, Communism, Fascism, and what for lack of a better term we may call Social Democracy. We cannot reverse the historic trend towards collectivism, but we can with intelligence and determination decide whether we will have some brand of Social Democracy rather than some brand of Socialism, Communism, or Fascism. It will clarify the issue to see how these various brands of collectivism emerged historically, in what respects they are alike, and in what respects they are different.

The various forms of collectivism have emerged during the last hundred years. They are all methods proposed or adopted for solving the social and political problems arising in the highly complex societies created by the Industrial and Technological Revolution of our time; and a brief historical sketch will serve to show what the nature of the problem is and how these forms of collectivism propose to solve it.

Modern democracy, in theory and as in fact established, was the result of opposition to the system of society and government that existed in most European countries in the seventeenth and eighteenth centuries. Most countries were then governed by kings who claimed absolute power by divine right, and whose power in fact rested upon the support of a small but influential class of privileged nobles, a few wealthy middle-class families, and an established state church, Protestant or Catholic. The mass of the people (chiefly peasant farmers) were oppressed and exploited and had few rights as we understand them—neither political freedom, nor freedom of religion, or of speech and the press, nor freedom to choose one's occupation or profession. Except in England, Holland, and the American colonies, citizens had no safeguard against arbitrary arrest and imprisonment, no right to trial by jury, no protection against search of their houses and possessions by the police. It was what we should call a highly "regimented" society governed by hereditary dictatorship. The English Revolution of 1688, and the American and French Revolutions at the end of the eighteenth century, were directed against this form of dictatorship, class privilege, and social regimentation; and by the end of the nineteenth century it had been replaced in most European countries and in America by some form of Liberal Democracy.

The theory or philosophy of Liberal Democracy was formulated in the seventeenth and particularly in the eighteenth century in a multitude of books and pamphlets, even though the authors ran the risk of having their works suppressed and of being themselves imprisoned or exiled. The classic expression of the philosophy is in the Declaration of Independence, written by Thomas Jefferson, and in the French Declaration of the Rights of Man and the Citizen, which was prefixed to the first French Constitution in 1789. The philosophy rested on the assumption that men had been too much and, above all, too arbitrarily governed. It was thought, rightly enough, that the chief oppressions and injustices from which men suffered were the result of governmental restraints upon the activities and thinking of men; and "liberty" was accordingly thought of as freedom for the individual from the restraints imposed by governments. The fundamental idea of the liberal democratic philosophy, therefore, was that the people could govern themselves better than kings and aristocrats and priests could do it for them; and that the best form of government was the one that governed least—the one that interfered as little as might be with the activities and thinking of the individual citizen. In the early nineteenth century writers on economics used two French words to express this idea—*laissez* (let) and *faire* (to do or to be). That is to say, governments should adopt the policy of *laissez faire*—should, as far as possible, let every man do what he wanted to do and be what he wanted to be. As applied to government, the philosophy might be called the do-nothing philosophy, and as applied to the citizen, the let-alone philosophy.

Of course this is putting it too baldly. There never was a time when anyone (except a few philosophical anarchists, such as Proudhon) believed that governments should do nothing, or that citizens should be allowed to do as they please. But in the early and middle nineteenth century it was the prevailing belief that governments should not "meddle in business." The sole duty of government, it was thought, was to protect life and property, maintain civil order, and safeguard the country against foreign aggression. All citizens would then be free to engage in whatever profession or occupation they preferred, and each man would find his natural level of ability and do the job he was best fitted to do. In that case the natural desire of everyone to make money and get on in the world would result in the maximum of effort and efficiency, and therefore in the maximum production of wealth; and free competition, keeping prices at the lowest possible level, would result in as equitable a distribution of wealth as the natural abilities and defects of men permitted. The general idea was that if each man attended to his own individual interests, a kind of harmony of all the several interests in the nation would more or less automatically emerge. "Private profit is a public benefit"—so the idea was briefly expressed.

This simple theory of *laissez faire,* of every man for himself and devil take the hindmost, would always work to the advantage of the strong against the weak. Even in the relatively simple societies of the eighteenth and the early nineteenth century it would work to the advantage of those few who by good fortune, superior intelligence, or lack of scruple were able to acquire wealth and use it to further their selfish interests by means of political "pressure": there would always be a sufficient number of not-too-good men to come to the aid of the party. But with the coming of power-driven machinery it soon became evident that unrestrained competition in industry would not work as well as economists and political philosophers thought it would. In England, in the 1830's, the manufacture of cotton cloth by the new machines was a most profitable industry. It was profitable, however, only to the owners of the industry and of the machines that did so much of the work. It was the reverse of profitable to the laborers, who had no share in the ownership or management of the industry and were forced to accept whatever wages the employers might offer. And since there were more laborers wanting jobs than could be employed, the owners of the industry had it all their own way, and the laborers found that freedom to choose their own occupation was limited to the necessity of working long hours for starvation wages at any job that might turn up.

The situation in the cotton factories became so scandalous that Parliament appointed a committee to investigate it. The members of the committee were appalled by what they found; and it is said that they decided not to mention the worst things for fear that if they did no one would believe anything they said. Even so, the conditions as reported by the committee were such as would not now be tolerated—underfed, anemic women and children working twelve hours a day, in foul, unsanitary, and dangerous shops, for wages that would barely sustain life. The public conscience was shocked by the report; and in 1833 Parliament passed an act to improve matters a little. The act provided that no children under nine years of age should be employed in factories; and that the hours of labor for children from nine to thirteen years should be limited to forty-eight hours per week, and for children from thirteen to eighteen years to sixty-nine hours per week.

Children nine years of age working eight hours a day, children fourteen years of age working twelve and a half hours a day—this was thought to be an improvement! And it was for that time. But the point is that this first "Factory Act" was passed on the ground that government must "meddle in business" in order to protect laborers who were not in a position to bargain on equal terms with employers. The further point is that this first Factory Act was only a beginning. From 1833 to the present time the English government has been constantly and increasingly "meddling in business," has passed innumerable laws designed to correct manifest injustices growing out of free competition in private business enterprise—laws relating to child labor, to hours of labor and to wages, to labor unions and strikes and collective bargaining, laws requiring employers to provide sanitary conditions in factories and making them responsible for accidents to laborers, laws basing taxation on ability to pay, and the like. Similar laws have been passed in other countries. Before Hitler came with his mania for destroying every good thing, Germany had what was regarded as the most comprehensive and the best code of social insurance in the world. Few countries have gone farther than Holland, Denmark, Norway, and Sweden in the regulation of private business enterprise for the purpose of equalizing opportunities and possessions. The United States, because of the easier conditions of life, has lagged behind European countries in this respect. But in 1873 laws were passed to protect farmers against excessive and unfair freight rates charged by the railroads; and the courts upheld the laws on the ground that "the state must be permitted to adopt such rules and regulations as may be necessary for promoting the general welfare of the people." Since then many laws have been passed in restraint or for the regulation of free competition. . . .

Many people seem to think that the New Deal is something brand-new. It is obviously not something new, but merely an acceleration of a trend that has been going on for a long time. In all democratic countries for the last seventy-five or one hundred years there has been an increasing amount of governmental regulation of unrestrained private business enterprise—an increasing amount of what is called "social reform" or "social legislation." Such legislation has been based on the assumption that it is the duty of government, not merely to protect life and property and maintain civil order, but to promote the general welfare by improving the conditions of life for the less fortunate classes at the expense if necessary of the more fortunate classes. It is the form of collectivism which I have called "Social Democracy." The results attained have been attained by the democratic method, by correcting specific evils as they appear by specific measures which the people will support. This is the slow way, the hard way of achieving Social Democracy. . . . The pre-war New Deal was a continuation of what Woodrow Wilson called the New Freedom, and what Theodore Roosevelt called the Square Deal. It was an attempt to solve what is called the "social problem," or what the Atlantic Charter refers to as "improved labor standards, economic adjustment and social security." What is needed for the solution of this social problem is easily stated: we need to have our industrial and agricultural enterprises working at full capacity producing the goods that are needed, and full employment of all the people at good wages so that the goods produced can be bought by the people that need or want them. How to bring about this result is far less easy to determine. The pre-war New Deal was an experiment—an effort to devise means of bringing it about which accomplished something, but not enough. Then the war came and forced us to adopt a wartime New Deal which makes the pre-war New Deal governmental intervention in business look like small potatoes, and which has very nearly attained the desired end of putting our industrial plants to work at full time and providing full employment for all the people.

The wartime New Deal has succeeded better than the pre-war New Deal for a variety of reasons. For two reasons more especially: first, because we know definitely what we have to do, which is to win the war; and second, because we are pretty thoroughly united in the desire and the determination to win it. But in order to fight and win the war it has been necessary, and generally recognized as necessary, to place in the hands of the government far more power than it has ever had in peacetime to regulate and co-ordinate the economic life of the country. The government has become a super-business enterprise, an over-all holding company, which determines what goods shall be produced and in what quantity, what men shall be employed by it in the armed services and government war jobs and what men must be "deferred" or reserved for war industries. All this calls for unlimited government spending, which means an unprecedented demand for goods and labor. According to Stuart Chase, the government was in June 1943 spending about eight billion dollars a month for goods and services. And it is for this reason that our industrial plants are now running at nearly full capacity, that unemployment has disappeared, and that the great majority of the people have much more money ("purchasing power") to buy what they need or want than they have had for a long time. The wartime New Deal is merely an extension of the pre-war New Deal—a more comprehensive and systematically planned intervention of government in the business enterprise and the economic life of the country.

But it will be said, and indeed is being said, that the war is a temporary emergency during which the government necessarily takes over, and when the emergency is ended the government ought to "stop meddling in business and let private business take over again"; government spending on the present mad scale must come to an end, and the "bureaucrats and college professors" down in Washington must stop messing things up and go home. So it is being said. But what would happen if on demobilization day the government stopped meddling in business, if overnight it stopped spending eight billion dollars a month and all the bureaucrats and college professors cleared up their desks and went home? The first thing that would happen is that forty-five million men now working directly or indirectly for the government would be out of a job, and a good proportion of them, including a good proportion of the twelve million soldiers, sailors, and airmen, would soon be on the street. And in no long time there would be an economic collapse which would make the Great Depression of 1929-33 look, by comparison, like a time of plenty and contentment.

When the war is over the government will necessarily cease to do many things which it is now doing, and no doubt it will cease to spend as much money. But there will still be an emergency, although of a different kind. There will be a demobilization emergency—the temporary emergency created by the necessity of getting back from a wartime to a peacetime economy. This will last for some time, and then will fade out into the old, familiar, permanent, and more difficult peacetime emergency which existed before the war began, and which the pre-war New Deal was an attempt to meet. To suppose that the peacetime emergency will be any less important or less insistent or less difficult than the wartime emergency, to suppose that the government will be able to by-pass this emergency and rely upon "business as usual" to maintain full production and full employment, is to be incredibly naive and incapable of learning anything from the experience of the last fifty years.

Whatever party is in power after the war will find that the government cannot cease spending or cease meddling. It might conceivably cease muddling. It will at all events be confronted with the same problem which the pre-war New Deal was an attempt to solve. But the pre-war New Deal was not enough for the situation before the war, and will be even less so for the situation after the war is over. It was an experiment from which, however, we can learn much. The wartime New Deal is another experiment from which we should learn still more. And it is to be hoped that, when we have learned much from these experiments, the demobilization emergency will prepare the way for a post-war New Deal which will avoid the most obvious defects of all previous new deals.

The chief defect of all our peacetime new deals, from Theodore to Franklin Roosevelt, is that they were all concerned primarily with particular measures designed to cure specific evils. When the banks were all on the verge of failure they were closed for a few days to tide them over. When millions of men were unemployed they were given temporary relief, or else jobs were rigged up to provide work for them. When farmers were desperate, mortgage foreclosures were forbidden temporarily, and in order to raise prices of farm products the raising of cotton and corn was restricted or the government bought the surplus and held it. And so on. But no adequate attempt was made to get at the underlying causes of the general collapse, and as a consequence there was no clear or agreed-upon idea of the ultimate end to be achieved. The chief defect of the pre-war New Deal was that it was too much concerned with curing particular evils and too little concerned with achieving some positive general good. It is an arresting and significant fact that the pre-war New Deal failed to abolish unemployment although that was its main object, whereas the wartime New Deal has virtually abolished unemployment although its main object was something else. The general object of the wartime New Deal is to win the war: the disappearance of unemployment is an incidental result of pursuing that general object. If I were Gilbert Chesterton I might say that the pre-war New Deal failed to cure unemployment because it tried to cure it, whereas the wartime New Deal succeeded in curing unemployment because it didn't try to.

This is something more than an amusing paradox. It means that if we could have a well-considered plan for promoting the national welfare—that is to say, for improving the standard of living for all the people—and were as united and determined in carrying it through as we are in winning the war, we could forget about business stagnation and unemployment. These evils would disappear as they have disappeared during the war; and their disappearance would be an incidental result of the effort to achieve a more positive and a more general object. Unfortunately, any nation is more easily united by the fear of an immediate and clearly discerned disaster than it is by the prospect of a debatable and uncertain future good. This is why it is easier to win the war than it will be to win the peace—that is to say, to solve the social problem. But at least a good starting-point for solving the social problem is to ask what specific things need to be done to raise the standard of living for all the people, and would be done if we were as united and militant for achieving that object as we are for winning the war.

Any comprehensive plan for raising the standard of living for all the people would obviously be concerned with such matters as sufficient food, clothing, shelter; adequate medical service; improved educational facilities, for vocational and professional training and for scientific research; extended facilities for recreation and amusement; disability and old-age insurance. What would this mean specifically? It would mean an enormous expansion in the production of food, clothes, houses, and all consumers' goods. It would mean a nation-state housing program, the abolition of slums, and the rebuilding of parts of a hundred or more cities to adapt them to the present and future conditions of business and transportation. It would mean a nation-state program for expanding, co-ordinating, and improving the system of transportation—highways, railroads, waterways, airways, and pipe lines. It would mean a nation-state program for the expansion and improvement of schools, colleges, and universities, for the building of public parks, recreation centers, museums, and art galleries. It would mean a nation-state program for building, equipping, and staffing more and better hospitals, asylums for the mentally defective, and centers for medical research. It would mean at least this; but such a systematic program would be capable of indefinite expansion.

It is obvious that such a comprehensive program could not be carried through, or even planned, without federal and state co-operation, supervision, and assistance all along the line. It would obviously require a good deal of governmental regulation of private business enterprise. But in carrying it through, the guiding principle should be to make the greatest possible use of private business enterprise. No program for promoting the national welfare can succeed unless it wins the support of the people—business men, farmers, and laborers—and no program will win the support of the business interests if it appears to business men in the light of measures which are primarily designed to restrict private enterprise. Capitalist business enterprise thrives only on expansion; and such a program for promoting the national welfare could succeed, therefore, only if and in so far as the agricultural and industrial interests could be induced to regard it as providing an opportunity for industrial and agricultural expansion. Only by uniting the private-profit motive with the desire to promote the national welfare could such a comprehensive program be carried through, but if that could be done the evils of business stagnation and mass unemployment would cease to trouble us.

I do not underrate the obstacles to carrying through any such comprehensive program. The chief difficulty would be to convince the industrial and agricultural interests and their representatives in Congress that it would be to their interests to support such a program, and even if that could be done there would be the inevitable conflict between regions and groups to get what they each thought was coming to them, which would be something more than their fair share. There would be, in short, the inevitable "pressure politics," and behind the pressure politics competition for private profit. The fundamental question is whether in the capitalist system the private-profit motive can ever be sufficiently reconciled with the desire for the general welfare. Perhaps not. But, at all events, apart from some such program it is difficult to foresee any situation which will provide business enterprise an opportunity for adequate and indefinite expansion. Failing such opportunity for expansion, we shall no doubt be forced to return to the policies and limited successes of the pre-war New Deal—mistaking symptoms for causes, attempting to abolish business stagnation and unemployment by giving subsidies to business men and relief checks to the unemployed. The chief difference is likely to be that the subsidies will have to be larger and the relief checks more numerous.

Supposing, however, that such a comprehensive program or something like it could be carried through; supposing that we succeed by whatever means in having full production and full employment—what then? Then we should have surplus goods to be sold abroad, which could not be sold abroad, however, unless foreign countries were in a position to pay for them and were permitted to pay for them in goods exported to this country. Full production and full employment can be maintained in an undeveloped country like Russia where the capitalist system has been abolished and the economic life of the community is entirely controlled by government decree. But it is difficult to see how it can be done in the United States, or any other country under the capitalist system, if the rest of the world is impoverished. It certainly cannot be done in the United States if the United States, as a chief creditor country, expects to sell goods and services abroad and at the same time erects a Hawley-Smoot tariff, which makes it impossible for foreign countries to pay by selling us their goods in exchange. If we return to that policy, or to anything like it, we shall only undermine our own export trade, alienate half the world, contribute to the collapse of world economy, and do our share to prepare the way for another global war.

It is as impossible for highly industrialized, capitalist countries to live in economic as in political isolation. The effort to make a new and better world at home is, therefore, inseparable in the long run from the making of a new and better world in international relations.

Alexander Meiklejohn

It is an apt coincidence that such a liberal thinker as Alexander Meikle-
john (1872-   ) should have been born in Rochdale, Lancashire, where
twenty-eight years earlier a handful of poor weavers had founded the
first co-operative society. He came to the United States in childhood,
attended Brown University, received a Ph.D. from Cornell, and returned
to Brown as Dean and Professor of Philosophy. In 1912 he became Presi-
dent of Amherst, where his bold innovations incurred criticism and
brought about his resignation. His most famous venture was the Experi-
mental College at the University of Wisconsin where, for twelve years,
he was free to work out new ideas in college education. He is today a
visiting professor at St. John's College and still, as the following essay
proves, a vigorous and original force.

EDUCATION AND THE FUTURE

IN the making of plans for international peace
and justice in the new world, three sets of factors must be dealt with. I list
them in order of increasing importance, which is also the order of increasing difficulty. They are first, economic; second, political; and third, educational. As to the first of these, all men now know that the time has come
when we must create and administer a unified economic world order. Economic chaos is no longer tolerable. It is no longer necessary. But second,
this ordering and controlling of our business activities imply and require
that we create and administer a unified political world order which shall be
equal in scope, but superior in power, to the forces of economic procedure.
The production and distribution of wealth must be under public control.
A world economy without a world government spells strife and disaster. But
third, political institutions in turn must be sustained and controlled by adequate education. The nature and quality of a government depend upon the
nature and quality of the intelligence of its citizens. The tragic experience
of Adolf Hitler has shown us that no dictatorship can endure unless it can
teach its people to be slaves. But, it is equally certain that no democracy can
endure unless it can teach its citizens to be free. A unified world economy,
authorized and controlled by a unified world government, implies, as a basic
postulate, a united system of world education.

When I speak of world unity in economics and politics and education,
I am not thinking of a unity which ignores or denies the facts of multiplicity. I am thinking, rather, of unity in multiplicity—a unifying activity

which, as it faces the varieties and complexities of human experience, endeavors to save them from sinking down into chaos and meaninglessness and brutish strife. What we must have in economics, in politics, in education, is an ordered multiplicity—an economic order, a political order, an educational order. These are three interdependent phases of a single human enterprise. They are three sides of that endeavor by which—if I may borrow a phrase from Rousseau—the human being "ceases from being a stupid and unimaginative animal and becomes an intelligent being, and a man."

Now, if what I have said is true, then two serious dangers beset the planning of the United Nations for post-war reconstruction. First, our economic experts working in isolation may be tempted, by "the bias of happy exercise," to devise an economic world order without placing it under the control of an adequate political world order. Second, our political experts, influenced by the same bias, may attempt to create and maintain political institutions without giving them a solid foundation in an adequate system of popular education. If those dangers are not avoided, then the outcome of our struggle for the four freedoms will be the establishment of more than four slaveries. Our economic arrangements will fail because they are not supported and controlled by adequate political institutions. Our political institutions will fail because they are not rooted in the understanding and good will of their citizens. If those evils are allowed to come upon us, catastrophe is inevitable. The greatness of our opportunity will be the measure of the greatness of our failure to meet it.

The economic danger of which I have spoken can be very simply though, on this occasion, very abstractly indicated. It has to do with the choice between public and private control of business. If we say that an economic world order is created, what we are really saying is that some human mind, or some group of human minds, has taken control of the economic forces of our civilization. Order, as here used, means control. To say that the play of economic forces has become orderly is to say that someone has taken charge of them. Someone has so studied them, so measured and charted them, that they can be directed to work together for the realization of assigned ends. Forces in themselves have no order. Order is a human contrivance. It is a human achievement. If, then, the world of business becomes a world of order, the first question to ask is: "Whose order is it? By what methods and toward what ends is it directed?"

As to that question two sharply different answers are possible. The control of the world's business may be in public hands or in private hands. It may be exercised with common consent or without common consent. It may belong to the common people or to the masters of the common people. If the first of these alternatives is adopted, if the production and distribution of the world's wealth is made subject to the common judgment, the common will of the citizens of the world, then world government, in some form or other, is established. But the danger which now threatens us is that our economic experts will lead us in the other direction. Men who through special knowledge have the inside track, and especially the shrewd and aggressive minds of our Anglo-American business world, will be sorely tempted, without the consent of their fellows, to take into their own hands the domination of the economic process. Such men do not always realize what they are doing. They commonly regard themselves not as our masters, but as the servants of natural forces which work through them. It is not by accident that the men who dominate our Anglo-American economic life have so generally believed in Natural Laws as governing human society. But that belief is, more or less unconsciously, simply a cover for the brutal fact of their own domination over the lives and fortunes of their fellows. These men, if they are not subjected to the authority of political institutions, will lead us into disaster. I do not on the whole challenge their good intentions. But I do challenge their understanding of what they are doing. I do not deny the need of economic leadership. But I do protest the futility of self-appointed, dictatorial leadership. Government, whether economic or political, must be by consent of the governed. If control is not public, then it is private. And a world economy in private hands means war—and war again. Only under a free, federated world government is a free, federated world economy possible. There is only one device by which human beings can escape the evils of dictatorship. That is by governing themselves.

But secondly, the enterprise of government has its own perplexities and dangers. If it be decided that an international economy is to be politically controlled, if its problems are to be dealt with by common consent, then all the difficulties of human education come rushing upon us. How shall the citizens of the world give consent, or refuse to give consent, to measures which they do not understand? Two thousand years ago, Epictetus stated the principle underlying this dilemma when he declared: "The rulers of the state have said that only free men shall be educated; but God has said that only educated men shall be free."

Here, then, is the second, the greater danger which threatens the plans which our experts are making for the organization of the world. To arrange that a world government shall be conducted by the consent of the governed implies and requires a system of world education. If we are to have a free world community, the citizens of the world must learn what free institutions are and how under actual conditions they can be achieved. To say this is not to deny that in the first instance the problems of an international society must be dealt with by "experts." These problems must be studied with all the finesse of scholarly investigation and with the wisdom which comes from wide political and economic experience. But for the purposes of free self-government such study is not enough. The same problems must be studied on the popular level. "Experts" may recommend. But "citizens" must decide. And that means that the citizens of a world order have much learning to do. They must become able to comprehend and to pass judgment upon what their leaders say. Even more important than that, they must learn to know each other, to think together, to understand the common enterprise. In the last resort, political institutions can succeed only as they grow out of and give expression to fundamental agreements of idea and purpose. But that implies mutual acquaintance, mutual understanding—in short, a common education. A free world government is possible only if from one end of the world to the other, free men and women are engaged in widespread, well-organized, and persistent study both of the *end* to be realized and of the *conditions* which are favorable and unfavorable to its realization. Just as a government must rule its business, so must a people rule its government. On any other basis than that we shall have dictatorship and with it the wars, the injustice, the slavery which dictatorship, whether open or concealed, inevitably brings.

2

If now we turn from the negative side of our problem to its positive side, from the dangers which threaten post-war reconstruction to ways of overcoming those dangers, I venture to suggest how a beginning might be made in the establishment of a system of world education adequate for our economic and political needs. I have in mind the creating of an International Institute of Education, somewhat analogous in kind, though differing in function, to the International Labor Office in the planning of the League of Nations. The positive considerations from which that suggestion springs are somewhat as follows:

1. It is I think essential that from the start international planning shall include as an organic element in its procedure provision for general popular education. And, especially, teaching must be devised for those mature persons who are to have the rights and responsibilities of world citizenship. As men plan for a world order, economic, political, and educational institutions must grow together. We cannot practice justice and freedom unless we can teach them. To impose economic and political arrangements upon citizens who do not understand them is to plan for the renewal of world conflict.

2. The international education which we need cannot be limited to provision for intellectual co-operation among scholars. Nor can the need be met by the establishment of one or more universities. Scholarship is essential. But it is not sufficient. The task which lies before us is that of cultivating among all the common people of the world such knowledge and good will as will weld them together into an international community.

3. It follows from what has just been said that, in its initial stages at least, international teaching must be done chiefly in the field of adult education. The citizens of the world must learn what it means to be a citizen

of the world. They must learn to use their minds, to enjoy using their minds, for the making of a free human society.

4. The education of which we are speaking must be, in the democratic sense, free. It must present to its pupils not the solution of a problem but the problem itself with all its perplexities. Such teaching forbids the use of propaganda. The common people of all countries must be led into a common study of a common enterprise in which they are together engaged.

5. It is equally certain—though the statement of the fact seems paradoxical—that in all countries the same basic education must be given. Amid all the varieties of circumstance, the same lessons are to be learned. Chinamen, Englishmen, Indians, Russians, Germans, Peruvians, Javanese—for all these the same fundamental problems must be presented, the same teaching methods applied, the same intellectual materials used. The first essential is that learners shall recognize that from one end of the world to the other the same human struggle to devise and maintain law and order is going on. To be educated is to be fitted to participate in that struggle.

On the basis of these considerations it is, I think, possible to draw in outline the form which an Institute of International Education might take. One can see also certain forms which it must not take.

1. The teaching we need cannot be given by the separate nations, acting separately. It must be given by the international organization itself as a fundamental part of its own procedure. All genuine education is initiation. It is the attempt of some social group to fit its members, old and young, for participation in the activities which the group is carrying on. The world government itself must study and teach what it is doing. No other group, no separate groups, can meet that responsibility.

2. It follows from what has just been said that the financial support of world teaching must come from the world government. That teaching must be free from all the restrictions and conditions which direct financial support from local or national sources might lay upon it. And in the same way the international organization must take direct and unqualified responsibility for the intellectual and administrative control of the teaching process. The world government must do its own studying, its own teaching.

3. The staff of an Institute of Education would be drawn in part from the administrative staff of the international organization. It would include also other scholars and teachers who are trained for the critical examination and interpretation of the principles of world order. If these two groups could be fused together into a unified faculty clearly aware of its responsibilities, we might achieve that integration of intellectual and practical activities which is so sadly lacking in much of the scholarly work, much of the teaching which is now going on.

4. The pupils of the Institute would be drawn from universities throughout the world. They would be young scholars who have completed in some

special field of study the intellectual training ordinarily required for admission to teaching on the university level.

5. These young scholars would have at least a year of training at the Institute. They would study there the work of the international organization, its aims and methods, its general principles and its specific problems, its successes and its failures, its hopes and its fears. They would be fitted to become, in the forms of adult education, interpreters of what the international organization is trying to do.

6. On the completion of their training, the Institute would send these young scholars throughout the world as teachers of its citizens. Acting in collaboration with local authorities, they would go from community to community, staying two or three or even four months in each place. But the Institute would keep them in close touch with each other and with itself. It would endeavor to make of them a well-integrated teaching body, clearly aware of its own purposes, ready to promote the realization of those purposes in the midst of all the differences of circumstance into which they might come. These international interpreters would learn as well as teach. In them and in their work, the motives, the ideas of world peace and world justice would find an approach at least to adequate expression.

3

Anyone who has engaged in actual teaching knows how fragmentary are the suggestions which I have made. The path of education is not an easy one. The task of devising and administering a scheme of education for the citizens of the world will be a long and perplexing one. And yet, fifty years of the achievements of adult education in many countries indicate the lines which we may at the beginning fruitfully follow. I mention here three of these:

1. As our teachers enter local communities, public meetings would be held at which various phases of the international enterprise would be presented, together with the intellectual materials bearing upon them. Such presentations would be supplemented by discussion at the meeting and on other occasions.

2. More important, however, than listening and discussion are the activities of careful and sustained study. To this end, small study groups would be formed in which leaders and pupils together would read and reflect upon the great books and the decisive documents in which international issues find their most enlightening formulations. The far-off goal of this method would be that every adult citizen of an international society should be an active member of such a group. That goal will not soon be reached. But only as we approach it are we making headway toward an international society.

3. In the new forms of communication and travel, the radio, the film,

et cetera, there are opening up vast new possibilities of teaching achievement. These must be tested and developed. They are for the first time in history making possible the creation in intellectual terms of a single, unified human society. In fact, so great are their promises and so great their dangers that they must not be allowed to develop without public criticism and control. They can be made to serve as instruments either for the elevation or for the degradation of the intelligence and generosity upon which in the last resort all human attempts at co-operation must rest. It would be a primary task of the Institute to explore and to develop the teaching possibilities of these agencies.

4

As I close this plea for an Institute of Education in the field of world government, two final words must be written. The need which I have presented is immediate and urgent. If adult education is to be ready to play its part in post-war reconstruction, decisive action must be taken at once. It will not do to wait until the experts in economics and politics have finished their work. The plans for teaching must modify and be modified by all other types of planning. The Institute of Education must take form and assume responsibilities step by step with all the other agencies which will appear as the general project moves forward. To that end, official and unofficial conferences should be now under way. Too much time has already been lost.

As we plan for the education or re-education of the nations of the earth, let us not think it is only our enemies who will have new lessons to learn. That theme has been much played in these days of bitter strife. But in sober fact it must be said that if, as we hope, we are to be the victors in the world conflict, it will be we, rather than our foes, who stand in greater need of teaching. Defeat brings its own lessons. But victory in battle has never been a good teacher. And we Anglo-Americans have been terrifyingly successful in the struggles of the modern world. Seventy-five years ago, Matthew Arnold told in bitter, hopeless words the impenetrability of the successful British mind to the forces of education. "One has often wondered," he says, "whether upon the whole earth there is anything so unintelligent, so unapt to perceive how the world is really going, as an ordinary young Englishman of our upper class."

I quote these words not because of their peculiar reference to the ruling class of England. They apply to all individuals who have won predominance over their fellows. The greatest danger to the United States is that as its power and success grow greater, there will come upon it the same blindness to its own need of education. The lessons of freedom and equality are not easy for nations accustomed to superiority and domination. It is the victors who must be educated. It is upon them that an International Institute of

Education must lavish its efforts. It is idle to plan for a free, federated world and, at the same time, to plan that we shall be masters of it. A free, federated world is a world of equals. All men, all nations must be educated.

Hu Shih

When the United States turned back the Boxer Indemnity to China as a scholarship fund, it was to receive rich dividends in the career of such men as Hu Shih (1891-   ). Born in Shanghai, he attended Cornell as a Boxer Indemnity student and received the degree of Ph.D. from Columbia, where he came under the influence of John Dewey. As Professor of Philosophy at the National University of Peking he was a leader in the promotion of popular education by breaking down the monopoly of the Mandarin dialect and fostering the literary use of the language of the people. Scholar, teacher, and man of letters, he has been called "The Father of the Chinese Literary Renaissance." From 1938 to 1942 he was his country's Ambassador to the United States and has since become honorary consultant to the Library of Congress on East Asiatic literature. In the essay which follows he offers a reasoned explanation of the differences between Chinese and Japanese cultures, and encourages one to believe that the democratic spirit of new China will eventually prevail in the East.

THE MODERNIZATION OF CHINA AND JAPAN

IN recent years I have published some of my reflections on the modernization of China and Japan. What I am now going to state is a summary and restatement of what I have been thinking on this fascinating subject during these years.

I

First of all, we must state the problem of our inquiry. What special aspect of the modernization of China and Japan arouses our curiosity and requires our study and explanation?

Generally speaking, there are two aspects of the question that have puzzled the outside world and demanded some explanation.

For many decades, down to very recent years, the question often asked was: Why was Japan so successful in her task of modernization, and why was China so unsuccessful? That is the first aspect of the question, which has called forth many explanations.

But in recent years, the problem has radically changed. After almost a century of hesitation and resistance, China has emerged as a modern nation, not sufficiently westernized (it is true) in her material aspects, but fully modern in her outlook on life and feeling completely at home in the modern world. On the other hand, Japan, after seventy years of apparently rapid modernization, is suddenly discovered by the outside world as having never been transformed in all the fundamental aspects of her national life. Professor G. C. Allen, one of the most sympathetic interpreters of Japan, said: "If the changes in some of the aspects of her [Japan's] life have been far-reaching, the persistence of the traditional in other aspects is equally remarkable. . . . The contrasts between these innovations and the solid core of ancient habit are as striking as ever they were." Professor Emil Lederer and Emy Lederer-Seidler, in their joint work on *Japan in Transition,* another most sympathetic interpretation of Japanese life, have dwelt on the most strange phenomenon in Japan, namely, her "immunity to the dialectic play of deep-lying evolutionary forces," her being "devoid of dialectic and dynamic" and her ancient civilization "offering strong resistance to the facile assimilation of foreign elements."

In short, the new problem is just the opposite of the older puzzle. It is: Why has China at last succeeded in overthrowing her old civilization and in achieving a Chinese Renaissance? And why has Japan, after seven decades of extraordinarily successful modernization, yet failed to break up her "solid core of ancient habit"? That is the second aspect of the problem.

Any theory that attempts to explain the first set of questions must also explain satisfactorily the second set of questions. And vice versa.

2

In 1933, I was trying to solve the first set of puzzles: Why and how has Japan succeeded, and China failed, to achieve a speedy and orderly cultural readjustment and bring about the modernization necessary for national survival in the new world? The explanation I offered then was that China and Japan had been going through two distinct types of cultural response. The modernization in Japan I described as the type of cultural transformation under centralized control, made possible by the existence of a powerful ruling class—the feudal militaristic caste—from which came the leaders of the Reformation who not only decided for the nation what to change and what not to change, but who also had the political power to carry out their decisions. On the other hand, I pointed out, China, because of the nonexistence of a ruling class and because of the thoroughly democratized social structure, could only go through the slow and often wasteful process of cultural transformation through the gradual and diffused penetration and assimilation of ideas and practices, usually initiating from a few individuals, slowly

winning a following, and finally achieving significant changes when a sufficient number of people are convinced of their superior reasonableness, convenience, or efficacy.

The advantages of the Japanese type of modernization under the centralized control of a ruling class are easy to see. It is orderly, economical,
continuous, stable, and effective. But, I point out, "it is not without very
important disadvantages. The Japanese leaders undertook this rapid transformation at so early a time that even the most far-sighted of them could
only see and understand certain superficial phases of the Western civilization. Many other phases have escaped their attention. And, in their anxiety
to preserve their national heritage and to strengthen the hold of the State
and the dynasty over the people, they have carefully protected a great many
elements of the traditional Japan from the contact and contagion of the new
civilization. . . . Much of the traditional medieval culture is artificially protected by a strong shell of militant modernity. Much that is preserved is of
great beauty and permanent value; but not a little of it is primitive and
pregnant with grave dangers of volcanic eruption."

The disadvantages of the Chinese type of cultural changes through
gradual diffusion and penetration are numerous: they are slow, sporadic, and
often wasteful, because much undermining and erosion are necessary before
anything can be changed.

But they have also undeniable advantages. They are voluntary. From
the lipstick to the literary revolution, from the footwear to the overthrow
of the monarchy, all has been voluntary and in a broad sense "reasoned."
Nothing in China is too sacred to be protected from the contact and contagion of the invading civilization of the West. And no man, nor any class,
is powerful enough to protect any institution from this contact and change.
In short, this process of long exposure and slow permeation often results in
cultural changes which are both fundamental and permanent.

3

This, in general, was my theory regarding the modernization of China
and Japan. Japan was modernized under the powerful leadership and control of a ruling class, and China, because of the nonexistence of such control
from above, was modernized through the long process of free contact,
gradual diffusion, and voluntary following.

We may ask, Can this theory satisfactorily explain all the four phases
of our main inquiry? Can it explain the marvelously rapid westernization
of Japan and at the same time the unchanging solid core of medieval Japan?
Can it explain both the long failures and the recent successes in China's
modernization? I think not only that it can, but that it is the only hypothesis
which can satisfactorily resolve all the apparent contradictions of the problem.

According to my theory, the early and rapid successes of the Meiji Reformation were brought about by the effective leadership and powerful control of the ruling class, which happened to coincide with the militaristic class of feudal Japan and which naturally was most anxious and at the same time best fitted to undertake the adoption of the Western armaments and methods of warfare. As Professor Lederer has pointed out, "It could hardly be foreseen at this early stage that in this case one step leads inexorably to a second." "Since a modern military state is possible only on condition that it is an industrialized state, Japan had to develop in that direction. But industrialization, by reason of the economic interrelationship between various types of production, means also the development of branches of industry which are not essential to the conduct of war. . . . Just as militarism reaches beyond itself into industry, so the technological system of industrialism has far-reaching implications for the social system." The leaders of Japanese westernization started out with the desire to adopt Western militarism and have thereby brought about what Professor Lederer calls the "militaristic industrial system."

Of all the non-European countries with which the European civilization has come into contact, Japan is the only nation that has successfully learned and mastered that one phase of the occidental civilization which is most coveted by all races, namely, its militaristic phase. Japan has succeeded where all these non-European countries have invariably failed. This historical mystery can only be explained by the fact that no other non-European country was so favored with the existence of a militaristic caste which has been the governing class of the country for over twelve centuries.

But this militaristic caste was not an enlightened or intellectual class. Its leaders were courageous, pragmatic, patriotic, and in some cases statesmanlike. But they were limited in their visions and in their understanding of the new civilization that had knocked at their shores. They thought, just as Lafcadio Hearn thought, that they could build up a Western war machine which should be made to serve as a protective wall behind which all the traditional values of Tokugawa Japan should be preserved unaltered.

Unfortunately for Japan and for the world, the military successes of Japan against Russia and China tended to vindicate these narrow-visioned leaders. The result has been an effective artificial protection and solidification of the traditional culture of medieval Japan against the "dangerous" contact and influence of the new ideas and practices of the ever-changing world. By the use of the modern means of rigidly controlled education, propaganda, and censorship, and by the use of the peculiarly Japanese methods of inculcating the cult of emperor-worship, Japan has succeeded in reinforcing and consolidating the "solid core" of unchanging medieval culture left over from the 250 years of Tokugawa isolation. It was the same centralized leadership and control which made possible the rapid and successful changes in militarization and industrialization and which has also deliberately protected and solidified the traditional values and made them "immune to the dialectic play of deep-lying evolutionary forces."

The same theory also explains the history of modernization in China. The early failures in the Chinese attempts at westernization were almost entirely due to the absence of the factors which have made the Japanese Meiji Reformation a success. The Chinese leaders, too, wanted to adopt the Western armaments and methods of warfare and to build up the new industries. Their slogan was "Fu Ts'iang" (Wealth and Strength). But there was in China neither the militaristic tradition nor an effective and powerful governing class to undertake the leadership and direction in such gigantic enterprises. China had come out of feudalism at least twenty-one centuries ago; the social structure had been thoroughly democratized; and governmental policy, religion, philosophy, literature, and social usage had combined to condemn militarism and despise the soldier. Whereas the Samurai was the most highly esteemed class in Japan, the soldier ranked the lowest in the Chinese social scale. Therefore the new Chinese army and the new Chinese navy of the eighties and nineties of the last century were doomed to failure. With the destruction of the Chinese navy in 1894-95, all the new industries—the shipyard, the merchant marine, the government-operated iron and steel industry—which were to feed and support the new war machine, gradually came to nought. The government and the dynasty were thus discredited in their early efforts in modernization. After the failure of the reforms of 1898 and the tragedy of the Boxer Uprising of 1900, the discrediting of the dynasty and the government was complete. From that time on, China's main endeavor was to destroy that center of ignorance and reactionism—the monarchy and its paraphernalia—and then to build up a new center of political authority and leadership.

Thus, while Japan's first successes in westernization were achieved under the leadership and control of her feudal-militaristic class, China has had to spend three or four decades in the effort of first removing the monarchy and later destroying the newly arisen militarists. It has been found necessary for China to bring about a political revolution as the precondition for her modernization.

In 1911-12, the revolution succeeded in overthrowing the alien rule and the monarchy together with its historical accompaniments. The political revolution was in every sense a social and cultural emancipation. In a country where there is no ruling class, the overthrow of the monarchy destroys the last possibility of a centralized control in social change and cultural transformation. It makes possible an atmosphere of free contact, free judgment and criticism, free appreciation, free advocacy, and voluntary acceptance.

What has been called the Chinese Renaissance is the natural product of this atmosphere of freedom. All the important phases of cultural change in China have been the result of this free contact and free diffusion of new ideas and practices, which are impossible in Japan under rigid dynastic and militaristic taboos. The net outcome is that modern China has undoubtedly achieved more far-reaching and more profound transformations in the social, political, intellectual, and religious life than the so-called "modern Japan" has ever done in similar fields.

I wish to cite one important and fundamental fact as illustration of the character of the cultural change in China. I refer to the spirit of free and fearless criticism which the leaders of China have applied to the study and examination of their own social, political, historical, and religious institutions. It is no accident that all the men who have exerted the greatest influence over the Chinese nation for the last forty years—Liang Ch'i-ch'ao, Ts'ai Yuan-p'ei, Wu Ching-heng, Chen Tushiu, and others— have been men who know our historical heritage critically and who have had the moral courage ruthlessly to criticize its evil and weak aspects and to advocate wholehearted changes. Neither Confucius, nor Lao-tse, nor the Buddha, nor Chu-hsi; neither the monarchy, nor the family, nor religion, is too sacred to be exempt from their doubt and criticism. A nation that has encouraged honest doubt and free criticism even in matters touching the sacred and most time-honored institutions is achieving a modernity undreamed of by its neighbors whose intellectual leaders are persecuted and punished for having taught thirty years ago a certain theory of constitutional law or for having suggested that certain Sacred Treasures at a certain shrine might be of doubtful authenticity.

To sum up, the modernization in China illustrates the view that, in the absence of centralized control from above, cultural changes of basic importance may take place through the process of free contact and slow diffusion. It is the reverse side of what has happened in Japan. The breakdown of the monarchy and its paraphernalia has removed the possibility of artificial protection and solidification of the old culture, which is then thrown open to the natural processes of cultural transformation through free contact and voluntary acceptance.

4

If I have any moral to present it is this: freedom or contact and choice is the most essential condition for cultural diffusion and change. Wherever two civilizations come into contact, there are natural tendencies (or laws) of one people learning and borrowing from the other what each lacks or recognizes as of superior utility or beauty. These natural tendencies of cultural diffusion will have free play if only the peoples are allowed free contact with the new ideas and practices.

Where such freedom is denied to a people, where artificial isolation and solidification are consciously and effectively carried out with regard either to a whole culture or to certain specially prized aspects of it, there arises the strange phenomenon of the "solid core of ancient habit" "devoid of dialectic and dynamic," such as has been found in present-day Japan.

There is really no mystery in this unchanging Japan after seventy years of marvelously rapid change in the militaristic industrial system. There is no truth in the theory, for example, that the Japanese civilization has been able to resist change because it has its peculiar vitality and has attained "the completed perfection of its forms." The fashion of men's dress in the Western world does not change so rapidly as that of women—can we say that men's dress has achieved special vitality and "the completed perfection of form"? In the same way, sitting on the floor, for example, was discarded in China so long ago that historians have difficulty in dating the first use of chairs and tables. But the Japanese to this day continue to sit on the floor. That does not mean the custom of sitting on the floor has any special "vitality" or has attained "completed perfection of form."

Nor is there much truth in the view that the Japanese are naturally clumsy in understanding and conservative in their outlook. Lack of understanding never prevents a people from accepting new fads. Japan probably never understood the various schools of Buddhism when she accepted them. (Certainly China did not understand some of them when she adopted them.) Besides, a people can always learn. European observers in the seventeenth century recorded that the Japanese knew "nothing of mathematics, more especially of its deeper and speculative parts." But we now know the Japanese can become accomplished mathematicians.

As to their native conservatism, the history of early Japanese contacts with Korea, China, and Europe only proves the contrary. They learned from these foreign peoples everything they could learn, not excluding things affecting their social, political, and religious institutions. In recording the success of the Jesuits in Japan, Sansom said: "Though a number of their converts were beyond all doubt genuine to the point of fanaticism and adhered to their new faith in the face of great danger, one cannot but suspect that it had, by one of those crazes which have often swept over Japan, become the fashion to ape the customs of foreigners, including their religion. We know that rosaries and crucifixes were eagerly bought and worn by many who were not Christians, even, it is said, by Hideyoshi himself; and it was modish to wear foreign clothes and to be able to recite a Latin prayer."

I cannot therefore escape the conclusion that it will be the element of freedom that may yet some day break down the "solid core of ancient habit" in Japan just as it has already broken it down in China.

Stuart Chase

Stuart Chase (1888-   ), in such books as The Tragedy of Waste, Your
Money's Worth, A New Deal, *and* Rich Land, Poor Land, *proves himself an incisive analyst of economic problems. One of these titles has become the slogan of a political program. Another,* The Tragedy of Waste,
*might express the main theme of Chase's earlier work, for he has been
relentlessly critical of the exploitation of American resources by a greedy
society. At the invitation of the Twentieth Century Fund he has undertaken a constructive series of monographs on the needs of post-war
America. Selected from these, the following discussion of housing has
the crispness of an engineering report plus the human touch which
Chase brings to every problem.*

SHELTER

HOUSING is a large and cloudy term. It be-
comes concrete when you look hard enough at one particular house. I want
to describe Uncle Henry's house in southeast Missouri. The description is
not flattering, but I do not think Uncle Henry will greatly mind.

My guide, Hans Baasch, drove me along a rutted dirt road which ran
east to the shore of the Mississippi River. The road led across the levee
and over a plain dotted with pools of swamp water. On the higher ground
cordwood was piled up, girdled trees were dying, and cotton was growing
between the stumps. We went over a crazy bridge with a sign "Unsafe."
"Well," said Hans, "we made it," and brought the car to a halt beside an
unpainted shack in a wilderness of girdled stumps. It was Uncle Henry's
place.

The house was perhaps eighteen feet square. It was set on wooden
posts, two of which had quietly decomposed, giving the whole structure
a distinct list to starboard. The roof of the porch had partially collapsed. A
stovepipe jutted crazily out of a hole in the back wall. Beyond stood a foul
privy with door askew and tar paper peeling off the roof.

Uncle Henry's rheumatism was so bad he could not get up to welcome
us. He sat in a broken-down armchair with springs coming out one way
and stuffing the other. His eyes lit up when he saw Hans. While they
talked I looked at Uncle Henry's house.

There were two rooms, the living-kitchen-dining room where we were,
and one bedroom. Through a sagging door, I could see a cast-iron bed, a
bureau, and a cracked mirror. There was no closet in either room.

The floor was of rough boards. It was a raw day and the wind was whistling through the cracks. Uncle Henry pulled the brown army blanket closer about him. "I don't feel good today," he said. Beside us was an iron stove with elaborate metal curlycues on the corners. It might once have belonged to some rich planter. It was cracked now and the pipe was smoking in time with the blasts of wind that came through the floor.

The walls of the rooms were made of unmatched vertical boards, insulated most ineffectively by pale-blue wrapping paper, peeling in long strips. Some repair work had been done with pages of the *St. Louis Post Dispatch*. I counted three broken panes in the two small windows. They were stuffed with old socks. In the corner stood an iron sink with a pail of water beside it; the pump was out in the yard. There was an old box half-full of firewood for the stove, a much-scrubbed wooden table holding an alarm clock and a year-old copy of the *Red Book,* a sewing machine, a shelf full of patent-medicine bottles, an insurance-company calendar, and a row of pegs hung with overalls, old coats and a battered hat.

When Hans had finished his business with Uncle Henry, we stood up to go. We both shook hands with the old man, shrunken in his blanket, his face grey with pain. "I guess I won't be here when you come next time, boy, but it was mighty nice to see you this time. And nice to see you, Mr. Chase."

"Oh, you're going to be all right," said Hans. "You're too tough to kill. You'll be chopping cotton again."

"Yes," said Uncle Henry, "I'm tough. You can't live here without being tough."

We had to drive up the road a bit before we could find a place to turn. I was mentally comparing Uncle Henry's cabin with the neat houses I had seen in the Farm Security project which Hans managed.

"Were all the houses like that when the government came in?" I asked.

"Some of them were worse," said Hans. "We took on a hundred families, and tore down ninety-four of the shacks. They were so rotten they hardly made decent firewood. Over three hundred kids were living in them. Up where I came from we wouldn't house a hog in such a place. We made an inventory of their furniture, clothes and tools. What do you suppose the average value was?"

"Judging from Uncle Henry's place, it couldn't have been much," I said.

"It was just twenty-eight dollars."

THE EXTENT OF THE HOUSING SHORTAGE

I liked Uncle Henry, but if I had to live in his house I would go out some dark night and jump in the Mississippi. I am not tough enough, and I doubt whether any human beings are really tough enough. But regardless of my personal opinion, when "housing" is discussed by learned statisticians, it is a good idea to have a clear picture in mind of Uncle Henry's house and others like it. A recent survey by the Department of Agriculture disclosed that at least 2,000,000 farmhouses are unfit for human habitation, while in Arkansas, Louisiana, Mississippi, Alabama and Georgia, the average value of farm dwellings is less than $500. It is also a good idea to think of the new houses in the project on the other side of the levee. We will come to them later.

In the meantime, let us go from Missouri cotton lands to a Massachusetts seaport. Learned statisticians and anthropologists from Harvard have been making an exhaustive survey of the town of Newburyport, at the mouth of the Merrimack River.[1] It used to be a shipping center and for a time it rivalled Boston. In that splendid era, captains and merchants built solid four-sided houses which make High Street perhaps the outstanding exhibit of colonial architecture in America. With the decline of shipping, Newburyport turned to the manufacture of textiles, boots and shoes, silverware. It never recovered its grandeur of sailing-ship days, but it never fell into such an economic backwater as did New Bedford and Fall River. Driving through, one gets an impression of a town housed above the average of New England towns. New England towns as a whole—perhaps due to a lack of economy in the use of white paint—give one the impression of being neater and in better repair than American towns generally.

The research staff from Harvard made a careful examination of the 12,424 houses in which the people of Newburyport lived. Here is what they found:

Houses in good repair	2,386 or 19 per cent of all
Houses in medium repair	4,938 or 40 per cent
Houses in bad repair	5,100 or 41 per cent

There were 403 large houses in good condition and 226 in bad condition. There were 1,107 medium-sized houses in good condition and 1,881 in bad. There were 876 small houses in good condition and 2,993 in bad. Well-to-do people lived mostly in the large houses, and poor people in the small houses, though the rule was not infallible.

From Newburyport we go to Washington, D. C. Within gunshot of the Capitol building you can find, if you know where to look for them, "Pork Steak Alley, Pig Alley, Goat Alley, Tin Can Alley, Coon's Alley, Tiger Alley, Moonshine Alley, Louse Alley and Chinch Row. These are Washington's Negro ghettos. Most of them are the back lots of the white residents of seventy years ago, and they were built to take care of the influx of refugee Negroes after the Civil War. The construction of alley dwell-

[1] Warner and Lunt, *The Social Life of a Modern Community.* Investigators were in Newburyport for a number of years.

ings was ended by law exactly fifty years ago, but most of the original shacks remain today. . . . The occupants of these alley shacks are a special brand of people, with their own customs, their own superstitions, and a notorious suspicion of outsiders. More than half the children born in the darkest alleys are illegitimate." [2]

The United States Census took an inventory of all the houses in the country, including Pork Steak Alley, Newburyport, and Uncle Henry's, in April 1940. The results speak for themselves.

There were then 37,327,000 dwelling units in the nation. This includes single houses, double houses counted as two, apartment houses counted for as many units as they contain.

Almost half of all American houses (49.2 per cent) were in need of major repairs or had no bath, or both. There were 6,414,000 houses needing major repairs. Out of more than 7,000,000 farm units reported, 6,500,000 had no bath, 6,000,000 had no running water, only 31 per cent had electric current. Under the best of conditions many farm families will continue to use outside privies, employ pumps instead of running water, and in lonely areas forego electric current. But any way you look at them the Census figures indicate a dreadful shortage of adequate shelter on the farms and in the cities. One does not need statistics to prove this, one needs only a pair of eyes.

In Arkansas there were 521,000 houses, according to the 1940 Census. Twenty-two thousand had one room, 90,000 had two rooms, 3,500 had ten rooms or more. Twenty-six per cent of all had four rooms; 46 per cent had less than four; only 28 per cent had more than four rooms. Arkansas is one of the states which is in direst need of adequate shelter.

Let us compare equipment in Georgia, Tennessee and Oregon, again using Census figures:

	Georgia	Tennessee	Oregon
Number of houses with electric light	46.6%	50.9%	85.8%
With mechanical refrigeration	24.7	27.7	43.4
With no refrigeration	45.6	44.5	47.8
With no central heating	93.1	86.7	65.2
With a radio	52.5	62.5	89.5

In houses with no refrigeration a large amount of food is likely to spoil. In the South, refrigeration is especially needed to keep the family healthy. Houses with no central heating may do in many Southern areas, but not so well in Oregon. Houses without radios are liabilities in a total war, where citizens need instant communication.

[2] W. M. Kiplinger, *Washington Is Like That,* Harper, 1942.

A TEN-YEAR BUDGET FOR SHELTER

The Census gives a dramatic picture of the vast task before the country in the department of shelter. To provide decent houses for all members of the Great Family cannot be done in any one year, but calls for a program stretching over a decade or more. There is no way to tell from these figures, or from any other figures, exactly how many homes need to be demolished as unfit for human habitation, how many need to be renovated from the foundations, how many can be salvaged by major repairs.

Various estimates have been made, however, of the total number of new units needed in the years before us to bring housing up to par. Miss Catherine Bauer, a noted expert in the field, estimated that between 1937 and 1950, sixteen million units ought to be built to care for the increase in families, and to replace the worst of the substandard structures. Mrs. Edith Elmer Wood, another recognized authority, estimated in 1938 that some 13 million units, not including farmhouses, should be built by 1950. This checks roughly with Miss Bauer's calculations. Both indicate a building program of more than 1,000,000 units a year. The best year we ever had, 1925, accounted for 900,000 new houses. In 1933, the number was down to 93,000. By 1940 it had climbed to 600,000.

Mr. C. F. Palmer, Federal Housing Co-ordinator, told a Fortune Round Table in the summer of 1941 that after the war we should build 1,600,000 non-farm units annually for ten years, to house the urban population properly. He thinks that private finance can swing a million of them, but that government subsidy will be required for 600,000 units a year. For the ten-year period, this would mean 6 million units subsidized for low-income families. Mr. Palmer reminds us that European governments, in the years before the war, subsidized 20 million urban units.

I think we can take it as demonstrated that the Budget [3] will call for somewhere between a million and two million dwelling units, over the whole country, every year, for at least ten years after the war ends. That will make the biggest single demand upon manpower of any project on the horizon—the largest pool for post-war work. According to Mr. Palmer, it will keep at least 1,600,000 construction workers busy; a high government source estimates 2,000,000 workers. It may mean two to three times the labor force which was building houses in 1940, when 600,000 units were constructed.

These estimates do not include labor for lumber and other materials, but only men on the job. On the average, it looks as if one man puts up one house in a year's time. When prefabrication goes into mass produc-

[3] The basic purpose of Chase's book is to draw up a "Budget" in which the needs of our population (food, clothing, shelter, education, health) are balanced against our potential production.

tion, it is probable that a house can be put up in a far shorter time, say a man month, or a man fortnight—the latter being the equivalent of a crew of seven putting the house up in two days. And although the factory cost of the prefabricated units will be greater than the factory cost of the lumber, nails, paint and other materials used at present—measured in man hours, or dollars, or any way you please—the total manpower required to meet the housing budget will be less than under pre-war conditions. By early 1942, the government had ordered 22,058 "demountable" or prefabricated houses for war workers. One San Francisco firm alone was given a contract for 5,000, the largest order for prefabrication ever placed!

OUR MOST BACKWARD INDUSTRY

The residential construction industry, as at present organized is, to quote Dr. Alvin H. Hansen and Guy Greer, "our most backward industry. In an age of mass production and assembly lines, it remains today, with a few noteworthy exceptions, a small-scale handicraft business which hardly deserves to be called an industry at all. It is made up of large numbers of contractors, subcontractors, material dealers, trade-unions, and so on. And, in spite of numerous honest carpenter builders and a few larger operators, it is shot through and through with graft, rackets and conspiracies. Topping all this, the manufacture of several important building materials and of much equipment is a virtual monopoly. The result is that every kind of dwelling costs far too much, even while the so-called industry is not, and has not been, prosperous for many years." Establishing our Budget might not only give us adequate houses, but conceivably it might clean up an Augean stable as well. No labor group has suffered more severely from unemployment than workers in the building trades, and few have suffered more from racketeering officials.

One reason why the construction industry is in such a deplorable state may be that it has been tied all along to the cart of land speculation. The men who have put up the money, by and large, have not been interested in houses for people to live in. They have been interested in developing property as an investment, or, as it has been described, in "buying by the acre and selling by the front foot." Now, with the prospect of population gradually levelling off, and real-estate values practically stationary from the same cause, we have a chance for the first time in our history to create a really efficient construction industry. No trouble is foreseen in finding the manpower, the materials and the skills to build 1,500,000 houses, or 2,000,000 houses per year, after the war. We built almost 900,000 urban units in 1925, under handicraft, racket-ridden methods. If the industry could be rationalized, its capacity would be greatly increased.

DEFINING ADEQUATE SHELTER

We have been talking about "houses," and "dwelling units." A better term for this department of the Budget is "shelter." Shelter can be defined as not only the floor, walls and roof of a house, but the land on which it stands, the furnishings and equipment inside it, and the services running into it—water, electricity, gas, telephone, waste disposal.

The first requisite of adequate shelter is a place where children can be reared in health and well-being. The child is my test of shelter. Will this house help his development or set it back? In such a test, the question of how many ice cubes the refrigerator can produce, or whether a Colonial design is to be preferred to a straight-line international job, sinks into insignificance. The province of the Budget is to give children and their parents a clean, healthy place to live in, not to help them keep up with the Joneses. On this standard, the size and construction varies with the size of the family and with the climate. A winter home in Maine must be a more solid affair than a winter home in Florida.

Allowing for the climatic differences over our great continent, a set of rough specifications for adequate shelter might read something like this:

A tight, honestly built structure, of reasonably good design, which can be kept adequately clean and warmed in winter.

Space enough for children to play. In city apartments this can be solved to a degree by playgrounds between the blocks. Land to grow flowers or vegetables or both, wherever possible.

Minimum equipment for sanitation, to include pure water, bathing facilities, screens, toilet facilities. For the latter, sanitary privies may be acceptable in some rural areas. In cities, flush toilets connected with the sewer system are mandatory for reasons of public health.

Electric lighting and refrigeration in most cases, and for most families a telephone.

Simple and substantial furnishings. There may be a great future for metal furniture after the war, to make use of our vast aluminum supply and bomber plants.

FARMHOUSES AT LA FORGE

When Hans and I got back to the Farm Security project at LaForge, I had a chance to see with my own eyes the kind of shelter I have been trying to outline above. Here were one hundred well-designed farm cottages on 5,000 acres of farmland. Sixty of them were occupied by white people and forty by Negroes, but there was no way of telling from the outside which house belonged to which. After the government bought the land in 1937 and decided to "resettle" the 100 sharecroppers then living on it, its first task was to dismantle the shacks and build some real shelter. Listen carefully to the way in which this task was accomplished. It may carry important suggestions for the post-war Budget.

Remembering certain sad experiences from rural resettlement projects in the past, where members were provided with electric refrigerators and flush toilets but no visible means of support, engineers of the Farm Security Administration designed a very modest house. They went into action and built 94 new houses in 100 days, at an average cost of $1,100 per house, a cost which fitted the return from the land. The whole project now comes close to paying its way. The FSA did it by an ingenious method of mass production, in which the project members did most of the work. Lumber was unloaded from freight cars in a field near the cotton gin. It was cut into standard sizes with power saws. The units were then nailed into sections—walls, roof trusses, partitions. The sections were loaded into trucks and taken to the site, where concrete posts had already been set up by another crew of LaForge men. In half a day or so the house was up, in another day or two it was painted. One day, on a bet, a crew put a house up in thirty minutes. A few skilled supervisors and carpenters kept the job moving on schedule.

We enter one of the houses, going through a screened porch into a good-sized living room with screened windows—which work—and a double floor. The walls are vertical tongue-and-groove stock, well-oiled, in natural wood. Furniture includes a stove for heating, a couch, chairs, a big table, a carpet, curtains at the windows. The kitchen beyond has an enameled sink but no running water. It has built-in cabinets, and a substantial cookstove, burning wood or coal. Wood may be had for the cutting, over beyond the levee. Electric current is in every house, but used mostly for lighting. Two bedrooms—in some cases three—open from the living room. The bedrooms have closets, double beds, a dresser, mirror and chairs. The cold north wind was still blowing, but every house I visited was snug, warm and clean. They lacked frills and gadgets but they did not lack cheer, in spite of getting down to the bare essentials of shelter in that climate.

Outside in the yard is a sealed well with pump, and, in the far corner, a sanitary privy. An earth-covered root cellar, full of homemade preserves and canned goods, and a small, well-built barn, complete the property. In the North, construction would have to be somewhat heavier, but beyond this I cannot conceive of a fairer, sounder minimum standard of rural shelter than this LaForge project. To come into it from Uncle Henry's place is to come from hell into heaven. If a hundred such units can be constructed by the people who are to live in them, why not a million?

Jawaharlal Nehru

Jawaharlal Nehru (1889-   ), scholar, lawyer, and politician, is one of the most influential natives in India. He was educated at Harrow and Cambridge and is a Barrister-at-Law of the Inner Temple. He has long been associated with Gandhi's Non-Cooperation Movement and the Nationalist, Labor, and Peasant Movements. Three times he has been President of the Indian National Congress. To pass the time during the sixth of his many imprisonments for political offenses he began a series of letters to his daughter for the purpose of instructing her in the story of mankind. The letter which follows is Number 196 and comes at the end of Glimpses of World History, *a volume of almost 1000 pages. In this beautiful valedictory he takes that long view of history which Irwin Edman advises in "Candle in the Dark."*

THE LAST LETTER

WE have finished, my dear; the long story has ended. I need write no more, but the desire to end off with a kind of flourish induces me to write another letter—the Last Letter!

It was time I finished, for the end of my two-year term draws near. In three and thirty days from today I should be discharged, if indeed I am not released sooner, as the gaoler sometimes threatens to do. The full two years are not over yet, but I have received three and a half months' remission of my sentence, as all well-behaved prisoners do. For I am supposed to be a well-behaved prisoner, a reputation which I have certainly done nothing to deserve. So ends my sixth sentence, and I shall go out again into the wide world, but to what purpose? *A quoi bon?* When most of my friends and comrades lie in gaol and the whole country seems a vast prison.

What a mountain of letters I have written! And what a lot of good *swadeshi*[1] ink I have spread out on *swadeshi* paper. Was it worth while, I wonder? Will all this paper and ink convey any message to you that will interest you? You will say, yes, of course, for you will feel that any other answer might hurt me, and you are too partial to me to take such a risk. But whether you care for them or not, you cannot grudge me the joy of having written them, day after day, during these two long years. It was winter when I came. Winter gave place to our brief spring, slain all too soon by the summer heat; and then, when the ground was parched and dry and men and beasts panted for breath, came the monsoon, with its

---

[1] Made in one's own country.

bountiful supply of fresh and cool rain-water. Autumn followed, and the sky was wonderfully clear and blue and the afternoons were pleasant. The year's cycle was over, and again it began: winter and spring and summer and the rainy season. I have sat here, writing to you and thinking of you, and watched the seasons go by, and listened to the pitapat of the rain on my barrack roof—

O doux bruit de la pluie,
Parterre et sur les toits!
Pour un cœur qui s'ennuie,
Oh! le chant de la pluie! [2]

Benjamin Disraeli, the great English statesman of the nineteenth century, has written: "Other men condemned to exile and captivity, if they survive, despair; the man of letters may reckon those days as the sweetest of his life." He was writing about Hugo Grotius, a famous Dutch jurist and philosopher of the seventeenth century, who was condemned to imprisonment for life, but managed to escape after two years. He spent these two years in prison in philosophic and literary work. There have been many famous literary gaolbirds, the two best known perhaps being the Spaniard, Cervantes, who wrote *Don Quixote,* and the Englishman, John Bunyan, the author of *The Pilgrim's Progress.*

I am not a man of letters, and I am not prepared to say that the many years I have spent in gaol have been the sweetest in my life, but I must say that reading and writing have helped me wonderfully to get through them. I am not a literary man, and I am not a historian; what, indeed, am I? I find it difficult to answer that question. I have been a dabbler in many things; I began with science at college, and then took to the law, and, after developing various other interests in life, finally adopted the popular and widely practised profession of gaol-going in India! . . .

I have given you the barest outline; this is not history; they are just fleeting glimpses of our long past. If history interests you, if you feel some of the fascination of history, you will find your way to many books which will help you to unravel the threads of past ages. But reading books alone will not help. If you would know the past you must look upon it with sympathy and with understanding. To understand a person who lived long ago, you will have to understand his environment, the conditions under which he lived, the ideas that filled his mind. It is absurd for us to judge of past people as if they lived now and thought as we do. There is no one to defend slavery today, and yet the great Plato held that slavery was essential. Within recent times scores of thousands of lives were given in an effort to retain slavery in the United States. We cannot judge the past from the

[2] From "Il Pleure dans mon Cœur," by Paul Verlaine: Oh, soft sound of the rain—On the ground and the roofs!—To the weary heart—Oh, the song of the rain!

standards of the present. Everyone will willingly admit this. But everyone will not admit the equally absurd habit of judging the present by the standards of the past. The various religions have especially helped in petrifying old beliefs and faiths and customs, which may have had some use in the age and country of their birth, but which are singularly unsuitable in our present age.

If, then, you look upon past history with the eye of sympathy, the dry bones will fill up with flesh and blood, and you will see a mighty procession of living men and women and children in every age and every clime, different from us and yet very like us, with much the same human virtues and human failings. History is not a magic show, but there is plenty of magic in it for those who have eyes to see.

Innumerable pictures from the gallery of history crowd our minds. Egypt—Babylon—Nineveh—the old Indian civilizations—the coming of the Aryans to India and their spreading out over Europe and Asia—the wonderful record of Chinese culture—Knossos and Greece—Imperial Rome and Byzantium—the triumphant march of the Arabs across two continents—the renaissance of Indian culture and its decay—the little-known Maya and Aztec civilizations of America—the vast conquests of the Mongols—the Middle Ages in Europe with their wonderful Gothic cathedrals—the coming of Islam to India and the Moghal Empire—the Renaissance of learning and art in western Europe—the discovery of America and the sea-routes to the East—the beginnings of Western aggression in the East—the coming of the big machine and the development of capitalism—the spread of industrialism and European domination and imperialism—and the wonders of science in the modern world.

Great empires have risen and fallen and been forgotten by man for thousands of years, till their remains were dug up again by patient explorers from under the sands that covered them. And yet many an idea, many a fancy, has survived and proved stronger and more persistent than the empire.

> Egypt's might is tumbled down,
>   Down a-down the deeps of thought;
> Greece is fallen and Troy town,
> Glorious Rome hath lost her crown,
>   Venice' pride is nought.
> But the dreams their children dreamed,
>   Fleeting, unsubstantial, vain,
> Shadowy as the shadows seemed,
> Airy nothing, as they deemed,
>   These remain.

So sings Mary Coleridge.

The past brings us many gifts; indeed, all that we have today of culture, civilization, science, or knowledge of some aspects of the truth, is a gift of the distant or recent past to us. It is right that we acknowledge our obligation to the past. But the past does not exhaust our duty or obligation. We owe a duty to the future also, and perhaps that obligation is even greater than the one we owe to the past. For the past is past and done with, we cannot change it; the future is yet to come, and perhaps we may be able to shape it a little. If the past has given us some part of the truth, the future also hides many aspects of the truth, and invites us to search for them. But often the past is jealous of the future and holds us in a terrible grip, and we have to struggle with it to get free to face and advance towards the future.

History, it is said, has many lessons to teach us; and there is another saying that history never repeats itself. Both are true, for we cannot learn anything from it by slavishly trying to copy it, or by expecting it to repeat itself or remain stagnant; but we can learn something from it by prying behind it and trying to discover the forces that move it. Even so, what we get is seldom a straight answer. "History," says Karl Marx, "has no other way of answering old questions than by putting new ones."

The old days were days of faith, blind, unquestioning faith. The wonderful temples and mosques and cathedrals of past centuries could never have been built but for the overpowering faith of the architects and builders and people generally. The very stones that they reverently put one on top of the other, or carved into beautiful designs, tell us of this faith. The old temple spire, the mosque with its slender minarets, the Gothic cathedral—all of them pointing upward with an amazing intensity of devotion, as if offering a prayer in stone or marble to the sky above—thrill us even now, though we may be lacking in that faith of old of which they are the embodiments. But the days of that faith are gone, and gone with them is that magic touch in stone. Thousands of temples and mosques and cathedrals continue to be built, but they lack the spirit that made them live during the Middle Ages. There is little difference between them and the commercial offices which are so representative of our age.

Our age is a different one; it is an age of disillusion, of doubt and uncertainty and questioning. We can no longer accept many of the ancient beliefs and customs; we have no more faith in them, in Asia or in Europe or America. So we search for new ways, new aspects of the truth more in harmony with our environment. And we question each other and debate and quarrel and evolve any number of "isms" and philosophies. As in the days of Socrates, we live in an age of questioning, but that questioning is not confined to a city like Athens; it is world-wide.

Sometimes the injustice, the unhappiness, the brutality of the world oppress us and darken our minds, and we see no way out. With Matthew Arnold, we feel that there is no hope in the world and that all we can do is to be true to one another.

> For the world which seems
> To lie before us like a land of dreams,
> So various, so beautiful, so new,
> Hath really neither joy, nor love, nor light,
> Nor certitude, nor peace, nor help for pain;
> And we are here as on a darkling plain
> Swept with confused alarms of struggle and flight,
> Where ignorant armies clash by night.

And yet if we take such a dismal view we have not learnt aright the lesson of life or of history. For history teaches us of growth and progress and of the possibility of an infinite advance for man. And life is rich and varied, and though it has many swamps and marshes and muddy places, it has also the great sea, and the mountains, and snow, and glaciers, and wonderful starlit nights (especially in gaol!), and the love of family and friends, and the comradeship of workers in a common cause, and music, and books and the empire of ideas. So that each one of us may well say:—

> Lord, though I lived on earth, the child of earth,
> Yet was I fathered by the starry sky.

It is easy to admire the beauties of the universe and to live in a world of thought and imagination. But to try to escape in this way from the unhappiness of others, caring little what happens to them, is no sign of courage or fellow-feeling. Thought, in order to justify itself, must lead to action. "Action is the end of thought," says our friend Romain Rolland. "All thought which does not look towards action is an abortion and a treachery. If then we are the servants of thought we must be the servants of action."

People avoid action often because they are afraid of the consequences, for action means risk and danger. Danger seems terrible from a distance; it is not so bad if you have a close look at it. And often it is a pleasant companion, adding to the zest and delight of life. The ordinary course of life becomes dull at times, and we take too many things for granted and have no joy in them. And yet how we appreciate these common things of life when we have lived without them for a while! Many people go up high mountains and risk life and limb for the joy of the climb and the exhilaration that comes from a difficulty surmounted, a danger overcome; and because of the danger that hovers all around them, their perceptions get keener, their joy of the life which hangs by a thread, the more intense.

All of us have our choice of living in the valleys below, with their unhealthy mists and fogs, but giving a measure of bodily security; or of climbing the high mountains, with risk and danger for companions, to breathe the pure air above, and take joy in the distant views, and welcome the rising sun.

I have given you many quotations and extracts from poets and others in this letter. I shall finish up with one more. It is from the *Gitanjali;* it is a poem, or prayer, by Rabindranath Tagore:—

Where the mind is without fear and the head is held high;
Where knowledge is free;
Where the world has not been broken up into fragments by narrow domestic
    walls;
Where words come out from the depth of truth;
Where tireless striving stretches its arms towards perfection;
Where the clear stream of reason has not lost its way into the dreary desert sand
    of dead habit;
Where the mind is led forward by thee into ever-widening thought and action—
Into that heaven of freedom, my Father, let my country awake.

Robert A. Millikan

Robert A. Millikan (1868-   ) was born in Illinois. After graduating from Oberlin College he studied at Columbia, Berlin, and Göttingen. He holds honorary degrees from some twenty institutions here and abroad. After teaching physics for twenty-five years in the University of Chicago he became director of the Norman Bridge Laboratory of Physics at the California Institute of Technology. In 1933 his world reputation was recognized by the award of the Nobel prize in physics. Aside from his many volumes of scientific research he has written a number of books which illuminate science for the layman. In the essay which follows, his is the voice of science, dispassionately and conservatively appraising man's present chances of survival and progress.

SCIENCE, FREEDOM, AND THE WORLD OF TOMORROW

EVEN though "prophecy is the most gratuitous form of mistake," and even though there is obviously the possibility that something so completely foreign to my thinking may happen as to make any prognosis that I may hazard now appear ridiculous in the years to come, yet I am going to be foolish and rash enough to forecast that, barring the return of the dark ages through the triumph the world over of tyranny over freedom, of the spirit of world conquest over the spirit of reason and peaceful change, life in America fifty or a hundred years hence will not differ nearly as much from the life of today as the life of today differs from that of a century or even a half century ago. The processes and techniques that have been responsible for the enormous changes of the last century will continue to improve our economic and social well-being, and to assure potentially a state of freedom for man, but the main changes will come from a more general understanding by the voting public of the nature of these processes and a more intelligent use of them. This will mean the gradual elimination of the effort to violate natural and social laws or, arithmetically stated, to make two plus two equal six, as we have been so ignorantly and so disastrously trying to do in much of our social floundering of recent years.

So long as one is considering only the physical or biological basis of change the informed and competent scientist has some reason for confidence in his analysis as to the general direction which progress can and must take. He at least knows a great many sorts of things that will *not* happen, and these are in the main the very things that the uninformed dreamers and wishful thinkers—the emotional pseudo reformers, not the real ones—hope and expect to see happen. Thus, we shall never be able to transform the energy released in the burning of coal or in the absorption of the sun's rays directly and completely into electrical energy. Indeed, we shall never be able to go very much farther in this direction than we have already gone.

Today the most efficient internal combustion engines transform into work 35 per cent of the heat energy released in the burning of the fuel, and it is safe to predict that in continuous operation we shall never be able to make very great advances beyond this limit. By that I do not mean that through improvements in details efficiencies in the neighborhood of say 50 per cent are completely out of the question. But in any case, the so-called second law of thermodynamics, which has now taken its place as a part of the core of established knowledge in physics, stands in the way of the realization of the dreams of the multitude of inventors and magicians who still want to transform the sun's heat rays directly and completely into work. Though the knowledge that it cannot be done is less than a hundred years old, it is about as firmly established as is the law of gravitation.

I have chosen the foregoing illustration because it lies at the very base of any correct analysis of what science has done and of what it is capable of doing in the future in bettering man's lot on earth. Let us look first at what it *has* done, for this will enable us to understand better what it can do. When in 1825 my grandfather loaded into a covered wagon his young wife, his Lares and Penates, and all his worldly goods, and trekked west from Stockbridge, Massachusetts, first to the Western Reserve in Ohio, and again in 1838 to the banks of the Rock River in western Illinois, the conditions of that migration, the motives prompting it, the mode of travel of the emigrants, their various ways of meeting their needs and solving their problems, their whole outlook upon life, were extraordinarily like those which existed four thousand years earlier when Abraham trekked westward from Ur of the Chaldees. In a word, the changes that have occurred within the past hundred years not only in the external conditions under which the average man, at least in this Western world, passes his life on earth, but in his superstitions, such as the taboo on the number thirteen or on Friday sailings (why, my own grandmother carried a dried potato in her pocket to keep off rheumatism), in his fundamental beliefs, in his philosophy, in his conception of religion, in his whole world outlook, are probably greater than those that occurred during the preceding four thousand years all put together. Life. seems to remain static for thousands of years and then to shoot forward with amazing speed. The last century has been one of those periods of extraordinary change, the most amazing in human history.

If, then, you ask me to put into one sentence the cause of that recent, rapid, and enormous change and the prognosis for the achievement of human liberty, I should reply, *It is found in the discovery and utilization of the means by which heat energy can be made to do man's work for him.* The key to the whole development is found in the use of power machines, and it is a most significant statistical fact that the standard of living in the various countries of the world follows closely the order in which so-called labor-saving devices have been most widely put into use. In other words, the average man has today more of goods and services to consume in about the proportion in which he has been able to produce more of goods and services through the aid of the power machines which have been put into his hands. In this country there is now expended about 13.5 horsepower hours per day per capita—the equivalent of 100 human slaves for each of us; in England the figure is 6.7, in Germany 6.0, in France 4.5, in Japan 1.8, in Russia 0.9, in China 0.5.[1] In the last analysis, this use of power is why our most important social changes have come about. This is why *we* no longer drive our ships with human slaves chained to the oars as did the Romans and the Greeks. This is why we no longer enslave whole peoples, as did the Pharaohs, for building our public structures and lash them to their tasks. This is why ten times as many boys and girls are in the high school today in the United States as were there in 1890—more than five million now, half a million then. This is why we have now an eight-hour day instead of, as then, a ten-, a twelve-, or sometimes a fourteen-hour day. This is why we have on the average an automobile for every family in the country. This is why the lowest class of male labor, i.e., unskilled labor, gets nearly twice as much in real wages in the United States as in England, three times as much as in Germany or France, and thirteen times as much

[1] These figures are substantially as given in Read, *An Economic Review,* 1933, p. 58; and in Hirshfeld, *Toward Civilization,* 1929.

as in Russia, and this is why the most abused class of labor in the world, domestic service, is even better off relatively in this country though completely unorganized, i.e., through the unhampered operation of economic laws, than is any other class of labor, skilled or unskilled, in other countries.

Do not think that these are the one-sided pronouncements merely of an enthusiastic scientist. Anyone can check them who will begin to study them. Listen to President Karl Compton's formulation of the results of his similar historical studies.[2] He says, "From the days of the cave man, all through history up to the modern era of science, there were only two primitive recipes for securing the materials desired for the more abundant life. One was to work hard and long in order to produce more, and the other was to take the good things of life from someone else, by theft, conquest, taxation or exploitation.

"To get the good things of life by taking them from others is a primitive instinct, undoubtedly developed by the age-old struggle for existence. We have all seen monkeys, or seagulls, or wolves, or pigs snatching food from each other, fighting to possess it, or shouldering each other away from the trough. When human beings carry this philosophy too far beyond the accepted standards, as did Jesse James and John Dillinger, we call them 'public enemies.' But this same philosophy of taking what we want from others, by violence and trickery, or by legalized strategy and force, has run all through human history.

"But, in recent times, modern science has developed to give mankind, for the first time in the history of the human race, a way of securing a more abundant life which does not simply consist in taking away from someone else. Science really creates wealth and opportunity where they did not exist before. Whereas the old order was based on competition, the new order of science makes possible, for the first time, a co-operative creative effort in which everyone is the gainer and no one the loser.

"For this reason, *I believe that the advent of modern science is the most important social event in all history*. It marks the point at which men have come to understand themselves and the world they live in well enough to begin systematically to control the hidden forces of nature to their advantage. Already science has done wonders to raise the standard of living and of knowledge, but these hidden forces are so great that we are assuredly only at the beginning of things possible.

"Some significant facts regarding the effect of the machine on the wages and employment of the worker are these: Counting 1840 as about the year in which power machinery came to be important in the United States, we find a steady increase since that date in the ratio of average wages to average prices of commodities, so that it is now about seven times what it was in

[2] *The Social Implications of Scientific Discovery,* delivered at the American Philosophical Society, Philadelphia, March 15, 1938 [Lancaster, 1938].

1840. In other words, the average wage earner in America can today buy seven times as much with his wages as he could in 1840; or more than twice as much as he could in 1910. Also despite increasing population and increasing use of labor-saving machinery, the percentage of our population gainfully employed increased 25 per cent between 1870 and 1930.

"More material progress has been made during the past one hundred and fifty years under the American system of business enterprise than during all the preceding centuries in world history. This record of achievement is a challenge to those who would radically change that system. . . . Under this system, the United States with a population of less than 7 per cent of the world's total controls about 40 per cent of the wealth of the world. One hundred years ago the average person had about 52 wants of which 16 were regarded as necessities. Today the wants number 484 on the average, of which 94 are looked upon as necessities." [3]

These facts, with their primary cause, are basic in enabling us to forecast the possibilities of improvement and of acquiring a state of true democratic liberalism in the century that is ahead. They make it well-nigh certain that we shall increase in economic well-being and in potential liberty in the future just as we have in the past in just the proportion in which we continue to apply science and engineering to our industries and thus produce more and more in goods and services per man hour, thus freeing more and more men, more and more time, and more and more brains for education, for research, for art, and thus for human freedom. There is a saturation point for automobiles and radios, but there is no such thing as saturation in education, in the service industries generally, or in liberty.

Civilization consists in the multiplication and refinement of human wants. It is a simple historical fact that these wants have actually developed with great rapidity wherever and whenever labor-saving machines have been rapidly introduced. In 1900 60 per cent of our population was on, or supported immediately by, the farm; in 1930 not over 25 per cent. Without serious unemployment in that period the millions of displaced farmers found their way into garages, service stations, newly created secretarial jobs, news reporting, a newly created telephone service, advertising, insurance, gardening, domestic service, and a thousand other service industries, and no serious or prolonged unemployment occurred until the enterprisers who normally create the new positions began to be suppressed, legislated against, and intimidated by unwise financial and political policies. The faster science and engineering are applied to industry the faster we ought to progress. There is literally no other way of comparable effectiveness to raise the standard of living, and the chief element in its effectiveness is in getting more power into the hands of the laborer so that he can produce

[3] This last paragraph of the quotation from Compton he in turn takes from a pamphlet distributed by the First National Bank of Boston.

more for himself, for in the last analysis the laborer taken as a whole gets under almost any modern social system practically all that he produces. According to the United States Department of Commerce, in 1936 labor received directly 66.5 per cent of the national income. Indirectly, it received nearly all the rest of it, since the idle rich represent an insignificant fraction of the population and they pass on practically all that they receive to workers of some kind.

My forecast of the future, then, must depend on what the future's sources of power are to be and on the cost of that power. That is why I began with a consideration of the possibility of getting more work out of a pound of coal. At present the main sources of power are coal and oil, with water playing a minor role and being in general more expensive. This situation will continue for a thousand years, for though the oil will perhaps be gone in fifty years, the coal will last for at least another millennium. The big steam plant is now nearly or quite as efficient as the best Diesel motor, but for small power purposes, motor vehicles and the like, the internal combustion engine is and will continue to be indispensable. However, we already know how to make liquid fuel from coal, so that when the oil is gone we shall still be able to get liquid fuel for our internal combustion engines. There are, I think, no other possible sources of power of comparable cheapness. When the oil and the coal are gone we shall get our power either directly from the sun through solar motors or windmills or tidal machines, or else indirectly through growing and burning plants; but it will then cost us more than it does now. So far as tapping the energy "locked up in the atoms" is concerned, we can dismiss that possibility. We can of course do it now in principle through radioactivity, but I see no possibility fifty years from now of supplying the world's power needs, or even a minute portion of them, from any such source.

For the foregoing reasons, then, fifty years from now the world will look to us, from the point of view of power, not so very different from what it looks now. Air travel will of course have increased, but the great bulk of the freight will go as now by surface vehicles or by steamships propelled in the essential particulars much as they are today. The art of communications, too, is already a pretty well perfected art, and though it may be considerably cheaper than now, more messages being simultaneously carried over a given cable, so far as the techniques used are concerned I do not expect any very radical or startling change.

Among the natural sciences biology has the opportunity to do the big new things so far as their immediate effect on human living is concerned, and I have no doubt that in the field of public health, the control of disease, the cessation of the continuous reproduction of the unfit, etc., big advances will be made, but here I am not a competent witness, and I find on the whole those who are the most competent and informed the most conservative.

The most burning and most uncertain situation about the future has to do with social and political matters, and it should be remembered that all the preceding forecast was based on the assumption that our present civilization would not be destroyed by man's present or prospective international wickedness, stupidity, and folly. I know of no direct way in which science can prevent that, for I see no prospect of our ever being able to turn some new type of ray upon a dictator filled with the lust for power and conquest and thus transform him into a humanitarian. Indirectly, however, the sciences of explosives and poison gases, of aerodynamics, of communication with its corollary, the rapid spread of knowledge among the people, are doing the work. The fact that the ultimate resources are in the democratic countries, as the science of geology has shown (something like three-fourths of the coal and the metals, the ultimate sources of power, being in these countries) and that these countries can be and have already been roused to arm to defend themselves—that is the great influence that gives promise that a permanent method of assuring peace may ultimately be worked out. But these countries must have the intelligence, the long-range selfishness to see the hopelessness, the folly at a time like this, of a policy of division and isolation. They must obviously, it seems to me, join their powers in time to show the international bandits the hopelessness of their spring at the throat of the world. If they, including ourselves, will do this then I stand by my prognosis of a golden age of human liberty and human dignity ahead through the further growth of science and its application to the well-being of mankind.

Robert Nathan

Robert Nathan (1894-   ) was born in New York of a distinguished ancestry which relates him to the founding of both Columbia University and Barnard College. His work as poet and novelist is marked by a disarming simplicity which often masks the play of ironic fantasy. Of his novels the best known are One More Spring, The Enchanted Voyage, *and* Portrait of Jenny. *Modern military nations bent on future glory may profitably recall the great Peloponnesian War of 431 to 404 B.C. The Athenians were conquered by the Spartans. So much for history. . . .*

431 B.C.

In Sparta, yes:
Here are the archers, the chariots, the Lacedaemonians,
The pure Doric, born and bred to be soldiers,
Taken at seven into the camps, the battalions,
To learn the spear and the sword, the thrust and the counter,
To learn to kill or to die, both or either in silence.

No more songs; this is a world of trumpets.
Let the dances be warlike. There is no need of statues
Or poems now. This is Sparta, the army with banners,
The men of might, the lions, those who have glory.
They do not need other joys, they do not need the silver
Sweet flute of love in the garden at evening,
The laughter of children, the wise caresses of women,
Gentle and loving, the advice of sages, the songs of the poets.
Let Athens make poems,
Let her build statues, temples, hold her elections,
They will not help her. A soft breed, the Athenians.
Athens will fall. There will only be Sparta left;
Only the sword, the force of arms, and the saying
That whatever succeeds, succeeds. Live then, or die, in the triumph.

So shall we be remembered, the Spartans, the heroes,
The pure breed, Doric, the race without fear, without pity,
Be praised and remembered.

Perish Athens. Be forgotten forever.

Carl Sandburg

The People, Yes, of which the following is Section 87, is a long, loose compilation of American sayings and yarns, broken by "the roar and whirl of street crowds, work gangs, sidewalk clamor," bound together and given poetic validity by the confident philosophy of a writer who believes in the destiny of the common man.

THE PEOPLE LEARN

The people learn, unlearn, learn,
a builder, a wrecker, a builder again,
a juggler of shifting puppets.
     In so few eyeblinks
     In transition lightning streaks,
the people project midgets into giants,
the people shrink titans into dwarfs.

     Faiths blow on the winds
     and become shibboleths
     and deep growths
     with men ready to die
for a living word on the tongue,
for a light alive in the bones,
for dreams fluttering in the wrists.

For liberty and authority they die
though one is fire and the other water
and the balances of freedom and discipline
are a moving target with changing decoys.

Revolt and terror pay a price.
Order and law have a cost.
What is this double use of fire and water?
Where are the rulers who know this riddle?
On the fingers of one hand you can number them.
How often has a governor of the people first learned to govern himself?

The free man willing to pay and struggle and die for the freedom of himself and others

Knowing how far to subject himself to discipline and obedience for the sake
of an ordered society free from tyrants, exploiters and legalized frauds—
This free man is a rare bird and when you meet him take a good look at
him and try to figure him out because
Some day when the United States of the Earth gets going and runs smooth
and pretty there will be more of him than we have now.

VII SEARCH FOR SIGNIFICANCE

WE approach the end of our modern pilgrim's progress. In its successive aspects—youth, marriage, work, play, citizenship—we have found the raw material out of which to make our judgment of life as it is lived in the middle years of the twentieth century. "Life, how and what is it?" muttered the dying Bishop in Browning's poem. By this time we know something of the *how*. It remains to find out the *what*.

What is life? What is God? What is man? What is man's relation to God? What, in short, is truth? Here we pass from the realm of the seen and the immediate into the realm of values, which is beyond space and time.

The way to ultimate truth is long. Man has been traveling it since the dawn of intelligence, yet the wisest minds which history records have failed to answer the ancient questionings. Perhaps, indeed, the way to truth is endless. Perhaps there is no final and permanent truth. Perhaps truth is forever relative and shifting. This is scarcely a new idea. The earliest of Greek philosophers taught that all things are in flux. And modern science, for all its sufficiency, is bound to agree. The Newtonian "laws" of the eighteenth century give place to the Einsteinian "laws" of the twentieth. "In science as in religion," wrote Sir Arthur Eddington, the physicist, "the truth shines ahead as a beacon showing us the path; we do not ask to attain it; it is better far that we be permitted to seek."

But if there is no final truth, why concern ourselves with the search? remarks the pragmatist. And Alice adds, with a sigh, "I think you might do something better with time than wasting it in asking riddles that have no answers." But thinking men and women have never acknowledged that thought is futile. In Hamlet's words,

> Sure, he that made us with such large discourse,
> Looking before and after, gave us not
> That capability and god-like reason
> To fust [1] in us unus'd.

What then are the ways by which men seek the meaning of life? There are only two, the not-Me and the Me. The first is the way of outward authority, such as the creed and dogma of a given church or group. The second is the way of inward guidance of mind and heart. Each way has its appeal.

[1] Grow moldy.

Which way we choose depends on what we are. The believer craves the serenity which comes of following a guide. The seeker requires the endless adventuring of the free spirit. But the second way is harder, its promises less assured.

To what extent we shall be led by reason, to what extent by intuition, is a question not to be disregarded, even in an age of science. Reason, mind, intelligence will carry us only part of the way to the truth. The biologist can take us back through the endless generations of organic life, but he stops at the point where, out of blind chemical forces, the genes "happened" to be formed. So much for the question, "What is man?" And the astronomer can tell us little more, except to take us even farther back into the nebulous fires of creation. The scientific reason tells us nothing of God, except by implication of the Unknown in the Known. "Thus far and no farther," says science. But we are loath to stop there. We feel like the disappointed mountain climbers in Bertrand Russell's parable who win the summit only to find there a refreshment pavilion, complete with radio, but entirely surrounded by fog.

Beyond the bounds of scientific knowledge we have to postulate God. But a postulate is cold comfort. Nobody ever died for a postulate. And so the intuitive mystery which we call the heart presents the more satisfying answer of God-through-faith.

> It is not wisdom to be only wise,
> And on the inward vision close the eyes,
> But it is wisdom to believe the heart . . .
> To trust the soul's invincible surmise . . .

By combining reason and faith, the wisdom of the mind and the vision of the heart, man can feel that he gains something against the darkness, that he approaches nearer the truth.

In terms of literature, prose is the language of the mind, poetry the language of the heart. Prose tends to be logical, poetry intuitive. Prose discusses the reasons for belief, poetry is belief speaking. Prose questions, defines, explores, argues. Poetry triumphantly affirms. Prose says what can be said, poetry says what can be felt. Prose asserts that two and two are four; poetry finds that two and two are four and something plus. Plus what? Even poetry cannot say. Only by exercise of the spiritual imagination can we dimly apprehend the something plus. Yet in that mystical remainder is hid the secret of all our inquiry.

In poetry we can see ourselves as wayfarers through the whistling void, where the strange star-fires burn to right and left, where night wheels relentlessly up the curving east, and youth and beauty pass. In fantasy, which is a sort of poetry, we begin to understand the nature of time, by which our lives are related to the farthest corner of space. By religious revelation, which is akin to poetry, we can approach the divine. And even scientific truth, transformed by the poetic imagination, permits us to penetrate the future, until the future becomes present to us. "Only poetry imagines, and imagining creates, the world that men can wish to live in and make true."

There is no one answer, certainly, to the question, What is truth? In the pages which follow are some attempted answers, mostly in poetry or fantasy. Out of them you have to start to fashion your philosophy, your system of ideas which you can believe, which you can live by. Here are means for shaping your private cosmos. In a disordered world it behooves us to seek the thread of meaning which binds life into a whole.

May your ends be good, though up ahead the way seems cloudy with uncertainties. One thing is clear: that into this future you take with you all those values which are true and honest and of good report. They will outlive war and change. They are the inextinguishable vision that gives hope and significance to life. They are the promise of the future that is assured to free men everywhere who face life unafraid.

Youth today need not be a lost generation. It need only think things through in order to travel beyond the Waste Land. It has only to remember Emerson's rebuke to the easily despairing: "You have allowed the sky to fall out of your landscape." In the counsel of a later philosopher we are reminded that the sky has not fallen, that "it never has done so; it never will."

To an air-minded generation: Try the sky!

William Saroyan

In the earlier pages of this volume we have been looking at life in its successive stages. Now we ask, What does it all mean? No one writer will give us the answer, but out of the thoughts of many writers we may reach some conclusions of our own. William Saroyan speeds our inquiry with these words of positive encouragement. They stand at the beginning of his successful play, The Time of Your Life, *a play which says, through all its fantastic action: "In the time of your life, live!"*

PROLOGUE

IN the time of your life, live—so that in that good time there shall be no ugliness or death for yourself or for any life your life touches. Seek goodness everywhere, and when it is found, bring it out of its hiding-place and let it be free and unashamed. Place in matter and in flesh the least of the values, for these are the things that hold death and must pass away. Discover in all things that which shines and is beyond corruption. Encourage virtue in whatever heart it may have been driven into secrecy and sorrow by the shame and terror of the world. Ignore the obvious, for it is unworthy of the clear eye and the kindly heart. Be the inferior of no man, nor of any man be the superior. Remember that every man is a variation of yourself. No man's guilt is not yours, nor is any man's innocence a thing apart. Despise evil and ungodliness, but not men of ungodliness or evil. These, understand. Have no shame in being kindly and gentle, but if the time comes in the time of your life to kill, kill and have no regret. In the time of your life, live—so that in that wondrous time you shall not add to the misery and sorrow of the world, but shall smile to the infinite delight and mystery of it.

Conrad Aiken

These familiar lines, from Part II of "Senlin: A Biography," are part of the "futile preoccupations" of Aiken's hero. And the hero is anyone that walks this world, occasionally conscious of the "whistling void" through which our planet so casually takes its way.

MORNING SONG

It is morning, Senlin says, and in the morning
When the light drips through the shutters like the dew,
I arise, I face the sunrise,
And do the things my fathers learned to do.
Stars in the purple dusk above the rooftops
Pale in a saffron mist and seem to die,
And I myself on a swiftly tilting planet
Stand before a glass and tie my tie.

Vine leaves tap my window,
Dew-drops sing to the garden stones,
The robin chirps in the chinaberry tree
Repeating three clear tones.

It is morning. I stand by the mirror
And tie my tie once more.
While waves far off in a pale rose twilight
Crash on a white sand shore.

I stand by a mirror and comb my hair:
How small and white my face!—
The green earth tilts through a sphere of air
And bathes in a flame of space.

There are houses hanging above the stars
And stars hung under a sea . . .
And a sun far off in a shell of silence
Dapples my walls for me . . .

It is morning, Senlin says, and in the morning
Should I not pause in the light to remember god?
Upright and firm I stand on a star unstable,
He is immense and lonely as a cloud.
I will dedicate this moment before my mirror
To him alone, for him I will comb my hair.
Accept these humble offerings, cloud of silence!
I will think of you as I descend the stair.

Vine leaves tap my window,
The snail-track shines on the stones,
Dew-drops flash from the chinaberry tree
Repeating two clear tones.

It is morning, I awake from a bed of silence,
Shining I rise from the starless waters of sleep.
The walls are about me still as in the evening,
I am the same, and the same name still I keep.

The earth revolves with me, yet makes no motion,
The stars pale silently in a coral sky.
In a whistling void I stand before my mirror,
Unconcerned, and tie my tie.

There are horses neighing on far-off hills
Tossing their long white manes,
And mountains flash in the rose-white dusk,
Their shoulders black with rains . . .
It is morning. I stand by the mirror
And surprise my soul once more;
The blue air rushes above my ceiling,
There are suns beneath my floor . . .

. . . It is morning, Senlin says, I ascend from darkness
And depart on the winds of space for I know not where,
My watch is wound, a key is in my pocket,
And the sky is darkened as I descend the stair.
There are shadows across the windows, clouds in heaven,
And a god among the stars; and I will go
Thinking of him as I might think of daybreak
And humming a tune I know . . .

Vine leaves tap at the window,
Dew-drops sing to the garden stones,
The robin chirps in the chinaberry tree
Repeating three clear tones.

James Norman Hall

James Norman Hall (1887-   ), a native of Iowa, has found plenty of experience to justify his faith in the worth of living. In the First World War he enlisted in the British Army, served for two years in the Lafayette Escadrille, and later entered the United States Army. In 1920 he went with Charles Nordhoff to study the native life of the Pacific islands, and with him wrote Mutiny on the Bounty *and other books of adventure. He married a native of Tahiti, in the Society Islands, where he lived for some years. The lines below were born of a perspective on life which today is unattainable even on the lonely shores of the South Seas.*

ON THE BEACH AT ARUÈ

Opinions framed for eight-and-twenty lines:
That men are nobler than their actions show;
That "Beauty is Truth" defined, and still defines,
As much of ultimate truth as we shall know.
That ever-questing Science yet may bare
Much that is strange and new, and after all
Her farthest quests, that man will stand and stare,
Awed and humbled, at the self-same wall
That barred the way when, first, he lived in trees.
That narrow bounds can make the happiest nation
For those who scorn to emulate the bees
In industry, the ants in population.

That of our crimes against ourselves, the latest,
Distance conquered, is among the greatest.

That love of power is the vilest weed
Growing in human hearts, and soon or late
The ruled and wronged of every class and creed
Will rise to curb their enemy, the State.
That those who make a very god of Reason
Are wanting it, if at her shrine they kneel,
Attending there both in and out of season,
Careless of what Unreason may reveal.
That dreams of peace, a full millennium hence,
Will still be dreams of peace, and cocks will crow
As blithely, then, upon the barnyard fence,
As now they do, regardless of our woe.
That life, for all the woe, is worth the living
Even today, and worth the risk of giving.

Thomas Hardy

Thomas Hardy (1840-1928) was the last of the Victorian novelists, the first of the modern poets. A native of Dorchester, he lovingly related the life of the Wessex countryside where he passed almost the whole of his long life. Most of his poetry was written after he had abandoned prose and when he was past sixty years of age. Hardy did not like to be called a pessimist. Not given to self-deception, he yet would allow to others a revelation of happiness which was denied to him.

THE DARKLING THRUSH

I leant upon a coppice gate
   When Frost was spectre-gray,
And Winter's dregs made desolate
   The weakening eye of day.
The tangled bine-stems scored the sky
   Like strings of broken lyres,
And all mankind that haunted nigh
   Had sought their household fires.

The land's sharp features seemed to be
   The Century's corpse outleant,

His crypt the cloudy canopy,
   The wind his death-lament.
The ancient pulse of germ and birth
   Was shrunken hard and dry,
And every spirit upon earth
   Seemed fervourless as I.

At once a voice arose among
   The bleak twigs overhead
In a full-hearted evensong
   Of joy illimited;
An aged thrush, frail, gaunt, and small,
   In blast-beruffled plume,
Had chosen thus to fling his soul
   Upon the growing gloom.

So little cause for carollings
   Of such ecstatic sound
Was written on terrestrial things
   Afar or nigh around,
That I could think there trembled through
   His happy good-night air
Some blessed Hope, whereof he knew,
   And I was unaware.

Edna St. Vincent Millay

In Conversation at Midnight *Miss Millay presents a group of men against a modern background talking of a wide diversity of subjects. In some of these subjects she is less convincing than in others; but in the words here quoted from the priest, Anselmo, she presents a clear statement of the Catholic position.*

From CONVERSATION AT MIDNIGHT

There is no peace on earth today save the peace in the heart
At home with God. From that sure habitation
The heart looks forth upon the sorrows of the savage world
And pities them, and ministers to them; but is not implicated.

All else has failed, as it must always fail.
No man can be at peace with his neighbor who is not at peace
With himself; the troubled mind is a trouble maker.

There is no freedom like the freedom of a man who sees his duty plain
And does it without demur; the edges of the torn brain
In him knit properly and heal;
The jangled bells are tuned, and peal
Once more from the sunny belfry in a morning clear and mild
Like to those mornings when he woke and wondered
What rapture was in store,—and it was only the simple day!
Bright mornings when he was a child.

How sweet when the battle is lost to unbuckle from the weary shoulders
The straps that cut and gall,
And let the heavy armor fall;
Let clatter to the floor and abandon where it lies
The shield whereon he took
All day shock upon shock
Of the opposing lance, his angel in disguise.

The act of complete submission to the Divine Will
Is to you an ignominious act,
An expedient of the cruelly pressed, an ugly pact
To save the soul at the expense of the soul's pride:
A mess of pottage in exchange for a princely heritage denied.
Can you not see that to surrender darkness to light is to be still
Valiant, and more valiant than before, and at length victor?
Or do you think so ill
Of light, as such, that it must walk in your Triumph as planned, and the
     way for it cleared
By a blind lictor?

✦

Anselmo said, and took in his brown hands
Quietly the small ebony crucifix
That hung between his knees, "Knowledge expands,
And men grow canny; yet if they cannot mix
Science and Jesus, they leave Jesus out—
Though Science, like the ogre on the mat,
Turns into fog, snake, demon, leaves in doubt
His face for ever; and Christ has not done that.
Out of such peace as can be troubled only
By your distress, I spoke; and I have erred.

You heard me through with deference; I saw plainly
You strove to get my drift—and got no word.
I am chagrined, like one who has defined
The colors of sunset to a friend born blind."

Irwin Edman

Out of the chaos caused by two world wars, thoughtful men turn to the consolations of philosophy. In "Candle in the Dark" the conflict between the hopes and the realities of our time is resolved. We see the present "at arm's length," we take the long-run view which only history and philosophy can give. We discover in the present all those good things by which men and women have always lived: play, friendship, work, the arts, creative thought, decency, kindliness. Ours are still the promises of science, of democracy, of co-operation, however the present may interrupt their fulfillment. The eternal is implicit in the present. "A vivid sense of the present is one of the best antidotes to despair."

CANDLE IN THE DARK

THE faiths by which men live are various, and some, like love, happiness, progress, and success, may hardly be recognized as faiths at all. But they are beliefs and men act on them. To sensitive human beings everywhere the most serious of casualties has already come. That casualty is the collapse of everything by which the hopeful spirit or the generous mind has lived. For the second time in a generation the brutal futility of war has broken out in the very heart of the civilized world, in lands that are the sources of ourselves and our culture. Whatever be the causes, whatever the necessity, the fact that there could be such causes and such necessity has already eaten like a canker into the bloom of every value we enjoy and every ideal we cherish. It has seemed to make a mockery of all our hopes, and nonsense of all our knowledge. It has turned the faith in education into an irony and has reduced to triviality the arts on which men have lavished their technical mastery and their lyric flame. It has made even private joys seem precarious and shame-faced. What do all these things avail, when they end in deliberate death and incalculable chaos? Men in the nineteenth century were sad that they could no longer believe in God. They are more deeply saddened now by the fact that they can no longer believe in man.

What, in the face of such overwhelming collapse, is there for us to escape to or to cling to or to lean on? Where may we turn, in Æ's wonderful phrases, from "the politics of time" to "the politics of eternity"?

✦

The first ray of hope, perhaps, lies in the discovery that the darkness may be not so absolute as we had supposed. Nihilism is a form of hysteria, and hysteria occurs where the patient, having no possible solution, moans incoherently in confused defeat. Bad as the present is, it seems worse than any past only by virtue of the fact that it has its sharp edge of being here and now. This is, of course, not the first time in the history of civilization that sensitive spirits, bred in a familiar culture, have declared, because that culture was changing, that all civilization was coming to an end.

This is not the first time in the history of the West that the good and the reasonable saw nothing to do but to die or to shudder. It is sobering to our too hysterical fears to take, under the guidance of competent historians, a historical perspective. It requires a hard, even a cruel effort at detachment to take the long view, but only by taking such a view can we see our present plight in something like its true proportions and find true proportions for our still persistent hopes. We shall, by so doing, discover that part of the nihilism that is in the air is the result of a strange—and absurd—conviction that we are living in a new kind of present, one without a past and without a future. Men in earlier ages, too, thought they were living at the end of the world. Nothing comes out of nothing, Lucretius once long ago informed his readers. No civilization ever ends. Let us calm ourselves a little by citing the words of an eminent historian of the Middle Ages:

The Middle Ages can be rightly understood only as a period of convalescence, slow at best, and with continual relapses, from the worst catastrophe recorded in the whole history of the Western World. . . . The break-up of the [Roman] Empire was followed by scenes of disorder, not only far more intense than what we have seen in the most unhappy districts of modern times, but prolonged for a period exceeding the worst that we can possibly fear as a result of the present international rivalries and class conflicts. . . . Generations later, when the barbarians had burst in and Alaric the Goth had even taken Rome, men felt as though the sky had fallen.[1]

The sky had not fallen; it never has done so; it never will. There is every evidence that the civilization of Western Europe as we men have known it for hundreds of years is in eclipse, in the sense that forces are coming to birth that will make it inconceivably different. What would Western culture be like without our familiar religions, arts, and aspirations? So much of our imaginative heritage is bound up with that world that radical changes in it seem very like an end, and that end very like a

[1] Coulton, *Medieval Panorama*, pp. 8-9.

tragedy. But though the Roman Empire collapsed, the elements of civilization it contained have survived. And if a complicated and decaying system of politics, finance, and privilege, blended with religion, is now passing away, that does not mean that all the past values it has enshrined are ended, or that they will not come to life again in a freer and more equitable world. The glory that was Greece continued to live in the grandeur that was Rome, and Rome endures today in our thoughts, emotions, our institutions and arts, in our laws and our languages. St. Augustine said the City of God lives on forever while the empires of man pass away. But all that counts in the City of Man, too, has survived; only the imperial matrix has vanished. Civilizations do not end; they change, and terrible as are the crises and disorders through which Western civilization has passed, it has never altogether ceased. We are too nihilistic. We prematurely and provincially assume that, because the present bodes an end to established empires, it is the end of all things. The world seemed to a good many Athenians, too, to have ended with the Peloponnesian War.

Historical-mindedness may rescue us, then, from the sense that we are living in a twilight of the gods. Perhaps our gods were not all gods, perhaps new gods are being born. But it may be argued that only from the point of view of astronomical coolness or geological leisure can one speak so calmly of the lapse of a civilization with which all the moral and esthetic and practical interests of contemporary lives are concerned. Nor can the actuality of present agonies be brushed away in such grandiose detachment. But to remember the past, to be historical-minded, if it does not give us too great expectations, at least removes us from a hysterical piling up of our worst fears and an exacerbated awareness of evil. We read of casualties by the thousand in undeclared wars in the Orient and of the tensions of the theater of war now closer to home in the West, of executions by the score in countries at peace, of starvation in lands of abundance. We ask, could anything at any time have been worse? The answer is that they could have been and that they have been. The collapse of the Roman Empire is not simply a graph in a later historian's pages. It meant actual painful disorder in the lives of millions of men for hundreds of years. Much later, the Thirty Years' War was one of the worst scourges, one of the most terrible and futile ravagings of European civilization, in recorded history. The news of it did not spread in hectic flashes instantly over the whole of mankind. But it was quite as acutely damaging to innocent and helpless individuals as anything men suffer today. The Thirty Years' War was but one among many times when the generous and reasonable could only lament and despair, if they were not themselves in too dire distress to look at that of others with either detachment or sympathy. It is not, I think, sentimentalism to point out that men have survived—certainly cultures and nations and races have survived—other crises, worse crises than even that of the national rivalries and class conflicts of today. It is true that the miseries of our own time are no less acute, its terrors no less frightening, because other ages had their share. But we need to be reminded of the epitaph of the shipwrecked sailor quoted in the Greek anthology:

> A shipwrecked sailor on this coast bids you set sail,
> Full many a gallant ship ere we were lost weathered the gale.

Our own tragedies are acutely our own, but they are not final in the universe, nor do they preclude a renascence of life in perhaps more liberal and intelligent forms. Vegetation dies every autumn but Nature does not die. So, too, with forms of human living. There will be springs again, and even now children are being born whose adult lives will begin when the storm is over, and when they may have learned to build better than we. And if the houses of their spirit have a different architecture, they may be no less beautiful; they may well be more solid and more roomy than our own inherited forms of shelter, and to the generations who will live in them quite as homely and familiar and as much the stimulus to affection and imagination as anything we have known.

But historical-mindedness has other uses than to show us that things were once worse or just as bad or just as portentous—or that Nature generates new ways of life for men. Its real uses are to show us the roots and sources of our worst evils and in the very revelation of their origins show us hints of their possible cures. This civilization itself, which we moan to see in collapse, contained, obviously, the very disease which produced the present crisis. We will not be quite so benumbed by the disaster if we see its long-range sources; we shall feel less a collectively suicidal impulse. Willy-nilly, we shall go on having expectations, for to live at all is to expect, but our hopes will be more sober and less treacherous. Historical-mindedness is important above all in giving us the habit of thinking in terms of causes and consequences. We shall see that, if not all our expectations were sober, neither were all our despairs. Why should we, in the long historical perspective, despair of science, democracy, and human nature itself?

✦

On the negative side, even the most bitter admit that physical science has been a triumphant and, as in the diabolical new technique of high explosives, sometimes a grimly spectacular success. So much have the miracles of the technique of physical science become familiar that they are banal. But we need to be reminded again how young a venture is scientific method and how limited the fields in which it has been tried. The present state to which civilization has come is not a cue to give up the hope of improvement of mankind through understanding. Rather it is brought home to us tragically to what a pass we are come when we leave human relations, private and public, to the devices of vested interests, fanatic formulas, and unin-structed passions. Small as is the area in which intelligence has been applied to social and human problems, it has been strikingly effective. Psychiatry is, in the modern sense, simply a child, yet it has begun to remake the souls of men. Where economic opportunity and stability have permitted it, educa-tion, too, for all its failures, has made thousands upon thousands of chil-dren—born, like children in any age, little bundles of animal savagery—into reasonable and decent human beings. Even in this disordered society there are thousands upon thousands of instances of relatively ordered and some-times beautiful lives. Scientific method is simply a name for the technique of human art applied to human problems. There is nothing but a challenge in the fact that the social and moral scene is still in chaos and threatens to be in worse disorder before it improves. . . .

That there is much to be done remains unquestioned; that there is much now seriously threatened no one in his senses could deny. But even under the dislocations of the past twenty years, now seen as a mere truce between wars, what *has* been done indicates what can be done. It is nothing less than hysteria or failure of nerve to believe that all is over because everything is interrupted. Indeed it would seem part of the very minimum of moral sanity today to keep in mind firmly that, however tragic and far-reaching the inter-regnum through which we are passing, it is an interregnum, even in Europe. It is to become a partner in the current madness that has overtaken the world to abet the madness by an abdication of just those interests and activities which in the long perspective make for the world's sanity. Nothing that mat-ters in an ordered time matters less now. The schools, the medicine, the research, the co-operative inquiry that are the only instruments of a better-ordered world are now more critically important than ever. It is not callous-ness but concern for the future of men that should urge us to keep alive the only enterprise working toward a more rational and equitable society. There is a parable in the story of the liberal French professor long ago imprisoned for his political opinions who returned after seven years to his class at the university and began, "As I was saying." Whatever men were saying or doing that made sense or was fruitful in life and society is no less sensible and fruitful now. It will not be less sensible or fruitful after the war is over. There is a chance, a bare chance, of course, that Europe will be an absolute chaos and shambles before peace comes. The peace that is arrived at may be no more than an armed truce. But even then men will have to begin again to rebuild, and it will only add to the destruction if the spirits and the minds of those not directly involved become a chaos and a shambles now. The methods of free inquiry and enlightened co-operative effort have been inter-rupted before. It would be foolish to the point of criminality to stifle them deliberately at a time when they are most threatened.

What holds true of the more directly scientific methods of social control holds true in equal, perhaps in greater, measure for those concerns that seem (but only superficially) the luxuries of the spirit. It is a striking historical fact that some of the quiet, powerful creations of the human race, works that have left their permanent liberating influence on mankind, were produced by men far from insensitive to the miseries of mankind, in times of apparent and of real dissolution and untold hurt to the bodies and souls of some of the best of their generation. Even in times of peace there is every temptation to be distracted and to let the noise of events in their hectic timeliness divert us from the arduous concerns of art and mind. It would do all of us some good in our hopeless moments of nihilism to recall what Pericles, according to Thucydides, said in the funeral oration over the bodies of those who had fallen in the war.

Our constitution does not copy the laws of neighboring states; we are rather a pattern to others than imitators ourselves. Its administration favors the many instead of the few; this is why it is called a democracy. If we look to the laws, they afford equal justice to all in their private differences; if to social standing, advancement in public life falls to reputation for capacity, class considerations not being allowed to interfere with merit; nor again does poverty bar the way; if a man is able to serve the state, he is not hindered by the obscurity of his condition. The freedom which we enjoy in our government extends also to our ordinary life. . . .

Further, we provide plenty of means for the mind to refresh itself from business. We celebrate games and sacrifices all the year round, and the elegance of our private establishments forms a daily source of pleasure and helps to banish the spleen; while the magnitude of our city draws the produce of the world into our harbor, so that to the Athenian the fruits of other countries are as familiar a luxury as those of his own. . . .

Nor are these the only points in which our city is worthy of admiration. We cultivate refinement without extravagance and knowledge without effeminacy; wealth we employ more for use than for show. . . .

In short, I say that as a city we are the school of Hellas; while I doubt if the world can produce a man who, where he has only himself to depend upon, is equal to so many emergencies, and graced by so happy a versatility as the Athenian. . . .

It was not of desolation or of misery that he spoke but of what Athens at its best meant.

If we cease to keep alive the things that are civilized in our society, our land is destroyed without a bomb bursting or an invader landing on our shores. There would not be much point in defending a civilization in which every civilized interest had lapsed. The arts and our intellectual activities need to be kept alive, not simply because, when they are most eloquent, clear, and free, they are the concentration of our best energies and of ourselves, but also because they are liberators and nourishers of life. It is true that, as Spinoza pointed out, the conditions of civil liberty are necessary to the preserving of intellectual freedom. But important also is the maintenance of the habit and the work of free speculation (free even from responsibility to the urgencies of the moment), for ideas permeate the atmosphere in which freedom is cherished. The arts and thinking become more somber and responsible and serious in a tragic time. They may seem irrelevant, but, paradoxically enough, their business becomes peculiarly urgent: to keep alive freedom and a deeper liberty, the play of mind and heart and imagination, in the living variety of human experience. Plato's *Republic,* Spinoza's *Ethics,* Dante's *Divine Comedy,* and Wordsworth's *Prelude* were not written when the world was quietly happy. Their pages outlived the troubled eras in which their authors lived, and have brought light and healing to men in other troubled eras. Creative art and creative thought are life-continuing and life-renewing beyond the immediate clamor, even while destruction is rampant. And their creation may renew life for generations knowing happier times or facing other perils. Out of tragedy, thinking may envisage a way to lessen the tragedy of other generations, or make images of a way of life less disastrous than our own.

+

The democracies have failed in Europe, we hear, meaning by democracy the pluto-oligarchy that has continued through constitutional forms. What makes us so certain that it could not function if it were tried? Probably three things: lack of faith in the common man, lack of belief that people could be deeply or effectively concerned with the common good, and, third, a sense that society could not be effectively planned without suppressing the liberty of individual living. . . .

God must have loved the common people, Lincoln remarked in an often-quoted utterance, because he made so many of them. The democratic hypothesis is simply that, given a chance, the common man may be a high, not a low, common denominator. For what we call the needs of the average man are those of everyone. He desires to eat, to sleep, to love. There is nothing that has happened to make us believe that those elements of decency and kindness, of living and letting live, which people exhibit if they are allowed to live without fear and insecurity, might not animate the decisions of mankind. We have not seriously tried to give the common man an adequate voice in the commonweal. It is the leaders of the democracies, not themselves democrats or brought up on a genuinely democratic concern, who have been complicitly instrumental in getting Europe into its present state. It is true now, possibly more than ever, that the generality of mankind, left to themselves, would live in amity and kindness. It is as much a challenge as ever to work for conditions of life under which people could come to be themselves, rather than to be stereotypes, or the victims of over-privilege, which makes them callous, or under-privilege, which makes them slaves.

Men and women are not angels, but they are not devils either. They are men and women. The experiment is young yet, that of arranging the conditions of life so that men and women can quietly be themselves and live decently shared lives. The community feeling in any village in Vermont, even the help and kindliness in a slum in London or New York, has shown what can be done in that direction. The battle against entrenched privilege, against authoritarianism, against snobbishness of race or caste, has been steadily going on. It is a battle quite as important in the long run as that in China or in Europe. Only when that subtler battle is successful will the bloodier battles disappear.

It is still argued in many quarters that private pleasures, private greeds, and private interests will prevent that co-operative concern for the common good which is most people's business. The average man, we are told, is too engrossed in his own little concerns, the great leaders too preoccupied by vast privileges and interests, to be occupied with the common good. I think this is largely because the common good has been conceived of as an abstraction. The common good is the good of each. But has not the war, have not totalitarian regimes, shown that a common concern, or what is pictured as being so, may be everyone's concern? Nor need private interests be sacrificed for it. It is possible, with proper education, to promote a moral equivalent for war. And many are discovering how thin are the private interests which are not shared. They have a tincture of poison in them. It is hard to realize how much moral loneliness and spiritual isolation there is in a society where people have no roots, no common bonds, no comradely concerns.

But suppose we put the worst face on it. Suppose we say that the hope for human nature, for scientific control, for co-operative sharing is not justified. As a matter of fact it is our only hope, for until the method of science and the organization of good will are made effective, we shall be paying in blood and in chaos as we have paid these tragic years. But suppose we grant that we are at the fatal turn, that every generous human hope is rendered nil. Is there anything else? There is—the present and the eternal. Bad as the present is, it is a good, as any future good must, in time, be a present, too. Whatever good it has is really good, just as good as it would be in a better time. Transitory, too, as the present is, it exhibits, as any present would, the eternal. And in the recognition of those present goods and manifestations of the eternal (for the eternal is always the same) lies a hint of what refuge we still have, if all our hopes founder.

✦

It may seem strange to the point of perversity to declare in an almost immitigably tragic time that a vivid sense of the present is one of the best antidotes to despair. But the fact is, so great is the impact of events upon us, that we are losing the capacity to realize the present at all. Even in quiet times most people live for the most part at second-hand, by labels and clichés passing for experience. In tense periods, such as that through which we are passing, we do not so much live as we are interrupted in living by dire intimations, by signals of death and darkness. We do not experience the present at all as a poet or any tree spirit or, in a word, any person completely alive feels it. Each moment is filled with such complex uncertainty that we are losing the capacity to take or to feel the moment as it is in itself—now. Haunted habitually by the thought of how all goods are threatened, we no longer have the freedom of spirit to be wholly or wholeheartedly acquainted with such goods of life as even now there are, such goods of life as persist, whatever ardors and endurances face men. These we experience at their fullest in art and play, in friendship and affection, or in our work (if we happen to be lucky), and in all those activities which release and enhance the sense of being and, with it, the sense of joy. . . .

The moments as they pass even now have their tang and character. They may yield even now the contagious joy of feeling and perception. Here are the familiar flowers, the music we love, the poetry by which we are moved. Here are the books and companions, the ideas and the relaxations, the gaieties and the co-operative tasks of our familiar world. These things may be threatened, they may be precarious, they may be ours only by the grace of God, or of geographical or economic accident. But undeniably, beckoningly, along with the portents and alarms, here they are. Here, in all tragic times, they always have been, affording challenge and delight to the senses, solace and nourishment for the affections, and friendly stimulus to the understanding.

Why should we feel that they are any less good, any less creditable, than in the past?

The days that make us happy make us wise,

John Masefield once wrote. They are instructions, by admirable instance, of what elements would go into a happy society. They are the first-hand realization of the extent to which civilization has achieved anything more than an abstract boast. That distant promised world of felicity—which we now find it so hard to believe in—what would it be in its eventual bright day but a bright day come to actuality for all mankind in the first-hand happiness men and women would experience in an eventual here and now? . . .

What better-planned economy of human hope could there be than one that took as its criteria such elements of delight and friendliness, and rationality, as are possible to the fortunate and, at moments, to the unfortunate, even now? These are paragraphs of the good life, tinctured only by the sense that such good fortune is very rare and that they are so scattered, so precarious, and that there is so little companionship in them. The awareness of these present paragraphs of the good life can be enhanced through education in the arts. Companionship in them can be increased through the still possible art of friendship even in an all-hating world. Education in delight and in the sharing of delight may be not only an antidote to the poison of despair. If made sufficiently contagious as an attitude toward life, it may be an instrument for removing the grounds for despair. If we learn now to see what the goods of life are and how they gain by being shared, the infinite possibilities of human intelligence and natural resources in the world may be organized for the common good. In the broad sense the arts will be an education in feeling, and the art of politics will be human friendship made a standard political practice.

Nor need there be any fear, I think, that the planning of the instruments of living in the interests of human happiness will be an enemy of human liberty. Planning the condition by which human beings can live at all and live together does not mean prescribing what that particular kind of happiness will be. The vaunted liberties of a democratic society have been too often the liberties of the already entrenched and privileged, the economic and moral slavery of the many. To organize the means of living for all is not to preclude the possibility of living well, or variously or individually, by each. To make and secure life for all is not to destroy liberty and happiness for each; it is to promote them. Only where "planning" becomes an end in itself, and the individual is a cog in a totalitarian machine, does organization by intelligence mean discipline by force.

A sense of the present thus has an important moral bearing, one might almost say a moral exaltation. A paradise on earth may not be impossible, for any such heaven would be composed of colors and joys and companionships such as we now in the worst of times have still been able to know. All the more reason to find the wit and the will to build a society in which these can be more generally and generously pervasive. We need not fear that human nature is incapable of such realization, for human nature is largely what its opportunities and circumstances make it. And even where its opportunities and circumstances have been extremely limited, it has broken through to heights of joy and accomplishment that should make us modify our suspicion that only cruelty and barbarism are in its heart. The history of civilization may be looked at as the history of selfishness and cruelty. But that history is the history also of saints, artists, and mystics. It ought not to be too much to believe, in the midst of disaster, that mankind can invent the conditions of human happiness, that mankind whose geniuses have invented and imagined so much, and whose simple people have enjoyed so much, under difficulty. And it is well to be reminded that such happiness is not impossible, for in the midst of violence and stupidity it has been achieved in the past; though clouded, it is being experienced fitfully even now.

✦

The eternal we have always with us and it is always at once a stimulant and an anodyne. Everyone recalls the preternatural lucidity of an autumn day, when every color, so soon to fade utterly, has for the moment the quality of timeless being. "The spirit lives in this continual sense of the ultimate in the immediate." To behold the recurrent types of energy and the spending of energy, of life and the passing of life, of hope and the disillusion that follows upon it, such beholding may—even if the energy, life, and hope be our own—raise us from the hurt and risk incident to existence in time to the peace of the eternal. To experience eternity does not take a long time. It may take an instant, as in the presence of a great work of art where the greatest number of energies are focused in the most intense concentration. On any basis of what we might wish existence to be, the prospects of our time may be very sad indeed. But would not the most peaceful society and the most secure material existence, the gayest association, have their inner voice of disillusion and disappointment, too? Does not even ecstasy of love or art borrow part of its poignancy from the hushed obbligato of fatality that hovers over it, the inner voice of futility that whispers in it? The death's head at the banquet is a grim but true image for the most radiantly happy life. But experience has half its venom removed when it is held at arm's length, with the detachment of contemplation. The crucial state of civilization at the present juncture has simply dramatized on a colossal scale the anxiety and indecision that cloud even the most auspicious turns of individual lives or the lives of nations and cultures. Life is always at some turning point. Great poets and seers have taught us in the past, they may teach us now, to behold the view. Stopping thus to behold it, its urgency, though not its tragedy, may be removed. And then we shall be enabled to behold what men have always beheld when they have raised their eyes to see: the serene, unending recurrences in Nature, the eternal forms and types of happiness and suffering, of cruelty and wisdom, of barbarism and saintliness, that perpetually return on the human scene. Even if our worst fears are realized, Nature will still breathe easily, and generate new men in new times to have hopes and fears again. While we live, at least, we can be alive in the perpetual music of the dream, the eternal note of the tragedy. And it is no small consolation to know, among these recurrences so regular as to be a kind of eternity, "the beginning, if not the fullness of beauty." That is something to have lived for, to live by, when all else fails.

If all else fails! One of the advantages of detachment is that it makes us see how hasty our despairs have been; how provincial, even on the human scale, our assumption of tragedy. The darkness now seems absolute. Men before us have forgotten that it hides the morning star.

Walter de la Mare

Walter de la Mare (1873-   ) was born in Kent and grew up in London. For eighteen years he was employed by a branch of the Standard Oil Company. Out of this experience incredibly flowered the luxuriant imaginings which fill more than a score of volumes of poems and stories. Though his earlier verses are for children, he later turns to deeper themes. The two poems which follow challenge the imaginative reader. Obviously "The Listeners" is a story of faithfulness in vain, and "The Old Angler" tells the frustration of the bright impossible dream. But implicit in De la Mare's magic are meanings to be reached only by that "suspension of disbelief" which is the approach to wonder.

THE LISTENERS

"Is there anybody there?" said the Traveler,
   Knocking on the moonlit door;
And his horse in the silence champed the grasses
   Of the forest's ferny floor.
And a bird flew up out of the turret,
   Above the Traveler's head:
And he smote upon the door again a second time;
   "Is there anybody there?" he said.
But no one descended to the Traveler;
   No head from the leaf-fringed sill
Leaned over and looked into his gray eyes,
   Where he stood perplexed and still.
But only a host of phantom listeners
   That dwelt in the lone house then
Stood listening in the quiet of the moonlight
   To that voice from the world of men:
Stood thronging the faint moonbeams on the dark stair
   That goes down to the empty hall,
Hearkening in an air stirred and shaken
   By the lonely Traveler's call.
And he felt in his heart their strangeness,
   Their stillness answering his cry,
While his horse moved, cropping the dark turf,
   'Neath the starred and leafy sky;

For he suddenly smote on the door, even
    Louder, and lifted his head:—
"Tell them I came, and no one answered,
    That I kept my word," he said.
Never the least stir made the listeners,
    Though every word he spake
Fell echoing through the shadowiness of the still house
    From the one man left awake:
Aye, they heard his foot upon the stirrup,
    And the sound of iron on stone,
And how the silence surged softly backward,
    When the plunging hoofs were gone.

THE OLD ANGLER

Twilight leaned mirrored in a pool
    Where willow boughs swept green and hoar,
Silk-clear the water, calm and cool,
    Silent the weedy shore:

There in abstracted, brooding mood
    One fishing sate. His painted float
Motionless as a planet stood;
    Motionless his boat.

A melancholy soul was this,
    With lantern jaw, gnarled hand, vague eye;
Huddled in pensive solitariness
    He had fished existence by.

Empty his creel; stolen his bait—
    Impassively he angled on,
Though mist now showed the evening late
    And daylight well-nigh gone.

Suddenly, like a tongueless bell,
    Downward his gaudy cork did glide;
A deep, low-gathering, gentle swell
    Spread slowly far and wide.

Wheeped out his tackle from noiseless winch,
    And furtive as a thief, his thumb,
With nerve intense, wound inch by inch
    A line no longer numb.

What fabulous spoil could thus unplayed
   Gape upward to a mortal air?—
He stoops engrossed; his tanned cheek greyed;
   His heart stood still: for there,

Wondrously fairing, beneath the skin
   Of secretly bubbling water seen,
Swims—not the silver of scale and fin—
   But gold immixt with green.

Deeply astir in oozy bed,
   The darkening mirror ripples and rocks:
And lo—a wan-pale, lovely head,
   Hook tangled in its locks!

Cold from her haunt—a Naiad slim.
   Shoulder and cheek gleamed ivory white;
Though now faint stars stood over him,
   The hour hard on night.

Her green eyes gazed like one half-blind
   In sudden radiance; her breast
Breathed the sweet air, while gently twined,
   'Gainst the cold water pressed,

Her lean webbed hands. She floated there,
   Light as a scentless petalled flower,
Water-drops dewing from her hair
   In tinkling beadlike shower.

So circling sidelong, her tender throat
   Uttered a grieving, desolate wail;
Shrill o'er the dark pool lapsed its note,
   Piteous as nightingale.

Ceased Echo. And he?—a life's remorse
   Welled to a tongue unapt to charm,
But never a word broke harsh and hoarse
   To quiet her alarm.

With infinite stealth his twitching thumb
   Tugged softly at the tautened gut,
Bubble-light, fair, her lips now dumb,
   She moved, and struggled not;

But with set, wild, unearthly eyes
   Pale-gleaming, fixed as if in fear,

She couched in the water, with quickening sighs,
   And floated near.

In hollow heaven the stars were at play;
   Wan glow-worms greened the pool-side grass;
Dipped the wide-bellied boat. His prey
   Gazed on; nor breathed. Alas!—

Long sterile years had come and gone;
   Youth, like a distant dream, was sped;
Heart, hope, and eyes had hungered on. . . .
   He turned a shaking head,

And clumsily groped amid the gold,
   Sleek with night dews, of that tangling hair,
Till pricked his finger keen and cold
   The barb imbedded there.

Teeth clenched, he drew his knife—"Snip, snip,"—
   Groaned, and sate shivering back; and she,
Treading the water with birdlike dip,
   Shook her sweet shoulders free:

Drew backward, smiling, infatuate fair,
   His life's disasters in her eyes,
All longing and folly, grief, despair,
   Daydreams and mysteries.

She stooped her brow; laid low her cheek,
   And, steering on that silk-tressed craft,
Out from the listening, leaf-hung creek,
   Tossed up her chin, and laughed—

A mocking, icy, inhuman note.
   One instant flashed that crystal breast,
Leaned, and was gone. Dead-still the boat:
   And the deep dark at rest.

Flits moth to flower. A water-rat
   Noses the placid ripple. And lo!
Streams a lost meteor. Night is late,
   And daybreak zephyrs flow. . . .

And he—the cheated? Dusk till morn,
   Insensate, even of hope forsook,
He muttering squats, aloof, forlorn,
   Dangling a baitless hook.

William Butler Yeats

William Butler Yeats (1865-1939), born near Dublin, spent his boyhood in the romantic western county of Sligo. At the age of twenty-three he published his first poems, the work of an extravagant romantic. He was profoundly stirred by the promise of the Irish Renaissance and became its leader. His later work cultivated a conscious austerity and a clear, hard simplicity very different from his beginnings. Of this later period "The Host of the Air" is a good example: a piece of Celtic magic "so delicate, so unobtrusive that the whole thing is like an improvisation . . . like the passing murmur of wind." As for meaning, that rests with the individual reader.

THE HOST OF THE AIR

O'Driscoll drove with a song
The wild duck and the drake
From the tall and the tufted reeds
Of the drear Hart Lake.

And he saw how the reeds grew dark
At the coming of night tide,
And dreamed of the long dim hair
Of Bridget his bride.

He heard while he sang and dreamed
A piper piping away,
And never was piping so sad,
And never was piping so gay.

And he saw young men and young girls
Who danced on a level place
And Bridget his bride among them,
With a sad and a gay face.

And the dancers crowded about him,
And many a sweet thing said,
And a young man brought him red wine
And a young girl white bread.

But Bridget drew him by the sleeve,
Away from the merry bands,

To old men playing at cards
With a twinkling of ancient hands.

The bread and the wine had a doom,
For these were the host of the air;
He sat and played in a dream
Of her long dim hair.

He played with the merry old men
And thought not of evil chance,
Until one bore Bridget his bride
Away from the merry dance.

He bore her away in his arms,
The handsomest young man there,
And his neck and his breast and his arms
Were drowned in her long dim hair.

O'Driscoll scattered the cards
And out of his dream awoke:
Old men and young men and young girls
Were gone like a drifting smoke;

But he heard high up in the air
A piper piping away,
And never was piping so sad,
And never was piping so gay.

A. E. Housman

Pessimistic as this poem may seem, it is yet a gallant defiance of "whatever brute or blackguard made the world" and a resolute summons to pick up the burden of living, as strong men have always done, whatever the odds of fate or stormy weather. Alfred Edward Housman (1859-1936) was a native of Worcestershire. His life was without notable events, and, as a biographer remarks, "He was averse to personal publicity." For ten years after attending Oxford he was a clerk in the Patent Office, London. Then he became a professor of Latin, and so continued the rest of his seventy-seven years. So he remains something of an enigma, a silent scholarly recluse whose three small volumes, A Shropshire Lad, Last Poems, and More Poems, carry the imprint of immortality. Where did he get the experience on which to build his thoughts of life and love and death? But the sources of genius are almost always obscure.

THE CHESTNUT CASTS HIS FLAMBEAUX

The chestnut casts his flambeaux, and the flowers
    Stream from the hawthorn on the wind away,
The doors clap to, the pane is blind with showers.
    Pass me the can, lad; there's an end of May.

There's one spoilt spring to scant our mortal lot,
    One season ruined of our little store.
May will be fine next year as like as not:
    Oh, ay, but then we shall be twenty-four.

We for a certainty are not the first
    Have sat in taverns while the tempest hurled
Their hopeful plans to emptiness, and cursed
    Whatever brute and blackguard made the world.

It is in truth iniquity on high
    To cheat our sentenced souls of aught they crave,
And mar the merriment as you and I
    Fare on our long fool's-errand to the grave.

Iniquity it is; but pass the can.
    My lad, no pair of kings our mothers bore;

Our only portion is the estate of man:
We want the moon, but we shall get no more.

If here today the cloud of thunder lours
Tomorrow it will hie on far behests;
The flesh will grieve on other bones than ours
Soon, and the soul will mourn in other breasts.

The troubles of our proud and angry dust
Are from eternity, and shall not fail.
Bear them we can, and if we can we must.
Shoulder the sky, my lad, and drink your ale.

Harry Emerson Fosdick

Harry Emerson Fosdick (1878-   ), born in Buffalo, is the liberal min-
ister of famous Riverside Church, New York, whose Gothic tower
showers the notes of its carillon from the heights above the Hudson
River. In this essay Dr. Fosdick frankly admits the validity of much that
science has urged against religion. But he makes a distinction between
the religions with which many people fool themselves and the sort of
religion which contains no element of self-deception; he spiritedly replies
to the scientists who, attacking this valid religion, would explain away
the deepest and noblest impulses of our nature.

ARE RELIGIOUS PEOPLE FOOLING THEMSELVES?

A FRESH criticism of religion is afoot, the sub-
tlety of which makes it difficult to counter. The gist of the contention is that
religion is a comforting fantasy. Finding ourselves in a ruthless universe, so
we are told, we imagine an illusory world of divine mercy and care and,
thus making our existence more tolerable, we cling to the subterfuge as a
sacred possession.

A wife who discovered that she had been worshipping an imaginative
construct of her husband instead of seeing clearly the real nature of the man,
once broke down in my presence with the cry "For all these years I have
supposed myself sincerely loved, but I was only fooling myself." Many today
entertain a similar suspicion about their relations with the universe. They
have believed it to be the work of a merciful God; they have seen it unified
by divine purpose and illumined by divine love; they have prayed to their
God, sung songs about him, found comfort and stimulation through faith

in him. Now, however, they wonder whether they are not fooling themselves. Is not religion the supreme example of the way mankind can enjoy an illusion?

It is time to expect this particular difficulty to arise. The physical and biological sciences are causing such radical readjustments of religious thought as will leave Christianity hardly recognizable by an ancient devotee but, while badly needing hospitalization in consequence, religion has kept its banners flying. The new universe of staggering distances is far less cozy a setting for the religious imagination to operate in than the old cosmology afforded, but it will take more than the new astronomy to banish God. Evolution has done to death some precious myths but, while landing painfully on sensitive spots, its weapons have not reached the heel of Achilles. The mathematical mechanism of natural processes has put religious thought on its mettle, but, as was pointed out long ago, hats made by machinery still fit human heads and a railroad train, mechanistic if anything is, still goes somewhere; mechanism and purpose are not antithetical, and a thoroughly mechanistic world may still be grounded in intelligence and guided by an aim.

The fresh criticism of religion starts where these old difficulties leave off. It asks why men so pertinaciously desire religious faith and so pugnaciously refuse to give it up. It inquires why religion exhibits such infinite capacity to recuperate from apparently fatal illnesses and even to revive after its obsequies have been publicly announced. This continuous ability of religion to escape from tight places, assume new forms, and settle down in strange intellectual environments must have an explanation within the nature of man himself. Man thus clings to religion, the solution runs, because he needs it. He needs it because the real universe is a Gargantuan physical process, which cares nothing for man or his values, knows nothing of him, and in the end will snuff him out. This world of fact is so intolerable that man refuses to live in it until he has overlaid it with a world of desire. Religion is thus a comforting illusion. It survives, not because it is true, but precisely because it is false; it is the world as man would like it, imaginatively superimposed on the world as it really is.

To be sure, this reduction of theology to psychology is not new; more than once in the long, running fight between religion and irreligion the completely subjective nature of God has been asserted, as, for example, by Feuerbach in the last century, but today this old method of attack has gained fresh poignancy. When it is Freudian, it posits the experience of the babe in his mother's womb as the most comfortable epoch in the human organism's existence—an experience of such sheltering care that unconsciously the adult forever wishes to return. Religion, then, with its God of love, is a psychological wish-fulfillment; it springs from the pathetic longing of the human organism in this inexorable universe to retreat to solace and peace.

No such special formulation, however, is indispensable to the interpretation of religious faith as a consoling mirage. Whether the mechanism by which it emerges is phrased in Freudian terms or not, faith can still be charged with being an illusion. Never did religion face hostile strategy more threatening. In the most dangerous hours of ascendent disbelief, when man's faith has been assailed as irrational and obsolete, it still has been possible to marshal evidence of the serviceable effects of religion on its believers, to enlarge on the comfort it confers, the doors of hope it opens, the sense of life's significance it imparts, the stimulating faiths it furnishes, the lives it invigorates and transforms. Now, however, all this is turned against the defenders of the faith.

To be sure, says the rejoinder, religion is comforting, stimulating, encouraging. That is the reason why folk are religious. This universe seen as modern science reveals it is utterly without encouragement or comfort.

> The world rolls round for ever like a mill;
> It grinds out death and life and good and ill;
> It has no purpose, heart or mind or will.

In such a cosmos the naked facts are too unendurably inhuman to be sustained with equanimity or lived upon with eagerness. But human beings, fortuitously emerging on this transient planet and living, as one astronomer puts it, like sailors who run up the rigging of a sinking ship, passionately desire to be at peace and to work with enthusiasm. Therefore, they make up religion. It springs from unconscious processes of emotional reaction. It is comparable to our concealment of the uncomfortable process of gestation under the friendly figure of the stork. It is the human organism's way of looking in another direction when the truth becomes intolerable, and there seeing what he wants to see. Religion no longer needs to be disproved; it is merely a psychological process to be explained.

By this strategy of attack some of the most potent religious artillery falls into the hands of the enemy. The more we insist on the beauty and usefulness of religious faith and extol it as a way to abundant living, the worse off, apparently, we are, for the more we lend color to the contention that religion rests on subjective desire rather than on objective fact. Thus losing so large a portion of our offensive armament, we find ourselves, as well, blasted from old defensive citadels. For in the past, no matter how difficult the intellectual readjustments may have been, we could insist that though God cannot be proved he cannot be disproved, that the path of faith is open to belief in a spiritual interpretation of the world. Now, however, the vanguard of the irreligious have no interest in disproving God; they simply explain him— he is a defense-mechanism by which we make a pitiless universe seem fatherly, a subjective fog-bank, hiding cruel facts of the real world, by calling which solid ground we make life more livable.

2

The first reaction of a religious man to this subtle and serious attack would better be frank recognition of the truth in it. Anyone acquainted with even the environs of modern psychiatry knows that not only religious imagination but every other function of the human mind is commonly used as a means of substituting desire for reality. "Anything to escape, to color the spectacles!" exclaims one of Warwick Deeping's characters. The psychiatrist suspects that human life is largely lived on that basis. Defense-mechanisms, rationalizations, and wish-fantasies, by which we sidestep the actual and escape into some desired fairyland, abound in the human mind. Indeed, tricks of evasion and self-deceit so infest our thinking that their presence in religion is only a small portion of the total problem which they represent.

"As one runs through the literature of the psychiatrist and the psychoanalyst of the day," writes Professor Gault, "one gains the impression that much of our behavior and almost every emotional reaction that one experiences is a defense." Drunkenness is a defense-mechanism by which we escape from humdrum conditions, boasting a compensatory device by which we elude a real sense of inferiority and simulate a superior attitude, daydreams a means of flight from a world of tiresome fact to a world of desire, hysteria a form of subconscious shirking, and a Micawberish faith that something will turn up, a familiar psychological alibi for directive thinking and hard work. The most difficult task in the world for most people is courageously to deal with reality. Our sanitariums are full of folk who, eluding constructive handling of their factual problems, have subconsciously betaken themselves to neurasthenia until neurasthenia has taken hold on them, and any one of us intelligently watching his own mind can catch it weaving its cunning subterfuges of escape. That is to say, the charge now made against religion, that it can be used and is being used as a substitute for facing real facts, is a charge that can be made against the whole mental life of man.

To be sure, religion is commonly employed as a means of retreat from disturbing facts! So are countless other things from cocaine, day-dreams, and detective stories, to music, poetry, and ordinary optimism. "Land sakes!" said one poor woman in Middletown, "I don't see how people live at all who don't cheer themselves up by thinkin' of God and Heaven." Many people's faith is thus a practical way of finding cheer when untoward circumstances press too ruthlessly upon them. Granted that such religion is naïve, not at all concerned with the philosophic truth about the universe, and taken for granted as a useful means of achieving solace in an uncomfortable world, one may say, even on this level, that, considering the various other defense-mechanisms popularly employed to cheer people up, we may be thankful that some folk still remain who reach the goal of inward joy by thinking about God.

While, however, this practical and largely unconsidered retreat upon religious faith because of its comforting effects is inevitably to be expected, intelligent exponents of religion cannot be complacent about the matter. Undoubtedly, many religious people are fooling themselves. Careless of the facts of the universe, they try by imaginative devices to wangle out of life a temporary peace of mind. They surround themselves with an impinging world of friendly saints and angels; believe what they wish to believe about the goodness of God, the spiritual significance of life, the hope of immortality; display militant impatience at any disturbance of their faiths and expectations. The impression they make on the detached observer is unfortunate. He is inclined to feel, like one young collegian, that "Religion is nothing but a chloroform mask into which the weak and unhappy stick their faces."

Obviously, such disparagement depends on an interpretation of religion in comfortable terms. No austere religion of self-renunciation would suggest this criticism. Our soft and sentimental modernism, therefore, must in this matter accept heavy responsibility, for it undoubtedly has led Christianity into the defile where this ambush could be sprung with deadliest effect. The old orthodoxy was by no means so susceptible of interpretation in terms of comfort. Men believed in a Calvinistic God who from all eternity had foredoomed multitudes of his children to eternal hell. Preachers drove women mad and made strong men cry out in terror by their pictures of God holding sinners over the infernal pit and likely at any moment to let go. One who, like myself, has now a long memory can recall those days when fear haunted the sanctuary. When I was seven I cried myself to sleep in dread that I was going to hell and when I was nine I was ill from panic terror lest I had committed the unpardonable sin. Had the idea been broached in those days that religion is merely a psychological device by which we solace ourselves, it would have been difficult to see the point.

Against this reign of terror in religion the new theology revolted. Judgment Day was allegorized; hell was sublimated; predestination was denied; God was sentimentalized. Whatever was harsh, grim, forbidding in the old religion was crowded to the periphery or thrust out altogether, and whatever was lovely, comforting, hopeful was made central. Religion became a song about the ideal life, the love of God, the hope of heaven. Many of the older generation still remember how like the water and bread of life this new interpretation seemed. It was part and parcel of the *Zeitgeist;* it accorded with the mid-Victorian attitude; it emerged in Browning's gorgeous optimism as well as in the sentimentality of gospel hymns. Skeptics might doubt and science pose difficult problems, but we knew that in this inspiring faith of religion—a good God, a morally trustworthy universe, an onward and upward march forever—we had found the secret of triumphant living. And now the ambush breaks upon this very position. Our strategy apparently has gone awry and the very battle-line we chose has given to the irreligious the best opportunity they ever had. They grant everything we say about the loveliness and comfort of our faith; they agree that it inspires, consoles, enheartens, and pacifies; they consent to the claim that it is emotionally satisfying and often practically useful. The fact that it is all this, they say, explains its emergence. It is a fantasy constructed for this very purpose. It is man's subjective method of making himself more comfortable in an uncomfortable world.

What we face today, therefore, is not only the universal tendency in human nature to sugarcoat stern fact with fantasy, but this tendency accentuated by a type of religion which lends itself readily to such saccharine use. The upshot is that multitudes of religious people are unquestionably fooling themselves. The chief engineer of the Eighth Avenue Subway recently told me that he had received a letter from a woman demanding that the blasting on the subway be stopped because it interfered with the singing of her pet canary. That woman's outlook illustrates much popular religion. Her ego had pushed itself into the center of the city's life; her pet canary's singing had become to her a crucial matter of metropolitan concern; the vast enterprises of the municipality should in her opinion turn aside for her pet. A similar frame of mind characterizes egocentric religion.

To be sure, some two billion years ago this little planet broke off from its parent sun and started on its orbit of six hundred million miles. To be sure, the sun itself is but a tiny thing—millions of it could be lost in a star like Betelgeuse. To be sure, there are extragalactic nebulae from which light speeding 186,000 miles a second has been travelling 140,000,000 years to reach us. The cosmos is a blasting operation on a titanic scale. This fact does not shut out the possibility that the Power behind the universe may ultimately be interested in personality. The Eighth Avenue Subway is concerned with personality; the welfare of persons is its object. Individual whimsies, however, do not count; pet canaries are not determinative. So our universe is a stern affair, and the God of it, as Jesus said in his parable, is like an "austere man." He has no pets, he plays no favorites, he stops no blasting for any man's canary. Law rules in this cosmos, not magic. There are no Aladdin's lamps. To forget that is to run with the egocentric multitude into a religion of illusion.

It is one thing, however, thus to grant that religious imagination, like every other mental functioning, is used to produce egotistically satisfying fantasies; it is another thing to claim that so obvious a fact finally disposes of religion. The latter is a much more weighty proposition than can be supported by any psychoanalysis of religious wish-fulfillments.

3

The claim that religion essentially is fantasy is just as strong or weak as the materialistic world-view with which it starts. For whether explicit or not, materialism, by whatever special name it may now be called to distinguish it from discredited predecessors, supplies these new strategists with their base of operations. They begin with a merely quantitative universe; they assume its metrical aspects to be original and creative; the cosmos, in their view, has emerged from the automatic organization of physical energy-units. With this for their beginning, their ending is inevitable: all man's qualitative life—his disinterested love of truth, beauty, and goodness—is purely subjective. In so far as his mind discovers quantitative facts, man may be knowing the outer world somewhat as it really is, but when, so we are told, man tries to externalize his esthetic and moral life, to posit a good God, or see artistry as a structural fact in the universe, or interpret social progress in terms of cosmic purpose, he is fooling himself. Nothing outside his own psychological processes corresponds with what he experiences as creative spiritual life. Since, therefore, there is neither goodness, purpose, intelligence, artistry, nor any other spiritual quality present in the universe external to man, all religion, in so far as it inspires man with the faith that his spiritual life is a revelation of the universal life, is fallacious. On that basis alone can the claim be erected that religion is essentially a fantasy. With that for a starting point one may go on to say with a character in a modern novel, "Man invents religion to hide the full horror of the universe's complete indifference, for it is horrible."

It is necessary to insist that this new psychological attack on religion does rest back on a materialistic foundation, and is just as steady or as shaky as its base. Too frequently these new strategists are unwilling to make a frank statement of their world-view. The number of thoroughgoing minds like Bertrand Russell's, saying straightly, "omnipotent matter rolls on its relentless way," and drawing the legitimate conclusion that religion is, of course, subjective finery with which we clothe an inexorable world, is small. Most of the humanists who elide all extrahuman elements from religion and reduce it to subjectivism discreetly draw a veil of silence over their world-view.

Once in a while some lucid mind, disliking clandestine dealing, states frankly what the upshot is to human life on this planet when his philosophy is granted. So Mr. Everett Dean Martin says: "At the end of all our strivings and efforts science sees our world a frozen clod whirling through emptiness about a cheerless and exhausted sun, bearing on its sides the marks of man's once hopeful activity, fragments of his works of art mixed with glacial debris, all waiting in the dark for millenniums until the final crash comes, when even the burned out sun shall be shattered in collision with another like it, and the story shall all be over while there is no one to remember and none to care. All will be as if it had never been." Obviously, in a universe where all spiritual values are thus casual, fortuitous, and transient, religion is an illusion. On that basis one might even say with Goncourt that "Life is a nightmare between two nothings," and add that religion is a subterfuge for inducing sweeter dreams. Most of the new strategists, however, never go through with their position to this logical conclusion but, forgetting their total world-view as best they can, like Mr. Lippmann they play around with such optimisms as happen to intrigue them. The fact is that when it comes to indulging in defense-mechanisms and fantasies the humanists practice it quite as commonly as the theists.

One editor, for example, rather desperately trying to be a humanist, says, "We ought to push gently aside the subject of cosmology for a season, and come to ontology. Not the universe, but man, is our proper study." The picture of this editor endeavoring "gently" to get the cosmos out of sight is one of the most priceless things that recent religious discussion has produced. Unfortunately this method of retreat from reality, this legerdemain by which the cosmos is "gently" secreted from view, is common. Nevertheless, the cosmos is important.

Indeed, the claim that religion is essentially a branch of pathological psychology is based upon gigantic assumptions about the cosmos. For example, it accuses the religious man who believes that the world has mind behind it and in it of constructing a fantasy to please himself, and in so doing it assumes that the world does not have mind behind it or in it, but is a potpourri and salmagundi of mindless forces. That is an immense assumption. As a matter of fact, this universe does not seem to be a non-mental process into which we import rationality as a comforting myth. The Woolworth Tower is no merely physical thing separable from mind; it is objectified thought. Abstract from it its mathematics, the ideas and plans which mind injected and without which it could not be understood at all, and the remainder would not be a tower. The very substance of the Woolworth Tower, the factors which make it cohere, are mental.

The mind's relationship with the intelligible universe as a whole is not altogether different from this. All the world of things we know lies within the apprehension of our minds. The very distances between the stars exist for us in our mental measurements. The realm of science, its formulations of law and its ideas of cause and effect are not directly given in our sensations of the outer world, but exist primarily in the world of thought. It is just as true to say that the cosmos exists in our minds as to say that our minds exist in the cosmos. So obvious is this that when Professor Jeans closes his essay, "Eos," setting forth the breath-taking marvels of modern astronomy, he decribes man as an infant gazing at it all and says, "Ever the old question obtrudes itself as to whether the infant has any means of knowing that it is not dreaming all the time. The picture it sees may be merely a creation of its own mind." Personally, I doubt that, but certainly the idea that physical energy-units have merely tossed us up into existence in a chance burst of energy and that our minds are aliens here in a non-mental world, fooling themselves by thinking there is sense in it, is no adequate account of the situation. The universe as we know it is thoroughly mental.

Harry Elmer Barnes recently wrote, "Astronomically speaking, man is almost totally negligible," to which George Albert Coe whipped back an answer, "'Astronomically speaking, man is' the astronomer." Quite so! There is no sense in claiming that astronomy belittles man when the astronomical universe which man marvels at is alike the discovery and the construct of man's mind.

These new strategists also accuse the religious man of wildly practicing fantasy when he reads the meaning of the cosmic process in terms of its highest revelation, personality. That accusation involves the assumption that personality is not a revelation of anything beyond itself, that while stars, rocks, and atoms are truth-tellers about the cosmos, the most significant thing we know, self-conscious being with powers of reflective thought, creative art, developing goodness, and effective purpose, has nothing to reveal. That is a gigantic assumption.

As a matter of fact, personality with its creative powers, spiritual achievements, developing civilizations, alluring possibilities, is here. However the world came into being, there must be somewhere the potency from which these consequences have emerged. "King Lear" cannot be explained by merely analyzing the play into the arithmetical points which constitute the hooks and dashes, which in turn constitute the letters, which in turn constitute the words, which in turn constitute the sentences, which in turn constitute the drama. If one tries to content oneself with such analysis, one must first by sleight of hand import into the original arithmetical points the potency of such self-motivation and self-arrangement as will bring the Shakspearean consequence. Just this the mechanistic naturalist does. When no one is looking, he slips into the universe's energy-units the potentiality— whatever that may mean—to become Plato's brain and Christ's character. If one is really desirous of getting rid of illusion one may well start with discontent at this mental legerdemain.

Such an interpretation assumes that the whole universe, including the human mind itself, is the result of casual cosmic weathering, and that any spiritual meaning supposedly found there is our fantasy. In Canon Streeter's phrase, it pictures the universe as "one gigantic accident consequent upon an infinite succession of happy flukes." As a serious attempt to understand a process which has issued in Beethoven's symphonies, Einstein's cosmology, and the Sermon on the Mount, to mention nothing else, this seems painfully inadequate.

If the universal process is thus nothing but the self-organization of physical energy, then the cortex of the human brain must be included. That also is the result of self-organizing energy-units working in mechanistic patterns, and mental determinism is the inevitable consequence. The universal energy, arranging itself into nebulae, solar systems, plants, and animals, has at last arranged itself into the human brain, and from the bottom to the top of this cosmic process everything is predetermined by mechanical necessity. This means that the functioning of physical cells, working in mechanistic patterns along lines of least resistance in the brain, predetermines everything we think—Freud's arguments as well as religion's answer, Voliva's idea that the earth is flat, as well as Jeans' astronomy. The mind's relation to the brain becomes, in such a case, as some have frankly said, like the shadow cast by a moving object. That is to say, all our apparent mental choices are predetermined activities of physical energy-units—not our reasoned reply to the world but only our automatic reaction.

To say that with such a world-view religion is an illusion is to state the consequence mildly; the serious meaning of reflective thought has also disappeared into mirage.

It is the distinguished virtue of a book like Mr. Joseph Krutch's *The Modern Temper,* that in it this fact is so clearly recognized and so honestly stated. Mr. Krutch is persuaded that religion is a comforting myth. It represents the world as man would like to have it in contrast with the world as man discovers it to be. It is born of desire and is clung to because, created by desire, it is more satisfactory than cruel fact. Mr. Krutch, that is, joins heartily in the new attack on religion. But he has a thoroughgoing mind. He sees that on that basis what is true of religion is true of all the intellectual and spiritual faculties of man, that scientific optimism is as unfounded as religious optimism, that not only is man "an ethical animal in a universe which contains no ethical element," but he is a philosophical animal in a universe which contains no philosophical element; that all man's finer life—art, romance, sense of honor—is as much an alien in this world as is religion and that, if the cosmos is basically physical, then through the entire range of man's mental and moral experience he faces "an intolerable disharmony between himself and the universe." This conclusion when the premises are granted seems to me logically inevitable. In a merely quantitative world all qualitative life is alien; we are then in a night where all cows are black.

If it be true that whatever arises in our experience by psychological processes in order that life may become more livable, is, therefore, suspect, then everything is suspect. Of course, religion meets psychological needs! Of course that is why it has arisen and has so tenaciously persisted!

Of course, like everything else, if religion had not aided the survival of the human organism, it long since would have disappeared. At its best it does inspire, encourage, and enrich life; it enables men to transcend their environments, rise above them, be superior to them, and carry off a spiritual victory in the face of them. And because of this, passing through many intellectual formulations, it still abides. In this it is at one with science, love, music, art, poetry, and moral excellence. This fact alone neither credits nor discredits anything in man's experience.

The great question on the answer to which all depends still remains: *why* a universe in which beings have evolved who cannot live without such spiritual values? The extraordinary datum to be dealt with is that, as a matter of fact, personalities exist, finding life intolerable without philosophy, ethics, art, music, and religion. The cosmos has produced us, has forced us, if we are to survive on honorable terms, to develop such spiritual faculties, has set a livable life as a prize not to be won without the creation and maintenance of these higher powers. It must require a particular kind of cosmos to act that way. The fact of personality, with its intellectual and spiritual needs, is the most amazing with which the universe faces us, and no detailed analysis of psychological mechanisms can seriously affect its explanation; it is the total fact which waits to be understood. That out of the cosmos has come a being too significant to find contentment without spiritual interpretations of his life is the basic datum on which intelligent religion rests its case.

<h3 style="text-align:center">4</h3>

The ultimate answer to this new attack, however, does not lie in the realm of intellectual discourse. The attack will continue until we popularly achieve a type of religion which does not come within its line of fire. Our real trouble is egocentric religion, which does egregiously fool its devotees. A comfortable modernism which, eliminating harsh and obsolete orthodoxies and making a few mental adjustments to scientific world-views, contents itself with a sentimentalized God and a roseate optimism will, if it continues, encourage the worst opinions of religion as a pacifying fantasy. Such a lush gospel will claim its devotees, but minds with any sinew in them turn away. Modern Christianity has grown soft, sentimental, saccharine. It has taken on pink flesh and lost strong bone. It has become too much flute and too little trumpet. It has fallen from the stimulating altitudes of austerity and rigor, where high religion customarily has walked. In consequence it is called a mere wish-fulfillment because it acts that way. "No completely healthy intelligent person," says one of our psychologists, "who has not suffered some misfortune can ever be truly religious." That is not so much intellectual judgment as peevishness, but the writer could easily claim that he had much to be peevish about.

The only adequate answer is a kind of religion which a "completely healthy intelligent person"—if there are any such—can welcome with the consent of all his faculties. At least three elements, I think, are crucially required.

A religion in holding which a man does not fool himself must take into full account the law-abiding nature of the world. Most popular religion is not yet within sight of that goal. Just as astronomy came out of astrology and on our back streets still displays the left-overs of its ancient superstition, or as chemistry came out of alchemy and labored for centuries to throw off its old credulities, so religion came out of magic. Primitive religion was magical and primitive magic was religious. The adhesive power of magical ideas is prodigious, and millions of people in the modern world retain a magical faith. They try to use God as a short-cut to get things they want because they want them, and not at all because they have fulfilled the law-abiding conditions for getting them.

To be sure, religious men do lip-service to the reign of law. They even acclaim it and quote stock arguments by which a law-abiding world can be conceived as under the governance of God. But too seldom have they grasped in either thought or practice the basic implication of the reign of law—that nothing can be won except by fulfilling the law-abiding conditions for getting it.

Especially does this magical attitude persist in prayer. Even the plain lessons of history are lost on multitudes of pious believers. They know or ought to know the story of the plagues that once devastated the Western world and of the prayers lifted in agonized desire and faith against them. They should know also that plagues continued their recurrent terror until sanitary conditions were fulfilled, and that even to this day wherever those conditions are neglected all the frenzied petitions of magical religion are of no avail.

This is a law-abiding world in which a man may not run to God saying, "Stop your blasting for my pet canary!" It is fortunate that such is the case. A cosmos in which we received what we wanted because we wanted it without fulfilling the conditions for getting it would be a fool's world that could produce only fools. "If wishes were horses, beggars would ride."

If we desire physical results we must fulfil physical conditions; if we desire mental results we must fulfil mental conditions; if we desire spiritual results we must fulfil spiritual conditions—that simple, basic, obvious fact would revolutionize popular religion if once it were apprehended. Let the pious trust God if they will, but it is fantasy to trust him to break his own laws. All supernaturalism is illusion. Even the pre-scientific New Testament says, "Be not deceived; God is not mocked: for whatsoever a man soweth, that shall he also reap," which translated into modern speech means, I suppose, "Don't fool yourself; this is a law-abiding world."

Intelligent prayer in particular is not magic; it is the inward fulfilling of spiritual conditions so that appropriate spiritual results are possible. It is the very soul of personal religion, but it is not whimsical, capricious, an affair of desperate exigency expressed in spasms of appeal. It is an inward life habitually lived in such companionship that the effective consequence follows.

A man whose religion lies thus in a spiritual life which, fulfilling spiritual conditions in a law-abiding spiritual world, achieves triumphant spiritual results, is not fooling himself.

Another element is bound to characterize a religious experience which escapes illusion—self-renunciation. The egocentric nature of much popular religion is appalling. The perspective is all wrong. Even God becomes a matter of interest to many believers largely for what they can get out of him. They treat the Deity as a kind of universal valet to do odds and ends for them, a sort of "cosmic bellboy" for whom they push buttons, and who is expected to come running. "God for us," is the slogan of their faith, instead of, "Our lives for God."

As a result, much current religion becomes what the new attack takes it to be—an auxiliary of selfishness. The centripetal force of a selfish life, when that life becomes religious, sweeps the whole cosmos in. God himself becomes a nursemaid for our pets, and religion sinks into a comfortable faith that we shall be fondly taken care of, our wishes fulfilled, and our egocentric interests coddled. Professor Royce of Harvard used to tell his students never to look for "sugar-plums . . . in the home of the Infinite." That injunction is critically needed in contemporaneous religion. Looking for sugar-plums in the home of the Infinite is precisely what popular religion is concerned about.

All great religion, however, starts with self-renunciation and there is no great religion without it. Such faith is austere, rigorous, difficult. It promises no coddling and expects no sugar-plums. It does not use God as a *deus ex machina* which in an emergency will do our bidding; it believes in God as the source and conserver of spiritual values, and dedicates life to his service.

Strangely enough, Christianity has been and still is interpreted as the supreme example of a coddling, comfortable faith. Jesus' dominant doctrine, the sacredness of personality, given a selfish twist, leads Christians to put each his own personality into the center of the cosmos and to see the divine purposes arrange themselves in concentric circles around him. Are not the very hairs of our heads numbered? Is it not the will of our Father that not one of these little ones should perish? Is not egoism bursting into songs like "That will be glory for me" the essential nature of Christianity?

It is amazing to find this flaccid interpretation of a faith whose symbol is the austere Cross. No one would be so astonished as Jesus himself at this rendering of his religion. He did believe in the sacredness of every personality, but to that truth he gave a self-renouncing turn. To give his life for the liberation and elevation of personality, asking as little as possible for himself and expending as much as possible of himself—to Jesus that was the upshot of believing that personality is sacred.

Indeed, as one listens to these Freudians and their various allies, one wonders why, if they really wish to know what religion is, they do not go to its noblest exhibitions. Would they judge music by jazz when there is Beethoven or architecture by automobile filling stations when there is Chartres? What the Freudians call religion Jesus of Nazareth called sin. Such religion was one of his first temptations, and the dramatic narrative of his rejection of it is on record. The Tempter took him to the temple top, so runs the story, and there said to him, "If thou be the Son of God, cast thyself down: for it is written, He shall give his angels charge concerning thee; and in their hands they shall bear thee up, lest at any time thou dash thy foot against a stone." That is to say, Jesus was tempted of the devil to have a religion for comfort only. He was allured by the devil toward a religion in which angels would protect him from the consequences of broken law, and from that Satanic suggestion that he practice religion as the Freudians describe it he turned decisively away.

Follow, then, this life that so began its ministry, until it comes to its climax in Gethsemane. Jesus did not want to bear the torture of the Cross; he had seen folk crucified. His prayer, however, was not the egoistic cry of popular religion, "My will be done," but the contrary prayer of self-renunciation, "Not my will, but thine, be done." Is such religion a compensatory device to make life comfortable? Is it a fantasy by which we overlay cruel fact with pleasing fiction? Is it a world of desire to which we escape for easy solace from a ruthless situation?

A man whose religion, conceived in the spirit of self-renunciation, is centered in God, not as a bed to sleep on but as a banner to follow, is not fooling himself.

Moreover, a religious experience that is not deceitful will be one in which a man does not endeavor to escape the actual world but to transform it. To be sure, much nonsense is talked today about the psychological devices by which we retreat from life. The very word "escape" in modern psychiatric jargon has an undesirable significance. As a matter of fact, escapes are among the most admirable of our activities. If some of us could not retreat to nature and re-orient ourselves amid her spaces and silences we should be undone. If some of us could not escape from the hurly-burly of our mechanistic age on the magic carpets of music and poetry to live for a while in the mansions of the spirit, we should collapse. If some of us could not retreat to friendship, life would not be worth living. These are "escapes" but they reëstablish us and return us to the world not less but better fitted to grapple with reality and throw it.

Suppose, then, that a man does not believe in atheism as the solution of the cosmic problem or think that this world is

> . . . a lost ironclad
> Shipped with a crew of fools and mutineers
> To drift between the cold forts of the stars.

Suppose that he is convinced that the cosmos is a law-abiding and progressive system, grounded in intelligence and patterned by a purpose whose deepest reality is revealed in spiritual life, shall he not retreat to that? To call that in an evil sense a defense-mechanism is to beg the question. If materialism in any of its forms is true, then, to be sure, religion is a deceptive defense-mechanism, and so are most beautiful things in human experience. But if the world really does have spiritual meaning, then such religion is one of those indispensable orientations of the soul in its real environment which steady, strengthen, and transform our lives.

Religion, however, is much more than retreat, even when retreat is elevated to its noblest terms. Comfort is a strong word—fort, fortress, fortification, fortitude, fortify are its near relatives—and a great religion always has brought and always will bring comfort. But great religion does so not by escaping from the actual world but by supplying faith and courage to transform it.

When, knowing religious biography at its best, one listens to the new strategists putting religion into the same class with drugs and day-dreams as a means of escape from life, patience becomes difficult. To be sure, cheap men have always held a cheap religion. So a Buddhist priest said to a friend of mine: "Religion is a device to bring peace of mind in the midst of conditions as they are." This attitude is not exclusively Buddhist; much contemporaneous Christianity is of the same breed. It is the ultimate heresy, hating which as a travesty on religion, one welcomes Freud and all his kind if they can make the case against it plainer and press the attack upon it more relentlessly. But to call that cheap article real religion is to forget the notable exhibitions of another kind of faith, from some ancient Moses linking his life to the fortunes of a slave people until he liberated them to some modern Grenfell forgetting himself into immortality in Labrador. Such religion is not akin to drugs and day-dreams; it means not escape from but transformation of the actual world.

It will be a sad day for the race if such religion vanishes. I see no likelihood of getting out of atheism the necessary faith and hope for social progress. Atheism pictures the universe as a crazy book in dealing with which we may indeed be scientific, may count the letters and note the method of their arrangement but may not be religious and so read sense and meaning in the whole. The human mind will not forever avoid the logical consequences of such a world-view if it prevails.

"It cannot be doubted," one of the new psychological assailants writes, "that God has been a necessity to the human race, that He is still a necessity, and will long continue to be." Indeed he will, and it is notable that even those who think him an illusion admit the fact. Religion has been described as mere superstition, a left-over from the age of magic, a deliberate device of priestcraft for controlling the masses, but today such external descriptions are outmoded. Whatever else may be true of it, religion is one of the most deep-seated responses of the human organism, part and parcel of personality's method of getting on in the world. To dismiss it as a branch of pathological psychology is too cavalier a method of disposing of a profound matter.

The Freudians, in this regard, are lifting their sails into a passing gust of wind. Often clouded by ignorance and wandering in uncertainty, using fantasy when fact gives out and mistaking wishes for reality, religion shares the common fate of all things human, but at its heart even the skeptic must at times suspect that it is dealing with truth—"no transient brush of a fancied angel's wing," as Martineau put it, "but the abiding presence and persuasion of the Soul of Souls."

Julian Huxley

Few scientists would care to be so outspoken regarding religion as Julian Huxley is in the following essay. Yet, in spite of a very different approach from Fosdick's, Huxley arrives at conclusions which, though not identical with Fosdick's, are strikingly similar.

THE CREED OF A SCIENTIFIC HUMANIST

I BELIEVE that life can be worth living. I believe this in spite of pain, squalor, cruelty, unhappiness, and death. I do not believe that it is necessarily worth living, but only that for most people it can be.

I also believe that man, as individual, as group, and collectively as mankind, can achieve a satisfying purpose in existence. I believe this in spite of frustration, aimlessness, frivolity, boredom, sloth, and failure. Again I do not believe that a purpose inevitably inheres in the universe or in our existence, or that mankind is bound to achieve a satisfying purpose, but only that such a purpose can be found.

I believe that there exists a scale or hierarchy of values, ranging from simple physical comforts up to the highest satisfactions of love, esthetic enjoyment, intellect, creative achievement, virtue. I do not believe that these are absolute, or transcendental in the sense of being vouchsafed by some external power or divinity: they are the product of human nature interacting with the outer world. Nor do I suppose that we can grade every valuable experience into an accepted order, any more than I can say whether a beetle is a higher organism than a cuttlefish or a herring. But just as it can unhesitatingly be stated that there are general grades of biological organization, and that a beetle *is* a higher organism than a sponge, or a human being than a frog, so I can assert, with the general consensus of civilized human beings, that there is a higher value in Dante's *Divine Comedy* than in a popular hymn, in the scientific activity of Newton or Darwin than in solving a crossword puzzle, in the fullness of love than in sexual gratification, in selfless than in purely self-regarding activities—although each and all can have their value of a sort.

I do not believe that there is any absolute of truth, beauty, morality, or virtue, whether emanating from an external power or imposed by an internal standard. But this does not drive me to the curious conclusion, fashionable in certain quarters, that truth and beauty and goodness do not exist, or that there is no force or value in them.

I believe that there are a number of questions that it is no use our asking, because they can never be answered. Nothing but waste, worry, or unhappiness is caused by trying to solve insoluble problems. Yet some people seem determined to try. I recall the story of the philosopher and the theologian. The two were engaged in disputation and the theologian used the old quip about a philosopher resembling a blind man, in a dark room, looking for a black cat—which wasn't there. "That may be," said the philosopher: "but a theologian would have found it."

Even in matters of science, we must learn to ask the right questions. It seemed an obvious question to ask how animals inherit the result of their parents' experience, and enormous amounts of time and energy have been spent on trying to give an answer to it. It is, however, no good asking the question, for the simple reason that no such inheritance of acquired characters exists. The chemists of the eighteenth century, because they asked themselves the question, "What substance is involved in the process of burning?" became involved in the mazes of the phlogiston theory; they had to ask, "What sort of process is burning?" before they could see that it did not involve a special substance, but was merely a particular case of chemical combination.

When we come to what are usually referred to as fundamentals, the difficulty of not asking the wrong kind of question is much increased. Among most African tribes, if a person dies, the only question asked is,

"Who caused his death, and by what form of magic?" The idea of death from natural causes is unknown. Indeed, the life of the less civilized half of mankind is largely based on trying to find an answer to a wrong question, "What magical forces or powers are responsible for good or bad fortune, and how can they be circumvented or propitiated?"

I do not believe in the existence of a god or gods. The conception of divinity seems to me, though built up out of a number of real elements of experience, to be a false one, based on the quite unjustifiable postulate that there must be some more or less personal power in control of the world. We are confronted with forces beyond our control, with incomprehensible disasters, with death; and also with ecstasy, with a mystical sense of union with something greater than our ordinary selves, with sudden conversion to a new way of life, with the burden of guilt and sin and of ways in which these burdens may be lifted. In theistic religions, all these elements of actual experience have been woven into a unified body of belief and practice, in relation to the fundamental postulate of the existence of a god or gods.

I believe this fundamental postulate to be nothing more than the result of asking a wrong question, "Who or what rules the universe?" So far as we can see, it rules itself, and indeed the whole analogy with a country and its ruler is false. Even if a god does exist behind or above the universe as we experience it, we can have no knowledge of such a power: the actual gods of historical religions are only the personifications of impersonal facts of nature and of facts of our inner mental life. Though we can answer the question, "What are the Gods of actual religions?" we can only do so by dissecting them into their components and showing their divinity to be a figment of human imagination, emotion, and rationalization. The question, "What is the nature of God?" we cannot answer, since we have no means of knowing whether such a being exists or not.

Similarly with immortality. With our present faculties, we have no means of giving a categorical answer to the question whether we survive death, much less the question of what any such life after death will be like. That being so, it is a waste of time and energy to devote ourselves to the problem of achieving salvation in the life to come. However, just as the idea of God is built out of bricks of real experience, so too is the idea of salvation. If we translate salvation into terms of this world, we find that it means achieving harmony between different parts of our nature, including its subconscious depths and its rarely touched heights, and also achieving some satisfactory relation of adjustment between ourselves and the outer world, including not only the world of nature, but the social world of man. I believe it to be possible to "achieve salvation" in this sense, and right to aim at doing so, just as I believe it possible and valuable to achieve a sense of union with something bigger than our ordinary selves, even if that something be not a god but an extension of our narrow core to include in a single grasp ranges of outer experience and inner nature on which we do not ordinarily draw.

But if God and immortality be repudiated, what is left? That is the question usually thrown at the atheist's head. The orthodox believer likes to think that nothing is left. That, however, is because he has only been accustomed to think in terms of his orthodoxy.

In point of fact, a great deal is left.

That is immediately obvious from the fact that many men and women have led active, or self-sacrificing, or noble, or devoted lives without any belief in God or immortality. Buddhism in its uncorrupted form has no such belief, nor did the great nineteenth-century agnostics, nor do the orthodox Russian Communists, nor did the Stoics. Of course, the unbelievers have often been guilty of selfish or wicked actions; but so have the believers. And in any case that is not the fundamental point. The point is that without these beliefs men and women may yet possess the mainspring of full and purposive living, and just as strong a sense that existence can be worth while as is possible to the most devout believers.

I would say that this is much more readily possible today than in any previous age. The reason lies in the advances of science.

No longer are we forced to accept the external catastrophes and miseries of existence as inevitable or mysterious; no longer are we obliged to live in a world without history, where change is only meaningless. Our ancestors saw an epidemic as an act of divine punishment: to us it is a challenge to be overcome, since we know its causes and that it could be controlled or prevented. The understanding of infectious disease is entirely due to scientific advance. So, to take a very recent happening, is our understanding of the basis of nutrition, which holds out new possibilities of health and energy to the human race. So is our understanding of earthquakes and storms: if we cannot control them, we at least do not have to fear them as evidence of God's anger.

Some, at least, of our internal miseries can be lightened in the same way. Through knowledge derived from psychology, children can be prevented from growing up with an abnormal sense of guilt, and so making life a burden both to themselves and to those with whom they come into contact. We are beginning to understand the psychological roots of irrational fear and irrational cruelty: some day we shall be able to make the world a brighter place by preventing their appearance.

The ancients had no history worth mentioning. Human existence in the present was regarded as a degradation from that of the original Golden Age. Down even to the nineteenth century, what was known of human history was regarded by the nations of the West as an essentially meaningless series of episodes sandwiched into the brief space between the Creation and the Fall, a few thousand years ago, and the Second Coming and the Last

Judgment, which might be on us at any moment, and in any case could not be pushed back for more than a few thousand years into the future. In this perspective, a millennium was almost an eternity. With such an outlook, no wonder life seemed, to the great mass of humanity, "nasty, brutish and short," its miseries and shortcomings merely bewildering unless illuminated by the illusory light of religion.

Today, human history merges back into prehistory, and prehistory again into biological evolution. Our time-scale is profoundly altered. A thousand years is a short time for prehistory, which thinks in terms of hundreds of thousands of years, and an insignificant time for evolution, which deals in ten-million-year periods. The future is extended equally with the past: if it took over a thousand million years for primeval life to generate man, man and his descendants have at least an equal allowance of time before them.

Most important of all, the new history has a basis of hope. Biological evolution has been appallingly slow and appallingly wasteful. It has been cruel, it has generated the parasites and the pests as well as the more agreeable types. It has led life up innumerable blind alleys. But in spite of this, it has achieved progress. In a few lines, whose number has steadily diminished with time, it has avoided the cul-de-sac of mere specialization and arrived at a new level of organization, more harmonious and more efficient, from which it could again launch out toward greater control, greater knowledge, and greater independence. Progress is, if you will, all-round specialization. Finally, but one line was left which was able to achieve further progress: all the others had led up blind alleys. This was the line leading to the evolution of the human brain.

This at one bound altered the perspective of evolution. Experience could now be handed down from generation to generation; deliberate purpose could be substituted for the blind sifting of selection; change could be speeded up ten-thousandfold. In man evolution could become conscious. Admittedly it is far from conscious yet, but the possibility is there, and it has at least been consciously envisaged.

Seen in this perspective, human history represents but the tiniest portion of the time man has before him; it is only the first ignorant and clumsy gropings of the new type, born heir to so much biological history. Attempts at a general philosophy of history are seen in all their futility—as if someone whose acquaintance with man as a species were limited to a baby one year old should attempt a general account of the human mind and soul. The constant setbacks, the lack of improvement in certain respects for over two thousand years, are seen to be phenomena as natural as the tumbles of a child learning to walk, or the deflection of a sensitive boy's attention by the need of making a living.

The broad facts remain. Life had progressed, even before man was first evolved. Life progressed further by evolving man. Man has progressed during the half million or so years from the first Hominidae, even during the ten thousand years since the final amelioration of climate after the Ice Age. And the potentialities of progress which are revealed, once his eyes have been opened to the evolutionary vista, are unlimited.

At last we have an optimistic, instead of a pessimistic, theory of this world and our life upon it. Admittedly the optimism cannot be facile, and must be tempered with reflection on the length of time involved, on the hard work that will be necessary, on the inevitable residuum of accident and unhappiness that will remain. Perhaps we had better call it a melioristic rather than an optimistic view: but at least it preaches hope and inspires to action.

I believe very definitely that it is among human personalities that there exist the highest and most valuable achievements of the universe—or at least the highest and most valuable achievements of which we have or, apparently, can have knowledge. That means that I believe that the State exists for the development of individual lives, not individuals for the development of the State.

But I also believe that the individual is not an isolated, separate thing. An individual is a transformer of matter and experience: it is a system of relations between its own basis and the universe, including other individuals. An individual may believe that he should devote himself entirely to a cause, even sacrifice himself to it—his country, truth, art, love. It is in the devotion or the sacrifice that he becomes most himself, it is because of the devotion or sacrifice of individuals that causes become of value. But of course the individual must in many ways subordinate himself to the community—only not to the extent of believing that in the community resides any virtue higher than that of the individuals which compose it.

The community provides the machinery for the existence and development of individuals. There are those who deny the importance of social machinery, who assert that the only important thing is a change of heart, and that the right machinery is merely a natural consequence of the right inner attitude. This appears to me mere solipsism. Different kinds of social machinery predispose to different inner attitudes. The most admirable machinery is useless if the inner life is unchanged: but social machinery *can* affect the fullness and quality of life. Social machinery can be devised to make war more difficult, to promote health, to add interest to life. Let us not despise machinery in our zeal for fullness of life, any more than we should dream that machinery can ever automatically grind out perfection of living.

I believe in diversity. Every biologist knows that human beings differ in their hereditary outfits, and therefore in the possibilities that they can realize. Psychology is showing us how different are the types that jostle each other on the world's streets. No amount of persuasion or education can make the extravert really understand the introvert, the verbalist understand the lover of handicraft, the nonmathematical or nonmusical person understand the passion of the mathematician or the musician. We can try to forbid certain attitudes of mind. We could theoretically breed out much of human variety. But this would be a sacrifice. Diversity is not only the salt of life, but the basis of collective achievement. And the complement of diversity is tolerance and understanding. This does not mean rating all values alike. We must protect society against criminals: we must struggle against what we think wrong. But just as in our handling of the criminal we should try to reform rather than merely to punish, so we must try to understand why we judge others' actions as wrong, which implies trying to understand the workings of our own minds, and discounting our own prejudices.

Finally, I believe that we can never reduce our principles to any few simple terms. Existence is always too various and too complicated. We must supplement principles with faith. And the only faith that is both concrete and comprehensive is in life, its abundance and its progress. My final belief is in life.

Theodore Spencer

Theodore Spencer (1902-   ), Professor of English at Harvard, is a Shakespearean scholar as well as a poet. His original and witty poems are to be found in The Paradox in the Circle *and* An Act of Life. *A number of them are included in an album of recordings made by the author, who says that they were written to be read aloud. Except for one line, "The Circus" would read like a glorified nursery rhyme, but: "Which is show and which is you?"*

THE CIRCUS; OR ONE VIEW OF IT

Said the circus man, Oh, what do you like
Best of all about my show—
The circular rings, three rings in a row,
With animals going around, around,
Tamed to go running round, around,
And around, round, around they go;
Or perhaps you like the merry-go-round,
Horses plunging sedately up,

Horses sedately plunging down,
Going around the merry-go-round;
Or perhaps you like the clown with a hoop,
Shouting, rolling the hoop around;
Or the elephants walking around in a ring
Each trunk looped to a tail's loop,
Loosely ambling around the ring;
How do you like this part of the show?
Everything's busy and on the go;
The peanut men cry out and sing,
The round fat clown rolls on the ground,
The trapeze ladies sway and swing,
The circus horses plunge around
The circular rings, three rings in a row;
Here they come, and here they go.
And here you sit, said the circus man,
Around in a circle to watch my show;
Which is show and which is you,
Now that we're here in this circus show,
Do I know? Do you know?
But hooray for the clowns and the merry-go-round,
The painted horses plunging round,
The live, proud horses stamping the ground,
And the clowns and the elephants swinging around;
Come to my show; hooray for the show,
Hooray for the circus all the way round!
Said the round exuberant circus man.
Hooray for the show! said the circus man.

E. B. White

With the scalpel of his wit, E. B. White uncovers the soul of his subject and reveals nothing more than an infinite and foolish satisfaction— Dr. Vinton's satisfaction with his world, his God, and particularly with himself. So keen is the blade and so deft the touch that the victim is not even aware of the vivisection that has taken place. But the reader will see the point: a merely fatuous search for significance will arrive at nothing but insignificance.

DR. VINTON

THE sea pleased Dr. Vinton as no other single element ever had. He was up very early the first morning of the voyage, all shaved and dressed and ready before the room stewards had finished wiping down the corridors. It was a calm morning, a steady morning, and the alleyways were humming with the faint note of progress that always fills a ship. Dr. Vinton was gratified to discover a calm sea through his porthole, and when he stepped forth from his state-room he was glad to find men already at work.

This feeling of satisfaction, of benignity, extended outward toward the world and toward his fellow men.

"Cleaning her up, eh?" he said, passing one of the stewards. Fraternization was good at any hour: it was particularly pleasing to Dr. Vinton before breakfast. He was glad, too, that he had remembered to refer to the ship as "her."

A pleasant conceit, making a ship feminine, he thought.

The forward deck was still wet when he stepped forth, but not so wet as to displease him. Spots of it were drying in the sun, and that gave promise of a fair, dry day, and of warm weather. The sea was a shining expanse of lovely blue in which the sun had already begun to cut a bright track. And the sea, by this time, was Dr. Vinton's favorite element.

At the moment the only other occupant of the deck was the ship's cat, which had made a quick trip to the scuppers and was on its way back to the forecastle, treading gingerly the wet path. "How free the sea stretches out," said the Doctor, aloud. "Like the thoughts of Man. Like *my* thoughts on this morning," he added. No one heard him. The look-out in the crow's nest saw him, but assumed he had come on deck to be sick. A gull swung low to the water. "Graceful, tireless, free," said Dr. Vinton.

His admiration of the gull became suddenly confused with his appreciation of his own words. Graceful, tireless, free. Those words might well be the outline of a sermon. Dr. Vinton tried to dismiss the thought, but it stuck. Graceful, tireless, free—and he could visualize the way the sermon would work out: there would be five minutes of introduction (a word-picture of a beautiful morning at sea), then he'd bring in the gull, graceful, tireless, free; then ten minutes setting up the gull as an example to Man, graceful (grace is beauty and our lives must be beautiful), tireless (tireless in the service of the Master), free (free of the bonds of temptation and sin). "Oh my friends . . ." said Dr. Vinton to the ship's cat, just as it disappeared below.

All things seemed to be conspiring to put the Doctor into as fine a mood as he had ever experienced. There was just enough motion to the ship to suggest a mysterious buoyancy. He read the name of the ship painted on a life preserver. *Amaryllis.* What a pretty name. A ship that was a flower. Dr. Vinton breathed deeply of the air that was all about him in inexhaustible quantities.

A slight scraping noise attracted his attention and he looked up to where a sailor was painstakingly cleaning the brass worm-gear of a lifeboat davit, so it wouldn't jam. The sailor's neck and face were a fine red color; the lifeboat was white; the worm-gear was beginning to shine in the sun. The whole scene seemed pleasant to Dr. Vinton, although it is doubtful if he caught its utilitarian significance. "Shining her up, eh?" he called, cheerily. The sailor paused an instant, made no reply, then rubbed again. "The sea," wrote Dr. Vinton in his diary that night, "makes men silent."

Breakfast was a continuation and a heightening of the bodily and spiritual well-being that had come over the Doctor.

He not only enjoyed the food, but he revelled in his ability to eat it; for he had come aboard with an abundant faith in God but with a certain dark fear of indigestion. Now it was clear that there was nothing to be afraid of. He liked the ship's coffee, and while sipping it recounted to the others at table the experiences of early morning—how pleasant it had been on deck while things were still wet and fresh with the new day, how he had seen a gull, how graceful and tireless it was (he did not mention how free it was, he thought he would save that one), and how the sailors were out early, shining the ship. Then he took another cup of coffee.

Dr. Vinton spent most of the morning forward, watching the sea. He noticed the look-out, and once, when a ship was sighted off the starboard bow, he saw the look-out report it to the bridge with a pull on the bell lanyard. That pleased him. The eyes of a ship, he thought. Always watching, in fog, in rain, in storm. He told his table companions about it later in the dining saloon, referring to the look-out as "the outlook." In the afternoon he played shuffleboard on the sunny boat-deck with Mrs. Lamont, from Nyack, and won. He could not recall ever having had a period of such sustained good feeling, such serenity.

Not even when he spoke sharply to a sailor who was reprimanding a little boy for throwing rubber quoits rapidly into the sea, did he lose his mellow humor. "You must remember," he said to the sailor, smiling, "that he is just a little boy." The sailor made no answer and again Dr. Vinton made a mental note that the sea makes men silent.

The *Amaryllis* was a modern ship. Fans sucked in air through ventilators and cooled every cabin with a forced draught. Dr. Vinton noticed with pleasure that, go where he would, he was gently followed by a little stream of fresh air. He noticed it particularly when he went to his stateroom to clean up for dinner and sat on the lounge for a moment, resting. The air came whispering through a small hole in the air shaft and bathed his face, refreshingly. Somehow this little draught of air seemed to epitomize human progress to him. It was no longer necessary to endure the discomforts of the unenlightened past. How far we had come from the slave ships of Roman days! We were free, not only of chains, we were free of unpleasantly hot state-rooms; we were coming to be a more graceful, tireless, free race of people. Nor did Dr. Vinton regard this new freedom entirely from a selfish point of view; he thought of the men tending the burners in the engine room below, and of how they, too, were cooled by a forced draught, and he was glad for them. He enjoyed dinner.

The next day was a repetition of his good feeling, and he found good in everything. The day after that was equally pleasant. On the evening of the third day, however, the *Amaryllis* ran into a heavy fog at ten-thirty o'clock, struck an iceberg, and sank with all on board—which was the first untoward incident of the entire voyage for Dr. Vinton.

I say sank with all on board—that is not precisely the case. Through an interesting circumstance Dr. Vinton did not go down with the ship. When the disaster occurred he was in the main social hall where the ship's concert was going on, an entertainment got up by the passengers. Dr. Vinton, much to his delight, had been chosen master of ceremonies for the occasion—"a rather signal honor" was the way he had expressed it in his diary. In his introductory speech he had stressed the point of friendship on shipboard, which he said was the keynote of this little gathering. "I look upon this fortunate gathering," he said, "as a sort of clearing house for friendship. I always think of a ship as a place where lasting friendships are made. I notice that our good purser has instructed each of us to apply for landing cards, that we may properly go ashore on our arrival overseas; but if *I* were the king or the president of a country, I think I should require each visitor to present a card testifying that he, or she, had made at least one *lasting friendship* whilst aboard ship."

Dr. Vinton smiled, and then introduced little Virginia Marsh, aged nine, who danced. After a few other numbers Mrs. Lamont sang *The Valley of Laughter.*

"I am sure," said Dr. Vinton, rising to his feet, "that we have all enjoyed Mrs. Lamont's singing of this beautiful song and that she will sleep extra soundly tonight for having given all of us so much pleasure." He smiled graciously at Mrs. Lamont and then announced that a plate would be passed, everyone being urged to contribute something, however small, to the Seamen's Institute.

It was just ten-thirty when the tin collection plate was returned, full of money, to Dr. Vinton. The *Amaryllis* was steaming along through the gathering fog; but the fog was not apparent in the brightly lighted social hall, and hence it had not displeased the Doctor. Holding the plate in both hands, he turned again to the audience. "Let us sing *Auld Lang Syne,*" he said, "and then swing naturally into *America.*" At this moment the *Amaryllis* struck the iceberg and sank.

The force of the collision threw Dr. Vinton through a large porthole, and he landed on a life-raft which had broken loose at the impact and fallen into the sea. It was such a neat piece of business that it scarcely hurt Dr. Vinton (merely a slight jar to his haunches) and would not indeed have hurt him at all had his hands been free to help break the fall. His hands still clutched the collection plate. It was all so neat that only one dollar bill was lost from the plate, and Dr. Vinton immediately replaced this with a dollar from his own pocket. Then he noticed that the ship had sunk, and that it was quite foggy. "I had better pray," he said; and he did, sitting cross-legged and quite alone in the middle of the ocean. It was the first time he had ever prayed sitting cross-legged, and it seemed both uncomfortable and disrespectful. He prayed for about an hour, and then slept.

Next morning he was up early. Although he could not shave or dress, he made a few minor adjustments in his attire and ate a peppermint, which Mrs. Lamont had given him and which he had put away in a pocket because he did not like peppermints. The fog had lifted from the sea, and Dr. Vinton noticed that the tiny deck of his raft was drying in the sun. That rather pleased him. He also discovered that it was possible to stand upright on the raft without upsetting it—even to take a step or two. So he walked up and down, stretching his legs, and was very careful not to go too near the edge. Then he sat down again and removed all the money from the collection plate, counted it to make sure it was all there, wrapped it tidily in his handkerchief, and placed it in the inside pocket of his coat for safe keeping in the event of heavy weather.

He looked at his watch, pleased to find that it was still running. Seven-thirty. Dr. Vinton remembered having seen a notice on the bulletin board of the *Amaryllis* saying the clocks would be set ahead forty minutes during the night, so he set his watch ahead forty minutes, wound it, and replaced it in his pocket.

The sea was a placid blue. A few hundred feet astern of the raft Dr. Vinton noticed the iceberg which had sunk the ship. Although the berg was, of course, considerably bigger and more substantial than his raft, he made no attempt to reach it, because he thought it would be too slippery to stand on and too cold to sit on—at least that was the way icebergs had always seemed to him. But the presence of the berg, so near, so shiny, and so blue, cheered him and emphasized his own good fortune. It reminded him, naturally, of the night's disaster, and tended to help him marshal his thoughts.

Certainly he could not ascribe to a mere Divine idiosyncrasy the inescapable fact of his having been honored, in a very unusual way, above all other people in the ship. They were all dead and he was alive. As a thinking man it was his duty to try and understand that, regardless of his immediate embarrassment. Possibly, he reasoned, I have been spared because of my being the person on the ship best fitted to pray for the salvation of those who have gone down. The logic of this contented him somewhat, although he found himself speculating on the inconsistencies which always seemed to shroud an omnipotent gesture. He even found himself bothered by one or two rather trite old matters: why, if Providence was so interested in the salvation of an entire passenger list as to provide them with a survivor with powers of intercession, had Providence not gone the whole hog and moved the iceberg a few yards to one side, out of the path of the ship? Mostly, he avoided such thoughts; for he knew from experience that he could not follow them through to their conclusion without impairing his general health, which, after three bracing days at sea, was very good.

Still, thought Dr. Vinton, as long as I do not fully understand my position, I suppose the only fair thing to do is to give the passengers the benefit of the doubt. With that he prayed for those who had gone down. He prayed aloud, in a normal speaking voice, for twenty-two minutes, and noticed to his satisfaction that he used several rather fresh phrases, particularly in the subaqueous passages. Then he followed with another short prayer for himself, for although he was comfortable on the life-raft (which he had renamed "Salvation," printing the letters neatly on the deck with his pencil), he felt that his position in the middle of the Atlantic was certainly not without some peril.

This latter prayer was answered with a promptness and dispatch which did credit even to omnipotency. In getting to a kneeling posture, the Doctor had up-ended the collection plate with his toe, and the sun, striking the tin plate, had shot a bright beam of light across the sea a distance of seven miles to where the look-out of a ship was scanning the horizon, and in less than an hour Dr. Vinton had been hauled aboard and given a drink of water. He visited the purser's office without delay and gave up the money in his pocket, directing that it be turned over to the Seamen's Institute.

On his return to America, Dr. Vinton experienced a new interest in, and appreciation of, dry land. Never had the hills, the fields, the roads around Vintondale, seemed so pleasing to eye and spirit. Occasionally, in the busy months that followed, his thoughts strayed back to the *Amaryllis* and the sea, but at such times he was reminded inevitably of his own good fortune and of the unique, almost Puckish, designs of the Creator.

And he frequently thought about the sermon on the seagull—the outline of which he recalled perfectly—but it occurred to him that it might be in better taste to allow a little time to elapse before using a marine subject in the pulpit. It was part of the Doctor's policy to avoid all discussions of the *Amaryllis* incident, either in church or out; for to discuss it at all meant that sooner or later the conversation would swing round to the possible significance of the event. His escape was palpably a miracle, and Dr. Vinton rather disliked getting mixed up in the miracles—which were properly both ancient and impersonal. As for the sermon on the seagull, he waited a year, and then delivered it, one lovely bright morning: it unfolded rhythmically, just as he had envisioned it on deck that day—the seagull, graceful (grace is beauty and our lives must be beautiful), tireless (tireless in the service of the Master), free (free of the bonds of temptation and sin). "Oh my friends . . ." said Dr. Vinton to his congregation.

Robert Frost

Robert Frost presents here a humorous portrait of a New England eccentric, one who makes his own set of values with divine disregard for practicality. So a poet: there is nothing very practical about a poem, yet it sometimes splits an idea in so many directions that all at once we see something beyond the present and the practical. We see light.

THE STAR-SPLITTER

"You know Orion always comes up sideways.
Throwing a leg up over our fence of mountains,
And rising on his hands, he looks in on me
Busy outdoors by lantern-light with something
I should have done by daylight, and indeed,
After the ground is frozen, I should have done

Before it froze, and a gust flings a handful
Of waste leaves at my smoky lantern chimney
To make fun of my way of doing things,
Or else fun of Orion's having caught me.
Has a man, I should like to ask, no rights
These forces are obliged to pay respect to?"
So Brad McLaughlin mingled reckless talk
Of heavenly stars with hugger-mugger farming,
Till having failed at hugger-mugger farming,
He burned his house down for the fire insurance
And spent the proceeds on a telescope
To satisfy a life-long curiosity
About our place among the infinities.

"What do you want with one of those blame things?"
I asked him well beforehand. "Don't you get one!"
"Don't call it blamed; there isn't anything
More blameless in the sense of being less
A weapon in our human fight," he said.
"I'll have one if I sell my farm to buy it."
There where he moved the rocks to plow the ground
And plowed between the rocks he couldn't move,
Few farms changed hands; so rather than spend years
Trying to sell his farm and then not selling,
He burned his house down for the fire insurance
And bought the telescope with what it came to.
He had been heard to say by several:
"The best thing that we're put here for's to see;
The strongest thing that's given us to see with's
A telescope. Someone in every town
Seems to me owes it to the town to keep one.
In Littleton it may as well be me."
After such loose talk it was no surprise
When he did what he did and burned his house down.

Mean laughter went about the town that day
To let him know we weren't the least imposed on,
And he could wait—we'd see to him tomorrow.
But the first thing next morning, we reflected
If one by one we counted people out
For the least sin, it wouldn't take us long
To get so we had no one left to live with.
For to be social is to be forgiving.

Our thief, the one who does our stealing from us,
We don't cut off from coming to church suppers,
But what we miss we go to him and ask for.
He promptly gives it back, that is if still
Uneaten, unworn out, or undisposed of.

It wouldn't do to be too hard on Brad
About his telescope. Beyond the age
Of being given one's gift for Christmas,
He had to take the best way he knew how
To find himself in one. Well, all we said was
He took a strange thing to be roguish over.
Some sympathy was wasted on the house,
A good old-timer dating back along;
But a house isn't sentient; the house
Didn't feel anything. And if it did,
Why not regard it as a sacrifice,
And an old-fashioned sacrifice by fire,
Instead of a new-fashioned one at auction?

Out of a house and so out of a farm
At one stroke (of a match), Brad had to turn
To earn a living on the Concord railroad,
As under-ticket-agent at a station
Where his job, when he wasn't selling tickets,
Was setting out up track and down, not plants
As on a farm, but planets, evening stars
That varied in their hue from red to green.

He got a good glass for six hundred dollars.
His new job gave him leisure for star-gazing.
Often he bid me come and have a look
Up the brass barrel, velvet black inside,
At a star quaking in the other end.
I recollect a night of broken clouds
And underfoot snow melted down to ice,
And melting further in the wind to mud.
Bradford and I had out the telescope.
We spread our two legs as we spread its three,
Pointed our thoughts the way we pointed it,
And standing at our leisure till the day broke,
Said some of the best things we ever said.
That telescope was christened the Star-splitter,

Because it didn't do a thing but split
A star in two or three the way you split
A globule of quicksilver in your hand
With one stroke of your finger in the middle.
It's a star-splitter if there ever was one,
And ought to do some good if splitting stars
'S a thing to be compared with splitting wood.
We've looked and looked, but after all where are we?
Do we know any better where we are,
And how it stands between the night tonight
And a man with a smoky lantern chimney?
How different from the way it ever stood?

Norman Corwin

Norman Corwin (1910-   ) was born and educated in Boston. Upon graduation from high school he became a newspaper writer but soon turned to radio broadcasting. Then he began to experiment with the possibilities of poetry and music in dramatic synthesis on a program called "Poetic License." By 1938 he was already a writer, director, and producer of a new kind of radio show, a sort of poetic documentation of ideas, employing a literary style, an unpredictable imagination, and every resource of radio engineering. Oddly enough his plays, aimed at a better than 12-year-old intelligence, were enormously successful: "We Hold These Truths" was said to have had more than sixty million listeners. An early interventionist, he found the direction of "This Is War" a congenial task. "An American in England" was a notable venture in short-wave broadcasting. "Good Heavens" was inspired by a visit to the Yerkes Observatory in Wisconsin and conveys, better than more conventional means, the authentic excitement of astronomy. Readers who are interested in production details or in the meaning of the Harvard Observatory telegram should consult the studio notes which accompany the play in More by Corwin.

GOOD HEAVENS

VOICE (*misterioso*). Schwassmann-Wachmann . . . one . . . comet . . . Thomas . . . 18 . . . 11 . . . 0 . . . September . . . 03355 . . . 21465 . . . 11141 . . . motion 10023 . . . 10001 . . . 74095 . . . suddenly brighter . . . spectra desirable!

Music: Suspense chord.

NARRATOR. That was code—and you're quite right, you're listening to a spy story. This is about men who want to get hold of the secret plans of the super nova. This is about the riddle of the White Dwarf. . . . Interested?

Music: Introductory cue.

SECOND NARRATOR. This show concerns astronomy. That code you heard a minute back is no gag. It's the actual wording of a telegram sent out by the head astronomer of Harvard to all observatories in America. What it means would take tall explaining. First, however, we must clear up for you the matter of what kind of life goes on at astronomical observatories.

Now there are a number of common misconceptions about the way serious astronomers spend their time. The interstellar comic strips and pseudo-scientific shocker magazines have encouraged most of us to believe that on a clear night in a telescopic observatory, this sort of thing goes on. . . .

Deep power hum as of a generator, in background.

HOTCHKISS. All right, Billingsgate, you've been looking long enough. Now give me a crack at it.

BILLINGSGATE (*excited*). Wait a minute, Hotchkiss, I think I see something moving!

HOTCHKISS. You do? (*To still another astronomer, across the room.*) Oh, I say, Dr. Dumke, Billingsgate has detected life on Mars!

BILLINGSGATE. Now, just a moment, Hotchkiss, I didn't say that at all. I merely said I thought I saw something moving.

DUMKE (*coming on*). Lemme see, lemme see.

HOTCHKISS. Me first. Lemme see, Billingsgate.

BILLINGSGATE. Here you are, Hotchkiss.

HOTCHKISS. Mm. (*Up.*) Increase the magnification two magnitudes.

A deep motor sound, cross-cut by the effect of a spark gap.

HOTCHKISS. Enough!

BILLINGSGATE AND DUMKE. What do you see?

HOTCHKISS. Nothing. Billingsgate, you were seeing things.

BILLINGSGATE. I resent that, Professor. I was only—

ADDINGTON (*the director, making an entrance*). Ah, good evening, gentlemen. What's up?

ALL. Good evening, Director. Good evening, Dr. Addington.

DUMKE. Nothing new. Still searching.

ADDINGTON. Very good. Keep your eye glued to Mars. And while you're at it, be on the lookout for exploding stars and new comets. We want to be the first to see them if there are any around.

HOTCHKISS. Right, sir.

ADDINGTON. Also, check a couple of constellations for weather predictions before it gets light.

BILLINGSGATE. Yes, sir.

ADDINGTON. I'm going back to the laboratory to continue work on the rocket ship; but in the meantime, Dumke, will you give Jupiter and Venus the once-over just in case there might be signs of life on them? (*Fading.*) Never can tell when something might show up.

DUMKE. Righto, Dr. Addington. (*Up.*) Swing 'er six degrees to the west!

VOICE (*off*). Swing 'er six degrees to the west.

Buzzer; then a bell; then a blast of compressed air; finally a tremendous sound of whirring. When it stops:

DUMKE. Hold it! Ah! Wonderful sharp focus!

HOTCHKISS. Yeah? What do you see?

DUMKE. Just a moment, now.

HOTCHKISS. Lemme see, lemme see.

BILLINGSGATE. Me first. I was first. . . . (*The squabbling fades under.*)

Music: A daft cue.

NARRATOR. No, that is not what goes on in an observatory of a clear night. Astronomers don't keep their eyes glued to their telescopes. They spend very little time gazing at the fancy showpieces of the skies. They hardly ever look at the rings of Saturn or the craters of the moon—they're not at all concerned with watching the planet Mars for signals to be flashed to earth, nor do they ever make weather predictions or have a desire to travel through space on rocket ships.

Do you want to know what really is typical of a night at a big observatory like Yerkes?

Music, please, for atmosphere.

Music: A night theme, fading under:

NARRATOR. It is night in the country. A dark observatory broods under the northern constellations. Off on the horizon there's a faint glow from a town in the valley. But here it is dark—and quiet, except for the scattered small talk of insects in the fields.

Night noises in.

We hear steps on stone; they advance up stone stairs. When they stop we hear the sound of a key in a lock.

NARRATOR. This man is an astronomer. He's alone. He's opening the door of the observatory. Observatories have doors with locks in them, like your house.

A door opens, closes; as it does so, the night sounds go out. Slowly the steps advance along a stone floor and upstairs. Then a metal door opens and closes.

NARRATOR. Now he enters the dome—a great vault full of echoes, dark and cold and draughty. It is solemn, like the inquisition chambers of comic-strip characters who commute between stars.

Echo chamber in for steps on metal stairs, then across a wooden hollow floor. We hear the flick of an electric switch; then more steps.

NARRATOR. A small light goes on now—enough to make out the great hulk of a telescope mounted on a massive pier, bigger-girthed and longer than the fiercest cannon.

　Now he pulls a cord which moves a shutter in the dome.

Shutter effect—a big Venetian-blind sound, off perspective, and with echo.

NARRATOR. And now the roof is slit, the heavens shining through.

Steps on a wooden floor.

NARRATOR. This done, he walks to a control board and pulls a lever.

A slight high-pitched skidding sound, as of a transmission belt being shifted.

NARRATOR. And the floor rises. . . .

A heavy motor sound—grinding—almost like a subway train at low speed. It stops.

NARRATOR. The floor has risen beneath his feet, risen three times his height. And now he pulls another lever, and the great refractor swings around to meet the open sector of the dome.

Another skidding sound and a slower grinding mesh of heavy gears; motor noises also. At length it stops.

NARRATOR. This telescope weighs twenty tons, and yet it can be moved by hand. Our friend now reaches up and pulls the eyepiece closer to his eye. Then, having found his field . . .

ASTRONOMER. Right ascension, three hours fifty-five minutes; declination, minus thirteen degrees forty-one seconds. . . .

NARRATOR. He trains it on the star 40 Eridani—40 for its order in the ascension, Eridani for the constellation in which it appears. . . . (This ascension and declination and parallax business is over our heads in more ways than one.) . . . But what is our astronomer doing now? He's twiddling screws to move cross-wires—reading a micrometer, to set the glass steady on its objective. Meanwhile a silent mechanism keeps turning the telescope westward exactly at the rate of the earth's rotation eastward. In this way the poised and balanced superspyglass follows automatically the pin-point in the sky which the astronomer has singled out.

And now, for a moment, the image of the star is studied. . . .

Music: Star theme in.

40 Eridani! It burns like some forgotten signal lantern at a junction of two skies. The naked eye is clothed now, and it senses something of the unimaginable force that throbs so many, many billions of miles away. It gathers in the long, pulsating rays; it feels the grave and mystic splendor of this numbered sphere whose light for more than sixty years has been traveling through space to keep this rendezvous.

Music: Out.

NARRATOR. He's noted all he needs to note, and now he disengages the eyepiece . . .

Small sound of metallic attachment.

NARRATOR. . . . and substitutes for it a camera plateholder. He's going to take a photograph which later will be studied under microscopes. Exposure? Say ten seconds, for dramatic license; it might well be closer to an hour. He sets an astronomical alarm-clock for the length of the exposure:

Clean, quiet ticking. After ten seconds, an ordinary alarm-clock rings.

NARRATOR. We'll leave the doctor now, while he takes his plate and goes inside a portable dark room to develop it. When he comes out he'll enter in a date book a log of observations concerning 40 Eridani. He will fill in right ascension, declination, date, observatory weather, the outside temperature, the temperature of the telescope tube, the barometric pressure. He will go home at two A.M. Another member of the observatory staff will come in at two and use the telescope till dawn. And when the dawn comes? . . .

A little dawn music, please.

Music: A dawn theme.

NARRATOR. Do practical-minded listeners want to know what good there is in all this? After the stars have been charted, weighed, their distances determined, their elements found out—so what, do you want to know? Well, in the first place, since when does the pursuit of a pure science have to apologize to practical men?

SCIENTIST (*very apologetically*). I say, Mr. Pennypacker, do you mind if I pursue my study of spectroheliography? It may take me a lifetime, and it may yield no commercially important results, but—er—uh—

NARRATOR. What does Pennypacker know about the possible practical results of spectroheliography? Pennypacker's busy packing pennies, and let him stick to it. Even if astronomy never meant a hoot toward the improvement of human existence, that would be no reason why its work should not persist, why it should require any statement of defense.

But consider some of astronomy's more practical applications—everyday ones:

ANNOUNCER. When you hear the musical note, the time will be exactly —— minutes and —— seconds past —— o'clock, Eastern Time.[1]

Chime.

WOMAN. It will be high tide at Sandy Hook at —— A.M. tomorrow.

NAVIGATOR. Our ship's position is latitude 56 degrees 9 minutes south, longitude 77 degrees 4 minutes west.

TECHNICIAN. The War Department has just ordered forty thousand more tanks of helium.

NARRATOR (*summarizing*). Time? The special province of astronomy. Tide? The pull of sun and moon upon the earth. Navigation? Largely a system of solar and lunar measurement. Helium? An element discovered on the sun before it was discovered in the earth. And moreover, Mr. Pennypacker—

ASTRONOMER. The sun and stars hold within them the secret of releasing tremendous quantities of energy from matter. We don't yet know the answer to the riddle of the sun's renewal. If we find out, the earth will never have to worry about exhausting fuel supplies, for the energy taken from an old tin can might move a ship around the world.

NARRATOR. Matter into energy? Here are some facts which may well raise a Pennypacker's hair:

QUESTIONER. Question: How much of the sun's total energy does the earth intercept? Do you think you can guess within 20 per cent?

A pause after each of these questions to give it time to sink in and to allow the listener a chance to guess.

[1] The announcer fills in the blanks with the actual time.

ANSWERER. Answer: One twenty-millionth of 1 per cent.

QUESTIONER. Question: Within a thousand degrees, what is the temperature of the sun's interior?

ANSWERER. Answer: Ten million degrees centigrade.

QUESTIONER. Question: According to Einstein's formula, the sun is losing four million tons of mass each second. At this rate, how soon will it be before it decreases by one-half of 1 per cent? See if you can guess within six months.

ANSWERER. Answer: Seventy-five thousand million years.

NARRATOR. Time for our time motif, orchestra.

Music: Time motif.

NARRATOR. Think you know a lot about time? Do you know the time of day? Do you know what year it is? You think it's 1943? That all depends on where you are. If you asked a citizen of Tokyo, he'd say—

JAPANESE. It's the year 2603.

NARRATOR. Note, please, that in our literal translation from the Japanese our actor doesn't say—

JAPANESE (*thick singsong*). It's the year 2603.

NARRATOR. Why do all foreign people in radio dramas speak broken English in their own countries? Oh, well . . . (*Gives up the line of inquiry.*) A Mohammedan would tell you—

MOHAMMEDAN. This is the year 1362 of the era of the Hegira.

NARRATOR. An orthodox Jew counts farther back than an orthodox gentile—

JEW. The new year, which commenced last week, is, according to our calendar, 5704.

NARRATOR. And an ancient Byzantine, returned to earth today, would calculate—

BYZANTINE. Why, this is the year 7452.

NARRATOR. Whereas an ancient Greek would figure it—

GREEK (*with a very phony Greek accent*). Year 2719 of the Olympiads or the third year of the six hundred eightieth Olympiad.

NARRATOR (*with disgust; he's against radio accents*). Et tu, Workshop. . . . That's all, brother.

NARRATOR (*withheld cue*).[2] Now then—let's talk about time: that which is so much a part of us, shaping our lives before we're born; that which we have so much of, yet so little. Time can be measured more easily than it can be defined. This thing, so common in our lives, defies description. For example, now, I'll ask at random two actors in the studio—they are not prepared for this. (*Addressing actor by name.*) ——, how would you define time?

[2] This part of the script should not be rehearsed or made known to the actors before the show takes the air. The idea of withholding the cue is to spring it as a surprise on the actors.

ACTOR. (*Answers.*)

NARRATOR. (*Asks another actor.*)

SECOND ACTOR. (*Answers.*)

NARRATOR. See what I mean? Even measurement is difficult. We count off seconds easily enough, but when it comes to aggregates of seconds, then we have trouble. The year is a big unit to us here on earth, and there's been considerable disagreement as to how to clock it. Between the Gregorian year, which we now employ, and the astronomical year, which astronomers use, there is a difference of twenty-six seconds—and this adds up to a full day every 3323 years.

Did you think our calendar just grew up by itself? Did you think Adam invented it? Why, once a famous pope suppressed ten days in order to straighten out our measurement of time. That's just what he did, and that's what made him famous. Three hundred sixty-one years ago, Pope Gregory the Thirteenth reformed a calendar which had been in service over fifteen hundred years, and which, because of errors in it, had begun to lag behind the solar year. So in order to make things come out even, Gregory suppressed ten days. . . .

GREGORY. Let it be ordained that the fifth day of October of this year of our Lord 1582 be designated as the fifteenth day of October.

NARRATOR. And that's the way it was suppressed.

We go around talking very loosely about time, as though there were only one kind of it.

VOICES. Good morning . . . good afternoon . . . good evening . . . good night . . . yesterday . . . tomorrow . . . when? . . . now . . . early? . . . late . . . soon . . . after . . . before . . . during . . . always . . . never . . .

NARRATOR. You'd think, by the commonness of these words, that time was absolutely uniform to our senses and our lives. But of course it's not. To each of us time's a sensation of a special sort, according to what occupies our consciousness at any given moment—

GIRL. Ooh my, the way the time's flown by—it seems like it was only yesterday we started on our honeymoon.

NARRATOR. Or else this sort of measurement—

MAN. You have no idea what a boring time we had! I thought they would never go home. Seemed like a thousand years to me.

NARRATOR. Outside our isolated solar system, time is relative in still another way—it's not what we think it is; no, not even the astronomers are sure of it. They argue theories with such impressive names as—

ASTRONOMER. The relativity of simultaneity.

NARRATOR. Time? That's a program by itself some night. It should have an all-star cast including—

VOICES. Greenwich mean time . . . nautical time . . . absolute time . . . mathematical time . . . empirical time . . . psychological time . . . sidereal time . . . Standard time . . . solar time . . . time-and-a-half . . . three-quarters time . . . time immemorial . . . time out of mind . . . time loan . . . time bomb . . . leisure time . . . hard times . . . time at bat . . . *Time* magazine . . . any old time . . .

NARRATOR. And, of course, time for the time motif.

Music: Time motif.

PROSECUTOR. Is there a doctor of philosophy in the house? Is there anybody listening who thinks he knows all the answers? If so, then let him take the stand.

VOLUNTEER (*off*). I'm no Ph.D. or genius, and there may be some answers I don't know, but I've had a decent education.

PROSECUTOR. Good. Would you care to come to the microphone, please?

Steps across the floor.

PROSECUTOR. Be seated, sir. Now tell me: Do parallel lines ever meet?

VOLUNTEER. No, of course not.

PROSECUTOR. Wrong. They do.

VOLUNTEER. I was taught they don't.

PROSECUTOR. Well, I was taught they do.

VOLUNTEER. By whom?

PROSECUTOR. By Einstein. . . . Question Number Two: Can a straight line be extended indefinitely?

VOLUNTEER. How's that again?

PROSECUTOR. If you draw a perfectly straight line, and if it runs off your paper and out of your window and into space—infinitely far—will it keep on going straight forever?

VOLUNTEER. Why, sure.

PROSECUTOR. Wrong. It would finally return to itself.

VOLUNTEER. Why?

PROSECUTOR. Because space is curved.

VOLUNTEER. Now, wait a minute—

PROSECUTOR. Does the sum of the angles of a triangle equal two right angles?

VOLUNTEER. Why, everybody knows that. I was taught that in high school. I suppose that's wrong too, is it?

PROSECUTOR. You're right, you're wrong.

VOLUNTEER (*hurt*). Wrong?

PROSECUTOR. Wrong, according to the laws of astronomy—the laws of the heavens—the laws of time and space.

VOLUNTEER. But we're not in space, mister, we're on solid earth.

PROSECUTOR. Wrong again. Not so very solid, sir. Why, every structure in the world—the granite mountain and the shapeless air—the very steel beams of this building are aquiver with atomic life, atremble with great systems of submicroscopic motion.

And what is light and color, what is sound, but more vibration?

VOLUNTEER. Look—you keep your atoms and molecules. I still say the earth is solid. It doesn't wiggle under my feet. It doesn't slip around. It turns smoothly on its axis, it minds its own business, it doesn't get carried away by every new theory that comes along.

PROSECUTOR. You don't have to get reactionary about it.

VOLUNTEER. I'm not getting reactionary.

PROSECUTOR. You are so.

VOLUNTEER. What authority have you got for what you're giving out here?

PROSECUTOR. Authority? Ha!—Will Astronomers Brown, Jones, Smith, and Doe take the stand, please?

Four pairs of footsteps.

PROSECUTOR (*sotto voce over sound of steps*). It's not for nothing that the Columbia Workshop hired me as prosecuting attorney. (*Up.*) Now, Professor Brown, tell the court: Does the earth wiggle under your feet?

BROWN. Yes, indeed, sir. The crust of the earth apparently slips relative to the terrestrial core. There are on the average of three hundred seventy earthquakes throughout the globe every year.

PROSECUTOR. Thank you. Dr. Jones—does the earth turn smoothly on its axis?

JONES. The axis of the planet does not hold fast, no. Its unsteadiness—

PROSECUTOR. Just a moment. (*Projecting.*) No photographs, please, until the hearing is over. . . . All right, go on, Dr. Jones.

JONES. In fact, the crust of the earth slips all the time. It produces complicated vibrations of latitude which bother us sometimes when we are trying to determine positions of stars accurately.

PROSECUTOR. Would you bear that out, Mr. Smith?

SMITH. Yes, sir. Moreover the rotation of the earth is not perfectly even, because the sun and moon drag on our equator, giving rise to certain intricate, though minor, motions. And also, the earth itself is changing its form.

PROSECUTOR. Now, Mr. Doe, your colleague speaks of the intricate motions of the earth. Can you name, offhand, the various directions in which our earth is gyrating or drifting?

DOE. Why, yes, sir, that's quite simple. There are six. First there's the daily rotation of the earth. The eastward rotation—night and day.

PROSECUTOR. Speed?

DOE. Oh, about a thousand miles an hour at the equator, seven hundred fifty miles an hour in the latitude of New York.

PROSECUTOR. Yes. Next?

DOE. Second, there's—

VOLUNTEER. All right, all right, the earth is moving in six directions at once. Okay. Now, can I cross-examine *you*?

PROSECUTOR. What was that?

VOLUNTEER. Can I cross-examine you?

PROSECUTOR. I don't get the name?

VOLUNTEER. Just change places with me here.

PROSECUTOR. Well—er—isn't that kind of irregular?

VOLUNTEER. So's our orbit, wise guy.

PROSECUTOR. Who's a wise guy?

VOLUNTEER. You.

PROSECUTOR. Me?

VOLUNTEER. Yes, you.

PROSECUTOR. You wouldn't like a pop on the nose, would you, quiz kid?

VOLUNTEER. Is that a dignified question to ask on a program dedicated to the Yerkes Observatory?

PROSECUTOR (*contritely*). No—I guess not. They won't think well of me at Yerkes, will they?

VOLUNTEER. Hardly.

PROSECUTOR. They'll think I'm a yerk!

VOLUNTEER. Step down, brother.

PROSECUTOR. I apologize. You may proceed to cross-examine me.

VOLUNTEER. Now, in the biblical book of Job, there is an allusion to the morning stars singing together.

PROSECUTOR. Morning stars singing together?

VOLUNTEER. Yes. Now, since you are full of astronomical lore, perhaps you can tell me what that sounded like.

PROSECUTOR. I can tell you what it didn't sound like.

VOLUNTEER. All right, what didn't it sound like?

PROSECUTOR. Like this—

Music: A quartet of girls singing "Daddy" in close harmony.

VOLUNTEER. I move that be stricken from the record.

PROSECUTOR. All right, strick it.

VOLUNTEER. Very well. Now you have attempted in this hearing to demonstrate that the average man entertains several misconceptions regarding the laws of time and space.

PROSECUTOR. Precisely.

VOLUNTEER. Did it ever occur to you that the ordinary man wishes to understand only those forces of nature which he encounters in his daily life?

PROSECUTOR. It occurred to me only yesterday, while I was shaving.

VOLUNTEER. And that he wishes to understand these only so far as it's necessary for him to keep alive and well?

PROSECUTOR. Well?

VOLUNTEER. Then let there be no easy assumption that the man in the street is naïve. It happens that the astronomer has access to far-reaching sources of information, and so *his* naïveté becomes relative—it's simply ignorance on a much higher plane.

PROSECUTOR. This is degenerating into a bull session.

VOLUNTEER. The astronomer knows things which stagger us—but the things he knows he *doesn't* know stagger *him!*

PROSECUTOR. Such as what? Name two.

VOLUNTEER. Such as the White Dwarfs.

PROSECUTOR. Snow White and the White Dwarfs?

VOLUNTEER. No. Dwarfed stars which, while smaller than the earth, have volumes greater than our sun. Their density is so great and their gravity so strong that a cigarette on their surface would weigh about two hundred thousand tons.

PROSECUTOR. What makes White Dwarfs, Daddy?

VOLUNTEER. Astronomers don't know.

PROSECUTOR. What else don't they know?

VOLUNTEER. They don't know the limits of the universe. They don't know why some stars flare up suddenly and die down again; they don't know what will happen when galaxies which are now rushing away from us at a rate of forty thousand miles a second accelerate their speed until they reach the speed of light, which is the greatest known speed. (*Fading.*) They don't know about the disintegration of matter. They don't know what happens to all the energy that has been radiated into space. (*He continues under Narrator.*) They don't know whether, when they are seeing two stars in a telescope, they are actually seeing two images of the same star, the light from which may have reached us by varying routes through the great curved voids of interstellar space. (*He is faded.*)

NARRATOR. He's speaking now of mysteries no earthbound Sherlock Holmes, no Moto, no Fu-Man-Chu can help to solve. These are the spiraled questions, the enigmas hung up in the purple sky. (*Music: Moon motif behind:*) They gaze down on the tortured face of our most pitiable planet, gaze down on us with the patience of a long and loping universe. These are the mysteries which our distant children in their clean and honorable and benign societies will still attempt to fathom, looking through the brighter glasses of a happier millennium. These are the passions of the good and goodly heavens—the fierce and holy matters of remoteness beyond the farthest tendrils of the outstretched mind.

Music: Out.

NARRATOR. O men who fish the luminescent and star-strewn seas of galaxy and nebula, of cluster and of constellation—men who silently, alone, patrol the shores of night, who track sidereal wanderers down and weigh and measure them and take their temperatures, you men who've traveled farther standing still than twenty billion Marco Polos, tell us:

Are we not brave and meaning animals? Do we not make a kind of plaintive music of our intermission here? Do we not clock War's baleful equinoxes by the rhythmic dripping of our blood? Are we not hopeful seekers after nebulae of Truth and patient watchers for the ray of Hope?

Tell us, astronomers of all the world's observatories: What is the magnitude of Man?

Music: Finale.

Archibald MacLeish

About three hundred years ago, a Puritan poet, Andrew Marvell, wrote a strangely un-Puritanical poem called "To His Coy Mistress." In it occur the lines (familiar to readers of Hemingway's A Farewell to Arms):

> But at my back I always hear
> Time's wingèd chariot hurrying near.

Urged by the same disturbing sense of time, MacLeish describes, in the imagination of a thinker, the relentless progression of night's shadow across the earth's surface.

YOU, ANDREW MARVELL

And here face down beneath the sun
And here upon earth's noonward height
To feel the always coming on
The always rising of the night

To feel creep up the curving east
The earthly chill of dusk and slow
Upon those under lands the vast
And ever-climbing shadow grow

And strange at Ecbatan the trees
Take leaf by leaf the evening strange
The flooding dark about their knees
The mountains over Persia change

And now at Kermanshah the gate
Dark empty and the withered grass
And through the twilight now the late
Few travelers in the westward pass

And Baghdad darken and the bridge
Across the silent river gone
And through Arabia the edge
Of evening widen and steal on

And deepen on Palmyra's street
The wheel rut in the ruined stone
And Lebanon fade out and Crete
High through the clouds and overblown

And over Sicily the air
Still flashing with the landward gulls
And loom and slowly disappear
The sails above the shadowy hulls

And Spain go under and the shore
Of Africa the gilded sand
And evening vanish and no more
The low pale light across that land

Nor now the long light on the sea—

And here face downward in the sun
To feel how swift how secretly
The shadow of the night comes on . .

Eric Knight

*If "Never Come Monday" seems, at first reading, to take us no great dis-
tance in the search for meaning, reflect on the idea of time as relative
which is implied in its extravagant invention. And what could be more
fantastic than relativity? Eric Knight (1897-1943) was born in Yorkshire. From the age of twelve he worked in the local mills, until he
came to the United States. Newspaper work was interrupted by the First
World War; then he returned to writing and eventually, at the age of
thirty-eight, published his first story. With* The Flying Yorkshireman
*Knight arrived. In his tales of "the Yorkshire Paul Bunyan" he attempted
two difficult feats, to make fantasy credible and to make his native dialect intelligible. Readers of "Never Come Monday" can judge how bril-
liantly he succeeded on both counts. His best novel,* This Above All, *was
called the first important novel of the Second World War. His* Lassie
Come Home *was effectively transferred to the screen. Believing that
every man should do his own fighting, he enlisted again at the age of
forty-five and met his death when the plane on which he was traveling
to North Africa crashed. "Maybe Sam Small was hovering over the falling transport," wrote the New York* Times, *"and maybe he gently
caught Eric Knight under one arm to save him from the final shock. It
would only have been turn about, one good turn for another."*

NEVER COME MONDAY

*Oh it's very, very nice,
Yes it's very, verrrry nice,
To get yer breakfast in yer bed
On Sunday mo-o-o-orning.*

THE first one to notice it was old Capper Wambley. And Capper was a
very important man. He was the knocker-up in the village of Polkingthorpe Brig—that is to say, he got up early every morning and went round
with his pole, tapping on the bedroom windows and waking up the people
in time for them to get to work. And this particular morning old Capper
knew there was something wrong.

He felt it first as he stepped outside his cottage and coughed in the
dark to clear his lungs, and looked up at the sky to see what kind of weather
it was. He felt that there was something wrong with the day, and then he
decided what it was. It was still Sunday.

For a moment or two he felt fair flabbergasted at this, for he remembered that the day before had been Sunday, too.

"Ba gum," Capper said to himself. "This is a champion do, it is an' all. No doubt summat should be done."

Now old Capper Wambley was very old, so he sat down on the edge of the curb, and after a while he came to the conclusion that what ought to be done was to think about it. So he began thinking about the very strange event.

"Now," he said to himself, "it don't seem reasonable and proper that we should hev two Sundays in a row. Let us see if we can get it sorted out. Now the thing for a chap to do to prove it, is to decide what is the difference between a Sunday morning and a weekday morning."

Old Capper thought and thought, and he saw that the only difference between the two was that on a weekday morning he wakened the people up, and on a Sunday morning he didn't.

"So, if Ah doan't wakken the village up this morning, it *is* a Sunday morning," he said to himself.

Of course, it took old Capper a long time to figure this out, because you can see it was no light matter. Here was one man, as you might say, who was holding the calendar in his hands. It was a very important decision. But once Capper had decided, he knew he must be right, for he was a Yorkshireman.

"Because Ah'm net wakkening onybody, it maun be a Sunday morning. And because it's a Sunday morning, Ah maun't wakken onybody up. So no matter which way a lad looks at it, the answer cooms out that it's Sunday."

But now he had decided it was Sunday, Capper saw that not wakening people up might not be sufficient. "Some of them may wake up of their own accord," he thought, "and not knowing this is the second Sunday in a row, will go walking down to the mill. And God knows they have to get up early often enough, and it would be a tarrible shame not to let them have this extra piece of rest that is so miraculously sent."

So old Capper got up slowly from the curb, and went stomping down the street, and stopped at his first call, which was the home of John Willie Braithwaite, who was the fireman at the mill. Old Capper got his long pole with the trident of wire at the end and lifting it so that the wire rested against the upstairs window pane, began twirling and twisting the pole in the palms of his hands so that the wire clacked and chattered fit to wake the soundest sleeper.

Soon the window went up, and John Willie Braithwaite's head popped out of the window.

"Ah'm wakkened," John Willie said. "Whet time is't?"

Now old Capper could see that John Willie wasn't awake, but was just moving in his sleep the way men did from their tiredness and weariness of getting up before dawn. But he knew it didn't matter this morning.

"Ah just wakkened ye to tell ye it's another Sunday morning," old Capper said. "Soa tha c'n goa on back to bed an' sleep i' peace."

At this John Willie Braithwaite closed the window and went back to bed and got in beside his wife without ever having really wakened up. Meanwhile old Capper was on his rounds, busily going up and down the village in the not-yet-dawn, rapping and tapping on all his customers' windows, and telling them they needn't get up because it was still Sunday.

Naturally, the news caused quite a little bit of a fuss. Some people gladly went back to sleep, but others woke up and got dressed, remembering that the day before had been Sunday. They packed their breakfasts and put on their clogs and their smocks and their shawls and went clacking up the streets until they got by the Green, and there they saw old Capper Wambley.

"Now, lad," they said, "whet's t'idea o' telling us this is another Sunday?"

"Well, it is," Capper said.

"How does'ta know it is?" Gollicker Pearson asked him.

"Ah can't explain it, but Ah'm full sure summat varry wonderful has happened, and it is," old Capper told them.

Some people were inclined to believe Capper, and some were not.

"Now lewk here, Capper," Gollicker said, "Ah doan't but admit that it does seem Sundayish, like, but how are we off to be sure?"

Old Capper thought a while. Then he saw the answer.

"Well, here's the way us can tell," he said. "Now if this be a weekday, the mill whistle'll blaw the fifteen minutes, wean't it?"

"Aye," they agreed.

"But if it be a Sunday, like Ah say, the mill whistle wean't blaw the fifteen minutes, will it?"

They all agreed that was true. So they stood round old Capper, who had one of the few watches in the village, and they waited. They all looked at his watch and saw it said twenty to six, then nineteen to six, then eighteen and seventeen and sixteen. And the second hand went round and finally it said quarter to six. But no whistle blew—largely because John Willie Braithwaite who was supposed to be there at 5:30 and get up steam and pull the whistle cord, was still home and sleeping warmly beside his wife.

"Well," old Capper says, "that shows it maun be a Sunday again, and now ye can all away hoam and get another hour's sleep."

So they all went home, glad to get another hour's sleep, and full of praises for old Capper because he had had the sense to perceive that it was another Sunday instead of a Monday morning.

Old Capper went off home himself, and was just making himself a little bit of breakfast, when Rowlie Helliker came in.

"Capper," Rowlie said, "Ah hear that tha discovered this is another Sunday."

"Aye, that's soa," Capper replied.

"Well," Rowlie went on, "isn't heving two Sundays in a row just a varry little bit irregular, as tha maught say?"

"It is that, lad," Capper told him. "But tha maun remember us is living in varry unusual times."

"We are that," Rowlie agreed. "And Ah'm glad tha discovered it in time. For if tha hedn't, Ah would ha' gone and rung the school bell like a gert lummox, thinking it were a Monday. But now Ah know it's a Sunday, Ah maun goa and ring the church bell."

"Ah should say that all sounds right and proper to me," old Capper agreed.

"Me too," Rowlie said. "And Ah thank thee for saving me from a gert mistake."

"Eigh, it's nowt, lad," old Capper said modestly.

So away went Rowlie, and Capper settled down to his breakfast, but he was soon interrupted again. Some of the villagers, all dressed in their Sunday clothes, came up and told him that people from other villages who worked at the Brig mill were at the mill gates insisting it was Monday. So Capper picked up a bit of bloater to eat on the way and went down there and told the people it was Sunday.

"But if it's Sunday in Polkingthorpe Brig, what day is it i' Wuxley Green?" someone asked.

"Aye, and i' Rombeck an' Holdersly an' Tannerley?" someone else added.

"Well, happen it's Sunday theer, too," Capper told them. "Only you didn't notice it. When two Sundays come in a row ye could hardly blame a chap for mistaking the second one for Monday. Soa Ah advise ye to goa back and enjoy Sunday."

"Well," said Tich Mothersole, "Ah'm reight glad to hev another day o' rest; but Ah wish Ah'd known it afore Ah started, because ma Mary Alice allus brings me ma breakfast to bed o' Sunday morning."

"Nay, if tha hurries tha's still time enow to gate hoam and pop back into bed," the Capper pointed out. "Then the minute thy wife sees thee theer she'll knaw it's a Sunday and she'll up and hev a bit o' bacon o't' fire i' noa time."

They were just ready to move away when Mr. Bloggs arrived. Mr. Bloggs was late, but then that didn't matter, because he lived in another town, and Mr. Bloggs owned the mill.

"'Ere, 'ere, 'ere, my good men," he said. "What's all this, 'ey? What's the idea you aren't all in the mill?"

So they explained to him that a second Sunday had arrived.

"Why, what nonsense," he said. "When I left 'ome it was a Monday. 'Ow can it be Sunday 'ere when it was a Monday in Puttersleigh?"

"Ah doan't knaw," old Capper said. "Unless," he added slowly, "it happens to be Sunday in Puttersleigh, too, and tha didn't realize it."

"It's Monday, I tell you. Come on in to work," Mr. Bloggs shouted. "How can it be two Sundays in a row?"

"It's Sunday," they said.

"It's not. It's Monday. And any man 'oo ain't in this mill in five minutes, is discharged."

"It's Sunday," they said.

"How can it be Sunday?" he shouted. "It's impossible."

He stared at them, and just then they heard the boom—boom—boom of the church bell ringing for Matins.

"That proves," they said, "it's a Sunday, and it'd be a sin to work on Sunday."

So they all turned round and went back to their homes, leaving Mr. Bloggs alone by his mill gates. He stood there, shaking his head, and finally he clumped upstairs and opened the office himself and sat down all alone at his desk to think the whole matter out.

Meanwhile in the homes of the village the people knew that since it was a Sunday, they would have to do all the things that one does on a Sunday. The men rested at home in comfortable chairs, and the women started mixing Yorkshire puddings for the big noontime dinner. The children were dressed in their nicest clothes and instead of going to school, they went up to the church for Sunday School. Ethel Newligate, who taught the Sunday School, went with them. Mr. Sims, the schoolteacher, hearing the church bell, knew it must be Sunday and off he went to play the organ. Rowlie Helliker was already there to pump the bellows. The church folk went up and stood in the pews. So the old Reverend Mr. Stoninghorn put on his cassock and surplice. He was a little puzzled as to whether it should be now the Fifth Sunday before Epiphany or the Fourth, but he compromised by giving the same service as he had done the day before, and preaching the same sermon. And many of the church folk said the sermon sounded a right lot nicer the second time than the first, because you could see just where it was going, in a manner of speaking.

All this time, of course, the mill was closed, but Mr. Bloggs wasn't idle. He picked up his telephone, which was the only one in the village, and asked the operator to get him the Greenwich Observatory. Mr. Bloggs always liked to be exact. When he got them he asked them what day it was, and they told him that it was Monday.

Armed with this fact, Mr. Bloggs went out and met the people just as they were coming out of church.

"Now see here," he said. "It's no use pretending. This is a Monday."

But they pointed out that they were just coming out of church, so how could it be Monday?

At this Mr. Bloggs got so angry that he shouted at them, and the noise brought the Rev. Mr. Stoninghorn to the church steps.

"You must not profane the Sabbath," he said, looking very handsome in his white surplice, and with his long white hair like a dandelion gone to seed.

Mr. Bloggs began to see he could get nowhere against Yorkshiremen by blustering, so he took another tack. He pointed out to the minister that while this might be Sunday, one would have to admit that it was a little bit unusual to have two Sundays in a row. Mr. Stoninghorn admitted this, and he agreed that a meeting ought to be called to look into the matter.

So it was announced through the village that a meeting was to be called at the school for four o'clock that afternoon. The Rev. Mr. Stoninghorn was asked to preside, but inasmuch as he was unsure whether or not it was the Sabbath, he declined. So Mr. Polkiby, the schoolmaster, agreed to take over the gavel and run a meeting in which everyone should have a chance to state his views on whether it was or wasn't Sunday.

At meeting time there wasn't a seat to be had, and after Mr. Polkiby rapped with the gavel, Mr. Bloggs got up and stated that it was Monday, and he could prove it because he had called up the Greenwich Observatory.

Then Taylor Huckle, the publican, got up and said it was Monday, because yesterday had been Sunday and the day after Sunday had always been Monday, for years and years, man and boy, as far back as he could remember.

After this there was a wait, because nobody liked to get up in front of so many people and put in their hap'orth; though a lot of people were dying to, because they knew Huckle was in favor of Monday for if it were Sunday he'd have to go on early closing hours.

So there was a long wait until somebody said: "Where's Sam Small?"

"Here Ah am," said a voice at the back of the hall, and they all spoke up and said: "Come on, Sam, let's hev thy opinion."

Now Sam was a man whose word was worth listening to at any time, and on any subject, not only as the inventor of the Sam Small Self-Doffing Spindle but because he was much traveled, having been not only to London and other parts but to foreign lands as well as on a cruise. So they waited politely as Sam walked down the aisle and clambered up on the stage.

"Well, lads," he said, "it's this way. A day's a day, but then again, it ain't, in a manner of speaking. The time Ah went round t'world, one day it were Tuesday, and the next morning the captain said it were Thursday—

and so it were, because Ah've nivver yet found that lost day. And on t'other hand, a lad on the ship told me if we'd gone round the world t'other way, we should of hed two Tuesdays. Now if we can have two Tuesdays when we're going round the world, Ah maintain we maught just as easy hev two Sundays when the world is going round us, which ivvery scientist knaws it is doing."

"Piffle," said Mr. Bloggs.

"Oh, aye?" asked Sam, his dander getting up. "Can tha tell me what day it is now i' Japan?"

"It's Monday," Mr. Bloggs said.

"Oh, pardon me, Mr. Bloggs," the schoolmaster said. "Just as a matter of academic accuracy . . ." and here he studied his watch carefully . . . "but in Japan now it is Tuesday."

"Tuesday?" roared Mr. Bloggs.

"There, tha sees," Sam said. "There don't seem to me to be noa sense to this day stuff. If it's Monday, as tha says, down i' Greenwich; and if it's Tuesday, as t'schoolmeaster says, i' Japan; then Ah say it's just as liable to be Sunday up here."

"Nonsense," yelled Mr. Bloggs. "I know what the matter is. You're all lazy and you wanted another day off. So you call it Sunday."

"Nay, lad," Sam replied. "There's six weekdays to one Sunday, so it seems to me like it were six to one i' thy favor that we'd hev an extra work-day i'stead of an extra restday. Simply because tha lost, tha maun't be a bad sport about it."

At this the people applauded Sam, and seeing he was at a good place to stop, he got down off the platform.

"Fiddlesticks," Mr. Bloggs said, now thoroughly angry. "If this is Sun-day, then what's tomorrow? Is it Monday or Tuesday? Or do we lose a day?"

"Happen Ah'm the man to clear that up," the Capper said, rising to his feet. "Us doesn't skip noa day at all. T'thing is that t'days o'to'week have gate tired o'turning, soa now they're stuck, like, and wean't goa no further, they wean't."

"How ridiculous," Mr. Bloggs snorted. "If that were so we'd get no further and tomorrow would be Sunday, too, wouldn't it?"

The Capper scratched his head and thought a moment. Then he looked up quickly.

"Ba gum, lad," he said. "Tha's hit t'nail o't'yead. Tomorrow *is* off to be Sunday."

At this the meeting broke up, and everyone started for home. They crowded round old Capper and asked him about the next day.

"Ah'm reight sure it'll be Sunday, lads," old Capper said. "But when Ah coom round to wakken ye up, Ah'll tell ye."

"Nay, Ah gate a better idea," John Willie Braithwaite said. "If it's a Sunday, it'd be a fair shame to disturb a little bit o' good extra sleep. That'd mak' it as bad as a weekday 'most. So supposing, if it's another Sunday, just thee doan't bother to coom round—and when tha doesn't coom we'll knaw for sure that way it's Sunday."

"Aye, that's fine," old Capper said, "but Ah'll lose all me collections that way."

They all saw that was so, but they agreed that even if it kept on being Sunday, they would pay old Capper just the same as if it had become the rotation of weekdays and he'd made his rounds.

"Nay, Ah couldn't tak' it," Capper protested.

"Nay, we'd like thee to," they protested.

"Well, if ye say," Capper agreed. "But how about lads i't'other villages? It's hard on them thinking it's a weekday and walking all the way here to find it's a Sunday."

"Well," John Willie said, "we'll form a committee, like, right now, and the members will each tak' a village and goa reight ovver theer and tell ivveryone that it's staying Sunday these days—that the days o't'week is stuck."

Everyone thought it a good and orderly idea, and so it was done.

The next morning people in the village woke up, and they lay abed and listened. But they heard no trident of wire chattering in the grayness of the morning, nor old Capper's voice wheezing: " 'Awf pest fower, ist'a oop?" They waited but they heard no clogs clattering on the cobbles, and no whistle at the mill saying that if they didn't get there in fifteen minutes they'd be locked out.

So they knew it must be Sunday again, and they went back to sleep, and the next thing they knew was the church bell ringing once more. So that made it Sunday and they were sure of it.

And in the other towns roundabout, the people didn't go to work, and so they knew it was Sunday, too. They put on their best clothes, and did a bit of gardening and the men mended things about the house and the children didn't go to school, and everyone had a fine rest so that their work-tired bodies began to grow glad and proud again.

The next day the news that the days of the week were stuck at Sunday had spread all over Yorkshire, and was percolating up to the Tyneside where the shipworkers were, and over into Lancashire where the youngsters worked before cotton mills and looms, and down into the black country where the men hauled at steel and went down into the mines, and down into Staffordshire where they toiled at the potteries and the car factories.

The newspapers sent men around to find out what had happened to the lost week days, and one of them came to the village and looked up old Capper. At first he laughed, until Ian Cawper came along. Ian just asked the newspaper lad for a penny, and then he bent the penny in two, and the newspaper lad stopped laughing.

"Nah, lad," Ian said. "Happen tha'd better tellyphone thy paper that this is Sunday."

"Indeed I will," the young man said, very appreciatively.

Now although the wonderful thing that it was still Sunday found great gratification in the hearts of all the men who worked long hours handling steel and wood and cotton and iron and glass and fabric and paper and silk, at furnaces and forges and foundries and looms and jennies and sides and presses and drills and lathes and assembly belts, there were some men who were quite upset by the miraculous happening. And in spite of the fact that everyone else in the country now saw that a beautiful series of Sundays had happened, these men kept on trying to persuade everyone that they were just ordinary days of the week that people merely *thought* were Sundays.

These men soon saw that if it kept on being Sunday they'd never be able to make any more battleships and gas bombs and motor cars and airplanes and radios and badminton rackets and all the rest of the things that are civilizing influences upon the world. And, to go further, if they didn't make those things, they wouldn't be able to go on making more money than they had already.

This was quite an abhorrent state of affairs. So they went to the Prime Minister about it.

"I yield my reverence for religion, especially the Church of England, to no one," one of them said. "In fact, I am thoroughly in accord with religion—one day a week."

"Hear, hear," the others said.

"But, Mr. Prime Minister, think of my stockholders! Many are orphans. Many are widows. If my factory doesn't make money, these poor people will be destitute—because always having drawn dividends, they've never had to learn how to work. We cannot let them suffer."

"Gentlemen," said the Prime Minister, "you may rest assured that His Majesty's Government will do all within its power to safeguard that industry and commerce which is the backbone of our nation—indeed, of our Empire."

Then the Prime Minister went away and thought. Being a Prime Minister he didn't think as you or I would. You or I, in the same case, might have said to ourselves: "Come, come now. What we've got to decide is whether this *is* Sunday or *isn't*." Which is probably why you and I will never be Prime Ministers.

This Prime Minister thought of a lot of things all at once. Suddenly, he called his secretary and said:

"Carrington-Smaithe. It is a Sunday today, I hear, and it will be a Sunday again tomorrow. Pack my things. We're going away for the week end."

"But, sir," said the secretary, "what about the International Crisis? We have two ultimatums which must be answered immediately."

"Dear me," said the Prime Minister. "That is a nuisance; but all the world knows the British week end is inviolate, and if this *is* Sunday, as it seems to me it must be, then I won't be able to answer till the week end is over."

"But when will it stop being Sunday, sir?"

"Well, Carrington-Smaithe, how long will it take our fastest cruiser squadron to get round to that troublesome part of the world?"

"Oh, about thirty-six more hours, sir."

"Hmmmph! Then I think it will stop being Sunday in about thirty-six more hours."

And with this the Prime Minister caught the five-fifteen train and went off to the country. And when the newspapers heard of it they printed it, and all the people in England—in fact, in all the world—knew that it was officially Sunday.

And back in Polkingthorpe Brig all the people were that proud of old Capper Wambley. For hadn't he been the first man in all the land to notice that the days of the week were stuck and every day kept turning up a Sunday?

And all over the land toil-weary people sighed with happiness at their escape from industrial chains. They rested their tired bodies. Some went to church every day. The men went walking with their dogs, or did odd jobs round the house, tinkering and gardening and cobbling and putting up shelves. In the cities people took buses out into the country and had picnics. The grownups lay in the sun and the children played in the fields, and the young men and women walked in the lanes and made love. There was only one flaw. The pubs had to go on Sunday closing hours, which allows no man to buy a pint of beer unless he is a legal traveler who has come so many miles. But this did good in a way, because many men walked the legal number of miles, and that way they saw parts of their own country they never would have seen otherwise, and they saw what other towns and villages looked like.

And all the time that went on, the Prime Minister sat in his garden and read detective novels, or snoozed in the sun with a couple of his favorite spaniels at his feet, until there came a wireless message.

"Sign here," said the boy.

So the Prime Minister signed, and then he got a code book and decoded the message. Immediately he had done so, he called his secretary and said:

"Carrington-Smaithe! What day is today?"

"Sunday, sir," the secretary said.

"Nonsense," said the Prime Minister. "I am tired of this blundering-through policy with its shilly-shallying. If this goes on, we shall have a Constitutional Crisis!"

"A Constitutional Crisis, sir?"

"Yes, Carrington-Smaithe. So you'd better pack and we'll get back to the City. We must act immediately. I shall issue a statement that His Majesty's Government hereby declares officially that today is Friday, and tomorrow shall be officially Saturday, and the days of the week must now go on officially in their regular and accustomed order."

"But isn't this really Sunday, sir? Hasn't a miraculous thing happened that has stopped the days of the week from arriving?"

"I don't know, my boy. But I do know this. Even if it is Sunday, and we all, everywhere, decide to call it Monday or Tuesday, then it becomes Monday or Tuesday because we all believe it is Monday or Tuesday."

"Yes, I see, sir."

And so the secretary packed, and the Prime Minister went back to London where he now could answer his ultimatums quite forcefully, and all the newspapers of the land carried the news that today was Friday and tomorrow would be Saturday—officially.

It wasn't until the next morning that this news reached Polkingthorpe Brig where it had all started. Mr. Bloggs got the news first, of course, and so he ordered the siren blown at the mill. So everybody hurried off to the mill because if you weren't there fifteen minutes after the siren went you were locked out and lost half a day's pay.

But as they trooped into the yard, old Capper stopped them.

"Hold on a minute, mates," he said. "Just what day is it?"

"Now come on in to work," Mr. Bloggs called. "It's Saturday."

"Nay," Capper said. "Yesterday were Sunday, so today maun be Monday, onless us's started slipping and now we're off to hev t'days backwards."

This remark of Capper's got everyone mixed up again and some said it was Saturday and some Monday while some still stuck to Sunday.

The upshot was that they decided to call Sam Small again to get his opinion. Sam arrived in about a half-hour, and heard all sides. Then he looked round, and spoke in the voice of one who is used to handling such matters.

"There's nobbut one thing to dew, lads," he said. "And Ah'm the chap that's off to dew it."

With that he walked into the office, and picking up the telephone, he said:

"Connect me with His Majesty, the King."

Before you could wink the connection was made.

"Is this His Majesty, the King?" Sam asked.

"Why Sammywell Small, lad!" said the King, recognizing the voice.

"If it doan't dew ma heart and sowl good to hear thy voice again. How's'ta been, Sam lad?"   ·

"Reight nicely, Your Majesty," Sam said.

"And how's that reight bonnie wife o' thine, Mully?" asked the King, who, as you will have noticed, spoke the dialects fluently. It is things like that, that make a good king. Little things like passing laws can be left to lads who have nothing but brains.

"Mully's reight well," Sam said. "And how's thy missus and bairns, if tha doan't mind the question?"

"Nay, Sam lad, Ah'm that glad tha axed ma," the King said. "My littlest 'un was a bit poorly last week. It's teethin', tha knaws. But she's feeling champion now."

"Well, Ah'm glad to hear that," Sam answered.

"Thanks," the King said. "Well, Sam, Ah doan't suppose tha called me oop just for idle barneying. Whet c'n Ah dew for thee, lad?"

"Well, it's this way, Your Majesty," Sam said. "Ah hoap tha'll net think ma gormless for axing, but could'ta tell me just whet day o' t'week it is for thee?"

"Eigh Sam," the King said, "Ah doan't monkey wi' things like that. Ah leave all that to ma ministers and such. But Ah've just gate official information from 'em that today's Sat'day."

"Your Majesty," said Sam, "if Sat'day's good enow for thee, then there's noa moar argyment. Thank you varry much."

"Net at all, Sam," the King said. "And by the way, Sam Small, it is our royal wish that tha doesn't wait soa long afore tha calls ma oop again. There's been sivveral things lately Ah would ha liked thy opinion on. When's'ta off to coom to Lunnon?"

"Nay, Your Majesty, Ah give oop traveling," Sam replied.

"Too bad, Sam. Too bad. Well, give me a ring soom time soon, will'ta?"

"That Ah will, lad."

"Well, so long," said the King.

"So long, Your Majesty," said Sam.

All during this conversation, of course, the people of the village had been crowding breathlessly round the door of the office, listening to Sam. And right in the forefront was Mr. Bloggs.

"Well, what did he say?" Mr. Bloggs breathed as Sam hung up.

"He said," said Sam, "that today is Sat'day."

"There, didn't I tell you?" Mr. Bloggs shouted. "Now, doesn't that make it Saturday?"

Everyone thought it did, but they weren't quite sure. They thought the matter over quite a while, and then John Willie Braithwaite said:

"T'only trouble is, it doan't *feel* like Sat'day to me."

"But I tell you it is officially Saturday," Mr. Bloggs cried.

"Wait a minute, lads," Sam Small put in. "Now Ah doan't wark here, soa Ah play no favorites. But Ah c'n tell yé for sure how ye'll all knaw it's a Sat'day."

"How can we tell?" they asked.

"Why, it's that simple," Sam replied. "Ye'all knaw that ivvery Sat'day morning at a quarter to twelve ye get paid a week's wages. Now if soa be this is Sat'day, Mr. Bloggs will begin paying each man a week's money exactly ten minutes from now. And, on t'other hand, then if he doan't start paying a week's brass i' ten minutes—it can't be Sat'day—and the chances are it's off to keep on being Sunday for a long time."

"Outrageous," Mr. Bloggs cried.

He argued and shouted, but they just stood and shook their heads and said that if it were a Saturday they'd draw a week's pay at exactly a quarter to twelve, as they always did on Saturday. And finally Mr. Bloggs, seeing no other way of getting the days of the week started properly again, gave in and paid off each man and woman and girl and boy.

By the time they were paid it was Saturday noon, and so they all trooped as usual down the stairs of the mill and into the yard to go home. And there old Capper stopped them.

"But if it's a Saturday today, lads and lasses, what day is it tomorrow?"

"It'll be Sunday," they all roared.

"Now ain't that champion," old Capper beamed. "If it's Sunday we'll all be able to lie abed late and get a bit o' extra sleep for a change."

Sir James Jeans

Sir James Jeans (1877-) is one of the most eminent living British scientists. He was educated at Trinity College, Cambridge. He has filled many distinguished posts and has received many honors. To Americans he is best known as Professor of Applied Mathematics for several years at Princeton University, as a Research Associate of the Mount Wilson Observatory, and as the author of The Mysterious Universe, The Stars in Their Courses, The New Background of Science, *and other books which give the layman an account of modern scientific research as trustworthy as it is engaging. This essay complements Muller's essay which follows it: both take the whole story of mankind within their scope, Muller biologically, Jeans astronomically.*

MAN IN THE UNIVERSE

INTEREST in scientific cosmogony is a recent, and still a very tender growth. Anthropologists and geologists tell us that man has existed on earth for something like 300,000 years; we must go this far back to meet our ape-like ancestry. Between them and us some 10,000 generations of men have walked the earth, most of whom have probably given some thought, in varying degrees, to the significance of their existence and the plan of the universe.

Of these 10,000 generations of men, the first 9990 unhesitatingly regarded the earth as the centre, and terrestrial life as the central fact, of the universe. As was suited to its majesty and dignity as the abode of man, the earth stood still while the celestial sphere spun round it, covering in the earth much as a telescope-dome covers in the telescope; and this dome was spangled with stars, which had been thoughtfully added so as not to leave the central earth unillumined at night. Ten generations at most have been able to view the problem of their existence in anything like its proper astronomical perspective.

The total age of the earth far exceeds the 300,000 years or so of man's existence. The evidence of geology, and of radioactivity in rocks in particular, shows that it must be something like 2000 million years, which is several thousand times the age of the human race. Old Mother Earth must regard man as a very recent apparition indeed; he has just appeared to burrow into her, burn her forests, put her waterfalls into pipes, and generally mar the beauty of her features. If he has done so much in the first few moments of his existence, she may well wonder what is in store for her in the long future ages in which he is destined to labour on her surface. For in all probability the life in front of the human race must enormously exceed the short life behind it. A million million years hence, so far as we can foresee, the sun will probably still be much as now, and the earth will be revolving round it much as now. The year will be a little longer, and the climate quite a lot colder, while the rich accumulated stores of coal, oil, and forest will have long been burnt up; but there is no reason why our descendants should not still people the earth. Perhaps it may be unable to support so large a population as now, and perhaps fewer will desire to live on it. On the other hand, mankind, being three million times as old as now, may—if the conjecture does not distress our pessimists too much—be three million times as wise.

Looked at on the astronomical time-scale, humanity is at the very beginning of its existence—a new-born babe, with all the unexplored potentialities of babyhood; and until the last few moments its interest has been centred, absolutely and exclusively, on its cradle and feeding-bottle. It has just become conscious of the vast world existing outside itself and its cradle; it is learning to focus its eyes on distant objects, and its awakening brain is beginning to wonder, in a vague, dreamy way, what they are and what purpose they serve. Its interest in this external world is not much developed yet, so that the main part of its faculties is still engrossed with the cradle and feeding-bottle, but a little corner of its brain is beginning to wonder.

Taking a very gloomy view of the future of the human race, let us suppose that it can only expect to survive for two thousand million years longer, a period about equal to the past age of the earth. Then, regarded as a being destined to live for three-score years and ten, humanity, although it has been born in a house seventy years old, is itself only three days old. But only in the last few minutes has it become conscious that the whole world does not centre round its cradle and its trappings, and only in the last few ticks of the clock has any adequate conception of the size of the external world dawned upon it. For our clock does not tick seconds, but years; its minutes are the lives of men. A minute and a half ago the distance of a star was first measured and provided a measuring-rod for the universe. Less than a quarter of a minute has elapsed since Professor Hertzsprung of Leiden and Dr. Shapley, now Director of Harvard Observatory, showed how the peculiar stars known as Cepheid variables provide a longer measuring-rod, and taught us to think in distances so great that light takes hundreds of thousands of years to traverse them. With the very last tick of the clock, Dr. Hubble, of Mount Wilson Observatory, using the same measuring-rod, has found that the most remote objects visible in the biggest telescope on earth are so distant that light, travelling 186,000 miles a second, takes about 140 million years to come from them to us.

Not only is our vision of the universe continually expanding, but also it is expanding at an ever-increasing rate. Is this expansion destined to go on for ever? So far as we can at present see, no; for a general guiding principle, that of generalised relativity, fixes a limit, which we are fast approaching. According to this theory, space cannot extend for ever; it has no limit, but is nevertheless finite like the surface of the earth. Without exploring and surveying the whole of the earth's surface, we can make a fair estimate of its total area by measuring its radius, which we can do by measuring its curvature at any one point. In the same way the total volume of space is fixed by a quantity, the curvature of space, which can be determined by measuring the density of distribution of matter in space. Space which contained no matter would go on for ever, but the parts of space we can survey with our telescopes contain enough matter to show that we already see an appreciable fraction of the whole of space. It is as though our baby, watching ships coming from over the horizon, concluded that the earth's surface was curved, and formed a general rough conception of its size by imagining the observed curvature continuing until the earth's surface rounded back on itself.

Exact figures are impossible, but Dr. Hubble has calculated that space is not likely to extend to more than about a thousand times as far as the farthest nebula visible in the biggest telescope. Nothing prevents our going on and on in space beyond this distance, but, if we do, we merely come back to ourselves. The possessor of a sufficiently sensitive wireless apparatus may emit signals and pick them up a seventh of a second later after they have travelled round the world. In the same way a not inconceivable increase in the size of our telescopes would take us round the whole of space, and we should see the stars surrounding our sun by light which had travelled round the universe, not of course as they now are, but as they were 100,000 million years ago.

Such considerations make it improbable that the expansion of the universe can continue at its present rate for much longer. Having grasped that the world is round, the infant speedily forms a fair idea of its size. Our particular infant, mankind, has made the great discovery of the existence of the outer world, has formed some conception of its size, and adjusted his ideas, not by a process of slow revelation, but by a brain-flash of the last few seconds. In his mature years and his staid old age he is no doubt destined to make many sensational discoveries, but he can never again live through the immortal moment at which he first grasped the immensity of the outer world. We only live through a few ticks of his clock, and fate might have ordained that they should be anywhere in the three days that the child has already lived, or in the seventy long, and possibly tedious, years yet to come. The wonderful thing is that she has selected for us what is, perhaps, in some ways the most sensational moment of all in the life of our race.

The child sets its newly awakened mind to work to adjust and co-ordinate a new array of facts. If the world was not made to surround its cradle, what purpose can it serve? If the lights of the great ships in the harbour were not designed to light its nursery at night, what can they possibly be for? And, most interesting problem of all, if the world is such a big affair, can there be other cradles and other babies?

THE BIRTH OF PLANETS

After their birth stars do not live entirely uneventful lives. They may meet with a variety of accidents and these result in different observed astronomical formations. A star may rotate too fast for safety, just as a flywheel may; when this happens it breaks into two, and the two stars so formed revolve endlessly about one another as a binary system. Two stars may run into one another, although this is very rare. A more common occurrence is for two stars to escape running into one another by a narrow shave. When this happens, huge tides are raised on the two stars involved, and these may take the form of long streamers of gas, which ultimately condense into "drops" just as did the gas in the outlying regions of the spiral nebulae. It seems reasonably certain that the planets were formed in this way.

The birth of the solar system, then, resulted from the close approach of two stars; if a second star had not happened to come close to our sun, there would have been no solar system. It may be thought that with a life of millions of millions of years behind it, one star or another would have been certain to come near enough at some time to tear planets out of the body of our sun. Calculation shows the reverse; even after their long lives of millions of millions of years, only about one star in 100,000 can be surrounded by planets born in this way. A quite unusual accident is necessary to produce planets, and our sun with its family of attendant planets is rather of the nature of an astronomical freak.

In the thousand million stars surrounding our sun there are, at a moderate computation, not more than ten thousand planetary systems, because there has not been time for more than this number to be born. They are of course still coming into existence; calculation suggests a birth-rate of about one per thousand million years. Thus we should have to visit thousands of millions of stars before finding a planetary system of as recent creation as our own, and, even if life similar to our own exists on other planets, we should have to visit millions of millions of stars before finding a planet on which civilization and interest in the outer universe were as recent a growth as are our own. Utterly inexperienced beings, we are standing at the first flush of the dawn of civilization. Each instant the vision before us changes as the rosy-fingered goddess paints a new and ever more wonderful picture in the sky, while on earth the rolling back of the morning mists discloses new, mysterious and unsuspected vistas to our bewildered gaze. We call it living in an age of progress.

In time the glory of the morning must fade into the light of common day, and this in some far distant age will give place to evening twilight presaging the final eternal night. But we children of the dawn need give but little thought to the far-off sunset.

It may be suggested that the creation of planetary systems is also only at its beginning, and that in time every star will be surrounded, like our sun, by a family of planets. But no; the stars will have dissolved into radiation or disappeared into darkness before there is time for this to happen. So far as we can judge, our part of the universe has lived the more eventful part of its life already; what we are witnessing is less the rising of the curtain before the play than the burning out of candle-ends on an empty stage on which the drama is already over. There is not time for many more planets to be born.

LIFE AND THE UNIVERSE

The planets are the only places we know where life can exist. The stars are too hot; even their atoms are broken up by the intense heat. Nebulae are in every way unsuitable; even if cool solid bodies exist in them, they would probably be so drenched with highly penetrating radiation as to render life impossible. . . . Life demands a special type of matter, such as does not produce intense light and heat by transforming itself into radiation. We find it only in the surfaces of the stars, which are too hot for life, and in the planets which have been pulled out of these surfaces.

On any scheme of cosmogony, life must be limited to an exceedingly small corner of the universe. To our baby's wonderings whether other cradles and other babies exist, the answer appears to be that there can at best be very few cradles, and there is no conceivable means of knowing whether they are tenanted by babies or not. We look out and see a universe consisting primarily of matter which is transforming itself into radiation, and producing so much heat, light, and highly penetrating radiation as to make life impossible. In rare instances, special accidents may produce bodies such as our earth, formed of a special cool ash which no longer produces radiation, and here life may be possible. But it does not at present look as though Nature had designed the universe primarily for life; the normal star and the normal nebula have nothing to do with life except making it impossible. Life is the end of a chain of by-products; it seems to be the accident, and torrential deluges of life-destroying radiation the essential.

There is a temptation to base wide-reaching inferences on the fact that the universe as a whole is apparently antagonistic to life. Other quite different inferences might be based on the fact of our earth being singularly well-adapted to life. We shall, I think, do well to avoid both. Each oak in a forest produces many thousands of acorns, of which only one succeeds in germinating and becoming an oak. The successful acorn, contemplating myriads of acorns lying crushed, rotten, or dead on the ground, might argue that the forest must be inimical to the growth of oaks, or might reason that nothing but the intervention of a special providence could account for its own success in the face of so many failures. We must beware of both types of hasty inference.

In any case, our three-days-old infant cannot be very confident of any interpretation it puts on a universe which it only discovered a minute or two ago. We have said it has seventy years of life before it, but in truth its expectation of life would seem to be nearer to 70,000 years. It may be puzzled, distressed, and often irritated at the apparent meaninglessness and incomprehensibility of the world to which it has suddenly wakened up. But it is still very young; it might travel half the world over before finding another baby as young and inexperienced as itself. It has before it time enough and to spare in which it may understand everything. Sooner or later the pieces of the puzzle must begin to fit together, although it may reasonably be doubted whether the whole picture can ever be comprehensible to one small, and apparently quite insignificant, part of the picture. And ever the old question obtrudes itself as to whether the infant has any means of knowing that it is not dreaming all the time. The picture it sees may be merely a creation of its own mind, in which nothing really exists except itself; the universe which we study with such care may be a dream, and we brain-cells in the mind of the dreamer.

H. J. Muller

H. J. Muller (1890-   ) was born in New York City and educated at Columbia University, where he received the degree of Ph.D. His researches in genetics have been conducted here and in Europe; at present he is a research fellow at the University of Edinburgh. Since 1911 he has patiently pursued breeding experiments on the fruit fly Drosophila, the amazing results of which are mentioned below. In this opening chapter of his Out of the Night *he reduces to its simplest terms the enormous complexity of modern bio-chemical teachings, and permits us to see as far as science can yet take us into the mystery of the life spark. Here the infinitely small contrasts with the infinitely vast of Jeans's essay, yet both writers arrive at the same staggering conclusions as to man's place in the universe. This is not easy reading; but the "tough-minded" reader will find the game well worth the candle. And it is light we are after.*

HOW HAS MAN BEEN MADE?

OUR ideas of what sort of progress is possible or desirable for man must depend in part at least upon our views of his nature, his manner of origination, the methods by which changes have occurred and can occur in him, and the relation which he bears to the rest of nature. It is a commonplace that these questions have, within the past two-thirds of a century, been thrown into an utterly new light—and an ever clearer one— by the findings of biology, supplemented by those of physical science. Yet there are a number of serious misconceptions afoot (even in semi-scientific circles) regarding the essential trends of the more recent biological work. It is, for instance, whispered, and later shouted, that "Darwinism is dead," that "materialism has proven inadequate," or that "acquired characters *are* inherited after all." And upon these fallacies are founded various spurious philosophies of life that profess to answer for us the questions "whence," "why," and "whither." The reader will see, therefore, that before we may consider fairly the topic of progress itself, we must pass briefly in review, in their most modern setting, the salient features of the basic biological principles therein involved. Indeed, a thoroughgoing recognition of these truths will itself carry with it a radical re-creation of our outlook upon human life, and, by the same token, it is to the interest of reactionaries everywhere (both in and out of science) to warp, to deny, or to belittle them.

In the establishment of these broader generalizations the earliest fruits of victory fell, as is well known, to the comparative anatomists. They showed beyond all doubt that in every discernible portion of his structure man is but an animal, no different in his inherent nature from other animals. It is true that in this conclusion their careful studies of morphology have merely corroborated at great length the casual observations which men in all times must have made, for it must have been obvious to anyone that, superficially at least, the differences separating a "higher" animal (such as a dog) from one of another grand division (such as an oyster or a sponge) are far greater than those separating any higher animal from man. The embryologists—naturalists of a somewhat more prying disposition—have added that this similarity between man and other animals extends, with even greater distinctness, to the development of all the parts from the egg. More recently the bio-chemists, immunologists, physiologists, psychologists, and other experimental workers, in a vast array of investigations, have come to the same conclusion with regard to the chemical composition and all the intricate workings of the elaborate organizations of man and beasts. And the searchers through the microscope confirm the finding for all essential features of the finest visible components, so far as microscopic eye can see. . . .

Now it is generally recognized by biologists that the workings of all the gross parts of animals—such as the liver, muscles, brain, etc.—and also the workings of plant parts, are entirely due to the reactions and interactions of the finer, microscopic units—the cells—of which all gross parts are composed. Beyond this, modern experimental and microscopic science is bringing forward striking evidence that all the operations of these cells are the resultant of the actions and interactions of still smaller particles within the cells—such as the "genes" of the "chromosomes," the "mitrochondria," "Golgi bodies," etc., as well as even more finely distributed and dissolved substances. And, according to the students of cell physiology, there seems no good reason to doubt that these constituent particles in turn, which are at or beyond the limits of microscopic vision, are formed of a complex system of what the physical chemists call "colloidal" bodies, and owe their entire behavior to the changes and movements which the latter undergo in their reactions with each other and with the dissolved substances lying about them. The colloidal bodies and the dissolved substances are necessarily beyond the range of the microscope, but they are certainly composed of the molecules of chemistry, and their properties depend upon the nature of these molecules and the manner in which the latter are combined. As the molecules are made up of atoms of familiar type, most complexly arranged and yet apparently not violating the laws of chemical combination, it appears as though all living things consisted, in the last analysis, of a superlatively complicated organization of atoms, in which each individual atom is identical with the atoms of inorganic substances and works wholly according to the same laws. The seemingly miraculous attributes of living things, such as their powers of growth, reproduction, compensation, regeneration, sense reception, nerve and muscle responses, mind, etc.—in a word, "adaption"—could then be referable, not to any extraordinary characteristics of their atoms in particular, nor to the intrusion of any mysterious "vital force" or new entity at any stage, but rather to the marvelously orderly complication in which the atoms of living matter are arranged, so as to form a stupendously intricate structure of harmoniously interacting parts.

The shortcoming of the early "mechanists" lay in their failure to realize sufficiently the transcendent complexity and the interwoven character of the life fabric, and the role played in its determination by a virtually infinite series of remote and involved historical processes. Compared with a living human cell, the mechanism of the most delicate chronometer is perhaps as coarse and simple as is the mechanism of a crowbar when compared with the chronometer itself. And we are composed of many trillions of cells of manifold types, put together in highly special ways. How fine and intricate the organization within an individual cell may be is best realized by thinking of the fact that in development an entire man (or other animal) automatically shapes itself, and grows, from a single cell (the fertilized egg cell), which therefore contains within itself the entire "machinery" to build a man—and that nevertheless the egg cell is itself so tiny that if we could collect together all the human eggs now existing which are going to form the next generation of mankind—two thousands of millions in number— we could pack them into a one-gallon pitcher! And all the fertilizing sperm cells, which equally with the egg cells determine the hereditary traits, would occupy only about half the amount of space of an ordinary aspirin tablet! As a matter of fact, the actual hereditary substance in the eggs would occupy only the same amount of space as the sperm; hence the hereditary substance of both eggs and sperm together would form just one tablet of the size of an aspirin tablet. It is hard to realize that in this amount of physical space there now actually lie all the inheritable structures for determining and for causing the production of all the multitudinous characteristics of each individual person of the whole future world population. Only, of course, this little mass of leaven today is scattered over the face of the earth in several billion separate bits. Surely, then, this cell-substance is incomparably more intricate, as well as more portentous, than anything else on this earth.

It is thus evident that before we can properly understand the living things of our world we must first learn to know the structure of that new world-of-the-small which within the past few decades has been opened to the mind of man. At first sight the attainment of such knowledge seems a fantastic dream, but modern genetics is already beginning to invade the ultra-microscopic land inside the eggs and sperm cells of the fly *Drosophila* and of some other forms of life; and to bring back from this survey what we actually call "maps," on which are shown, within the chromosomes of an individual germ cell, the locations of hundreds of the separate hereditary particles or "genes" that help to determine the various visible characters of the individual growing from that germ cell. After all, the latter—though tremendously more complicated—is by no means so minute a mechanism as that with which the inorganic chemist works. To gain adequate control over the world of things of our own size, then, we must first seek knowledge and control of the very small world. The same conclusion is being reached today, with equally great force, in the realms of inorganic chemistry and of physics. And surely we cannot hope to conquer successfully the great masses in the sphere of very large things until we have control over those of our own size. The precept therefore follows that, for man, the road to the macrocosm lies through the microcosm.

Concerning the manner of origin of this staggeringly involved fabric of organic nature, all its features bear witness, and countless secondary tokens testify, that it has arisen most gradually through the operation of natural forces no different in kind from those which are working within it today, and which are ultimately referable to the mode of combination of its atoms.

For many millions of years blind chemical forces must have acted and interacted in early times to build up ever different and more complicated organic compounds and systems of compounds; but a turning point was reached when from these shifting combinations those materials which we call "genes" happened to become formed. Genes are self-propagating— that is, growing, multiplying particles within the organic system, which may by their chemical activity affect the characteristics of the system in all sorts of ways: its chemical properties, its shape, its size, its internal and external structure (fine and gross), and its behavior. The genes are themselves subject to occasional internal chemical alterations, or "mutations," which do not deprive them of their power to grow but do change the nature of their action upon the system. From the time of the birth of these mutable genes onward, the different genes (or the little systems of organic matter containing an association of genes) would necessarily enter into a destructive competition for growth and multiplication against each other. Relatively few of all that were produced in the multiplication process would now be able to survive, and to increase still further; indeed this would occur only in the case of those rare ones in which mutations had happened to result in genes whose action was especially favorable for the growth and multiplication of the gene itself and of the organic system (or "protoplasm") containing it. The other organic corpuscles, containing genes that had not mutated, or that had mutated in ways unfavorable to their growth, were meanwhile weeded out. By the repetition of these events, times without number, a more and more complexly efficient organization became built up within those protoplasmic masses which did manage to persist and multiply. So, step by step, through mutation (the alteration of genes) and heredity (the multiplication of genes) the millions of marvelously fashioned species of animals and plants which now exist were differentiated and integrated.

It should be distinctly realized that, in all of this, there is no evidence of an internal principle in organic nature causing beneficial, adaptive, admirable, or desirable changes to occur, rather than deleterious ones. In fact, the author has found that in the flies the harmful mutations far outnumber the beneficial ones, and this finding is being confirmed in other organisms. Thus, in spite of the great preponderance of detrimental variations, what we call progress ensues in the end, simply because, as Darwin pointed out (and we are not overthrowing Darwin in modern biology, but rather are building ever higher upon the basis that he laid down), the harmful variants perish in the struggle, whereas the accidentally beneficial ones survive. As this happens repeatedly, beneficial characters accumulate in the race. But we can see here that immeasurably more germ plasms finally die than manage to continue, and we owe all our wonderful frame to the cruelty of nature, which from step to step allowed the animals carrying our ancestral genes to multiply only at the cost of a life-and-death struggle in which the others, usually the vast majority, finally perished miserably.

Note, then, that though the evolutionary process may be described as a "progress" in complexity or adaptation, it does not necessarily result in an increase in the well-being or the happiness of the competing individuals, because it provides all survivors with increasingly deadly weapons in a great world war that not only pits species against species, but still more makes the individuals of the same species (in some cases, of different groups of the species) competitors of each other. The latest upstart, man, has been able partly to thwart this tendency only because, along with other advances, he has succeeded to some extent in limiting the growth of his naturally slow-breeding population, and in temporarily and occasionally amplifying his means of subsistence faster than his population has grown. Note also that although the creatures which were allowed to survive in any given age were those which happened, at that time, to fit, this did not by any means imply that they would be found to fit in the long run. Every germ plasm, every species, including man, is still thus on probation; and if—as much more often happens—it does not chance to have (or to acquire by mutation) genes so useful as those of the best competing species, it is eventually snuffed out ruthlessly.

Now this peculiar creature, man, has as yet had only a very short probationary period. Recent findings in radioactive rocks have given testimony that the entire process of organic evolution on the earth has taken something like a thousand million years, at least—possibly even several times as long. Only by comparisons can we grasp such immensities, so let us imagine this period symbolized by a distance along a cord, each yard of which stands for 10,000 years, and which ends, in the present time, at some established point of reference—say the center of the private desk of J. P. Morgan in his office in Wall Street, New York City. To represent the beginning of organic evolution we should have to start the string many miles away— probably at least as far off as New Haven, possibly as far as Boston.

It is of interest to note that, on this scale, a human generation (from one birth to the next) would occupy somewhat less than an eighth of an inch, and that, if our symbolic cord were taken as about three-eighths of an inch wide (a small rope), the portion included within one generation would then be a disc-shaped cross-section having the approximate dimensions of an ordinary aspirin tablet. Now this is just equal to the volume of hereditary material which actually is contained in one generation of mankind, and which is to be passed on to the next generation (as was explained on page 708). Hence our cord now acquires a further symbolic significance, in that it may be taken as representing in a certain real physical sense the evolving germ plasm of ourselves and our ancestors—though it would not everywhere be of equal width, as the numbers of the population change. Within this cord the fine fibers represent the chromosomes themselves, which are in fact filamentous bodies that intertwine, separate, and reunite in diverse ways as they pass along from generation to generation in the varying combinations resulting from sexual reproduction. In this cord, then, there would be represented, in one long line of ancestry, all the material which, from the beginning, has continued to make generation after generation of progressing forms. Their bodies (or soma), which constituted a vastly greater volume, may be considered as a series of excrescences about the cord, formed under the influences emanating from the by-products of the cord's chemical activity. The evolutionary changes manifested in their multitudinous characteristics are but reflections of primary changes occurring within the potent particles (genes) composing the tiny filaments of the cord itself. While the cord in question shows our particular line of ancestry, the lines of the millions of other living species would be shown by other, parallel cords— some thin, some thick, some branching as time goes on and as species diverge from one another, and many coming to an early end as species become extinct; but practically all the "higher" forms, at any rate, tracing back their origin to one original cord in the beginning. At any given place there is but a single one, out of all the mass of cords, which has led on so as finally to issue in our branch; this may be distinguished, in our figurative representation, by giving it a red color. It is this red cord which may be regarded as the red "thread of destiny," in a rather literal sense. Its free end is even now being spun further, being transfigured by mutation, being twined and interwoven, to give a new sort of living world, dependent on its new properties.

Let us now start at the beginning of the mass of life cords—say at New Haven—and follow along them on their long way towards their present destination in New York City, observing what forms are assumed by their bodily outgrowths (soma) as we travel forward. Except to the trained biologist, it will prove a dreary trip for much the greater part of the distance. For in this whole journey there will be no actual "beasts" as we ordinarily think of them (four-footed land animals) until we are well within the limits of New York City. Not until we are passing through Harlem shall we see any creatures with fur or feathers—i.e., mammals or birds. And note that even at that stage in our journey tremendous reptiles—dinosaurs —are still crashing over the earth; they long remain dominant over the few little warm-blooded pioneers, and they do not disappear until after we cross Forty-second Street. Not far below that point monkeys make their first appearance; but from that point southward the records show nothing higher than an ape until, having turned the corner of Wall Street, we actually confront our terminal building. There, about 100 feet from the end of the cord, are found the relics of the famous "missing link"—Pithecanthropus— not yet a man, but passed beyond the ape. Well within the building, and only about 15 feet from the desk in question, stands that stoop-shouldered lowbrow, the Neanderthal man, whom we do not dignify by classification in our species—the species self-styled *Homo sapiens,* "man the wise."

Our own *Homo sapiens* leaves his first known remains within the private office, only seven and a half feet from the desk. The earliest known "civilization" (not over 14,000 years ago, according to maximum estimates) leaves its crockery a yard and a half from the desk. On the desk, one foot from the center, stands old King Tut. Five and a half inches from the center we mark the Fall of Rome and the beginning of the Dark Ages. Only one and a half inches from the present end of the cord come the discovery of America and the promulgation of the Copernican theory— through which man opens his eyes for the first time to the vastness of the world in which he lives and to his own relative insignificance. Half an inch from the end of the cord there start the first faint reverberations of the Industrial Revolution, which set this desk here and which is now completely transforming man's mode of existence. A quarter of an inch from the end Darwin speaks, and man awakes to the transitory character of his shape and his institutions.

Since we men are, in our present forms, such recent comers upon the battle-field of the earth, what are the characteristics that have made us successful in so short a time as all this indicates? The answer is clear: the combination of intelligence and social behavior—or, we may say, of cunning and cooperation—whose product is "tradition." Man cannot outrun, outbite, or outclaw the animals; but, making tools and traps, he can outwit them. His native intelligence, to be sure, is neither different in kind nor many times greater than that of some other animals. Individually and un-taught, he scarcely has the wits to fashion the simplest tools. There seems to be needed a fairly definite critical amount of intelligence (and possibly of the impulse to imitate) before numerous experiences and customs are naturally transferred from one animal to another. Man was the first animal —at least the first *gregarious* animal—to just overstep this critical level of intelligence. Accordingly, since he does have the social impulse to band with others of his kind, one little happy discovery after another, or one slight beneficial modification of usage—generally hit upon by the most intelligent —has been passed along from man to man, and from woman to child, in the progress of the ages, till finally the average individual's cranium carries packed within it the fruit of the combined experiences of many generations of the most superior meddlers and tinkerers—engrafted in it not by heredity at all (since there is no inheritance of acquired characters), but by that usually informal kind of education called "tradition." This process of accumulating tradition we call "social evolution."

Among the important useful traditions that in this way accumulated gradually among early men were language (which was especially impor-tant in accumulating more tradition and for which a special gift was needed), the processes of making and using implements, the customs in regard to fire, food, bodily covering where necessary, and shelter, and moral codes. And so, in spite of a concomitant load of disadvantageous traditions —some of them derived from useful traditions that became outworn or perverted, others doubtless based on misconceptions from the start—it has happened that the not excessive intelligence of man has, after numberless generations (though, geologically speaking, in an extremely short time), been multiplied to far beyond its native magnitude, thus "artificially" set-ting the capabilities of most groups of man at an immeasurable distance above those of the cleverest animals and enabling him to dominate the earth.

Stephen Vincent Benét

Stephen Vincent Benét (1898-1943) was born in Pennsylvania of an Army family and grew up in Army posts. He attended Yale at the same time as Archibald MacLeish and Thornton Wilder, and began to publish poetry before he had graduated. The writing of John Brown's Body, *a book-length account of the Civil War in narrative verse, was made possible by a Guggenheim Fellowship: it became a best-seller and won the Pulitzer Prize for 1928. In spite of this success, he was never free from worry in the effort to make a living by writing. The sheer bulk of* John Brown's Body *somewhat overshadows his versatile accomplishment in shorter poems, especially ballads, and short stories. Of the latter, "The Devil and Daniel Webster" promises to be an American classic. In his later years he developed an intense concern for the American destiny and, when the war came, gave his talents without reserve to its prosecution. His death resulted from overwork. He left unfinished a long poem,* Western Star, *on which he had been working for years. "Metropolitan Nightmare" is a superb example of his fabulous imagination. Its conclusion is not without a parallel in the last lines of "The Hollow Men" by T. S. Eliot.*

METROPOLITAN NIGHTMARE

It rained quite a lot, that spring. You woke in the morning
And saw the sky still clouded, the streets still wet,
But nobody noticed so much, except the taxis
And the people who parade. You don't, in a city.
The parks got very green. All the trees were green
Far into July and August, heavy with leaf,
Heavy with leaf and the long roots boring and spreading,
But nobody noticed that but the city gardeners
And they don't talk.

              Oh, on Sundays, perhaps, you'd notice:
Walking through certain blocks, by the shut, proud houses
With the windows boarded, the people gone away,
You'd suddenly see the queerest small shoots of green
Poking through cracks and crevices in the stone
And a bird-sown flower, red on a balcony,
But then you made jokes about grass growing in the streets
And politics and grass-roots—and there were songs
And gags and a musical show called "Hot and Wet."

It all made a good box for the papers. When the flamingo
Flew into a meeting of the Board of Estimate,
The new Mayor acted at once and called the photographers.
When the first green creeper crawled upon Brooklyn Bridge,
They thought it was ornamental. They let it stay.

There was the year the termites came to New York
And they don't do well in cold climates—but listen, Joe,
They're only ants and ants are nothing but insects.
It was funny and yet rather wistful, in a way
(As Heywood Broun pointed out in the *World-Telegram*)
To think of them looking for wood in a steel city.
It made you feel about life. It was too divine.
There were funny pictures by all the smart, funny artists
And Macy's ran a terribly clever ad:
"The Widow's Termite" or something.
                              There was no
Disturbance. Even the Communists didn't protest
And say they were Morgan hirelings. It was too hot,
Too hot to protest, too hot to get excited,
An even, African heat, lush, fertile and steamy,
That soaked into bone and mind and never once broke.
The warm rain fell in fierce showers and ceased and fell.
Pretty soon you got used to its always being that way.

You got used to the changed rhythm, the altered beat,
To people walking slower, to the whole bright
Fierce pulse of the city slowing, to men in shorts,
To the new sun-helmets from Best's and the cops' white uniforms,
And the long noon-rest in the offices, everywhere.
It wasn't a plan or anything. It just happened.
The fingers tapped the keys slower, the office-boys
Dozed on their benches, the bookkeeper yawned at his desk.
The A. T. & T. was the first to change the shifts
And establish an official siesta-room,
But they were always efficient. Mostly it just
Happened like sleep itself, like a tropic sleep,
Till even the Thirties were deserted at noon
Except for a few tourists and one damp cop.
They ran boats to see the big lilies on the North River
But it was only the tourists who really noticed
The flocks of rose-and-green parrots and parrakeets
Nesting in the stone crannies of the Cathedral.
The rest of us had forgotten when they first came.

There wasn't any real change, it was just a heat spell,
A rain spell, a funny summer, a weather-man's joke,
In spite of the geraniums three feet high
In the tin-can gardens of Hester and Desbrosses.
New York was New York. It couldn't turn inside out.
When they got the news from Woods Hole about the Gulf Stream,
The *Times* ran an adequate story.
But nobody reads those stories but science-cranks.

Until, one day, a somnolent city-editor
Gave a new cub the termite yarn to break his teeth on.
The cub was just down from Vermont, so he took the time.
He was serious about it. He went around.
He read all about termites in the Public Library
And it made him sore when they fired him.
                                        So, one evening,
Talking with an old watchman, beside the first
Raw girders of the new Planetopolis Building
(Ten thousand brine-cooled offices, each with shower)
He saw a dark line creeping across the rubble
And turned a flashlight on it.
                          "Say, buddy," he said,
"You better look out for those ants. They eat wood, you know,
They'll have your shack down in no time."
                                    The watchman spat.
"Oh, they've quit eating wood," he said, in a casual voice,
"I thought everybody knew that."
                              —and, reaching down,
He pried from the insect jaws the bright crumb of steel.

Kirtley F. Mather

Kirtley F. Mather (1888-), Professor of Geology, has been at Harvard since 1924. His interests, by no means confined to science, include propaganda analysis, children's museums, adult education; in 1935, he led the opposition to the "teachers' oath" law in Massachusetts on the ground that such compulsion was a denial of academic freedom and would make teachers subservient to the State.

THE FUTURE OF MAN AS AN INHABITANT OF THE EARTH

DURING the first decade or two of the current century, geologists, astronomers, and physicists engaged in many discussions concerning the future of the earth as an abode for life. Some believed that "the end of the world" was relatively close at hand; others, that the prospect for the future was to be measured in terms of hundreds of thousands if not of millions of years. As usual in scientific circles, there has emerged from the conflict of ideas during the years of discussion a general unanimity of opinion, and today the geologic outlook for the future of the earth is quite clear.

Since the turn of the century new methods of measuring the length of geologic time have been discovered and applied. New concepts of the nature and sources of energy have been proposed and tested. New data concerning astronomic space and the distribution of the stars have been obtained. Innumerable details of earth history have been deciphered to give a trustworthy record of the changes that the earth and its inhabitants have undergone in the past. The key to unlock the secrets of the future is now available in this knowledge of the past, and with our present understanding of the processes of nature that key may be intelligently used. All the evidence combines to lead us unmistakably to the conclusion that for many scores, if not for hundreds of millions of years to come, the earth will continue to be a comfortably habitable abode for creatures like ourselves.

Surface temperatures of the earth, the most important item in any consideration of its long-range habitability, are determined by the receipt of solar energy distributed through atmospheric agencies. For any given area of land the annual contribution of heat from the earth's interior, hot though it may be, is just about equal to the warmth received from the sun in 20 minutes by an equal area in equatorial latitudes under a clear sky at mid-

717

day. The nineteenth-century picture of an earth, initially fiery hot but progressively cooling so that yesterday it displayed a glacial climate and tomorrow it will be too frigid to support life, may now be thrown into the discard. The earth will "grow old and die" only as a result of failure to receive adequate supplies of radiant energy from the sun. The prospect that the sun will "burn itself out" in a decrepit old age is so remote as to baffle all attempts to date that untoward event even by those who are expert in manipulating astronomic figures. Nor is there any likelihood that the space relations between earth and sun will change appreciably within scores of millions of years and put the earth either too close to the sun or too distant from it for comfort.

The lurid pictures of a sudden catastrophic debacle resulting from collision with some other heavenly body—comet, planet, star, or what you will —are products of a vivid imagination wholly without foundation in astronomic fact or theory.

The only plausible alternative to the conclusion that earth and sun will continue the even tenor of their ways for an inconceivably long period of time is that the sun will some day imitate the supernovae occasionally detected among the stars and terminate the existence of the entire solar system by a gigantic explosion. Precisely one such supernova has been observed within the galaxy of the Milky Way and several such in all the other galaxies of stars during the past few decades. The astronomers could, therefore, calculate for us the chances on a statistical basis that any individual star—the sun, for example—would suffer such a fate within any given period of time. The result would be a figure so infinitesimal as to set at rest the mind of even the most jittery of questioners. Pending the discovery of the kind of premonitory symptoms displayed by stars about to blow themselves to atoms, the best that can be done is to rest content in history. Since the earliest records of living creatures were left as fossils, if not indeed since the earliest sedimentary rocks were formed, the sun has faithfully maintained its energy output within a fairly narrow range and has given no evidence of any fluctuations that might suggest any significant change in its behavior.

The geologist may, therefore, turn with confidence from the long perspective of geologic past with its 1½ to 2 billion years of recorded earth history to a similarly long prospect for the future. Time is one of the most overwhelming resources of our universe.

It should not be inferred, however, that the earth will continue in the future to display the same environmental conditions as those which we enjoy today. The history of mankind thus far has been enacted against a background that in the full perspective of earth history is truly extraordinary. The geologic period in which we live is a time of unusually rugged and extensive lands, with notably varied climate ranging from the glacial cold of Greenland and Antarctica to the oppressive warmth and humidity of certain equatorial regions. Such conditions have apparently recurred many times at long-spaced intervals since the oldest known rocks were formed, but added together the time thus represented cannot be as much as a fourth of geologic time. Much more characteristic of earth history as a whole have been the conditions illustrated by those periods when corals thrived in shallow seas occupying the site of Baffin Land and North Greenland, and coal-forming plants flourished on Antarctica. The probability is strong that eventually, say in 5 or 10 million years, the earth will display again the physical conditions of many past geologic periods that were characterized by broad low lands, wide shallow seas, and uniform genial climate.

But most of us have a greater interest in the next few centuries than in the subsequent millions of years. Minor changes in climate will doubtless occur just as they have in the last few thousand years. Unfortunately, or perhaps fortunately, there is no basis for prediction concerning their nature, whether for better or for worse. There is really no good reason for referring to the present as "a post-glacial epoch"; it may prove to be an interglacial epoch. But our ancestors weathered ice ages in the past, and presumably we are better equipped for such contingencies than they were. Should the average annual temperature of the earth as a whole be reduced something like 10° F. and remain at that lower level for a few millennia, it is likely that once more the greater part of Canada, the northern United States, and the Scandinavian countries would be buried beneath great ice sheets. But in consequence of the removal of water from the sea as vapor to form the snow to produce the glacial ice, considerable areas now shallowly submerged along the coast lines in middle and equatorial latitudes would emerge as dry land. Indeed, it is likely that the area of land suitable for human abode would be nearly or quite as great at the climax of a glacial period as it is today.

By the same token, the disappearance of existing bodies of glacial ice as a result of rapid amelioration of climate in the not-distant future would, if it occurred, be a decidedly mixed blessing. Return to the sea the water now imprisoned in the ice on the Arctic islands, Greenland and Antarctica without any compensating changes in crustal elevation, and sea level would be raised 150 to 160 feet the world around. Considering the number of people who now work or sleep in buildings in metropolitan communities not over 150 feet above sea level, the importance of such a change is readily apparent. But from the geologists' point of view these are relatively trivial matters. With due deference to the nature of the climatic variations and geologic changes which are certain to occur in the next few thousand years, there is nothing to be expected from such sources that would seriously deter the human species from maintaining a comfortable existence on the surface of the earth for an indefinitely long period of time—a period to be measured in millions rather than in mere thousands of years.

2

At last, it is generally understood that man is a part of nature. He may be something more than an animal (that depends largely upon definition), but he is none the less truly a part of the animal world. Like the other inhabitants of the earth, man is a product of evolutionary processes operating on this particular planet.

We may be the latest product of the creative forces displaying themselves in the organic development taking place in this particular portion of the cosmos, but we have no reason to assume that we are the last achievement of those forces. Nor does the fact that man has arisen from a lowly origin through processes of evolution validate the optimistic inference that he will necessarily continue his progress to ever higher levels of activity. Evolution does not guarantee progress; it merely guarantees change. The change may be for the better or the worse, depending upon the conditions of time and place and the vitality of the individuals concerned.

The pages of Mother Earth's diary reveal an amazing and thought-provoking record of the progress of living creatures throughout the long eras of earth history. Again and again, in the procession of the living, dynasties of animals or plants have arisen from a humble origin to a position of world supremacy, maintained for a comparatively brief period and then lost forever. Some have disappeared entirely as their paths have led them off into blind alleys. Others have sunk to a low level and have continued a degenerate existence to the present day. A few have given rise to other and more efficient forms of life that superseded their predecessors as leaders in the procession. Gradually we are discovering some of the reasons for success and failure along the path of life. Beyond question, man may profit from these experiences of the past, if he uses the intellectual and moral resources which are available for him.

From the point of view attained through knowledge of geologic life development, man has today a unique opportunity to gain continuing security for himself and his progeny on the face of the earth, but whether or not he takes advantage of that opportunity is to be determined largely by himself. So far as we can tell, man is the first animal possessing the power to determine his own evolutionary destiny, but there is nothing in the record which guarantees that he will use that power wisely.

The animal species that in the past have been able to maintain their existence for more than 2 or 3 million years are relatively few in number. Most of them were comparatively simple types belonging to the less highly organized branches or phyla of the animal kingdom. Many were inhabitants of the sea where environmental conditions were remarkably stable throughout long periods of time. Among placental mammals, the major subdivision of the vertebrates to which man belongs, there is no similar record of longevity. Except under extraordinary conditions of geographic isolation, no species of placental mammal has persisted more than 2 or 3 million years. No matter how successful it may have been temporarily in multiplying and spreading over the face of the earth, each has become extinct in a geologically brief span of time. Perhaps a half million years might appropriately be taken as the average "life" of a species in this group of highly organized and notably complex creatures.

But extinction does not necessarily mean failure; it has frequently indicated the acme of achievement. For example, some of the now extinct three-toed horses and four-toed camels passed on "the torch of progress" to their descendants, the one-toed horses and two-toed camels, and thus gained long-continuing security for their kind.

What then does the future hold for mankind? Genus *Homo* has already existed for 3 or 4 hundred thousand years; the species *Homo sapiens* has about 50 thousand years to its credit. If the average applies, we may expect nearly or quite a half million years more of existence for our kind and then either oblivion as we reach the end of a blind alley or progressive development into some type of descendant better adjusted than we to the total environmental factors of the time.

3

But does the average apply? Must man exit from the scene through either of the doors, that which closed behind the dinosaurs and titanotheres or that which opened before the three-toed horses and notharctines?

Most creatures have gained security by specializing in adjustment of structure and habit to particular environmental conditions, whereas man is a specialist in adjustability of structures and habits to a variety of environments. No other vertebrate can live as can he on Antarctic ice cap, in Amazonian jungle, beneath the surface of the sea, or high in the air.

Furthermore, man is the world's foremost specialist in transforming environments to bring them within the range of his powers. Far more efficient than the beaver or the mound-building ant, he drains the swamp, irrigates the desert, tunnels the mountain, bridges the river, digs the canal, conditions the air in home, factory, and office.

As a matter of fact, adjustability to environment is accomplished more by controlling surroundings than by modifying internal organs or essential functions of the body. When we ascend with Major Stevens into the stratosphere, or dive with Dr. Beebe 500 fathoms deep off Bermuda, or live with Admiral Byrd through the long night of Little America, we take along with us a sample of sea-level atmosphere and temperate climate that is our real environment in a situation otherwise unbearable. Fur-lined parkas and tropical linen suits are but a medium for ensuring an immediate environment as nearly as possible like that of middle latitudes when living in polar or equatorial surroundings.

But regardless of interpretation of procedure, the result is clear. Man has placed himself in control of external conditions to an extent immeasurably greater than any other creature. He has practically "drawn the teeth" of environment.

Although we know little of the details, it is certain that most of the creatures of the past, who "have had their day and ceased to be," were forced into extinction by changes of one sort or another in their environment, changes which came with such relative speed that they were unable to make adjustment to them in time. Man need have no fear on that score.

4

It is, however, immediately apparent that man's conquest of his surroundings has resulted from his clever use of ·things. Unless there is a ceaseless flow of cotton, flax, and wool, of coal, iron, and petroleum, of copper, lead, and tin, from ground to processing plant to consumer, he becomes a puny weakling. It is because he uses certain resources provided by his environment that he is freed from slavery to his environment. Are these resources adequate to keep him supplied with what he needs to maintain indefinitely the sort of existence to which he has accustomed himself?

There are two fundamental sources of the goods and the energy that man uses in the grim business of obtaining the sort of living that he apparently desires. On the one hand there is the farm and the waterfall, on the other there is the mine and the quarry. Things which grow in the field or forest, and power produced by falling water are in the category of annual income. Now that scientific research has made available the limitless quantity of nitrogen in the air for use as fertilizer, the resources of the plant and animal kingdoms are renewable; we use them, but we need never use them up. In startling contrast, the resources of the mineral kingdom are nonrenewable; they are in the category of accumulated capital. Petroleum and coal, copper and iron, lead and vanadium, these and many other prerequisites of modern civilization have been accumulated by nature through hundreds of millions of years of geologic activity. Thanks to scientific research, man is exhausting that store of mineral wealth in a few hundred, or at most a few thousand, years. That inescapable fact is at rock bottom one of the most fundamental causes of economic distress, of war between nations, and of strife between classes.

Fairly accurate estimates of the world stores of many nonrenewable resources are now available. Take petroleum as an illustration. The known available reserves of petroleum beneath the surface of the United States total at present approximately 17 billion barrels. Experts differ in their guesses as to the quantity of petroleum that may be discovered in the future in areas that have not yet been adequately explored with the drill, or in known fields by discovery of deeper reservoirs not yet reached by the deepest wells in those fields. There are also many varying shades of optimism and pessimism concerning the possibility of increasing materially the percentage of recovery of the oil present in a reservoir rock when penetrated by drilling operations. Estimates of the quantity to be added to our petroleum reserves from those two sources range from 7 or 8 billion barrels to 15 or 20 billion. I would incline toward the larger figures, considering them as maxima that are extremely unlikely to be exceeded. On that basis, the present store of available petroleum beneath the surface of the United States is 25 to 35 billion barrels. That is only about 30 times the annual domestic consumption of petroleum in recent years. The average annual production of petroleum in the United States during the 5 years from 1934 through 1938 was almost 1 billion 100 million barrels, and the 1939 production exceeds $1\frac{1}{4}$ billion barrels. At the present rate of withdrawal, the domestic stores of this essential raw material would, therefore, be exhausted in less than a third of a century.

Data are not nearly so precise for the majority of foreign countries as for the United States. It is, however, fairly safe to conclude that the world stores of petroleum will last only something like 75 years at the present rate of withdrawal. With the possible exception of Mexico, no other country has been as successful as the United States in the attempt to exhaust its petroleum resources in the shortest possible period of time, but rapid progress toward that result is now being made in many regions.

Lest we become too pessimistic in response to such unwelcome figures, we should promptly note that substitutes for petroleum are already known. Gasoline, fuel oil, and lubricating oil can now be manufactured from coal and other rocks rich in carbon, by processes of hydrogenation and polymerization. These are expensive processes and their products cannot now compete with the products from petroleum even in countries far removed, both geographically and psychologically, from the more productive oil fields. They will, however, come into use more and more in the next few decades.

Enough bituminous and subbituminous coal is known to be available within the United States to meet the present annual demand for coal, plus enough to manufacture gasoline and fuel oil in sufficient quantity to meet current demands for at least 2,000 years. In addition there is enough oil shale—a rock rich in carbon but containing little or no oil—to meet present needs for petroleum products for at least 3,000 or 4,000 years.

Although petroleum affords an excellent illustration of the relation of nonrenewable resources to the activities of man, it is by no means typical of the items comprising nature's accumulated capital. For nearly all of the important nonrenewable resources, the known world stores are thousands of times as great as the annual world consumption instead of less than a hundred times. But for the few which like petroleum are not known to be available in such vast quantities, the story is much the same. Substitutes are already known, or potential sources of alternative supply are already at hand, in quantities adequate to meet our current needs for at least 2,000 or 3,000 years. There is, therefore, no prospect of the imminent exhaustion of any of the essential raw materials, so far as the world as a whole is concerned, provided our demands for them are not multiplied rapidly in the future.

That, of course, raises another question. Will the demand for non-renewable resources increase materially in the future and thus hasten their exhaustion? Recalling the fact that the human population of the earth has increased almost fivefold in number in the last 300 years, we might well be fearful on that score. The study of current population trends, however, makes it readily apparent that the next few hundred years will by no means duplicate that record of the past. If present trends continue, the all-time maximum population of the United States will be attained about the year 1970 and will total little more than 150 million souls. Thereafter, except for possible influx of immigrants from other countries, no further increase in numbers is to be expected.

Accurate figures are available for only a few other countries, such as England, France, and Germany, but there is a strong probability that the all-time maximum for the white races will be reached during the last third of the twentieth century and for the entire population of the earth before the end of the twenty-first century. Although the human family has doubled its numbers since 1860, it is extremely unlikely that it will ever reach twice its present number of approximately 2 billion. The pressure of demand for nonrenewable resources will not, therefore, become acute because of the increase in population in the near future. Mother Earth is a very wealthy benefactress, and our heritage of physical resources is far greater than ordinarily supposed.

There is, however, another reason why current consumption of non-renewable resources cannot be taken as the basis for computing the "life" of such stores of basic materials. The demand for automobiles, telephones, radios, airplanes, and zippers, is today very unevenly distributed. Only a small fraction of the human population uses such things in any large amount. Other peoples are beginning to demand them and will do so increasingly as they become acquainted with the "benefits of civilization."

In a few decades, unless we return to savagery, the world demand for many nonrenewable resources will be twice or thrice that of today.

Taking all these things into consideration, it would appear that world stores of needed natural resources are adequate to supply a basis for the comfortable existence of every human being who is likely to dwell anywhere on the face of the earth for something like a thousand years to come.

Even so, there may be found here an excuse for the policy of "grabbing while the grabbing is good" which motivates many individuals and nations at the present time. That excuse might, of course, be offset by the suggestion that there is no need to take thought for a morrow a thousand years hence, if we have any respect for the ingenuity of our remote offspring. There is, however, another phase of current trends in human history that should not be overlooked in this connection.

One hundred years ago, something like 80 per cent of all the things man used had their source on farms; most of the energy used to do the work of the world came from the muscles of living beings and from falling water. Today only about 30 per cent of the things man uses come from things that grow; most of the energy with which work is done comes from petroleum and coal. For a century or more, the policy has been to use relatively less of the annual income and more of the stored capital.

Now comes the change. Automobile steering wheels are made from soy beans; piano keys from cottage cheese; innumerable articles fashioned of plastics are produced in part from corncobs and alfalfa; multitudinous metal and rubber substitutes are synthesized from various farm crops. Energy is transmitted at high voltages for hundreds of miles from hydroelectric turbines. A considerable portion of the annual budget for research is being devoted to progress in the direction of using more of the renewable resources—man's annual income, and less of the nonrenewable resources—nature's stored capital.

What this new policy will mean is readily apparent. With progress along such lines, the pressure for political control of metalliferous ore deposits, coal fields, and oil pools is lessened. Much of the physical basis for international jealousy is liquidated. At last the intelligence of science may make it truly practical to beat our "swords into ploughshares, our spears into pruning hooks."

Again comes the insistent question from the pessimistic critic. Is there land enough? Is there sufficient fertile soil to provide adequate food and in addition the plant materials for the ever-expanding chemical industries? And again we hear the same reply. Yes, there is enough and to spare. J. D. Bernal computes from apparently valid data that the cultivation of 2 billion acres of land by the methods now in vogue in Great Britain would provide an optimum food supply for the entire population of the earth. "Two billion acres is less than half the present cultivated area of 4 billion 200 million acres, itself hardly 12 per cent of the land surface of the earth." And in this calculation no account is taken of the increased yields that may confidently be expected from the continuing research of agronomists, plant breeders, and experts in animal husbandry, not to mention recent developments in the new science of the soilless growth of plants. Evidently, the predictions of Malthus notwithstanding, mankind need have no fear that increasing populations will place an impossible burden upon the available sources of food. Human ingenuity, intelligent use of renewable resources, wise adjustment of structures and habits to environmental conditions, seem competent to dispel that dread shadow.

But these optimistic conclusions concerning the relation of man to the nonrenewable and renewable resources essential for comfortable existence are based upon world statistics. Obviously they do not apply with equal force to the economy of individual nations. No nation, not even the Soviet Union, Brazil, or the United States of America, embraces within its political frontiers a sufficient variety of geologic structures to give it adequate supplies of all the various metalliferous ores necessary as raw materials for modern industrial operations. The United States, for example, must import nickel, tin, antimony, chromium, and platinum if American manufacturers are to use those metals in the fabrication of articles essential to what we are pleased to call the civilized way of life. Likewise, no nation enjoys a sufficient variety of climatic conditions to permit all kinds of foodstuffs to be grown on its farms and fields or gathered from its forests, and to allow the growth of all the various plants contributing raw materials to industry. The United States, again the most significant example for us, is forced to import all the bananas, coffee, tea, camphor, coconuts, flax, jute, quinine, rubber, and shellac consumed in this country, either from foreign countries or its own overseas possessions. It is entirely possible that, within a few decades, substitutes of domestic origin may be available to take the place of many, or even all, of such commodities or that plant breeders and agronomists may find a practical way of extending the geographical limits of some of the plants whose products are considered essential so that any nation occupying a large fraction of any continent may actually be self-sufficient. But for the present and probably for a long time to come it is evident that every nation is dependent upon many other nations for the raw materials that it needs for its own industrial prosperity.

Perhaps the most important fact concerning the life of man today is this fact of interdependence. No nation, community, or individual can gain any lasting measure of security without taking that fact into consideration. The resources that man must utilize, if he wishes to escape the fate of his less intelligent relatives now known only by their fossil remains, are unevenly distributed and locally concentrated. The techniques of discovering and utilizing them are now fairly well known, but satisfactory procedures for making them and their products available to all members of the human family are not close at hand.

The very solution of the physical problems which man encounters in his attempt to maintain his foothold upon the earth brings him all the more forcefully into bruising contact with psychical and spiritual problems that must also be solved if he is to continue his existence on this planet. The critical question for the twentieth century is: How can 2 or 3 billion human beings be satisfactorily organized for the wise use and equitable distribution of resources that are abundant enough for all, but are unevenly scattered over the face of the earth? Clearly, the future of man depends upon finding and applying the correct answer to that specific but far-reaching question.

Man is not only a specialist in the art of coordinated activity, but the trend toward organization is recognizable in the entire development of cosmic administration. Electrons, neutrons, and protons are organized into atoms, atoms into molecules, molecules into compounds. Some of the compounds prove to be cells, and these are organized to form individual plants and animals. Latest of all in the history of creative evolution certain individuals have been organized into societies. Transcending all that has gone before is the development of human society, obviously the most difficult, but at the same time potentially the most glorious organization yet attempted.

Two antagonistic alternatives present themselves as possible bases for this organization. The issue between the two has never before been so clearly drawn as it is today. The social group, whether it be the family, the industrial or commercial company, or the political unit, may be organized on the principle of regimentation, or it may be developed according to democratic principles. Both methods are being tried under a variety of conditions, and each has something to be said in its favor. But both cannot be equally conducive to the continuing existence of mankind. One or the other must be selected as the basis for the future security of man.

If regimentation be the choice, then the great mass of humankind must be trained for obedience—blind, unquestioning, but superbly skillful obedience. The educator becomes the intellectual and spiritual counterpart of the drill sergeant in the army. This is no menial task, nor is its objective a mean one. Skill is a commodity of which there is never likely to be an oversupply. On the other hand, if democracy be the choice, the great mass of humankind must be trained for wise, self-determined cooperation. Precisely those qualities of mind and heart which have long been extolled in Christian doctrine must be developed to the fullest possible extent. Not only skill but also the ability to govern oneself, the eternal prerequisite for freedom, must be developed in each member of the group.

Insofar as physical existence is concerned, there would seem to be little or no choice between these alternatives. Human nature being what it is today, perhaps the regimentation of society may temporarily be the more efficient method. But the full circle of organic law embraces more than mere existence. From the continuity of the evolutionary process, there has emerged a creature who is aware of vivid values in life that may be found beyond the goods necessary for comfortable existence. Ideas and ideals are powerful determining factors in the world today, and among them the ideal of freedom for the individual in the midst of social restraint is the most vital and compelling of all. Though it baffle our scientific tools for measurement, it is nonetheless a reality.

It is in the yearning for freedom, the love of beauty, the search for truth, the recognition of moral law and in the awareness of spiritual forces that human nature is distinguished from all other sorts of nature. Man shares with other animals the need for satisfactory economics, for adequate food and shelter, for the goods essential to existence, but his needs transcend these physical factors because his nature differs from theirs. Probably nine-tenths of all the words that have been used since the dawn of speech in reference to "human nature" have referred to those elements in the nature of man that are shared with other animals rather than to those that are man's unique possession. It would be far better to concentrate upon the latter and thus to distinguish human nature from animal nature.

Regimentation may be good for man as an animal; through that type of social organization his need for goods may be efficiently supplied. But regimentation is certainly not good for human nature as thus distinguished. Experience verifies what wisdom foresees; regimentation stultifies the spirit, destroys personality, standardizes thought and action. Worst of all, regimentation means stagnation of the creative process and, as we have seen, stagnation among the more complexly organized vertebrates has led inevitably to extinction. If man attempts to live by bread alone, mankind commits collective suicide. Apparently the best and perhaps the only chance for mankind to succeed in the quest for security is through progress in the art of living on a high spiritual plane rather than through exclusive attention to the science of existence on a purely physical level.

5

To put this same thought in more specific terms, it means that coordinated activity directed toward efficient organization of individuals must become cooperative activity directed toward the enrichment of personality within an efficiently organized society. This requires both intelligence and good will.

Fortunately, these characteristics are uniquely developed in the species of placental mammal with which we are preeminently concerned. Man is a specialist in the use of both. The trend of the past 5,000 years may well continue, despite numerous temporary setbacks, throughout the next few centuries at least.

It is sometimes suggested that because man has specialized in brains, brains may cause his downfall, just as presumably the overspecialization in external armament contributed to the downfall of certain herbivorous dinosaurs. That argument by analogy is, however, heavily punctuated with fallacies. There is as yet no evidence that mankind is weighted down with a superabundance of intelligence. On the contrary, it is failure to act intelligently that endangers individuals and groups in the midst of competition. To see in advance the remote consequences of contemplated action is an ability that ought to be increasingly cultivated rather than scouted as a menace.

There seems to be no good reason why a sound mind should not be accompanied by a sound body. If the number of psychopathic individuals is increasing in this high-speed, technologic age, it is a challenge to be met not by bemoaning the imminent collapse of civilization but by intelligent adjustment of habits and activities to the new demands of the new times.

Once the commitment is made to the belief that the cooperative way of life offers the best chance for the future security of man as an inhabitant of the earth, the need is greater for intelligence to be used as a guide for good will, rather than for good will to be applied as a brake on any possible increase in intelligence.

The roots of self-centered individualism may be traced backward for at least 600 million years in the record of geologic life development, whereas our heritage of social consciousness dates from a time only about 60 million years ago when gregarious instincts became clearly evident among placental mammals. That trend is, however, especially apparent in the group from which mankind has stemmed.

Man is still in the stage of specific youth. His golden age, if any, is in the future rather than in the past. Human nature is still sufficiently plastic and pliable to permit considerable change, notably in this important area of attitudes and relationships wherein the increase of good will as a motive for action seems most likely to result in beneficial adjustments to the new factors in the environment.

In thus seeking a satisfactory coordination of intelligence and good will, it becomes necessary for research scientists to give more thought than has been customary in the past to the social consequences of their work. They share with statesmen, politicians, educators, and all molders of public opinion the responsibility for determining the uses to which the new tools provided by scientific research are put. As scientists, they should continue to seek truth regardless of its consequences and to increase human efficiency in every possible way, but as members of society, as individual representatives of a species seeking future security as inhabitants of the earth, they must also do their utmost to ensure wise use of knowledge and constructive application of energy.

There is a real difference between the so-called social sciences and the natural and physical sciences that has an important bearing here. It is not that there is anything unnatural about the social sciences. Man is a part of nature, and the study of human society is just as truly natural science in the real sense of the term as any other study. The difference arises from the peculiar factors and particular functions pertaining to the cooperative way of life. Whereas the scientific use of things may be achieved through the efforts of a very small minority of the citizens, provided with adequate facilities for research, the scientific organization of society in a democracy can be achieved only when the majority of its citizens have the scientific attitude toward social problems and act in accordance with that attitude of mind. In other words, only a few physicists, chemists, and technologists are required for the mastery of our physical environment, but for victory in the struggle with ourselves every man must be his own sociologist.

Although this places upon the forces of education a Herculean task, it is not nearly so impossible an assignment as at a first glance it might appear to be. In the first place, the responsibility upon the individual citizen is rarely that of designing a new social structure or charting a new program for society. Almost invariably it is his duty merely to select from many plans, programs, or proposals the one that seems to him most likely to produce the most desirable results for all concerned. In the second place, scientific habits of mind have already been developed to a greater extent than is ordinarily recognized. The garage mechanic attacks the problem of a balky automobile in a truly scientific manner. The salesman uses psychology in planning his approach to a difficult prospect. The housewife thinks scientifically when about to concoct a new dessert or redecorate the living room. In most cases, it is only necessary to apply in the area of social relationships the same habits of mind that have been followed in the area of individual behavior.

6

In conclusion, the outlook for the future of man as an inhabitant of the earth is far from pessimistic. If certain tendencies already developing are encouraged and certain resources already available are capitalized to the full, there is good reason to expect that mankind will maintain existence and even live happily for an indefinitely long period of time. The opportunity is his to demonstrate the intrinsic worth of biologic phenomena and thus to justify the vast expenditure of time and energy involved in organic evolution. With greater emphasis upon the development of intelligence and good will, he may achieve that which the temporarily triumphant dynasties of the past have failed to achieve. Thus the geologist may turn from the long perspective of geologic history to the enticing vista of the geologic future of earth and man with high hope and even with confident assurance.

Conrad Aiken

The poets have the last word. Only poetry can make finality beautiful and so make it bearable. Conrad Aiken and the poets who follow have set regret to music.

ALL LOVELY THINGS

All lovely things will have an ending,
All lovely things will fade and die,
And youth, that's now so bravely spending,
Will beg a penny by and by.

Fine ladies all are soon forgotten,
And goldenrod is dust when dead,
The sweetest flesh and flowers are rotten
And cobwebs tent the brightest head.

Come back, true love! Sweet youth, return!
But time goes on, and will, unheeding,
Though hands will reach, and eyes will yearn,
And the wild days set true hearts bleeding.

Come back, true love! Sweet youth, remain!
But goldenrod and daisies wither,
And over them blows autumn rain,
They pass, they pass, and know not whither.

Thomas Hardy

*In "Afterwards" Hardy reveals himself as a man of unexpected tender-
ness and sensibility. The new leaves of May, the hawk's flight, the hedgehog, the stars, the broken cadence of a tolling bell—these were some of
the little things which he loved and would be remembered for.*

AFTERWARDS

When the Present has latched its postern behind my tremulous stay,
  And the May month flaps its glad green leaves like wings,
Delicate-filmed as new-spun silk, will the neighbors say,
  "He was a man who used to notice such things"?

If it be in the dusk when, like an eyelid's soundless blink,
  The dewfall-hawk comes crossing the shades to alight
Upon the wind-warped upland thorn, a gazer may think,
  "To him this must have been a familiar sight."

If I pass during some nocturnal blackness, mothy and warm,
  When the hedgehog travels furtively over the lawn,
One may say, "He strove that such innocent creatures should come to no
    harm,
  But he could do little for them; and now he is gone."

If, when hearing that I have been stilled at last, they stand at the door,
  Watching the full-starred heavens that winter sees,
Will this thought rise on those who will meet my face no more,
  "He was one who had an eye for such mysteries"?

And will any say when my bell of quittance is heard in the gloom,
  And a crossing breeze cuts a pause in its outrollings,
Till they rise again, as they were a new bell's boom,
  "He hears it not now, but used to notice such things"?

Robert Frost

The two poems which follow, though published in different volumes of Frost's work, may almost be regarded as companion pieces. Two moods, two whole philosophies, are compressed into these simple and tender lines. The second poem answers the mood of the first.

RELUCTANCE

Out through the fields and the woods
   And over the walls I have wended;
I have climbed the hills of view
   And looked at the world, and descended;
I have come by the highway home,
   And lo, it is ended.

The leaves are all dead on the ground,
   Save those that the oak is keeping
To ravel them one by one
   And let them go scraping and creeping
Out over the crusted snow,
   When others are sleeping.

And the dead leaves lie huddled and still,
   No longer blown hither and thither;
The last lone aster is gone;
   The flowers of the wich-hazel wither;
The heart is still aching to seek,
   But the feet question "Whither?"

Ah, when to the heart of man
   Was it ever less than a treason
To go with the drift of things,
   To yield with a grace to reason,
And bow and accept the end
   Of a love or a season?

733

ACCEPTANCE

When the spent sun throws up its rays on cloud
And goes down burning into the gulf below,
No voice in nature is heard to cry aloud
At what has happened. Birds, at least, must know
It is the change to darkness in the sky.
Murmuring something quiet in her breast,
One bird begins to close a faded eye;
Or overtaken too far from his nest,
Hurrying low above the grove, some waif
Swoops just in time to his remembered tree.
At most he thinks or twitters softly, "Safe!
Now let the night be dark for all of me.
Let the night be too dark for me to see
Into the future. Let what will be, be."

Elinor Wylie

*Elinor Wylie (1885-1928) was born in New Jersey of a family long fa-
mous in Pennsylvania history. She was educated at Bryn Mawr. Her
beauty, her romances, her scholarship, and her literary virtuosity have
already become almost a legend of American letters. But the novels, such
as* The Venetian Glass Nephew *and* The Orphan Angel, *and her poems,
sumptuously issued in a collected edition, survive to testify to the intricate dexterity, the metaphysical subtlety, the brittle exquisiteness of this
late descendant of John Donne.*

FAREWELL, SWEET DUST

Now I have lost you, I must scatter
All of you on the air henceforth;
Not that to me it can ever matter
But it's only fair to the rest of earth.

Now especially, when it is winter
And the sun's not half so bright as he was,
Who wouldn't be glad to find a splinter
That once was you, in the frozen grass?

Snowflakes, too, will be softer feathered,
Clouds, perhaps, will be whiter plumed;
Rain, whose brilliance you caught and gathered,
Purer silver have reassumed.

Farewell, sweet dust; I was never a miser:
Once, for a minute, I made you mine:
Now you are gone, I am none the wiser
But the leaves of the willow are bright as wine.

Maxwell Anderson

At the end of Winterset, *a tragedy inspired by the Sacco-Vanzetti case,
the aged Esdras, speaking by way of chorus to the action, sadly regards
his daughter Miriamne and her lover Mio, killed by the gangsters' bullets; and mindful of the brave way they died he speaks with passionate
finality of man's victorious courage in face of "the endless dark."*

From WINTERSET

Oh, Miriamne,
and Mio—Mio, my son—know this where you lie,
this is the glory of earthborn men and women,
not to cringe, never to yield, but standing,
take defeat implacable and defiant,
die unsubmitting. I wish that I'd died so,
long ago; before you're old you'll wish
that you had died as they have. On this star,
in this hard star-adventure, knowing not
what the fires mean to right and left, nor whether
a meaning was intended or presumed,
man can stand up, and look out blind, and say:
in all these turning lights I find no clue,
only a masterless night, and in my blood
no certain answer, yet is my mind my own,
yet is my heart a cry toward something dim
in distance, which is higher than I am
and makes me emperor of the endless dark
even in seeking! What odds and ends of life
men may live otherwise, let them live, and then

go out, as I shall go, and you. Our part
is only to bury them. Come, take her up.
They must not lie here.

John Holmes

Address to the Living, *the first book of John Holmes* (1904-   ), *fulfills the promise of its title. With the confidence of youth he praises the
experiences of this world, holds the certainties of the present against the
secrets of the future, and proclaims simply, "Life is enough."* Map of My
Country, *a later book, shows a sharpening of perceptions, a deepening
of tone. In its notable introduction the author tells what he has learned
as a teacher of English at Tufts College guiding beginners in the writing art, and talks freely of his own purposes as a poet.*

TESTAMENT

There are too many poems with the word
Death, death, death, tolling among the rhyme.
Let us remember death, a soaring bird
Whose wing will shadow all of us in time.

Let us remember death, an accident
Of darkness fallen far away and near.
But, being mortal, be most eloquent
Of daylight and the moment now and here.

Not to the name of death over and over,
But the prouder name of life, is poetry sworn.
The living man has words that rediscover
Even the dust from whence the man was born,

And words that may be water, food, and fire,
Of love and pity and perfection wrought,
Or swords or roses, as we may require,
Or sudden towers for the climbing thought.

Out of the beating heart the words that beat
Sing of the fountain that is never spent.
Let us remember life, the salt, the sweet,
And make of that our tireless testament.

THEME ASSIGNMENTS

THE following theme assignments supplement and loosely parallel the reading assigned in the text. Many of these assignments are not directly related to a particular piece of reading but fall within the student's own frame of reference. His reading provides a mood, a springboard, a range of ideas from which, indirectly, he may derive his impetus. The actual content of his theme is best drawn from the deep springs of his own thoughts, emotions, studies, conversations, and experiences—in short, his personal history. In the later assignments the student will find a preponderance of subjects outside his first-hand knowledge, and then he will have to learn the judicious use of works of reference.

Note that this is no mere list of titles, such as "My Pet Ambition" or "Why I Am Going to College." The assignments provide sufficient specifications to give the student-writer some preconception of his task. Often he is presented with a situation which he must figure out for himself. The conditions are given. He must do the rest.

These assignments are no more than samples. They cannot be otherwise if they are to be fresh and timely and immediate. They ought to be related to the morning's headlines, the evening's broadcast, no less than to last week's reading in *Present Tense*. They must be applicable to the students who use them, and the requirements of the student in the mid-West are widely different from those on the East Coast or the West Coast or in Canada. Somewhat different assignments may be needed for men and for women. In short, these samples should be adapted to the particular circumstances under which they are used.

The editor gratefully acknowledges the assistance of his colleagues, especially Dr. I. J. Kapstein, who suggested assignments and tested them in their classes.

I. FIRST PERSON SINGULAR

1. Try to imagine meeting yourself as you were at nine years old. What traits would you rediscover in the boy or girl that was you? (A Boy I Knew)

2. If you could meet the child that was you, what would you talk about? Reproduce the conversation. (A Boy I Knew)

3. In a conversation with your parents tell the earliest experiences of your life as you remember them—and as they remember them.

4. Remembering the games and deviltries of your childhood, compare them with the activities of children in the 1880's. (Introduction to the Universe)

5. You are swapping experiences with one of your new classmates: tell him an episode from your childhood which still stands out vividly in your memory.

6. If you no longer live in your childhood home, try to recall its features for the benefit of a friend who knows you only in your present environment.

7. A group of students are describing the most completely carefree and irresponsible thing they ever did, and its consequences. Add your contribution. (The Circus)

8. Assume that a local broadcasting station (or the college radio network) is sponsoring a contest for accounts of "My Most Embarrassing Moment." Write your entry, telling how you got into an embarrassing situation during secondary school years, and how you got out of it. (Calf Love)

9. During your last year in high school you have invited your girl to the Senior dance, but a distant cousin arrives unexpectedly for a visit and your mother insists that you take her instead. Complicating the situation is the fact that your girl is sensitive to slights. Write her and explain everything!

10. For a magazine addressed to the high-school age write an article, based on your own experience, in which you explain how to train an animal. (I Get a Colt to Break In)

11. If you are a student of music or some other art, discuss the place of the artist in modern society. (Young Archimedes; Whatever Hope We Have)

12. In a letter to a friend who will enter your college next year describe several members of the faculty against the background of the campus on a particular day. (Fine Morning)

13. You and a new friend of the opposite sex are getting acquainted. Tell your friend some of your early ambitions for a career, how you came to dream them, and what happened to them.

14. Describe two dances, one which you enjoyed and one which you did not enjoy, and show clearly the reasons for your reactions.

15. You have a classmate who has come to college with misgivings as to the value of higher education; he is discouraged by the necessity of earning his way through college. Talk over his problems with him and show him how college looks to you in prospect.

16. Troubled by the uncertainties of the future and disheartened by low grades in his first courses, your roommate is thinking of leaving college and getting a job. Help him to think his way through his problem.

17. Write two brief treatments of the same topic of campus opinion: one wholly favorable, the other wholly unfavorable.

18. "We do not know what the humanities are, we do not know why we teach them, and we do not know what results to expect from them, when they are taught." After a careful reading of "The Place of the Humanities in American Education" write a letter to the president of your college in which you attempt a definition of the humanities, show why you think they should (or should not) be stressed, and discuss what results you expect to get from your college studies.

19. You are continually questioning whether college is good enough for you. But are you good enough for college? Have you the maturity, the intellectual background, the clear purpose which success in college requires?

20. Stephen Leacock sees in the mounting complexity of knowledge an unfortunate lengthening of the period of education. If you see a solution to this dilemma write an article on education as it might be; do not try to plan an actual curriculum, but indicate what, in general, would be a good education without unreasonable expenditure of time. (Education Eating Up Life)

21. Your college daily is holding a symposium on the subject: "Who gets the more from college, the student who must count every cent or the student who has an adequate allowance for all expenses?" Write your contribution. Refer to your experience and observation. (Forty Rubles a Month)

22. In a democracy equal opportunity should be open to all. Do you think that the federal government should support universal college education as a democratic ideal?

23. Have you learned more during the past semester inside or outside the classroom? Document your answer with actual experiences.

24. Write a feature article for your former school paper telling in what ways (aside from matters of routine) college life differs from school life and how far college fulfills your expectations. Take pains to make the article lively and amusing.

25. "The lack of leisure on an American campus is its greatest curse, but fraternity membership encourages not leisure but idleness." Explain the distinction between leisure and idleness, and comment on the quotation.

26. Before you left for college your crabbed old uncle Ezra told you: "'Tisn't worth it! The only real education is the one you get in the school of hard knocks." Now that you have had time to test the truth of his opinion, write him what you think of college education. Be tactful but sincere.

27. "The American undergraduate," bumbled the chapel orator, "lives a happy, carefree existence, protected from the harsh realities of the world beyond the college gates." Write a chapel address of your own in which, on the basis of your own experience, you agree or disagree with this view.

28. Your roommate is a skeptical Sophomore who declares that college has taught him nothing. Show him how college has already taught you some one specific skill or idea or way of thinking which will be valuable to you in the kind of world you expect to live in.

29. Write a report to your faculty counselor on the most important events that have happened to you in college thus far.

30. In a letter to the editor give your personal estimate of the campus daily as a publication and as an organ of undergraduate opinion.

31. You have just listened to a radio commentator who said that the younger generation today is insensitive, realistic, cynical. Write him a letter in which you agree or disagree with any or all of his charges. Back your opinions by examples from your own acquaintance.

32. What was the first time in your life that you felt a real sense of achievement? Tell the circumstances.

33. Tell how you taught yourself something: a good habit, a skill, an attitude toward life or people.

II. FIRST PERSON PLURAL

34. If it were spring and you were faced by the same dilemma as Crazy Willie, what would you do about it? How do you think your plans would come out? Tell your own story. (Spring over Brooklyn)

35. Retell the story "Spring over Brooklyn" from Dolly's point of view.

36. As Chapter III of your unwritten autobiography, discuss the influence of your family and friendships upon your attitude toward certain problems, social, political, or moral.

37. Describe a personal encounter with wild life, not a hunting episode. Don't neglect the background of the experience. (Two Look at Two)

38. You are still swapping experiences with your new classmate. Now you have got well enough acquainted to tell him of the first friendship (boy or girl) that has really meant something to you and of how it came about.

39. Write the body of a letter to an old friend back home describing your roommate or some other newly made friend (boy or girl) at college.

40. You are inviting your roommate to go home with you next week end. He has never met your family. Tell him what the visit will be like and introduce him to the members of your family in advance.

41. You have just arrived at your summer home or camp for the vacation. Tell about the experience of coming back in a conversation with your nearest neighbor, a native, who drops in on the following day.

42. An aunt whom you have never seen comes to visit your home. Through a misunderstanding, the rest of the family have gone to meet her at the train and you are alone when she arrives at the house. Tell her something of your family life so that she will feel at home, and try to make the best of an awkward situation.

43. To a newly arrived Jugo-Slavian describe the traditions and superstitions which surround a wedding in the United States. Put all this into the story of an actual wedding which you have attended. (Wedding in Carniola)

44. Describe some celebration, procession, or custom which you have observed in a foreign community either here or abroad.

45. If you have ever plowed a field, try to explain to a city-born classmate what the experience feels like, in the morning, at noon, at supper-time. (These Acres; A Peculiar Gift)

46. Describe and contrast several of the domestics who have worked in your family from time to time—a saga of the sink.

47. Your best friend, a bride who scarcely knows how to boil water, is giving a dinner for her husband's fastidious relatives. Tell her what to prepare and how, without resorting too freely to the can-opener.

48. Do you think that the housewife leads a pleasanter life than the career woman? What do you mean by "pleasant"? (These Acres; People from Out of Town)

49. A student writes: "Girls have as much spending money as fellows, and the living expenses of both sexes are about equal. If the girl shared the expense of the date by paying her own way, the financial burden on her escort would be

cut in half. With the cost of dates reduced, the average man would feel able to go out more often, know more girls, and get more fun out of life." Was the writer a girl or a boy? Do you share the opinion expressed?

50. Describe a day in the home life of the most interesting old couple you have known. (Blinker Was a Good Dog)

51. Write the body of a letter to a student of your own age living in a co-operative community in Palestine. Tell him what you think he would like to know about your life, and ask him questions about his life. (A Peculiar Gift)

52. The college psychiatrist has asked you whether you have ever led an imaginary existence. If a boy, you may have permitted yourself dreams of athletic or military distinction; if a girl, you may have pictured yourself as the subject of a glamorous romance. Tell the doctor your story and its consequences. (The Secret Life of Walter Mitty)

53. An old friend in a distant city has written you: "The firm is transferring me next month to open a new branch in your home town. How do you think I am going to like the place?" In reply try to convey to him the special quality, character, spirit, which distinguishes your community or region and tell him how his family are going to fit into it. (Our Town)

54. "Very ordinary town, if you ask me. Little better behaved than most. Probably a lot duller." So says Mr. Webb of Grover's Corners. Yet his town furnishes the matter for a famous play. Consider the dramatic possibilities of your own home town. Perhaps you could write a one-act play about some of the people in it. Perhaps you could defend it in a letter to a friend who has never seen it but who has heard that it is very dull indeed. (Our Town)

55. If, like Emily, you could relive a single day out of your past life, which day would you choose? (Our Town)

56. Describe the personal appearance, history, and reputation of one of the least successful citizens of your home town, or of the town where you spend your summers.

57. "Every street is a mirror of the people who live in it." Contrast two streets in your town to show how they illustrate the truth of this quotation.

58. The Chamber of Commerce in your home town proposes to tear down a historical landmark in order to relieve traffic congestion. Write a letter to the secretary of the Chamber opposing the project.

59. Are you an individualist or a conformer? Illustrate your attitude toward society by a significant example of your conduct.

60. What person has had the most important influence on your life? Show the nature of this influence and its effect upon your development.

III. MANPOWER

61. If you have ever worked on a farm at harvest time describe a typical day's routine. (Kansas; Planting and Harvest)

62. To a city boy who is visiting your country home describe some activity of farm life which you know at first hand; for example, raising chickens, caring for a horse, running a dairy, calling a square dance, celebrating a holiday, being

your own handy-man, growing apples, planning a kitchen garden. If the visitor is a girl she will be interested in most of these activities and such other things as putting up preserves, making butter, feeding country appetites, braiding a rug.

63. If you have ever held a steady job, write for your course in social science a report describing the job, your personal feelings about it, the relations of worker to worker, of worker and employer, and any other comments which seem pertinent to an understanding of the conditions of employment in the given industry.

64. Write a letter of instruction for the guidance of an inexperienced worker who is to take the job which you are leaving.

65. Write a letter of application for a job in work for which you are already experienced; or assume that you have finished the training for the vocation in which you seek employment.

66. Describe and explain the operation of a mechanical device with which you are familiar. Supplement your knowledge with such reference information as may be necessary (with proper acknowledgments). Note that it is usually undesirable to separate completely the technical description of a device from some exposition of process. Sample topics: surveyor's level, canal lock, milking machine, storage battery, camera, chicken incubator, turret lathe, thermostat, oil-burner furnace, radio network, washing machine, jet-propulsion plane, turbine.

67. Explain some simple industrial or commercial process which you know from experience or observation. Make use of both description and narration. Choose a reader who would be totally unfamiliar with the subject. Suggestions: selling men's clothing, mixing soft drinks, laying a cement foundation, operating a lathe, making an omelet, operating a filing system, taking inventory.

68. A woman Senior has her choice of these alternatives after graduation: marriage and the life of a housewife, a professional career in college teaching, newspaper work. Give her your advice for whatever it is worth.

69. Assume that you are applying for a spare-time job during the college year. Explain to your prospective employer why you consider yourself qualified for it.

70. "All work is noble." So the philosophers and poets acclaim the glories of honest toil. But we all know that today the way to succeed is not working hard but knowing the right people. Or is it?

71. Write a report to some agency of your local government on social conditions in your home town which you believe should be corrected; for example, factory conditions, housing, child labor, sharecropping, racial discrimination, municipal lodging for vagrants, poor farm. It may be necessary to do some firsthand investigation. (The Leaden-Eyed; The Mouse That Gnawed the Oak-Tree Down)

72. Through the exertions of a consumers' lobby, Congress has legislated advertising out of existence. Describe the effects, good or bad. Should we know what to eat, drink, smoke, wear? how to amuse ourselves? how to keep our health and beauty?

73. For *Fortune* write a popular exposition of a manufacturing process of which you have first-hand information. (To One-Millionth of an Inch)

74. Write an informal essay in which you compare the "nearly right" of the Chinese with the near-perfection of an American manufacturing process. (To One-Millionth of an Inch; The Importance of Loafing)

75. Using the narrative-journalistic method (but not necessarily the style) of *Time,* retell the story of some famous scientific discovery of the past, such as the telephone, the airplane, radium, insulin, the steam engine, the automobile, vaccination, ether. (Twentieth Century Seer)

76. For *Time* write a "man of the week" article which tells the life story and important achievements of a scientist, inventor, political leader, military leader, or other public figure. Name the sources from which you take your facts. (Twentieth Century Seer)

77. An American scientist discovers a formula for the most powerful explosive in the world. Instead of turning his discovery over to the government he destroys the formula. What do you think of his action? Write in the form of a narrative in which, perhaps, the scientist justifies himself.

78. How may the post-war world benefit from the scientific advances occasioned by World War II? Stick to facts.

79. Your freshman science course is opening a new world to you. Write home to your mother, who has never studied such a course, telling her what you are getting out of it and sharing the experience with her.

80. As a student of science, how do you view the fact that science destroys in war the lives which it saves in time of peace? Take this question as the subject for a speech before a meeting of your science club.

81. In the factual style of an engineer's report, describe some federal or state project of which you have personal knowledge, which has benefited your home region; for example, an airport, a dam, a conservation project, a reservation, a superhighway, a postoffice, a fish hatchery. (TVA Is Power)

82. For *The New Yorker* write a profile of the most eccentric character you have ever known. (Professor Sea Gull)

83. For a magazine which emphasizes personalities, write an account of someone whom you know well and admire.

IV. PURSUIT OF HAPPINESS

84. A friend of yours whose father has died has had to leave college and go to work. In a rather discouraged letter he has written you how tedious he finds his job. Tell him how, on some occasion, you learned to combine vocation with avocation. (Two Tramps in Mud-Time)

85. Your father, a successful scientist, has hoped that you would follow his profession. After arriving at college you decided to enroll for the degree of Bachelor of Arts, and expect to include courses in literature, art, and music. Write him a letter in which you fully explain and justify your decision.

86. Who are the wise, the loafers or the hustlers? After considering Lin Yutang's answer, give your own opinion, with suitable illustrations, in a courteous letter to Dr. Lin. (The Importance of Loafing)

87. Write an article for one of the better magazines on the following: If you

were free to choose a life of adventure and action or a life of quiet uneventfulness, which would you do, and why? Keep your plans within the bounds of plausibility.

88. Discuss the mechanical age as it affects life in your own home and state whether you sincerely believe that machinery is a blessing or not.

89. There are many ways in which people try to escape from boredom: music, the theater, country life, books, games, and so forth. If you are one of these would-be escapists, what method of escape do you recommend?

90. Write in narrative form a character study of some relative whom you have known as intimately as Mrs. Damon knew Grandma Griswold. (Grandma Reads Thoreau)

91. After reading at least the first and second chapters of *Walden,* write an analysis of Thoreau's character as revealed in his ideas. (Grandma Reads Thoreau)

92. If, like Fadiman, you have ever conducted reading experiments with yourself as subject, write a report on the results. (My Life Is an Open Book)

93. Write the body of a letter to Mrs. Buck in which you describe some book which you have read and which, you believe, meets her requirement that good literature contributes to our understanding of life. Explain the reasons for your choice. (Literature and Life)

94. A magazine is conducting a contest on the subject: The best book I ever read. Write your entry, fully describing the book and convincingly explaining why you consider it better than any other.

95. Is fact stranger than fiction? Support your opinion by reference to two books which you have read: a novel and a true account of war experiences.

96. "There is no frigate like a book to take us lands away." Show how, in your reading experience, you have learned the truth of these lines. Refer to a specific book or books.

97. "I like to have a man's knowledge comprehend more than one class of topics, one row of shelves. I like a man who likes to see a fine barn as well as a good tragedy." Attempt an imaginary portrait of the sort of man who said this.

98. Write, for one of the better magazines, a character study of some figure in history whose biography you have read. Draw your facts from the biography and re-state them in your own words. Name your source.

99. You and several friends are discussing the relative literary merits of your favorite magazines, especially the pro and con of the "digest." Give the discussion.

100. For a textbook in literature to be used by high-school Seniors write your explanation of the meaning of one of the poems in *Present Tense.* Suggestions: These Acres, Not Marble nor the Gilded Monuments, Speech to a Crowd, The Great and Marching Words.

101. Write a letter to a friend who is convalescing from an illness and, seeking intellectual entertainment, has asked you to recommend some good reading or a good author.

102. If you have ever met a great artist or if you have ever felt the thrill of contact with great art (a painting, a piece of sculpture, a building, a piece of

music, a ballet, etc.), describe the experience in the form of a personal narrative. (Rodin and Paris)

103. Visit your local art museum: select any one object in the galleries which appeals to you and study it carefully. Then, in an imaginary conversation with the artist who created it, tell why you were attracted by it.

104. If you could choose a good colored reproduction of any picture in the world to hang in your room, what picture would you choose and why?

105. Which, to your taste, is the more beautiful: an airplane or a racing yacht? Justify your preference.

106. When Americans turn to the culture of their own country, what do they find? Write a continuation of Edman's article in which you discuss the worth of the particular contribution of your own section of the United States to some one art. (Look Homeward, America!)

107. Select a group of three moving pictures that are widely popular and try to analyze the secret of their appeal to the public. Does the popularity of such films constitute damaging evidence regarding the quality of our civilization? Discuss both sides of the question and present your own conclusions. Do not give mere summaries of the pictures.

108. "All the resources of science are applied in order that imbecility may flourish and vulgarity cover the earth. That they are doing so must be obvious to anyone who glances at a page of comic strips, attends the movies, or listens to the radio." Discuss the truth of this somewhat sweeping indictment.

109. Write the body of a letter to one of the broadcasting companies protesting against some one type of program which you believe the radio could do with, out. Tell what type you would prefer and give your reasons.

110. One of your friends, a swing fan, has ridiculed your attendance at symphony concerts (or purchase of symphony recordings). Defend your taste. (On Hearing a Symphony of Beethoven)

111. Play one of the following recordings several times, carefully noting your reactions as you listen: Dvořák's New World Symphony; Smetana's The Moldau; Gershwin's Rhapsody in Blue; Mendelssohn's The Hebrides (Fingal's Cave); Ravel's Bolero; Sibelius's Finlandia; Debussy's La Mer; Prokofiev's Lieutenant Kije Suite; Beethoven's Seventh Symphony, Second Movement. Describe the experience or translate the resulting mood into an imaginary narrative. (On Hearing a Symphony of Beethoven)

112. If you had fifty dollars to spend on phonograph recordings, what would you buy and why?

113. From recent numbers of Life select several examples of good art in photography. Explain why you consider them good from a technical and professional standpoint. Do not write on this subject unless you know a good deal about photography.

114. You have been asked to plan a community center for your home neighborhood. In a report to the committee describe the layout, including sketches.

115. For a course in government, prepare a report on the state of Liberia, its history and its possibilities for the future. Give your sources. (What Is Africa to Me?)

116. For a student discussion group prepare a talk on the Zionist movement, emphasizing its human rather than its legalistic aspects. (A Peculiar Gift; By the Waters of Gideon)

117. If you have had flying experience, write the body of a letter to a friend who has never flown and convey to him some of the actual sensations of flying. Don't attempt too much: Mrs. Lindbergh spends seven pages on the description of a take-off. (Listen! the Wind Is Rising; Wings Across the Andes)

118. Though you have never flown across the Andes or been shipwrecked on Greenland you have learned how to find the qualities of adventure in the more familiar experiences of daily life. Tell your roommate, who is bored with the routine, how to do it. (Wings Across the Andes; Shipwreck, etc.)

119. Write an account, in the form of a journal, of an exciting experience from your own life. (Shipwreck)

120. Did you ever have an experience so perfect and so true that you wished it might always remain that way? Tell your story. (The Bear)

121. To a beginner in some sport in which you excel try to convey the special sensations which you have got from it. (The Feel; European Saga; Mountain Speed)

122. Assume that you are preparing a popular handbook on some sport, skill, hobby, or craft; write an introduction to the book in which you describe the *personal qualities* necessary for success in the activity which you are about to present.

V. AMERICAN HERITAGE

123. Visit a railroad station, bus station, or commercial airport at a time when traffic is heavy and make notes on the spot to serve as setting for a chapter of a story. Write the chapter. Or develop as an essay on the spirit of American life. (American Landscape)

124. Study *Fortune's* article, "The U. S. A.," to discover and report on the changes which have come about in your section of the country since it was written.

125. For a course in United States history write a report describing the geography of your home region and showing how it has affected the history and economic development of the region. (The U. S. A.)

126. For a course in economics make a factual analysis of the products of your home region to show how they are the natural result of conditions in the background of the region. (The U. S. A.)

127. John Buchan has told us how the United States looks to a visitor from England. In the same spirit of friendly interpretation describe the features of life in Canada, Mexico, England, or some other country which you have visited. (My America)

128. Democracy "is primarily a spiritual testament, from which certain political and economic orders naturally follow." Explain what you, personally, understand by democracy as a "spiritual testament." (My America)

129. "It is only out of the dirt that things grow." Apply Buchan's words to democracy and illustrate. (My America)

130. "Democracy, after all, is a negative thing. It provides a fair field for the Good Life, but it is not in itself the Good Life." Explain this quotation from Buchan. (My America)

131. Watch the crowd wandering along Main Street on a Saturday night, buying groceries in the chain store, going to the movies, shopping in the five-and-ten, playing bingo, listening to juke-boxes, waiting for buses. Then reflect that these are the voters. Ask yourself whether you have enough faith in the democratic ideal to believe in the infallibility of the majority in choosing our legislators and determining our destiny. Write an editorial which treats with hope or with misgiving the working of democratic government. (What Is Freedom?)

132. Visit a regular meeting of the City Council or other governing body of your community and report, on the basis of notes, your impressions of democracy in action.

133. "But do they really count the ballots?" exclaims a bewildered ex-Fascist as he listens to an account of an American presidential campaign. Give him a fair and frank account of political methods in the United States.

134. A foreign agent in the United States is required to send his superiors a report explaining the functioning of our democratic system. Write the report for him.

135. How can capitalism flourish in a democracy? A careful definition of terms is involved in the answer to this question. (The Rise of the Democratic Idea in the United States; Democracy in the Making)

136. For your course in political science prepare a talk in which you explain your party affiliation; if you are an independent, explain why you do not belong to one of the parties and how your views differ from theirs.

137. Read the Declaration of Independence and show how the principles there enunciated are still valid in your own thinking.

138. Compare the preambles of the several party platforms in the last national election in an effort to discover their real meanings.

139. Write an article for the general reader in which you try to make clear the meaning of some abstract term (such as democracy, capitalism, free enterprise, nobility, morality). Explain, illustrate, give specific examples, eliminate what you do not mean.

140. "To provide for the economic well-being of our inhabitants, only three attributes, which are not beyond the reach of the average person, are necessary—honesty, industry, and thrift." Draw the character of the statesman who held this kind of philosophy.

141. For a course in economics prepare a report on the history of the co-operative movement in Nova Scotia. (Democracy in the Making)

142. "Our young people are starving for real tasks and vital opportunities. Many of them live like sleepwalkers, apparently in contact with their environment, but actually dead to everything but the print of the newspaper, the blare of the radio, or the flickering shadows on the screen." These words were written by Bruce Bliven before the United States entered World War II. Assuming that

they become true again after the war, is compulsory military training of young men a satisfactory remedy for the conditions described? or have you an alternative to suggest and defend? (Notes on the American Character)

143. Choose a single feature of the American character as identified by Bliven and develop it into a full article. (Notes on the American Character)

144. In an article for one of the better magazines describe a person of your acquaintance whose ideas and behavior seem to you typically American. (Notes on the American Character)

145. Somewhere there may be a spot that you love best, a woods road, a river bank, a hilltop. Describe it and tell how it gained its importance for you. (Lost Road)

146. In an article for your home-town newspaper tell in what way, however small, the history of your town has played a part in the making of the nation.

147. A publisher has asked you to write a novel about a period of American history that reveals the best in the American character. Write him a letter telling what period you have chosen and why.

148. For a newspaper contest write an answer to the question: "If you could have lived at any other period of your country's history, which period would you choose and why?"

149. Lewis Mumford writes: "But in its best sense, patriotism is always narrow and intense: close to one's family, one's village or city and the land around." Forgetting all conventional definitions of patriotism, ask yourself what specific things you love in American life. What are the actual roots of your patriotism? (Roots in the Region)

150. If your parents entered the United States as immigrants, get them to tell you some of their early experiences in a strange country. Then retell the best of them as a short story. (The Citizner; Mr. Kaplan and Shakespeare)

151. To a friend of yours who is ashamed of his racial background (which is the same as yours) write a strong letter telling him what your racial group has contributed to the United States.

152. One of your classmates is a refugee from a European country. He has had no opportunity to travel in the United States. So far as you have experience of American life explain to him what it means to be an American. (The Citizner)

153. "A union of the two strange worlds must be." After thoughtful study, give your own solution for the problem of the Negro in America. (What Is Africa to Me?; For My People; Colossal Bronze; American Ideals and the American Conscience)

154. Clip from a recent newspaper a story revealing some social injustice in American life. Write an editorial condemning the condition, discussing its causes, and suggesting remedies.

155. Clip from a recent newspaper an editorial which criticizes some social condition in American life. Write the news story which might have prompted the editorial. For material draw upon your own first-hand observations.

156. Write a letter to your Senator in which you tell him what you think of some pending measure of reform legislation.

157. An eccentric uncle has died and left you a large sum of money on the

condition that you can convince his lawyer that you have a sound plan for using half of this sum in some project for social betterment. Write a letter to his hard-headed lawyer in which you describe your plan.

158. Write an editorial on some one element in American civilization which you think contradicts the American Creed. (American Ideals and the American Conscience, page 499)

159. In a letter to your home-town newspaper, which has been critical of the present Administration, tell from personal experience or observation something which the federal government has done for the good of the people in your community or in any other community with which you are familiar.

160. In a letter to a friend in a foreign country describe a personal experience that has made you say to yourself: "I'm proud to be an American!" (Two for a Penny)

VI. PORTRAIT OF A WORLD

161. Tell, in the form of a short story, a personal experience which has given you an understanding of the real meaning of Liberty, Democracy, or Sacrifice. (The Great and Marching Words)

162. Write a letter to Henry Wallace in which you agree or disagree with his declaration that the century which comes out of the war must be "the century of the common man." Note that Julian Huxley refers to "the Age of Social Man." (The Price of Free World Victory; On Living in a Revolution)

163. "College students are sick of the constant harping on the same dull subjects: America, democracy, politics, world problems. After all, these matters are of no concern to them. Later on, perhaps; but right now football games and dances are a lot more important and a lot more pleasant to think about. And after all, there's nothing kids can do about that stuff anyway." Give your own opinion on this question.

164. "The majority of undergraduates look at national politics with contempt, at international planning with distrust. It is their firm conviction that government and corruption are inseparable, that wars are inevitable, that foreign powers are not to be trusted. And it is upon their generation that the hope of the world rests!" Can you answer this criticism of your generation?

165. Describe an example of government planning or control with which you are familiar; give your reasons for approving or disapproving. (On Living in a Revolution)

166. "It is entirely wrong to equate democracy with a system of free individual enterprise." Write an editorial agreeing or disagreeing with Julian Huxley. (On Living in a Revolution; The Rise of the Democratic Idea in the United States)

167. Warburg declares that class conflict is inevitable in the United States unless we all "make up our minds to abolish the injustice which causes the class conflict to exist." Point out some of the principal injustices and tell how you would remove them. (Domestic Prerequisites to Peace)

168. "That which a nation chuses to do it has a right to do." What do you

think Tom Paine meant by these words? Do you think that he might qualify them to answer to present-day realities?

169. After adequate research and thought write a magazine article on some one of the Four Freedoms which you think is not being lived up to in the United States today. (Pan-Humanism)

170. Should you be willing to see your taxes raised in order that "Freedom from Want" might become a reality in China? Write a letter to your Congressman in which you square your opinion with your allegiance to democracy. (Pan-Humanism)

171. Write a biographical sketch about one of the four "world citizens" mentioned by Friedrich: Tom Paine, Thomas Jefferson, Benjamin Franklin, Lafayette. Give the sources of your information. (Pan-Humanism)

172. "What are the common patterns of conduct that will enable the world's common men to join forces in solving their common problems? Is there a basis for a world community?" With these large and difficult questions Friedrich concludes his article. How would you answer them? (Pan-Humanism)

173. As a young man or woman with a stake in the future of this country, write a letter to your Senator or Representative telling him what you expect of Congress in relation to a certain specified issue of present or future in which you have a personal concern.

174. "When the war is over the government ought to stop meddling in business and let private business take over again; ought to stop spending on such a mad scale; and ought to send all the bureaucrats and professors home again." Do you agree or disagree? (What Kind of Collectivism Do We Want?)

175. The war has been over for some time and you can write again to a friend in one of the European countries. Describe for him what living was like under full wartime restrictions of food, clothing, transportation, luxuries, and so on. Did you discover any advantages in going without?

176. You have been asked to speak at a post-war symposium on peace. Prepare a speech in which you state what you believe to be *one* important requirement for a lasting peace.

177. Select from the following list one respect in which a dictatorship is more efficient than a democracy; show why this is so; explain how democracy can overcome this particular shortcoming: ownership of property, preparation for war, foreign trade, love of country, youth movement, sports, legal justice, education, recreation, distribution of wealth, public health, housing, public works.

178. Prepare a report for Meiklejohn's "Institute of Education" on the teaching possibilities of radio or film or travel in post-war reconstruction. (Education and the Future)

179. If you have undergone some fundamental change in your beliefs as the result of your education, would you say that it is possible to re-educate Nazi youth into acceptable citizens of a democracy?

180. "Why should the young people not have their first experience of public service on work that serves for local improvement? It is our youngsters nearing military age who should be toughened off in lumber camps, on fishing boats, behind the hay-wagon and the threshing machine, on the road gang and in the

quarry."—Mumford. Give your opinion. If you wish to look the subject up further before writing on it, see "The Moral Equivalent of War" in *Memories and Studies* by William James. (Roots in the Region)

181. For a magazine of opinion write an analysis of the Japanese character which undertakes to explain why Japan attacked the United States. (The Modernization of China and Japan)

182. Write a letter to an imaginary student who will enter your college ten years from now. Describe to him your hopes for the future as plainly intimated in present developments in some one field of activity (education, housing, transportation, industrial relations, the fine arts, international relations, etc.)

183. In what respects do Lin Yutang and Hu Shih agree as to the Chinese character? (The Importance of Loafing; The Modernization of China and Japan)

184. If you live near a modern housing project, write a magazine article similar to Chase's in which you describe, on the basis of actual visits, a new model dwelling and a typical dwelling of the sort which it supplants. (Shelter)

185. Write a letter to your local newspaper proposing a slum clearance project and specifying the type of housing which should be provided. Some study of source material may be necessary. (Shelter)

186. After a careful reading of "The Last Letter" and if possible some reading of the author's autobiography, attempt a character sketch of Nehru.

187. Just before the beginning of the rise of power machinery in the United States the average person had about 16 wants that were considered necessities; today he has 94. What would Henry Thoreau (who died in 1862) say to this record of "progress"? (Science, Freedom, and the World of Tomorrow; Grandma Reads Thoreau)

188. "Civilization consists in the multiplication and refinement of human wants." So says Millikan. "Will the time come when the population will prefer to stabilize the standard of living at a certain level rather than to continue with vast extension programs?" So says Lamont. What do you think? (Science, Freedom, and the World of Tomorrow; The Principles of Planning)

VII. SEARCH FOR SIGNIFICANCE

189. Write a brief paraphrase of one of the poems in this section and explain its meaning for you. Suggestions: Morning Song, Conversation at Midnight, The Listeners, The Chestnut Casts His Flambeaux, The Circus or One View of It, Winterset, Testament.

190. Some of the poems in this section, such as "On the Beach at Aruè," give an optimistic view of life; others, such as "The Chestnut Casts His Flambeaux," are pessimistic. Where do your own sympathies lie?

191. Who do you think has the better of the debate between religion and science in the conflicting views of Fosdick and Huxley? Why do you think so? (Are Religious People Fooling Themselves?; The Creed of a Scientific Humanist)

192. Summarize the findings of the astronomers regarding man's place in time and space and compare them with the findings of the biologists. (Good Heavens; Man in the Universe; How Has Man Been Made?)

193. What does geology teach as to the past and the future of the earth? (The Future of Man as an Inhabitant of the Earth)

194. A Freshman asks the question: "How does one develop a sense of values? Why not live for the moment—take a short-range view of life—for tomorrow we die? What's the use of all the talk about right and wrong? What does it matter, eventually?" Can you advise him?

195. You and a friend at another college have occasionally discussed religion in your letters. One of you is more than ever convinced of the rightness of his beliefs; the other is rapidly losing most of the beliefs with which he entered college. You now write him a letter in which (taking either side) you discuss how college is affecting your religious views.

196. "Beyond the will to believe, there must be, first of all, the will to doubt. He who has no doubts can never be educated. Education does not try to create the believer; it strives to create the understander. If you don't understand, your beliefs are of little value anyway." Do you agree or disagree? Compare the views of Anselmo in "Conversation at Midnight."

197. Since entering college, have you come to any religious or moral conclusions contrary to those held by your parents and, previously, by yourself? What caused the change in your opinions?

198. Walter Lippmann writes: "Our ancestors thought they knew their way from birth through all eternity; we are puzzled about the day after tomorrow." What has caused the change? (The Creed of a Scientific Humanist)

199. You and several classmates have been discussing your attitudes toward the church and religion. Somebody asks whether the church has anything to offer except the same old phrases, the same meaningless practices, the same far-off thing called religion. What can you tell him?

200. "If a man doesn't have a God, he creates one." Think over the full implications of this quotation before you express your opinion of it.

201. "Religion is all right in its place, but you can't mix it with war or business or politics." Just where does religion belong?

202. "Fatalism and faith represent two classic attitudes with which men have faced hard and rigorous times." Where do you stand? (The Chestnut Casts His Flambeaux; Conversation at Midnight)

203. Out of your whole life thus far what memory should you like to keep longest? (All Lovely Things; Afterwards; Reluctance)

ACKNOWLEDGMENTS

The editor of *Present Tense* is indebted to the following authors and publishers, who have courteously permitted the use of the selections indicated, all rights in which are reserved by the owners of the respective copyrights.

ANDERSON HOUSE: For "Whatever Hope We Have," by Maxwell Anderson, from *The Essence of Tragedy.*
For an excerpt from *Winterset,* by Maxwell Anderson.

THE ANNALS OF THE AMERICAN ACADEMY OF POLITICAL AND SOCIAL SCIENCE: For "What Is Freedom?" by Gaetano Salvemini. By permission of the editors and the author.

BRUCE BLIVEN: For "Notes on the American Character," by Bruce Bliven, from *The New Republic,* November 8, 1939. By permission of the author.

BRANDT & BRANDT: For "Metropolitan Nightmare," by Stephen Vincent Benét. From *Selected Works of Stephen Vincent Benét,* published by Farrar & Rinehart. Copyright, 1933, by Stephen Vincent Benét.
For excerpt from *Conversation at Midnight,* published by Harper & Brothers. Copyright, 1937, by Edna St. Vincent Millay.
For "On Hearing a Symphony of Beethoven," by Edna St. Vincent Millay. From *The Buck in the Snow,* published by Harper & Brothers. Copyright, 1928, by Edna St. Vincent Millay.

ZECHARIAH CHAFEE, JR.: For "Give Your Minds Sea Room."

COWARD-MC CANN, INC.: For "Our Town," by Thornton Wilder. Copyright, 1938, by Coward-McCann, Inc. This play may not be reprinted in part or in whole without permission in writing from the publishers. All inquiries about any performance whatsoever must be addressed to the author's agent, Harold Freedman, 101 Park Avenue, New York, N. Y.

THE JOHN DAY COMPANY, INC.: For "The Last Letter," by Jawaharlal Nehru, from *Glimpses of World History.*
For "The Importance of Loafing," by Lin Yutang from *The Importance of Living.*

STEPHEN DAYE PRESS: For "European Saga," by David J. Bradley. Reprinted from the *American Ski Annual,* 1939-40.

DODD, MEAD & COMPANY, INC.: For "Education Eating Up Life," from *Too Much College* by Stephen Leacock. Copyright, 1939, by Dodd, Mead & Company, Inc.

DOUBLEDAY, DORAN & COMPANY, INC.: For "Forty Rubles a Month," from *Madame Curie*: A Biography, by Eve Curie. Copyright, 1937, by Doubleday, Doran and Company, Inc.

E. P. DUTTON & COMPANY, INC.: For "Man in the Universe." Taken from *Eos, or The Wider Aspects of Cosmology* by Sir James Jeans. Published and copyright by E. P. Dutton & Co., Inc., New York. (Courtesy of George Routledge & Sons Ltd. for Canada.)

IRWIN EDMAN: For "Look Homeward, America!" by Irwin Edman.

ENGLISH LEAFLET of the New England Association of Teachers of English: For "The Place of the Humanities in American Education," by Howard Mumford Jones. Reprinted by permission of the editor and the author.

FARRAR & RINEHART, INC.: For "Speech to a Crowd" from *Public Speech* by Archibald MacLeish, copyright 1936, and reprinted by permission of Farrar & Rinehart, Inc., publishers.

FORTUNE: For "The U. S. A.," reprinted from *Fortune,* February, 1940, copyright, Time, Inc., 1940.

For "To One-Millionth of an Inch," reprinted from *Fortune,* October, 1943, copyright, *Time,* Inc.

JAMES NORMAN HALL: For "On the Beach at Aruè."

HARCOURT, BRACE AND COMPANY, INC.: For "What Is Africa to Me?" from *Dusk of Dawn,* by W. E. B. DuBois, copyright, 1940, by Harcourt, Brace and Company, Inc.

For "The Modernization of China and Japan," by Hu Shih, from *Freedom: Its Meaning,* edited by Ruth N. Anshen, copyright, 1940, by Harcourt, Brace and Company, Inc.

For "Listen! the Wind Is Rising," from *Listen! the Wind,* copyright, 1938, by Anne Morrow Lindbergh.

For "Education and the Future," by Alexander Meiklejohn, from *Beyond Victory,* edited by Ruth N. Anshen, copyright, 1943, by Harcourt, Brace and Company, Inc.

For "Science, Freedom, and the World of Tomorrow," by Robert A. Millikan, from *Freedom: Its Meaning,* edited by Ruth N. Anshen, copyright, 1940, by Harcourt, Brace and Company, Inc.

For "Roots in the Region," by Lewis Mumford, from *Faith for Living,* copyright, 1940, by Lewis Mumford.

For "A Day's Work," by Katherine Anne Porter, from *The Leaning Tower and Other Stories,* copyright, 1944, by Katherine Anne Porter.

For "Mr. Kaplan and Shakespeare," from *The Education of Hyman Kaplan* by Leonard Q. Ross, copyright, 1937, by Harcourt, Brace and Company, Inc.

For Section 47 and Section 87 from *The People, Yes,* by Carl Sandburg, copyright, 1936, by Harcourt, Brace and Company, Inc.

For "The Circus," by William Saroyan, from *My Name Is Aram,* copyright, 1937, 1938, 1939, 1940, by William Saroyan.

For "Prologue" from *The Time of Your Life* by William Saroyan, copyright, 1939, by Harcourt, Brace and Company, Inc.

For "I Get a Colt to Break In," from *The Autobiography of Lincoln Steffens,* copyright, 1931, by Harcourt, Brace and Company, Inc.

For "The Secret Life of Walter Mitty," by James Thurber, from *My World— and Welcome to It,* copyright, 1942, by James Thurber.

For "Domestic Prerequisites to Peace," from *Foreign Policy Begins at Home* by James P. Warburg, copyright, 1944, by Harcourt, Brace and Company, Inc.

HARPER & BROTHERS: For "Wedding in Carniola," from *The Native's Return* by Louis Adamic. Published by Harper & Brothers.

For "Are Religious People Fooling Themselves?" from *As I See Religion* by Harry Emerson Fosdick. Published by Harper & Brothers.

For "Young Archimedes," from *Young Archimedes and Other Stories* by Aldous Huxley. Published by Harper & Brothers.

For "On Living in a Revolution," from *On Living in a Revolution* by Julian Huxley. Published by Harper & Brothers.

For "Never Come Monday," from *Sam Small Flies Again* by Eric Knight. Published by Harper & Brothers. Copyright, 1942, by Eric Knight.

For "American Ideals and the American Conscience," from *An American Dilemma,* Volume I, by Gunnar Myrdal. Published by Harper & Brothers.

For "Dr. Vinton," from *Quo Vadimus?* by E. B. White. Published by Harper & Brothers.

HENRY HOLT AND COMPANY, INC.: For "Good Heavens," by Norman Corwin, from *More by Corwin*. Published by Henry Holt and Company, Inc.

For "The Listeners," by Walter de la Mare, from *Collected Poems*. Published by Henry Holt and Company, Inc.

For "The Old Angler," by Walter de la Mare, from *The Veil*. Published by Henry Holt and Company, Inc.

For "Two Tramps in Mud-Time," by Robert Frost, from *A Further Range*. Published by Henry Holt and Company, Inc.

For "The Star Splitter," "Reluctance," "Acceptance," and "Two Look at Two," by Robert Frost, from *Collected Poems*. Published by Henry Holt and Company, Inc.

For "Testament," by John Holmes, from *Address to the Living*. Published by Henry Holt and Company, Inc.

For "The Chestnut Casts His Flambeaux," by A. E. Housman, from *Last Poems*. Published by Henry Holt and Company, Inc.

HOUGHTON MIFFLIN COMPANY: For "Democracy in the Making," from *Pursuit of Happiness* by Herbert Agar. By permission of the publishers, Houghton Mifflin Company. (Courtesy of Herbert Agar for Canada.)

For "My America," from *Pilgrim's Way* by John Buchan. By permission of the publishers, Houghton Mifflin Company.

For "Lost Road" and "These Acres," from *These Acres* by Frances Frost. By permission of the publishers, Houghton Mifflin Company.

For "Not Marble nor the Gilded Monuments," "Eleven," and "You, Andrew Marvell," from *Poems, 1924-1933* by Archibald MacLeish. By permission of the publishers, Houghton Mifflin Company.

ROCKWELL KENT: For "Shipwreck" from *N. by E.*

ALFRED A. KNOPF, INC.: For "What Kind of Collectivism Do We Want?" from *How New Will the Better World Be?* by Carl Becker. By permission of and special arrangement with Alfred A. Knopf, Inc.

For "Tne Feel" from *Farewell to Sport* by Paul Gallico. By permission of and special arrangement with Alfred A. Knopf, Inc.

For "The Negro Speaks of Rivers" from *The Weary Blues* by Langston Hughes. By permission of and special arrangement with Alfred A. Knopf, Inc.

For "Introduction to the Universe" from *Happy Days, 1880-1892* by H. L. Mencken. By permission of and special arrangement with Alfred A. Knopf, Inc.

For "431 B.C." from *A Winter Tide* by Robert Nathan. By permission of and special arrangement with Alfred A. Knopf, Inc.

For "Playmates" from *Lanterns on the Levee* by William Alexander Percy. By permission of and special arrangement with Alfred A. Knopf, Inc.

For "To Youth" from *To Youth* by John V. A. Weaver. By permission of and special arrangement with Alfred A. Knopf, Inc.

For "Farewell, Sweet Dust" from *Collected Poems* by Elinor Wylie. By permission of and special arrangement with Alfred A. Knopf, Inc.

CORLISS LAMONT: For "The Principles of Planning" from *You Might Like Socialism.*

BEN HUR LAMPMAN: For "Blinker Was a Good Dog," reprinted from *The Atlantic Monthly.*

LITTLE, BROWN & COMPANY: For "Pan-Humanism" from *The New Belief in the Common Man,* by Carl J. Friedrich. Reprinted by permission of Little, Brown & Company.

For "Calf Love" from *As I Remember Him: The Biography of R. S.* by Hans Zinsser. Reprinted by permission of Little, Brown & Company.

DAVID LLOYD: For "Literature and Life" by Pearl S. Buck. Copyright, 1938, by Pearl S. Buck.

ARCHIBALD MACLEISH: For "The Western Sky."

THE MACMILLAN COMPANY: For "The Darkling Thrush" and "Afterwards" from *Collected Poems* by Thomas Hardy. By permission of The Macmillan Company, publishers. ("The Darkling Thrush" by permission of the Trustees of the Hardy Estate and Macmillan & Co. Ltd. for Canada.)

For "Kansas," "The Leaden-Eyed," and "The Mouse That Gnawed the Oak-Tree Down" from *Collected Poems* by Vachel Lindsay. By permission of The Macmillan Company, publishers.

For selection from *Tristram* by Edwin Arlington Robinson. By permission of The Macmillan Company, publishers.

For "The Coolin" from *Collected Poems* by James Stephens. By permission of The Macmillan Company, publishers.

For "Requisites for Social Progress" abridged from *Science and the Modern World* by Alfred North Whitehead. By permission of The Macmillan Company, publishers.

For "The Host of the Air" from *Collected Poems* by William Butler Yeats. By permission of The Macmillan Company, publishers. (Courtesy of A. P. Watt & Son, and by permission of Mrs. W. B. Yeats and Messrs. Macmillan & Co. Ltd. for Canada.)

KIRTLEY F. MATHER: For "The Future of Man as an Inhabitant of the Earth," by Kirtley F. Mather. Reprinted from *Sigma Xi Quarterly* (now the *American Scientist*) by permission of the author and editors.

MCKEOGH & BOYD, INC.: For "The Great and Marching Words," by Christopher La Farge. Reprinted from *The Saturday Review of Literature* by permission of the author and the editors.

NEW DIRECTIONS: For "The Circus; or One View of It" from *The Paradox in the Circle* by Theodore Spencer.

W. W. NORTON & COMPANY, INC.: For "Planting and Harvest" from *R.F.D.,* by Charles Allen Smart, published by W. W. Norton & Company, Inc., New York.

HAROLD OBER: For "The Bear," by William Faulkner. Copyright 1942 by the Curtis Publishing Company. Reprinted by permission of the author.

G. P. PUTNAM'S SONS: For "A Peculiar Gift" from *Children of Abraham* by Sholem Asch. Courtesy of G. P. Putnam's Sons.

RANDOM HOUSE, INC.: For "Wings Across the Andes" from *South by Thunderbird* by Hudson Strode. Reprinted by permission of Random House, Inc.

THE READER'S DIGEST: For "A Boy I Knew," by E. B. White.

SYDNEY A. SANDERS: For "Spring over Brooklyn," by Zachary Gold. Copyright by The Saturday Evening Post, 1939.

THE SATURDAY REVIEW OF LITERATURE: For "Roark Bradford's Revenge," by David L. Cohn.

WINFIELD TOWNLEY SCOTT: For "Fine Morning" from *Wind the Clock*.

CHARLES SCRIBNER'S SONS: For "All Lovely Things," "Morning Song," and "The Road" from *Selected Poems* by Conrad Aiken.

For "Rodin and Paris" from *Heads and Tales* by Malvina Hoffman.

For four lines from Sonnet III in *Poems* by George Santayana.

For "American Landscape" from *Of Time and the River* by Thomas Wolfe.

SIMON AND SCHUSTER, INC.: For "Grandma Reads Thoreau," from *Grandma Called It Carnal* by Bertha Damon.

For "My Life Is an Open Book," from *Reading I've Liked* by Clifton Fadiman. Copyright 1941 by Simon and Schuster, Inc.

For "The Creed of a Scientific Humanist," from *I Believe* by Julian Huxley.

For "The Door" by E. B. White, from *Short Stories from The New Yorker*.

SURVEY GRAPHIC: For "The Rise of the Democratic Idea in the United States," by Charles A. Beard. Reprinted by permission of the editors and the author.

TIME: For "Twentieth Century Seer," by permission of Time, Inc.

TWENTIETH CENTURY FUND: For "Shelter" from *Goals for America* by Stuart Chase. Copyright 1942, by Twentieth Century Fund, Inc.

THE VANGUARD PRESS, INC.: For "How Has Man Been Made?" from *Out of the Night, A Biologist's View of the Future,* by H. J. Muller. By permission of the publishers, The Vanguard Press.

THE VIKING PRESS, INC.: For "Candle in the Dark" (abridged) from *Candle in the Dark* by Irwin Edman. Copyright 1939 by Irwin Edman. By permission of The Viking Press, Inc., New York.

For "By the Waters of Gideon" from *The World I Knew* by Louis Golding.

Copyright 1940 by Louis Golding. By permission of The Viking Press, Inc., New York.

For "The Sexes" from *Here Lies* by Dorothy Parker. Copyright 1930, 1933, 1939 by Dorothy Parker. By permission of The Viking Press, Inc., New York.

For Chapter 15 from *The Grapes of Wrath* by John Steinbeck. Copyright 1939 by John Steinbeck. By permission of The Viking Press, Inc., New York.

For "TVA Is Power" from *My Native Land* by Anna Louise Strong. Copyright 1940 by Anna Louise Strong. By permission of The Viking Press, Inc., New York.

For "Colossal Bronze" from *While Rome Burns* by Alexander Woollcott. Copyright 1934 by Alexander Woollcott. By permission of The Viking Press, Inc., New York.

HENRY A. WALLACE: For "The Price of Free World Victory."

YALE UNIVERSITY PRESS: For "For My People" from *For My People* by Margaret Walker.

GEOFFREY WINTHROP YOUNG: For "Mountain Speed."

LOUIS ZARA: For "The Citizner," by Louis Zara. By permission of the author.

GENERAL INDEX